Handbook of International Trade Agreements

International trade has, for decades, been central to economic growth and improved standards of living for nations and regions worldwide. For most of the advanced countries, trade has raised standards of living, while for most emerging economies, growth did not begin until their integration into the global economy. The economic explanation is simple: international trade facilitates specialization, increased efficiency and improved productivity to an extent impossible in closed economies. However, recent years have seen a significant slowdown in global trade, and the global system has increasingly come under attack from politicians on the right and on the left. The benefits of open markets, the continuation of international co-operation, and the usefulness of multilateral institutions such as the World Trade Organization (WTO), the International Monetary Fund and the World Bank have all been called into question. While globalization has had a broadly positive effect on overall global welfare, it has also been perceived by the public as damaging communities and social classes in the industrialized world, spawning, for example, Brexit and the US exit from the Trans-Pacific Partnership.

The purpose of this volume is to examine international and regional preferential trade agreements (PTAs), which offer like-minded countries a possible means to continue receiving the benefits of economic liberalization and expanded trade. What are the strengths and weaknesses of such agreements, and how can they sustain growth and prosperity for their members in an ever-challenging global economic environment?

The Handbook is divided into two parts. The first, Global Themes, offers analysis of issues including the WTO, trade agreements and economic development, intellectual property rights, security and environmental issues, and PTAs and developing countries. The second part examines regional and country-specific agreements and issues, and PTAs and developing countries. The second part examines regional and country-specific agreements and issues, including NAFTA, CARICOM, CETA, the Pacific Alliance, the European Union, EFTA, ECOWAS, SADC, TTIP, RCEP and the TPP (now the CPTPP), as well as the policies of countries such as Japan and Australia.

Robert E. Looney is a Distinguished Professor in the National Security Affairs Department at the Naval Postgraduate School, Monterey, California, USA. He received his PhD in Economics from the University of California, Davis. He specializes in issues relating to economic development in the Middle East, Latin America and Africa. He has published 22 books, including *Economic Policymaking in Mexico: Factors Underlying the 1982 Crisis* (Duke University Press), and *Iraq's Informal Economy: Reflections of War, Sanctions and Policy Failure* (the Emirates Center for Strategic Studies and Research). He has also edited four Routledge International Handbooks: *Handbook of US-Middle East Relations* (2009), *Handbook of Oil Politics* (2012), *Handbook of Emerging Economies* (2014), and *Handbook of Transitions to Energy and Climate Security* (2016). He is also the editor of the Routledge Europa Emerging Economies series.

Handbook of International Trade Agreements

Country, regional and global approaches

Edited by Robert E. Looney

LONDON AND NEW YORK

First published 2019
by Routledge
2 Park Square, Milton Park, Abingdon, Oxon OX14 4RN

and by Routledge
711 Third Avenue, New York, NY 10017

Routledge is an imprint of the Taylor & Francis Group, an informa business

© 2019 Robert E. Looney for selection and editorial material; individual chapters, the
contributors; Chapter 34 © Peterson Institute for International Economics.

The right of Robert E. Looney to be identified as the author of the editorial material, and of
the authors for their individual chapters, has been asserted in accordance with sections 77 and
78 of the Copyright, Designs and Patents Act 1988.

All rights reserved. No part of this book may be reprinted or reproduced or utilised in any
form or by any electronic, mechanical, or other means, now known or hereafter invented,
including photocopying and recording, or in any information storage or retrieval system,
without permission in writing from the publishers.

Trademark notice: Product or corporate names may be trademarks or registered trademarks, and
are used only for identification and explanation without intent to infringe.

Europa Commissioning Editor: Cathy Hartley

Editorial Assistant: Eleanor Catchpole Simmons

British Library Cataloguing in Publication Data
A catalogue record for this book is available from the British Library

Library of Congress Cataloging in Publication Data
Names: Looney, Robert E., editor.
Title: Handbook of international trade agreements : country, regional and global approaches /
    Edited by Robert E. Looney.
Description: New York, NY : Routledge, 2018.
Identifiers: LCCN 2018015591| ISBN 9781857439151 (hardback) | ISBN 9781351046947
    (webpdf) | ISBN 9781351046930 (epub) | ISBN 9781351046923 (mobi/kindle)
Subjects: LCSH: Commercial treaties. | Foreign trade regulation. | International trade.
Classification: LCC K4600 .H37 2018 | DDC 382/.9–dc23
LC record available at https://lccn.loc.gov/2018015591

ISBN: 978-1-85743-915-1 (hbk)
ISBN: 978-1-351-04695-4 (ebk)

Typeset in Bembo
by Taylor & Francis Books

For Pamela

Contents

List of illustrations	*xi*
The Editor and Contributors	*xiii*
Preface	*xxv*
Acknowledgements	*xxvii*
Acronyms and Abbreviations	*xxviii*

PART I
Global Themes 1

1 Introduction 3
Robert E. Looney

2 Regional trade agreements: Myths and misconceptions 9
Kati Suominen

3 The WTO and regional/bilateral trade agreements 17
Kimberly Ann Elliott

4 International agreements on intellectual property rights: TRIPS
and beyond 29
Keith E. Maskus

5 The spread of international trade agreements: A dynamics towards the
'spaghetti bowl' phenomenon? 41
Zakaria Sorgho

6 The economic effects of FTAs 56
Holger Breinlich

7 Trade agreements and economic development 67
Christopher Stevens

vii

Contents

8 The investment component of trade agreements 79
Wolfgang Alschner

9 Trade agreements and national security: An economic approach 91
Ryan Garcia and Jonathan Lipow

10 Economic reform and service liberalization in developing countries: Can preferential trade agreements help? 101
Leonardo Baccini

11 Gender rights and trade agreements 112
Sophia Price

12 Trade agreements and the environment 122
Inkyoung Kim

13 Neoliberal globalization and its opponents 134
Anne L. Clunan

PART II
Regional/Country Analysis 145

14 NAFTA 147
Robert A. Blecker

15 CAFTA-DR: diverging trajectories and uneven development 166
Mary Finley-Brook

16 CARICOM 181
Lester Henry

17 Mexico's approach to preferential agreements 192
Luz Maria de la Mora Sanchez

18 CETA 209
Kurt Hübner

19 Mercosur 218
Walter Antonio Desiderá Neto

20 The Pacific Alliance 230
Gian Luca Gardini

Contents

21 ALBA 241
Asa Cusack

22 The European Union 251
Christian Schweiger

23 TTIP 261
Christoph Scherrer

24 EFTA 271
Marius Vahl and Aslak Berg

25 Eastern Partnership countries 282
Inmaculada Martínez-Zarzoso

26 Trade agreements and regional integration: The European Union
after Brexit 296
Annette Bongardt and Francisco Torres

27 The GCC trade agreements: regional integration challenges
and opportunities 307
Joseph A. Kéchichian

28 Liberalization without integration: Egypt and PTAs (1990–2010) 322
Amr Adly

29 The African Union and the European Union: Trade reciprocity and/or
economic development? 335
Mark Langan

30 ECOWAS: An economic commitment that needs political strengthening 348
Osaore Aideyan

31 SADC: Towards a deeper and wider union? 359
Donald L. Sparks

32 COMESA: A case study 372
B. Seetanah, R. V. Sannassee, S. Fauzel and Paul Okiira Okwi

33 RCEP and Asian economic integration 384
Ganeshan Wignaraja

34 The TPP: Origins and outcomes 401
Jeffrey J. Schott

ix

Contents

35 Japan's approach to preferential trade agreements   412
    Gregory P. Corning

36 Australia's approach to PTAs   423
    Richard Pomfret

Index   *434*

Illustrations

Figures

3.1	Proliferation of RTAs, 1948–2018	20
3.2	Physical RTAs in force, participation by region	21
5.1	Evolution of ITAs globally, 1995–2016	42
5.2	ITAs in force by region (including intra- and cross-regional ITAs), 1948–2017	48
5.3	Comparative evolution of ITAs and intra-trade within the ITA blocs, 1995–2016	49
5.4	Number of state interventions affecting global trade per year, 2009–17	50
14.1	Total employment in Mexican manufacturing by industry, 2007 and 2016	151
14.2	Exports of goods to the other NAFTA members as a percentage of each country's total exports of goods, 1993–2016	154
14.3	Imports of goods from other NAFTA members as a percentage of each country's total imports of goods, 1993–2016	155
14.4	Trade balances of NAFTA members with non-NAFTA countries, 1993–2016	156
14.5	Mexican foreign direct investment inflows as a percentage of GDP, 1980–2016	156
14.6	Mexico's labour productivity and per caput GDP as percentages of US levels, 1950–2014	160
14.7	Hourly compensation of Mexican production workers, in real terms and as a percentage of the US levels, 1994–2016	161
16.1	CARICOM's main trade partners, 2014 (%)	182
21.1	SUCRE trade volumes (US $) 2010–16	246
21.2	Total ALBA trade (US $000) and Organization of the Petroleum Exporting Countries (OPEC) basket price ($) 2005–16	248
24.1	The two-pillar EEA structure	274
25.1	Democracy, 1994–2012	284
25.2	Freedom of the press, 1995–2012	285
25.3	Key determinants of transition to market economy, 2012	286
25.4	Ease of doing business, 2007–17	287
25.5	Corruption, 2007–17	288
25.6	Trust, 2007–17	289
25.7	Exports of goods and services, 1995–2016 (% of GDP)	290
25.8	Exports of manufactures, 1995–2016 (% of total merchandise exports)	290
25.9	Direction of trade in 2012 (% of total)	291

25.10	Exports and imports to EU-28, 2005–14	292
32.1	Share of value added to GDP, 2016	376
32.2	COMESA key export market shares, 2015	379
32.3	Logistics Performance Index, 2012–16	381
33.1	Global importance of RCEP, the TPP-11 and the EU in 2016	387
33.2	Gains from a goods-only RCEP	389
33.3	Gains from a comprehensive RCEP	390

Tables

15.1	Economic Freedom Index	169
15.2	Foreign balance of goods and services	169
15.3	Top trade partners, 2015	170
15.4	Trade balance with the USA (US $ millions)	170
15.5	Demographic characteristics, 2005–15	171
15.6	Economic indicators by country, 2005–14	172
15.7	Employment indicators by country, 2005–14	173
15.8	Inequality and vulnerability, 2015	174
15.9	Environmental indicators, 2015	174
16.1	CARIFORUM tariff liberalization schedule	186
16.2	Shares of exports to various CARICOM trading partners, 2007–16	190
17.1	Mexico's network of RTAs	194
17.2	Mexico's trade with RTA partners, 2016 (US $, billions)	194
17.3	Mexico's network of BITs	195
17.4	Mexico's network of ECAs under ALADI	199
24.1	EFTA trade in goods, 2016 (value in US $ billion)	278
27.1	GCC countries' economic growth rates (GDP)	310
27.2	Bahrain's trade partners, 2015	314
27.3	Oman's trade partners, 2015	315
27.4	India's trade with GCC countries (in US $ million)	318
30.1	Background information	350
30.2	Internal trade liberalization provisions	351
30.3	Common external tariff	351
30.4	General trade-related provisions	352
31.1	Intra-SADC trade (% of total trade that is with members)	364
32.1	COMESA states	373
32.2	Average GDP growth rate for member countries between 2005 and 2016	375
32.3	Global COMESA trade, 2003–2016, values in US $ millions	377
32.4	Intra-COMESA trade, 2015	377
32.5	Value of intra-group trade, 2015 (exports in US $ millions)	378
32.6	COMESA's major export trade markets, 2003–12, values in US $ million	380
33.1	Selected economic characteristics of RCEP members	387
33.A1	Overview of BCEP negotiating rounds	396
34.1	Indicators of diversity, TPP-12, 2016	403
34.2	TPP-12 vs TPP-11: real income gains	405
36.1	Australia's Pacific Island partners	425
36.2	Australia's 21st-century trade agreements, to the end of 2016	427

The Editor and Contributors

Robert E. Looney is a Distinguished Professor in the National Security Affairs Department at the Naval Postgraduate School, Monterey, California. He received his PhD in Economics from the University of California, Davis. He specializes in issues relating to economic development in the Middle East, Latin America and Africa. He has published 22 books including *Economic Policymaking in Mexico: Factors Underlying the 1982 Crisis* (Duke University Press, 1985), and *Iraq's Informal Economy: Reflections of War, Sanctions and Policy Failure* (the Emirates Center for Strategic Studies and Research). He has also edited four previous Routledge Handbooks: *Handbook of US-Middle East Relations* (2009), *Handbook of Oil Politics* (2012), *Handbook of Emerging Economies* (2014), and *Handbook of Transitions to Energy and Climate Security* (2016). He is currently the editor of the Routledge Europa Emerging Economies series. Dr Looney is on the board of editors of the *International Journal of World Peace* and the *Journal of Third World Studies*. In addition, he has published over 300 articles in numerous professional journals and is a regular contributor to the *Milken Institute Review* and the *World Politics Review*. As an international consultant, Dr Looney has provided advice and assistance to the governments of Iran, Saudi Arabia, Japan, Mexico, Panama and Jamaica as well as to the World Bank, the International Monetary Fund, the International Labor Office, the Inter-American Development Bank, the Stanford Research Institute, and the RAND Organization.

Amr Adly is a researcher at the Middle East Directions Program at the European University Institute. He worked as a non-resident scholar at the Carnegie Middle East Center, where his research centred on political economy, development studies, and economic sociology of the Middle East, with a focus on Egypt. Adly has taught political economy at the American University in Cairo and at Stanford University. He has been an economic researcher at the Ministry of International Cooperation in Egypt and a Director of the Social and Economic Justice Unit at the Egyptian Initiative for Personal Rights. Adly has also worked as a Project Manager at the Center on Democracy, Development, and the Rule of Law at Stanford University, where he was a Postdoctoral Fellow. Adly is the author of *State Reform and Development in the Middle East: The Cases of Turkey and Egypt* (Routledge, 2012). He has been published in a number of peer-reviewed journals, including *Business and Politics*, the *Journal of Turkish Studies*, and *Middle Eastern Studies*. Adly is also a frequent contributor to print and online news sources, including Jadaliyya, Alshorouk, Ahram Online, and Egypt Independent.

Osaore Aideyan is an assistant professor in the Department of Politics and Government at Illinois State University. He earned a BS and MS in Sociology and Political Science from Universities in Nigeria. He also earned an MA in International Studies and a PhD in Political Science from Claremont Graduate University, California. His areas of teaching and research are comparative and international politics, African politics, and the politics of development and underdevelopment. His most recent article and book chapter on trade and development appear in Politics and Policy, and International Norms, Normative Change, and The UN Sustainable Development Goals.

Wolfgang Alschner is an Assistant Professor at the University of Ottawa's Common Law Section and a former researcher at the Graduate Institute of International and Development Studies in Geneva and the World Trade Institute in Bern. He worked for UNCTAD's International Investment Agreements Section as an individual contractor for several years and has been published in peer-reviewed journals on WTO law, regionalism as well as investment law and arbitration. His current research focuses on the empirical and computational analysis of international economic law. Wolfgang holds a PhD in International Law and a Master of Law from Stanford Law School.

Leonardo Baccini (PhD, Trinity College Dublin) is an Assistant Professor in the department of Political Science at McGill University. Before joining McGill, he was an Assistant Professor at the London School of Economics and Political Science and a Research Fellow at Princeton University and at New York University. His research interests lie in the area of international political economy and comparative political economy with a focus on trade. He is the author of *Cutting the Gordian Knot of Economic Reform: How International Institutions Promote Liberalization* (Oxford University Press, 2014) and of several articles published in leading journals. Information on his published articles and working papers can be found at https://sites.google.com/site/leona rdobaccini/. His research has been funded by British, Irish, Italian and US grants. He is an Associate Editor of the journal *Economics and Politics* and he serves on the steering committee of the Virtual International Political Economy Society.

Aslak Berg is the Economic Officer at the EFTA Secretary-General's Office in Geneva, where he is responsible for economic analysis and statistics in addition to supporting EFTA's third country activities. Prior to joining EFTA, he spent six years at the Norwegian Agriculture Agency working on agricultural trade policy, including agricultural trade negotiations between Norway and the EU. He also had secondment with the Directorate-General of Trade at the European Commission in 2011–12 and worked for Statistics Norway in 2008–10. He holds a BA in Economics and Political Science from Vassar College and a Master of Arts in Law and Diplomacy from the Fletcher School of Law and Diplomacy at Tufts University.

Robert A. Blecker is a Professor in the Department of Economics, College of Arts and Sciences (CAS), and Affiliate Faculty of the School of International Service (SIS) and Center for Latin American and Latino Studies (CLALS), at American University, Washington, DC. He is a member of the editorial boards of the *European Journal of Economics and Economic Policies: Intervention, International Review of Applied Economics, Investigación Económica, Metroeconomica*, and the *Review of Keynesian Economics*. His books include *Fundamentals of US Foreign Trade Policy: Economics, Politics, Laws, and Issues* (co-authored with Stephen D. Cohen and Peter D. Whitney, 2nd edition, Westview, 2003). His articles have appeared in numerous refereed academic journals as well as in edited books and conference volumes published by Cambridge University Press, Oxford University Press, University of Michigan Press, Routledge, Palgrave Macmillan and Edward Elgar, among others. His research includes work on open economy macroeconomics, international trade theory and policy, economic integration in North America, global imbalances and the US trade deficit, the Mexican economy, and export-led growth.

Professor Blecker received his BA in Economics from Yale University and his MA and PhD in Economics from Stanford University. He also studied on the Masters programme in Economics at El Colegio de México, Mexico City, under a Fulbright scholarship.

Annette Bongardt is currently a Visiting Senior Fellow in Political Economy at the European Institute of the London School of Economics and Political Science. She has been a Senior and SCR Member of St Antony's College, Oxford University, and a Visiting Fellow at the Robert Schuman Centre for Advanced Studies of the European University Institute (EUI) in Florence. She has been long-standing Professor and Head of European Studies at the Portuguese National Institute for Public Administration and Associate Professor at University Fernando Pessoa in Portugal. After receiving her PhD in Economics from the EUI in 1990, she was Schuman Fellow of the European Commission at the Centre for European Policy Studies (CEPS), Assistant Professor (eq.) at the Rotterdam School of Management and Senior Research Fellow at ICER (Turin). She was also Visiting Professor at the Universities of Aveiro, Pisa, Rome (II) and Victoria, BC, Canada, and Católica, Lisbon, among others, as well as Academic Visitor and consultant of the European Commission.

Holger Breinlich is Professor of International Economics at the University of Nottingham. He is also a Research Fellow at the Nottingham Centre for Research on Globalisation and Economic Policy, a Research Associate at the Centre for Economic Performance and a Research Fellow at the Centre for Economic Policy Research. He received his PhD from the London School of Economics and Political Science in 2006. Professor Breinlich's main area of research is empirical international trade. He has published articles in leading international journals such as the *Economic Journal*, the *Journal of International Economics*, the *Journal of the European Economic Association* and the *Journal of Development Economics*. He has worked extensively on the determinants of firm and country export patterns, export promotion, trade in services, and on the effects of trade agreements on economic activity. He has received a number of awards, including the European Economic Association's Young Economist Award. His research has been funded by the British Academy, the Economic and Social Research Council, the European Union, the German Science Foundation and the Leverhulme Trust. In addition to his academic research, Professor Breinlich has carried out projects for OECD, the UK's Department for Business, Innovation and Skills, the European Union and UK Trade and Investment (UKTI), and has acted as an external academic advisor on several occasions.

Anne L. Clunan is Associate Professor of National Security Affairs at the Naval Postgraduate School, Monterey, California. Her interests focus on globalization, governance, and non-state actors, international status, rising powers and identity politics, and emerging technologies, competitiveness and national security. She has published on non-state actors and ungoverned spaces; Russian identity and national security; international status and rising powers; globalization and sovereignty; biological weapons and biotechnology; nanotechnology and national competitiveness, and terrorism financing. Her work has appeared in *Communist and Post-Communist Studies*, the *Political Science Quarterly*, and *Perspectives on Politics*, and elsewhere. She is the author of *The Social Construction of Russia's Resurgence: Aspirations, Identity, and Security Interests* (Johns Hopkins, 2009) and co-editor of two edited volumes, *Ungoverned Spaces: Alternative Governance in an Era of Softened Sovereignty* (Stanford, 2010) and *Terrorism, War or Disease?* (Stanford, 2008). Clunan also has 20 years' experience leading international non-governmental organizations in countries transitioning from communism. She has worked in the US Senate, the US Department of State, and the British Houses of Parliament. She is the recipient of the Velvet Revolution Award from the Czech and Slovak governments and the US Defense Threat

The Editor and Contributors

Reduction Agency Director's Award for Outstanding Service. She earned her PhD in Political Science at the University of California, Berkeley.

Gregory P. Corning is Associate Professor and department Chair in the Department of Political Science at Santa Clara University. His current research explores the politics of trade and investment agreements in the Asia-Pacific. He is the author of *Japan and the Politics of Techno-Globalism* (M. E. Sharpe, 2004) and of articles in journals including *Asian Survey, East Asia, Pacific Affairs*, and the *Pacific Review*. A former Fulbright-Hays Fellow at Tokyo University, Corning served as Associate Dean of the College of Arts and Sciences from 2005 to 2011.

Asa Cusack is Managing Editor of the LSE Latin America and Caribbean blog, Honorary Research Associate of University College London, and Associate Fellow of the Institute of Latin American Studies, University of London. He holds a PhD in Latin American and Caribbean Political Economy from the University of Sheffield, UK. His research focuses on international affairs in Latin America and the Caribbean, particularly regional integration and its relationship to the political economy of Venezuela, Ecuador, the Eastern Caribbean, and the wider 'Left Turn'. He is author of *Venezuela, ALBA, and the Limits of Postneoliberal Regionalism in Latin America and the Caribbean* (Palgrave Macmillan, 2018) and editor of *Understanding ALBA: Progress, Problems, and Prospects of Alternative Regionalism in Latin America and the Caribbean* (Institute of Latin American Studies, 2018).

Luz María de la Mora Sanchez is Affiliate Professor in the International Studies Division at the Center for Economic Research and Teaching (CIDE) in Mexico City. Dr de la Mora is an expert in foreign trade relations and international public policy, has held multiple posts within the Mexican government representing its interests in foreign trade negotiations. She has served as Undersecretary for Economic Relations and International Cooperation in Mexico's Ministry of Foreign Affairs and as Assistant Undersecretary for International Trade Negotiations in Mexico's Ministry of Economy. She headed Mexico's trade offices in Brussels and Montevideo, and worked at the NAFTA office in Washington, DC. She has been NAFTA Chapter 19 panellist and was part of the Mexican government negotiation group for the NAFTA negotiations (1990–92). She has a BA in International Relations from El Colegio de México, an MA in International Political Economy from Carleton University in Ottawa, and a PhD in Political Science from Yale University. She has been a Fulbright Scholar, a Government of Canada award holder, a Ford Foundation award winner and a Research Fellow at both the Center for US-Mexican Studies (San Diego, California) and the Woodrow Wilson International Center for Scholars in Washington, DC. She is the author of the book *Apertura con reciprocidad* (CIDE, 2012), which analyses Mexico's trade negotiations policies, and has written extensively on Mexico's trade policy and trade negotiations. She is a board member of Mexico's Foreign Affairs Council (COMEXI).

Walter Antonio Desiderá Neto is an International Relations PhD candidate at the University Complutense of Madrid (UCM), Spain (2016–), developing a thesis about the Brazilian foreign policy of Dilma Rousseff's administration (2011–2016). He has a Masters degree in International and Comparative Politics (University of Brasília, 2014), with research interests on South American integration, South-South cooperation and Brazilian foreign policy, and has been a researcher in the International Studies, Political and Economic Relations Department (Dinte) of the Institute for Applied Economic Research (IPEA), Brazil, since 2010.

The Editor and Contributors

Kimberly Ann Elliott is an independent trade consultant and a Visiting Fellow at the Center for Global Development. She is the author or co-author of numerous books and articles on trade policy and globalization, economic sanctions, and food security. Her most recent book is *Global Agriculture and the American Farmer: Opportunities for US Leadership* (Center for Global Development, 2017), a follow-on to *Delivering on Doha: Farm Trade and the Poor* (Peterson Institute for International Economics, 2006). Her co-authored publications include *Economic Sanctions Reconsidered, Can Labor Standards Improve under Globalization*, and *Reciprocity and Retaliation in US Trade Policy, Third Edition* (Peterson Institute for International Economics, 2009). She is a member of the Research Consortium on Targeted UN Sanctions and has served on a number of official advisory committees, including the State Department's Working Group on Economic Sanctions, the National Research Council committee on Monitoring International Labor Standards, the USDA Consultative Group on the Elimination of Child Labor in US Agricultural Imports, and the National Advisory Committee for Labor Provisions in US Free Trade Agreements. She has an MA, with distinction, from the Johns Hopkins University School of Advanced International Studies and, in 2004, Austin College named her a Distinguished Alumna.

Sheereen Fauzel is a senior lecturer at the University of Mauritius. Having completed a Bachelors degree in Economics and Finance and a Masters degree in Banking and Finance, her areas of expertise are international economics, development economics and related areas. She has participated in international conferences and has published in notable international business and economics journals. She is a reviewer for a number of refereed journals including *Current Issues in Tourism* and the *Journal of Hospitality Marketing and Management*, among others. She also has a PhD in International Economics from the University of Mauritius.

Mary Finley-Brook, PhD, is an Associate Professor of Geography, Environmental Studies, and International Studies at the University of Richmond, Virginia. She has published articles on free trade in journals such as *Geopolitics, Latin American Perspectives*, and *Mesoamérica*. For the past 30 years, she has worked to publicize concerns shared by Central American civil society and scholars and to support advancement of economic, social and environmental justice in Latin America and the Caribbean.

Ryan Garcia is an Assistant Professor in the Defense Resource Management Institute (DRMI) at the Naval Postgraduate School, Monterey, California. He received a BA in Political Science and Economics from the University of California, Berkeley, and a PhD in Political Science from Yale University. Prior to joining DRMI, Dr Garcia was a faculty member at the Rochester Institute of Technology and a research fellow at the Center for Risk and Economic Analysis of Terrorism Events (CREATE). His research interests are primarily in the areas of Decision Analysis, Program Evaluation, Civil-Military Relations, and National Security Studies.

Gian Luca Gardini is Professor of International Relations and Chair of International Business and Society Relations (with a focus on Latin America) at the Friedrich Alexander University in Germany. Professor Gardini obtained his PhD in International Relations from the University of Cambridge. His main research interests cover the international relations of Latin America, foreign and trade policy analysis, comparative regional integration, and issues of international power, order and institutions. Among his recent books are *Latin America in the 21st Century* (Zed Books, 2012), and *Foreign Policy Responses to the Rise of Brazil* (Palgrave Macmillan, 2016). Professor Gardini has also acted as a practitioner of International and EU affairs. He was

xvii

The Editor and Contributors

Representative to the EU of the Italian Confederation of Industry, and International Trade Advisor to EUROCHAMBRES, the European Association of Chambers of Commerce and Industry. In 2012 he participated in the team that organized the EU-Community of Latin American and Caribbean States summit.

Lester Henry is Senior Lecturer in Economics at the University of the West Indies at St. Augustine. He holds a PhD in Economics from the University of Massachusetts, Amherst (USA). He also did graduate studies at the University of California, San Diego. His undergraduate studies were done at the University of Wisconsin at Madison and at Brooklyn College where he obtained his Bachelors degree in Economics with Mathematics and Computer Science. He was the recipient of a graduate fellowship of the American Economics Association. Dr Henry has taught at Brooklyn College (CUNY) and at the Fashion Institute of Technology in New York and was a Summer Fellow at the Center for Advanced Study in the Behavioral Sciences at Stanford University. His areas of teaching and research include Capital Flight, Monetary Issues in Economic Development, Trade and Exchange Rate Policies.

Kurt Hübner received his PhD in Economics and Political Science from the Freie Universität Berlin. He holds the Jean Monnet Chair for European Integration and Global Political Economy, as a Professor in the Political Science Department at the University of British Columbia. For the past few years he has acted as the Director of the Institute for European Studies. He has published and edited 12 books and numerous journal articles. His most recent books are *Europe, Canada, and the Comprehensive Economic and Trade Agreement* (Routledge, 2011) and *Global Currency Competition and Cooperation* (Routledge, 2018). He is also an Adjunct Professor at Ben-Gurion University in the Negev. He has also been a visiting researcher at the Hebrew University in Jerusalem, the University of Birmingham, the National University Singapore, LUISS University Rome, and Sciences Po in Grenoble.

Jonathan Lipow is an Associate Professor of Economics at the Defense Resources Management Institute located at the Naval Postgraduate School in Monterey, California. He received a BA in Political Science from UCLA (1984), an MA in International Development from American University (1989), and a PhD in Agricultural and Resource Economics from the University of California, Berkeley (1994). His research interests are primarily in public economics and national security studies. His most recent book is *Survival: The Economic Foundations of American National Security* (Lexington Books, 2016).

Joseph A. Kéchichian is Senior Fellow at the King Faisal Center for Research & Islamic Studies in Riyadh, Saudi Arabia, and the CEO of Kéchichian & Associates, LLC, a consulting partnership that provides analysis on the Arabian/Persian Gulf region, specializing in the domestic and regional concerns of Bahrain, Iran, Iraq, Kuwait, Oman, Qatar, Saudi Arabia, the United Arab Emirates and the Yemen. He held the post of Senior Writer with the Dubai-based *Gulf News* between 1 January 1995 and 31 August 2017, and served as the Honorary Consul of the Sultanate of Oman in Los Angeles, California, between 2006 and 2011. Kéchichian received his doctorate in Foreign Affairs from the University of Virginia in 1985, where he also taught (1986–1988), and assumed the Assistant Deanship in International Studies (1988–1989). Between 1990 and 1996 he worked at the Santa Monica-based RAND Corporation as an Associate Political Scientist, and was a lecturer at the University of California in Los Angeles. He is the author of 14 books. His latest titles are *The Attempt to Uproot Sunni-Arab Influence: A Geo-Strategic Analysis of the Western, Israeli and Iranian Quest for Domination* (a translation of *Istihdaf*

Ahl al-Sunna [Targeting Sunnis], by Nabil Khalifé; Sussex Academic Press, 2017); *From Alliance to Union: Challenges Facing Gulf Cooperation Council States in the Twenty-First Century* (Sussex, 2016); *'Iffat Al Thunayan: An Arabian Queen* (Sussex, 2015); *Legal and Political Reforms in Sa'udi Arabia* (Routledge, 2013); as well as *The Arab Nationalist Advisor: Yusuf Yassin of Sa'udi Arabia* (Sussex, forthcoming).

Inkyoung Kim is an Assistant Professor at the Political Science Department of Bridgewater State University (BSU), USA. She received her PhD in Political Science at the University of Massachusetts, Amherst. Before joining BSU in 2016, she taught at Clark University and Reed College. She teaches global environmental politics, international relations, comparative government, and East Asian politics. Her research interests include regional environmental cooperation, transboundary pollution, regionalism, government and politics in East Asia, and sustainable consumption patterns. She has published three journal articles: 'Free Trade Agreements for the Environment? Regional Economic Integration and Environmental Cooperation in East Asia' (with In Tae Yoo, 2016) and 'Messages from a Middle Power: Participation by the Republic of Korea in Regional Environmental Cooperation on Transboundary Air Pollution Issues' (2014) both in *International Environmental Agreements: Politics, Law and Economics*, and 'Environmental Cooperation of Northeast Asia: Transboundary Air Pollution' (2007) in *International Relations of the Asia-Pacific*. Her book chapter, entitled 'Push and Pull by Japan for Regional Environmental Cooperation: Transboundary Air Pollution in East Asia', is forthcoming in the Routledge *Handbook of Japanese Foreign Policy*. She is working on a book project on regional environmental cooperation on transboundary air pollution in East Asia.

Mark Langan is Senior Lecturer in International Politics at Newcastle University. His research focuses upon EU trade and development cooperation with former colonies in Sub-Saharan Africa and the Maghreb. He has recently published a monograph entitled *Neo-Colonialism and the Poverty of 'Development' in Africa* (Palgrave Macmillan, 2017). He is also the author of *The Moral Economy of EU Association with Africa* now available in paperback (Routledge, 2017).

Inmaculada Martínez–Zarzoso holds a PhD in International Economics from the University of Birmingham, UK. She has been full Professor of Economics at the University Jaume I (Spain) since 2012 and a member of the Institute of International Economics (Spain) since 1995. Currently, she is Apl Professor at the University of Göttingen (Germany) and chair of the U4 Network on Social Sciences Economics and Law. She is Research Fellow at the Center for Statistics and the Center for European Governance and Economic Development Research from the same university and board member of the European Network for Economic Research (INFER). She has advised the World Bank, OECD, the German Ministry of Development, and the Spanish Ministry of Transport and Infrastructure. Her fields of research include international economics, environmental economics and development economics. She is the author of numerous articles in international journals including the *Journal of International Economics*, the *Review of International Economics, Ecological Economics, Environmental and Resource Economics*, and the *Journal of Common Market Studies*, among others. Her current research interests are in the areas of environmental provisions in trade agreements, migration and remittances, networks and trade and sustainable global value chains.

Keith E. Maskus is Arts and Sciences Professor of Distinction in Economics at the University of Colorado, Boulder, USA. He was Chief Economist of the US State Department from 2016 to 2017. Maskus has also been a Lead Economist in the Development Research Group at the

World Bank. He is a Research Fellow at the Peterson Institute for International Economics and a consultant for the World Trade Organization and the World Intellectual Property Organization. Maskus received his PhD from the University of Michigan. He has written extensively about various aspects of intellectual property rights, international trade and investment, and technology. His most recent book is *Private Rights and Public Problems: The Global Economics of Intellectual Property in the 21st Century* (Peterson Institute for International Economics, 2012).

Paul Okiira Okwi is a development economist at Canada's International Development Research Centre (IDRC). Prior to joining IDRC, Paul worked for the World Bank in Kampala, the International Livestock Research Institute (ILRI) in Nairobi and was a lecturer at Makerere University. Paul has a PhD in Economics from the University of Cape Town. He has published extensively on welfare and income inequality, poverty mappings, geographic determinants of poverty, health and natural resource economics.

Richard Pomfret has been Professor of Economics at the University of Adelaide since 1992, and is Adjunct Professor of International Economics at the Johns Hopkins Bologna Center. For 2017–20, he holds a Jean Monnet Chair on the Economics of European Integration. He previously worked at the Johns Hopkins University School of Advanced International Studies in Washington, DC, Bologna and Nanjing, at the Concordia University in Montréal and the Institut für Weltwirtschaft in Kiel. In 1993 he was seconded to the United Nations for a year, acting as adviser on macroeconomic policy to the Asian republics of the former Soviet Union. He has been a consultant for OECD, UNDP, the World Bank, the Asian Development Bank, and the EU. His research interests centre on economic development and international economics, and he has published over 100 papers and 20 books, including *The Economics of Regional Trading Arrangements* (Oxford University Press, 2001), *The Central Asian Economies since Independence* (Princeton University Press, 2006), and textbooks on international trade and development economics.

Sophia Price, PhD, is Head of Politics and International Relations at Leeds Beckett. Her research focuses on feminist political economy, pro-poor development strategies and the external relations of the European Union, particularly its trade and aid relations with the Africa, Pacific and Caribbean Group of States.

R. V. Sannassee is a Professor in the Department of Finance at the University of Mauritius. He holds a PhD in Economics from the University of Reading, UK, and currently lectures on international business at undergraduate and postgraduate level. In addition, Dr Sannassee has contributed to several publications in the areas of finance, economics and trade. He is also the Director of Programme for the MSc in Social Protection Financing, a joint initiative by the University of Mauritius and the ILO, funded by the International Development Research Centre. In addition, Dr Sannassee is also a Co-Chair of the WTO Chairs Programme, an initiative by the WTO. Finally, Dr Sannassee has also acted as a consultant for various international organizations including the World Bank, UNDP, UNCTAD, UNECA and the AfDB, among others.

Christoph Scherrer is full Professor of Globalization and Politics, Executive Director of the International Center for Development and Decent Work (ICDD) at the University of Kassel, and a member of the Steering Committee of the Global Labour University. He holds PhDs in Political Science from the Freie Universität Berlin (Dr habil) and the University of Frankfurt

(Dr phil) and an MA in Economics (University of Frankfurt). He is Chair of the Graduate School of Socio-Ecological Research and Development, University of Kassel and he directs two English-language Masters programmes: the MA in Global Political Economy and Development and the MA in Labour Policies and Globalization. He has received the Excellency in Teaching Award of the State of Hessia and the Excellence in Development Cooperation Award from the Deutscher Akademischer Austauschdienst (DAAD – German Academic Exchange Service). His international experience includes most recently a visiting professorship at the University of the Philippines as well as the position of Visiting Fellow YCIAS, Yale University (2004), Kennedy Memorial Fellow, Harvard University (1996/97). He is an Adjunct Member of the Graduate Faculty Rutgers University – New Brunswick.

Jeffrey J. Schott joined the Peterson Institute for International Economics in 1983 and is a senior fellow working on international trade policy and economic sanctions. During his tenure at the Institute, Schott also has taught at Princeton University (1994) and at Georgetown University (1986–88). He was formerly a senior associate at the Carnegie Endowment for International Peace (1982–83) and an official of the US Treasury Department (1974–82) in international trade and energy policy. During the Tokyo Round of multilateral trade negotiations he was a member of the US delegation that negotiated the GATT Subsidies Code. He is co-chair of the Trade and Environment Policy Advisory Committee of the US Trade Representative's office and a member of the Advisory Committee on International Economic Policy of the US Department of State. He also is a member of the Advisory Council of the Department of Economics of Washington University in St Louis. Schott is the author, co-author, or editor of numerous books on trade, including *The Trans-Pacific Partnership: An Assessment* (2016); *From Drift to Deals: Advancing the WTO Agenda* (2015); *Local Content Requirements: A Global Problem* (2013); *Understanding the Trans-Pacific Partnership* (2013); *Payoff from the World Trade Agenda* (2013); *NAFTA and Climate Change* (2011); *Figuring Out the Doha Round* (2010); *Economic Sanctions Reconsidered* (3rd edition, 2007); and *NAFTA Revisited: Achievements and Challenges* (2005) (All of the above are published by the Peterson Institute for International Economics). Schott holds a BA degree magna cum laude from Washington University, St Louis (1971) and an MA degree with distinction in International Relations from the School of Advanced International Studies of Johns Hopkins University (1973).

Christian Schweiger is Visiting Professor of Comparative European Governance Systems in the Institute for Political Science at Chemnitz University of Technology in Germany. His research concentrates on the comparative study of political systems, economies and welfare states of the member states of the European Union (particularly the UK, Germany and transformation in the Central and Eastern European countries), the political economy of the EU Single Market, economic globalization and transatlantic relations. His most recent publications include the jointly edited collection with José M. Magone and Brigid Laffan, *Core-periphery Relations in the European Union: Power and Conflict in a Dualist Political Economy* (Routledge, 2016) and the monograph *Exploring the EU's Legitimacy Crisis: The Dark Heart of Europe* (Edward Elgar, 2016).

Boopen Seetanah is an Associate Professor at the University of Mauritius (UoM) with research interest in tourism and transport, international trade and finance and development economics. He is currently the Faculty Research Advisor and the Co-Chair of the WTO Chair (UoM). Dr Seetanah has acted as a consultant for the local government and also numerous international

The Editor and Contributors

organizations including UNEP, UNDP, the World Bank, the ADB, the ILO and the Mauritian Regional Multidisciplinary Centre for Excellence (RMCE), among others.

Zakaria Sorgho is currently a Research Fellow in the Department of Economics at HEC Liège (Belgium). He is an Associate Researcher at the Centre for Inter-disciplinary Studies on International Trade and Investment (CISIT) in Québec (Canada). He has been Scientific Collaborator at the Centre for Research on the Economics of Environment, Agri-food, Transport and Energy (CREATE), and Lecturer in the Department of Economics, at the Laval University (Canada). He holds a PhD in International Studies, specializing in International Economics and WTO Law from the Graduate Institute (HEI) of the Laval University in Québec (Canada). He obtained a Masters in Macroeconomics from the University of Ouagadougou, Burkina Faso, and then a Masters in International Development from the Graduate Institute Geneva (IHEID) in Switzerland. Sorgho has gained considerable experience from different organizations (international organizations, public and private sectors). He is a co-founder of the African Centre for International Trade and Development (ACITD) based in Ouagadougou (Burkina Faso). His broad research areas are related to global studies and development studies, implying an interaction between political economy and economic development. His works generally tackle macroeconomic topics, in particular the analysis or assessment of policy related to trade, environment and/or development. He has several publications, including papers in scientific peer-reviewed journals, books, book chapters, etc. Using an innovative multidisciplinary approach, Sorgho tries to address through his publications some complex research questions, for which a disciplinary approach would be limited.

Donald L. Sparks is Professor of International Economics at the Citadel in Charleston, SC, USA (where he has been named MBA Professor of the Year three times) and University Lecturer in International Business at the Management Center Innsbruck, Austria. Dr Sparks has served as a Senior Consulting Associate in the Bureau of Intelligence and Research at the US Department of State. He has been a Fulbright Professor of Economics at the University of Swaziland and at the University of Maribor, in Slovenia. He was also a Fulbright Senior Specialist at the University of Swaziland. In 2017 he was a Fulbright Specialist in Economics at the African Union Commission's Department of Economic Affairs in Addis Ababa, Ethiopia. He was the Department Chairman and Visiting Professor of Economics at the American University in Cairo. Before beginning his academic career, Dr Sparks served as the Regional Economist for Africa in the Office of Economic Analysis at the US Department of State in Washington, DC, and as a Staff Assistant to Senator Ernest F. Hollings. Dr Sparks has published widely, including authoring the 'Economic Trends' chapter of *Africa South of the Sahara* (Routledge) for each edition for the past 30 years. He has been a consultant for a number of international organizations, including UNIDO, the UN Council for Namibia, the International Union for Conservation of Nature and Natural Resources, and the Economist Intelligence Unit.

Christopher Stevens is a trade expert with more than 35 years of experience working on trade, regional integration and trade agreements. Currently a Senior Research Associate at the Overseas Development Institute, London (where he was formerly Director of International Economic Development) he has accumulated a substantial knowledge of the details of free trade agreements (notably those involving the EU, most of which he has analysed). He has used this to explain their implications for different socio-economic groups in the signatories, the key features that determine this impact, and the policy levers that can alter undesirable effects. He has now turned his attention to the implications of Brexit for UK trade policy towards developing countries. A former Head of Graduate Programmes in the Institute of Development Studies at the University of Sussex (where he was a Fellow) he has developed numerous training programmes and manuals on the sustainability impact assessments of free trade agreements. Recent work includes an assessment of the fiscal impact of Economic Partnership Agreements (for the European Parliament) and a meta-analysis published by the UK Department of International Development on the impact of free trade agreements on economic

Kati Suominen is Founder and CEO of Nextrade Group, a data and AI company that helps governments and Fortune 500s to optimize public policies and investments in trade and ecommerce worldwide; Founder of TradeUp Capital Fund, a growth capital platform for globalizing tech companies acquired by Nextrade in 2017; Founder of Business for eTrade Development, a non-profit backed by leading global companies on a mission to advance ecommerce in developing nations; and lead coordinator and Co-Founder of the new Singapore-based Digital Standards for Trade (DST) aimed at digitizing international trade transactions end-to-end. She was Adjunct Fellow at the Center for Strategic and International Studies (CSIS), where she founded the Digital Trade programme; and Adjunct Professor at UCLA Anderson School of Management. Her tenth book is *Making Trade Great Again: How Disruptive Technologies Open Opportunities for All* (Stanford University Press, 2018). She is the 'ideas woman' behind such international initiatives as eTrade for All which is now championed by the United Nations and the RTA Exchange, a global dialogue forum on regional trade agreements led by the Inter-American Development Bank with the International Centre for Trade and Sustainable Development. She has spoken extensively on trade, e.g. at Davos, the World Trade Symposium, the Global Trade Review, the World Bank, WTO, etc. She is a Life Member of the Council on Foreign Relations. She holds an MBA from Wharton, and a PhD from the University of California, San Diego.

Francisco Torres is Visiting Senior Fellow in European Political Economy at the LSE and Visiting Professor of European Political Economy at the Católica Lisbon School of Business and Economics. He is also a Political Economy of Financial Markets (PEFM) Research Associate at St Antony's College, Oxford University, and an EU Steering Committee Member of the European Consortium for Political Research (ECPR). Before moving to Oxford and London in 2012, where he teaches European (and International) Political Economy, he had taught, among others, at the universities of Victoria, Canada, Rome (Tor Vergata), Bolzano and Aveiro (where he was Associate Professor for five years), and especially at the Catholic University, both at the Economics Department and at the European Studies Institute, of which he was Director and Research Coordinator for a decade. He was a Visiting Fellow at the EUI, Florence, the ESC, Oxford University, and was the first Robert Schuman Fellow of the European Commission at CEPS, Brussels. He holds a PhD in European Political Economy (Católica, Lisbon), an MSc in Economics (Nova, Lisbon) and a 'licenciatura' also in Economics (Católica, Lisbon). He also studied Economics at the EUI in Florence (PhD programme) and holds an MA in International Affairs from the Johns Hopkins University (SAIS).

Marius Vahl is Head of EEA Policy Coordination at the EFTA secretariat in Brussels working on the management of the agreement on the European Economic Area. Having joined EFTA in 2006, since 2011 he has been responsible for the preparation and organization of the EFTA standing committee, the EEA joint committee and the EEA council. In 2013 he was a seconded national expert in Directorate-General Enterprise and Industry in the European Commission, working on the development of EU innovation programmes. From 2000 to 2006 he was a

The Editor and Contributors

Research Fellow at the Centre for European Policy Studies (CEPS) in Brussels, focusing on EU foreign and neighbourhood policies. His main areas of research are EU relations with neighbouring countries and regions in Eastern Europe (Russia, Ukraine, Moldova, the Black Sea region) and Western Europe (Norway, Switzerland). He has a BA in Political Science, History and Economics from the University of Oslo, Norway, and received an MA in International Relations and International Economics from the School of Advanced International Studies (SAIS) of the Johns Hopkins University in Bologna, Italy and Washington, DC, USA in 1999.

Ganeshan Wignaraja is the Chair of the Global Economy Programme at the Lakshman Kadirgamar Institute of International Relations and Strategic Studies in Sri Lanka. He is also a Senior Research Associate at the Overseas Development Institute in London. During a career spanning over 25 years he has held senior positions at the Asian Development Bank, the Commonwealth Secretariat, OECD, Oxford University, the United Nations University Institute for New Technologies and a UK consulting firm. He has published 16 books on international economics, regional integration, small and medium-sized enterprises, development economics and development finance. He holds a DPhil in Economics from Oxford University and a BSc in Economics from the London School of Economics and Political Science.

Preface

For decades international trade has been central to economic growth and improved standards of living for nations and regions around the world. For most of the advanced countries, trade has raised standards of living, while for most emerging economies their 'economic miracles' did not begin until their economies were integrated into the global economy. The economic explanation is simple. International trade facilitates specialization, increased efficiency and improved productivity to an extent impossible in closed economies.

Recent years, however, have seen a significant slowdown in global trade. Because historical evidence shows a clear a clear link between trade liberalization, trade expansion and higher GDP growth, there is mounting concern over the ability of the international economic/financial system to assure continued prosperity on a global scale.

With the slowdown in trade, the global system has increasingly come under attack from politicians on the right as well as on the left. International trade is an easy target for all the ills of the world. From a political perspective it plays into the intuitive populist, zero-sum view – if another country we trade with is prospering, it must somehow be at our expense. The spread of this perspective throughout Europe and the USA over the past few years has called into question the benefits of open markets, the continuation of international co-operation, and the usefulness of multilateral institutions such as the World Trade Organization, the International Monetary Fund and the World Bank

The backlash against globalization should not come as a surprise. While globalization has had a broadly positive effect on overall global welfare, it has also been perceived by the public as damaging communities and social classes in the industrialized world. This perception sees 'good jobs' migrating to lower-wage economies and regions, only to be replaced by low-paid and precarious forms of employment or by unemployment. As the argument goes, globalization has undermined wage structures in the advanced countries, while enriching the top 1 per cent of elitists in the advanced countries. With international trade, stagnant wages have become the 'new normal'.

In recent years, the 'left behind' have lent their support to populist movements, mostly but not exclusively on the political right. So far, populist movements have spawned Brexit and the US exit from the Trans-Pacific Partnership (TPP) with additional threats to tear up other trade treaties such as NAFTA.

Is the whole global system becoming unravelled with nothing to replace it but economic nationalism, trade wars and xenophobic migration policies? Fortunately, there are still significant segments of populations and national leaders who still believe in a liberal world economy and global co-operation. Others such as the Chinese continue to view globalization as a means of assuring that country's future rates of improved prosperity.

Preface

While global cooperation on a scale immediately following the formation of the WTO in the mid-1990s is mostly out of the question, regional preferential trade agreements offer like-minded countries a possible means to continue receiving the benefits of economic liberalization and expanded trade.

The purpose of this volume is to examine these agreements. While most economists would consider preferential trade agreements (PTAs) a 'third best' alternative to free global trade and the rules-based WTO, they now represent the only cooperative trade option available. What are the PTAs' strengths, weaknesses and ability to sustain growth and prosperity for their members in an ever-challenging global economic environment?

The overall picture is encouraging. While the WTO is no doubt dead, most parts of the world having envisioned an alternative reality of economic nationalism and trade wars, have rediscovered the benefits produced by trade. Better-designed trade agreements that address many of the excesses that brought on the populist wave in the first place are the hope for prosperity in the coming years. The future is clear. Those countries creative enough to gain the benefits of trade while compensating the 'losers' will continue to grow and prosper. Those that turn inwards will stagnate.

Acknowledgements

A book of this scope and sheer length could not have come to completion without the contributions of many individuals. In addition to the volume's many contributors, special thanks go to my department Chairman, Mohammed Hafez, for his continued support and encouragement. Thanks also go to the many students who have taken my international economics class over the past few years. The international students, in particular, have often challenged US trade policies and forced me to view developments in the global economy from many different perspectives. Greta E. Marlatt of the Naval Postgraduate School Knox Library went far beyond the call of duty to keep me informed of the latest oil developments throughout the course of the writing of the manuscript – a task only she could perform. A special thanks to Alison Phillips for her tireless efforts and professionalism in copyediting the entire manuscript. Most of all, thanks go to Cathy Hartley, Europa Commissioning Editor, who conceived of the original study, provided ongoing guidance and most importantly offered good cheer and positive encouragement throughout the project.

Acronyms and Abbreviations

ALBA	Bolivarian Alliance for the Peoples of Our America
APEC	Asia-Pacific Economic Cooperation
ASEAN	Association of Southeast Asian Nations
CAFTA-DR	Dominican Republic–Central American Free Trade Agreement
CARICOM	Caribbean Community
CETA	Comprehensive Economic and Trade Agreement
COMESA	Common Market for Eastern and Southern Africa
CPTPP	Comprehensive and Progressive Agreement for Trans-Pacific Partnership
DCFTA	Deep and Comprehensive Free Trade Agreement
EaP	Eastern Partnership
ECOWAS	Economic Community of West African States
EEA	European Economic Area
EFTA	European Free Trade Association
EPA	Economic Partnership Agreement
EU	European Union
FTA	free trade agreement
FTAA	Free Trade Area of the Americas
GATS	General Agreement on Trade in Services
GATT	General Agreement on Tariffs and Trade
GCC	Gulf Cooperation Council
GDP	gross domestic product
ILO	International Labour Organization
IPRs	Intellectual Property Rights
Mercosur/Mercosul	Southern Common Market
MFN	most-favoured-nation
NAFTA	North American Free Trade Agreement
OAS	Organization of American States
OECD	Organisation for Economic Co-operation and Development
PTA	preferential trade agreement
PTIA	preferential trade and investment agreement
RCEP	Regional Comprehensive Economic Partnership
RTA	regional free trade agreement
SADC	Southern African Development Community
TPP	Trans-Pacific Partnership
TRIPS	Agreement on Trade-Related Aspects of Intellectual Property Rights

TTIP	Transatlantic Trade and Investment Partnership
UK	United Kingdom
UN	United Nations
UNCTAD	United Nations Conference on Trade and Development
UNDP	United Nations Development Programme
US(A)	United States (of America)
WTO	World Trade Organization

xxx

Part I
Global Themes

2

1
Introduction

Robert E. Looney

Even before the recent tendency towards anti-globalization in the advanced countries, and the stalling of the World Trade Organization (WTO)'s Doha Development Round, bilateral and regional free trade agreements (RTAs) were becoming an essential alternative to the WTO's multilateral approach. Many of these preferential trade agreements (PTAs) involve trade between 'like-minded' countries, thus avoiding the conflicts associated with large numbers of nations engaged in multilateral negotiations.

The narrowing of country coverage has enabled modern RTAs and PTAs (the two are used interchangeably throughout the volume, with both often taking the form of free trade agreements or FTAs) to become increasingly sophisticated in their content and coverage. Not only do most PTAs include market access commitments in goods and services, but they are also accompanied by provisions on rules of origin, trade remedies (anti-dumping, countervailing and safeguards). Increasingly, core provisions concern investment, intellectual property rights (IPRs), competition, labour and the environment.

The current challenge for PTAs is making growth more inclusive so that it benefits workers across all economic sectors. Unfortunately, there are no clear-cut policy choices that assure broad-based benefits from trade. The challenge has not only to do with economic incentives but also social, regional, ethnic and cultural factors that require local solutions.

Several themes flow through the entire volume. How have PTAs been affected by and adjusted to significant changes in the global economy? How has the WTO handled PTAs and are these agreements undermining the authority of the WTO? How do the leading PTAs differ from each other and what are the general reasons for undertaking concessionary contracts? How have decisions involving PTAs been impacted by populist and anti-globalization attacks?

The Handbook addresses these issues in two main sections. The first 12 chapters explore the key themes from a general perspective, across all countries. The next 23 chapters assess the major individual PTAs and specific national approaches towards trade agreements. What were the factors motivating the agreements? To what extent have the agreements fulfilled their promise of improved trade and investment flows? Were there significant impediments in this regard? What is the potential for the existing agreements to facilitate more inclusive sustained growth for member countries? Might modifications to existing agreements improve their effectiveness towards this goal?

The volume starts off with an examination of the seven central myths and misunderstandings surrounding these trade agreements. Drawing on rigorous empirical analysis, rather than that of 'armchair empiricism' and political rhetoric, Chapter 2 provides a solid refutation to each. Chapter 3 asks if RTAs can lead the way to deeper integration and lay the foundation for new rules in new areas at the WTO. Or will RTAs prove to be a substitute, rather than a complement, leading to increased discrimination and undermining of the multilateral trade system?

Recent years have seen significant increases in global protection of IPRs in history. This shift has been the outcome of the Agreement on Trade-Related Aspects of Intellectual Property Rights (TRIPS) at the WTO. However, Chapter 4 notes that TRIPS alone failed to address significant new technological issues, such as copyright protection for digital goods on the internet, nor did it meet the needs of the global pharmaceutical and biotechnology industries. Thus, recent PTAs negotiated by the USA and the European Union (EU) have added stronger standards through a process commonly called 'TRIPS-Plus.'

Since the completion of the WTO's Uruguay Round in the mid-1990s, the world trade system has seen a proliferation of PTAs. Overlaid on a map the boundaries of these agreements resemble a 'spaghetti bowl'. This bewildering range of geographical configurations of PTAs at regional and extraregional level containing a tangle of rules of origin (RO) prompts worries about the inefficiency of the so-called spaghetti bowl phenomenon. Chapter 5 finds that the multiplication of PTAs might result in trade diversion effects owing to higher transaction costs caused by a mass of overlapping rules.

Since most economists consider PTAs such as FTAs a 'second-best' solution, with the multilateral WTO agreement being the most efficient in providing economic benefits, it is interesting to determine the likely consequences of these agreements. The broad picture that emerges (Chapter 6) is one of positive long-term effects, accompanied by often substantial short-term adjustment costs. While some concerns about appropriate measurement remain, FTAs seem to increase trade flows, profitability and economic efficiency. At the same time, however, trade agreements can lead to substantial wage and employment losses, at least in the short term.

On the other hand, with regard to development, the jury is still out (Chapter 7) on the effects that FTAs have on investment, employment and income distribution. Given the areas that they address, most FTAs signed during the last 20–25 years are about investment just as much as trade, with many taking on the title of preferential trade and investment agreements (PTIA). As Chapter 8 points out, even though the future inclusion of investment rules in trade agreements, at least in some parts of the world, is uncertain, PTIAs are likely to remain a central means through which to reform and update investment rules.

PTAs (or PTIAs), of course, can have a number of effects in addition to altering trade and investment flows. One neglected area in the literature concerns the national security implications of PTAs. As Chapter 9 notes, bilateral and RTAs serve both to promote ties between friendly states and to isolate rivals. The authors then go on to offer some conceptual arguments on how trade agreements can enhance signatories' ability to defend themselves from their enemies and rivals. Trade agreements also have implications for economic reforms (Chapter 10), and there is evidence that North-South PTAs involve microeconomic reform in Southern countries.

A relatively new aspect of PTAs involves the incorporation of gender. However, the measures to address gender equality and rights have been relatively limited (Chapter 11). In addition to gender issues, PTAs are increasingly addressing environmental issues. Chapter 12 draws on the 'precautionary principle' in examining how different RTAs, particularly in Europe, North America and Asia have resolved the differences between trade interests and environmental protection.

Part I concludes with an assessment (Chapter 13) of the effect of the anti-globalization movement on existing PTAs and their prospects for the future. This chapter develops a picture of globalization from its opponent's perspective. Three core concerns are identified – popular self-determination, collective cultural autonomy, and global social justice – that motivate this diverse set of actors and how these concerns have been put into practice in the 21st century. Specifically, these critiques have helped to champion the development agenda that many developing countries and the sustainability goals environmentalists and human rights activists have long advocated. They have also successfully impeded the US entry to the Trans-Pacific Partnership (TPP), by making what had been a non-issue a central focus of the US presidential election of 2016 in which the candidates of both parties swore to reject membership if elected. The message is clear. Until countries in which populism is on the ascendency find creative ways of addressing the perceived damages associated with globalization, the prospects for future PTAs or even the retention of some existing PTAs is seriously in doubt.

Part II introduces the various regional PTAs beginning with those in North America. Of these, the North American Free Trade Agreement (NAFTA) is by far the most important in terms of volumes of trade and investment. NAFTA reduced or eliminated trade barriers (with exceptions in specific sectors) between Canada, Mexico and the USA. NAFTA also broke new ground by incorporating provisions related to the property rights of foreign investors, IPRs and dispute settlement mechanisms. Trade and investment flows between the three member countries have mushroomed since NAFTA's creation in 1994, but as Chapter 14 notes the impact of NAFTA on employment, wages, productivity and inequality remains controversial. Although most economists view NAFTA as a significant success story, US politicians have also held the agreement responsible for many of the country's problems. As of 2017, the three members had begun a process of renegotiating NAFTA at the behest of US President Donald Trump. The outcome of this process is very uncertain and could lead to a US withdrawal from NAFTA with unpredictable consequences.

None of the chapters contained in this volume focus entirely on US PTA policies. As the NAFTA experience to date suggests, US policies well into the Trump Administration are still in a state of flux with little progress made. However, as of early 2018, with economic realities setting in, the Administration appears to be backing away from its campaign rhetoric of extreme economic nationalism.

Another significant North American agreement is that of the Central American Free Trade Agreement-Dominican Republic (CAFTA-DR) with the USA which entered into force in 2006 (Chapter 15) Regional integration objectives target securitization, infrastructure and natural resource management. CARICOM does not include the USA, with its members confined mainly to the Caribbean region. However, as Chapter 16 documents, the various trade agreements negotiated by CARICOM do little to suggest that the region has been benefiting directly from more magnificent trade creation. However, treaties with the EU, for example, have brought considerable benefits in the form of development and technical assistance.

The Mexican experience with PTAs (Chapter 17) is instructive. Since the 1990s Mexico has adopted an open regionalism strategy that has made it a key player in international trade having consolidated a network of 12 FTAs with 46 countries. Mexico's open regionalism created a dynamic export sector which has made the country the eighth largest exporter and importer worldwide. Trade is a critical element of Mexican economic growth and job creation. The Trump Administration's protectionist trend has reinforced Mexico's commitment to an open trading regime and the search for new export markets. Finally, the region's most recent PTA, the Comprehensive Economic and Trade Agreement (CETA) between Canada and the EU provisionally came into effect in September 2017. The agreement (Chapter 18) will reduce tariff lines to zero, open up public procurement markets, entail forms of regulatory cooperation and provide a new investor-state-dispute regime.

PTAs in South America began on a large scale in 1991 with the creation (Chapter 19) of the Southern Common Market (Mercado Común del Sur – Mercosur). In sharp contrast with the

Pacific Alliance (Chapter 20), Mercosur is more inward-oriented, with a considerable degree of effort devoted to increasing trade between the member countries (Brazil, Argentina, Uruguay, Paraguay and Venezuela – until the latter was suspended in 2016). The Pacific Alliance consisting of Chile, Colombia, Mexico and Peru came into effect in April 2011. As Chapter 20 documents, this PTA breaks new ground for Latin American economic integration through its commitment to free trade and entrepreneurship as well as the belief in investments and competitiveness as the best way to pursue societal development and international inclusion. Distinctively, the initiative was designed as a means of reaching out to the Asia-Pacific region, a novel approach to integration in Latin America.

The Bolivarian Alliance for the Peoples of Our America (Alianza Bolivariana para los Pueblos de Nuestra América – ALBA) was officially launched in December 2004 by Hugo Chávez's Venezuela and Fidel Castro's Cuba. ALBA emerged as an explicit alternative to the hemispheric Free Trade Area of the Americas (FTAA). Chapter 21 finds that despite its initial promise, poor implementation has robbed the agreement of much of its potential effectiveness. Whereas ALBA once made significant and innovative contributions to the regional political economy, its descent into political posturing suggests increasing irrelevance in future.

The EU remains the most prominent global trading power in Europe and Eurasia despite having come under increasing pressure from competitors in Asia and lingering crisis conditions. The effects of the 2008 global financial crisis and the eurozone crisis have deepened the already existing economic and social cleavage within the EU and dramatized the divergence of national preferences on trade. As Chapter 22 documents, growing public doubts about the legitimacy of the EU's decision-making processes and the breakdown of the pro-market consensus has resulted in increasing scepticism towards the EU's free trade agenda. Doubts over the future of the EU centre on the combination of the already noticeable absence of the United Kingdom (following its decision to leave the EU, referred to as Brexit), and the growing uncertainty about the future of transatlantic trade relations with the USA (Chapter 23). Consequently, the EU currently stands at a crossroads between further disintegration and a new post-Brexit impetus for a revitalized common trade agenda.

One opportunity for moving ahead with further integration is the proposed Transatlantic Trade and Investment Partnership (TTIP). As its name suggests, the accord would not only eliminate remaining tariffs on trade in goods but also facilitate investments among the trading partners. As Chapter 23 notes, TTIP would lead to an even more profound integration of the already intensely enmeshed economies on both sides of the Atlantic, which account for roughly 47 per cent of global gross domestic product, one-third of world trade flows and more than half of foreign direct investment. Unfortunately, after 15 rounds of negotiations, the TTIP project became embroiled in the US presidential election of 2016; its prospects dimmed considerably with the election of Donald Trump to the presidency.

The European Free Trade Association (EFTA), established in 1960, is unique in some regards. As Chapter 24 shows, its four current members – Iceland, Liechtenstein, Norway and Switzerland – do not trade that much with each other. Instead, the strength of EFTA lies in its ability to bring the member countries together as a bloc to negotiate package deals on more favourable terms.

The Eastern Partnership initiative (EaP) was launched by the EU in 2009 as a means of providing a forum in which the Union could discuss with the post-Soviet states of Armenia, Azerbaijan, Belarus, Georgia, Moldova and Ukraine issues related to trade agreements and economic collaboration between the EaP and the EU. Chapter 25 presents the main developments that the EaP countries have made regarding the quality of institutions, trade and economic integration in the last decade and evaluates the main effects of these agreements regarding increasing trade.

When Brexit takes place in 2019, the UK will pass from EU membership with associated full rights and obligations to third country status. The UK announced its intention to leave both the single market and the EU customs union, albeit only after a transition period. Furthermore, the UK's membership of all EU trade agreements will end automatically on the day of Brexit. Chapter 26 considers the political economy of Brexit. It focuses on the EU after Brexit and notably on implications for regional integration and trade agreements. It also critically assesses the UK's stated aim to become a global trading nation post-Brexit.

Preferential trade agreements in the Middle East are much less numerous than in other parts of the world. Trade between individual countries has always been less than that usually associated with countries with similar incomes and sizes of population. In this regard, the Gulf Cooperation Council (GCC) comprising Bahrain, Kuwait, Oman, Qatar, Saudi Arabia and the United Arab Emirates (UAE) stands out. The GCC was established in early 1981 with the promise of close trade relationships that would bind conservative rulers and their societies together. However, as Chapter 27 demonstrates, the GCC states have confronted two sets of economic integration challenges: bilateral free trade agreements favoured by Bahrain and Oman, and multilateral commitments envisaged by Saudi Arabia, Bahrain, Kuwait and the UAE. While the majority supported coordinated trade activities as a regional organization, multilateral FTAs with other economic entities produced mixed results.

Egypt has by far the region's largest number of PTAs. However, as Chapter 28 shows, the country's path towards integration into global trade proved rather poor. The chapter goes on to examine why Egypt ended up with so many PTAs and why they have failed to produce the desired effects.

In sharp contrast with the Middle East, Africa has seen the development of a broad spectrum of PTAs. Chapter 29 documents the way in which the EU has increasingly engaged the African Union on matters of trade and economic development. In doing so, it examines the parallel negotiations for Economic Partnership Agreements (EPAs) and Deep and Comprehensive Free Trade Agreements (DCFTAs) in Sub-Saharan Africa and the Maghreb, respectively.

Chapter 30 examines the role of institutional design factors in providing the basis for the successful implementation of a common market and currency for the Economic Community of West African States (ECOWAS). It concludes that addressing the cooperation and coordination of problems in the region would not only strengthen individual economies but also foster the region's global competitive position.

The origins, objectives, primary functions and evolution of the Southern African Development Community (SADC, formerly known as the Southern African Development Co-ordination Conference) are of particular interest. SADC, established in 1992, includes 16 members: Angola, Botswana, Comoros, the Democratic Republic of the Congo, Lesotho, Madagascar, Malawi, Mauritius, Mozambique, Namibia, Seychelles, South Africa, Swaziland, Tanzania, Zambia and Zimbabwe. Chapter 31 assesses this agreement by asking whether the community wants to, and can, become both 'deeper' (i.e. achieve increased convergence and harmonization in a variety of economic, political and social areas) and 'wider' through the addition of new additional members.

Finally, the Common Market for Eastern and Southern Africa (COMESA) was established in 1994. There are 19 member countries which have the overarching aim of fostering economic prosperity. However, this initiative has proven beneficial for some countries, but not for all. As Chapter 32 argues, there are still grounds for optimism, especially with the increasing drive by member countries to implement trade facilitation initiatives and to increase cooperation with other African trading groups.

For good reasons, much of the world's attention is focused on a series of trade agreements, the Regional Comprehensive Economic Partnership (RCEP) and the TPP, which involve Asia. Covering about three billion people across 16 diverse economies, the People's Republic of

China-led RCEP is the most extensive FTA in the world. While concerns exist about the depth of the final preferential agreement, RCEP can support Asian economic integration and global recovery. As Chapter 33 contends, a priori reasoning and model-based studies show that a comprehensive RCEP agreement can bring substantial economic gains for Asia and the world economy. However, several potential risks could reduce the extent of these benefits.

Chapter 34 traces the TPP from its origins to the initial agreement. Despite fears of its demise when the Trump Administration withdrew the USA from the agreement, the remaining 11 TPP countries have moved ahead to finalize a newly branded Comprehensive and Progressive Agreement for Trans-Pacific Partnership (CPTPP) comprised mainly of the original TPP text. The chapter concludes by noting that the US withdrawal from the TPP was a mixed blessing for China. It set back efforts to forge a US-China consensus on pathways to regional integration based on regional arrangements including the TPP and RCEP, but it also opened the door for China to assert a more pronounced leadership role in the region via its own bilateral trade pacts and regional investment arrangements such as the Belt and Road Initiative. In the short term, however, China is more likely to give priority to deepening its ties with its Asian neighbours before engaging with the TPP.

Of the major industrial countries, Japan has entered into the fewest PTAs. As documented in Chapter 35, the pressure of political and economic competition forced Japan to begin the negotiation of bilateral PTAs at the close of the 1990s, but the ambitious aims of this policy have been constrained by weak political leadership and by a strong farm lobby that is resistant to liberalization. Japan has pursued a cautious and reactive policy negotiating agreements that offer minimal agricultural concessions while seeking to eliminate trade diversion and counter the rising influence of China. However, the Trump Administration's withdrawal from the TPP has unexpectedly thrust Japan into the unusual role of leading talks to liberalize trade and investment in the Asia-Pacific.

Finally, Australia has pursued a unique approach towards trade agreements. As Chapter 36 shows, Australia's approach to PTAs started with surrounding Pacific island nations, before turning to the 21st-century pattern of proliferating trade agreements outside the WTO. The trend is occurring as part of Australia's desire for economic diversification beyond primary product exports in a world that is becoming increasingly fragmented along ever more complex international value chains.

When this volume was ordinally conceived in the latter part of 2016, Brexit had just occurred, and populism in Europe and the USA seemed to be on the ascendency. At the time, a tide of protectionism, economic nationalism and anti-trade policies appeared to be intensifying to the point where the old post-Second World War international order appeared to be crumbling. For the most part, Brexit aside, the chapters in this volume paint a more optimistic picture. The TPP is not dead, and the Trump Administration is even considering possible membership thereof.

Of the possible NAFTA scenarios – capitulation by one side or another, constructively upgrading and modernization of NAFTA, withdrawal, or muddling through – the latter is by far the most likely. In future, NAFTA may not be called NAFTA, but US/Mexico trade will not decline significantly and may even continue its logical expansion.

If anything, the realities of Brexit and the possible US withdrawal from the international system has served as a reality check. While US intentions remain unclear, most countries appear inclined to respond with creative solutions to fix the existing system rather than merely to withdraw from it.

2

Regional trade agreements
Myths and misconceptions[1]

Kati Suominen

Regional trade agreements (RTAs) have proliferated around the world over the past decades. As of June 2017 445 RTAs had been notified to the World Trade Organization (WTO), of which 279 are in effect. All members of the WTO belong to at least one RTA. The share of world trade that flows between pairs of countries that share an RTA is well over 40 per cent. For the most prolific integrators such as Chile, Peru, Mexico, the Republic of Korea (South Korea) and Singapore, RTAs govern most of their trading relationships. RTAs matter to world trade, and they are here to stay.

The proliferation of RTAs has reshaped the patterns of economic integration. In the past, most RTAs were north–north agreements negotiated among advanced economies. Over the past two decades, however, RTAs have grown to include a wide variety of north–south and south-south agreements. In addition, RTAs have over time grown deeper – more liberalizing and more encompassing in trade disciplines. Following the conclusion in 1994 of the North American Free Trade Agreement (NAFTA), which included extensive binding commitments across issue areas such as market access for goods, investment, trade in services, intellectual property rights (IPRs), and competition policy, the number of such deep agreements has grown significantly. Today, more and more RTA partners are test-driving rules also for the digital era, such as on ecommerce regulations, data privacy rules, and intellectual property of digital products. RTAs, in short, are continuing as laboratories for trade disciplines that countries are very hard-pressed to agree to multilaterally at the WTO.

Granted, there have been major challenges of late, reflecting a sour mood around globalization. The Trump Administration famously pulled the USA out of the Trans-Pacific Partnership (TPP) that had already been signed by the Obama Administration, while the Transatlantic Trade and Investment Partnership (TTIP) talks are on ice. A new leading trader, the People's Republic of China, is forging agreements in Asia, most notably the Regional Comprehensive Economic Partnership. Although none of these agreements is moving as fast as free traders would wish, it is a fact that the trade policymaking of most countries and companies, RTAs and plurilateral agreements command a central position.

It is not new that RTAs are politically contentious – most RTAs result from hard-won battles among various coalitions, perhaps most famously export-driven companies and labour unions fearing import penetration. RTAs have also survived many long-standing

9

Myth 1: RTAs are formed owing to lack of progress at the WTO

Remarkably, General Agreement on Tariffs and Trade (GATT) and WTO members have been forming RTAs while concluding seven multilateral trade rounds and establishing the WTO in 1994, and, since 2001, negotiating the Doha Round. One common explanation for the wildfire-like spread of RTAs over the past two decades is the lack of substantial progress in the WTO system since its establishment. Members have struggled to make progress under the WTO's standard negotiating modality, the single undertaking principle, whereby nothing is agreed until everyone agrees to everything. Also complicating multilateral talks and the Doha Round, in particular, is the changing political economy among WTO members, spawned by the rise of large emerging powers whose interests differ quite significantly from those of the main advanced economies.

This might lead one to conclude that RTAs happen because the WTO struggles. It is absolutely the case that RTAs offer countries a way out of the deadlock at multilateral level: they enable countries to make progress on trade liberalization and new rules during impasses at the WTO. Yet there are many more reasons why countries make RTAs – and why they would probably make RTAs even if WTO talks prospered. After all, unlike the WTO, RTAs enable countries to deepen access to their key markets and to customize trade rules with their specific trading partners, as well as to experiment with new rules that respond to the emerging needs of their exporters or importers. Many developing countries ask large countries such as the USA to form trade agreements as a means to attract foreign direct investment – by putting in place world-class investor protections and freeing bilateral trade.

There are countless further theories to explain the proliferation of RTAs that have nothing to do with the WTO, such as geopolitical considerations.[2] And, of course, RTAs encourage RTAs: as more and more RTAs are forged, outsiders face an urgent need to form agreements of their own so as not to miss out on the benefits that RTAs confer to others. Offering Mexico preferential access to the US market was attractive to US manufacturers, and caused NAFTA to drive Central America and Chile to ask for and make RTAs with the USA.

Moreover, the link between the WTO and RTAs could also be revisited. RTAs may have prospered because of the success, not the failure, of the multilateralism in liberalizing trade, which has empowered export lobbies and led them to demand deeper and faster integration with regional partners.

Myth 2: RTAs are bad for the WTO

A decades-old question concerning RTAs is whether they help or hinder multilateralism and most-favoured-nation (MFN) treatment. This is also a very important question. Incompatibilities between RTAs and the multilateral trading system could be interpreted as violating international trade law.

The 1948 GATT allows member countries to grant each other preferential treatment under free trade agreements (FTAs) or customs unions as long as certain conditions are met. These conditions were defined mainly in GATT Article XXIV, but also in the General Agreement on Trade in Services (GATS), other WTO agreements, and the so-called Enabling Clause, which exempts developing countries from MFN obligations in RTAs they form with each other. GATT Article XXIV stipulates that members notify their RTAs to what is now the WTO and that RTAs liberalize 'substantially all trade' among members 'in reasonable length of time' and not introduce new 'restrictive rules on commerce'.[3] The Article also demands open regionalism, thus preventing RTA members from raising barriers vis-à-vis third parties when liberalizing trade with each other.

Have WTO members complied with Article XXIV? The answer is negative in the sense that numerous RTAs among developing countries are exempted. But it also depends on how exactly the multilateral disciplines governing RTAs are interpreted. WTO members' interpretations of the Article vary widely.[4] For example, 'substantially all trade' has at least two different interpretations: a quantitative approach, geared towards a statistical benchmark, such as a percentage of trade between RTA parties, commonly suggested as 90 per cent, 85 per cent, or 80 per cent; and a qualitative approach, stipulating that no sector (or at least no major sector) should be kept from liberalization, with definitions of 'sector' varying widely.

Empirically, most agreements do meet some of these most common interpretations of 'substantially all trade' and 'reasonable length of time' – liberalization of 90 per cent of tariff lines and about the same amount of trade by year ten into the agreement.[5] However, there are also a number of outlier RTAs (in general among developing countries) that do not want to single out product categories (particularly sensitive sectors, such as agriculture, textiles and apparel, and footwear) that have prolonged tariff phase-outs and/or non-tariff barriers.

There also is no clear agreement on what constitutes 'other restrictive regulations of commerce'. RTAs have several rules that can qualify the extent of market access that tariff liberalization provides, such as tariff-rate quotas; special safeguards; anti-dumping regulations; non-tariff measures; and rules of origin. Such disciplines are often put in place for political reasons, as governments may be more willing to engage in deep tariff liberalization in RTAs when defensive instruments are also available. Complex rules of origin have been found to divert trade: by tying final goods producers to using intra-RTA sourcing even if it is inefficient, stringent rules of origin can ultimately augment intra-RTA production costs to the point where compliance costs exceed the benefits that RTA tariff preferences confer.[6] The jury has long been out, and is still out, on whether rules of origin violate Article XXIV. But the consequences of this debate are likely to be mild: no WTO member wants its RTAs to be scrutinized by other members, so none will raise questions about the RTAs of other members.

Taking a step further back, although RTAs have been blamed for sapping energy from the multilateral trading system, they have helped to save the global trading system in times of crisis. RTAs have emerged as incubators of new trade and trade-related rules in such areas as services trade, investment regulations, customs procedures and trade facilitation, environmental norms, IPRs, and ecommerce. In many of these areas, RTAs are unquestionably more advanced and sophisticated than the multilateral trading system, helping member countries to test-drive new rules matching today's market realities.

Myth 3: RTAs divert trade

Economists have long engaged in a contentious debate on whether RTAs are 'building blocks' or 'stumbling blocks' to multilateral trade liberalization. The building block camp argues that RTAs fuel the liberalizing logic of the multilateral system and enhance RTA members' trade with outsiders, while the stumbling block camp maintains that RTAs are discriminatory instruments that lead to trade diversion, by 'artificially' incentivizing companies in the RTA region to source from and export to RTA partners. Concerns over the impact of RTAs on outsiders have strengthened of late in the context of mega-regional agreements such as the TPP and the TTIP, as these agreements do not include most of the small developing countries that are keen to access regional and global supply chains.

While the empirical literature supports both the building and stumbling block camps, the scales have been long tilting in favour of the building block thesis. Recently, Mattoo *et al.* found that comprehensive, deep RTAs that substantially liberalize all trade show no trace of trade diversion; rather, they found that the inclusion of MFN provisions increases trade with non-member countries and lowers the negative impact from RTAs' relative tariff preferences on outsiders.[7] To the extent that RTAs stimulate growth and demand in the member economies, they tend to increase trade with outsiders as well – for example, the TPP can swell China's trade with TPP members due to the agreement's impact on demand in the member economies. Moreover, the concern that RTAs discriminate against outsiders has also been diluted as multilateral, regional and unilateral trade liberalization has progressed over recent decades.

RTAs have also been found to help to generate goodwill and greater economic interaction among members, which can be conducive to deeper integration and efforts that benefit *all* countries trading with any of the RTA members, such as infrastructure development, or harmonization of product standards across the entire trading block (e.g. NAFTA) or integrating national export promotion efforts and stock markets (e.g. the Pacific Alliance). RTAs have also helped to relax the political economy constraints in countries to trade liberalization in general by aggregating national pro-trade forces in the participating nations, as well as cementing political and strategic ties among the member economies.

However, there is some evidence of trade diversion in RTAs. This has occurred in some south-south RTAs where members have failed to commit to open regionalism and to liberalize trade with outsiders. Typically, however, trade diversion, if it happens, is sectoral. For example, sectors with restrictive rules of origin have been found to divert trade to the insiders, as they disincentivize the use of cheaper inputs from outsiders to RTAs. Blyde *et al.* estimate that, on average, countries source 15 per cent more of their foreign value added from members of a common RTA than from non-members, often thanks to restrictive rules of origin.[8]

Myth 4: RTAs hurt jobs

In marshalling votes against RTAs, some policymakers and unions have long loved to argue that RTAs kill jobs, either by resulting in import penetration or by inducing companies to move their manufacturing hubs to RTA partner markets to take advantage of low-cost labour or shoddy environmental protections. This debate, especially when it touches blue-collar factory workers, has been vicious in the USA; in such counties as Japan and South Korea, it is the rural labour force that has been fiercely lobbying against RTAs.

When implemented well, RTAs should have impacts – and result in some reallocation of labour and other resources to sectors where countries have comparative advantages. Yet the most important point about RTAs and jobs is that RTAs are only one and a relatively limited factor among the great many factors that shape job churn, employment patterns, employment levels, and wages. The drivers of job losses include major factors such as technological progress, with robots taking over manufacturing labour and increasingly also some white-collar jobs, recessions and lack of economic growth, imposition of rigid labour market regulations, and so on. In turn, one of the main determinants of wage levels is productivity, which is particularly determined by human capital and technology utilization. There are many other factors driving wages that have nothing to do with RTAs. For example, consider that US auto workers' salaries dropped by 40 per cent during the first decade of NAFTA implementation. It would be tempting to argue that NAFTA caused the salary drop. Yet the wage drop was not because of NAFTA; it was because of the shift of the US auto industry from northern states to the southern states that had lower union membership in auto manufacturing and thus less power in wage bargaining with auto manufacturers.[9]

Even when trade is to blame for job losses, an RTA may not be at fault. After all, RTAs are typically just one element in countries' trade and trade policy. The distributional impacts of trade have been textbook: dispersed gains and concentrated losses. Numerous studies indicate that every American is roughly US $3,000 richer *each year* because of America's post-war liberalization – unilaterally, multilaterally and in RTAs. The most striking evidence that trade does hurt some groups was produced by economists Daron Acemoglu, David Autor, David Dorn and Gordon Hanson, who found that net US manufacturing job losses due to the rise in import competition from China in 1999–2011 were as high as 2.4 million in the USA. That is not insignificant considering that net manufacturing job losses totalled 5.7 million.[10] But this is still a small share of the annual labour market churn of some 50 million hires and almost as many separations plus layoffs. The pressure on US jobs by Chinese imports may be due in part to China's accession to the WTO in 2001. However, there was no RTA in place between the USA and China. In short, among many other factors, trade, and sometimes RTAs, can undermine or kill some jobs, while generally benefiting most firms and all consumers. And it needs to be born in mind that imports do create jobs, even if their contribution is seldom calculated. For example, imports from China created many US jobs in logistics, transportation, warehousing and retail. Also, growth in US exports to China created jobs.

So, while RTAs may occasionally hurt some workers, they are very far from being the leading cause of job losses or declining wages, and typically their benefits far outweigh the gains.

Myth 5: RTAs create an unmanageable 'spaghetti bowl'

RTAs' impact on members and outsiders' trade volumes is not a straightforward calculation. One reason is that each new RTA adds complexity. Rather than centring production activities in a few locations, since the 1990s companies have segmented and spread production over a wide range of international sites. While RTAs are designed to lower the costs of cross-border business and global distribution networks, the 'spaghetti bowl' of multiple overlapping RTAs has created transaction costs to companies that operate global supply chains. Furthermore, small business exporters seeking to trade across many different markets, each with its own RTA, are mired in a maze of rules.

To be sure, there are 'RTA families' in which different RTAs have rather similar rules – this would be the case for the respective trade agreements of the EU and the USA which make the use of RTAs easier for US and EU companies than for companies in countries with a very diverse range of trade deals, such as the RTAs formed by Singapore or Mexico. However, it is true that the proliferation of RTAs has amplified the 'spaghetti bowl' problem. Studies indicate that some 60–80 per cent of large companies in diverse countries such as Peru, Singapore, Thailand, and Mexico would much prefer a single set of rules of origin to the numerous rules of origin regimes included in the RTAs signed by their respective governments.

The differences in rules across RTA theatres is one reason why the implementation of RTAs by customs and governments and the application of RTAs by firms is still suboptimal. Easing some of these transaction costs could yield major economic gains, particularly for smaller economies. It could also lead to higher preference utilization rates in RTAs. While preference utilization has improved over the past few years, it is far from optimal – a recent estimate puts it on average at 50 per cent.[11] However, there are great variations in preference utilization across companies of different sizes and export intensities, and also across sectors, with preferences in sectors with wide preference margins being more utilized than those where the preferential margin is closer to zero. There is also some learning by doing – so that preference utilization improves over time as firms learn to comply with rules of origin and other RTA rules.

In the near future, there may be similar 'spaghetti bowl' concerns regarding RTA rules of ecommerce: digital and ecommerce regulations that vary widely across RTA partner markets can add complexity to companies seeking to engage in digital trade across their countries' various RTAs, and discourage them from taking the full advantage of RTAs to globalize their digital businesses.

Myth 6: RTAs will forever Balkanize the global trading system

One of the critical challenges that lies ahead is how the WTO system and the RTA system can be made more synergistic and help to deepen and enhance each other. Given that the WTO's 'one size fits all' single undertaking approach no longer works, plurilateral agreements – broad-based agreements among subsets of the WTO membership – offer a path forward. They also provide a means to pioneer entirely new rules and market access in an otherwise clogged system.

Plurilateral agreements among large coalitions of the willing can be the right vehicles to enable a greater number of countries to sign on to tried and tested rules incubated in RTAs, and to sort out the RTA spaghetti – essentially creating dishes of lasagne. Forging larger integration zones can yield major economic gains, particularly for smaller countries. Michael Gasiorek and Patricia Augier have studied the Paneuro system – a vast system of cumulation implemented in 1999 across all of the bilateral FTAs the EU had with the various Eastern European nations – finding that cumulation increased trade between the Eastern European spokes by between 7 per cent and 22 per cent, and that the increase was between 14 per cent and 72 per cent for affected sectors. Harris and Suominen take the idea further to examine the effects of cumulation zones over the past 50 years, finding that adding partners representing 10 per cent of world output to a 'cumulation zone' was associated with a 3 per cent increase in the bilateral trade of small countries.[12] Importantly, this is a net effect that includes any reduction in trade due to trade diversion.

Plurilaterals are hardly pie in the sky. There are ongoing plurilateral negotiations towards a Trade in Services Agreement (TiSA) taking place outside the WTO. There are also calls for plurilateral agreements in areas such as investment as well as data flows, and ideas are being put forward for negotiating a 'sustainable' plurilateral and an agreement aimed at enabling global value chains.

One difficult question in driving for more multilateral application of RTAs' disciplines is dispute settlement. Many RTA disciplines have not been multilateralized, and, typically, they extend only to RTA members – and are not covered by the WTO's dispute settlement system. It is not clear where the locus of dispute settlement lies as world trading system pursues more plurilaterals.

Myth 7: RTAs should not be renegotiated

With the Trump Administration's insistence on renegotiating NAFTA, there have been concerns that NAFTA 2.0 would undermine the economic gains from the agreement and disrupt supply chains that companies have formed over the past few years – something that could have a major negative impact on countless US companies, in particular. However, the notion that trade agreements should be revised over time is meaningful. After all, 25 years ago, when the NAFTA talks were finalized, the priority for trade negotiators was, and has since been, to accommodate corporate supply chains by freeing trade and securing national treatment for foreign investors around the world.

Today, however, new technologies such as ecommerce, the cloud, 3D printing, and the Internet of Things are revolutionizing world trade and production, and creating new challenges for policymakers in areas such as intellectual property of 3D printed designs, regulation of cross-border data flows, and taxation of digital trade. If trade agreements are truly instruments for helping cross-border business, then trade agreements should indeed be upgraded to accommodate both the technology which facilitates trading and the precise make-up of the goods and services that are traded in this modern era.

One method to upgrade trade deals is to reopen them, as was the case with NAFTA; another, better method, is to build on commitments that already exist rather than reopening texts that have already been agreed. For example, the Pacific Alliance countries (Chile, Colombia, Mexico and Peru) have joined forces recently to negotiate as a bloc a trade agreement with Australia, Canada, New Zealand and Singapore, updating members' work especially on digital trade, small and medium-size enterprises (SMEs), and issues related to women's inclusion in trade. Still another method to upgrade RTAs is the mounting a new agreement that upgrades multiple trading relationships simultaneously, as has been the case of the TPP (which would have revised NAFTA de facto had the USA stayed in).

A bigger question is whether the traditional, multi-year, and hard law trade negotiations that are carried out to form RTAs serve the purpose they did in the past: rules agreed to today may prove outdated tomorrow, given the rapid technological changes. As such, the technology for negotiating trade agreements will probably need to change. For example, future commitments may more appropriately be developed as norms and codes of conduct.

Going forward there can also be constructive, flexible ways to engage new players in trade. For example, ecommerce has also opened up new opportunities for small businesses to engage in trade; the TPP has to that effect established a special committee to focus on SME issues, to ensure that policy aligned with technology is helping not hindering SMEs' trade.

There are also broader concerns related to RTA negotiations' transparency. While RTA negotiations require a certain degree of confidentiality, the lack of transparency during the ratification process risks becoming the main focus and could derail approval. Whatever the modality for future trade talks, those who talk need to find ways to do more information sharing as well.

Conclusion

This chapter has examined and mostly debunked the popular concerns surrounding RTAs. I have found that RTAs have in many ways greatly facilitated world trade. At times when multilateral talks have failed, RTAs have enabled countries to open access to new markets and emerge as incubators of new trade-related rules in such areas as services trade, investment regulations, IPRs, e-commerce, customs procedures and trade facilitation, and labour and environmental standards. RTAs have also propelled export-oriented, efficiency-seeking investment, fuelled the formation of value chains, and paved the way for cooperation among members in trade-related areas, such as customs modernization and infrastructure integration. In addition, RTAs have been found to help to relax the political economy constraints to further trade liberalization in participating nations and to cement national economic policies in areas such as competition policy.

This is not to say that the RTA architecture could not be better – it could certainly be streamlined and simplified to accommodate companies big and small in trade, such as via large mega-regional plurilaterals. In addition, the negotiation of RTAs, just like any other trade agreements, need to be rethought and streamlined in an era in which technologies change fast, and reshape the patterns, players and possibilities in trade.

Notes

1 This chapter draws on some of the conclusions of K. Suominen (2016) 'Enhancing Coherence and Inclusiveness in the Global Trading System in the Era of Regionalism', E15 Expert Group on Regional Trade Agreements and Plurilateral Approaches, Geneva: World Economic Forum, Geneva, January (online).

2 The literature is huge and only some representative studies are highlighted here. For more exhaustive literature reviews, see L. A. Winters (1996) 'Regionalism versus Multilateralism', World Bank Policy Research Working Paper No. 1687, Washington, DC: World Bank; R. Baldwin (2006) 'Multilateralising Regionalism: Spaghetti Bowls as Building Blocs on the Path to Global Free Trade', *World Economy*, 29(11): 1451–518; J. Bhagwati (2008) *Termites in the Trading System: How Preferential Agreements Undermine Free Trade*, New York: Oxford University Press; E. D. Mansfield (1998) 'The Proliferation of Preferential Trading Arrangements', *Journal of Conflict Resolution*, 42(5): 523–43; World Bank (2000) *Trade Blocs*, Oxford: Oxford University Press; World Trade Organization (2011) *World Trade Report 2011: The WTO and Preferential Trade Agreements: From Co-existence to Coherence*, Geneva: WTO; M. Schiff and A. L. Winters (2003) *Regional Integration and Development*, Washington, DC: World Bank; A. Estevadeordal and K. Suominen (2009) *The Sovereign Remedy: Trade Agreements in the Globalizing World*, Oxford: Oxford University Press.

3 For the purposes of Article XXVI, a customs union is understood as 'the substitution of a single customs territory for two or more customs territories, so that (i) duties and other restrictive regulations of commerce (except, where necessary, those permitted under Articles XI, XII, XIII, XIV, XV and XX) are eliminated with respect to substantially all the trade between the constituent territories of the union or at least with respect to substantially all the trade in products originating in such territories, and, (ii) … substantially the same duties and other regulations of commerce are applied by each of the members of the union to the trade of territories not included in the union'. A free trade area is 'a group of two or more customs territories in which the duties and other restrictive regulations of commerce (except, where necessary, those permitted under Articles XI, XII, XIII, XIV, XV and XX) are eliminated on substantially all the trade between the constituent territories in products originating in such territories'.

4 A. Estevadeordal and K. Suominen (2009) *The Sovereign Remedy: Trade Agreements in the Globalizing World*, Oxford: Oxford University Press.

5 Ibid.

6 As such, demanding rules of origin are akin to a tariff on the intermediate product levied by the country importing the final good. See R. Falvey and G. Reed (2000) 'Rules of Origin as Commercial Policy Instruments', Research Paper No. 2000/18, Centre for Research on Globalization and Labor Markets, University of Nottingham; P. J. Lloyd (2001) 'Rules of Origin and Fragmentation of Trade', in L. K Cheng and H. Kierzkowski (eds) *Global Production and Trade in East Asia*, Boston, MA: Kluwer Academic. However, whether specific rules of origin are actually restrictive depends on the availability of inputs in the RTA region and the ex ante production patterns.

7 A. Mattoo, A. Mulabdic and M. Ruta (2017) 'Trade Creation and Trade Diversion in Deep Agreements', Policy Research Working Paper WPS8206, Washington, DC: World Bank.

8 J. Blyde, A. Estevadeordal and K. Suominen (2013) 'Are Global Value Chains Really Global? Policies to Accelerate Countries' Access to International Production Networks', Think Piece for the E15 Initiative on Global Value Chains (December). Available at http://e15initiative.org/publications/a re-global-value-chains-really-global-policies-to-accelerate-countries-access-to-international-p roduction-networks/.

9 Gary Hufbauer, Cathleen Cimino-Isaacs and Tyler Moran (2014) 'NAFTA at 20: Misleading Changes and Positive Achievements', Policy Brief 14-14, Peterson Institute for International Economics, May.

10 D. Acemoglu, D. Autor, D. Dorn, G. Hanson and B Price (2014) 'Import Competition and the Great US Employment Sag', Working Paper (August), available at https://economics.mit.edu/files/10590.

11 Kazunobu Hayakawa, Kimura Fukunari and Nuttawut Laksanapanyakul (2015) 'Simple Measure of Preference Utilization: The Tariff Exemption Ratio', Working Paper. Available at www.jsie.jp/Annua l_Meeting/2015s_Hannan_Univ/pdf/A-2.pdf.

12 P. Augier, M. Gasiorek and C. Lai-Tong (2005) 'The Impact of Rules of Origin on Trade Flows', *Economic Policy*, CEPR, CES and MSH, 20(43): 567–624; J. Harris and K. Suominen (2008) *Connecting Regional Trade Agreements: What Are the Trade Effects?* Inter-American Development Bank, Washington, DC: Mimeo.

3

The WTO and regional/bilateral trade agreements

Kimberly Ann Elliott

For most of the 20th century, following the Second World War, non-discrimination and multilateralism were core pillars of the international, rules-based trading system. From in the early 1990s onwards, however, the number of regional and bilateral trade agreements in force increased more than ten-fold, from the low 20s to 279 in 2017. Moreover, the qualitative nature of these agreements changed, beginning with the USA dropping its staunch support for multilateralism and joining the trend. Later, the revolution in information and communications technology (ITC) allowed increased fragmentation in trade and the further globalization of supply chains, which raised a host of new issues that trade negotiators struggle to address.

The take-off in regionalism coincided with the launch of the World Trade Organization (WTO), which was designed to institutionalize and more effectively enforce the rules and negotiating processes of the General Agreement on Tariffs and Trade (GATT). The concerns about the impact of regional trade agreements (RTAs) on the multilateral trading system include the potential for excluded parties to suffer trade losses, as well as broader questions about the systemic impact. The GATT/WTO rules aim to mitigate potential negative effects, but the core question remains – can multilateralism and regionalism coexist peacefully?

Non-discrimination and multilateralism in the post-war trading system[1]

The USA and the United Kingdom began negotiating the rules and institutions they hoped would prevent another Great Depression and promote post-war reconstruction and economic prosperity well before the end of the Second World War. Along with the International Monetary Fund and the World Bank which were tasked with governing international financial markets and providing finance, they created the GATT to govern trade. The very first GATT article codified the so-called most-favoured-nation (MFN) principle as a core pillar of the rules-based trading system. Contrary to what the phrase might seem to suggest, the MFN principle promotes non-discrimination by requiring that each GATT signatory treat all other GATT parties in the same way as its 'most favoured' trade partner. US Secretary of State Cordell Hull had used this principle in bilateral negotiations to help to unwind the 1930s protectionist binge that deepened and lengthened the Great Depression.[2] Under MFN, any tariff cuts negotiated among two or more GATT parties are automatically extended to all other GATT members.

Along with Article III's national treatment principle, which requires that imports be treated similarly as domestically produced goods once past the border, MFN cemented non-discrimination's place at the centre of the multilateral trading system.

From the beginning there were exceptions, however. While the USA was a strong proponent of non-discrimination, the UK wanted to retain preferential trade arrangements with the Commonwealth. British negotiators eventually agreed to include non-discrimination as a core principle in what became the GATT, but they also insisted on an exception for imperial preferences. In explaining the shift, John Maynard Keynes, a prominent economist and member of the UK delegation negotiating the Bretton Woods arrangements for the post-war global economy, argued before the House of Lords:

> [The proposed policies] aim, above all, at the restoration of multilateral trade ... The basis of the policies before you is against bilateral barter and every kind of discriminatory practice. The separate blocs and all the friction and loss of friendship they must bring with them are expedients to which one may be driven in a hostile world where trade has ceased over wide areas to be cooperative and peaceful and where are forgotten the healthy rules of mutual advantage and equal treatment. But it is surely crazy to prefer that.[3]

Anticipating post-war efforts to promote integration in Europe, the GATT also included a broader exception, embodied in Article XXIV, permitting the negotiation of customs unions and free trade agreements (FTAs) under certain conditions.[4] The exception was initially limited to customs unions, which are relatively harder to negotiate than FTAs because the parties must agree on a common external tariff, as well as eliminating tariffs on trade among themselves. US negotiators agreed to expand Article XXIV to allow FTAs, reportedly because they were involved in FTA negotiations with Canada, something that would not come to fruition for four decades.[5] As of 2010, only a quarter of the regional agreements reported to the WTO were customs unions.[6]

Jagdish Bhagwati (op. cit.) reports that supporters of multilateralism and non-discrimination were willing to accept the exception for FTAs and customs unions because they believed that the conditions contained in Article XXIV would make these arrangements relatively rare. The aim of the conditions was to steer such agreements in the direction of maximizing trade creation among the parties to them and minimizing trade diversion at the expense of outsiders. The key conditions are that 'substantially all trade' should be covered, and that implementation of liberalization should occur over a relatively short period. With respect to customs unions, the new common external tariffs applying to third parties should not 'on the whole' be more restrictive than that which the parties had in place prior to the customs union.[7] Article XXIV also permits 'interim agreements' as long as they result in a customs unions or FTA within a 'reasonable time'.

However, the GATT did not clearly define these conditions and, in practice, they have been only loosely enforced. This was partly due to the USA prioritizing European integration for foreign policy reasons over the legal niceties of the GATT. Writing two decades after the GATT's creation, legal scholar Kenneth Dam concluded that only one of the dozen or so regional arrangements notified to the GATT met the requirements of Article XXIV (e.g. UK-Ireland).[8] Yet neither the GATT nor the WTO has ever rejected an RTA for inconsistency with Article XXIV.[9]

Although not the major focus of this chapter, it is worth considering two other types of 'plurilateral' agreements that are attracting attention. They are potential alternatives to multilateral negotiations that are subject to the WTO's consensus rule, by which any member can block agreement, or to bilateral and regional agreements that are outside the WTO. Exploration of these options has intensified since the Doha Round of WTO negotiations, launched in 2001, fell into its current zombie-like state – not alive but also not fully dead and buried.

One type of plurilateral involves a weakening of the norm of *unconditional* MFN. For the first three decades, GATT negotiations focused on cutting tariffs and they took place primarily among the so-called Quad: Canada, the European Economic Community (EEC), Japan and the USA. Less developed countries offered few if any concessions yet were able to benefit from tariff cuts made by the Quad via the (unconditional) MFN principle. As certain developing countries became more important actors in international trade in the 1960s and 1970s, and as GATT members turned their attention to non-tariff barriers, American negotiators (in particular) were increasingly frustrated by what they perceived as free riding. They sought a way to restrict the benefits of certain agreements to countries that were willing to accept the obligations of those agreements.

This led to what legal scholar John Jackson calls 'code-conditional' MFN during the Tokyo Round of multilateral trade negotiations (1973–79).[10] Under the Government Procurement Agreement, for example, signatories agreed to open procurement by designated public agencies to import competition, but only from signatories to the agreement that also agreed to open their procurement markets. As Jackson (op. cit.) notes, these codes do not explicitly limit MFN to signatories but they allow countries to impose conditionality on the benefits. Key WTO members are currently trying to negotiate further liberalization of trade in services using a similar plurilateral approach, with the expectation that any resulting market access benefits would be restricted to signatories. It remains unclear whether such an agreement could be brought under the WTO umbrella because that would require consensus from all members, whether they are parties to the agreement or not.

Another type of plurilateral agreement that is easier to incorporate under the WTO's rules is illustrated by the Information Technology Agreement. This is basically a sectoral version of the original GATT negotiating mode whereby a critical mass of countries – those accounting for the vast majority of trade in the relevant products – negotiate tariff cuts that are then extended to all WTO members on an unconditional MFN basis. WTO members have been working on a similar agreement on environmental goods for several years, but, as of early 2018, had been unable to agree on the scope of products to be included.

Trends in regionalism

For several decades, the major exception to trade multilateralism was the entity that began as the EEC. This six-member customs union expanded its geographic and functional scope to eventually become the 28-member single market now known as the European Union (EU). Over the years, the EU also negotiated RTAs with neighbours, such as Switzerland, Norway, and Iceland in the north, and Turkey in the south. It also negotiated RTAs with former colonies and members of the British Commonwealth, including in Africa, the Middle East, and, most recently, Canada. The EU has a range of other RTA negotiations in progress.

From 1990 onwards regional and bilateral trade agreements proliferated rapidly, with the USA finally participating. According to the WTO, there were 279 RTAs in force as of 20 June 2017 (combining goods, services, and accessions). The WTO also reports that notifications about all bilateral and regional arrangements increased from 124 during the period 1948–94, applying to goods only, to over 400 arrangements covering trade in goods or services (counted separately) just since 1995. The degree to which the expansion of Article XXIV to include FTAs became a major loophole is demonstrated by the fact that of the 242 agreements (excluding accessions) notified to the GATT/WTO, only ten are customs unions. And of those, only the EU is economically significant.[11] Figure 3.1 illustrates the sharp upward trend in RTAs beginning in the early 1990s and accelerating in the early 2000s.

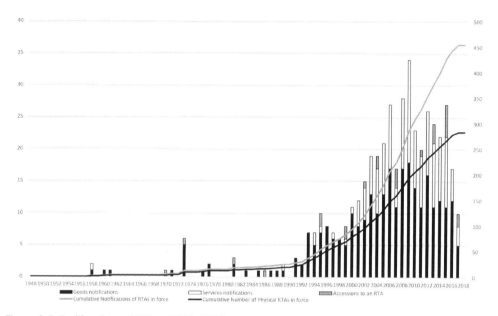

Figure 3.1 Proliferation of RTAs, 1948–2018
Source: WTO, Regional Trade Agreements Information System (RTA-IS). Available at https://rtais.wto.org/UI/PublicMaintainRTAHome.aspx (accessed 4 January 2018).

For much of the post-war period, the USA acquiesced in European integration efforts for foreign policy reasons, but itself eschewed bilateral and regional trade agreements. In the early 1980s US frustration built up over the failure to launch new GATT negotiations to address issues not resolved in the Tokyo Round (1973–79). American negotiators concluded the first bilateral FTA with Israel in 1984 and then launched negotiations that culminated in a more economically significant FTA with Canada in 1988.[12] The latter was expanded a few years later to include Mexico and become the North America Free Trade Agreement (NAFTA). The USA is now party to 14 FTAs with 20 countries. All but the agreements with Israel and Canada were concluded after 1990 and 12 of them are with neighbours in North and South America (Canada and Mexico; five Central American countries plus the Dominican Republic; Chile, Colombia, Panama and Peru). There is a cluster in North Africa and the Middle East, negotiated after the 11 September 2001 terrorist attacks perpetrated on the US mainland (Bahrain, Jordan, Morocco and Oman), plus Australia, the Republic of Korea and Singapore. Had President Donald Trump not rejected the Trans-Pacific Partnership (TPP) when he entered office in 2017, the number would have expanded to 25 (Brunei, Japan, Malaysia, New Zealand and Viet Nam, plus six others with whom the USA already had FTAs). President Trump also abandoned negotiations towards a Transatlantic Trade and Investment Partnership (TTIP) that his predecessor, Barack Obama, had launched.

Following notification of the Japan-Mongolia FTA in 2016, the WTO reports that every member is now party to at least one regional or bilateral trade agreement.[13] The EU is the most active RTA negotiator, with nearly 100 agreements in force, followed by East Asia with 80 RTAs. Other regions, with the exception of South America (57), are all below 50 in the number of RTAs in force (Figure 3.2).

It is important to note, however, that these agreements vary widely in terms of breadth and depth, and in the impact they have on trade and their potential effect on the multilateral trading system.

The WTO and trade agreements

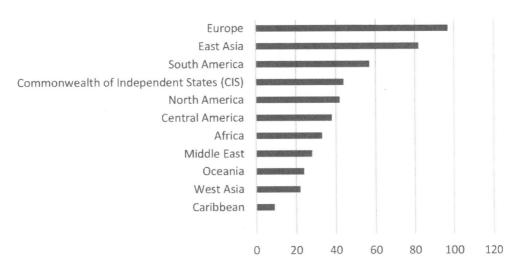

Figure 3.2 Physical RTAs in force, participation by region
Source: WTO, Regional Trade Agreements Information System (RTA-IS). Available at https://rtais.wto.org/UI/PublicMaintainRTAHome.aspx (accessed 4 January 2018).

WTO responses to the proliferation in RTAs[14]

Although members have challenged specific RTA provisions, neither the GATT nor the WTO has ever rejected one of these arrangements. Under the GATT, members appointed ad hoc working parties to review and debate the consistency of RTAs with Article XXIV conditions, but there was no standing body for ongoing monitoring and assessment. In response to growing concerns about the impact of proliferating RTAs on the multilateral system in the 1980s and early 1990s, GATT members adopted an understanding to clarify 'the criteria and procedures for the assessment of new or enlarged agreements' as part of the Uruguay Round agreement (1986–93). WTO members have continued since then to work to improve the transparency and beef up the monitoring of these agreements, including potential impacts on the multilateral system as a whole.

Moreover, the understanding specified that the 'reasonable time' before agreements are fully implemented should not be more than 10 years, unless there are exceptional circumstances. The understanding does not attempt to define a minimum standard for 'substantially all trade', but it does reiterate the importance of that criterion and notes that the exclusion of 'any major sector' reduces the trade-creating benefits of preferential arrangements.

With respect to customs unions, the understanding charged the WTO Secretariat with assessing the potential impact of the common external tariff on outsiders. Importantly, members agreed that the calculation should use applied rather than bound tariffs, which gives a more realistic picture of potential impact in the case of developing country parties that have bound tariffs at levels well above those they normally apply. The understanding also clarified the procedures that countries should follow in negotiating compensation for third parties whose exports face increased tariffs as a result of the new customs union. And it affirms that members can have recourse to dispute settlement procedures in cases that cannot be resolved through negotiation.

In February 2006 WTO members created a Committee on Regional Trade Agreements to examine agreements notified under Article XXIV, to develop procedures for doing so more effectively, and to 'consider the systemic implications of such agreements … for the multilateral trading system and the relationship between them'.[15] But continued disagreements over the interpretation of Article XXIV, inadequate information from FTA parties, and the fact that Committee reports had to be approved by all WTO members (including those party to FTAs under review), meant that no reports were formally adopted.

In December 2006 the WTO General Council adopted, on a provisional basis, a new mechanism to enhance the transparency of RTAs that the new Committee on Regional Trade Agreements would oversee. Under the mechanism, members are to expeditiously notify the WTO Secretariat about new RTA negotiations and provide information about the timing and scope of the agreement, including the text of the agreement and any annexes once they are completed. FTA parties are also required to provide detailed data on tariff changes under the agreement that the Committee can use to assess the impact on third parties. The WTO also created a special website to make available the texts and other information about RTAs.

Implications of regionalism

There are two aspects to the potential costs and opportunities of RTAs from a WTO perspective: the net impact on global trade and welfare, and the political impact on the strength and credibility of the multilateral system itself. The WTO's primary role (and that of the GATT before it) is to promote freer global trade. But its role in establishing a multilateral rules-based system founded on non-discrimination is of at least equal importance for smaller, usually poorer, developing countries that would otherwise be subject to the protectionist whims of larger, more powerful trade partners. Moreover, the poorest countries are seldom invited to join economically significant RTAs and could find themselves disadvantaged in major markets.

The two key questions about regionalism are, therefore, whether it is leading toward freer global trade (on net), and whether it is complementing or competing with the WTO. The answers depend to a large degree on why it is occurring. Are RTAs laboratories for experimenting with rules in new areas that facilitate deeper economic integration and lay the foundation for multilateral agreement in the future? Or is the trend primarily driven by frustration with the stagnation of negotiations at the WTO and are regional negotiations seen as an *alternative* to the multilateral system?

Economic welfare and trade effects of regionalism

The net welfare effects of RTAs are only positive if the trade created among the parties is not primarily diverted from more efficient external producers. And even when the trade creation effects are positive for the parties, there will still be negative effects for third party exporters facing increased discrimination. As RTAs proliferate, the economic effects also depend on the balance between the reductions in tariffs and other trade barriers, and the transactions costs associated with increased complexity – a phenomenon frequently called the 'spaghetti bowl' effect. Richard Baldwin and Phil Thornton note that this 'spaghetti bowl' can be a significant problem in a world of global supply chains where trade is increasingly fragmented.[16] Since both the economic and 'spaghetti bowl' effects of RTAs are addressed in detail in Chapter 5 in this volume, I discuss them only briefly here.

As noted, the conditions imposed by Article XXIV are designed to promote customs unions and FTAs which create more trade than they divert. When such objectives are achieved economists generally conclude that these arrangements will improve the welfare of the countries participating with limited damage for third parties and could, therefore, contribute positively to the goal of freer global trade. Although it is difficult to isolate the effect of trade agreements, it

The WTO and trade agreements

is also possible that RTAs increase growth and thereby increase trade and confer benefits on outsiders as well. A detailed analysis of 76 RTAs in the mid-2000s found that most were meeting the Article XXIV conditions of eliminating barriers on 'substantially all' trade (defined in this case as at least 90 per cent of tariff lines), and were doing so in ten years or less. This and other studies also find, however, that the agriculture sector frequently is an exception.[17]

When it comes to the third core requirement, that generally barriers to third parties should not go up, things become more complicated. Given that FTAs are far more common than customs unions, it might not seem that this should be the case. With FTAs, there is no need to negotiate a common external tariff and the tariff applied to non-parties generally should not change. But there are other channels through which discrimination against outsiders can increase under FTAs. The first potential problem arises when developing countries apply tariffs below the maximum levels they are committed not to exceed under WTO rules. That gives them the flexibility to raise barriers against third parties while implementing or maintaining preferential tariffs for FTA partners. A prominent example is Mexico's trade policy response to the peso crisis in 1994 when it did exactly that in the wake of implementing NAFTA.[18] Other studies have found that FTA partners use remedies against allegedly unfair trade (anti-dumping and countervailing duties) more often against outsiders than one another.[19]

FTA partners also often discriminate against outsiders by manipulating rules of origin. These agreements need rules of origin to prevent goods produced elsewhere from being exported to the lowest-tariff FTA party and then being re-exported duty-free to a party with a higher external tariff on those goods. FTA partners often craft rules of origin to protect sensitive industries. US agreements, for example, typically require that apparel exporters in partner countries use American (or other regional) yarn and fabric before the final product is considered eligible for duty-free treatment. EU trade arrangements often use a slightly less restrictive 'double transformation' rule for apparel, meaning that the fabric (but not the yarn) must be sourced in the EU or regionally.[20] Protectionist rules of origin raise production costs for parties to the agreement and divert trade from others. Even when not protectionist, differing rules across often overlapping agreements contribute to the 'spaghetti bowl' problems discussed below.

Writing two decades ago, Jeffrey Frankel concluded that the weight of the evidence suggested that RTAs were generally consistent with freer global trade because RTA members 'have tended to increase trade with nonmembers even as they intensify trade (even more) with one another'.[21] A decade and a half later, and with many more RTAs in place, WTO economist Jo-Ann Crawford concluded there was little evidence 'to suggest that increased market access in merchandise goods [among RTA partners] leads to a more favourable trading environment for third parties'.[22]

Pravin Krishna concluded that, while there was evidence in a number of studies showing trade diversion from RTAs, they might not have important effects on trade overall.[23] He noted that, while the WTO's 2011 *World Trade Report* showed that intra-PTA trade had roughly doubled between 1990 and 2007 to 35 per cent (excluding intra-EU trade), that was not a good measure of preferential trade. The WTO report noted that a significant portion of global trade already takes place on an MFN-zero basis, thanks to past liberalization. As a result of that, and the fact that there are often exceptions for sensitive products, the amount of trade under RTAs that is potentially preferential is only 16 per cent and the share that benefits from preference margins greater than 10 per cent was less than 2 per cent (4 per cent if intra-EU trade is included). The report also found that two-thirds of tariffs over 15 per cent are not lowered under PTAs.[24]

As RTAs have proliferated, however, other questions have come to the fore. One important debate is over the impact of RTAs on increasingly fragmented global supply chains. An argument in favour of RTAs is that they are a more efficient way of making progress on 'deep integration' issues that these modern supply chains need in order to function well. That benefit is undercut, however, by the increased transaction costs associated with overlapping and inconsistent RTAs with different tariff rates for the same product and different rules of origin. According to Baldwin and Thornton (summarizing a conference on regionalism co-organized by the WTO), the 'spaghetti bowl' effect has become a major concern for the international business community.[25]

Since Frankel's relatively positive analysis in the mid-1990s, RTAs have proliferated while WTO negotiations have been largely moribund. This gives increased salience to the political economy concerns that RTAs are more likely to be stumbling blocks than building blocks for the non-discriminatory, rules-based multilateral trading system.

Systemic implications of regionalism[26]

As with the net economic effects of trade creation and diversion, the effects of regionalism on the multilateral trading system depend in part on the particular features of each RTA and the economic and political effects of the resulting changes in trade policy within the area. Beyond that, there are two other arguments for why RTAs are seen as supportive of the multilateral system, or at least of global trade integration. The first is that regional negotiations have in important instances triggered 'competitive liberalization' episodes whereby excluded parties pursue multilateral negotiations to offset the discriminatory effects of RTAs. The more recent argument in favour of RTAs, particularly the 'mega-regional' agreements that President Barack Obama was negotiating with partners throughout the Pacific and across the Atlantic, is that they are more likely than the WTO to make progress on 'deep integration' issues that should be at the centre of 21st-century trade policy.

At country level, the political economy arguments about the effects of RTAs on support for multilateral liberalization tend to centre around the effects of preference erosion and the potential for diversion of negotiating resources. If special interests are powerful enough to influence negotiations so as to protect themselves, for example with restrictive rules of origin, they then have a strong incentive to avoid multilateral liberalization that could undermine that advantage. In north-south RTAs, developing countries are often negotiating to preserve their access to important developed country markets. Once inside that preferential zone, their exporters will be leery of further liberalization – either multilaterally or regionally – that could erode the advantage they have vis-à-vis third party competitors. Another practical concern is that negotiating resources in most countries are limited and a shift to focusing on regional or bilateral negotiations will inevitably distract from multilateral negotiations.

The Article XXIV conditions are designed to weaken the manipulation of RTAs for protectionist purposes in ways that could weaken the incentives for also pursuing multilateral trade liberalization. And, if those conditions are fully implemented, regional free trade could have the effect of weakening import-competing sectors, which might reduce their political influence while strengthening that of exporters who gain from regional liberalization and could gain even more from further multilateral liberalization.

Because they are inherently discriminatory, even when fully compliant with Article XXIV, RTAs might also spur third party exporters to push for multilateral trade openings to reduce the degree of discrimination they face. C. Fred Bergsten is one of the strongest proponents of regional negotiations as a positive global force via 'competitive liberalization.' He argues that the NAFTA negotiations, along with the efforts by President Bill Clinton to pursue regional trade liberalization through the Asia-Pacific Economic Cooperation process, demonstrated that the USA had alternatives to GATT negotiations and thereby helped to bring the struggling

Uruguay Round (1986–93) to a successful conclusion.[27] Others note that European integration efforts, though supported for foreign policy reasons, repeatedly spurred US negotiators to seek multilateral liberalization under GATT auspices.

Another form of competitive liberalization can occur when outsiders seek to offset trade discrimination by joining an RTA from which they were initially excluded. It has been argued that, in theory at least, this process could ultimately lead to global free trade as new countries successively seek to join. 'Open regionalism', which makes it relatively easy for third parties to accede to RTAs, has also been proposed as a means of promoting this form of competitive liberalization and turning the 'spaghetti bowl' into a 'plate of lasagna'. Some economic models, however, show this process stopping well short of global free trade and, instead, ending in a handful of competing blocs that, collectively, lower global welfare.[28] In practice, outside of the EU, accessions to existing RTAs or customs unions have been relatively rare.

Another impetus for RTAs has been the desire to modernize trade agreements and develop disciplines in new areas that would help global supply chains to operate more efficiently. The dramatic fall in the cost of ICT permitted corporations to lengthen their supply chains, sourcing components and assembling them into final products wherever it was most cost-effective to do so. But this fragmentation also puts a premium on reducing trade costs beyond tariffs as it often involves cross border investment and access to financial and other services, as well as the need to move physical inputs around the world. Richard Baldwin argues that this 21st-century regionalism is fundamentally different from that of the 1990s and that it has quite different implications for the global trading system.[29]

These 'deep integration' agreements strive to go beyond and strengthen WTO rules that open services markets and protect intellectual property and foreign investment, as well as negotiating issues not yet broached at the WTO, such as competition policy, digital trade, regulatory cooperation, labour standards, and environmental protection. The WTO 2011 *World Trade Report* shows that the former issues, called WTO+, are increasingly included in RTAs and are often enforceable. RTAs also increasingly include issues in the beyond WTO categories, often called WTO-X, but they are more often hortatory and emphasize cooperation, rather than being legally enforceable.[30]

The main argument for pursuing deep integration agreements regionally or bilaterally is that the Doha Round of WTO negotiations is stuck on less and less important 20th-century issues, and that members cannot even reach agreement on those. Progress on emerging 21st-century issues should, therefore, be pursued by plurilateral groups of like-minded countries that can progress faster. Proponents also argue that these deep integration agreements are unlikely to pose serious problems for outsiders, and could even have benefits, because many of these provisions are of a regulatory nature and are likely to be implemented on an MFN, non-discriminatory basis. They also argue that if these rules are part of 'mega-regional' trade agreements, such as the proposed TPP and TTIP, that cover a large amount of global trade, then they can serve as templates for global trade rules when other WTO members are ready to negotiate them.

In early 2018 this rosy scenario seemed less likely than it did in 2016 when the USA and 11 other Pacific nations signed the TPP. One of the first actions that President Trump took on assuming office in January 2017 was to withdraw the USA from the TPP and stop negotiating TTIP. The other 11 TPP parties are trying to adapt and adopt the TPP among themselves. But even if they succeed, it will have far less global significance without the USA. And, even if a future American president decides to rejoin the TPP and bring TTIP to a successful conclusion, the result is unlikely to provide a clear basis for global rules. The TPP largely reflects US preferences, while the differences between the USA and the EU on key issues are significant. The likely result is a TTIP that diverges in important ways from the TPP, thereby confusing rather than clarifying what global rules could look like.[31]

The relatively greater utility of RTAs, including the mega-regionals, in addressing deep integration thus remains to be seen. There is no question that RTAs have pushed beyond the WTO in liberalizing traditional trade barriers (at least outside of agriculture) and, to some degree, in opening services markets, reducing barriers to foreign investment, and protecting intellectual property. It should be noted, however, that these agreements often involve asymmetric bargaining power with smaller developing countries accepting provisions that they had (collectively) resisted in multilateral negotiations. In some cases, developing countries are willingly embracing provisions in RTAs in the hope that they will reinforce domestic economic reforms and send a positive signal to potential foreign investors. In other cases, such as stronger patent protection for pharmaceuticals, the benefits for developing countries are questionable.

In the WTO-X areas, and especially in the behind the border, regulatory areas purported to be so important for global supply chains, progress has often been tentative. As noted in the WTO 2011 *World Trade Report*, the provisions in WTO-X areas are frequently unenforceable. Rather, they are often hortatory and call for little beyond information sharing and cooperation to address unintended obstacles to trade created by differences in regulatory approaches.[32]

Whither trade policy?

The WTO's 2011 *World Trade Report* concluded that neither theory nor empirical evidence could show definitively whether the proliferation of RTAs had been good or bad for the multilateral system. The weight of the evidence suggests that major RTAs have been trade-creating, and therefore positive for participants, while trade diversion at the expense of outsiders has been relatively modest. But over the past decade, RTAs have proliferated while the WTO's ability to negotiate anything more than narrow agreements on relatively minor issues has seemingly unravelled. These parallel trends underscore the concerns that regionalism could be an alternative, rather than a complement, to the WTO.

Richard Baldwin argues instead that the 21st-century trade regime will need to be a 'two-pillar' system that relies on both multilateral and regional/plurilateral approaches in order to work smoothly. The WTO would stay focused on shallow integration – continuing to monitor, enforce and further liberalize rules on traditional trade barriers – while mega-regionals or other plurilaterals (such as the negotiations on a new Trade in Services Agreement) address deep integration issues that are important for global value chains.[33] The WTO would also still have a role in promoting transparency and assessing the impact of RTAs to ensure that they minimize negative effects.

At the end of the second decade of the 21st-century, however, both trade negotiating pillars seem shaky. The Doha Round is dead but not buried, and this is blocking a new set of more up-to-date negotiations. The TPP is going ahead, but without the USA, and TTIP has disappeared for the moment. Unlike in the Great Depression, the trading system largely held during and after the Great Recession of 2007–09, but not without strains that continue to undermine political support for trade in key countries. The relevant question may not be whether regionalism or multilateralism offers the best path forward, but whether conflict will replace cooperation as the dominant force in international trade relations.

Notes

1 In recalling this history, I benefited particularly from John Jackson's seminal work (1991), *The World Trading System: Law and Policy of International Economic Relations*, Cambridge, MA: MIT Press, particularly chs 2 and 6.

The WTO and trade agreements

2 A brief history of the MFN principle can be found in Jeffrey A. Frankel (1997) *Regional Trading Blocs in the World Economic System,* Washington, DC: Institute for International Economics, pp. 2–3.

3 Quoted in Jagdish Bhatwati (2008) *Termites in the Trading System: How Preferential Agreements Undermine Free Trade,* A Council on Foreign Relations Book, New York: Oxford University Press, pp. 2–5.

4 World Trade Organization (2011) *World Trade Report,* Geneva: WTO, p. 51.

5 Bhagwati, *Termites in the Trading System,* ch. 2.

6 I have chosen to adopt the WTO approach of using regional trade agreements to encompass a variety of preferential trade agreements, even though they do not always involve countries from the same region. I will also use it to refer to both customs unions and free trade agreements, unless there is a reason to distinguish the two.

7 Jackson, *World Trading System,* p. 141.

8 Cited in Bhagwati, p. 23.

9 Frankel, *Regional Trading Blocs,* p. 4; WTO, *World Trade Report,* pp. 183–84.

10 Jackson, pp. 136–38, 55–57.

11 WTO (2011) 'Some Figures on Regional Trade Agreements Notified to the GATT/WTO and in Force', Summary Tables from the Regional Trade Agreements database. Available at www.coursehero.com/file/p6afvl2/Some-Figures-on-Regional-Trade-Agreements-notified-to-the-GATTWTO-and-in-force/ (accessed 4 January 2018).

12 Jackson, pp. 146–47. See also I. M. Destler and Marcus Noland, 'Constant Ends, Flexible Means' (pp. 25–26) and Gary Clyde Hufbauer and Jeffrey J. Schott, 'Trade Policy at the Institute: 25 Years and Counting' (pp. 41–42), both in Michael Mussa (ed.) (2006) *C. Fred Bergsten and the World Economy,* Washington, DC: Peterson Institute for International Economics.

13 See the WTO topics page on RTAs at www.wto.org/english/tratop_e/region_e/region_e.htm (accessed 4 January 2018).

14 This section draws on WTO, *World Trade Report,* pp. 183–85 and the WTO website page on RTAs.

15 WTO, Committee on Regional Trade Agreements, WT/L/127, Geneva, 7 February 1996.

16 Richard Baldwin and Phil Thornton (2008) *Multilateralising Regionalism: Ideas for a WTO Action Plan on Regionalism,* Geneva: The Graduate Institute; Swiss National Centre of Competence in Research, Trade Regulation, Centre for Economic Policy Research.

17 Ibid., pp. 12–13. Also see Jo-Ann Crawford, 'Market Access Provisions on Trade in Goods in Regional Trade Agreements', Staff Working Paper ERSD-2012–20, Geneva: WTO, 2012, pp. 11–12.

18 Bhagwati, pp. 53–54.

19 Thomas J. Prusa and R. the (2010) 'Protection Reduction and Diversion: PTAs and the Incidence of Antidumping Disputes', NBER Working Paper No. 16276, Cambridge, MA: National Bureau of Economic Research; WTO, *Report,* pp. 180–81.

20 Kimberly Ann Elliott (2016) 'Rules of Origin in Textiles and Apparel', in Cathleen Cimino-Isaacs and Jeffrey J. Schott (eds) *Trans-Pacific Partnership: An Assessment,* Washington: Peterson Institute for International Economics.

21 Frankel, p. 209.

22 Crawford.

23 Pravin Krishna (2012) 'Preferential Trade Agreements and the World Trade System: A Multilateralist View', NBER Working Paper No. 17840, Cambridge, MA: NBER.

24 WTO, *Report,* pp. 64, 73, 125.

25 Baldwin and Thornton, ch. 5. For more on the rules that 21st-century global supply chain trade demands, see Richard Baldwin (2011) '21st Century Regionalism: Filling the Gap between 21st Century Trade and 20th Century Trade Rules', WTO Staff Working Paper, No. ERSD-2011–08, Geneva: WTO.

26 This section draws on Frankel (ch. 10), Bhagwati (pp. 86–88), and WTO, *Report* (Part II.E).

27 C. Fred Bergsten (1996) 'Competitive Liberalization and Global Free Trade: A Vision for the 21st Century', Working Paper 96–12, Washington, DC: Institute for International Economics.

28 Frankel, pp. 221–23; see also Baldwin and Thornton.

29 Baldwin, '21st Century Regionalism'.

30 WTO, *Report,* pp. 128–33, based on the typology in Henrik Horn, Petros Mavroidis and André Sapir (2010) 'Beyond the WTO? An Anatomy of EU and US Preferential Trade Agreements', *World Economy,* 33(11): 1565–88.

31 Todd Allee and Andrew Lugg (2016) 'Who Wrote the Rules for the Trans-Pacific Partnership?' *Research and Politics,* July–September: 1–9; Kimberly Ann Elliott (2016) 'How Much 'Mega' in the

Mega-Regional TPP and TTIP: Implications for Developing Countries', CGD Policy Paper, Washington, DC: Center for Global Development.

32 See also Elliott, 'How Much "Mega"'.

33 Richard Baldwin (2016) 'The World Trade Organization and the Future of Multilateralism', *Journal of Economic Perspectives*, 30(1), Winter: 95–116. See also Kyle Bagwell, Chad P. Bown and Robert W. Staiger (2015) 'Is the WTO Passé?' Policy Research Working Paper 7304, Washington, DC: World Bank.

4

International agreements on intellectual property rights

TRIPS and beyond

Keith E. Maskus

Introduction[1]

The period since 1995 has seen the greatest expansion of global protection for intellectual property rights (IPRs) in history. This fundamental policy shift covers multiple dimensions, including bringing most of the world comprehensively into a more harmonized system, extending legal standards and enforcement expectations across virtually all areas of intellectual property, and tightly linking such regulations to international trade and investment policy. It is no exaggeration to state that IPRs have been elevated from an obscure bit of backwater regulatory policy to the top rank of international structural concerns. Policymakers in nearly all countries now posit that effectively protecting IPRs is a *sine qua non* for promoting economic growth and a shift towards more innovative economies.

This major regime change is the outcome of several international policy initiatives, beginning with the Agreement on Trade-Related Aspects of Intellectual Property Rights (TRIPS), a foundational component of the World Trade Organization (WTO). Policy emphasis on international protection of IPRs quickly migrated to other international organizations, particularly the World Intellectual Property Organization (WIPO) and, especially, to regional trade agreements negotiated chiefly by the USA and the European Union (EU). On the strength of such accords, rights holders generally enjoy stronger and more harmonized global protection for their patents, copyrights and trademarks.

These changes are the focus of this chapter. The next section describes the primary elements of TRIPS and how it has transformed protection in the developing world. The third section addresses the importance of preferential trade agreements (PTAs) in pushing the protective agenda forward. A final concluding section briefly mentions the mixed empirical evidence on how effective the new global regime seems to be in encouraging innovation and trade in technology, key objectives of such agreements.

TRIPS and the WTO

The TRIPS Agreement, adopted as Annex 1C of the single undertaking establishing the WTO, is the most important global accord on IPRs for three reasons. First, it is by far the most comprehensive agreement ever reached regarding policy standards and government responsibilities in this realm. Second, because membership in the WTO is virtually universal it establishes minimum protection norms on a global scale. Third, because TRIPS is covered by the WTO's dispute resolution mechanism it is the only multilateral accord on IPRs that can be enforced through legal action and trade sanctions.[2] TRIPS is therefore the bulwark of the international regime and the basis on which most national legal systems are constructed.

Before considering specific elements of TRIPS, two basic principles about IPRs as regulatory devices should be clarified. First, the standards and policies defining the scope of IPRs are commercial regulations applying to all entities using them. They differ considerably from tariffs and other elements of border trade regulations. Such restrictions are widely recognized as inefficient and costly. Their reduction or removal generally increases welfare in all trading partners, even if it redistributes income within countries. In contrast, there is no clear standard of optimality in the case of IPRs. A country that broadens its patent or copyright protection may generate gains in technology transfer and innovation but may also suffer losses in access and higher-cost imitation. Even this trade-off depends on numerous socio-economic factors, including national income levels and technological developments. Countries vary widely in their attitudes towards IPRs and an agreement to raise standards globally may benefit some trading partners but harm others.

Second, although TRIPS is a multilateral agreement, countries retain considerable ability to determine the precise specifications by which IPRs are protected according to their own legal systems and practices. Patents, copyrights, trademarks and other provisions are *national* rights, not *international* rights. Definitions of patentable subject matter vary across countries, as do limitations on patent scope. There are different national limitations and exceptions (L&Es) on the scope of copyrights. Some countries bar unauthorized reimportation of goods protected by IPRs, while others do not.

Although IPRs are nationally determined, TRIPS does mandate that WTO member nations establish and enforce a set of minimum legal standards, including in such untraditional areas as computer software and geographical indications. These requirements have prompted policy changes in many nations, especially in the developing world. Nonetheless, there remain numerous so-called TRIPS flexibilities that remain widely discussed in public debates. For example, WTO members may deploy measures needed to protect public health and to pursue the public interest in sectors deemed critical to social and technological development.

Such flexibilities notwithstanding, TRIPS markedly raises the average level of protection in the world and holds countries more accountable.[3] In that context, it is unlikely that many of its stipulations would have been voluntarily adopted in the bulk of developing countries, given their continuing status as importers of intellectual property.[4] Many developing countries were willing to accede to TRIPS in return for improved market access for their exports and the expectation that it would raise inflows of investment and technology.[5]

Major requirements of TRIPS[6]

TRIPS requires WTO members to have IPRs laws and procedures that are non-discriminatory, applying both the national treatment and most-favoured-nation (MFN) principles, subject to minor exceptions. Under MFN, any country adopting stronger protection for intellectual property must immediately and unconditionally apply those new standards to entities of all WTO partners. This principle applies to the so-called TRIPS-Plus standards that countries may adopt through a preferential trade agreement, making such protection available beyond the PTA members alone.[7] This feature means that recent PTAs have ratcheted upward the protection of IPRs globally.

Copyrights

The TRIPS Agreement expanded the scope of copyright protection for authors, composers and other creators, and introduced new protected subject matter. For example, it requires countries to offer copyrights for a minimum period covering the life of an author or creator plus 50 years, or, where no author is identified, for 50 years. WTO members are free to adopt longer protection, as many have done. For example, the basic period in the USA is life of the author plus 70 years, or 120 years from creation for works developed for hire or made anonymously.

TRIPS introduced significant new global standards beyond duration. For example, it requires that computer programs be copyrighted as literary expressions. It also mandates that compilations of data be protected where their accumulation and arrangement can be considered intellectual creations. However, the Agreement does not require that new software be patented, as in the USA and the EU.[8] Neither does it obligate governments to provide patent-like protection for databases, as exists in the EU. TRIPS does require that copyright owners be permitted to exclude films and computer programs from rental markets. Finally, TRIPS clarifies that artists may prevent recording and broadcasting of their performances; music producers may deny reproduction of recorded works; and broadcasters may deter unauthorized use of their works, such as television programmes.

Despite these changes, TRIPS failed to deal effectively with issues of copyright protection in the digital age, which largely arrived after 1995. Thus, the music, film, game and software industries have worked tirelessly in the intervening period to expand and sharpen their rights to limit unauthorized downloading and file-sharing, both in national legislation and as a component of PTAs. Opposition to expanding such rights has been raised by certain civil society groups and university and public libraries.

Patents

TRIPS ushered in several notable minimum standards regarding patent protection. First, patents must be awarded for at least 20 years, making TRIPS the first international agreement with a minimum patent length. Second, patents must be available for both products and processes, addressing the long-standing problem that many developing economies had only offered the latter for pharmaceuticals and chemicals. Third, all fields of technology must be eligible for protection, with exceptions for inventions that may harm public order, threaten human, animal or plant health, or seriously harm the environment. Countries may also exclude surgical, diagnostic and therapeutic treatments, and may refuse patents for plants and animals other than microorganisms and for methods of biological reproduction, except for microbiological processes. These provisions on patenting life (Article 27.3(b)) remain controversial even after more than two decades of application.

Trademarks and geographical indications

The trademark provisions in TRIPS essentially incorporate legal practices, found in the major developed economies, to address misleading or fraudulent use of registered marks. One challenge in some developing nations has been to implement laws protecting well-known international trademarks, even without local registration. What makes a trademark well known is sometimes vague, leading currently to variability in protection standards.

More controversial was the TRIPS requirement that geographical indications be protected. These devices identify goods, such as Bordeaux wines or Gruyere cheese, as being produced in a particular region, where the product's quality is particularly associated with that location.[9] WTO members are required to establish procedures permitting owners of geographical indications to prevent misleading or unfair use of their place names. At the time of TRIP's implementation, the EU demanded that a stronger set of requirements be put into place for wines and spirits, although prior use in good faith remains permissible under some circumstances.

Plant variety rights (PVRs)

TRIPS requires countries to provide developers of qualifying new plant varieties exclusive rights to control use of their propagating material (primarily seeds) and harvested products. Such rights are important for seed companies and developers of agro-biotechnological inventions. They were relatively rare in developing countries prior to TRIPS and the international obligation to register and protect PVRs was new.

Countries were obliged to implement either a *sui generis* system of protection, patents for new plant varieties, or both. Regarding the former, developing nations could model their laws on provisions of two versions of the UPOV Treaty.[10] Under UPOV 1978, countries could implement the farmers' privilege, which permits farmers to retain seeds for their own use and to exchange them outside normal commerce, and the breeders' exemption, which allows developers to experiment with protected varieties without the need for a licence. The UPOV 1991 Treaty disallowed this non-commercial exchange of seeds and required breeders to obtain authorization for experimenting with protected varieties. The majority of developing countries implemented PVRs systems based on the earlier version, which is no longer open for accession. Others formally joined UPOV 1991, adopting its more rigorous provisions, often in the context of negotiating a PTA with the USA or the EU.

Trade secrets and confidential test data

TRIPS does not set out any substantive obligations regarding trade secrets or confidential business information. It does, however, require governments to let firms take legal measures to prevent their disclosure through dishonest means. Thus, countries had to enact laws that define unfair practices and to establish judicial processes to determine whether methods of unauthorized disclosure were legal.

Far more controversial was the obligation (Article 39.3) that member governments protect confidential testing data, submitted to achieve marketing approval for pharmaceuticals and agricultural chemicals, against disclosure and ensure that the data could not be used unfairly for commercial purposes. Thus, TRIPS certifies that clinical trials data should be protected for some period of time in order to give originator firms a lead time advantage over generic rivals. However, the agreement does not stipulate a minimum period of protection, leaving authorities free to legislate for their own chosen period. This issue has featured prominently in debates over TRIPS-Plus provisions in PTAs.

Enforcement expectations

TRIPS states that there must be an administrative and judicial system permitting IPRs owners to enforce their rights effectively against suspected infringement. The enforcement procedures must include remedies to prevent and deter infringing activity, including fines, disposal of infringing products, and criminal penalties in the case of wilful counterfeiting and piracy at a commercial level. However, TRIPS does not define 'effective' enforcement, nor does it require countries to establish processes that go beyond their general framework for law enforcement.

Intellectual Property Rights and TRIPS

There also need to be measures to address infringement at the border, permitting customs authorities to prevent exports of suspect goods and ensure that imported counterfeit products are not released into the market. Some safeguards are stipulated to avoid abuses that could turn such measures into illegitimate barriers to trade. TRIPS is the first international agreement to set out expectations for national enforcement of IPRs.

Residual policy space

The TRIPS Agreement undoubtedly ushered in stronger global standards and expectations concerning IPRs protection. However, it also attempted to reach a balance between the needs of private rights holders and the importance of sustaining access for users of new products and technologies, whether to support competition or facilitate acquisition of public goods. This sub-section briefly discusses the primary flexibilities permitted in the agreement in order to understand the policy space remaining for member countries.[11]

One key element is the treatment of *exhaustion and parallel imports*. A country's exhaustion doctrine establishes conditions under which a rights holder loses the ability to prevent further distribution of a good.[12] For physical commodities, these rights are typically exhausted upon domestic first sale. Digital products are the exception, for when someone legally acquires a movie or a computer program, the transaction is a licensing agreement that prevents resale by the consumer.

Exhaustion is an international trade issue because IPRs are national in scope, and a country may choose to bar parallel imports (i.e. imports outside the authorized distribution channel) of goods that were legitimately placed on the market in another country. In the USA, for example, it is generally illegal to import for commercial distribution products that are protected by US patents, designs and copyrights – a policy of national exhaustion.[13] The EU follows regional exhaustion, permitting free parallel trade among its members but preventing it from outside the single market area. Many developing countries follow international exhaustion, where distribution rights end upon first sale anywhere in the world.

The TRIPS Agreement states (Article 6) that this policy choice is up to individual governments and there is no obligation to permit or prevent parallel trade. After an initial period of debate about the meaning of this provision, a consensus now exists that WTO members are free to regulate parallel trade as they see fit.

A second critical element is the freedom of governments to issue *compulsory licences* so that domestic firms may use patented technologies without authorization by the rights owners. Authorities in developed countries have long retained the right to permit such unauthorized uses, whether to encourage competition through early working and research exceptions, to discipline anti-competitive behaviour by firms with technological dominance, or to ensure government use for public and non-commercial purposes.[14]

The TRIPS Agreement has a general exceptions clause (Article 30), permitting governments to sustain exceptions to exclusive rights so long as they do not unreasonably conflict with the legitimate interests of the patent owner, or unreasonably interfere with his or her ability to exploit a patent. Many developing countries interpret Article 30 as a broad platform on which to establish limitations on the private exercise of patent rights, including through compulsory licences.

TRIPS also has extensive language (Article 31) setting out conditions under which governments may award non-voluntary licences to third parties. These provisions essentially require that reasonable efforts have been made to license the technology in the market, but without success, that the government-authorized use will be temporary, that the licence is non-exclusive, and that adequate compensation is paid. TRIPS also permits compulsory licences of dependent patents and as remedies for anti-competitive licensing practices by patent owners.

33

The most controversial TRIPS provision in this context is Article 31.f, which states that a compulsory licence may only be authorized for production and sale aimed predominantly at the domestic market. This provision was entered at the request of countries with multinational companies seeking to maximize the international profitability of exploiting their patents, because it precludes competition from non-voluntary licensees in global markets. However, the rule was quickly recognized as problematic, because it eliminated the possibility that small countries, with little domestic production capacity, could issue compulsory import licences in medicines. This difficulty was addressed in 2005 through the adoption of an Amendment to TRIPS under which other countries could authorize exports of essential medicines to poor countries lacking such production capacity under compulsory import licences.[15]

A survey of 49 developing countries found that virtually all had adopted provisions for issuing compulsory licences by the early 2000s.[16] Most of these laws established that the failure of a rights owner to work the patent by providing adequate domestic supply within three or four years was sufficient grounds to compel licensing. A smaller number recognized that such licences could be issued on grounds of the public interest, national security and public health. Fewer than half listed the need to remedy anti-competitive practices or the failure of domestic firms to acquire production rights.

A third factor is the ability to issues *limitations and exception (L&Es) on the scope of copyrights*. The reach of copyrights has long been limited by permissible L&Es, such as the fair use doctrine sustained in the USA. Thus, TRIPS permits countries to adopt L&Es on exclusive copyrights under certain conditions. Examples include making limited personal copies, permitting teachers to use portions of copyrighted works for educational purposes, allowing libraries to reproduce works for preservation purposes, and supporting free access by persons with disabilities, such as the sight-impaired.[17] Such provisions vary widely across nations.

The TRIPS Agreement permits considerable latitude to countries in setting their L&Es on copyrights. For example, while TRIPS requires that computer programs be protected by copyrights at a minimum, it does not address whether program code may be copied and decompiled for purposes of reverse engineering and interoperability. It also permits governments, under certain circumstances, to issue compulsory licences for copying imported works published abroad.[18]

Dispute settlement

By the end of 2017 37 disputes involving TRIPS rules or enforcement had been notified to the WTO dispute settlement body, although panels were formed in just a subset of those cases.[19] While each case is interesting, only five are mentioned briefly here in order to conserve space. These cases illuminate important points with respect to TRIPS obligations.

First, in 1997 Brazil established a local 'working requirement' that firms had to meet in order to sustain exclusive patent rights. This law required either that the patented product be manufactured locally or that full use of the patented process be made within a certain time period. Failure to comply would subject the patent to a possible compulsory licence. In 2000 the USA complained that requiring local production, rather than importation, to satisfy access needs was inconsistent with TRIPS. Brazil countered that its law complied with the Agreement. In July 2001 the parties reached a settlement and the USA withdrew the complaint. Brazil promised not to grant a compulsory licence against an American-held patent, based on inadequate domestic production, without engaging in prior consultations with the US government. This case suggests that countries may have production-based working requirements, despite the language in TRIPS Article 27.

Second, in 1997 the European Community (EC) challenged two provisions of Canada's Patent Act insofar as they applied to pharmaceuticals. Under its regulatory review exception, the Canadian law permitted generic competitors to use the drug, without authorization, to demonstrate that their versions were effective and safe, thereby gaining marketing approval upon patent expiration. The law also allowed generic firms to produce and stockpile quantities of patented drugs so that they could be sold immediately upon expiration. The dispute panel found that the regulatory review exception is acceptable under TRIPS but the stockpiling exception was an inappropriate use of the product during the patent term. This case clarified that experimental use during the patent term was acceptable, so long as it did not support stockpiling in marketable quantities. Such exceptions provide an important means through which generic firms can gain rapid entry into the market, and are widely in place in developing nations.

Third, in 1999 the EC challenged Section 110(5) of the US Copyright Act. That provision contains a 'business exemption', permitting small bars and restaurants to play radio and television broadcasts freely and without authorization. An accompanying 'homestyle exemption' allowed the same uncompensated use if establishments utilized equipment like that found in private homes. The EC argued that the business exemption applied to the majority of US restaurants and bars, and to nearly half the retail stores in the country, and therefore interfered with the legitimate exploitation of copyrights. In 2000 the panel found that the business exemption violated TRIPS because it was not a minor limitation on the economic value of copyrights. However, the homestyle exemption was found to be acceptable. The USA has yet to amend the law in the light of this ruling; rather, it paid the EC US $3.3 million in compensation for lost royalties of European music and television rights holders. This was the first instance of monetary compensation being paid as a resolution of a WTO dispute.

In a fourth case, in 1999 the USA, later joined by Australia, requested consultations with the EC over its registration procedures with respect to geographical indications. These countries complained that certain regulations and administrative procedures discriminated against firms outside the EU, violating the national treatment and MFN requirements of TRIPS. The ensuing WTO panel in 2005 ruled substantively for the complainants, finding that the procedures did not provide national treatment, primarily because they made geographical indication registration dependent on the domestic government of the applicant adopting a protection system identical and reciprocal to that in the EU. The EU adopted a new regulation in 2006 that it claimed complied with the ruling, but the USA and Australia argued that it did not reach full compliance and continue to press the case.

A final case was the US dispute with the People's Republic of China regarding aspects of its IPRs protection and enforcement, launched in 2007. The USA charged that China's criminal penalties against trademark counterfeiting and copyright piracy were an ineffective deterrent and that the customs authorities were failing to dispose of seized goods properly outside commercial channels. Separately, the USA argued that the denial of copyrights in China to works that were not approved for local distribution was inconsistent with TRIPS. The WTO panel report essentially split these claims. The criminal penalty thresholds were found not to be a TRIPS violation, largely because the agreement is not prescriptive in that regard, but the public auctioning of seized goods was deemed inappropriate. Furthermore, China's denial of copyright protection to works not approved for distribution was found to be inconsistent with TRIPS. In 2010 China revised its copyright law and customs regulations to comply with these rulings.

The panel's findings in the US-China dispute essentially affirmed that countries retain sovereignty over the scope of penalties associated with enforcing IPRs, so long as procedures are consistent with the overall legal framework. However, authorities cannot unreasonably interfere with the market opportunities of IPRs owners, nor can they use other forms of regulation, such as censorship, to deny copyright protection.

Keith E. Maskus

The Role of preferential trade agreements and the TRIPS-Plus agenda

Despite the comprehensive nature of TRIPS, it did not take long after its introduction for major producers of intellectual property to realize that it failed to achieve a number of their objectives.

WIPO copyright treaties

An initial example was that the copyright provisions of the agreement did not anticipate the subsequent emergence of the internet and how it would facilitate the unauthorized use of software and other forms of digital content. Thus, not long after the WTO's foundation this issue was addressed initially by the negotiation of two treaties at the World Intellectual Property Organization (WIPO). These were the WIPO Copyright Treaty (WCT) and the WIPO Performance and Phonograms Treaty (WPPT), both aimed at setting a framework for securing digital copyrights. These treaties have attracted widespread adherence around the world, in part because the USA and the EU demand such accession by partners in the PTAs they negotiate.

Briefly, the WCT states that authors of copyrighted works have exclusive rights to authorize the communication to the public of those works by wire or wireless methods and that protection must be provided against circumvention of technological methods used by rights owners to prevent digital copying and retransmission. It also requires that countries have effective remedies against the removal or disablement of the systems deployed to protect these rights. The WPPT recognized the right of performers and publishers of music and other digital products to authorize recordings of their performances and communication of those recordings and published works over the internet or other channels. These entities were given rights to compensation for the use of their works.

Thus, these WIPO accords set out broad obligations to deal with the problems that are inherent in trading digital products and services, including unauthorized downloading and circumvention of digital rights management. As such, they have improved the framework for trading digital content among member nations. However, many countries have taken advantage of the limitations and exceptions they permit, consistent with the earlier discussion of general copyrights. Both treaties also state that nations may select their own policy towards exhaustion of copyrights in software, databases, recordings and other digital products, so that markets may remain open to parallel imports, even through electronic means.

Preferential trade agreements

From the standpoint of digital content providers these WIPO treaties did not go far enough to meet their evolving needs in a dynamic technological market. That many countries chose to adopt weak provisions (or chose not to enforce stronger rules) for disciplining circumvention of digital copyrights and unauthorized file-sharing was a major frustration for content providers. Other intellectual property concerns remained dissatisfied with the flexible elements of TRIPS itself, such as the ability to exclude certain technologies from patent eligibility, the unclear obligations for test data protection, and the near absence of substantive provisions for addressing trade secrets.

As a consequence, both the USA and the EU soon adopted the strategy of expanding the scope of IPRs beyond TRIPS through negotiating stronger standards in bilateral and multilateral PTAs. This focus on demanding TRIPS-Plus standards is a central priority of American and European trade policy, albeit with somewhat different emphases. US policy strives to raise standards primarily in the areas of pharmaceuticals, biotechnology and digital copyrights, while the EU adds protection of geographical indications.[20]

Thus, for example, in recent US-negotiated PTAs a key demand has been to provide patent-term extensions for drugs and agricultural chemicals in cases where health authorities issued marketing approvals with undue delays. Another is for authorities to grant 'second use patents', or protection for existing drugs that are shown to be effective in treating indications beyond the initial claims. Yet another is to limit experimental use of patented materials and also to restrict their use by generic firms in preparation for entry as patents expire.

A major change compared to TRIPS is the requirement in some PTAs that local health authorities ban the registration of any generic drugs during the lifetime of a patent. This 'linkage rule' precludes approval of any generic medicine until the regulatory authority can certify that no patent would be violated by it. Strong provisions of this type ban generic entry without linkage notifications in the US agreements with Chile, Morocco, Singapore, the Republic of Korea (South Korea) and others.

Regarding protections against unfair use of confidential test data, the USA successfully negotiated the adoption of its own legal standard of five years for pharmaceutical products and ten years for agricultural chemicals in all recent PTAs. These periods begin from the date on which the original applicant, which submitted the data, is granted marketing approval. This provision means that exclusive marketing rights exist in such circumstances, even if a patent is not granted. It can also effectively extend patent rights in cases where they are granted, if marketing approval comes late in the patent period.

Turning to copyrights, the USA has consistently negotiated a term of protection of life plus 70 years for authors and 70 years for works of institutional authorship. These terms exceed the TRIPS protection periods of life plus 50 years and 50 years, respectively. As for digital copy-rights, the basic level of protection arises from the WIPO treaties, which each PTA partner is required to ratify. Thus, in addition to protecting performers, publishers and broadcasters from unauthorized copying, partners must enact laws against circumvention of technological access controls and digital rights management. Some PTAs with the USA also feature TRIPS-Plus restrictions on the ability to deploy particular L&Es in copyrights. More recent agreements have added language on the protection of satellite broadcasts, the responsibilities of internet service providers, and additional scope for civil and criminal penalties for infringing digital copyrights.

That PTAs have become the preferred method for raising global intellectual property rights standards may be seen from reading the intellectual property chapters in succeeding agreements over time. In the early US-Israel FTA there was just a single paragraph committing both sides to act without discrimination. Each succeeding agreement reached increasingly complex and lengthy chapters, which may be illustrated by the US-Korea Free Trade Agreement, which entered into force in 2012. Chapter 18, covering IPRs, stretches over 35 pages and 12 substantive articles, covering nearly all elements of standards, administration and enforcement expectations.

Even more expansive was the language on IPRs agreed in the Trans-Pacific Partnership (TPP), the massive PTA negotiated among 12 countries of the Asia-Pacific region, across a mix of developed and developing economies. This agreement, as originally negotiated, would have extended the US model for protecting intellectual property to a large swathe of the global economy. The draft text added numerous substantive requirements going well beyond TRIPS and existing US-led PTAs. For example, it called for patent eligibility for plants, animals, medical therapies and surgical procedures, and clarified the need for issuing second-use patents and delaying generic entry. The IPRs chapter also introduced a period of protection for con-fidential test data in new forms of drugs, called biologics. It further harmonized minimum protection periods for copyrights, placed limits on fair-use provisions, and issued strong expectations for administrative and criminal enforcement. The TPP also brought in an expectation that countries add criminal penalties to wilful violation of confidential business information, or trade secrets – a novel concept in global IPRs agreements.

Thus, the TPP, had the USA not famously withdrawn from it early in the Trump Administration, would have institutionalized a set of standards considerably elevated from global norms. It remains to be seen how much of this expansion may remain as the other 11 countries decide whether to ratify a modified agreement, but the draft TPP set a baseline that is likely to sustain stronger protection, even without US participation.

Conclusion

When negotiated, the TRIPS Agreement was, and remains, the most comprehensive global agreement covering standards of protection and enforcement norms in IPRs. Numerous developing and emerging nations implemented significant legal reforms over time, according to the allowable transition periods.[21] At the same time, developed economies have continued to advance their own standards, particularly in the areas of digital protection, medical and biological patents, geographical indications and trade secrets. Furthermore, recent bilateral and regional PTAs with successively stronger IPRs chapters have ratcheted global protection upwards. Together, these changes, despite the policy flexibilities inherent in TRIPS, have strongly increased the global scope of protection for patents, copyrights and related rights.

Whether this new global regime has achieved an appropriate balance between incentives for innovation and licensing on the one hand, and the need for access to new goods and information on the other, remains an open question. A positive note is that there is solid empirical evidence that this regime is encouraging the formal transfer of new technologies to emerging countries through enhanced trade and investment in high-technology sectors.[22] Furthermore, innovation seems to be growing in major emerging economies that have introduced markedly stronger patent laws, as measured by the development of new products, additional research and development investments, and foreign patenting.[23] And the introduction of domestic patents is correlated with more rapid introduction of new global pharmaceuticals into developing markets.[24] In this sense, TRIPS and the broader system seem to be improving the global landscape for technology transactions and the use of information.

However, there are reasons to remain cautious about the overall impacts of these policy shifts. First, there is little evidence to date that technology transfers, even through outsourcing within supply chains, are increasing to the poorest developing economies. It appears that reforming IPRs protection by itself is not particularly effective in connecting such countries to the global technological structure. Second, there is no indication that innovative enterprises in the advanced or emerging economies are investing more in products and technologies that would meet the specific needs of consumers and patients in poor countries. This is particularly unfortunate, for the development of such incentives was touted as a key reason for developing economies to support TRIPS in the first place. Put briefly, stronger international patent protection is not sufficient to overcome other market difficulties that may prevent such innovation and technology diffusion.

Perhaps most importantly, stronger IPRs raise fundamental, and as yet unanswered, concerns about the ability of governments and international organizations to procure essential public goods at reasonable cost.[25] Private property rights in information do not seem to be an adequate global solution to such problems as procuring and distributing essential medicines, transferring green technologies, or diffusing scientific knowledge into the developing world. In this sense, the international system remains controversial and subject to further revisions.

Notes

1 This chapter draws in part on material in Keith E. Maskus (2012) *Private Rights and Public Problems: The Global Economics of Intellectual Property in the 21st Century*, Washington, DC: Peterson Institute for International Economics.

2 Interestingly, TRIPS included a moratorium on so-called non-violation complaints, which effectively remains in place.

3 Maskus, *Private Rights and Public Problems*, reviews various measures of increased protection around the world.

4 This argument is developed in Gene M. Grossman and Edwin L.-C. Lai (2004) 'International Protection of Intellectual Property', *American Economic Review* 94(5): 1635–53.

5 See Maskus, *Private Rights*; Joseph E. Stiglitz and Andrew Charlton (2005) *Fair Trade for All: How Trade Can Promote Development*, Oxford: Oxford University Press; Keith E. Maskus (2004) *Encouraging International Technology Transfer*, Geneva: International Center for Trade and Sustainable Development, Issue Paper 7.

6 There are numerous detailed descriptions in the literature. An extensive discussion can be found in International Center for Trade and Sustainable Development (2005) *Resource Book on TRIPS and Development*, Geneva: International Center for Trade and Sustainable Development. See also Maskus, *Private Rights and Public Problems*; and Carolyn Deere (2009) *The Implementation Game: The TRIPS Agreement and the Global Politics of Intellectual Property Reform in Developing Countries*, Oxford: Oxford University Press.

7 For descriptions of the TRIPS-Plus process within PTAs, see Carsten Fink and Patrick Reichenmiller (2005) *Tightening TRIPS: the Intellectual Property Provisions of Recent U.S. Free Trade Agreements*, Washington, DC: World Bank, Trade Note 20, and Pedro Roffe and Christoph Spennemann (2006) 'The Impact of FTAs on Public Health Policies and TRIPS Flexibilities,' *International Journal of Intellectual Property Management* 1(1–2): 75–93.

8 These jurisdictions vary markedly in this regard. The EU essentially requires that computer programs be implemented in order to effect a useful outcome within a tangible product to be protected, while the USA permits utility to be found within the program itself.

9 For further analysis see Carsten Fink and Keith E. Maskus (2006) 'The Debate on Geographical Indications at the WTO', in Richard Newfarmer (ed.) *Trade, Doha and Development: A Window into the Issues*, Geneva: World Bank, pp. 197–207.

10 Union internationale pour la protection des obtentions végétales (UPOV, International Union for the Protection of Varieties of Plants).

11 Further analysis may be found in Carolyn Deere, *The Implementation Game*; International Center for Trade and Sustainable Development, *Resource Book on TRIPS and Development*, and several chapters in Keith E. Maskus and Jerome H. Reichman (eds) (2005) *International Public Goods and Transfer of Technology under a Globalized Intellectual Property Regime*, Cambridge: Cambridge University Press.

12 See Mattias Ganslandt and Keith E. Maskus (2008) 'Intellectual Property Rights, Parallel Imports and Strategic Behavior', in Keith E. Maskus (ed.) *Intellectual Property, Growth and Trade*, Amsterdam: Elsevier-North Holland.

13 Recent decisions by the US Supreme Court suggest that national exhaustion may no longer hold for patented goods (*Impression Products, Inc. v. Lexmark International, Inc.*, 2017) and copyrighted textbooks (*Kirtsaeng v. John Wiley and Sons*, 2013). However, the full reach of these rulings remains unclear.

14 For fuller analysis see Jerome H. Reichman and Catherine Hazensahl (2003) *Non-Voluntary Licenses of Patented Inventions: Historical Perspective, Legal Framework under TRIPS, and an Overview of Practice in Canada and the United States*, Geneva: International Center for Trade and Sustainable Development.

15 This amendment has rarely been used, for reasons that are not altogether clear. See Maskus, *Private Rights and Public Problems*.

16 See Sisule Musungu and Cecilia Oh (2006) *The Use of Flexibilities in TRIPS by Developing Countries: Can they Promote Access to Medicines?* World Health Organization Study on Intellectual Property Rights, Innovation and Public Health, Geneva: WTO.

17 See Ruth L. Okediji (2006) *The International Copyright System: Limitations, Exceptions and Public-Interest Considerations for Developing Countries*, Geneva: International Center for Trade and Sustainable Development, Issue Paper 15, and also Deere, *The Implementation Game*.

18 Despite its complex structure, many WTO participants did not see TRIPS as a finished agreement and there were subsequent calls for its revision within the Doha Round. Key issues included clarification of

Article 27.3(b) on patenting of life forms, an international registry of geographical indications, disclosure of origin of genetic resources in patent applications, and the meaning of Article 66.2 (mandating affirmative actions of developed countries to encourage technology transfer to least developed countries). For further discussion see Maskus, *Private Rights and Public Problems*.

19 See 'Disputes by Agreement', available at www.wto.org/english/tratop_e/dispu_e/dispu_status_e.htm. Maskus, *Private Rights and Public Problems*, offers fuller analysis of these disputes.

20 Roffe and Spenneman, 'Impact of FTAs on Public Health Policies and TRIPS Flexibilities', is an early analysis of TRIPS-Plus measures in pharmaceuticals. Maskus, *Private Rights and Public Problems*, details the US approach while a comprehensive discussion of the EU strategy may be found in the chapters of Josef Drexl, H. Grosse Ruse Khan and S. Nadde-Phlix (eds) (2013) *EU Bilateral Trade Agreements and Intellectual Property: for Better or Worse?* Heidelberg: Springer-Verlag.

21 Many of the poorest economies have yet to come into compliance in particular ways.

22 See the review in Maskus, *Private Rights and Public Problems*. Recent papers with such findings include Lee Branstetter, Raymond Fisman, C. Fritz Foley and Kamal Saggi (2011) 'Does Intellectual Property Rights Reform Spur Industrial Development?' *Journal of International Economics*, 83(1): 27–36; and Olena Ivus (2010) 'Do Stronger Patent Rights Raise High-Tech Exports to the Developing World?' *Journal of International Economics*, 81(1): 38–47.

23 See Yi Qian (1978) 'Do National Patent Laws Stimulate Domestic Innovation in a Global Patenting Environment? A Cross-Country Analysis of Pharmaceutical Protection, 1978–2002,' *Review of Economics and Statistics*, 89(3): 436–53; Yonmin Chen and Thitima Puttitanun (2005) 'Intellectual Property Rights and Innovation in Developing Countries', *Journal of Development Economics*, 78(2): 474–93; and Branstetter *et al.*, 'Does Intellectual Property Rights Reform Spur Industrial Development?'.

24 See Margaret K. Kyle and Yi Qian (2014) *Intellectual Property Rights and Access to Innovation: Evidence from TRIPS*, National Bureau of Economic Research, Working Paper 20799, Cambridge MA: NBER.

25 See various chapters in Maskus and Reichman, *International Public Goods*.

5

The spread of international trade agreements

A dynamics towards the 'spaghetti bowl' phenomenon?

Zakaria Sorgho[1]

Introduction

Trade policy refers to the regulations and agreements that control imports/exports to/from foreign countries. In general, the design of trade policy, similarly to the negotiation of an international trade agreement (ITA), is subject to economic and political considerations. New political economy of trade policy emphasizes the political interaction of self-interested subjects (politicians, economic lobbyists, voters, etc.) in an institutional context of decision–making. Trade policy is viewed as being determined jointly by the objectives of policymakers, the influence over policy exerted by the would-be winners and losers from that policy including free trade policy and by the institutional setting governing the interaction between policymakers and by those affected by protection.[2]

An ITA[3] is a wide-ranging tax, tariff and trade pact that often includes investment issues. The most common ITAs are of the preferential and free trade type concluded in order to reduce (or eliminate) tariffs, quotas and other trade restrictions on items traded between members. ITAs are an exception to the non–discrimination rule, one of the fundamental principles of the World Trade Organization (WTO)'s law and policy. Indeed, ITAs are conceived as an exception to the most-favoured–nation (MFN) clause to cater to the specific needs of developing as well as developed countries (Article XXIV of the General Agreement on Tariffs and Trade – GATT). The multilateral trading system is based on the MFN principle which states that any special favours (such as lower tariffs or technical measures) granted to a member of the WTO must also be extended to all other WTO members (Article I of GATT). Therefore, ITAs have become a ubiquitous feature of global trade – almost all countries have signed ITAs.[4]

Historically, prior to the creation of the WTO in 1995, two waves of ITAs could be discerned: the first took place in the 1960s and 1970s and did not spread beyond Western Europe, while the second wave started in the 1980s when the USA switched its trade policy from multilateral approach to liberalization of trade and then to regional liberalization of trade within ITAs.[5] Thus, there were only 124 ITAs which were notified prior to the establishment of the

WTO (i.e. during the period 1948–94), whereas over 400 additional arrangements were notified after 1995 (under the WTO). In particular, the failure to complete a new multilateral trade deal has meant that policymakers hoping to liberalize trade have turned to ITAs as a way of achieving their policy goals. By the end of 2016 the WTO noted that it had received a total of 654 notifications of ITAs, of which over 200 were notified after 2001. Regionalism is sweeping through the multilateral trade system like wildfire while WTO talks advance at a glacial rate.

Since 2001 global trade has witnessed a drastic increase in ITAs (see Figure 5.1). Overall, the formation of RTAs between countries has evolved. For a long time, most RTAs were regional in focus with members being geographically close to each other (e.g. the EU, NAFTA, ECOWAS, ASEAN, etc.).[6] Nowadays, countries or regional blocs sign or negotiate RTAs with diverse and geographically distant partners (e.g. EPAs, CETA, the TPP, TTIP).[7] The number of this latter group of ITAs is also important. Thus, world trade flows are increasingly occurring between countries that grant each other tariff preferences via ITAs. By 2013 about 15 per cent of country pairs shared an ITA and nearly half of world trade took place within ITA trading blocs for each year between 1981 and 2013.[8]

Even if there is a wide consensus in the empirical literature that ITAs have had a positive impact on trade flows, the effectiveness of ITAs on economic welfare remains controversial in policy debates. From a welfare perspective, ITAs are viewed as the second-best option– not the first best. Contrary to intuition, not all trade liberalizations are desirable and in particular the preferential liberalizations (as in the case of ITAs) may harm the liberalizing country.[9] They may lead to trade creation (i.e. an increase in imports replacing less efficient domestic production) and trade diversion (whereby imports shift from an efficient outside supplier to a less efficient supplier due

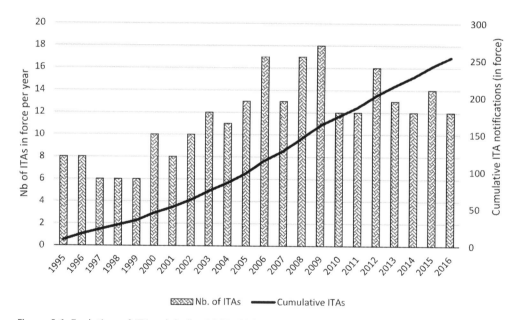

Figure 5.1 Evolution of ITAs globally, 1995–2016
Source: Author's calculations taken from WTO database, available at http://rtais.wto.org. Data only consider ITAs on goods (including/excluding services) and account for all accessions (enlargement of an ITA or accession of a country).

to the preferences granted to the latter); the former can be associated with welfare improvement and the latter with welfare reduction.[10] By eliminating tariffs within an ITA trading bloc, trade may be diverted away from more efficient extra-ITA countries and towards less efficient intra-ITA countries. Some of the goods that a country would have imported from outside the ITA will be imported from countries within the ITA. Also, without tariffs on imports, some of a country's domestic production will be replaced by imports from a more efficient producer among the ITA trading partners.[11] Thus, trade diversion has an ambiguous impact on a country's welfare depending on whether or not the consumer gains outweigh the losses to producers and to the government tax revenues.[12] In sum, ITAs can have either positive or negative effects on global welfare depending on the magnitude of the effects of trade creation and trade diversion.

Moreover, ITAs are a threat to multilateralism.[13] They have proved not to be the building blocks[14] towards global free trade, but rather stumbling blocks towards the generation of free trade because they restrict such privileges to members of the ITA. A major drawback of this free trade regime has been identified, which is that ITAs have proliferated at the cost of the dilution of multilateral agreements. Thus, preferential trading blocs limit global trade liberalization due to high external trade barriers.[15] For instance, one-way ITAs can be viewed as measures taken by stronger trading countries against weaker ones (i.e. developing countries) in order to influence the latter to avoid the kind of multilateralism encouraged by the WTO.[16]

The way in which the ITAs around the globe are now configured has resulted in a tangle of trading relationships resembling a 'spaghetti bowl'. The system of ITAs could further complicate trading even among the members of ITA through the requirements of local content and rules of origin.[17] The excessive complexity of rules of origin (for a given country) caused by the overlapping of ITAs in which it is involved can create an artifact production network of countries that would not be necessarily consistent with the principle of economic efficiency. This is what Jagdish Bhagwati[18] called the 'spaghetti bowl' phenomenon of ITAs. By this he was referring to 'the manner in which half-finished products and parts go around various FTA networks using tariff differentiation in an effort to export finished products to the consumer countries at the lowest price'. He visualized this as 'crisscrossing lines' and likened these strings of lines to 'strands of spaghetti tangled in a bowl'.[19]

This chapter re-examines the relationship between ITAs and this inefficient trading situation, known as the 'spaghetti bowl' phenomenon (SBP). Its concern is not to show empirically whether ITAs cause a SBP in the world economy through econometrical modelling, but to discuss the evidence of the SBP by surveying relevant empirical studies and ITAs and analysing data. The remainder of this chapter comprises three sections. The second section presents the political economy of trade agreements by reviewing the reasons behind their formation, and giving some justification for their proliferation. The third section looks at the data analytics on ITAs and trade, relating to the existing studies, to highlight the evidence for the trade diversion of ITAs. The final section concludes the chapter, suggesting that one way of avoiding the SBP in the long term is to implement laws and regulations in accordance with the strictest of multiple agreements and apply them to all countries.

Political economy of ITAs

In the literature, there is no clear-cut definition of an ITA. That is not surprising! Indeed, there are other motives and goals associated with ITAs beyond simply improving economic welfare. In general, they are often embodied into the vague concept of economic integration, whose main objective is to increase welfare within a trading bloc. For instance, one definition views ITAs as both a process and a state of affairs, involving the removal of trade discrimination between different states.[20] In the same vein, ITAs can be viewed as an efficiency in resource use, caused by the freedom of movement of goods and factors of production and an absence of discrimination among members.[21] An extension to these two definitions refers to economic integration as the discriminatory removal of all trade impediments between participating nations and the establishment of cooperation and coordination among members.[22]

For the purposes of this chapter, I consider an ITA to be a treaty that seeks to form a preferential trading bloc in which nations commit to eliminating trade barriers on goods and/or services among participating states. This definition views ITAs as the gradual elimination of 'economic frontiers' between two or more economies.[23] Among other things, these 'economic frontiers' include trade barriers and policies between exporting countries such as quotas, tariff barriers, anti-dumping actions, countervailing duty (charged to counter export subsidies), sanitary and phytosanitary measures, etc. Thus, the establishment of a preferential trading bloc through an ITA is a means of removing these trade barriers in order to free trade between ITA members, and this is expected to increase welfare for each signatory party. Therefore, an ITA can be perceived as a process of eliminating trade barriers so as to reduce trade costs in order to increase welfare.[24] However, how effective ITAs are in improving welfare among all trade bloc members, and in particular the impact that this has, remains controversial?

Economic welfare of ITAs

The traditional economic theory asks two questions relating to trade liberalization and the formation of an ITA: (1) what is the welfare impact on each member country, the preferential trading bloc as a whole and the rest of the world? (2) Can two or more countries form a preferential trading bloc such that it makes the rest of the world worse off? These two questions have been tackled in the trade literature since 1950, and remain as valid today.[25]

These questions have been discussed by Jacob Viner,[26] a pioneer in the use of the concepts of trade creation and trade diversion in the economic analysis of ITAs. On the one hand, trade liberalization with certain trade partners generates positive effects as high-cost products in the home country can be substituted for low-cost products from the partner countries (known as the trade creation effect). One the other hand, given that preferential integration is discriminatory, countries outside the agreement face higher tariffs than the bloc members (trade diversion effect). Associating trade creation with gains in welfare and trade diversion with decreases in welfare, Viner stresses that although trade creation is beneficial, since it does not affect the rest of the world, trade diversion is harmful. Thus, he concludes that the net welfare impact of an ITA depends upon the relative magnitude of trade creation and trade diversion. The products from a non-member country will instead be imported from member countries that do not face tariffs, even though they are not the most efficient producers. Indeed, trade diversion has an ambiguous impact on a country's welfare depending on the net magnitude of consumer gains, the losses to producers and the government tax revenues.[27]

In 1955 James Meade[28] published the first welfare theoretic analysis of trade blocs. Using a general equilibrium model, he pointed out that the relative magnitudes of trade creation and trade diversion alone are insufficient to determine the welfare effect of a bloc on world welfare because the benefits of preferential liberalization depend not only upon the extent of trade creation but also on trade costs. Thus, losses are determined not just by the amount of trade diversion but also the magnitude of the increase in costs due to trade diversion. An ITA member could individually lose on account of adverse income distribution effects arising from tariff revenue redistribution, even if the trading bloc as a whole benefits.

Furthermore, welfare brought about by ITAs is not seen as the best, but as the second best. The general theorem of the second best states that if a constraint is introduced into a general equilibrium setting which prevents the attainment of one of the Pareto conditions, other Pareto conditions, although still attainable, are in general no longer desirable.[29] Prior to the development of the theory of the second best, preferential trading blocs implemented by ITAs were considered to be a step closer to the theoretical concept of free trade (no trade distortions), and therefore they increased welfare. Indeed, Adam Smith and David Ricardo viewed ITA policy and the unimpeded movement of factors as the 'first best' policy in a world which does not have any distortions. This implies that the Pareto optimality – a situation where there are no trade distortions (tariffs, subsidies, taxes, monopolies and any others trade barriers) – is satisfied. This optimal situation is unrealistic, particularly in the field of international trade. The theorem of the second best addresses this issue by stating that, in the presence of distortions, if all the conditions for Pareto optimality cannot be satisfied, then the removal of some of the distortions does not necessarily increase welfare, nor does the addition of other distortions necessarily decrease it.[30] From this theorem, welfare comparisons between economic states are ambiguous when some Pareto optimum conditions are met while others are not. Welfare comparisons need to be done so that no one is left worse off.

Why are ITAs spreading?

The world trade system has noted that the number of ITAs has spread since the end of the Uruguay Round in the mid-1990s (with the institutionalization of trade regulation by the WTO). Prior to 1995 only 124 ITAs had been notified to the WTO. This number has rapidly increased with more than 500 additional ITAs reaching a total notification of 646 (whether in force or not) at the end of 2016, and a number of ITAs in preparation but not yet notified.[31] There are many reasons why countries have negotiated, and continue to form, so many preferential trading blocs. ITAs implemented around the world are thus different from one another because countries have different objectives when they negotiate them.

Traditionally, the economic theory states that the formation of an ITA should promote trade and investment between members by lowering or eliminating trade barriers as well as guaranteeing investment (i.e. the traditional gains from ITA formation). This motive is used to support the assertion that ITAs are spreading because of 'slow multilateralism'. Thus, the multiplication of ITAs may be due in part to the frustration of negotiators attempting to achieve multilateral free trade. Nations are increasingly eager to negotiate the removal of barriers bilaterally because multilateralism talks progress so slowly.[32, 33] For instance, during the Doha Round, the latest round of trade negotiations among the WTO membership, members (particularly developing countries) have made it clear that they are unwilling to negotiate on other topics until a suitable agreement on agriculture exists.[34] ITAs may facilitate deeper integration by eliminating non-tariff barriers including technical standards, food safety concerns, and domestic regulations – where the WTO has made very little progress – on 'substantially' all trade within the preferential trading bloc, and since they are easier to conclude because involving fewer negotiating parties, countries prefer bilaterally or regionally negotiated preferential trading blocs. In sum, the multi-memberships of ITAs may generate duty-free market access and zero-tariffs on imports with many trading partners and can hence be an appealing alternative to national policymakers as a substitute for multilateral free trade.[35]

Beyond these traditional gains from trade and capital flows, there are other reasons[36] for which nations negotiate ITAs. Some countries, for example smaller ones, see ITAs with larger partners as a way of securing their access to larger markets. Other uses of ITAs reflect tactical considerations, such as increasing states' power in multilateral negotiations with international organizations such as the WTO. Certain ITAs seek to strengthen some members' domestic policy reforms. Others provide underpinnings to strategic alliances, and hence implicitly promote security arrangements (maintaining of peace) among the countries involved, in particular in Europe.[37] From an institutional perspective, the multiplication of ITAs can be explained by the need to disseminate some political ideologies such as democracy,[38] and the quest for geopolitical stability.[39]

All the previous explanations for the spread of ITAs do not take into account third-nation effects. Thus, seeking the causal relationship between ITAs, recent studies provide evidence of an interdependence between ITAs (i.e. a 'contagion effect' or a 'domino effect'). The domino theory posits that the signing of an ITA induces outside nations to sign new ITAs that they have previously shunned since the trade diversion effect of the first ITA creates new political economy forces in excluded nations.[40] A pre-existing ITA is an important determinant that increases the probability of belonging to another ITA.[41] Thus, the multiplication of preferential trading blocs is partly driven by 'defensive' ITAs. Countries sign ITAs in reaction to third-nation ITAs in order to reduce discrimination created by the latter.[42]

As already discussed, countries can seek to achieve various goals by signing ITAs. It is therefore complicated to evaluate the overall welfare of a ITA for its members. The conventional trade creation and trade diversion are not the entire story in deciding on the welfare outcome for an individual member of a trade bloc.[43] However, for the purposes of this chapter, I am only interested in the trade effects of ITAs. Does the proliferation of ITAs matter? Can a country really benefit from all the agreements to which it is a signatory? Does the ITAs' overlapping – due to the participation of a country in various trading blocs – really promote trade? Does the signing of multiple ITAs increase trade for each individual member?

The proliferation of ITAs went on to create a so-called SBP in global trade.[44] The 'spaghetti bowl' is a metaphor to illustrate the numerous and criss-crossing ITAs, in which innumerable applicable tariff rates and a multiplicity of rules of origin must coexist. This situation imposes higher transaction costs on firms and distorts trade and investment flows.[45] Thus, the SBP could be considered as a trade-diverting or a status quo situation (similar to the MFN situation) within a new ITA area, dependent on the number of previous ITAs signed individually by each member.

Evidence of the 'spaghetti bowl' phenomenon

As mentioned above, the term 'spaghetti bowl' phenomenon (SBP) refers to the tangle of rules of origin induced by the bewildering range of geographical configurations of ITAs at regional and extraregional level.[46] Overlapping rules of origin (i.e. determining the country from which a product comes) can make it difficult to determine the actual country of origin, resulting in higher business and administration costs (increasing trade costs) and making it more expensive to comply with those rules. In the presence of overlapping ITAs, firms may strategically choose not to comply with the minimum rules of origin requirements. Instead, the firm may choose to comply with a rules of origin level that is higher than required, or pay the MFN tariff instead without enjoying tariff exemption by the ITA in the new country.[47] Such unintended outcomes of ITAs are called the 'spaghetti bowl' effect.

Empirical studies

These trade diversion effects of ITAs have not been thoroughly examined empirically in the academic literature.[48] In particular, the specific literature investigating the evidence on the SBP is scarce, which is not surprising. Note that the preferential network is, in reality, more complex, and includes many overlapping preferential trade relations often involving a tangle of rules of origin requirements at different levels; this complexity makes it difficult to properly investigate the SBP in the trading system. However, there are a number of empirical studies concerned with the SBP.

The overlapping of ITAs increases the trade growth rate for members by 5.57 per cent[49] due to the 'hub-spoke' structure,[50] and this is essentially for 'hub' countries. Indeed, as part of the 'backbone' in a trading bloc, a 'hub' country has the capacity to trade more in several ITAs, and this is not the case for the 'spoke' countries. A recent study finds significant trade impacts of pre-existing ITAs for countries that belong to another ITA.[51] More precisely, it finds that trade creation between member countries is always positive, but weaker (the dilution effect)[52] in this situation, whereas trade diversion is mitigated (the shielding effect).[53] Thus, trade within pre-existing ITAs is potentially subject to trade diversion from new ITAs. However, this trade diversion is becoming increasingly irrelevant as a concern for new trade deals because it is steadily declining with the increasing number of ITAs and the falling level of tariffs.[54] Moreover, trade creation is higher for original members of ITAs than for new members, and bilateral trade within a new ITA increases more than within a pre-existing ITA.[55] Accordingly, multimembership of several ITAs is less beneficial than membership of only one ITA.[56]

The 'spaghetti bowl' effect might bring about a potential negative transaction cost resulting from ITA proliferation. Using cross-sectional data on intra-Africa bilateral trade flows for 53 African countries, a 2011 study did not find any robust evidence for the hypothesis of a negative trade effect caused by the SBP.[57] Another study sought to quantify the impact on trade caused by the proliferation of ITAs. Using cross-sectional data, it found a significant trade creation effect for ITAs of between 1.76 per cent and 3.80 per cent and a trade diversion for SPB-like ITAs estimated at between -0.76% and -1.39%, depending on the model specification.[58] Using the same methodology with large panel data, a recent paper showed that an additional ITA concluded by one of both countries decreased trade by 12.1 per cent, all else being equal.[59] Moreover, it found that participation in another ITA with the USA or the EU leads to a trade diversion effect (on average 3 per cent), whereas there is no evidence for the SBP in north-north, south-south and north-south preferential trade.

Data insights

The data used here on ITAs come from the WTO which only lists trade agreements that have been officially notified by members.[60] Taking into consideration ITAs that have entered into force only after 1 January 1995 (the date of the establishment of the WTO), the data give a cumulative total of 254 ITAs notified (and still in force) during the period 1995–2016 (see Figure 5.1).[61] During the same period about 40 per cent of the ITAs under consideration were signed by EU countries or the USA. More than 45 per cent of ITAs involve at least one Organisation for Economic Co-operation and Development (OECD) country, and more than 40 per cent involve at least one BRICS country.

Figure 5.2 shows that ITA activity (including intra-/extraregional deals) is strongly led by European countries (which were involved in 105 ITAs in force), followed by East Asian countries (82 ITAs), South America countries (60 ITAs) and the Commonwealth of Independent States with 46 ITAs. The most active among WTO members in term of ITAs are the EU (40 ITAs), the European Free Trade Association) with 26 ITAs, Chile (30 ITAs), Singapore (22 ITAs) and Turkey (22 ITAs), far ahead of direct competitive countries such as the People's Republic of China (15 ITAs), the USA (14 ITAs), Canada (13 ITAs) and the Russian Federation (12 ITAs).

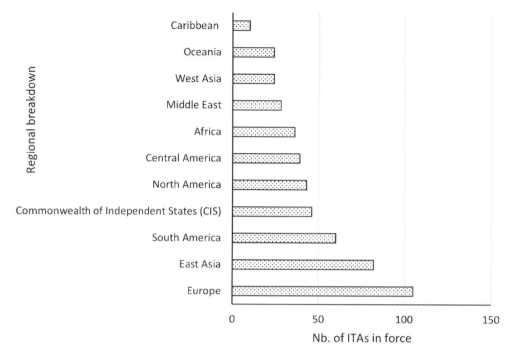

Figure 5.2 ITAs in force by region (including intra- and cross-regional ITAs), 1948–2017
Source: Author's calculations taken from WTO database, available at http://rtais.wto.org. Data only consider ITAs on goods (including/excluding services) and account for all accessions (enlargement of an ITA or accession of a country).

Following the spread of ITAs, the percentage of world trade covered by them has expanded sharply. As Figure 5.3 shows it, since 2003 more than half of world trade in goods is conducted through ITA blocs. That is consistent with the conclusion that trade diversion has not been a major concern for most ITAs.[62] In 85 per cent of cases, an ITA is estimated to generate more trade creation than trade diversion.[63] However, about 22 per cent of bilateral ITA relations have no impact on trade.[64] Indeed, ITAs have a larger impact on trade flows when they are between countries that are similar.[65] The relative size of trade creation and trade diversion depends on trade elasticities with the trading partners.[66] Theoretically, the amount of trade creation is directly related to a country's import demand elasticity. If import demand is more elastic, eliminating tariffs with a trading partner is expected to generate more trade creation because the country's total imports rise by a greater amount. When a country signs a new ITA, it tends to reduce other nations' exports to the country, however, and this latter effect is greater the larger the foreign nations' export supply elasticities are. Similarly, if the export supply elasticities are much larger in magnitude, the expected values for trade diversion would be much larger.

The majority of countries around the world are no longer vulnerable to trade diversion from new ITAs because most of their imports already come from ITA partners and because MFN tariffs are relatively low.[67] Partly due to ITAs, the global trade in goods has been boosted by the reduction in import tariffs over the past few decades. In general, all countries have joined at least one ITA, under which they promise to give another country's products lower tariffs (duty-free access) than their MFN rate. Thus, the average tariff applied by WTO members stands at 9 per cent (including preferential tariffs), whereas the average bound rate is as high as 39 per

The 'spaghetti bowl' phenomenon

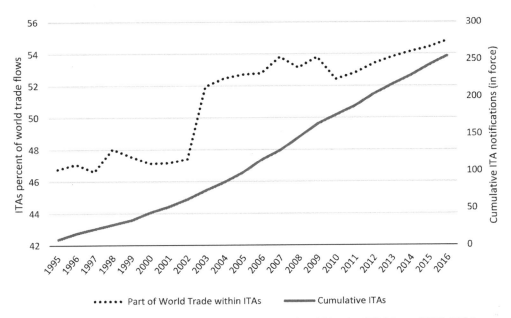

Figure 5.3 Comparative evolution of ITAs and intra-trade within the ITA blocs, 1995–2016
Source: Author's calculations taken from WTO database, available at http://rtais.wto.org. Data only consider ITAs on goods (including/excluding) and account for all accessions (enlargement of an ITA or accession of a country).

cent.[68] The global dynamics of the multilateral trading system shows that the application of MFN tariffs are less important in restricting trade; however, non-tariff barriers or non-technical measures are more commonly used in trade relations. Cumulatively, since 2009 more than 5,000 government interventions on trade have been implemented, including 3,734 'harmful' interventions as opposed to 1,364 'liberalizing' interventions (see Figure 5.4).

There is a tendency of ITAs 'to design stricter rules of origin, while detecting concomitantly the inclusion in modern preferential rules of origin of flexibilities that provide, through the rules of origin themselves, a preference beyond the lower tariff rate resulting from the preferential treatment and mechanisms that allow the integration of third-parties into preferential rules of origin regimes'.[69] Beyond the coverage of ITAs, it is their effective implementation that poses a challenge to economic operators. The analysis of the effects of rules of origin on preferential trade flows appears to give rise to a dual reality; namely a relatively high use of preferences in certain instances coexisting with preferences failing to attain their potential in other cases. Accordingly, rules of origin in ITAs seem be more trade-inhibiting than the tariffs that they have replaced. For example, the average tariff ad valorem equivalent (AVE) of rules of origin in the ASEAN free trade area is 3.40 per cent across all instruments and sectors.[70]

Conclusion

This chapter has investigated the effects of ITAs by looking at whether the proliferation of ITAs has led to an inefficient trading situation, i.e. the trade-diverting so-called SBP. Through a survey of relevant empirical studies coupled with data analysis, we can conclude that the multiplication of ITAs might result in trade diversion effects owing to higher transaction costs due to a mass of overlapping rules. Even if the percentage of world trade covered by ITAs has

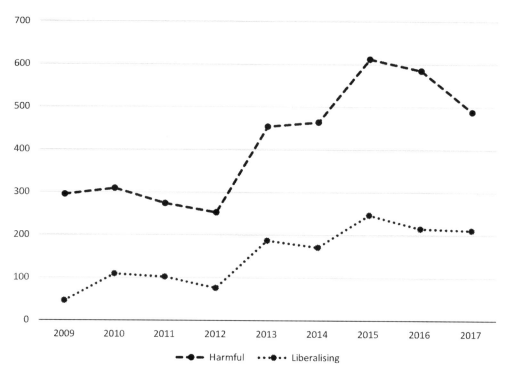

Figure 5.4 Number of state interventions affecting global trade per year, 2009–17
Note: 'harmful' refers to state interventions that have been implemented and almost certainly discriminate against foreign commercial interests; 'liberalizing' refers to state interventions that benefit foreign commercial interests by liberalizing market access.
Source: Global Trade Alert database. Available at www.globaltradealert.org/.

expanded sharply, and suggests the creation of trade, the multiplication of ITAs nevertheless diverts trade even when including many bilateral ITA relations that do not impact on trade.

The relative size of trade creation and trade diversion depends on trade elasticities between the trading partners. Thus, ITAs have a larger impact on trade flows when they are between countries that are more similar. This chapter is intended to show policymakers which countries would make good preferential trading partners. There are three ways to address trade diversion due to multi-membership: (1) countries should choose ITA partner countries whose imports will not displace imports from other non-ITA countries; (2) a country interested in signing an ITA can minimize trade diversion by signing a new trade deal with a large bloc of partner countries or by negotiating several bilateral agreements simultaneously; (3) a country can minimize the possibility of trade diversion (caused by third-nation ITAs in which it is non-member) by reducing its MFN tariffs still further (at WTO level).[71]

However, most countries around the world are no longer vulnerable to trade diversion from new regional agreements (related to their tariff barriers) because MFN tariffs are relatively low. Accordingly, applied tariffs are less important in restricting trade. The non-tariff barriers or non-technical measures are more commonly used in trade relations which can discriminate against the commercial interests of trading partners despite the presence of an ITA. However, it is difficult to precisely measure the various forms of non-tariff barriers that have replaced tariffs as the primary tools of trade policy.[72] In addition to non-tariff barriers, benefiting from a ITA requires the compliance of rules of origin. Thus, a multiplicity of ITAs gives a country the problem of the rules of origin becoming entangled.

The *raison d'être* of rules of origin in the ITAs is to avoid trade deflection or 'free riding'. In other words, the rules of origin preclude the movement of goods or components of goods from a third country outside the ITA bloc to a member of an ITA; thus producers from non-signatories cannot benefit from trading preferences. However, the practice in ITAs has diluted this objective and it would seem that preferential rules of origin are increasingly becoming an economic, political and trade instrument. The restrictiveness of rules of origin is found to be beyond the levels that would be justified to prevent trade deflection, suggesting exploitation by special interest groups.[73] In particular, the multiplication of ITAs with extensive provisions of rules of origin raise the trade-diverting effects due to the complex problems relating to the correct management of rules of origin and the compliance costs for economic operators. In the long term, all that needs to be done – to control the negative effects of the SBP of ITAs – is to implement laws and regulations in accordance with the strictest of multiple ITAs (signed by each other) and apply them to all countries in the case of new trade agreements.

For instance, that can be interestingly implemented in the case of the Asia-Pacific Region for a Trans-Pacific Partnership (TPP) Agreement, currently between 11 parties (excluding the USA); in the Regional Comprehensive Partnership Agreement between ASEAN members and six other WTO members; in the Pacific Alliance in Latin America currently between Chile, Colombia, Mexico and Peru; and in the Tripartite Agreement between parties to COMESA, EAC and SADC in Africa.[74] Such plurilateral agreements, once in force, have the potential to reduce the SBP of ITAs especially if they supersede existing bilateral agreements and develop common rules (such as for rules of origin) to be applied by all the parties to the agreement. Moreover, deep integration clauses in these cross-regional agreements, in particular the mutual recognition of conformity assessment procedures, will substantially reduce the price-raising effect of non-tariff measures, possibly reflecting lower compliance costs.[75]

The SBP affects both law and commercial issues. If we consider the SBP as referring to the entanglement of domestic rules and regulations, the term is applicable to other fields such as intellectual property regulation, investment regulation, etc. With regard to intellectual property regulation, the SBP is defined as a situation in which ITAs include provisions for intellectual property rights (IPRs) and if such provisions differ from one ITA to another, domestic rules and regulations for the protection of IPRs get entangled. In the area of investments where more than 2,200 agreements have been concluded worldwide the criss-crossing of investment rules is causing a certain problem. However, the problem is merely an extremely technical issue concerning arbitration procedures and it is completely different in nature from the aforementioned problem of criss-crossing laws and regulations.

Notes

1 I thank Joe Lamesch for his careful reading of the manuscript and helpful comments and suggestions.
2 Arye L. Hillman (1989) *The Political Economy of Protection*, London: Harwood Academic Publishers.
3 I take an ITA to denote any trade agreement between countries, meaning any preferential access for members. Thus, in this context the term ITA is used to encompass the terms free trade agreement (FTA), preferential trade agreement (PTA) and regional trade agreement (RTA) that includes customs union, common market, and other arrangements related to trade. In practice, there are some differences between these categories of ITA. For instance, in a FTA group, members enforce their own external trade restrictions outside the FTA trading bloc, but they have a free trade pact between them. With respect to PTAs, only those where countries give each other trade preferences (two-way PTAs) are considered here as ITAs; this excludes the PTAs whereby a country can unilaterally grant

preferences to a group of countries under required conditions by the World Trade Organization's agreements (one-way PTA). In a RTA, countries belonging to the same region (or geographical space) decide to create a reciprocal trade preferences bloc by restricting such privileges to the countries that are members of the RTA (e.g. the European Union, NAFTA, ECOWAS, ASEAN, etc.). In a customs union group, members adopt a common set of external trade restrictions, while, in a common market area, the movement of factors must be unrestricted, while fiscal, monetary and other economic policies must be harmonized between members. To avoid linguistic confusion, I refer to all of them (FTAs, PTAs, RTAs, customs unions, common markets, and other trade deals) as ITAs.

4 Christopher S. P. Magee (2017) 'The Increasing Irrelevance of Trade Diversion', *KYKLOS* 70(2): 278–305.

5 Jagdish Bhagwati (1993) 'Regionalism and Multilateralism: An Overview', in Jaime de Melo and Arvind Panagaryiya (eds) *New Dimensions in Regional Integration*, Cambridge: Cambridge University Press, pp. 22–51.

6 European Union (EU), North American Free Trade Agreement (NAFTA), Economic Community of West African States (ECOWAS), Association of Southeast Asian Nations (ASEAN).

7 The Economic Partnership Agreements (EPAs) are between the EU and the Africa-Caribbean-Pacific (ACP) group (agreement pack partially completed). The Comprehensive Economic and Trade Agreement (CETA) is between the EU and Canada (agreement in force). The Transatlantic Trade and Investment Partnership (TTIP) was planned to be negotiated between the EU and the USA, but has now been suspended. The Trans-Pacific Partnership (TPP) is being negotiated between Brunei, Chile, New Zealand, Singapore, the USA, Australia, Peru, Viet Nam, Malaysia, Mexico, Canada and Japan (but the agreement is not yet in force) – Taiwan, the Republic of Korea, Colombia, Indonesia, the Philippines and Taiwan announced their interest to join the TTP trading bloc. On 23 January 2017 US President Donald Trump signed a presidential memorandum to withdraw the USA from the TPP.

8 Magee, 'Increasing Irrelevance of Trade Diversion'.

9 As first demonstrated by Jacob Viner (1950) *The Customs Union Issue*, New York: Carnegie Endowment for International Peace.

10 Sanjay Pandey (2006) 'Spaghetti Bowl Phenomenon and Crucification of Multilateralism: Task Ahead for WTO' (10 December). Available at http://ssrn.com/abstract=951392 or http://dx.doi.org/10.2139/ssrn.951392 (accessed on 17 November 2017).

11 Richard Lipsey (1957) 'The Theory of Customs Unions: Trade Diversion and Welfare', *Economica* 24 (93): 40–46.

12 In a ITA, if the price of the imported goods falls, consumers gain from trade diversion while domestic producers lose out. The standard economic analysis shows that the gain to consumers outweighs the loss to producers. Trade diversion also means that the importing country loses tariff revenue because goods are now imported without tariffs from inside the regional bloc. Thus, trade diversion can either raise or lower a country's welfare. See Magee.

13 As pointed out by Jagdish Bhagwati, David Greenaway and Arvind Panagariya (1998) 'Trading Preferentially: Theory and Policy', *Economic Journal*, 108: 1128–1148.

14 As argued in Jagdish Bhagwati (2008) *Termites in the Trading System: How Preferential Agreements Undermine Free Trade*, Oxford: Oxford University Press.

15 Elina Fergin (2011) *Tangled up in a Spaghetti Bowl: Trade Effects of Overlapping Preferential Trade Agreements in Africa*, Bachelor Thesis in Economics, Lund University, School of Economics and Management.

16 Pandey, 'Spaghetti Bowl Phenomenon and Crucification of Multilateralism'.

17 Local content requirements are policies imposed by governments (generally in an ITA framework) that require firms to use domestically manufactured goods or domestically supplied services in order to operate in an economy. Rules of origin are the criteria used to define where a product was made. The rules of origin are also used to compile trade statistics, and for 'made in' labels that are attached to products. These requirements are complicated by globalization and the way a product can be processed in several countries before it is ready for the market; compliance with these requirements could lead to an inefficient trading situation for the economy.

18 Jagdish Bhagwati (1995) 'U.S. Trade Policy: The Infatuation with Free Trade Areas', in Jagdish Bhagwati and Anne O. Krueger (eds) *The Dangerous Drift to Preferential Trade Agreements*, Washington, DC: AEI Press, pp. 1–18.

19 Pandey.

20 Bela Balassa (1962) *The Theory of Economic Integration*, London: George Allen & Unwin.

21 Peter Robson (1987) *The Economics of International Integration* (3rd edn), London: George Allen & Unwin.

22 Ali M. El-Agraa (1994) *The European Union: Economies and Politics* (4th edn), London: Harvester Wheatsheaf.

23 That is also view of authors such as Jacques Pelkmans (2006) *European Integration: Methods and Economic Analysis* (3rd edn), London: Prentice Hall; and Willen Molle (1990) *The Economics of European Integration*, Aldershot: Dartmouth.

24 Thomas S. Snorrason (2012) 'The Theory of Trade Agreements, Economic Integration, Size of Economies, Trade Costs and Welfare', in *Asymmetric Economic Integration: Contributions to Economics*, Heidelberg: Physica.

25 In the first research, few studies explicitly distinguish trade blocs as customs unions involving internal free trade and a common external tariff (e.g. Viner, *The Customs Union Issue*; and Jaroslav Vanek (1965) *General Equilibrium of International Discrimination: The Case of Customs Unions*, Cambridge, MA: Harvard University Press). Other contributors do not explicitly define ITAs, using instead a general term to denote internal free trade whereby members retain their original tariff levels against non-members.

26 Viner.

27 Magee.

28 James Meade (1955) *The Theory of Customs Unions*, Amsterdam: North-Holland.

29 Snorrason, 'Theory of Trade Agreements'. Pareto efficiency, or Pareto optimality, is a concept developed by the economist Vilfredo Pareto who used it to study economic efficiency and income distribution (i.e. the allocation of resources). Thus, a Pareto optimality is a state of allocation of resources from which there does not exist another feasible allocation in which some agents would be better off (in a welfare sense) but none would be worse off. In trade theory, Pareto optimality is achieved exclusively under free trade such that other cases where there are distortions – e.g. tariffs, subsidies, taxes, monopolies etc. – are suboptimal.

30 Ibid.

31 In 2017 ITAs continued to proliferate. According to the WTO Secretariat (RTA Section), 13 ITAs 'were notified to the WTO in the first half of 2017, bringing the total number of ITAs in force and notified to the WTO to 279 by the end of June 2017'. Some ITAs are in force that have not yet been notified at the WTO. See www.wto.org/english/tratop_e/region_e/rtajan-june17_e.pdf (accessed 17 November 2017).

32 See Paul Krugman (1993) 'Regionalism versus Multilateralism: Analytic Notes', in Jaime de Melo and Arvind Panagariya (eds) *New Dimensions in Regional Integration*, Cambridge: Cambridge University Press, pp. 58–84; and Bhagwati, *Termites in the Trading System*.

33 The Bilateralism/Regionalism phenomenon may also be explained by idiosyncratic events (such as the USA's opening of the US-Canada FTA talks in 1996, the break-up of the USSR in 1991, and the Asian Crisis of 1997) and by some institutional needs (such as democracy, transparency and geopolitical stability). Cf. Richard Baldwin and Dany Jaimovich (2012) 'Are Free Trade Agreements Contagious?' *Journal of International Economics*, 88: 1–16.

34 Jason H. Grant and Dayton M. Lambert (2008) 'Do Regional Trade Agreements Increase Members' Agricultural Trade?' *American Journal of Agricultural Economics*, 90: 765–82.

35 Maurice Schiff and Alan Winters (2003) *Regional Integration and Development*, Washington, DC: World Bank.

36 These reasons are discussed in John Whalley (1998) 'Why Do Countries Seek Regional Trade Agreements?' in J. Frankel (ed.) *The Regionalization of the World Economy*, Chicago, IL: University of Chicago Press, pp. 63–90.

37 See e.g. Vincent Vicard (2012) 'Trade, Conflicts and Political Integration: Explaining the Heterogeneity of Regional Trade Agreements', *European Economic Review*, 56: 54–71.

38 See e.g. Edward Mansfield, Helen Milner and Peter Rosendorff (2002) Replication, Realism, and Robustness: Analyzing Political Regimes and International Trade', *American Political Science Review*, 96: 167–69.

39 See e.g. Philippe Martin, Thierry Mayer and Mathias Thoenig (2008) 'Make Trade not War?' *Review of Economic Studies*, 75: 865–900.

40 Baldwin and Jaimovich, 'Are Free Trade Agreements Contagious?'.

41 Peter Egger and Mario Larch (2008) 'Interdependent Preferential Trade Agreement Memberships: An Empirical Analysis', *Journal of International Economics*, 76: 384–99; and M. Xiaoyang Chen and Joshi Sumit (2010) 'Third-Country Effects on the Formation of Free Trade Agreements', *Journal of International Economics*, 82: 238–48.

42 Leonardo Baccini and Andreas Dür (2015) 'Investment Discrimination and the Proliferation of Preferential Trade Agreements', *Journal of Conflict Resolution*, 59: 617–44; and Baldwin and Jaimovich.

43 Jagdish Bhagwati and Arvind Panagariya (1996) 'Preferential Trading Areas and Multilateralism: Strangers, Friends of Foes?' in Jagdish Bhagwati and Arvind Panagariya (eds) *The Economics of Preferential Trade Agreements*, Washington, DC: AEI Press, pp. 1–78.

44 Bhagwati, 'U.S. Trade Policy'.

45 Bhagwati *et al.*, 'Trading Preferentially'.

46 Innwon Park and Park Soonchan (2011) 'Best Practices for Regional Trade Agreements', *Review of World Economics*, 147(2): 249–68.

47 S. Hee Lee, K. Soo Park and Y. Won Seo (2017) 'Multinational Firm's Production Decisions under Overlapping Free Trade Agreements: Rule of Origin Requirements and Environmental Regulation', *Sustainability*, 9: 1–42.

48 Mian Dai, Yoto V. Yotov and Thomas Zylkin (2014) 'On the Trade-Diversion Effects of Free Trade Agreements', *Economics Letters*, 122: 321–25.

49 Jung Hur, Joseph D. Alba and Donghyun Park (2010) 'Effects of Hub-and-Spoke Free Trade Agreements on Trade: A Panel Data Analysis', *World Development*, 38: 1105–13.

50 A 'hub' country is defined as a country that participates to a given ITA with at least two 'spoke' countries, that belong to another ITA without the hub (i.e. between 'spoke' countries).

51 Juyoung Cheong, Do Won Kwak and Kam Ki Tang (2015) 'Heterogeneous Effects of Preferential Trade Agreements: How Does Partner Similarity Matter?' *World Development*, 66: 222–36.

52 A pre-existing ITA with a third country decreases the trade with a member country of a new ITA. In other words, countries continue to trade with trading partners in a former ITA, but to a lesser extent because of the new adhesion to a PTA.

53 Members of a pre-existing ITA have a higher level of trade compared with members of a new PTA due to the trade-promoting effect reducing the trade diversion.

54 Magee.

55 Jong-Wha Lee, Innwon Park and Kwanho Shin (2008) 'Proliferating Regional Trade Arrangements: Why and Whither?' *World Economy*, 31: 1525–57.

56 Ibid.

57 Fergin, *Tangled up in a Spaghetti Bowl*.

58 Fukunari Kimura, Arata Kuno and Kazunobu Hayakawa (2006) 'Does the Number of RTAs Matter? Empirical Analysis on the Spaghetti Bowl Phenomenon', Working Paper, Faculty of Economics, Keio University. Available at https://faculty.washington.edu/karyiu/confer/GJ06/papers/kimura-kuno-hayakawa.pdf (accessed 17 November 2017).

59 Zakaria Sorgho (2016) 'RTAs' Proliferation and Trade-Diversion Effects: Evidence of the "Spaghetti Bowl" Phenomenon', *World Economy*, 39: 285–300.

60 See database at http://rtais.wto.org/UI/PublicAllRTAList.aspx (accessed 17 November 2017).

61 Data only consider ITAs on goods (including/excluding services) and account for all accessions (the enlargement of regional economic blocs or the accession of countries). Note that, in the WTO database, some ITAs were in force many years after being notified at the WTO: for example, the accession of Egypt to the Common Market for Eastern and Southern Africa (COMESA) dates from February 1999 despite the fact that it was only notified in January 2017, or the trade agreement between India and Thailand dates from September 2004, but was notified in June 2017. Using the WTO database, my data pay attention to these details (notification *post* date-in-force) by only taking into account ITAs in force in a given year.

62 Caroline Freund and Emanuel Ornelas (2010) 'Regional Trade Agreements', *Annual Review of Economics*, 2: 139–66.

63 Magee.

64 Ibid.

65 Cheong *et al.*, 'Heterogeneous Effects of Preferential Trade Agreements'.

66 Magee.

67 Ibid.

68 WTO, ITC and UNCTAD (2016) *World Tariff Profiles 2016*, Geneva: WTO.

69 Abreu M. Donner (2016) Preferential Rules of Origin in Regional Trade Agreements', in Rohini Acharya (ed.) *Regional Trade Agreements and the Multilateral Trading System*, Cambridge: Cambridge University Press, pp. 58–110.

The 'spaghetti bowl' phenomenon

70 Olivier Cadot and L. Yan Ing (2016) 'How Restrictive Are ASEAN's Rules of Origin?'. *Asian Economic Papers*, 15: 115–34. Cadot and Ing's study assesses the non-tariff barriers induced by rules of origin within the ASEAN FTA. The objective is to emphasize that even if the commercial tariffs have disappeared, there is an 'invisible' tariff through the rules of origin. This non-tariff barrier is at least equal to the commercial tariff eliminated with the creation of the free trade zone.

71 These recommendations are consistent with those of Magee.

72 Pinelopi K. Goldberg and Nina Pavcnik (2016) 'The Effects of Trade Policy (Chapter 3)', in Kyle Bagwell and Robert W. Staiger (eds) *Handbook of Commercial Policy*, vol.1(A), Amsterdam: North-Holland, pp. 161–206.

73 Olivier Cadot and Jaime de Melo (2007) 'Why OECD Countries Should Reform Rules of Origin', *World Bank Research Observer*, 23: 77–105.

74 Association of Southeast Asian Nations (ASEAN), Common Market for Eastern and Southern Africa (COMESA), East African Community (EAC) and Southern African Development Community (SADC).

75 Olivier Cadot and Julien Gourdon (2016) Non-Tariff Measures, Preferential Trade Agreements, and Prices: New Evidence, *Review of World Economics*, 152: 227–49.

6

The economic effects of FTAs

Holger Breinlich

Introduction

The two decades since the creation of the World Trade Organization (WTO) in 1995 have seen a surge in the formation of reciprocal free trade agreements (FTAs). Between 1995 and 2017 the number of FTAs notified to the WTO increased from around 50 to over 320.[1] While earlier agreements focused on the elimination of bilateral tariffs, modern FTAs usually include a large number of additional provisions focusing on non-tariff barriers and behind-the-border policies such as state aid or competition policy, as well as measures that are only indirectly linked to trade such as human rights or consumer protection.[2]

Against this background, a large body of research has tried to assess the effects of FTAs. This chapter summarizes the literature, with a focus on the economic impact of FTAs. Section 2 starts with the effect of FTAs on trade volumes, Section 3 looks at the effect on companies and labour markets, and section 4 focuses on their impact on consumers and overall economic welfare. Throughout the chapter, the focus is on reciprocal FTAs in which all partners grant improved access to their markets. The literature on preferential trade agreements (e.g. the General System of Preferences) and unilateral trade liberalizations undertaken by individual countries is only discussed when it is of relevance to understanding the effects of reciprocal agreements. I also do not look at the underlying determinants of the existence and design of FTAs, their interaction with the WTO-based multilateral trading system, or at their effects on non-economic variables such as human rights or environmental and geopolitical outcomes.[3]

Effects on trade

The most direct impact of trade agreements is on trade flows, and a substantial amount of research effort has been devoted towards measuring such effects. The key challenge in this literature is to disentangle the effects of FTAs from the myriad of other factors that also influence bilateral trade flows. By far the most important tool to address this problem is the so-called gravity equation which models trade flows between two countries as a log-linear function of exporter- and importer-specific regressors (e.g. the countries' gross domestic products) and bilateral variables such as distance. Gravity equations can be used to predict the 'normal' level of trade between two countries, and to show the extent to which FTAs increase trade flows over and above that level. In principle, this could be done by including a number of variables measuring the different provisions of an FTA in a gravity equation. In practice, however, it is often hard to quantify the individual components of FTAs and the sheer number of provisions introduces severe multicollinearity problems. Hence, the most common solution is to simply include a dummy variable for whether two countries are part of the same trade agreement.

Earlier estimates of the trade impact of FTAs based on the gravity equation framework produced a wide range of results and often found that there were zero or even negative effects of trade agreements. For example, a meta-analysis carried out by the World Bank in 2005 looked at 17 studies and 362 estimates.[4] While the average estimated effect of trade agreements on the partner countries' bilateral trade was positive and large (indicating an FTA-induced trade increase of over 100 per cent), the estimates' standard deviation was very high. Consequently, just over 50 per cent of the estimates were statistically significant and positive, while 12 per cent were negative and significant. Given that the primary purpose of FTAs is to enhance bilateral market access, this absence of robustly positive effects raised questions about the validity of these studies and led to important methodological advances. Some of the problems identified in earlier papers included small and too-selective samples, omission of important country-specific control variables, and endogeneity resulting from the selection of country pairs into trade agreements.[5]

Following important contributions by James Anderson, Eric van Wincoop, Scott Baier and Jeffrey Bergstrand, most recent papers have included exporter-year and importer-year fixed effects to control for multilateral price terms and other country-specific omitted variables.[6] The issue of selection has also received increased attention, although it is fair to say that no consensus has been reached as to the best way of accounting for the fact that countries do not choose their FTA partners randomly. One approach is to find suitable instrumental variables that are correlated with the likelihood of FTA formation but do not directly influence trade between the partner countries. However, authors such as Scott Baier and Jeffrey Bergstrand have argued that in practice it is difficult to find credible exclusion restrictions, as determinants of trade agreements are usually also likely to have a direct impact on trade.[7] As an alternative they suggest using country-pair fixed effects to control for endogeneity. This is justified if selection is based on time-invariant omitted variables such as geographic proximity or the general potential for FTA-induced trade increases. However, if countries systematically sign trade agreements with countries with those where they have seen strong increases in bilateral trade (or where they expect such increases in the near future), controlling only for country-pair fixed effects will exaggerate the true effect of FTAs.

Another important innovation that has influenced the literature on the trade effects of FTAs is the use of gravity estimation methods other than ordinary least squares (OLS). In an influential paper, J. M. C. Santos Silva and Silvana Tenreyro pointed out that OLS estimation of log-linear gravity equations is likely to result in biased estimates.[8] Because trade flows are non-negative, the gravity equation's stochastic error term will in general be heteroskedastic and log-linearization will introduce correlation between the regressors and the error term. Santos Silva and Tenreyro propose using Poisson pseudo-maximum likelihood (PPML) estimation to overcome this issue.

While newer contributions to the FTA literature have only adopted these methodological innovations to varying degrees, the broad consensus is that recent estimates are more reliable and more consistently positive. For example, a widely cited study by Baier and Bergstrand uses a panel of around 100 countries for the period 1960–2000 and estimates gravity equations controlling for country-year and bilateral fixed effects.[9] Their findings indicate that FTAs approximately double a country pair's trade after ten years.[10] A recent meta-analysis by Keith Head and Thierry Mayer uses estimates from 159 papers published between 2006 and 2012 in highly ranked journals and also finds a positive mean effect of FTAs on trade flows of around 80 per cent, and a median effect of 60 per cent.[11] Importantly, while the mean effect reported by Head and Mayer is slightly lower than that of the earlier World Bank meta study (80 per cent as opposed to 120 per cent), the standard deviation of the estimates also declined substantially (from 1.3 to 0.5), reinforcing the view that more recent estimates are more reliable.

While the recent literature thus finds that FTAs have a strong, positive effect on trade, one important caveat is that these estimates capture the effects of both trade creation and trade diversion. This is because they are based on a comparison of trade with FTA partners and trade with other countries. So, a positive coefficient can indicate the displacement of domestic production by imports from the FTA partner (trade creation) or the diversion of trade with other countries to FTA partners (trade diversion). Earlier studies often included a dummy variable taking the value of one if a country had a trade agreement with *any* other country. When included in addition to the usual bilateral FTA dummy, this variable captured changes in trade volumes with non-partner countries. However, the inclusion of country-year fixed effects precludes this approach because the additional dummy is not separately identified from these fixed effects. Instead, newer studies often rely on general equilibrium models of the global economy to capture trade diversion.[12] First, a gravity equation is used to estimate the direct effect of FTAs on bilateral trade. This estimate is then converted into an *ad valorem* equivalent using an appropriate trade elasticity. Finally, the model is solved with and without the FTA-induced change in trade cost between countries, and the resulting counterfactual trade flow changes for each country pair are computed. Of course, different modelling frameworks will lead to different estimates but the findings from multi-country Armington-type models (that assume products traded internationally are differentiated by country of origin) suggest that trade diversion effects are unimportant relative to trade creation effects.[13]

Embedding gravity estimates in explicitly specified economic models also makes it possible to predict the general equilibrium effects of trade agreements that work through changes in domestic income levels and prices. Because FTAs improve market access and increase competition, prices in the partner countries fall, thus partially offsetting the direct trade-creating effect of lower barriers. Recent research by Keith Head and Thierry Mayer suggests that this offsetting effect can be quantitatively important although the exact extent of this does of course again depend on the model used.[14]

The vast majority of studies on the trade effects of FTAs focus on merchandise trade and exclude trade in services. This is despite the fact that the share of commercial services in total world trade has been steadily increasing over the past 30 years and now stands at 22 per cent, or US $4.97 trillion.[15] At the same time, a growing share of FTAs include legally enforceable provisions on the liberalization of trade in services. Whereas only approximately 30 per cent of FTAs signed prior to the creation of the WTO contain such provisions, 55 per cent of agreements signed after 1995 do.[16] One problem facing research in this area is that services trade is inherently more difficult to measure than trade in goods. High-quality data is still mostly restricted to Organization of Economic Co-operation and Development (OECD) countries and so is the scope of most of the existing studies. For example, Fukunari Kimura and Hyun-Hoon Lee estimate traditional gravity equations based on the trading patterns of ten OECD countries with 47 OECD and non-OECD partner countries. They find that FTAs increase bilateral trade by around 30 per cent for both goods and services.[17] Peter H. Egger, Mario Larch and Kevin E. Staub use a sample of 16 European OECD countries and find a direct effect of liberalization on trade in goods of about 49 per cent and on trade in services of close to 220 per cent.[18] While they use modern estimation techniques (PPML with country-year fixed effects), their identification mainly comes from EU accessions, making the external validity of their results to non-European contexts less clear. This view is confirmed in recent work by Monique Ebell.[19] She uses cross-sectional data for 42 rich and emerging economies in 2014 and finds that membership of the European Economic Area (EEA) is associated with 182 per cent more trade compared to trade between countries which do not have any trade agreements in place. However, no statistically significant effects are found for other FTAs covering services.

Overall, the recent literature thus finds that trade agreements do have strong, if sometimes uneven, impacts on trade in both goods and services. This raises the question of what the associated impacts on other economic variables are. In the next section, I describe impacts on firms and labour markets, and turn to the effect of FTAs on consumers and overall welfare in section 4.

Effects on firms and labour markets

There is a large and growing body of literature covering the effects of trade policy on firms as well as on the associated labour market effects. Here, I focus more narrowly on trade policy changes brought about by FTAs, although I also review evidence from unilateral trade liberalizations where necessary. I do not discuss the related and even more voluminous body of research on the effects of trade on growth and income levels that relies on aggregate cross-country data. This research has been plagued by measurement and endogeneity problems and more recent work has tended to focus on individual liberalization episodes and has used more disaggregated data such as firm- or household-level information.[20]

The company performance measure that has attracted the most attention in the literature is productivity, measured as either labour or total factor productivity and usually computed on a revenue basis. One mechanism through which FTAs can increase industry-level productivity is by reallocating market shares from less to more productive firms. This can occur because reductions in the FTA partner's trade barriers increase sales by domestic exporters which tend to be larger and more productive, or because increased competition from foreign producers leads to the exit of less productive domestic firms.[21] The best available evidence for these FTA-induced reallocation processes comes from the 1988 Canada-US Free Trade Agreement (CUSFTA). Work by Jen Baggs shows that Canadian tariff reductions sharply increased exit rates, while Alla Lileeva has demonstrated that this increase was concentrated among non-exporting firms.[22] Daniel Trefler estimates that CUSFTA helped to improve Canadian manufacturing productivity by 5.8 per cent over an eight-year period, and that market share reallocations accounted for most of this increase.[23] These findings are consistent with a number of papers which have demonstrated similar effects in the context of unilateral trade liberalization. For example, Nina Pavcnik has studied firm-level adjustment in the wake of the Chilean trade liberalization and found that two-thirds of the observed 19 per cent increase in productivity was due to a market share reallocation towards more efficient producers.[24] Work by Ana Fernandes also finds that market share reallocation was an important driver of productivity growth in Colombia between 1977 and 1991, a period that saw significant variation in external trade barriers.[25]

FTAs can also enhance the productivity of existing firms through a number of channels. First, better exporting opportunities increase the size of the market available to a firm and hence boost returns to innovation. Consistent with this idea, Daniel Trefler and Alla Lileeva show that CUSFTA led to in-plant productivity increases that went hand-in-hand with productivity-enhancing investments, and were concentrated among Canadian plants that started exporting to the USA in response to the agreement.[26] Similarly, Paula Bustos finds that Argentinian manufacturing firms and industries with larger tariff reductions in the wake of Mercosur increased their investments in technology more rapidly.[27] Second, trade liberalization can also improve access to foreign intermediate inputs.[28] Third, increased import competition can force plants to reorganize production processes and product ranges. For example, John Baldwin and Wulong Gu show that CUSFTA induced Canadian manufacturers to increase the length of their production runs, and Andrew Bernard, Stephen Redding and Peter Schott find that US firms increasingly focused on core products following the signing of the agreement.[29]

While the existing literature thus provides ample evidence for the productivity-enhancing effects of FTAs, one important caveat is that most studies are unable to distinguish between revenues and physical productivity (output per inputs). This is because productivity is usually computed as the residual in a firm-level regression of revenues on factor input expenditures.[30] So, if trade liberalization leads to changes in input or output prices, this will lead to changes in measured productivity even if technical efficiency has not changed. Initial research focused on output prices and showed that trade liberalization in Turkey and Côte d'Ivoire led to decreases in mark-ups as domestic firms were exposed to tougher competition.[31] However, in more recent work Jan De Loecker *et al.* warn that this effect does not easily generalize to other trade reforms.[32] They show that mark-ups actually increased as a consequence of the Indian trade liberalization of 1991, because cost reductions due to cheaper imported intermediate inputs were not fully passed on to output prices. While they also find that the liberalization had pro-competitive effects, these were dominated by the mark-up increase due to incomplete cost pass through. As noted by De Loecker and Pinelopi Goldberg, the fact that mark-ups can both increase or decrease after trade liberalization makes the interpretation of earlier studies difficult.[33]

The existing literature has also studied the impact of trade agreements on a number of additional firm-level variables. I have already briefly summarized evidence that FTAs can lead to changes in firms' innovation incentives, production processes and product ranges. Another variable that has attracted attention is firm-level profits. Studying profit responses seems worthwhile because they are an important part of the overall welfare impact of lower trade barriers and also help to understand the political economy aspects of FTAs, such as lobbying responses by firms. One way of approaching this topic is to look at accounting profits. For example, Jen Baggs and James Brander have regressed measures of accounting profitability on tariff changes following the signing of CUSFTA and found that lower Canadian import tariffs reduced the profits of Canadian firms, whereas lower US tariffs increased them.[34] One potential criticism of this approach is that accounting profits might only be loosely linked to profitability in an economic sense.[35] Hence, an alternative approach in the literature is to use stock market reactions to unexpected FTA-related announcements. Christoph Moser and Andrew Rose study price reactions to over 200 FTA announcements and find that during the two-and-a-half-week period following announcement of an agreement there are on average positive and statistically significant abnormal returns, and this is consistent with the view that FTAs increase overall company profits.[36] Holger Breinlich looks at unanticipated changes in the likelihood of CUSFTA's implementation and finds that prices of companies operating with larger future Canadian tariff cuts experienced negative abnormal returns when CUSFTA became more likely.[37] By contrast, stronger future cuts in intermediate input tariffs were associated with higher abnormal returns. Future US tariff cuts only benefited the stock prices of larger firms, possibly because these firms are more likely to be exporters. Making a number of assumptions about market efficiency and the underlying model of stock price determination, Breinlich also estimates the implied change in firm profits. He finds that CUSFTA increased total yearly profits of Canadian manufacturing firms by approximately 1.2 per cent.

The final set of outcomes that the literature on trade liberalization has studied are labour market variables such as wages and employment, both at the level of sectors and individual firms. The literature in this area is extensive and still growing, but surprisingly few studies look at the effects of bilateral trade agreements on labour market outcomes. Instead, most evidence comes either from unilateral trade liberalizations in developing countries or the effect of import competition more generally.[38] An exception is Daniel Trefler's work on CUSFTA in which he finds that the tariff changes mandated by that agreement reduced manufacturing employment in Canada by 5 per cent. Most of the job losses were concentrated in the one-third of industries with the largest Canadian import tariff reductions. By contrast, U.S. tariff reductions did not lead to statistically significant employment changes in Canada. While lower US tariffs increased employment at exporting plants, they were also associated with job losses at purely domestic plants, with the net effect being close to zero. One important question arising from these findings is to what extent the overall estimated job losses represented short-term adjustment costs or whether they had more long-term negative consequences. Noting that employment levels in Canada remained constant during CUSFTA's implementation period and that manufacturing employment even increased slightly, Trefler concludes that employment reductions must have been of a short-term nature, with displaced workers being re-employed quickly. At the same time, his findings suggest that CUSFTA had a positive, if small, effect on earnings and did not lead to increases in inequality.

Studying the North American Free Trade Agreement (NAFTA), Shushanik Hakobyan and John McLaren reach much less optimistic conclusions.[39] Their findings show that US sectors producing tradable goods that were exposed to steeper US import tariff reductions saw lower wage growth, with less-educated workers being particularly negatively affected. They also find that US locations that specialized in the tradable goods sectors most affected by tariff reductions experienced lower wage growth more generally. One explanation for this is that displaced manufacturing workers do not move to other, less affected, locations, but compete with workers in non-tradable sectors, hence depressing wages. Again, these location-specific effects seem to be particularly severe for less-educated workers and non-existent for college graduates.

One concern with these results is that they do not take into account improved exporting opportunities to Mexico.[40] By contrast, Brian McCaig focuses exclusively on the effects of better access to the US market following the 2001 US-Vietnam Nam Bilateral Trade Agreement. He shows that provinces with greater shares of workers in industries that experienced larger US tariff cuts saw significantly faster reductions in poverty rates.[41]

The evidence base directly relevant for the effects of bilateral trade agreements is clearly still somewhat limited. However, many of the findings outlined above echo the conclusions of the much larger literature on unilateral trade liberalizations and the effects of import competition. For example, Petia Topalova studies the effects of the 1991 Indian trade liberalization and finds that rural districts with production sectors that were more exposed to import tariff reductions experienced slower declines in poverty and lower consumption growth.[42] In the context of Brazil's trade liberalization in the 1990s, Brian Kovak shows that regions facing larger liberalization-induced price drops experienced larger decreases in wages.[43] David Autor, David Dorn and Gordon Hanson look at the impact of Chinese import competition on local labour market outcomes in the USA and find that changes in Chinese imports are correlated with higher unemployment, lower labour force participation, and reduced wages.[44] By contrast, studies relying on cross-industry variation of trade policy reach more mixed conclusions regarding the wage effects of trade liberalization, mirroring the diverging findings of Trefler and Hakobyan and McLaren discussed above.[45] Research into the firm-level effects of liberalization also confirms Trefler's findings that exporters and non-exporters react very differently to improved exporting opportunities, with the former increasing wages relative to the latter.[46] Potential explanations include positive productivity effects of exporting, possibly linked to technology upgrading or rent-sharing between exporters and their employees.[47]

Effects on economic welfare

Arguably the most important impact of FTAs is their effect on economic welfare. Put differently, the reason why we care about the effects of FTAs on variables such as trade and productivity is because of the associated changes in welfare, usually measured as the percentage change in real consumption of a representative consumer.[48] Leaving aside for now the question of whether this measure is indeed a good guide for evaluating the effects of FTAs, the key challenge is to find ways to link changes in trade barriers to changes in welfare.

In an important recent contribution, Costas Arkolakis, Arnaud Costinot and Andrés Rodríguez-Clare demonstrate that for a range of modern trade models, the welfare effects of a change in trade costs can be evaluated using just two pieces of information – the change in the share of expenditure on domestic goods caused by the change in trade cost and the elasticity of imports relative to domestic demand with respect to trade costs (henceforth, the trade elasticity).[49] Arkolakis *et al.* focus on models featuring a single sector, one production factor, no tradable intermediate inputs and constant elasticity of substitution (CES) utility but their results have been generalized across all these dimensions.[50] While the exact formula for computing welfare changes needs to be adapted accordingly, the basic idea that the consequences of trade cost changes (including changes in import tariffs) can be evaluated using simple macro-level sufficient statistics continues to apply.

Given the simplicity of Arkolakis *et al.*'s approach it is surprising that there does not seem to be any work applying their insights to the evaluation of trade agreements. One would need credible estimates of the trade elasticity as well as the FTA-induced changes in domestic goods' expenditure shares; however, given the progress of the literature on the trade effects of FTAs discussed in section 2, the latter would seem to be clearly feasible, and trade policy changes themselves could serve as sources of variation to identify the trade elasticity.[51]

Of course, the question remains to what extent the numbers predicted by combining modern 'middle-sized' trade models with the Arkolakis *et al.* formula are credible. These models all predict gravity-type functional forms for trade flows, ensuring that they tightly fit cross-sectional trade data; however, the evaluation with respect to the prediction of out-of-sample trade flows and additional relevant variables such as factor prices or technical efficiency remains in its infancy.[52] It should be noted, however, that similar concerns plague older large-scale computable general equilibrium (CGE) models that have been the workhorse for applied trade policy analysis for the past decades. If anything, a small number of recent evaluations have shown that the more recent, middle-sized models that are the focus of Arkolakis *et al.* tend to perform better in terms of out-of-sample predictions.[53]

An alternative to estimates based on fully specified models is to remain agnostic about the supply side of an economy and focus on the welfare effects that can be computed based on assumptions about consumer demand only. The classic paper in this literature is by Christian Broda and David Weinstein who try to quantify the gains to US consumers from increases in the number of imported varieties.[54] They find that if such gains were taken into account in the computation of the US import price index, measured import prices would have been 28 per cent lower during the period 1972 to 2001. Importantly, these results only require the specification of a demand system (nested CES in this case) and an estimate of the elasticity of substitution across foreign varieties.[55]

Again, demand-side approaches such as that of Broda and Weinstein have rarely been applied to actual trade liberalization episodes. An exception is recent work by Giuseppe Berlingieri, Holger Breinlich and Swati Dhingra who try to measure the consumer price effects of the trade agreements negotiated by the European Union (EU) between 1993 and 2013.[56] They first decompose the overall change in import prices into price changes, quality changes and changes in the number of imported varieties. They then estimate the impact of FTAs on each of these components by comparing imports of trade agreement partners with a control group of other countries. Aggregating across products and time, they find that the cumulative effect of the EU's trade agreements was to lower consumer prices by −0.13 per cent which translates into savings for EU consumers of around €13 billion per year from 2013 onwards. Similarly to Broda and Weinstein, these results only require the specification of a demand system, as well as the usual assumptions underlying the empirical difference-in-differences estimation strategy. One downside of this approach is, however, that they have to abstract from a number of additional gains from trade, such as reduced mark-ups of domestic firms or cheaper and better intermediate inputs.[57]

Overall, recent approaches towards measuring the welfare gains from trade certainly seem promising although applications to actual trade policy changes are still rare. This raises the question as to whether future research efforts should be directed more squarely at estimating the welfare effects of trade agreements, and away from more traditional topics such as the impact on trade, productivity and labour market outcomes. After all, isn't welfare what policy makers should care about? Here, there are reasons to remain sceptical. One reason is of course that we might not have sufficient confidence in the predictions of what are still relatively stylized models. By contrast, reduced-form estimates of the effects of trade agreements on variables such as employment or productivity are generally considered to be more reliable.[58] But there are also reasons to doubt whether aggregate consumer welfare is really the best measure of the effects of trade agreements. For example, the assumption of a representative consumer assumes away many of the real world distributional issues that have been so relevant to the recent public debates about the benefits of globalization.[59] At a more fundamental level, a well-known criticism of consumer welfare is that it simply equates well-being with greater consumption opportunities.[60] It stands to reason that citizens and their elected representatives also care about other economic variables, including employment opportunities and life chances more generally. Hence, it seems that aggregate welfare effects in the sense of this section will remain only one, albeit an important, indicator of the economic success of trade agreements.

Conclusion

The literature on the economic effects of trade agreements has made important progress over the past two decades. The key finding is that FTAs have a substantial impact on numerous facets of economic activity, ranging from trade flows to productivity and employment. The broad picture that emerges is one of long-term gain for short-term pain. While some concerns regarding appropriate measurement remain, FTAs seem to increase profitability and economic efficiency. At the same time, however, trade agreements can lead to sometimes substantial wage and employment losses, at least in the short term. Empirically, there also seems to be an important difference between tougher import competition triggered by domestic tariff reductions and better access to foreign markets and intermediate inputs. Further disentangling these different channels of impact, in particular in the context of labour market outcomes, remains an important area of future work. Another area that clearly requires more research effort is the quantification of the numerous provisions of modern FTAs that go far beyond tariff reductions.

Most of the existing work discussed here focuses on the latter but it is unclear whether measures such as regulatory harmonization, mutual recognition of qualifications or investment liberalization have similar effects. Harmonization of standards, in particular, might interfere with domestic regulation aimed at the reduction of market failures and could have less clear-cut welfare consequences than the elimination of tariffs. Given that the proliferation of modern bilateral and unilateral agreements is expected to continue for now, these issues will occupy researchers and policymakers for many years to come.

Notes

1 See www.wto.org/english/tratop_e/region_e/rta_pta_e.htm for a list of all reciprocal trade agreements notified to the WTO.
2 See C. Hofmann, A. Osnago and M. Ruta (2017) 'Horizontal Depth: A New Database on the Content of Preferential Trade Agreements', Policy Research Working Paper 7981, Washington, DC: World Bank.
3 Chapters 7, 9, 11, 12 and 14 in this Handbook review the key non-economic aspects of FTAs in more detail.
4 See World Bank (2005) 'Regional Trade Agreements: Effects on Trade,' in *Global Economic Perspectives: Trade, Regionalism, and Development*, World Bank: Washington, DC, ch. 3.
5 See N. Limão (2016) 'Preferential Trade Agreements', in Kyle Bagwell and Robert W. Staiger (eds) *Handbook of Commercial Policy*, Amsterdam: Elsevier.
6 J. Anderson and E. van Wincoop (2003) 'Gravity with Gravitas: A Solution to the Border Puzzle', *American Economic Review*, Vol. 93(1): 170–192.
7 S. Baier and J. Bergstrand (2007) 'Do Free Trade Agreements Actually Increase Members' International Trade?' *Journal of International Economics*, 71: 72–95.
8 J. M. C. Santos Silva and S. Tenreyro (2006) 'The Log of Gravity', *Review of Economics and Statistics*, 88 (4): 641–58.
9 Baier and Bergstrand, 'Do Free Trade Agreements Actually Increase Members' International Trade?'.
10 In recent work, Nuno Limão replicates their study using data up to 2010 and a more comprehensive list of trade agreements and finds a similarly large effect. See Limão, 'Preferential Trade Agreements'.
11 See K. Head and T. Mayer (2014) 'Gravity Equations: Workhorse, Toolkit, and Cookbook', in G. Gopinath, E. Helpman and K. Rogoff (eds) *Handbook of International Economics*. Amsterdam: Elsevier.
12 See, for instance, P. Egger, M. Larch, K. E. Staub and R. Winkelmann (2011) 'The Trade Effects of Endogenous Preferential Trade Agreements', *American Economic Journal: Economic Policy*, 3: 113–43.
13 Ibid., section VI.
14 See Head and Mayer, 'Gravity Equations: Workhorse, Toolkit, and Cookbook', Table 6. The median direct FTA effect in their sample is 32 per cent but declines to just 13 per cent when taking into account price adjustments. Furthermore, allowing for income changes again increases the trade effect to 21 per cent.
15 Figures for 2014, based on author's calculations using the WTO's *Time Series in International Trade*. WTO (n.d.) 'WTO Time Series on International Trade'. Available at http://stat.wto.org/Home/WSDBHome.aspx?Language=.
16 Author's calculations based on the World Bank's Content of Deep Trade Agreements database. A simple explanation for this increase is that FTAs often reaffirm commitments made under the General Agreement on Trade in Services (GATS). However, some of the more recent FTAs, such as the EU-Canada and EU-South Korea agreements, go considerably beyond GATS liberalization commitments.
17 F. Kimura and H.-H. Lee (2006) 'The Gravity Equation in International Trade in Services', *Review of World Economics*, 142(1): 92–121.
18 P. Egger, M. Larch and K. Staub (2012) 'Trade Preferences and Bilateral Trade in Goods and Services: A Structural Approach', CEPR Discussion Paper 9051. London: Centre for Economic Policy Research.
19 M. Ebell (2016) 'Assessing the Impact of Trade Agreements on Trade', *National Institute Economic Review*, 238: R31–R42.
20 See A. Harrison and A. Rodríguez-Clare (2010) 'Trade, Foreign Investment, and Industrial Policy for Developing Countries', in D. Rodrik and M. Rosenzweig (eds) *Handbook of Development Economics*, vol. 5, for a comprehensive recent review.

21 See A. Bernard, B. Jensen, S. Redding and P. Schott (2007) 'Firms in International Trade', *Journal of Economic Perspectives*, 21(3): 105–30.

22 See J. Baggs (2005) 'Firm Survival and Exit in Response to Trade Liberalization', *Canadian Journal of Economics*, 38(4): 1364–83; A. Lileeva (2008) 'Trade Liberalization and Productivity Dynamics: Evidence from Canada', *Canadian Journal of Economics*, 41(2): 360–90.

23 D. Trefler (2004) 'The Long and Short of the Canada-U.S. Free Trade Agreement', *American Economic Review*, 94(4): 870–95.

24 N. Pavcnik (2002) 'Trade Liberalization, Exit and Productivity Improvements: Evidence from Chilean Plants', *Review of Economic Studies*, 69: 245–76.

25 A. Fernandes (2007) 'Trade Policy, Trade Volumes and Plant-Level Productivity in Colombian Manufacturing Industries', *Journal of International Economics*, 71: 52–71.

26 A. Lileeva and D. Trefler (2010) 'Improved Access to Foreign Markets Raises Plant-Level Productivity ... for Some Plants', *Quarterly Journal of Economics*, 125: pp. 1051–99.

27 P. Bustos (2011) 'Trade Liberalization, Exports, and Technology Upgrading: Evidence on the Impact of MERCOSUR on Argentinian Firms', *American Economic Review*, 101: 304–40.

28 See, for example, M. Amiti and J. Konings (2007) 'Trade Liberalization, Intermediate Inputs, and Productivity: Evidence from Indonesia', *American Economic Review*, 97(5): 1611–38.

29 J. Baldwin and W. Gu (2009) 'The Impact of Trade on Plant Scale, Production-Run Length and Diversification', in T. Dunne, B. Jensen and M. Roberts (eds) *Producer Dynamics: New Evidence from Micro Data*. Chicago, IL: University of Chicago Press; A. Bernard, S. Redding and P. Schott (2011) 'Multiproduct Firms and Trade Liberalization', *Quarterly Journal of Economics*, 126: 1271–318.

30 See J. De Loecker and P. Goldberg (2014) 'Firm Performance in a Global Market', *Annual Review of Economics*, 6: 201–27.

31 J. Levinsohn (1993) 'Testing the Imports-as-Market-Discipline Hypothesis', *Journal of International Economics*, 35(1): 1–22; A. Harrison (1994) 'Productivity, Imperfect Competition and Trade Reform: Theory and Evidence', *Journal of International Economics*, 36(1): 53–73.

32 J. De Loecker, P. Goldberg, A. Khandelwal and N. Pavcnik (2016) 'Prices, Markups and Trade Reform', *Econometrica*, 84(2): 445–510.

33 De Loecker and Goldberg, 'Firm Performance in a Global Market'.

34 J. Baggs and J. Brander (2006) 'Trade Liberalization, Profitability, and Financial Leverage', *Journal of International Business Studies*, 37: 196–211.

35 See R. Schmalesee (1989) 'Inter-Industry Studies of Structure and Performance', in R. Schmalensee and R. Willig (eds) *Handbook of Industrial Organization*, Vol. II, Amsterdam: North Holland.

36 C. Moser and A. Rose (2014) 'Who Benefits from Regional Trade Agreements? The View from the Stock Market', *European Economic Review*, 68: 31–47.

37 H. Breinlich (2015) 'The Effect of Trade Liberalization on Firm-Level Profits: An Event-Study Approach', CEPR Discussion Paper 11011, London: Centre for Economic Policy Research.

38 See, for example, P. Goldberg and N. Pavcnik (2007) 'Distributional Effects of Globalisation in Developing Countries', *Journal of Economic Literature*, Vol. XLV: 39–82. One reason for the lack of research on bilateral trade agreements is the complexity of modern FTAs which makes the quantification of trade barrier reductions difficult. As discussed, one solution is to simply use dummy variables for whether two countries are part of the same trade agreement. But this prevents identification using cross-sectional or regional variation in trade barrier reductions for a single country, which is the preferred method in the literature we are about to discuss.

39 S. Hakobyan and J. McLaren (2016) 'Looking for Local Labour Market Effects of NAFTA', *Review of Economics and Statistics*, 98(4): 728–41.

40 Hakobyan and McLaren's conclusions also seem to be sensitive to whether or not agriculture is included among the tradable goods sectors and whether initial tariffs are controlled for in their regressions (see ibid., n. 15 and Table 4).

41 B. McCaig (2011) 'Exporting Out of Poverty: Provincial Poverty in Vietnam and U.S. Market Access', *Journal of International Economics*, 85: 102–13.

42 P. Topalova (2010) 'Factor Immobility and Regional Impacts of Trade Liberalization: Evidence on Poverty from India', *American Economic Journal: Applied Economics*, 2: 1–41.

43 B. Kovak (2013) 'Regional Effects of Trade Reform: What Is the Correct Measure of Liberalization?' *American Economic Review*, 103(5): 1960–76.

44 A. Autor, D. Dorn and G. Hanson (2013) 'The China Syndrome: Local Labor Market Effects of Import Competition in the United States', *American Economic Review*, 103(6): 2121–68.

45 See, for example, N. Pavcnik (2011), 'Globalization and Within-Country Income Inequality', in M. Bacchetta and M. Jansen (eds) *Making Globalization Socially Sustainable*, Geneva: International Labour Office.

46 See, for example, J. Frías, D. Kaplan and E. Verhoogen (2012) 'Exports and Within-Plant Wage Distributions: Evidence from Mexico', *American Economic Review: Papers & Proceedings*, 102(3): 435–40; M. Amiti and D. Davis (2011) 'Trade, Firms, and Wages: Theory and Evidence', *Review of Economic Studies*, 79: 1–36.

47 See Lileev and Trefler, 'Improved Access to Foreign Markets Raises Plant-Level Productivity'; Bustos, 'Trade Liberalization, Exports, and Technology Upgrading'; Amiti and Davis, 'Trade, Firms, and Wages'.

48 Real consumption is measured as consumer expenditure deflated by a suitable theoretical price index (usually a CES price index).

49 C. Arkolakis, A. Costinot and A. Rodríguez-Clare (2012) 'New Trade Models, Same Old Gains?' *American Economic Review*, 102(1): 94–130.

50 See A. Costinot and A. Rodríguez-Clare (2014) 'Trade Theory with Numbers: Quantifying the Consequences of Globalization', in G. Gopinath, E. Helpman and K. Rogoff (eds) *Handbook of International Economics*, Amsterdam: Elsevier.

51 See P. Goldberg and N. Pavcnik (2016), 'The Effects of Trade Policy', in Kyle Bagwell and Robert W. Staiger (eds) *Handbook of Commercial Policy*, Amsterdam: Elsevier.

52 See Costinot and Rodríguez-Clare, 'Trade Theory with Numbers'; and H. Breinlich and A. Cuñat (2016) 'Tariffs, Trade and Productivity: A Quantitative Evaluation of Heterogeneous Firm Models', *Economic Journal*, 126(595): 1660–702.

53 For a critical evaluation of older CGE models, see T. J. Kehoe (2005) 'An Evaluation of the Performance of Applied General Equilibrium Models of the Impact of NAFTA', in T. J. Kehoe, T. N. Srinivasan and J. Whalley (eds) *Frontiers in Applied General Equilibrium Modeling: Essays in Honor of Herbert Scarf*, Cambridge: Cambridge University Press, pp. 341–78. For a newer 'mid-sized' model that predicts trade flow changes after NAFTA, see L. Caliendo and F. Parro (2012) 'Estimates of the Trade and Welfare Effects of NAFTA', *Review of Economic Studies*, 82(1): 1–44.

54 C. Broda and D. E. Weinstein (2006) 'Globalization and the Gains from Variety', *Quarterly Journal of Economics*, 121(2): 541–85.

55 An important caveat to Broda and Weinstein's result is that their data do not allow them to estimate the loss of domestic varieties in response to import competition. Indeed, C.-T. Hsieh, N. Li, R. Ossa and M.-J. Yang (2016) 'Accounting for the New Gains from Trade Liberalization', NBER Working Paper 22069, Cambridge, MA: National Bureau of Economic Research, show that in the case of the US-Canada Free Trade Agreement of 1988, changes in the group of firms serving the Canadian market had a negative effect on Canadian welfare owing to the agreement.

56 G. Berlingieri, H. Breinlich and S. Dhingra (2018) 'The Impact of Trade Agreements on Consumer Welfare: Evidence from the EU Common External Trade Policy', *Journal of the European Economic Association*, 16, February.

57 By making additional assumptions about technology and market structure, Berlingieri *et al.* also quantify the impact of intermediate inputs and show that this raises the price-reducing effect of the EU's FTAs to −0.24 per cent for their baseline specification.

58 See, for example, the discussion in M. Melitz and D. Trefler (2012) 'Gains from Trade when Firms Matter', *Journal of Economic Perspectives*, 26(2): 91–118.

59 A recent exception to the standard representative-consumer framework is P. Fajgelbaum and A. Khandelwal (2016) 'Measuring the Unequal Gains from Trade', *Quarterly Journal of Economics*, 131(3): 1113–180.

60 See, for example, D. Hausman (1992) *The Inexact and Separate Science of Economics*, Cambridge: Cambridge University Press.

7

Trade agreements and economic development

Christopher Stevens

Introduction

Trade agreements are very popular: some 260 regional trade agreements have been notified to the World Trade Organization (WTO).[1] And grand claims (both positive and negative) are made about their impact on economic development. It is widely assumed that they will result in increased trade: a typical example of this is the European Commission's very precise forecast that over a period of ten years the European Union (EU)-Singapore free trade agreement (FTA) would result in a 3.6 per cent increase in Europe's exports to Singapore and a 10.4 per cent rise in its imports.[2] Some claims are also made about broader development impacts. One forecast about the Norway-China FTA was that it might result in 'win-win' (trade and environment) and 'win-win-win' (trade, environment, development) opportunities and avoid environmentally harmful consequences of commitments.[3] But the opposite is also claimed: a bleak (and also suspiciously precise) forecast about the US-Colombia FTA argued that its impact on the Colombian small farm sector would be critical for the 28 per cent of small-scale producers (whose total income would fall by up to 45 per cent) and serious for 13 per cent of producers (whose total income would fall by 16 per cent).[4]

Yet there have been few rigorous analyses of the actual development impact of such agreements. While the effects on the volume of goods traded have been assessed to some extent, other development-related impacts of trade agreements are subject to hardly any rigorous *ex post* analyses. The impact of international trade agreements on employment, genderized income distribution between socio-economic groups and on the environment is so poorly documented that the implications for 'development' must be inferred from quite fragmentary data.

This chapter examines what is known about the effects of trade agreements, the reasons for gaps in knowledge and what all this means for forecasting big events such as the potential wholesale shuffling of trade agreements consequent upon the United Kingdom's departure from the EU (known as Brexit). It focuses on analyses of those accords notified to the WTO as regional trade agreements (which involve liberalization by all parties). But when discussing Brexit it also covers preferential accords listed by the WTO under which some states, mainly in the north, offer unreciprocated preferential access for a number of goods imported from some developing countries.

The anticipated effects of trade agreements

As explained in more detail elsewhere in this volume the effects of international trade agreements are contested because they are an exercise in partial trade liberalization and rule making (towards a limited number of partners). Supporters argue that, as with any form of liberalization, the removal of barriers to trade will result in an increase in the aggregate welfare of both parties. The rules within the agreements are also perceived as providing a more predictable policy environment (and thereby fostering economic activity and investment) and as being a 'cement' that binds together regional integration schemes. The assumed beneficial impact on development is considered to flow directly and indirectly from this range of gains.

However, the agreements are also criticized from both sides. Some trade liberals identify potential negative effects as the result of partial liberalization. The essence of the liberal critique is that trade may be diverted as well as created. The former is welfare reducing and, if it is relatively large, it may significantly reduce (or completely offset) the latter which is welfare enhancing.

- Trade creation occurs when the removal of trade barriers results in more efficiently produced imports replacing some goods that previously were produced domestically albeit relatively inefficiently. It creates 'adjustment problems' for displaced domestic producers but gains for consumers (including industries for which the good is an input).
- Trade diversion can occur when the goods in question were already being imported – from a globally efficient source. As a result of the removal of trade barriers to some partners but not others, these 'efficient' imports from a country that is outside the FTA are displaced by 'less efficiently produced goods' from a country inside the FTA because it faces lower tariffs.

Because of this, it is not enough, even from a liberal perspective, to discover that trade has expanded between partners to judge the impact of an agreement on aggregate welfare, let alone on economic development more broadly defined. It is also important to know how much of the growth is 'created' and how much is 'diverted'. Too much trade diversion relative to trade creation can reduce rather than increase both economic welfare and gross domestic product (GDP).

Critics of the liberal case argue that liberalization will worsen inequality since adjustment to increased imports will be borne mainly by the poor and vulnerable whose alternative employment opportunities are the most limited while any gains accrue to the rich and powerful. Aggregate figures, whether for trade created or welfare gains, are an insufficient guide to development impact; for critics it is the distribution of these gains that is crucial.

A second line of criticism is that governments need to retain the flexibility to shield some domestic producers (or public goals, such as protection of the environment) from import competition and that over-rigid rules remove this necessary 'policy space'. The broader and more detailed the agreement's rule book, the more rigid a straightjacket it is to future policy initiatives.

Concerns about loss of policy space owing to over-rigid agreement rules are particularly marked in the case of north-south trade agreements. These are seen by critics as locking the southern trade partner into a liberal policy regime that may be detrimental to development. For this reason such agreements are often treated more as symbols than as discrete policies with finite boundaries, with the conclusions drawn being heavily influenced by the analysts' underlying views on the relative merits of predictability and non-interventionism compared with flexibility and government support. Forecasts of the broader development impact of agreements are consequently inferred from the expected effects of this gain in predictability or loss in policy space on socio-economic and gendered income distribution, employment, and the environment.

Why they may not happen

But a prior question is: how great are the direct effects of the agreements (from which any indirect effects will flow)? The minimum expected impact of an international trade agreement is that it will increase the flow of goods across borders. All of the agreements notified to the WTO include provisions to reduce barriers to trade in goods. A detailed review of 144 studies on specific agreements covering two-thirds of all fully implemented north–south FTAs found that in most cases trade was estimated to have increased.[5] But it failed to find any significant assessments of growth in services trade despite an increasing number of FTAs containing commitments to services.[6]

Although trade in goods was generally found to have grown there was a wide range of outcomes between different agreements. One survey article of 24 EuroMed studies indicated an impact on GDP that varied between +8.9 per cent and −1.6 per cent and on exports of between +54.1 per cent and −0.9 per cent.[7] Big differences were found even between studies on a single country. In the case of Morocco, for example, the estimated impact on GDP ranges from +12.2 per cent to −1.6 per cent.

There is evidence in the literature about the factors contributing to this variability. They confirm the reasonable expectation that the trade effects will be greater if the FTA text removes more rather than fewer trade barriers, provided that the barriers removed are not offset by other trade-related policies that are unaffected by the agreement, and also that the partners' economies are sufficiently flexible to respond to the new opportunities that have been created. One accord may effectively liberalize more trade than another for three basic reasons. The formal text may provide for the removal/reduction of trade barriers on a larger proportion of traded goods in one of them. Even if formal barriers are effectively removed they may be offset by the small print of the accord or replaced by new barriers not covered by the agreement. Furthermore, implementation of that which has been agreed may be faster or slower.

For those agreements notified to the WTO under Article 24 for goods (and under GATS Article 5 if they cover services) there exist disciplines that in theory determine the proportion of trade that is to be liberalized. But these are contested because the language used is vague: in an FTA 'duties and other restrictive regulations of commerce' must be 'eliminated on substantially all the trade' between the parties to the agreement.[8] The EU, for example, has interpreted this requirement quantitatively, arguing that it is fulfilled if tariffs are removed on a basket of goods accounting for 90 per cent of the value of trade between the parties. One consequence is that very heavily protected sectors, in which barriers are so high that they suffocate trade, can be excluded relatively easily precisely because they account for a very small percentage of trade. For this reason, WTO members such as Australia argue that all sectors must be covered in order for an FTA to be deemed as covering substantially all trade.

Even for goods that are liberalized, the small print may limit their commercial value. All FTAs include rules of origin to determine whether a good containing imported inputs qualifies for preferential access to partners' markets. These may be drafted lightly, to do no more than avoid trade deflection, or more onerously to require the use of methods that might not be commercially necessary. Even the 'light' rules can become 'heavy' as global production arrangements change. FTA uptake will be restricted by any rules of origin that firms cannot meet without investment and/or shifting the global value chain within which they operate (which may or may not be commercially viable). The extent to which compliance with rules of origin or other FTA administrative arrangements deters firms from using a trade agreement is related to the scale of the benefits to be obtained. Surveys of firms generally identify as a limiting factor the cost of utilizing FTA provisions, which is often perceived to be disproportionately high compared with the tariff preference on offer.[9]

Not all trade agreements are notified to the WTO under its Article 24; those between states in the south can be notified under the Enabling Clause which contains no disciplines over the share of trade that is to be covered. This need not mean that there is little regional integration. The East African Community (EAC), for example, one of the most successful African regional integration schemes, was notified under the Enabling Clause. But it may mean a dilution in the stimulus to development foreseen by supporters of trade agreements for which governments do adopt binding rules.

Within the EAC, for example, many trade barriers remain. All of the member states except Rwanda have replaced some intra-regional tariffs with 'charges of equivalent effect': taxes on cross-border movements of goods that, while not described as tariffs, have the same effect as a tariff.[10] And in cases where both tariffs and charges having equivalent effect have been eliminated in theory, there still exist some problems for commerce in practice because of the way in which rules of origin are applied. Implementation is incomplete in some areas. For example, customs procedures have not been fully harmonized by member states, nor do they have documentation requirements.[11] There also exist substantial gaps in trade-related legislation and technical barriers to trade are still prevalent.

Whatever the provisions of an agreement, implementation often slips. GATT/WTO Article 24 (para. 5c) specifies that agreements must be completed 'within a reasonable length of time' which 'should exceed 10 years only in exceptional cases'.[12] But the inclusion of the word 'exceptional' has justified implementation periods in many north-south agreements that extend to 15 or up to 25 years for the most sensitive items.

Even prolonged implementation periods may slip. The Caribbean-EU Economic Partnership Agreement (EPA), for example, has not yet formally entered into force a decade after it was signed in 2008 as it has not been ratified by all parties. A review in 2016 noted that, although it was being applied provisionally pending full ratification, many critical development cooperation programmes had yet to come on stream as a result of the delay in ratification. Projects that would allow Caribbean economic operators to harness the opportunities under the EPA were adversely affected.[13] Limited legislative capacity was seen as a key bottleneck.

This concern about harnessing opportunities is important because, most fundamentally, a trade agreement may not boost welfare as much as is hoped if there are supply-side constraints limiting one or more partners' capacity to respond to any new incentives. Such constraints include not only government policies but also the country's physical and institutional infrastructure, its human resources and all the other elements that determine the short-term flexibility of an economy. The rigorous literature assessing the impact of FTAs provides only modest quantification for the contribution of supply-side constraints in cases where trade effects are limited. This is partly because many of the very wide range of constraints fall outside the ambit of an FTA trade analysis.[14] But some case studies flag up specific examples of supply-side constraints such as weakness in transport-related infrastructure services, administrative red tape and, more broadly, major difficulties with respect to an increase in the generation of domestic employment.[15]

Problems with assessing impact

For these reasons international trade agreements may often have a smaller impact than either supporters or critics claim – but there will still often be *some* effects to be assessed. Yet the literature provides only a very patchy assessment of how far pre-agreement claims have been realized in practice.

One major reason is that it is very hard to make such an assessment. According to a United States (US) Congressional Research Service report, 'Estimating the economic impact of trade agreements is a daunting task'.[16] Among the key problems are the following:

Trade agreements and economic development

- Trade and economic development are not synonymous, even though they are related, and the many intervening variables leave wide scope for reasonable, well-informed analysts to differ over causality and impact.
- This problem is exacerbated by the extended transition period of many trade agreements and crab-like implementation.

  a If the analysis is done in the early years of implementation it may be misleading because parties typically defer the most sensitive changes to the end. An early assessment will cover only the least substantial changes (such as liberalizing goods that were already duty-free or faced very low tariffs). It may also be misleading if, as often is the case in north-south agreements, the signatories are liberalizing asymmetrically, with one party removing barriers faster than the other.

  b If the assessment is made after 15–25 years, when the most contentious elements have finally been implemented, so much will have happened to a country's broader economic and social environment that it may be hard to disentangle the specific impacts of the FTA.

- Like any other policy reform, implementing an FTA will create winners and losers and produce effects in different arenas (including potential trade growth and diversification, job creation in some sectors and losses in others, investment and technology transfer). Any given household may be affected in several different (possibly conflicting) ways and the net effect on individuals will also be affected by power relations within the household. Analysts can reasonably differ over the relative priority they accord to these differential effects and to the role played by external variables.

In addition to these technical reasons for the gaps in knowledge there are other causes that can be labelled political and territorial. While international trade agreements are under negotiation there is intense interest in their potential provisions from industrial and civil society lobby groups. Once the deal is done, interest wanes. Of the 144 studies on FTAs assessed in one review, 59 per cent were undertaken before the final details of the accord were agreed and only 6 per cent were studies of fully implemented agreements.[17] And most of the latter were undertaken by trade economists and, hence, focused on aspects that fell neatly within their disciplinary ambit. There have been few rigorous analyses of the specific impact of trade agreements by scholars concerned primarily with distribution and the environment, possibly because their field of view is much broader than trade policy.

Limited evidence on non-trade impacts[18]

For all of these reasons the jury is still out on the impact of FTAs on investment, employment, income distribution and the environment. Trade agreements are often credited with encouraging investment and with it technology transfer both directly (as a result of the increased economic activity induced by the removal of barriers to trade) and indirectly (from increasing investor confidence as a consequence of 'locking in' government policies). Hopes are also expressed that FTAs will increase employment (as a result of increased economic activity corresponding to the partners' comparative advantage) and that the dialogue between parties will help to improve labour and environmental policy.

Critics fear the reverse. They argue that there could be dis-investment as the newly opened markets are supplied by producers in the more developed partner countries. They fear that unemployment will increase since labour displaced when inefficient domestic industries are out-competed by the newly 'created trade' will not be fully absorbed elsewhere because of structural rigidities in the economy. And they are concerned that governments will be forced to discontinue social and environmental policies in the face of commercial pressure from their partners.

Although there is some evidence in the literature that FTAs can encourage investment, technology transfer and firm upgrading, it is not definitive. Similarly, the limited analysis that exists suggests that neither the hoped for nor the feared socio-economic and environmental effects of trade agreements are inevitable: much depends on the precise provisions of the agreement and the characteristics of the partners.

Rigorous *ex post* literature is similarly silent on the issue of 'policy space'. There is very limited guidance on whether FTA signatories have been unable (for good or ill) to adopt new policies because they were prohibited in the treaty. Those studies that do focus on aspects of policy space tend to be broadly assertive rather than precisely analytical and fail convincingly to demonstrate a plausible causal link between the actions (or, more usually, inactions) that concern them and FTA provisions.

Effects of trade agreements on government revenue

But there is one area in which data do exist, albeit not from the literature on international trade agreements: the effects of trade agreements on government revenue. Owing to the ease of collection, many developing country governments rely heavily on trade taxes for a significant share of their revenue. Figures for 97 low- and middle-income countries (1975–2000) indicate that trade taxes contributed between one-quarter and one-third of total tax revenue.[19]

Although many of the potential consequences of international trade agreements are contested, the broad fiscal effects are relatively straightforward to identify: removing tariffs on substantially all imports must result by the end of the implementation period in a loss of substantially all tariff revenue on imports from partners. This revenue effect will be compounded by any 'trade diversion' whereby importers switch their sources of supply towards countries inside the trade agreement in order to benefit from the tariff cut. The effect will be to reduce tariff revenue on goods currently imported from countries unaffected directly by the FTA.

The potential scale of the impact is high in some cases.[20] A meta-analysis of some 30 studies forecasting the revenue effects in Africa of EPAs with the EU found that the consequences could be very serious in some countries depending on the importance of tariffs in government revenue and the share of imports sourced from the EU.[21] It identified eight countries in which total tax revenues could fall by between 6 per cent and 43 per cent, and a further 15 countries for which the fall could be between 3 per cent and 16 per cent.

Losing one source of tax does not necessarily mean an equivalent reduction in total government revenue. Indeed, a shift from tariffs to other sources of government revenue has much to commend it from an economic perspective. The case for tax diversification is made in several analyses of revenue loss as well as in the broader literature. One succinct formulation is that 'a strategy of increasing domestic consumption taxes (slightly less than) one-for-one with tariff cuts has the attractive properties of leaving consumers better off (because the consumer price falls), preserving the production efficiency gain from the tariff reform, and increasing the government's revenue (since consumption is a wider tax base than imports).[22]

But the literature also makes it clear that the process takes considerable time and requires a strong commitment from the implementing government as well as from donors. One analysis of seven country case studies made by the Organisation for Economic Co-operation and Development (OECD) and the International Trade Center (ITC) concludes that tax system 'reform is a long-term process which often implies steps forward and back'.[23] Inputs of 'hard infrastructure' have to be married to 'soft infrastructure' if they are to have the desired outcomes.[24]

Despite the potential scale of the problem and the difficulty of shifting tax bases within FTA implementation timetables the question of whether countries that have liberalized have actually recovered from other sources the revenues lost 'surprisingly … seems to have received virtually no attention'.[25] Impact assessments of mature trade agreements fail to cover how they affect government revenue and what consequences may follow, but some studies do exist on the revenue effects of broader liberalization (for example as a result of structural adjustment or GATT Rounds). And their findings are cautionary.

Based on panel data for 111 countries obtained over 25 years one analysis finds that whereas rich and middle-income states have largely replaced from other sources tariff revenue lost, low-income countries 'have on average recovered no more than around 30 cents of each lost dollar'.[26] Other studies using the same database have come to similar conclusions.[27]

Apart from the lower collection efficiency of alternative taxes, their distributional effects may be different from those of an equivalent level of tax derived from tariffs. An analysis of 125 countries found that in those cases where it proved possible to fill the gap left by declining tariff revenue, the principal vehicles were domestic consumption taxes as well as income taxes.[28] When switching to other consumption taxes, customs officials simply stop collecting a tariff and start collecting sales tax/value-added tax (VAT) on the same goods. But this tax applies equally to imports from FTA partners and from other states which still pay the non-liberalized tariff. And, while it is common to have different rates of sales tax/VAT on different goods, such fine-tuning tends to be less extensive than is the case with tariffs. The consequence is that relative prices are likely to change: some may go down (if the sales tax rate is lower than the tariff it is replacing) while others go up (if the sales tax is additional to the tariff or on domestic production). Since different socio-economic groups have different consumption baskets there could be knock-on effects on poverty.

Applying the lessons – the case of Brexit

Understanding how existing trade agreements influence economic development provides lessons for the future. Normally this has been thought of as influencing the design of new agreements, but the contemporary scene sees a new situation: one in which established agreements are under close scrutiny such that some existing preferential trade regimes may be replaced by non-preferential ones. In North America the USA has questioned the future of the North American Free Trade Agreement (NAFTA) and in Europe Brexit will result in a wholesale shuffling of the EU's extensive network of trade agreements. How might the loss of a trade agreement affect development?

The Brexit case is particularly interesting because it involves two sets of actions that are analytically separate and, possibly, will also be temporally distinct with one occurring before the other. The first is the potential departure of the UK from all of the EU's extensive set of trade agreements. The second is the forging of new agreements between a post-Brexit UK and some or all of the countries with which it currently has preferential trade relations by virtue of its EU membership. If these two events do occur consecutively rather than concurrently, what might be the effects on economic development in the states with which the EU has trade agreements?

As is usually the case during the negotiation of individual trade agreements, such questions cannot be answered definitively because so much is uncertain. But with Brexit this uncertainty has been taken to a new level in three areas. First, there is uncertainty over UK and European policy: the UK's post-Brexit relationship with the remaining EU members (EU-27) and its future independent trade regime for developing countries. Second, there is uncertainty over how the EU's trade agreement partners will respond to the potential departure of the UK from these accords. And finally, there is uncertainty over business response: how firms might react to any change in relative market access or to any new regulations affecting the transshipment to the UK of goods initially imported into an EU-27 port. Critically, this commercial uncertainty extends to the timing for when firms must react. How long in advance of Brexit are their trading decisions made? Two years from the date that the UK formally notified Brussels of its decision to leave or during any transition period once the terms and length of this are known, or only a fraction of these periods? The answers will vary for different firms and different goods.

Such uncertainty puts a premium on understanding what different options might mean for development so that, as events unfold and doors are opened or closed, an appreciation already exists on what opportunities or challenges are being created for which countries. These will be determined both by what happens to the UK's import policy and to the regime that UK exporters encounter in their markets.

The scope for a UK trade policy that is significantly more development-friendly than that of the EU's will depend on how far UK and EU-27 trade-related and regulatory policies diverge over time. While it is almost certain that on the day after Brexit the UK will inherit trade-related regimes that are (almost) identical to those of the EU-27 (even if it leaves both the customs union and the single European market), what happens next depends on the nature of the post-Brexit relationship after any agreed transition period. If the break is reasonably harmonious, resulting in very close trade relations between the UK and the EU-27, there will be intense political pressure to retain regulatory equivalence in order to facilitate UK exports to Europe. Maintaining very similar market conditions reduces the need for close checking of goods moving across the border. Lowering tariffs or setting more flexible rules of origin for developing countries could undermine these efforts. It could raise concerns (legitimate or invented) among the EU-27 that goods from states favoured by the UK are circumventing the barriers that the EU imposes on them by trade deflection via the UK. Only strict border controls on goods arriving from UK would weed out the deflected trade.

This link between UK and EU-27 policies may be asymmetrical. While the EU-27 might be concerned if the UK has lower tariffs or less stringent rules of origin, instances of less liberal UK trade policy would not cause any such concerns about trade deflection. Past experience suggests that when there are difficult trade-offs to be made within any country between lobby groups, some of whom are trying to protect their current margins or who fear increased import competition, an easy way to square the circle is to offer domestic producers some of the market share currently supplied by developing country and other third-party producers.

Such political manoeuvring becomes all the more likely because there is no route that maintains the status quo for all developing countries in a way that is both simple and incontestably consistent with the UK's global obligations, notably within the WTO.[29] At present, imports from developing countries into the UK obtain preferential access through one of two windows each of which is justified in a different way by the WTO. The first is if they are parties to a trade agreement with the EU (which is covered by WTO Article 24 and its equivalent for services). The other is if their exports obtain reduced or duty-free access under one of the EU's non-reciprocal regimes that form part of its Generalised System of Preferences (GSP) and are pegged on the WTO Enabling Clause.

The simplest option for the UK would be to extend the status quo unilaterally, at least for a transitional period. By definition, this would formally leave relative market access unchanged. However, the UK government might consider the risk of a WTO challenge too great, although some 'defences' are possible.[30] If the UK used one of the two WTO pegs allowing members to treat some trade partners more favourably than others it would not be adequate for many developing countries, and the feasibility of the other peg is not guaranteed.

The GSP would be fine for least developed countries (LDCs) because the EU's 'Everything but Arms' regime is as good as it gets for merchandise. And the UK government has announced that LDCs will continue to enjoy their current terms of access.[31] However, market access under the EU's 'standard GSP' is less favourable than that currently obtained by many developing countries.[32] Hence, many non-LDC states would suffer a severe deterioration in market access if the UK merely transcribed the EU's GSP into domestic law. But avoiding this by amending the GSP would involve either a substantial improvement in the liberality of a UK 'standard GSP' available to all (resulting in 'preference erosion' for states that are currently most favoured), or a special regime that attracted WTO attention because it gave the most liberal treatment to groups of countries not currently recognized as sharing common characteristics.

It might be possible to sidestep this if the UK somehow remains a member of all of the EU's FTAs. But this would require the assent of all the other members (European and non-European alike) – which may not be practical within the Brexit timetable. In its absence (or the implausible negotiation of new trade agreements between them and the UK before Brexit) these partners' imports from the UK will be subject after Brexit to their standard most-favoured-nation tariffs. This would relieve, to a degree, any of those development problems noted above (on revenue, employment, etc.) but it could exacerbate trade diversion.

In the absence of one of these solutions being applied before commercial firms start to take purchasing and selling decisions in anticipation of Brexit, there is a risk that those states in a trade agreement with the EU will continue to obtain the benefits and bear the costs in respect of their trade with 27 European states but will face non-preferential trade with the UK. This might be a temporary state of affairs until a more stable post-Brexit trade regime has been agreed with the UK. But markets might already have been lost before any new regime is in place.

How might such a change affect the balance of perceived advantages and costs from trade agreements? The direct trade effects of the agreements will continue but at a reduced scale depending on the relative importance of trade with the EU-27 and with the UK. The revenue effects may be reduced but only to the extent that there is less than full trade diversion with importers shifting supplies from a UK to an EU-27 source. But the indirect effects (arising from locking in/loss of policy space, and changes in relative prices) are unlikely to be greatly affected.

Conclusion

The literature is good at estimating the effect of FTAs on the parties' trade flows: international trade agreements tend to have had positive effects in at least some cases. But the picture is mixed and the range of estimated effects is wide. In some cases, the estimated trade effect was substantial; in others, it was modest and some partners were found to have gained nothing. There is also limited, but partly contradictory, evidence that FTAs can encourage investment, technology transfer and firm upgrading which is valuable because of the importance of supply capacity.

Robust explanations have been given for the key factors that influence the scale of effect – many of which are within government control (although some only in the longer term). They include the following:

- The specific features of the trade agreement: how deep and broad are its provisions and how much policy change do they herald – and how fast? Unsurprisingly, deeper broader rapid change produces a bigger effect. Firms are less likely to incur additional administrative costs if the tariff advantage provided by the FTA is small. And a 'small' advantage can result not only from 'residual protectionism' (if the FTA fails to cut some tariffs) but also from 'broad liberalism' (if tariffs outside the FTA are already low).

- What the wider 'trade-related' environment looks like and the small print of the agreement (such as on rules of origin). The FTA impact will be greater if the impediments to trade removed by the agreement are large relative to those that remain untouched.
- The most fundamental factor is the capacity of an economy to increase supply of products for which the agreement has boosted demand. This 'supply-response' is touched on only briefly in the literature because it is determined by a wide range of factors. They include not only government policies but also the country's physical and institutional infrastructure, its human resources and all the other elements determining the short-term flexibility of an economy.

The minimum lesson that can be drawn from the patchy literature is that in most cases international trade agreements are neither 'a golden bullet' that will automatically destroy impediments to trade nor – at an aggregate level – a potent source of harm. International trade agreements tend to result in an increase in trade between partners compared to the counter-factual of what would have happened in their absence. And it may be a large increase for some partners. But the scale is heavily dependent on the factors identified above that may limit the trade effects of any accord.

However, the operative words are 'at an aggregate level' – particularly, though not exclusively, as regards the potential for harm. Some of the best studies do assess the effects of FTAs on trade at a disaggregated level.[33] But the main impact may be on small socio-economic groups and/or on gender relations within a household the distinct features of which are homogenized in the aggregation that is inevitable when assessing the performance of complex agreements over many products for one or more decades.

There is one sense in which the absence of evidence could be considered as suggestive. The fact that few critics of the liberal agenda have attempted substantial assessments of the actual impact of the limited changes created by FTAs might suggest that any impacts have been insufficiently sharp to attract attention. It might be reasonable to infer, therefore, that any adverse effects are small scale and/or dissipate over time which is why they are not picked up.

But, fundamentally, the absence of negative findings cannot be taken as evidence of a positive outcome. Not only is there a strong asymmetry between the number of sources assessing the potential effects of FTAs before they are signed (large) and the number that assess impact after the agreements have been in force for some time (small), but also the latter overlook important concerns (such as the effects on income distribution) expressed in the former.

So why are international trade agreements so popular, particularly among developing countries in which the supply-side characteristics that are so important in determining impact are relatively weak? Despite the recent spate of north-south FTAs, south-south trade agreements are numerous, and many are analysed in this volume.

One reason may be that they aim to achieve political as much as economic or development goals. They are a tangible expression of a desire to increase co-operation between neighbours. Trade commitments, to the extent that they are applied in practice, provide a cement to bind co-operation. And there are respectable precedents: the EU, for example, and its antecedents has always been as much a political as an economic project. But there are also dangers, as attested by the 'spaghetti bowl' of overlapping and partly incompatible trade agreements that Africa is currently trying to rationalize. Trade agreements that are unimplemented may create as much tension between neighbours as solidarity. And, because they create winners and losers, the implementation of trade agreements is always politically sensitive.

Notes

1 The exact number depends on how multi-state agreements are treated. For example, the EU's EPA with the Eastern and Southern Africa group could be considered as one agreement or four separate ones (between the EU and each of the African signatories).

2 EC (2013) *The Economic Impact of the EU-Singapore Free Trade Agreement. An Analysis Prepared by the Directorate-General for Trade*, Luxembourg: Publications Office of the European Union. Available at http://trade.ec.europa.eu/doclib/docs/2013/september/tradoc_151724.pdf.

3 O. K. Fauchald and H. Vennemo (2012) 'Environmental Impacts of a Free Trade Agreement between China and Norway', *FNI Report 1/2012*, Lysaker, Norway: Fridtjof Nansen Institute, p. 58. Available at http://fni.no/doc&pdf/FNI-R0112.pdf.

4 L. J. G. Salamanca, F. B. Gómez and I. C. Landínez (2009) *Impact of the US-Colombia FTA on the Small Farm Economy in Colombia*, Oxfam America Research Report, Bogotá: Oxfam America.

5 C. Stevens, M. Irfan, I. Massa and J. Kennan (2015) *The Impact of Free Trade Agreements on Economic Development in Developing Countries: A Rapid Evidence Assessment*, London: Department for International Development.

6 The poor quality of statistics on bilateral services trade flows raises substantial methodological problems. As noted in an Asian Development Bank manual for FTA impact assessment, 'the methods to assess the impact of investment and services liberalization have not been well established … and data on services and investment is insufficient to conduct rigorous analysis'. See M. G. Plummer, D. Cheong and S. Hamanaka (2010) *Methodology for Impact Assessment of Free Trade Agreements*, Mandaluyong City, Philippines: Asian Development Bank, p. 3. Available at http://aric.adb.org/pdf/FTA_Impact_Assessment.pdf.

7 N. Péridy and N. Roux (2012) 'Why Are the Trade Gains from the Euro-Mediterranean Partnership so Small?', *Journal of World Trade*, 46(3): 571–96, Table 1.

8 World Trade Organization (1994a) *General Agreement on Tariffs and Trade 1994*. Geneva: WTO, Article 24.8.b. Available at www.wto.org/english/docs_e/legal_e/ursum_e.htm#General.

9 Stevens *et al. The Impact of Free Trade Agreements on Economic Development in Developing Countries*.

10 World Bank and EAC (2014): *East African Common Market Scorecard 2014*, Washington, DC and Arusha, pp. 78–86. Available at. http://documents.worldbank.org/curated/en/799871468194049251/Main-report.

11 World Trade Organization (2012) *Trade Policy Review: Report by the Secretariat; East African Community*, WT/TPR/S/271, Geneva: WTO (17 October), p. 14.

12 World Trade Organization (1994b) *Understanding on the Interpretation of Article XXIV of the General Agreement on Tariffs and Trade 1994*, Geneva: WTO, Article XXIV:5 para. 3.

13 Commonwealth Secretariat (2015) 'The Commonwealth in the Unfolding Global Trade Landscape', *Commonwealth Trade Review 2015*, London: Commonwealth Secretariat.

14 Stevens *et al.*

15 Ibid.

16 M. A. Villarreal and I. F. Fergusson (2014) 'NAFTA at 20: Overview and Trade Effects', Congressional Research Service Report prepared for Members and Committees of Congress, Washington, DC: Congressional Research Service, p. 10. Available at https://fas.org/sgp/crs/row/R42965.pdf.

17 Stevens *et al.*

18 The evidence supporting the statements made in this section can be found in Stevens *et al.*

19 International Monetary Fund (2005) 'Dealing with the Revenue Consequences of Trade Reform', *Background Paper for Review of Fund Work on Trade*, Fiscal Affairs Department International Monetary Fund, Washington, DC: IMF (February).

20 C. Stevens and I. Massa (2016) *Addressing Developing Countries' Challenges in Free Trade Implementation*, Brussels: European Parliament.

21 S. Bilal, M. Dalleau and D. Lui (2012) 'Trade Liberalisation and Fiscal Adjustments: The Case of EPAs in Africa', ECDPM Discussion Paper No. 137, Maastricht: European Centre for Development Policy Management (November). Available at www.ecdpm.org/dp137.

22 A. Baunsgaard and M. Keen (2005) 'Tax Revenue and (or?) Trade Liberalization', IMF Working Paper, WP/05/112, Washington, DC: IMF (June), p. 3.

23 OECD and ITC (2015), 'Examples of Successful DRM Reforms and the Role of International Co-operation', Discussion Paper (July), Paris: OECD, p. x.

24 Commonwealth Secretariat, 'The Commonwealth in the Unfolding Global Trade Landscape', section 3.4.

25 Baunsgaard and Keen, 'Tax Revenue and (or?) Trade Liberalization', p. 4.

26 Ibid., p. 22.

27 See, for example, G. Glenday (2006) *Towards Fiscally Feasible and Efficient Trade Liberalization*, mimeo (May). Available at: https://fds.duke.edu/db/attachment/828; and IMF, 'Dealing with the Revenue Consequences of Trade Reform'.

28 IMF, ibid.

29 See C. Stevens and J. Kennan (2016) 'Trade Implications of Brexit for Commonwealth Developing Countries', Trade Hot Topic 133, London: Commonwealth Secretariat. Available at www.thecomm onwealth-ilibrary.org/; C. Stevens and J. Kennan (2017) 'Be Prepared: Trade Policy Research for Brexit', in Sangeeta Khorana and Brendan Vickers (eds) *Navigating Uncertainty: Towards a Post-Brexit Trade and Development Agenda?* London: Commonwealth Secretariat; and Traidcraft Exchange (2018) 'How Should the UK Trade with Developing Countries after Brexit?', Traidcraft in-depth blog, London: Traidcraft (27 February). Available at https://traidcraftindepth.org/2017/02/27/how-should-the-uk-trade-with-developing-countries-after-brexit/.

30 T. Y. Soobramanien and M. A. Razzaque (2017) 'Staging Brexit at the WTO', *Trade Hot Topic* 138, London: Commonwealth Secretariat.

31 Department for International Trade (2017) *Preparing for Our Future UK Trade Policy*, London: DIT.

32 Stevens and Kennan, 'Trade Implications of Brexit for Commonwealth Developing Countries'; Traidcraft Exchange, 'How Should the UK Trade with Developing Countries after Brexit?'.

33 Stevens *et al.*

8

The investment component of trade agreements

Wolfgang Alschner

Introduction

Most preferential trade agreements (PTAs) signed over the past two decades should more appropriately be called preferential trade and investment agreements (PTIAs). Not only do investment chapters form an integral part and signature element of deep economic partnership treaties that follow the design of the North American Free Trade Agreement (NAFTA) and its more recent counterparts, but investment plays a major role in the rules, political economy and public perception of trade agreements. Even though by mid-2017 only a quarter of the 450 preferential trade treaties notified to the World Trade Organization (WTO) contained an investment chapter, measured in words, investment provisions occupied more space in the corpus of trade agreements than any other issue area, thus reflecting the high level of attention devoted to it by states.[1] In part, this is a reflection of the growing importance of including investment norms in trade governance instruments, as global value chains require both trade liberalization and asset protection in order to thrive. At the same time, investment rules have also rendered trade agreements more controversial. Investment chapters typically allow private investors to sue sovereign host states and have their cases ruled on by international arbitration tribunals potentially winning damages valued at many millions of dollars. Criticized for privileging the interests of wealthy multinational companies over those of taxpayers, this potent enforcement mechanism is one of the most contentious elements of trade agreements today. In short, any consideration of trade agreements would be incomplete without an assessment of their investment component.

This chapter will thus introduce the rules, issues and controversies raised by investment provisions in trade agreements. The first section provides an overview of investment commitments in trade agreements. Section two sets out the wider policy context in favour of and against the inclusion of such investment rules. Finally, section three discusses the main normative issues raised by investment provisions in trade agreements both in their substantive and procedural dimension as well as in relation to their interaction with parallel and often overlapping bilateral investment treaties (BITs).

Overview: investment rules in trade agreements

Several sets of rules in trade agreements affect investment, including those that we would ordinarily define as trade obligations. For instance, trade-related investment measures (TRIMs) or the supply of services through commercial presence ('mode 3') of the General Agreement on Trade in Services (GATS) can impact investment transactions. In this chapter, however, we consider a narrower scope of rules, namely those that are found in the investment chapters of PTIAs. This section provides a brief overview of the scope of these rules and offers a typology of trade agreements based on the depth of their investment commitments.

The scope of investment provisions in trade agreements

Investment provisions in trade agreement cover four main areas: investment protection, liberalization, promotion and facilitation. Investment protection is the most important area. Investors face a variety of political risks abroad that range from expropriation to discrimination, unfair treatment and limitations on a firm's operation or its hiring decisions. These risks drive up investment premiums and are thus seen as impeding the efficient flow of capital across borders.[2] As a result, most investment rules seek to protect investors against these risks and thereby lower the cost of capital. Moreover, since local courts can be biased or inexperienced in the application of investment protection obligations and home states are often disinclined to turn ordinary commercial disputes into inter-state disputes, investor–state dispute settlement (ISDS) before international arbitral tribunals has emerged as the preferred mechanism to enforce investment protection obligations in trade agreements.[3]

Investment liberalization, in contrast, is only an ancillary goal of investment provisions in trade agreements. Whereas the inflow of foreign goods requires strong market access rules to overcome domestic pressure for protectionism from import-competing industries, countries generally welcome the inflow of foreign capital with the expectation that it will create employment, transfer technology and generate wealth. Nevertheless, investment protectionism does exist. Since foreign investment often leads to foreign control over domestic assets, countries put in place screening procedures, limitations of ownership stakes, or ban foreign takeovers on national security grounds. While most bilateral investment treaties leave the admission of capital to the discretion of host states, many PTIAs contain investment liberalization rules to ensure market access for capital imports. Lists of non-conforming sectors and measures that the states parties have excluded from liberalization accompany such market access or pre-establishment national treatment rules.[4]

Investment promotion, understood as state-sponsored encouragement of investment flows, is an oft-stated goal of investment rules in PTIAs, but is also one that is rarely realized through specific obligations.[5] Investment treaties historically treated investment promotion as a corollary of protection under the assumption that reduced political risk would quasi-automatically spur investment flows. Empirical research has provided scant support for this hypothesis.[6] Active incentives for home countries to export capital, though, are rarely enshrined in trade agreements although a few agreements foresee the provision of investment financing, guarantees and risk insurances to capital exporters or they permit collaboration between investment promotion programmes.[7] Regarding incentives by host countries, many trade agreements even discipline excessive investment promotion by following NAFTA Article 1114(2) in preventing states from relaxing labour or environmental standards to attract investment inflows.

Investment facilitation provisions, defined as clauses aimed at the reduction of transactional investment costs, are more often found in trade agreements than those relating to active investment incentives. States often agree, albeit typically in hortatory terms, to exchange information about investment opportunities, to facilitate the approval of permits or to create a treaty-based committee that is tasked with drawing up elaborate strategies to encourage mutual investment flows.[8]

A typology of trade agreements with investment provisions

Leaving aside those agreements that are silent on investment matters, one can distinguish between three types of trade agreements based on whether they cover rudimentary, moderate or comprehensive investment provisions.

First, trade agreements with rudimentary investment provisions put in place a framework for discussion on investment promotion and facilitation. However, they leave the substantive and procedural protection and liberalization of foreign investment to parallel investment treaties. Typically, such agreements combine hortatory language encouraging investment cooperation with a negotiation mandate for the conclusion of separate investment protection treaties.[9] In some instances, the outcome of such negotiations will subsequently be incorporated, *mutatis mutandis*, into the trade agreement.[10] Where a prior BIT already exists, such PTIAs typically reaffirm its investment protection provisions and add language on investment cooperation.[11]

Second, a minority of trade agreements put in place basic investment protection provisions that are more ambitious than the above-mentioned language on investment cooperation, but fall short of offering protection equivalent to that found in most BITs. The investment chapter in the Canada-US FTA (1988), for instance, offers protection against discrimination and expropriation, but neither protects against denial of justice nor offers recourse to investment arbitration for investors. Similarly, several PTIAs concluded by the European Free Trade Association (EFTA) group of states protect against discrimination, regulate the entry of investment-related personnel, and offer free transfer of funds, but omit protection against expropriation and do not grant access to arbitration.[12]

Third, the majority of modern PTIAs devote a lengthy chapter to the protection of foreign investment and create a framework that is substantively and procedurally equivalent to that of BITs. Between the conclusion of Chapter 11 of NAFTA in 1992 and the finalization in 2016 of Chapter 8 of the Comprehensive Economic and Trade Agreement (CETA), there have been more than 70 such PTAs with comprehensive investment chapters that protect foreign investors against discrimination, expropriation and unfair treatment, and these are enforceable through investor–state arbitration. It is this latter group of agreements that this chapter focuses on.

Context: regulating investment protection through trade agreements

This section will situate the interplay between trade and investment rules in their wider historical, political and legal context. Even though investment and trade rules are linked by their common origins, related economic considerations and recent normative convergence, the future of investment rules in trade agreements seems highly uncertain.

Common origins, distinct paths, recent convergence

Long before the signing in 1959 of the first bilateral investment protection agreement between Germany and Pakistan, trade agreements already secured the possessions and legal rights of natural persons abroad alongside other commercial interests. The Friendship, Commerce and Navigation (FCN) Treaty signed between Paraguay and the USA in 1859, for instance, provided in Article IX that citizens in the territory of the other party 'shall enjoy full and perfect protection for their persons and property, and shall have free and open access to the Courts of

Justice for the prosecution and defence of their just rights'.[13] Over time the protection of property of foreigners abroad became an ever-more important feature of trade agreements.[14] Following the Second World War, FCN treaties explicitly protected the property of companies abroad against discrimination, expropriation and limitations on the transfer of funds.[15] Predating the first BITs by almost a decade, these post-war FCN agreements have consequently been referred to as the 'first' investment treaties.[16]

Despite their common origins, trade and investment regulations began to follow different paths from the 1960s onwards.[17] Based on the insight that 'the attempt to address very complex issues in the context of such a broad spectrum of relations detracted from the utility of the FCN as an investment protection device',[18] the USA, the primary proponent of FCN treaties, abandoned the practice of concluding comprehensive trade and investment agreements and instead followed the strategy of European states to negotiate specialized investment treaties.[19] After efforts collapsed at the Organisation for Economic Co-operation and Development (OECD) to conclude a multilateral investment treaty in the 1960s, all major developed states as well as many developing countries including the People's Republic of China began signing BITs in the ensuing decades.[20] At the same time, trade negotiations shifted to the multilateral arena with several rounds of tariff negotiations that followed the creation of the General Agreement on Tariffs and Trade (GATT) in 1947. Investment and trade concerns were thus regulated through different instruments and on different levels.

In the late 1980s the modes of trade and investment governance began to converge again. In 1988 the USA and Canada signed a comprehensive economic agreement (CUSFTA) that not only lowered tariffs, but also protected investment through a dedicated chapter that included provisions on national treatment, expropriation, free transfer of funds and prohibitions on performance requirements.[21] Yet, in contrast to most BITs, CUSFTA provided only for partial inter-state dispute settlement, but not investor-state arbitration.[22] It was only four years later, following the conclusion of NAFTA between Canada, Mexico and the USA, that a PTIA provided an investment chapter enforceable through investor-state arbitration.

The importance of NAFTA and its investment provisions in Chapter 11 can hardly be overstated. First, NAFTA expanded the protective scope of investment protection beyond that provided by CUSFTA, thus considerably adding provisions on the minimum standard of treatment, most-favoured nation (MFN) treatment and the entry and sojourn within the other countries by investment-related personnel, as well as providing for compulsory investor-state arbitration.[23] This made NAFTA's Chapter 11 substantively and procedurally equivalent to investment protection offered by BITs. Second, NAFTA was the first modern investment agreement to involve two major developed countries, thus expanding investment law's traditional purview beyond the asymmetric relations between northern capital exporters and southern capital importers.[24] Third, as a corollary of that expansion, investment arbitration between developed countries became more likely.[25] Indeed, the investment arbitration regime owes much of its existence to trade agreements since investment arbitration claims only started to proliferate after the conclusion of NAFTA as industrious Canadian and American lawyers exploited Chapter 11 to launch the first major wave of investor-state disputes.[26] This led to a series of influential investment awards that laid the jurisprudential foundations of the field and turned investment arbitration into a distinct practice area.[27] By November 2017 98 investment claims, or 12 per cent of all 817 treaty-based investment disputes, had been brought pursuant to investment provisions in trade agreements. Under NAFTA alone, 59 claims had been brought making it the second most exploited investment treaty after the Energy Charter and equivalent to the cumulative claims brought under the four most heavily litigated BITs combined.[28] Finally, NAFTA's treaty design developed into a model for states around the world. Canada and

Mexico signed PTIAs that were closely modelled on NAFTA with Central and South American countries, and these, in turn, concluded NAFTA-type agreements among themselves as well as with third countries in South-East Asia.[29] Commentators thus routinely speak of the successful diffusion of the 'NAFTA model',[30] a 'NAFTA-ization'[31] or a convergence towards NAFTA.[32] In short, NAFTA marked the beginning of a new breed of deep economic agreements that covered both trade and investment through ambitious commitments turning PTAs into PTIAs.

The political economy debate surrounding investment rules in trade agreements

Whether investment rules should be included in trade agreements is hotly debated in political economy circles. Richard Baldwin, in his book *The Great Convergence*, makes a forceful conceptual argument for the joint regulation of trade and investment by distinguishing different phases of economic globalization.[33] In the 20th century, globalization could be viewed as an unbundling of production and consumption – goods were produced in one country and shipped for consumption to another country, thus making tariff reductions and market access liberalization the most important trade governance instruments. In the 21st century, however, information technology has facilitated an unbundling of production processes that used to take place within the same factory. As a consequence, global value chains have emerged that spread development, manufacturing and assembly of the same product across different countries creating the need for a new regulatory framework that Baldwin labels the 'trade-investment-service-intellectual property nexus'.[34] Since global value chains are highly vulnerable to regulatory changes, companies not only require predictable rules about market access, but also need to know that their investments and intellectual property rights are secured. As a result, modern trade agreements need to address trade and investment concerns jointly.

Sceptics of the need to include investment rules in trade deals do not dispute the proliferation and importance of global value chains, but doubt the need and utility of today's investment rules. Empirically, it is still an open question whether investment rules actually help to increase investment flows.[35] Moreover, political risk insurance and investment contracts with binding third party dispute settlement are viable alternatives for investors to price-in and mitigate political risk in host states.[36] At the same time, some of the traditional justifications for investment protection lose credibility in the context of 21st-century trade. While a host state may have had an incentive to expropriate a mine or an oilfield owned by a foreign investor in order to internalize profits, investments in global value chains owe their value to their participation in global production networks that are likely to be disrupted or diverted following a state's intervention. Finally, bringing an investor-state arbitration claim against a state is extremely expensive, typically takes several years and, in the process, sours relations with the host state. Investor-state arbitration has thus become an exit strategy unavailable to all but the most deep-pocketed investors. Furthermore, the absence of investment claims against China, for instance, which has signed 150 BITs and PTIAs, but which exerts tight control over the involvement of foreign capital, or the case of Brazil, which has received high foreign investment inflows, but which has not ratified an investment agreement with investor-state arbitration, place doubt on the effectiveness of current investment protection rules and, consequently, the need to include them in trade agreements to support global value chains.

In addition to this debate among economists, the inclusion of investment rules in trade agreements has become a sticky political issue at a time when trade agreements are already becoming increasingly controversial. Opposition by the regional parliament of Wallonia to the investment chapter in the CETA between Canada and the European Union (EU) almost prevented the conclusion of that treaty.[37] Similarly, New Zealand's opposition to investment arbitration almost led to the collapse of negotiations to revive the Trans-Pacific Partnership.[38] Investment provisions have thus made trade agreements more controversial at a time when the benefits of trade, accepted by the vast majority of economists, are increasingly questioned by major Western democracies, the first and foremost of these being the USA where the Trump Administration is blaming trade agreements for shipping American jobs abroad.[39] Commentators have thus suggested excluding investment protection rules and arbitration from trade agreements so as to not jeopardize the latter.[40]

The legal debate surrounding investment rules in trade agreements

In the legal realm, the case for the inclusion of investment rules in trade agreements is also a mixed bag. On the one hand, commentators point to the increasing convergence of trade and investment law. Not only do both systems of law share common norms such as national or MFN treatment, but many real-life disputes have both a trade and an investment dimension. Major NAFTA Chapter 11 investment arbitration claims are, in fact, trade disputes involving, for instance, importation bans (*Ethyl Corporation v. Canada*), trade remedies (*Canfor Corporation v. United States of America*) and trade countermeasures (*Corn Products v. Mexico*). Other disputes such as the legal challenges against Australia's plain cigarette packaging legislation have been brought before investment tribunals and WTO panels simultaneously.[41] Just as trade and investment transactions have become increasingly intertwined through global value chains, trade and investment dispute settlement mechanisms seem to offer different means to similar ends. This normative convergence between both regimes makes trade agreements a natural place to situate investment rules.

On the other hand, the convergence between investment and trade rules should not be overstated, as important differences remain that can militate for their regulation in different instruments. While the same norms, e.g. on non-discrimination, may be found in trade and investment treaties, their interpretation can vary starkly due to their differing legal and structural contexts.[42] Similarly, while disputes may overlap factually, they differ legally. Only states can bring trade cases before WTO panels whereas private investors can enforce investment rules. Moreover, the remedies offered under both routes are very different. Investment tribunals can award monetary damages, but cannot overturn a national law; trade panels, by contrast, can ask a country to change its law to bring it into compliance with trade obligations, but cannot award damages for past harm.[43] Given these remaining structural differences, trade and investment rules may be contained in the same treaty, but, in effect, regulate two distinct normative regimes.

Whether the future of trade and investment rules lie in more convergence or greater separation remains to be seen. Efforts spearheaded by the EU to replace traditional investment arbitration by a court-like system that through its dual structure of a panel and appeal stage mirrors the design of the WTO dispute settlement mechanism could result in greater convergence or even integration of the trade and investment regimes.[44] At the same time, the European Court of Justice has made it clear that while the EU has exclusive competence over virtually all aspects of modern trade agreements, investor-state arbitration is part of the competence shared with the EU member states.[45] In consequence, the EU Commission seems intent on excluding investment rules from trade agreements in order to benefit from an accelerated ratification process for the latter.[46]

In conclusion, at this point it is an open question whether the inclusion of investment rules in trade agreements, which in their modern dimensions began with NAFTA, will firm up further in the future, or whether the current joint regulation is merely a transient phase with the

The investment component of trade agreements

prospect of a greater separation of both regimes on the horizon. There is historical, political economy and legal justification for either path. The existence of these different points of view, however, highlights the fact that trade and investment rules, even if formally integrated in PTIAs, are still sufficiently distinct to make the continued presence of investment provisions in trade agreements everything but a foregone conclusion.

Norms: legal issues raised by PTIA's investment chapters

Investment chapters in trade agreement broadly track the core substantive and procedural investment protection standards included in freestanding investment agreements. Consequently, debates and controversies surrounding BITs are also mirrored in trade agreements. Nevertheless, some legal issues are also unique to PTIAs. This section will also discuss the increasing problem of treaty overlap with multiple investment agreements protecting the same investment but through different rules.

Core investment protection provisions in trade agreements

PTIAs that follow the design of BITs provide for a set of core investment protection standards that are typically, but not always, enforceable through investor-state arbitration provisions. This section will be limited to a concise overview of these provisions and the normative issues they raise. Excellent textbooks exist that review these clauses in greater detail.[47]

Substantive protection provisions

Investors benefit from both relative and absolute standards of protection in PTIA investment chapters. Relative standards of protection ensure the non-discriminatory treatment of a foreign investment compared to its domestic counterpart (national treatment) and a foreign investment of third parties (MFN treatment). In addition to guaranteeing equal treatment of all foreign investors before the host country's regulators, MFN clauses have an additional function of levelling the playing field when it comes to varying the treaty obligations that a host state has agreed to. Investment tribunals have routinely allowed investors to rely on MFN clauses to invoke more beneficial treatment accorded to investors under third treaties.[48] This practice has generated an ongoing controversy, particularly in relation to the incorporation of more favourable dispute settlement provisions through MFN clauses that would cut waiting periods before a claim becomes admissible or extend the jurisdiction of a tribunal.[49]

Absolute standards, on the other hand, offer protection that is independent of that granted to domestic or third-party investors. The most well-known absolute standard concerns the direct or indirect expropriation of investment. Investment rules do not prohibit expropriation; rather, they regulate its use, namely by requiring it to be for a public purpose, implemented in non-discriminatory manner, under due process of law, and subject to prompt, adequate and effective compensation paid to the foreign investor. The more important absolute standard of protection in practice, however, is the obligation to provide 'fair and equitable treatment' (FET) to foreign investors. According to the United Nations Conference on Trade and Development (UNCTAD)'s database on treaty-based investment cases, 83 per cent of claims on which data is available involve an alleged FET violation.[50] Given the ambiguity of equity and fairness, states have sought to clarify the norm's content by linking it to the customary international law minimum standard of treatment that is generally understood to impose a higher liability threshold (the conduct must be 'egregious' or 'shocking') and by explicitly spelling out illegal conduct, such as denial of justice.[51] In addition to these two standards found in the great majority of investment treaties, a set of other absolute protection clauses exists that is less common in treaties and also less frequently invoked in litigation, which includes the obligation to provide full protection and security and the commitment not to impair investment through arbitrary measures.

A third group of substantive protection obligations ensures that investments can be operated without undue state interference. Key commitments in this respect include the free transfer of funds and the repatriation of profits, the entry and sojourn of investment-related personnel and board of directors as well as the prohibition of performance requirements such as mandatory local content requirements. One reason why these provisions have attracted less litigation is that they are typically accompanied by exceptions and reservations that limit their protective scope.

A final group of norms brings contractual commitments entered into between the host state and the foreign investor under the protection of the treaty. These so-called umbrella clauses are relatively common in BITs, but are less frequent in PTIAs, although they do exist.[52] The USA, for instance, lists investment agreements concluded between covered investors and host states as an independent jurisdictional basis for bringing an arbitration claim pursuant to its PTIAs. Umbrella clauses are controversial because they can be used to circumvent the dispute settlement procedure agreed upon in the contract.

Investor-state dispute settlement

Early trade and investment treaties made investment rules exclusively subject to state-to-state dispute settlement. Following the creation of the International Centre for Settlement of Investment Disputes (ICSID) in 1965, BITs then started to additionally provide for investor-state arbitration either on the basis of ICSID or through alternative arbitration rules whose awards were then subject to the New York Convention on the Recognition and Enforcement of Foreign Arbitral Awards. Starting with NAFTA, investor–state arbitration made its way into the investment chapters of trade agreements. Interestingly, apart from few exceptions, such as the USA-Australia FTA (2004), investment arbitration mechanisms were also inserted in PTIAs, thus connecting countries with highly developed judicial systems, often under the premise that it would be difficult to convince trading partners in the developing world to subscribe to ISDS if the same rules were not also applied between developed countries.

Investor-state arbitration has been criticized on numerous grounds including in relation to (1) the financial interests of arbitrators in reappointments that may result in a pro-investor bias in adjudication; (2) practices of double-hatting whereby individuals act as counsel, arbitrator or expert witness in different proceedings; (3) judicial lawmaking and unchecked discretion facilitated by overly vague treaty language; (4) fears of chilling public interest regulation by allowing investors to threaten and bring claims; and (5) inconsistent or erroneous decisions without the possibility of appeal.[53]

These growing concerns with investor–state arbitration have led to a series of reform efforts in recent years. Some states prefer to tweak the existing arbitration structure through greater transparency and stricter codes of conduct for arbitrators as was the case in the Comprehensive and Progressive Agreement for the Trans-Pacific Partnership (CPTPP). By contrast, the EU has proposed a major overhaul of the system. Together with Canada, the EU foresees the creation of a permanent tribunal structure with appellate review as enshrined in CETA. Eventually, the EU envisages generalizing this structure into a multilateral investment court.[54] Another group of states has been exploring non-judicial alternatives to arbitration such as the creation of focal points or ombudsmen that are tasked with preventing disputes from escalating and with mediating in case of disagreements.[55] At the point of writing, it is an open question which of these paths to reforming ISDS will dominate future treaty-making.

Differences, overlap and interaction between BITs and PTIAs

Even though investment chapters in PTIAs largely mirror the provisions of BITs, there are some differences between them that derive from their differing formats. First, investment rules in PTIAs are embedded in the wider architecture of a trade agreement. On the one hand, that means that investment-related rules are not confined to the investment chapter. While BITs often have individual provisions on financial regulations, general exceptions or inter-state dispute settlements, PTIAs tend to have dedicated chapters on these matters that often apply to the entire agreement including its investment provisions. On the other hand, even if rules in BITs and PTIAs are identical, other chapters can serve as context for the purposes of treaty interpretation affecting the meaning of investment provisions.[56] Furthermore, in contrast to BITs whereby northern capital exporters tend to act as rule-makers while southern capital importers serve as rule-takers resulting in treaties that consistently follow developed countries' treaty templates,[57] PTIAs are often negotiated by two or more rule-makers, like Canada and the EU in the case of CETA, which then results in more varying investment chapters as parties with strong bargaining power and diverging models seek to find a compromise.[58]

Irrespective of their structural differences, BITs and PTIAs together form one investment regime. In fact, both types of agreement often overlap between the same set of states parties. In 2015 it was estimated that every fourth inter-state relationship governed by investment rules was subject to two or more investment treaties.[59] Think of the future CPTPP that, for Canada alone, will coexist with NAFTA in relation to Mexico and with the BITs that Canada has signed with the Philippines (1995) and Thailand (1997). Between some country pairs as many as four parallel layers of investment treaties are in force at the same time.[60] Regional investment initiatives in Asia (e.g. the Regional Comprehensive Economic Partnership) and Africa (e.g. the Tripartite Free Trade Area) will add further layers to the already complex 'spaghetti bowl' of overlapping BITs, bilateral PTIAs and regional PTIAs.

What makes this overlap of agreements problematic is that the interaction between treaties remains largely unregulated, which can have serious consequences.[61] First, investors can pick and choose the treaty that offers the most protection. Canadian tobacco companies excluded from ISDS under the CPTPP can thus bring a claim against the Philippines or Thailand under the respective BITs instead. Parallel treaties thereby undercut innovations and limitations enshrined in later PTIAs. Second, depending on how the consent to arbitration is framed, investors can have a second bite of the apple by bringing a claim under a parallel treaty after their first claim has been rejected. Third, parallel treaties give rise to conflicts of norms whereby the same issue is regulated differently in overlapping agreements leading to confusion over compliance and adding to the complexity of litigation. In short, since only few states use PTIAs to consolidate or phase out pre-existing BITs, the proliferation of PTIAs adds a second (or third and fourth) layer of protection on top of already existing treaties, which further complicates an already complex system.

Conclusion

Investment rules form a critical component of trade agreements. Even so, the future of investment chapters in PTAs is uncertain. On the one hand, investment protection and trade liberalization have become closely intertwined and are complementary forces of trade governance that sustain and facilitate the growth of global value chains. On the other hand, investment rules have also become a liability making trade agreements more controversial in the eyes of the public and more difficult to ratify. Hence, whether we see more or fewer investment rules in trade agreements in the future is an open question.

Yet since every fourth trade agreement notified to the WTO has an investment chapter, PTIAs are here to stay for some time to come. Solving the numerous challenges facing investment law is therefore not only paramount for the future of the investment regime, but also for international trade governance. This calls, first and foremost, for a reform of ISDS. Whether or not one agrees with its critiques, there is a real risk that opposition to investment arbitration will escalate into a wider opposition to trade agreements at a time when the achievements of decades of trade liberalization are already being cast into doubt. Moreover, the issue of overlapping treaties needs to be addressed more thoughtfully. Adding layer after layer of investment protection commitments creates confusion and complexity and is therefore, ultimately, in nobody's interest. With the number of new BITs in decline and no multilateral investment agreement in sight, PTIAs need to be the medium through which these challenges are addressed and the investment rules of the future are crafted.

Notes

1 See the PTA Issue Area Explorer. Available at http://mappinginvestmenttreaties.com/rta/areas (accessed 10 November 2017).
2 Jürgen Voss (1982) 'The Protection and Promotion of Foreign Direct Investment in Developing Countries: Interests, Interdependencies, Intricacies', *International and Comparative Law Quarterly*, 31: 686.
3 For a critical engagement with the conceptual foundations of investment protection rules, see Jonathan Bonnitcha, Michael Waibel and Lauge N. Skovgaard Poulsen (2017) *The Political Economy of the Investment Treaty Regime*, Oxford: Oxford University Press.
4 See generally Wolfgang Alschner (2017) 'Investment Barriers-to-Entry', in Thomas Cottier and Krista Nadakavukaren Schefer (eds) *Elgar Encyclopedia of International Economic Law*, Cheltenham: Edward Elgar.
5 United Nations (2008) *Investment Promotion Provisions in International Investment Agreements*. Geneva and New York: United Nations.
6 UNCTAD (2009) *The Role of International Investment Agreements in Attracting Foreign Direct Investment to Developing Countries*, Geneva: United Nations.
7 See, for instance, the Cotonou Agreement between the EU and the African, Caribbean and Pacific Group of States (2000), Arts. 75–77; or (more limited) the Belize-Guatemala FTA (2006), Article 37.
8 For examples, see United Nations (n 5) 15–26.
9 See, for example, the Lomé III Convention (1984), Arts. 240–247; the EFTA-Lebanon FTA (2006), Art. 26; or the Framework Agreement on Comprehensive Economic Cooperation between the Association of Southeast Asian Nations and the People's Republic of China (2002), Art. 5.
10 See, for example, the China-Singapore FTA (2008), Art. 84; or the ASEAN-Japan FTA (2008), Art. 51.
11 See, for instance, the Iceland-China FTA (2013), Chapter 8.
12 See, for instance, the EFTA-Ukraine FTA (2010), Chapter 4; the EFTA-Hong Kong FTA (2011), Chapter 4; the EFTA-Colombia FTA (2008), Chapter 5; or the EFTA-Peru FTA (2010), Chapter 5.
13 Similar provisions were included, for instance, in Article 13 of the Colombia-USA Treaty (1846) and in Article 3 of the Brunei-USA FCN Treaty (1850).
14 Kenneth J. Vandevelde (1988) 'The Bilateral Investment Treaty Program of the United States', *Cornell International Law Journal*, 21(201): 205–07.
15 Herman Walker (1956) 'Provisions on Companies in United States Commercial Treaties', *American Journal of International Law*, 50: 373; Herman Walker (1957) 'Modern Treaties of Friendship, Commerce and Navigation', *Minnesota Law Review*, 42: 805.
16 Kenneth J. Vandevelde (2017) *The First Bilateral Investment Treaties: U.S. Postwar Friendship, Commerce and Navigation Treaties,* Oxford: Oxford University Press; Herman Walker (1956) 'Treaties for the Encouragement and Protection of Foreign Investment: Present United States Practice', *American Journal*

of Comparative Law, 5: 229; Wayne Sachs (1984) 'New U.S. Bilateral Investment Treaties', *International Tax & Business Lawyer*, 2: 192.

17 Tomer Broude (2011) 'Investment and Trade: The "Lottie and Lisa" of International Economic Law?' *Transnational Dispute Management*, 2.

18 M. S. Bergman (1983) 'Bilateral Investment Protection Treaties: An Examination of the Evolution and Significance of the US Prototype Treaty', *NYUJ Int'l L. & Pol.*, 16: 1, 7.

19 See Pamela B. Gann (1985) 'The U.S. Bilateral Investment Treaty Program', *Stanford Journal of International Law*, Vol. 21: 373; Vandevelde, *The First Bilateral Investment Treaties*, n. 14; K. S. Gudgeon (1986) 'United States Bilateral Investment Treaties: Comments on Their Origin, Purposes, and General Treatment Standards', *Int'l Tax & Bus. Law*, 4: 105. At the same time, the FCN heritage left a lasting imprint on US BITs that affected the subsequent development of international investment law; see Wolfgang Alschner (2013) 'Americanization of the BIT Universe: The Influence of Friendship, Commerce and Navigation (FCN) Treaties on Modern Investment Treaty Law', *Goettingen Journal of International Law*, 5: 455.

20 Stephan W. Schill (2009) *The Multilateralization of International Investment Law*, Cambridge: Cambridge University Press, pp. 35–44; UNCTAD (2000) *Bilateral Investment Treaties: 1959–1999*. Available at http://unctad.org/en/docs/poiteiiad2.en.pdf (accessed 3 June 2015).

21 The Canada-U.S. Free Trade Agreement (1988, Chapter 16). Available at www.international.gc.ca/trade-commerce/assets/pdfs/agreements-accords/cusfta-e.pdf (accessed 10 November 2017). See also Jean Raby (1990) 'The Investment Provisions of the Canada-United States Free Trade Agreement: A Canadian Perspective', *American Journal of International Law*, 84: 394.

22 CUSFTA, Art. 1608.

23 Daniel M. Price (1993) 'An Overview of the NAFTA Investment Chapter: Substantive Rules and Investor-State Dispute Settlement', *International Lawyer*, 27: 727.

24 On the traditional asymmetry, see Jeswald W. Salacuse (1990) 'BIT by BIT: The Growth of Bilateral Investment Treaties and Their Impact on Foreign Investment in Developing Countries', *International Lawyer* (ABA), 24: 655, 663.

25 Armand De Mestral (2017) *Second Thoughts: Investor State Arbitration between Developed Democracies*, Waterloo, ON: CIGI Press.

26 Wolfgang Alschner (2017) 'The Impact of Investment Arbitration on Investment Treaty Design: Myth Versus Reality', *Yale Journal of International Law*, 42: 37–38.

27 Ibid.

28 These figures are based on UNCTAD's Investment Dispute Settlement Navigator. Available at http://investmentpolicyhub.unctad.org/ISDS (accessed 10 November 2017).

29 Wolfgang Alschner, Julia Seiermann and Dmitriy Skougarevskiy (2017) 'Text-as-Data Analysis of Preferential Trade Agreements: Mapping the PTA Landscape', UNCTAD Research Paper No 5, UNCTAD/SERRP/2017/5, Geneva: UNCTAD. Available at https://papers.ssrn.com/abstract=2999800 (accessed 10 October 2017).

30 Andreas Dür, Leonardo Baccini and Yoram Z Haftel (2015) 'Imitation and Innovation in International Governance: The Diffusion of Trade Agreement Design', in Andreas Dür and Manfred Elsig (eds) *Trade Cooperation*, Cambridge: Cambridge University Press. Available at http://ebooks.cambridge.org/ref/id/CBO9781316018453A015 (accessed 27 April 2017).

31 Axel Berger (2013) 'Investment Rules in Chinese PTIAs: A Partial "NAFTA-Ization"' (Social Science Research Network) SSRN Scholarly Paper ID 2171765. Available at http://papers.ssrn.com/abstract=2171765 (accessed 4 August 2013).

32 Filippo Fontanelli and Giuseppe Bianco (2014) 'Converging towards NAFTA: An Analysis of FTA Investment Chapters in the European Union and the United States', *Stan. J Int'l L.*, 50: 211.

33 Richard Baldwin (2016) *The Great Convergence: Information Technology and the New Globalization*, Cambridge, MA: Belknap Press of Harvard University Press.

34 Ibid.

35 Karl P. Sauvant and Lisa E. Sachs (eds) (2009) *The Effect of Treaties on Foreign Direct Investment: Bilateral Investment Treaties, Double Taxation Treaties, and Investment Flows*, Oxford: Oxford University Press.

36 Jason Webb Yackee (2007) 'Conceptual Difficulties in the Empirical Study of Bilateral Investment Treaties', *Brooklyn Journal of International Law*, 33: 405.

37 'Belgian Politicians Drop Opposition to EU-Canada Trade Deal', *The Guardian*, 27 October 2016. Available at www.theguardian.com/world/2016/oct/27/belgium-reaches-deal-with-wallonia-over-eu-canada-trade-agreement (accessed 10 November 2017).

38 *Jacinda Ardern Lays Ground for Defeat on TPP Investor Dispute Clauses, New Zealand Herald*, 10 November 2017. Available at www.nzherald.co.nz/business/news/article.cfm?c_id=3&objectid=11942488 (accessed 30 November 2017).

39 'Trump Wants to Renegotiate NAFTA: Here's What You Need to Know', *Business Insider*, 5 February 2017. Available at www.businessinsider.com/what-is-nafta-is-it-good-for-america-2017-2 (accessed 10 November 2017).

40 Jason Yackee (2015) *New Trade Agreements Don't Need ISDS*, Washington, DC: Cato Unbound, 10 May. Available at www.cato-unbound.org/2015/05/19/jason-yackee/new-trade-agreements-dont-need-isds (accessed 10 November 2017).

41 Sergio Puig (2016) 'Tobacco Litigation in International Courts', *Harvard International Law Journal*, 57: 383.

42 Nicholas DiMascio and Joost Pauwelyn (2008) 'Nondiscrimination in Trade and Investment Treaties: Worlds Apart or Two Sides of the Same Coin?' *American Journal of International Law*, 102: 48.

43 Alan O. Sykes (2005) 'Public versus Private Enforcement of International Economic Law: Standing and Remedy', *Journal of Legal Studies*, 34: 631.

44 Naboth van den Broek and Danielle Morris (2017) 'The EU's Proposed Investment Court and WTO Dispute Settlement: A Comparison and Lessons Learned', *European Investment Law and Arbitration Review Online*, 2: 35.

45 CJEU, Opinion 2/15 of the Full Court, Opinion pursuant to Article 218(11) TFEU – Free Trade Agreement between the European Union and the Republic of Singapore, 16 May 2017, ECLI:EU: C:2017:376, para. 293.

46 'Juncker's Risky Bid to Rescue EU Trade Policy', *Politico*, 12 September 2017. Available at www.politico.eu/article/juncker-trade-sotu-risky-bid-to-rescue-eu-trade-policy/ (accessed 10 November 2017).

47 See, for instance, Andrew Newcombe and Lluís Paradell (2009) *Law and Practice of Investment Treaties: Standards of Treatment*, Alphen on the Rhine: Kluwer Law International; Rudolf Dolzer and Christoph Schreuer (2012) *Principles of International Investment Law*, 2nd edn, Oxford: Oxford University Press.

48 See generally Stephan W. Schill (2009) 'Mulitilateralizing Investment Treaties through Most-Favored-Nation Clauses', *Berkeley Journal of International Law*, 27: 496.

49 See generally Tony Cole (2012) 'The Boundaries of Most Favoured Nation Treatment in International Investment Law', *Michigan Journal of International Law*, 33: 537.

50 UNCTAD, ISDS Navigator (n. 27).

51 See Federico Ortino (2013) 'Refining the Content and Role of Investment "Rules" and "Standards": A New Approach to International Investment Treaty Making', *ICSID Review*, 28: 152.

52 See, for example, Japan-Singapore FTA (2002), Art. 86 (2).

53 See, for example, UNCTAD (2013) *World Investment Report 2013. Global Value Chains: Investment and Trade for Development*, Geneva: UNCTAD, p. 112.

54 European Commission (2015) *Commission Proposes New Investment Court System for TTIP and Other EU Trade and Investment Negotiations*, Brussels: EC, 16 September. Available at http://europa.eu/rapid/press-release_IP-15-5651_en.htm (accessed 10 November 2017).

55 C. Titi (2016) 'International Investment Law and the Protection of Foreign Investment in Brazil', *Transnational Dispute Management*, 13. Available at www.transnational-dispute-management.com/article.asp?key=2330 (accessed 1 December 2017).

56 See also Freya Baetens (2103) 'Preferential Trade and Investment Agreements and the Trade/Investment Divide: Is the Whole More than the Sum of Its Parts?' in Rainer Hofmann, Christian Tams and Stephan W. Schill (eds), *Preferential Trade and Investment Agreements: A New Ordering Paradigm for International Investment Relations?* Frankfurt: Frankfurt University Press.

57 Wolfgang Alschner and Dmitriy Skougarevskiy (2016) 'Mapping the Universe of International Investment Agreements', *Journal of International Economic Law*, 19.

58 Alschner, Seiermann and Skougarevskiy, 'Text-as-Data Analysis of Preferential Trade Agreements', n 29.

59 Wolfgang Alschner (2017) 'Regionalism and Overlap in Investment Treaty Law: Towards Consolidation or Contradiction?' *Journal of International Economic Law*, 17: 271.

60 Ibid.

61 For an in-depth discussion see ibid.

9

Trade agreements and national security

An economic approach

Ryan Garcia and Jonathan Lipow

It has long been understood that trade, and trade deals, are intimately entwined with considerations of national security. Consider, for example, the Schuman Declaration of 9 May 1950, which laid the groundwork for the establishment of the European Coal and Steel Community (ECSC), the predecessor to the European Union (EU):

> The coming together of the nations of Europe requires the elimination of the age-old opposition of France and Germany. Any action taken must in the first place concern these two countries.
>
> With this aim in view, the French Government proposes that action be taken immediately on one limited but decisive point.
>
> It proposes that Franco-German production of coal and steel as a whole be placed under a common High Authority, within the framework of an organization open to the participation of the other countries of Europe. The pooling of coal and steel production should immediately provide for the setting up of common foundations for economic development as a first step in the federation of Europe, and will change the destinies of those regions which have long been devoted to the manufacture of munitions of war, of which they have been the most constant victims.
>
> The solidarity in production thus established will make it plain that any war between France and Germany becomes not merely unthinkable, but materially impossible.[1]

Bilateral and regional trade agreements such as the ECSC serve as a means both to promote ties between allies and friends, and to isolate enemies and rivals. In the case of the ECSC, the goal was to take advantage of the temporary opening created by the Allied occupation of Germany to establish institutional arrangements that would permanently *transform* into allies two seemingly implacable enemies – France and Germany. They had fought no less than nine wars against each other between 1700 and 1950.

Sometimes, as demonstrated by the ECSC, the promotion of security-related goals is the *explicit* objective of an agreement. In other agreements, such as the Trans-Pacific Partnership (TPP), the agreement's role in promoting security objectives is *tacit*, but widely understood:

Perhaps more important, though, the TPP – regardless of its original intent – has developed an overtly strategic dimension in the past two years. It means to lay the foundation of future competition in the Asia-Pacific, a set of rules that China, unsurprisingly, is unlikely to accept. From the United States and Japan's point of view, the deal is a means to try to force China to get onboard with their interests or risk isolation.[2]

This chapter asks both why and how bilateral and regional trade agreements – such as the North American Free Trade Agreement (NAFTA) and the TPP – create conditions that enhance the national security of signatories. On balance, the literature that examines the role of trade deals in promoting national security focuses on the *political* dimension. Yet trade deals are first and foremost *economic* transactions. Hence, this chapter will examine the relationship between international trade and national security by offering some conceptual, if not mathematized, arguments for how trade agreements can enhance signatories' ability to defend themselves against their enemies and rivals.

This chapter is divided into six sections. In section two, we review the literature concerned with international trade, alliances and conflict. In section three, we discuss the relationship between the size of a country's economy and its ability to defend itself. The chapter then moves on to an illustration of how a trade deal, if properly thought out, can be used to increase the size of signatories' economies at the expense of the economies of non-signatories excluded from the deal. Section four applies the neoclassical theory of trade driven by factor endowments to examine how not only the sizes, but also the structures of economies, affect international trade. This section considers all types of trade that result from such a framework, including traditional trade in goods and services, foreign direct investment, and migration. It shows that trade agreements that directly affect the flow of goods and services can be used to indirectly affect flows of capital and labour in ways that enhance signatories' military capability at the expense of non-signatories' capability. Section five explores the 'new trade theory' approach to trade whereby goods are characterized by increasing returns to scale or product differentiation. It argues that armament industries exhibit such characteristics, and shows why a country's economic and strategic interest in exporting armaments to a potential ally would lead it to pursue a bilateral agreement to liberalize trade with that country. Section six concludes the chapter.

International trade, alliances and conflict

The literature that examines the relationship between international trade agreements and national security can be divided into two main subcategories: the effect of international trade on conflict and the effect of alliances on international trade. Research that analyses the relationship between international trade and conflict advances a number of competing arguments about the relevance of international trade to national security. The liberal school of thought argues that economic interdependence is instrumental to the reduction of conflict in the international system. Conversely, many realists would argue that interstate trade is irrelevant to the propensity of interstate disputes, and some neo-realists and neo-Marxists argue that asymmetrical trade relationships can lead to dependency and conflict.[3]

The quantitative literature that supports the pacifying qualities of international trade have their basis in the opportunity cost framework proposed by Polachek.[4] The opportunity cost framework advances the notion that states are reluctant to initiate conflict with trading partners due to resulting welfare reduction associated with terminating the trading partnership. Recent studies on this generally have found that bilateral trade reduces dispute propensity between dyadic state pairs.[5] In addition to the pacifying effects of bilateral trade, Russett and Oneal find that general economic openness (the total trade-to-GDP ratio) leads to reduced risk of dyadic conflict. However, Martin *et al.* contest this result as they find that while bilateral trade lowers the probability of bilateral conflict, multilateral trade openness results in a higher probability of bilateral war. Martin *et al.* argue that multilateral trade reduces the opportunity cost associated with bilateral conflict because diversified trade relations diffuse the welfare costs of the termination of trade with any one country.

While the international trade and conflict literature examines the direct impact of trade on a state's relative level of security (i.e. its likelihood of experiencing conflict), the literature that analyses the impact of alliances on trade is indirectly related to a state's national security through the potential expansion of its economy, which can then be used to enhance its military capability. The linkage of alliances with international trade is important because alliances incentivize trade cooperation by extending the 'shadow of the future', reducing the pay-offs associated with immediate defection and thereby incentivizing long-term cooperation.[6]

States that have both an alliance and preferential trading agreements have been found to trade at a much higher level than do states that have one or the other, but not both.[7] Moreover, states that agree to alliance treaties that specify economic cooperation have been found to have higher levels of trade than alliances that do not.[8] Not only do alliances impact the volume of trade between two states, but alliances also impact the type of goods that are favoured by trading states. For instance, Gowa and Mansfield demonstrate that goods produced under conditions of increasing returns to scale are more likely to benefit from alliances than goods produced under constant returns to scale.[9] Finally, alliances and international trade institutions such as the General Agreement on Tariffs and Trade (GATT)/the World Trade Organization (WTO) can also impact a state's national security through stabilizing trade volatility.[10] This stabilizing effect is important because trade volatility has been found to negatively affect economic growth and, as a result, can lead to domestic conflict.[11]

A classical economic analysis of trade agreements

As mentioned in the introduction to this chapter, a trade deal is first and foremost an economic transaction. Hence, the most important question that has to be asked regarding trade agreements' impact on national security is whether they promote economic conditions that enhance signatories' ability to deter, and if necessary defeat, potential military adversaries. The first step in answering this question is to identify the economic conditions that actually do enhance national security.

There is a wide consensus that the most important measure of a country's economic ability to defend itself – its' latent military power – is embodied in its ability to mobilize, equip and supply as large a military force as possible. In warfare, numbers matter more than anything. For example, a study by Ralph Rotte and Christoph Schmidt that covered 625 battles, fought between 1600 and 1973, concluded that 'our estimation results indicate that numerical superiority has retained its crucial role for battlefield performance throughout history'.[12]

In their seminal text on defence economics, Charles Hitch and Roland McKean draw a connection between aggregate economic output and the size of the military that a country can field, writing that 'even if it does not measure total satisfaction or welfare accurately, full-employment GDP appears to be a useful index of physical production possibilities – a useful indicator of the flow from which resources for national defense must be diverted'.[13] Furthermore, Lipow makes the connection between aggregate output and latent military power explicit, writing that output 'goes up when there is an increase in either its intensive (wealth per citizen) or extensive (total number of citizens) margins. That is important, because having more people implies the potential to field more combatants, and having more wealth implies the potential to arm those combatants with better equipment.'[14] Taking a cue from these studies, the argument advanced below will assume that, to a good first approximation, aggregate output defines a country's latent military capability. It then follows that a bilateral or regional trade agreement should promote national security if it results in increased aggregate output.

This section now turns to examining whether this will be the case in the classical Ricardian model of comparative advantage. In the Ricardian model, two autarkic countries – A and B – differ in terms of their relative ability to produce two goods – X and Y. Country A is relatively efficient in producing X while country Y is relatively efficient in producing Y. This difference leads to different relative prices for X and Y in the absence of trade. In country A, X will be cheaper relative to Y than it will be in country Y. Trade is then 'opened'. Country A exports its cheap X in return for precious Y, while country B exports its cheap Y for precious X. The relative prices of X and Y in both countries converge, and output measured in financial terms is higher in both countries. This analysis compares autarky and completely free trade, but the results hold just as well for any shift from a relatively constrained trade regime to a less regulated 'freer' one.

It is a nice story, but it only goes so far. Intuitively, one would expect a reduction or elimination in barriers to trade between two countries to boost aggregate output in both. That is often, but not always, the case. First, the relative benefit from Ricardian trade depends on the degree to which prices change after trade is opened. If country A is vastly larger than country B, it is likely that its' relative prices of X and Y will not budge after trade is opened. As a result, country A's aggregate output does not change and it does not benefit from trade (although it isn't harmed either). Instead, all of the benefits flow to country B.

When the autarkic economies are distorted, these relationships become even more complicated. Perhaps X is actually cheaper than Y in country B as a result of some ill-advised subsidy offered by its government to producers of X. In that case, country B would end up exporting X instead of Y when trade is opened, even though it is relatively inefficient in the production of X. Perversely, country B would be better off if it stayed autarkic rather than opening trade with country A. This is an application of a result – articulated in Lipsey and Lancaster (1956) – known as the 'theory of the second best'.[15] The theory shows that once there are distortions in an economy that lower output and/or social welfare, an additional distortion may actually benefit the economy by skewing output in the direction that would have resulted had the economy not been distorted in the first place.

The 'second best' ensures that it is easy to construct hypothetical trade deals that leave one or even both parties to the agreement worse off. That said, it is reasonable to assume that almost all bilateral and regional trade deals that are actually implemented enhance the aggregate output of all signatories, and this is what the chapter assumes going forward.

There is an additional consideration to take into account when analysing a country's ability to defend itself. Nothing illustrates this better than the old joke about two hunters who encounter a lion at close range in the bush. The first says to the second: 'Let's run!' The second sensibly responds: 'You cannot outrun a lion!' And the first even more sensibly explains: 'I don't have to. All I have to do is outrun you.' The moral of the story is that if having a high aggregate output leads to greater latent military capability, then engaging in trade can be a double-edged sword. A trade agreement will generally boost the aggregate output – and hence the latent military capability – of all the countries that sign it. If some of those countries are rivals or enemies, the overall impact on national security becomes ambiguous.

Economists generally fail to recognize the potential negative externalities associated with international trade. They see that trade liberalization will boost all signatories' output and declare that deals to reduce barriers to trade cannot be opposed by any reasonable person. But such arguments miss the wisdom embedded in the story of the hunters and the lion. While all signatories to a trade deal may benefit in terms of living standards, countries whose *relative* military capability is negatively impacted may balk at the terms.[16]

As a result, it is much easier for countries to implement trade deals with countries that – due to history, culture or ideology – are firm allies. They may see trade with allies as making a positive contribution to national security. After all, the ally's higher aggregate output will translate into a greater ability to contribute to the alliance's defence. Taken together, these two results constitute the strongest explanation for why countries enter into bilateral or regional trade agreements that are almost exclusively with allies or at a minimum, potential allies.

A neoclassical economic analysis of trade agreements

The Ricardian model of trade is built upon the idea of comparative advantage, but offers no real explanation for the origin of that comparative advantage. The neoclassical model of trade addressed this by offering a very simple and intuitive explanation for the origin of comparative advantage.[17] The neoclassical model offers additional insights into trade, and the impact of trade agreements, that have significant implications for national security.

The model, which is often referred to as the H-O model in recognition of Heckscher and Ohlin, assumes that there are two countries (A and B) that can produce two goods (X and Y) using two factors of production – capital and labour (K and L). Technology and consumer tastes are the same in both countries, and the two goods are manufactured using production processes that exhibit constant returns to scale (and hence diminishing marginal returns to each factor of production) in perfectly competitive markets. Good X requires relatively more K to produce than good Y, and is thus designated the capital-intensive good. Countries A and B differ from each other in only one way – country A is richer than country B. In other words, A has more K per worker than B. As a result, trade is absent, the return on capital in A is relatively low, wages are relatively high, and the price of the capital-intensive good X is relatively low.

No less than three types of trade could result when markets are opened between A and B: A might export X to B in return for imports of Y, capitalists in A may seek out investments in B where the return to investment is higher; or workers in B may seek to migrate to A in search of higher wages. In the basic H-O model, any or all of these types of trade will take place, resulting in convergence in the prices for goods and the rates of return on capital.

In the generic H-O model articulated above, trade in goods or either of the factors of production are completely interchangeable. It does not matter which goods, labour or capital flow where. In practice, however, it is widely recognized that flows in goods, capital and labour cannot fully substitute for each other. First, there are transaction costs, which tend to be low for trade in many types of goods but high for flows of capital and extremely high for flows of labour (for example, many people *die* while migrating from one country to another). Second, there is a powerful complimentary relationship between flows of capital and flows of goods. If a national invests abroad, he or she expects to get paid! The foreign money that is earned on overseas investments is only worth something if it can purchase goods abroad and facilitate their shipment home to the purchaser. A flow of labour, however, remains an effective substitute for trade in goods or a flow of capital. Quite simply, a migrant also expects to be paid. But the foreign money that a migrant earns can be used immediately to purchase goods since he or she now lives in that foreign country.

The next question to consider in the neoclassical analysis of trade agreements is how a trade deal that lessens barriers to trade in goods and services will affect the economy and national security. The examination of this question requires a distinction that was not made above in the discussion of aggregate income and its role in promoting latent military power. Aggregate national income is measured in two different ways – gross national product (GNP) and gross domestic product (GDP). GNP is the total sum of the wages and profits earned by a country's citizens and firms *owned by a country's citizens*. These wages and profits can be earned anywhere on the planet. GDP, however, is the total sum of the wages and profits earned by workers and firms *within a country's borders* – including workers who are not citizens and firms owned by foreigners.

Normally, the distinction between GNP and GDP does not matter very much and is of little policy significance. When addressing considerations of national security, however, the distinction is very important. Hitch and McKean hint at this when they write that 'full-employment GDP appears to be a useful index of physical production possibilities – a useful indicator of the flow from which resources for national defense must be diverted'.[18] Note that Hitch and McKean say GDP and not GNP. That is significant because at the time *The Economics of Defense in the Nuclear Age* was published, GNP was the dominant metric of aggregate output among American economists. It was not until 1991 that US national accounts switched to reporting GDP and use of the term became widespread.[19]

Lipow fleshes out why it is GDP and not GNP that matters in terms of national security:

> Each type of trade – in labor (migration), capital (foreign investment), and goods and services – differs radically in terms of its effect on national security. When an American firm invests abroad, for example, the result can boost US GNP as long as the investment in profitable. At the same time, it will lower America's GDP, since the additional income earned by Americans is being earned outside US borders.
>
> In a traditional economic analysis, such distinctions do not matter. But when there are military conflicts, such distinctions matter a lot! American capital investment in Germany and Japan, for example, contributed to the war effort during World War II. Unfortunately, this contribution was made to the war efforts of Nazi Germany and fascist Japan, rather than to the war effort of the democracies. Many of the trucks used by the Wehrmacht, for example, rolled off assembly lines that had been built by Ford in Germany. Meanwhile, ethnic Germans and Japanese who had migrated to the United States also contributed to the war effort – of the United States. During wartime, the country that physically controls the means of production – the machines and the workers – enjoys a huge advantage.[20]

The following analysis applies this distinction between GNP and GDP to trade deals. First, consider a world comprised of two countries. Recall that section three demonstrated that in a Ricardian model, a large country might refrain from liberalizing trade with a smaller country because the result would boost the small country's aggregate output but not the aggregate output of the large country. Something a bit different takes place in the H–O model. Should trade in goods and services be opened between the two countries, it becomes attractive for capital to flow from the rich country to the poor country, regardless of each country's size. That will lower the rich country's GDP while raising that of the poorer country. As a result, it is the rich country rather than the large country that may refrain from liberalizing trade in goods and services due to considerations of national security, and it may do so even if it is a small country likely to benefit in terms of GNP as a result of a trade agreement.

Now, consider a situation where there are three countries and two are military allies while the third is a rival. In this situation, the Ricardian model suggests that the allies would both benefit in terms of national security by liberalizing trade between them, even if one was much larger than the other. Simply put, if both countries are going to fight together, what matters is the aggregate output of the alliance as a whole. In the H–O model, however, the incentive to cut trade deals with allies and not potential enemies is even more intense for a country if it is rich relative to its rivals. In such a situation, the country would never want to facilitate trade with – and hence investment in – the rival country. Those investments could be harnessed to facilitate the rival's war effort should the two countries experience hostilities with one another. Better to retain a large differential in wages that will encourage workers from the rival country to migrate – and if the rival is an authoritarian regime, force it to divert considerable military forces to patrol its borders and limit that migration. Opening trade with a friendly but poorer country, however, would remain a good security move, since aggregate output of the alliance as a whole would go up and the investments in the poorer country would still contribute to the security of both allies.

To illustrate this, consider American trade policies towards two of its neighbours – Canada and Cuba. Does it really matter to US national security if American firms open factories in Canada? Obviously not. But it is easy to see that US factories in Cuba might not end up contributing to an American war effort. When it comes to Cuba, the trade 'maths' is pretty clear. From a national security perspective, America does not want factories in Cuba, or even Cuban cigars. It wants Cubans to become Americans. Limiting trade, and hence investment, is the most effective way of assuring that Cubans are a lot poorer than Americans, and that large numbers of them want to migrate to the USA.

A 'new trade' theory analysis of trade agreements

In the 1980s two influential papers introduced a new model often called 'new trade theory', 'strategic trade theory', or even the 'B–S model'.[21] What distinguished the B–S model was its relaxation of the assumption of perfect competition that was built in to the H–O model. Of course, various forms of market power – monopolies, oligopolies and imperfect competition – all distort the economy and push it away from its optimum. Hence, the theory of the second best applies, and it is no surprise that the B–S model identifies a wide variety of situations where government intervention in trade could enhance social welfare.

What really *is* surprising is the type of intervention that is generally indicated by the B–S model. Rather than traditional trade interventions such as tariffs and import quotas, strategic trade theory calls for *subsidies* directed at promoting the export of goods whose production is subject to market power due to product differentiation or increasing returns to scale. Not only are there conditions under which such subsidies could benefit the exporting country, but when adopted, the subsidies would actually move the world as a whole closer to an efficient allocation of its resources. This represents a radical departure from earlier models, where trade interventions could under certain circumstances boost a country's economy, but only as part of a zero-sum or negative sum game.

One particular formulation of the B–S model is of considerable interest in terms of national security. In this version, there are three countries. All three countries produce a generic consumption good with constant returns to scale technology in a competitive market. Two of the countries, however, also produce a good which exhibits increasing returns to scale in production, and hence is traded in markets that are not perfectly competitive. The model shows that each of those two countries will, holding the other country's actions constant, enhance its welfare by subsidizing the purchase of this good by the third country. In the Cournot-style equilibrium that results, both exporters offer subsidies, aggregate welfare at global scale is enhanced, and the benefits are captured by the importing country. This model, sometimes called 'Boeing vs Airbus', is of direct relevance to national security.

Consider a similar model in which there are three countries. Two – country A and country B – are military rivals and each has a defence industry that produces weaponry. Since armament production generally exhibits increasing returns to scale and product differentiation, each country's defence industry enjoys market power. The two countries also produce a generic good subject to constant returns in a competitive market. As such, there will be no trade between A and B – neither is interested in exporting weapons to its rival, and therefore neither would be able to import the generic good from the other. After all, what product could they sell in return for it?

The third country – country C – is neutral, and only produces the generic good. C would be interested in importing armaments in return for exports of the generic good, and both A and B are eager to sell weapons to C. Indeed, A and B's motivation to subsidize the export of weapons to C would be more intense that that which is suggested by the Brander and Spencer model. First, A and B will want to harm each other's economy for reasons that were addressed in section three. Given that the export of weaponry promotes aggregate output in this model, country A will see the subsidization of armament exports not only as a boon to its own economy, but as snatching away sales that would have benefited the economy, and hence the latent military capability, of its rival. Second, both A and B recognize that there is some possibility that C will one day become an ally or an enemy. Due to the benefits of inter-operability and simplified logistics, allied militaries are more capable in the field if they are using the same equipment. Hence, by selling their weaponry to C, the military effectiveness of an alliance with C is enhanced. For the same reason, should C make an alliance with a rival, its contribution to the enemy's military capability will be degraded. As a result, both A and B can be expected to offer unusually generous export subsidies to their defence industries.

Now, consider how trade agreements would fit into such a scenario. Such agreements should reduce trade barriers between countries. In this model, however, formal trade barriers between A and B are irrelevant. The refusal to export armaments to the other assures that there will be no trade between them. But what about trade barriers between one of the arms-exporting countries, say country A, and C? In such a situation, the only meaningful trade barriers would be impediments that country A had imposed on imports of the generic good from country C. Such impediments could be in the form of tariffs, or non-tariff barriers such as quotas. One of the adages of trade theory is that 'a tax on imports is a tax on exports'. Imposing a tariff or quota on imports of the generic good from C will make it more difficult for C to purchase weapons from A. The reason is simple – C can only finance the purchase of weapons from A by exporting the generic good to A. If the trade barrier lowers C's exports to A, it has to lower C's imports from A as well.

Of course, it is possible for country A to overcome this by increasing the size of the export subsidy relative to what it would offer absent trade barriers. If, for example, the barrier is an import tariff, the resultant tax revenue can be used to partially offset the cost of the export subsidy. But since no government shuffles funds with 100 per cent efficiency, there will no doubt be some costs associated with taxing imports and then turning around and subsidizing exports in order to offset the negative impact of the import tax. It would be more efficient not to impose the tariff in the first place! Thus, countries may tend to enter trade agreements with allies and potential allies because they want to export weapons to these countries in order to capture the resultant economic rents as in the B-S model, while denying those rents to rival countries. Additionally, such agreements enhance the operational effectiveness in combat should their trade partner become an ally, and erode operational effectiveness should their trade partner become an enemy.

Conclusion

Common sense suggests that countries should seek to maximize trade with allies and potential allies while limiting trade with rivals and potential enemies. This is indeed what is observed worldwide, and as has been demonstrated, there are sound reasons for this. While many of the explanations that have been advanced in the literature to explain this phenomenon focus on the diplomatic and political dimensions of trade – for example, the use of alliances to incentivize trade cooperation by extending the 'shadow of the future' – the economic dimension has received less attention.

This chapter addressed the economic dimension by considering whether the strategy of shifting trade towards friends and away from enemies makes sense in terms of its effect on the balance of latent military power, as measured by GDP. For all three dominant paradigms of trade – the Ricardian, the neoclassical, and the strategic – the result was essentially the same. Liberalizing trade through bilateral or regional agreements with allies and potential allies enhanced, for a variety of reasons, the latent or actual military capability of the bloc of allied countries as a whole. Given the beneficial economic effects of bilateral and regional trade agreements in terms of national security, it is hardly surprising that such agreements have been aggressively pursued, and for decades formed a central tenet in the national security strategies of the major Western powers.

With Britain's planned exit from the EU, and the American insistence on renegotiation of the NAFTA accords, important agreements that the USA and its many allies depend upon to execute their shared trade strategy are under unprecedented stress. Meanwhile, the proposed TPP – developed as an important weapon to contain Chinese ambitions in Asia – is defunct. Given current global security conditions that can be characterized as the worst since the end of the Cold War, it is unfortunate – and even dangerous – that the strategy of steadily integrating the economies of the Western allies through liberalized trade at bilateral and regional level seems to have been abandoned precisely when it is needed the most.

Notes

1 Schuman Declaration of 9 May 1950. See https://europa.eu/european-union/about-eu/symbols/europe-day/schuman-declaration_en.

2 See https://worldview.stratfor.com/article/trading-tpp-deal-chinas-making.

3 For a review of the international trade and conflict literature see Katherine Barbieri and Gerald Schneider (1999) 'Globalization and Peace: Assessing New Directions in the Study of Trade and Conflict', *Journal of Peace Research*, 36(4): 387–404.

4 Solomon W. Polachek (1980) 'Conflict and Trade', *Journal of Conflict Resolution*, 24(1): 57–78.

5 Solomon W. Polachek (1997) 'Why Democracies Cooperate More and Fight Less: The Relationship between International Trade and Cooperation', *Review of International Economics*, 5(3): 295–309; Bruce Russett and John Oneal (2001) *Triangulating Peace: Democracy, Interdependence, and International Organizations*, New York: W.W. Norton & Company; Philippe Martin, Thierry Mayer and Mathias Thoenig (2008) 'Make Trade Not War?', *Review of Economic Studies*, 75(3): 865–900.

6 Robert Axelrod (1984) *The Evolution of Cooperation*, New York: Basic; Robert Axelrod and Robert O. Keohane (1985) 'Achieving Cooperation under Anarchy: Strategies and Institutions', *World Politics*, 38 (1): 226–54; Michael D. McGinnis (1986) 'Issue Linkage and the Evolution of International Cooperation', *Journal of Conflict Resolution*, 30(1): 141–70; Joanne Gowa and Edward D. Mansfield (1993) 'Power Politics and International Trade', *American Political Science Review*, 87(2): 408–20.

7 Edward D. Mansfield and Rachel Bronson (1997) 'Alliances, Preferential Trading Arrangements, and International Trade', *American Political Science Review*, 91(1): 94–107.

8 Andrew G. Long and Brett A. Leeds (2006) 'Trading for Security: Military Alliances and Economic Agreements,' *Journal of Peace Research*, 43(4): 433–51.

9 Joanne Gowa and Edward D Mansfield (2004) 'Alliances, Imperfect Markets, and Major-Power Trade', *International Organization*, 58(4): 775–805.

10 Edward D. Mansfield and Eric Reinhardt (2008) 'International Institutions and the Volatility of International Trade', *International Organization*, 62(4): 621–52; Benjamin Bagozzi and Steven T. Landis

(2015) 'The Stabilizing Effects of International Politics on Bilateral Trade Flows', *Foreign Policy Analysis*, 11(2): 51–171.

11 Dani Rodrik (1998) 'Why Do More Open Economies Have Bigger Governments', *Journal of Political Economy*, 106(5): 997–1032; Dani Rodrik (1999) 'Where Did All the Growth Go? External Shocks, Social Conflict, and Growth Collapses', *Journal of Economic Growth*, 4(4): 385–412.

12 Ralph Rolfe and Christoph Schmidt (2003) 'On the Production of Victory: Empirical Determinants of Battlefield Success in Modern War', *Defense and Peace Economics*, 14(3): 175–92.

13 Charles J. Hitch and Roland N. McKean (1960) *The Economics of Defense in the Nuclear Age*, Santa Monica, CA: Rand.

14 Jonathan Lipow (2016) *Survival: The Economic Foundations of American National Security*, New York: Lexington, pp. 20.

15 R. G. Lipsey and Kelvin Lancaster (1956) 'The General Theory of Second Best', *Review of Economic Studies*, 24(1): 11–32.

16 Kenneth Waltz (1979) *Theory of International Politics*, New York: Random House. See also Joseph M. Grieco (1988) 'Anarchy and the Limits of Cooperation: A Realist Critique of the Newest Liberal Institutionalism', *International Organization*, 42(Summer): 485–529.

17 Bertil Ohlin (1933) *Interregional and International Trade*, Cambridge, MA: Harvard University Press; Wolfgang F. Stolper and Paul A. Sameulson (1941) 'Protection and Real Wages', *Review of Economic Studies*, 9(1): 58–73; Paul A. Samuelson (1948) 'International Trade and the Equalisation of Factor Prices', *Economic Journal*, 58(230): 163–84; T. M. Rybczynski (1955) 'Factor Endowment and Relative Commodity Prices', *Economica*, 22(88): 336–41.

18 Hitch and McKean, *The Economics of Defense in the Nuclear Age*, p. 32.

19 Bureau of Economic Analysis, U.S. Department of Commerce (2017) 'Concepts and Methods of the U.S. National Income and Product Accounts'.

20 Lipow, *Survival*, p. 88.

21 Barbara J. Spence and James A. Brander (1983) 'International R & D and Industrial Strategy', *Review of Economic Studies*, 50(4): 707–22; James A. Brander and Barbara J. Spencer (1985) 'Export Subsidies and International Market Share Rivalry', *Journal of International Economics*, 18(1–2): 83–100.

10

Economic reform and service liberalization in developing countries
Can preferential trade agreements help?

Leonardo Baccini

Introduction

This chapter offers a survey of the literature exploring the effect of preferential trade agreements (PTAs) on economic reform. More specifically, I discuss recent studies showing that the formation of North–South PTAs is associated with the implementation of microeconomic reforms – the privatization of state-owned enterprises, for instance – in developing countries. One of the key goals of the chapter is to pin down the mechanisms of the PTA-reform nexus. I do so by covering theories which argue that PTAs act as an instrument of power used by Northern countries to exploit concessions from Southern countries or to act as a signalling device or a credible commitment. I devote particular attention to the last mechanism, showing that PTAs allow leaders to tie their hands when it comes to reform.

In an effort to explore down to the micro-foundation of the PTA-reform nexus, I also discuss recent findings showing that US services firms lobby cohesively in favour of PTAs, which remove restrictions in (previously protected) partner countries and, in turn, facilitate the entry of competitive US services firms into Southern markets.[1] A case study on services is particularly compelling to show that North–South PTAs affect policy changes in Southern countries, because the USA has a clear comparative advantage in services and competitive services firms are interested in the removal of behind-the-border barriers rather than in tariff cuts to enter into foreign markets.

The association between PTAs and reform helps to explain why PTAs have increasingly included provisions that liberalize investment and services, protect investment, and regulate government procurement and competition policies. By including a plethora of trade-related provisions in the treaty, developing countries commit to changing regulations and policies at home, lowering behind-the-border restrictions, reducing state intervention, and moving to free market economies. In short, I argue that PTAs in general, and North–South PTAs in particular, are an instrument of global governance rather than a mere tool of trade liberalization.

Leonardo Baccini

Given that there is a large literature on the relationship between international cooperation and domestic reform, some caveats apply. First, in surveying the literature, I will focus only on the 'new regionalism', i.e. the wave of preferential liberalization that has taken place since the 1990s. Second, my literature review is biased in favour of studies published in political science journals. In particular, the bulk of the studies surveyed in this chapter are from scholars working in international political economy. Third, much of the material covered in this chapter comes from my own work on trade agreements in collaboration with several co-authors.

The remainder of the chapter is organized as follows. The second section provides background information on the political economy of reform. The third section surveys the literature exploring the PTA-reform nexus. The fourth section discusses the case of services liberalization in the context of US trade agreements. A final section concludes the chapter.

The problem of reforming

During the past two decades governments across the developing world have implemented many liberal economic reforms. To begin with, Southern countries embarked on ambitious trade liberalization by either cutting tariffs unilaterally or joining international trade agreements, i.e. the World Trade Organization (WTO) and PTAs. Moreover, going beyond macroeconomic reform, such as anti-inflation measures, governments have implemented liberal microeconomic policies that reduce direct state intervention in different industries. These reforms have changed the face of global business. Low most-favoured-nation (MFN) and preferential tariffs, capital account liberalization, stringent rules for the protection of intellectual property rights (IPRs), and liberal investment rules have overhauled the economies of dozens of developing countries.

Yet liberal reforms have also provoked intense political controversy. Their detractors mobilize against the implementation of reforms and campaign to depose national leaders who promote these reforms. Take Algeria, for instance: President Abdelaziz Bouteflika signed a trade agreement with the European Union (EU) in 2004, which encountered the strong opposition of a large number of firms due to the fear of competition from European countries.[2] Even a very popular president like Nelson Mandela faced fierce opposition from the Congress of South African Trade Unions when his government implemented neoliberal economic reforms in the late 1990s. In short, economic reform can be a dangerous strategy for some political leaders. Why do some leaders implement economic reforms, while others fail to do so? Given the importance of the topic, there is no shortage of explanations for this question.

Why do leaders implement economic reform in the first place? In political economy, two prominent explanations have been put forward by the previous literature. First, economic reform increases the probability of leaders' survival in democratic regimes. Building on the seminal work by Bueno de Mesquita *et al.*,[3] several studies argue that as countries become more democratic, leaders need the support of the median voter to stay in power. In this context, economic reform is a form of public good, which remunerates the large majority of the population and increases the probability of a leader keeping the office.[4] Second, economic reforms are instruments to benefit constituencies that are pivotal to support the political leader in power. As opposed to from the first stream of research, this body of the literature does not assume that reforms are welfare-enhancing for the entire population, i.e. they increase economic growth. Conversely, economic reforms serve here the dual purpose of empowering those interest groups whose support is pivotal for the leader's survival and of weakening the opposition.[5]

When such benefits are present, why do some leaders choose not to implement reform? In explaining why some governments and political leaders fail to implement reform, several studies focus on its cost, which is borne by a segment of the population and some interest groups. For instance, in the case of trade liberalization, import-competing industries are usually against tariff reductions because they fear the competition of cheap goods from foreign markets.[6] Recent studies have also shown that trade liberalization benefits large, productive firms at the expense of small, less productive firms, which are forced to leave the market or face a substantive reduction of their revenue.[7] These recent findings go to the heart of the problem of reform: policy changes produce stark distributional consequences. Thus, even if the aggregate effects of reform are positive, individuals and interest groups may have incentives to oppose it due to the uncertainty concerning distributional benefits.[8]

For reformers there is another problem: even if the economic benefits materialize eventually, their timing is uncertain. In exploring the effect of the North American Free Trade Agreement (NAFTA), Trefler finds that preferential trade liberalization produced large negative effects on employment in both Canada and the USA in the short term, while the positive effect on productivity that had been predicted by trade models arose only in the long term.[9] Timing poses a serious threat to the effort to reform. If a large chunk of the population is disappointed with the results of economic reform in the short and medium term, then there is a concrete risk of reform reversal.[10] In turn, this risk of reversal may reduce the probability of successful reform because it deters investors from capitalizing on the opportunities that reform provides. If economic reforms fail to create confidence among investors, liberalization may fail to generate economic benefits.

Given these difficulties, it does not come as a surprise that governments and political leaders have used international institutions to carry out unpopular and controversial reforms. This is particularly true for developing countries, whose economies are more protected than those of developed countries and which have fewer resources to compensate the losers. Indeed, the number of PTAs signed by developing countries has increased sharply over the past two decades and the large majority of developing countries are now members of the WTO. The next section explores the record of international institutions in general, and trade agreements in particular, when it comes to economic reform in developing countries.

Trade agreements and economic reform

In a seminal work published in 1998, Ethier advances the argument that trade agreements are not about trade liberalization, since tariffs are already quite low to begin with.[11] Indeed, more than 40 per cent of MFN tariffs are already at zero before the formation of a PTA and the average tariff cut in North-South PTAs is rather small, i.e. about 3 per cent.[12] On the contrary, Ethier observes some specific features of the new regionalism: (1) PTAs are made between a large country and a small one; (2) they are usually 'deep', i.e. they do not only remove tariffs but also harmonize policies and regulations; and (3) liberalization is usually one-sided, i.e. the small country liberalizes significantly more than the large country. These simple facts opened the door to a large number of studies that explore other gains from preferential liberalization in addition to an increase in trade flows and investment.

Fernandez and Portes were among the first to provide an extensive analysis of non-traditional gains from PTAs.[13] In particular, they claim that PTAs act as signalling devices to show that member countries are committed to free market policies. This signal is of particular help to developing countries seeking to attract investment and, more generally, to improve their reputation in the eye of the international economic system. Moreover, Fernandez and Portes argue that PTAs solve the time inconsistency problem related to trade policy, i.e. the temptation to raise tariffs in the case of adverse circumstances. In this regard, PTAs offer a credible commitment to stick with trade openness even in the case of negative terms-of-trade shocks.[14] Several studies have subsequently explored the roles of signalling and credible commitment in the context of international institutions.[15] Here I focus on two bodies of work that use the signalling and credible commitment arguments and explicitly apply them to explain the relationship between PTAs and reform.

Signalling

Gray's work represents one of the best applications of the signalling model to trade agreements.[16] Her argument is that North–South trade agreements help developing countries that implement ambitious economic reform to receive the seal of approval from major economic actors and, in turn, boost their confidence in these emerging markets. In her article published in the *American Journal of Political Science*, Gray tests her argument on the post-communist European countries, which implemented ambitious economic reform to move from state-led to free market economies in order to enter into the EU. Gray shows that spreads on sovereign debts substantively decreased when Eastern European countries closed negotiation chapters on domestic economic policy, which indicates that policy reforms were acceptable to the EU. In other words, joining a trade agreement with Western European countries reduced perceptions of default risk in post-communist countries.

In her book *The Company States Keep: International Economic Organizations and Investor Perception*, Gray expands this compelling argument and provides a wider range of empirical evidence. In particular, she shows the importance of 'the company a country keeps' in international cooperation. Indeed, while cooperation with responsible countries (for which read Northern countries) makes emerging markets less risky, cooperation with low–reputation countries increases sovereign spreads, i.e. the risk premium that a portfolio investor demands for holding a country's debt. In Gray's work, the role of the design of international institutions is secondary compared to the importance of member states, a point to which I will return below. As deep cooperation arises usually with northern (virtuous) countries, disentangling the effect of membership from design is empirically quite challenging.

Credible commitment

In our book *Cutting the Gordian Knot of Economic Reform: When and How International Institutions Help* and in a series of articles, Urpelainen and I show that PTAs made possible some of the most important reforms in developing countries, by allowing leaders to credibly commit to liberal policies and by creating domestic political support for reform.[17] Empirically, we show that leaders have used PTAs with the EU and the USA, which prescribe unusually deep economic reforms in many sectors of the national economy, to promote liberal economic policies.[18] Specifically, PTAs help leaders to overcome two distinct obstacles to economic reform: lack of credibility and domestic political opposition.

First, PTAs contain legally binding provisions that tie leaders' hands in relation to economic reform. For example, if the leader of a developing country were to renege on commitments to implement economic reforms that have been enshrined in a PTA, such as a commitment to enact new legislation to protect IPRs, the leader would be in breach of the PTA. The PTA contains reciprocal commitments and is enforced by the EU or the USA. The EU and the USA are major powers with the ability to withhold trade concessions of substantial value to exporters in the developing country. They are also willing to negotiate PTAs that contain reform commitments, because these reform commitments allow them to influence economic policies in partner countries. A leader who reneges on a PTA induces retaliation by the EU or the USA, and thus pays a high domestic political cost. Given the anticipation of a costly punishment, the leader's incentive to renege in the first place is diminished. Moreover, this diminished incentive to renege also applies to future leaders, so an EU or US PTA can enhance the credibility of reform beyond the current leader's own tenure.

Second, PTAs can help the leader to create domestic political support for economic reform. In the absence of preferential liberalization, reform is difficult if the constituencies and interest groups that stand to lose from economic reform are more vocal than those that expect gains. PTAs can tilt the balance in favour of the reformers. The rules of PTAs cannot be implemented without economic reform, and if these rules are not implemented, PTAs do not produce benefits for domestic constituencies. Therefore, the leader of a developing country can strategically use the international institution to create benefits for influential constituencies and interest groups as well as enabling side payments for the losers.[19] In turn, these constituencies support economic reform to ensure the implementation of the rules of the international institution.

A PTA with an economic giant is particularly helpful. Although nominally trade agreements, EU and US PTAs contain a range of provisions that prescribe deep economic reforms across the board. These treaties constrain public subsidies to domestic companies, expand the coverage of patent protection, mandate dispute resolution between foreign investors and the state upon a dispute between the two, and pry open the financial sector for European and American banks. Unless a developing country complies with these reform requirements, it cannot reap the benefits of enhanced market access to the EU and the USA. Similarly, failure to comply means that the developing country foregoes the benefits of increased foreign direct investment (FDI). The combination of market access and legally binding commitments to economic reform allows leaders to simultaneously enhance the credibility of reform and build domestic political support for liberalization. And since the EU and the USA have a clear interest in promoting liberalization in developing countries, the door to negotiation is usually open, which makes PTA negotiations a flexible strategy for promoting liberalization at home.

We test this argument using a combination of quantitative methods and case studies on Colombia, Chile, Croatia and South Africa. Our main findings are two-fold. First, we show that leaders of developing countries pursue PTA negotiations with the EU and the USA when these leaders believe their political-economic fortunes would be improved by economic reform, but they face political difficulties in the implementation of economic reform. Specifically, newly elected leaders in democratizing countries are significantly more likely to sign PTAs with the EU and the USA compared to established leaders in countries that are not going through a democratization process.[20] Second, we find that the formation of a PTA with the EU and the USA is associated with major changes in the economic policies of developing countries that form these PTAs. In particular, we demonstrate that PTAs with the USA and EU correlate with passing pieces of legislation to protect IPRs, to liberalize investments, and to privatize state-owned enterprises.

The role of power

While previous studies provide evidence that PTAs are linked to reform, it is difficult to pin down the exact mechanism(s) at play. As described above, Baccini and Urpelainen emphasize preferences of leaders in developing countries as well as the institutional environment in explaining why leaders form PTAs and then implement reform.[21] On the contrary, other studies rely on an argument based on power to explain the association between PTAs and reform. For instance, Gruber argues that Mexico was forced into NAFTA by the need to secure an important importing market for its products, especially after the trade agreement between Canada and the USA in 1988.[22] Similarly, Shadlen claims that the Central American Free Trade

Agreement (CAFTA) was imposed on Central American countries that were in desperate need of exporting textile goods to the USA.[23]

While putting forward different arguments, these studies have a common denominator: power asymmetries among countries explain the association between PTAs and reform. Without denying the importance of power in international cooperation, there are problems with this argument. Examples of relatively small countries walking away from negotiations with the EU and the USA abound. For instance, Ecuador abandoned negotiations for the formation of a PTA with the USA under Rafael Vicente Correa's presidency.[24] Similarly, Malaysia stopped negotiating a PTA with the USA because of the latter's support for the Israeli invasion of Gaza.[25] African countries have repeatedly delayed the formation of economic partnership agreements (EPAs) due to disagreements with the EU.[26]

Moreover, while the design of EU and US PTAs tends to be similar,[27] there are some important variations in the inclusion of specific provisions. For instance, Jordan was able to obtain from the USA a positive list showing which products or services the countries in the agreement would lower tariffs on (or decrease non-tariff barriers on), whereas CAFTA countries opposed the inclusion of provisions allowing the movement of people in the service and investment chapters. Similarly, the design of EU PTAs with Middle Eastern and North Africa countries is usually shallower than the design of EU PTAs with Mexico and Chile. That seems evidence against a take-it-or-leave-it approach from major powers. Finally, in my aforementioned book, I interviewed several negotiators from Chile, Colombia, Croatia and South Africa as well as from the EU and the USA, and these practitioners never mentioned power asymmetry as the decisive factor in explaining the negotiations' outcomes.[28]

Window dressing?

A key component of the mechanism linking reform to PTAs hinges on the design of trade agreements. Indeed, the inclusion in PTAs of a large number of provisions regulating investment, services, IPRs, government procurement and competition is supposed to trigger policy changes in member countries. While the majority of the literature agrees that the design of PTAs matters,[29] some recent studies cast doubts on that. In a series of articles co-authored with Slapin, Gray shows that the effectiveness of trade agreements is quite low, not only with respect to trade, but also to other issue areas.[30] In testing the effectiveness of PTAs, Gray and Slapin rely on expert survey of a rather limited pool of agreements. Leaving aside methodological problems related to the use of export survey, their work points out an important issue: *de jure* design is not equivalent to *de facto* design. In other words, the fact that PTAs include a large number of provisions does not automatically imply their enforcement.

Perhaps the most convincing analysis casting doubts on the effectiveness of PTAs is a recent article by Gray, in which she shows that roughly 50 per cent of international economic organizations are either dead or are 'zombies'.[31] To assess the vitality of these organizations, Gray tests their effect on trade flows and checks whether they hold at least one meeting per year. Her results are interesting, but ultimately not surprising. The bulk of ineffective organizations is made up of South-South regional economic agreements, which are usually underperforming compared to North-North and North-South PTAs and are often merely instruments of patronage. The take-home message from this stream of research is that PTA enforcement is more likely to happen when major powers are members of the agreement than when they are not part of PTAs. Indeed, major powers help to solve the coordination problem by providing the supply side of cooperation.[32] This finding would reconcile a realist view of how international cooperation operates with a neoliberal institutionalist view.

Building on the insights of literature surveyed in the first part of the chapter, the next section will explore the effect of US PTAs on reforming a key sector of the economy in partner countries: services. Services are an ideal laboratory in which to explore the effect of PTAs on reform. Indeed, differently from merchandise, services liberalization is about changing regulations rather than cutting tariffs.

Reforming services: evidence from US PTAs

Services are the most important sector of the economy in every developed country, but also in many emerging markets. Over the last three decades, services have grown from roughly 58 per cent of GDP to almost 75 per cent across the Organisation of Economic Co-operation and Development (OECD) countries.[33] Moreover, services currently represent more than two-thirds of the global GDP. Furthermore, according to the WTO, services make up 21 per cent of global exports and are increasingly tradable. Indeed, services are also the fastest growing component of international trade, having grown on average by 7.9 per cent since 1980 (compared to 6.6 per cent average growth in goods trade).[34] Strikingly, with few exceptions, previous studies have largely ignored the relationship between PTAs and services.[35]

In a recent paper co-authored with Osgood and Weymouth, I explore the level of political engagement of US services in relation to PTAs and its implications for reform in this sector of the economy in partner countries.[36] We start from three simple facts. First, data on service exports indicates a US comparative advantage in services. Indeed, the USA is currently running a growing trade surplus in services, in contrast to the widening deficit in goods. Second, and not unrelatedly, according to standard indicators of openness, the US level of services restrictions are quite low compared to those of developing countries, but are also low compared to those of other high-income countries.[37] Third, US trade agreements are the deepest in the world in terms of commitments to liberalize services. According to Desta,[38] they include provisions that are significantly more ambitious than the PTAs signed by the EU, the closest competitor, and they go well beyond General Agreement on Trade in Services (GATS) commitments.[39]

Armed with these basic facts, we argue that US services firms are expected to be particularly interested in and in favour of trade agreements, because they are on average significantly more competitive than firms in partner countries and because PTAs remove barriers in protected markets. Using the entire sample of lobbying activities related to the implementation of US PTAs,[40] we find that services firms' lobbying contributions in favour of trade agreements is comparable with those of merchandise. This is quite remarkable, given that many services are non-tradable. Moreover, we find that services firms are more likely to lobby in favour of trade agreements and more likely to lobby as industry trade associations rather than as individual firms, compared to other sectors. This second finding implies that there is very little disagreement among services firms operating in the same industry when it comes to pushing for the implementation of PTAs. This is in stark contrast with what we observe in manufacturing, in which there is significant disagreement among firms in the same industry.

Once it has been shown that services are a political engine of preferential trade liberalization in the USA, the key question addressed in this chapter remains: do PTAs produce policy changes facilitating the entry of US services firms into partner countries? Roy *et al.* argue that 'the US ... has gotten very significant access in various services where its industry sees particular interest, e.g., financial services, express delivery, distribution, [and] audiovisual'.[41] Take the agreement with Costa Rica, for instance: it included commitments to liberalize the insurance sector, which was under a state-owned monopoly, in two stages by 2011. Similarly, Cameron and Tomlin[42] argue that liberalization of the Mexican financial sector was 'an essential

Leonardo Baccini

component of NAFTA', whereas Manger claims that US firms used NAFTA to gain market access to the telecommunications industry in Mexico.[43] Moreover, in line with the credible commitment mechanism, there is also evidence that US PTAs helped lock in existing openness and pre-empt demand for trade restrictions in the future.[44]

We can also draw simple correlations between the occurrence of US PTAs and services liberalization in partner countries, using the newly compiled I-TIP Services database.[45] For instance, Bahrain liberalized telecommunications on 1 July 2014, just before the signing of its PTA with the USA. Moreover, Colombia removed some restrictions related to foreign companies in banking and insurance on 15 July 2009, in between signature and ratification of its PTA with the US. Similarly, Honduras implemented some liberalization of financial services on 24 September 2004, in between signature and ratification of its PTA with the USA. In all these cases, PTA treaties explicitly required the partner countries to liberalize the services industries facing policy changes.[46] In the last two cases, the timing of the implementation of reform is in line with the argument developed by Baccini, according to which Southern countries strategically time reform to occur between signature and ratification in order to influence a 'yes' vote from the US Congress.[47]

While only suggestive, the empirical evidence shows some support for an association between PTAs and reform in services. The occurrence of services liberalization in markets that were previously protected explains why US services firms donate generous lobbying contributions towards the implementation of PTAs.[48] Given that the studies surveyed so far have been mostly focused on the incentives of developing countries, these results also help to explain why Northern countries are interested in forming PTAs with developing countries. In sum, the last generation of PTAs is a perfect example of an issue linkage strategy in international cooperation. Since US trade partners are usually small export-dependent economies, the USA requires them to liberalize their services in exchange for preferential access to its large rich markets in manufacturing and agriculture as well as for generous inflows of FDI.

Conclusion

This chapter provided a survey of the main contributions to the literature linking PTAs to economic reform in developing countries. The main take-away messages are two-fold. First, there is evidence that North-South PTAs are associated with microeconomic reform in Southern countries. In other words, PTAs do not just affect tariffs, but also regulations and trade-related policies. The main mechanism proposed here is that PTAs help leaders to tie their hands in relation to reform. Second, bringing the preferences of Northern countries into the picture, services are important actors in promoting preferential liberalization in the USA: they donate generously through lobbying contributions and they are always in favour of PTAs. Since services are typically not affected by tariffs, this result is in line with the argument that PTAs produce changes in policies and regulations in developing countries. In turn, these changes help competitive US services firms to enter into these liberalizing markets, as several studies have shown.

While the literature surveyed in this chapter has offered convincing evidence of the PTA-reform nexus, many important debates remain unsettled. First, the mechanism(s) at play are still unclear. Some studies emphasize the incentives of developing countries, and leaders in particular, to form PTAs to implement unpopular and controversial reform. However, since the PTA-reform nexus is particularly strong in the case of North-South cooperation, power can also explain this association. Indeed, it may be that Southern countries are forced into reform by Northern countries, leveraging on the size of their economies. Moreover, there is still a debate on the enforcement of PTAs. Indeed, including provisions to protect investments and IPRs does not automatically imply their enforcement. Similarly, implementing policy changes does not necessarily translate into their fulfilment. Shedding light on these important issues would require more research.

A final issue concerns causality. In surveying the literature, I have been very careful to use the words 'association' and 'correlation' when discussing the PTA-reform nexus. Indeed, virtually all the studies covered in this chapter struggle to provide evidence of the *causal* effect of PTAs on reform. It may well be that the arrow of causality runs in the opposite direction: countries that implement reform are then more likely to form PTAs. Similarly, it could be that there are underlying characteristics that explain both the formation of PTAs and the implementation of reform. Indeed, Ethier has already noted that the typical country forming North-South PTAs has recently made or is currently making significant unilateral reforms.[49] In short, the literature is severely plagued by the identification problem. Future studies should take up the challenge, using a more sophisticated research design and novel microanalysis or should move away from observational data.

Notes

1 In this chapter, I use the expression 'developing countries' and 'Southern countries' as well as 'developed countries' and 'Northern countries' interchangeably. For the purpose of this chapter, a developing country is every country that is not high income, according to the World Bank classification.

2 *Maghrebia* on 23 January 2008.

3 Bruce Bueno De Mesquita, Alastair Smith, Randolph M. Siverson and James D. Morrow (2005) *The Logic of Political Survival*, Cambridge, MA: MIT University Press.

4 Fiona McGillivray, and Alastair Smith (2004) 'The Impact of Leadership Turnover on Trading Relations between States', *International Organization*, 58(3): 567–600.

5 Oona A. Hathaway (1998) 'Positive Feedback: The Impact of Trade Liberalization on Industry Demands for Protection', *International Organization* 52(3): 575–612; Hector E. Schamis (1999) 'Distributional Coalitions and the Politics of Economic Reform in Latin America', *World Politics* 51(2): 236–68; Helen V. Milner and Keiko Kubota (2005) 'Why the Move to Free Trade? Democracy and Trade Policy in the Developing Countries', *International Organization* 59(1): 107–43.

6 Milner and Kubota, 'Why the Move to Free Trade?'

7 Marc J. Melitz (2003) 'The Impact of Trade on Intra-Industry Reallocations and Aggregate Industry Productivity', *Econometrica* 71(6): 1695–725.

8 Raquel Fernandez and Dani Rodrik (1991) 'Resistance to Reform: Status Quo Bias in the Presence of Individual-Specific Uncertainty', *American Economic Review*, 81(5): 1146–55.

9 Daniel Trefler (2004) 'The Long and Short of the Canada-U.S. Free Trade Agreement', *American Economic Review*, 94(4): 870–95.

10 Adam Przeworski (1991) *Democracy and the Market: Political and Economic Reform in Eastern Europe and Latin America*, New York: Cambridge University Press; Stephan Haggard and Robert R. Kaufman (1997) 'The Political Economy of Democratic Transitions', *Comparative Politics* 29(3): 263–83.

11 Wilfred J. Ethier (1998) 'The New Regionalism', *Economic Journal* 108(449): 1149–61.

12 Leonardo Baccini, Andreas Dür and Manfred Elsig (forthcoming) 'Intra-Industry Trade, Global Value Chains, and Preferential Tariff Liberalization', *International Studies Quarterly*.

13 Raquel Fernandez and Jonathan Portes (1998) 'Returns to Regionalism: An Analysis of Nontraditional Gains from Regional Trade Agreements', *World Bank Economic Review*, 12(2): 197–220.

14 Maggi and Rodriguez-Clare have formalized the credible commitment argument in the context of multilateral trade cooperation. See Giovanni Maggi and Andres Rodriquez-Clare (1998) 'The Value of Trade Agreements in the Presence of Political Pressures', *Journal of Political Economy*, 106: 574–601; Giovanni Maggi (2007) 'A Political-Economy Theory of Trade Agreements', *American Economic Review* 97, September: 1374–406.

15 Edward D. Mansfield, Helen V. Milner and B. Peter Rosendorff (2002) 'Why Democracies Cooperate More: Electoral Control and International Trade Agreements', *International Organization* 56(03): 477–513; James Raymond Vreeland (2003) *The IMF and Economic Development*, Cambridge: Cambridge University Press; Randall W. Stone (2004) 'The Political Economy of IMF Lending in Africa',

American Political Science Review, 98(4): 577–91; Jon. C. Pevehouse (2005) *Democracy from Above: Regional Organizations and Democratization*, Cambridge: Cambridge University Press; Tim Büthe and Helen V. Milner (2008) 'The Politics of Foreign Direct Investment into Developing Countries: Increasing FDI through International Trade Agreements?' *American Journal of Political Science*, 52(4): 741–62. Tim Büthe and Helen V. Milner (2014) 'Foreign Direct Investment and Institutional Diversity in Trade Agreements: Credibility, Commitment, and Economic Flows in the Developing World, 1971–2007', *World Politics*, 66(01): 88–122.

16 Julia Gray (2009) 'International Organization as a Seal of Approval: European Union Accession and Investor Risk', *American Journal of Political Science*, 53(4): 931–49; Julia Gray (2013) *The Company States Keep: International Economic Organizations and Investor Perceptions,* Cambridge: Cambridge University Press.

17 Leonardo Baccini and Johannes Urpelainen (2012) 'Strategic Side Payments: Preferential Trading Agreements, Economic Reform, and Foreign Aid', *Journal of Politics*, 74(4): 932–49. Leonardo Baccini and Johannes Urpelainen (2014a) *Cutting the Gordian Knot of Economic Reform: When and How International Institutions Help*, New York: Oxford University Press; Leonardo Baccini and Johannes Urpelainen (2014b) 'International Institutions and Domestic Politics: Can Preferential Trading Agreements Help Leaders Promote Economic Reform?' *Journal of Politics*, 76(1): 195–214.

18 To capture the design of PTAs, we rely on the Desta dataset. See Andreas Dür, Leonardo Baccini and Manfred Elsig (2014) 'The Design of International Trade Agreements: Introducing a New Dataset', *Review of International Organizations*, 9(3). Data is available at www.designoftradeagreements.org/.

19 Baccini and Urpelainen, 'Strategic Side Payments', show that foreign aid from the EU and the USA increases after the formation of PTAs with these two major powers.

20 See a follow-up paper with Chow that shows that incentives to form PTAs are heterogeneous even among authoritarian countries, depending on the credibility of the new autocratic leader and the probability of her facing a coup. Leonardo Baccini and Wilfred M. Chow (2017) 'The Politics of Preferential Trade Liberalization in Authoritarian Countries', *International Interactions*, 45: 189–216.

21 Baccini and Urpelainen, *Cutting the Gordian Knot of Economic Reform*; Baccini and Urpelainen, 'International Institutions and Domestic Politics'.

22 Lloyd Gruber (2000) *Ruling the World: Power Politics and the Rise of Supranational Institutions*, Princeton, NJ: Princeton University Press. For an analysis of the diffusion of the new regionalism, see Leonardo Baccini and A. Dur (2012) 'The New Regionalism and Policy Interdependence', *British Journal of Political Science,* 42: 57–79.

23 Kenneth C. Shadlen (2008) 'Globalisation, Power and Integration: The Political Economy of Regional and Bilateral Trade Agreements in the Americas', *Journal of Development Studies*, 44(1): 1–20.

24 www.toboc.com/tradenews/ecuador-president-rejects-international-trade-agreement-with-us/722.aspx.

25 ww1.utusan.com.my/utusan/info.asp?y=2009&dt=0113&pub=Utusan_Malaysia&sec=Muka_Hadapan&pg=mh_03.htm.

26 www.reuters.com/article/us-africa-trade/east-african-community-says-will-delay-signing-trade-deal-with-eu-idUSKCN11E1UM?il=0.

27 Leonardo Baccini, Andreas Dür and Yoram Z. Haftel (2014) 'Imitation and Innovation in International Governance: The Diffusion of Trade Agreement Design', in Andreas Dür and Manfred Elsig (eds) *Trade Cooperation: The Purpose, Design and Effects of Preferential Trade Agreements*, Cambridge: Cambridge University Press, pp. 167–94.

28 See Baccini and Urpelainen, *Cutting the Gordian Knot of Economic Reform*, chs 7 and 8.

29 Mark Manger (2009) *Investing in Protection: The Politics of Preferential Trade Agreements between North and South*, Cambridge: Cambridge University Press; Dür *et al.* 'The Design of International Trade Agreements', pp. 353–75; David H. Bearce, Cody D. Eldredge and Brandy J. Jolliff (2016) 'Does Institutional Design Matter? A Study of Trade Effectiveness and PTA Flexibility/Rigidity', *International Studies Quarterly*, 60(2): 307–16.

30 Julia Gray and Jonathan B. Slapin. (2012). 'How Effective are Preferential Trade Agreements? Ask the Experts', *Review of International Organizations*, 7(3): 309–33; Julia Gray and Jonathan B. Slapin (2013) 'Exit Options and the Effectiveness of Regional Economic Organizations', *Political Science Research and Methods* 1(2): 281–303; Jonathan B. Slapin and Julia Gray (2014) 'Depth, Ambition and Width in Regional Economic Organizations', *Journal of European Public Policy*, 21(5): 730–45.

31 Julia Gray (2018) 'Life, Death, or Zombies?: The Vitality of Regional Economic Organizations', *International Studies Quarterly*, 62, March: 1–13.

32 Walter Mattli (1999) *The Logic of Regional Integration: Europe and Beyond*, Cambridge: Cambridge University Press.

PTAs and economic reform

33 Joseph Francois and Bernard Hoekman (2010) 'Services Trade and Policy', *Journal of Economic Literature*, 48(3): 642–92.

34 www.wto.org/english/res_e/statis_e/services_training_module_e.pdf.

35 Kerry A. Chase (2008) 'Moving Hollywood Abroad: Divided Labor Markets and the New Politics of Trade in Services'. *International Organization*, 62(4): 653–87.

36 Leonardo Baccini, Iain Osgood and Stephen Weymouth (2017) 'The Service Economy: Understanding Sectoral Differences in Patterns of Lobbying for Trade in the United States', working paper.

37 The main indicators of services restrictions are the World Bank's Services Trade Restrictions Database (STRD), the OECD's Services Trade Restrictiveness Index (STRI), and the measure capital account and financial current account restrictions developed by Dennis P. Quinn and A. Maria Toyoda (2008) 'Does Capital Account Liberalization Lead to Growth?' *Review of Financial Studies*, 21: 1403–49.

38 Available at www.designoftradeagreements.org/.

39 Martin Roy, Juan Marchetti and Hoe Lim (2007) 'Services Liberalization in the New Generation of Preferential Trade Agreements (PTAs): How Much Further than the GATS?' *World Trade Review*, 6 (2): 155–92.

40 We rely on the LDA dataset, available from Song Kim (2017) 'Political Cleavages within Industry: Firm-Level Lobbying for Trade Liberalization', *American Political Science Review*, 111: 1–20. Available at www.lobbyview.org.

41 Roy *et al.* 'Services Liberalization in the New Generation of Preferential Trade Agreements (PTAs)', p. 182.

42 Maxwell A. Cameron and Brian W. Tomlin (2000) *The Making of NAFTA*, Ithaca, NY: Cornell University Press, p. 83.

43 Manger, *Investing in Protection*.

44 Roy *et al.*; Manger.

45 Martin Roy (2016) 'Charting the Evolving Landscape of Services Trade Policies: Recent Patterns of Protection and Liberalization', in Pierre Sauvve and Martin Roy (eds) *Research Handbook on Trade in Services*, Research Handbooks on the WTO series, Camberley: Edward Elgar, ch. 1.

46 In the case of Bahrain, Chapter 12 regulates liberalization of telecommunications. In the case of Colombia and Honduras, Chapter 12 regulates financial services.

47 Leonardo Baccini (2014c) 'Before Ratification: Understanding the Timing of International Treaty Effects on Domestic Policies', *International Studies Quarterly*, 58(1): 29–43.

48 Reservations included in the annexes (usually Annexes 1 and 2) pose some exceptions to services liberalization. On average, the number of these reservations is larger for partner countries than for the USA, unveiling the difficulties faced by the USA in liberalizing services in partner countries.

49 Ethier, 'The New Regionalism', p. 1151.

11

Gender rights and trade agreements

Sophia Price

Introduction

Gender has not traditionally been a focus of trade agreements, as the assumptions underpinning trade liberalization have been that it creates benefits for all and that its impacts will be gender neutral. This position has been contested, notably by feminist economists who argue that liberalization has differentiated gendered impacts, and that these can intensify and exacerbate existing gender inequalities. A spotlight has been put on women's experiences as workers, consumers and producers and the impact of trade liberalization on these, and a range of responses have been developed. Certain initiatives such as the Fairtrade movement have sought to address gender inequalities by setting institutional principles and standards in relation to paying a fair wage, equal employment opportunities, and financial and technical support for female producers. Programmes such as Grown by Women encourage women's participation in export markets and global supply chains, supported by gender-related initiatives such as education and training programmes, and improved access to water, health and childcare facilities. In addition, a range of non-governmental organizations (NGOs) and activist movements have advocated reform of international trade policies and agreements, arguing that these should reflect broader international commitments to gender equality and human rights. However, attempts to incorporate codified gender rights into trade agreements have been contested processes, with arguably more success seen recently in bilateral relations than in the regulation of global trade. This chapter will explore these trends first through an exploration of the gender-trade nexus. It will then chart attempts to incorporate gender rights into trade agreements and conclude with a discussion of recommendations for future gender-aware and gender sensitive trade policies.

The gender-trade nexus

At the heart of the gender-trade nexus are gendered inequalities experienced on a global scale. This is the starting point of the World Trade Organization (WTO)'s 2017 publication *Gender Aware Trade Policy: A Springboard for Women's Economic Empowerment*, which cites key empirical data in relation to gender inequality; for example, in most countries women earn only 60–75 per cent of men's wages; that only 15 per cent of exporting firms are led by women; that between 1995–2015 there has been a decrease in the participation of women in the labour force from 52.4 per cent to 49.6 per cent; and that economic and social discrimination against women costs Africa 6 per cent of the continent's gross domestic product. The WTO therefore proposes that trade policies should address these fundamental inequalities and be an agent for the empowerment of women. In doing so it not only emphasizes the positive impact of gender empowerment on economic growth and poverty reduction, but argues that this has a 'snowball effect' on development, as women tend to invest most of their income in their families, particularly through spending on health and education, which in turn improves societal living standards. Moreover, the economic empowerment of women brings concomitant political and social empowerment, as control over financial resources strengthens the position of women in decision-making, in both their households and communities. According to Roberto Azevêdo, Director of the WTO and International Gender Champion, 'action is needed to better integrate women into the international trading system. All evidence suggests that giving an equal chance to women is not only economically important; it results in beneficial outcomes for society as a whole.'[1]

Unsurprisingly, the WTO favours trade liberalization as a route to gender equality and women's empowerment. It argues that trade liberalization creates job opportunities and better salaries for women, encouraging skills and education development and increasing financial independence. In particular, it states that the jobs created through trade liberalization are concentrated in export-orientated industries which tend to have higher rates of remuneration than domestic-orientated jobs and work in the informal sector. It points to the high levels of female employment in exporting companies and in export processing zones (EPZs), citing a figure of 90 per cent female employment in EPZs in many developing countries, and argues that these offer better and more stable jobs, with higher and fairer incomes and better work conditions. The WTO also highlights that the service sector, including tourism, finance, health and education, is the largest source of employment for women, citing a figure of 62 per cent of female employment in this sector in 2015 (rising to 70 per cent in some parts of Latin America and Europe). The WTO argues that the development of this sector, along with global value chains, technological development, online platforms and e-commerce all offer significant opportunities for the increase in women's employment and better incorporation into global markets.

This positive assessment of trade liberalization is contended by feminist economists and various NGOs and activists. They argue that trade liberalization relies on, reproduces and exacerbates existing gender inequalities. Feminist economists such as Elson argue that the impacts of trade liberalization are gendered because men and women occupy different positions in the economy and in relation to economic resources, and as such gender-based inequalities may impact trade policy outcomes in ways that are not predicted by standard trade theory.[2] To some extent this has been conceded by the WTO which states that women are particularly vulnerable to changing economic circumstances and 'disruptions', although it does not relate these directly to trade liberalization.

The Women and Development Network, recognizing that the impacts of trade are not uniform and that various sectors are affected differently, outlines a number of ways trade liberalization negatively impacts on women, as workers, producers and consumers.[3] In contrast to the position of the WTO, they argue that in reality export-orientated firms exploit existing gender inequalities to provide women with lower wages and inferior working conditions, as a form of competitive advantage. They also contend the WTO's analysis of the working conditions in EPZs, highlighting evidence that points to workers earning less than industrial sector minimum wages and to the suppression of union rights. Moreover, there is evidence of the segregation of women into unskilled positions that do not benefit from training and skills development. In their analysis of the gendered impact of trade liberalization, Papyrakis *et al.* find that for developing countries the evidence points to a beneficial impact of trade expansion on female employment, both relative to male employment and in absolute terms, but that this is largely in unskilled manufacturing. In contrast, however, they cite a 'bulk' of evidence of a widening gender wage gap as a result of trade liberalization.[4] Moreover, the Women and Development Network points to a 'defeminization' of employment as countries move into manufacturing higher value-added goods.

While the focus on the negative impacts of trade liberalization has tended to be on women in developing countries, these are experienced on a global scale. The employment gains from the expansion of export-orientated industries in certain sectors in developing countries can come at the cost of women working in developed countries, experienced as job losses and increased precarity. Negative impacts are also felt by women-led small and medium-sized enterprises (SMEs) and by women farmers, who face great competitive pressures from trade liberalization. In the agricultural sector, where women in the Global South tend to be small-scale subsistence farmers who are not engaged in global markets, trade liberalization can threaten their livelihoods and undermine household incomes.

The gendered impacts of liberalization are not solely experienced in the workplace or in private enterprises. The reduction in government incomes through the loss of tariffs has a negative impact on the ability of the state to generate budgetary resources which can affect the allocation of public funds to gender equality and the forms of social spending that support women and families in particular. This is exacerbated by the liberalization of trade in services, which facilitates the privatization of essential public services. The Women and Development Network points to the way in which the shift towards commercial providers in service provision can mean either the introduction or increase of user fees that can have a particular impact on women. This is because traditional gender roles ascribed to women mean that they are relied upon to fill the gap left by the privatization of social provision, and as the burden of household labour is intensified so it follows that their ability to engage in the labour market is reduced. This can negatively affect household incomes, health and well-being. In addition, the protection of intellectual property rights in international agreements can hamper access to affordable medicines, which have particularly gendered impacts, not only due to women's health requirements (notably in relation to reproductive health) but also due to women's disproportionate experiences of poverty, gender-based violence and harmful traditional practices which exacerbate their vulnerability to ill health.

Arising from this critique of liberalization there have been calls for a review of international trade policies and agreements, and for a new phase of gender-aware trade policies to be introduced. Of specific concern is that trade policy should move beyond the focus on the social impact of trade (e.g. economic growth and improved market access) to the social content of trade, namely the context of trade policy in terms of gender, class and race. As intersectional inequalities undermine the predicted benefits of trade liberalization, it is argued that trade policy needs to address these in order to achieve its aims. As part of these debates it has been highlighted how women who work in the household tend not to be included in discussions about trade policy and trade liberalization, and their labour is largely excluded from consideration in trade initiatives. Moreover, the discussion of gender and trade and the impacts of liberalization tend to rely on the binaries of men and women, with little explicit focus put on the differential impact of trade on LGBTQ+ (lesbian, gay, bisexual, trans and queer+) people.

Campaigns to ensure that trade agreements become more gender-aware and sensitive are given weight by the commitments to gender equality as a right that have been enshrined in various international conventions and agreements, particularly since the 1979 United Nations Convention on the Elimination of all forms of Discrimination Against Women (CEDAW). While these commitments are not specifically applied to trade, the concept of non-discrimination is foregrounded in each, and is applied to the economic realm, which de facto includes international trade. This gives strong endorsement within the international community for specific commitments to gender equality in trade, and has been the basis of calls to codify gender rights in trade agreements.

The codification of gender rights in trade agreements

Historically, the issue of gender rights has not been part of the international trade agenda. The focus has been on the processes to support trade liberalization and overcoming the barriers to trade. The codification of gender rights at an international level has been mainly concentrated within the UN, in regional organizations such as the European Union and by states at the national level. There has been a range of approaches taken by different states to the codification of gender rights, although in general gender equality legislation is a relatively recent phenomena. For example, it was not until the 1970s that the United Kingdom passed a raft of workplace gender equality legislation, such as the Equal Pay Act of 1970 and the Sex Discrimination Act of 1975. In 2016 a World Bank report found that of the 173 countries surveyed, 90 per cent had at least one law impeding women's economic opportunities.[5]

At international level the United Declaration of Human Rights encompasses commitments to labour and gender equality rights, including the right to work and rest (which are equally applied to women and men) and emphasizes the principle of non-discrimination. The subsequent 1966 UN International Covenant on Economic, Social and Cultural rights (ICESCR), which translates the principle of the Declaration into legally binding form, emphasizes the equal right to work and the right to equal remuneration for work of equal value, along with various provisions in relation to equality in working conditions (although it allows for the gradual realization of these). The CEDAW, which was adopted at a time of increased focus on the economic and social rights of women and their reflection in feminist movements across the world, sought to address persistent gendered inequality in a more fundamental way. The Convention recognized discrimination as an obstacle to full participation in the economy and the limitations this placed on realizing women's potential. Importantly, the Convention moved beyond the commitment to workplace rights to the elimination of social and cultural forms of discrimination, which relegate women to an inferior position and replicate stereotyped gendered roles, and also contained a commitment to equal access to education and vocational training. CEDAW entered into force in 1981 and represented the comprehensive codification of international legal standards for women. However, there have been numerous violations of its provisions and reservations have been imposed by various parties.

There has been an ongoing movement to incorporate the commitments to gender equality and gender rights represented in CEDAW more broadly into a range of international-level agreements, including trade agreements. In 1995 the fourth UN World Conference on Women (the Beijing World Conference) established the principle of 'gender mainstreaming' as a global strategy for promoting gender equality. This required that in all areas and levels of legislation, policymaking and programmes, including those related to trade, the implications for women and men of any planned action had to be assessed. As such, the issue of gender equality, and the assessment of gendered impacts of decision-making, were to be placed at the heart of policymaking in all political, economic and social spheres, with the Beijing Platform of Action promoting active and visible gender mainstreaming. This was reflected in the 2001 International Labour Organization (ILO) Action Plan on Gender Equality and Gender Mainstreaming which aimed to ensure that gender analysis and planning was introduced into all areas of ILO activities. The mainstreaming of gender and prioritization of gender equality in all forms of international agreements was also reflected in the commitments contained in the UN Millennium

Development Goals, most notably MDG 3 – the promotion of gender equality and empowerment of women. This was further augmented in the subsequent 2015 Sustainable Development Goals, including SDG 5 which aims to achieve gender equality and empower all women and girls, and SDG 8 which aims to promote inclusive and sustainable economic growth, employment and decent work for all. The target for this is that by 2030 there will be full and productive work for all women and men and equal pay for work of equal value.

It is in this context that the WTO produced its 2017 publication *Gender Aware Trade Policy: A Springboard for Women's Economic Empowerment*. In doing so it recognized that there are significant obstacles that reinforce gendered inequalities in the global economy. These can range from barriers to building and financing private enterprises, for example legal impediments to registering property ownership and difficulties in accessing credit, to gender biases which can create vulnerabilities and unfavourable working conditions for women, and/or limit the skills development and education of the female population. However, there has been a reluctance within the membership of the WTO to specifically incorporate gender rights into its framework in order to address these gendered barriers. This institutional reluctance reflects the wider debates about the inclusion of labour rights and standards into its framework. As a regulatory organization for trade liberalization, there are contending normative positions about the extent to which the WTO should protect labour and other human rights. The size and scope of the WTO has led some observers to argue that it should adopt and enforce rules relating to labour standards. However, for others this goes beyond the intended remit of the WTO, as an organization created to regulate trade relations between states but not state-society relations, and therefore it is not appropriate for it to implement or enforce labour standards and human rights.

These contending debates were reflected in the original negotiations for the creation of the WTO and the issues of the inclusion of a social clause. There was concern, particularly among some developing counties, that such measures might countervail exports on the grounds of violations of labour standards and human rights, and that the inclusion of a social clause might provide for the imposition of economic sanctions in situations in which standards are not respected. The WTO identified four key questions that were explored in the negotiations in relation to the incorporation of labour rights into global trade rules, the operation of labour standards and the potential for protectionism.[6] First, do countries with lower standards of labour rights experience unfair export advantages and if so does this create an incentive for a lowering of standards (and therefore a race to the bottom). Second, if there were a race to the bottom should countries only trade with those of a similar standard. Third, should WTO rules allow governments to pressure others to comply with their standards. Fourth, is the WTO the appropriate vehicle for the setting and enforcement of rules on labour rights. Those in favour of the inclusion of a social clause as a means of raising and generalizing higher labour standards on a global scale argued that it would incentivize the inclusion of labour laws at a national level and bring about the harmonization of a codified set of rights and standards. Moreover, that these reforms would be supported by those engaged in the export sector. Those against the inclusion of a social clause argued that these measures could be enacted for protectionist economic interests, would interfere with the domestic political economies of the member states, and that trade sanctions were not the appropriate mechanisms through which to enforce labour standards. Moreover, rather than improving working and living conditions, the threat and imposition of embargoes and sanctions could harm employees and the general population. A number of parties, especially a number of developing countries, therefore rejected the use of the WTO to set and enforce such rules, regarding this as an attempt by the developed countries to undermine the competitiveness of their low-wage trading partners and ultimately their economic development potential.

Gender rights and trade agreements

As a consensus was not reached on these issues the WTO negotiations were concluded without the inclusion of a social clause nor the provision of trade defence measures in response to human rights violations. Currently, therefore, WTO Councils and Committees do not undertake direct work on gender and labour rights, although the WTO has stated that among its member states there is a clear consensus on and commitment to a relatively narrow set of internationally recognized 'core standards' of freedom of association: no forced labour, no child labour, and no discrimination at work (including gender discrimination).[7] At the 1996 Singapore Ministerial Conference it was agreed that the ILO was the appropriate body to negotiate labour standards, although the WTO and the ILO coordinate their activities in order to ensure coherence in global economic policymaking.

The ILO has explicit aims in relation to gender equality and gender rights and employment, including the creation of more opportunities for both men and women to secure decent employment and income. The main mechanisms for the promotion of labour rights are the conventions that are binding on the members that have ratified them with the key conventions on equality: the 1951 Equal Remuneration Convention; the 1958 Discrimination (Employment and Occupation) Convention; the 1981 Workers with Family Responsibilities Convention; the 1981 Maternity and the 2000 Protection Convention.[8] Importantly also the ILO Declaration on Fundamental Principles and Rights to Work includes a provision that labour standards should not be used for protectionist trade purposes and that the comparative advantage of a country should not be called into question by the Declaration.

In the intervening years since the creation of the WTO there have been ongoing debates and conflicts about the inclusion of labour standards and gender rights in its framework, for example the wave of social protest unleashed in 1999 in Seattle, USA. In response to growing social pressure to incorporate gender concerns into the international trade framework, as well as international commitments to mainstream gender into all areas of global economic policymaking, the WTO has increasingly adopted gender-aware policies, including the development of gender equality rules and procedures in relation to the operation of the organization itself. The WTO produces an *Annual Diversity Report* which monitors women's employment in the organization. The latest report shows that 53 per cent of all WTO staff and 45 per cent of professional staff are female.[9] Given the levels of gender parity it is perhaps unsurprising that there is increasing interest in prioritizing gender parity in the WTO.

In 2017 the WTO created a Gender Focal Point, tasked with coordinating its work on gender issues and has also presented its Gender Aware Trade Policy which outlines various measures to address the structural barriers to the inclusion of women in the global economy. However, in contrast to its own expansive analysis of the various social, economic and political barriers to the participation of women in international trade, it proposes a relatively narrow set of measures to combat these. These include general measures such as trade facilitation and trade finance, and measures such as the Standards and Trade Development Facility and the Enhanced Integrated Framework.[10] These measures, while not solely focused on gender equality, are framed by the WTO's Gender Aware Trade Policy as having an impact on the role of women in the global economy. The policy places great emphasis on the provisions to support private enterprise and encourage the integration of women into the global economy, but does not include gendered labour rights, for example for women to be employed on equal terms to men, to be paid equally for work of equal value, nor provisions aimed at domestic labour and care. This failure to include the codification of gender rights within WTO trade agreements reflects the ongoing institutional barriers facing the organization. Therefore, while the WTO regards international trade policy as an appropriate vehicle to address gender issues, it is currently limited in relation to its approach and is reluctant to employ the range of potential policy tools at its disposal.

While this has been the case at global level, the focus on gender mainstreaming, alongside the activism of social movements and feminist organizations, has provoked an increased focus on and promotion of the incorporation of gender rights and equality into bilateral and multilateral trade agreements. The positive reception by some trade policymakers to this pressure can be explained by a number of factors, including the increased participation of women in trade policymaking and in the number of women trading in international markets, coupled with the work of advocacy campaigns and the research undertaken in international organizations and academia in raising gender awareness. As a result, a range of existing trade agreements have been amended to reflect a commitment to gender equality and mainstreaming, while others have been negotiated with commitments as part of the original agreement.

Allied to the provisions on gender equality and rights, many trade agreements focus Aid for Trade (AfT) funds on gender equality and particularly support for women entrepreneurs. For example, the relationship between the EU and the African Caribbean and Pacific (ACP) Group of states, which was renegotiated and reframed in 2000 as the Cotonou Partnership includes gender-related issues in the preamble and as a cross-cutting theme[11], based on a commitment to respect international conventions on gender equality and to uphold a gender perspective in all areas of cooperation, supported by AfT provision. The Cotonou Partnership in turn sets the framework for the creation of free trade areas (economic partnership agreements – EPAs) between the EU and regional organizations throughout Africa, the Caribbean and the Pacific, which have also included a focus on gender. The EPA between the EU and the Caribbean Forum affirms the commitment of the signing parties to full and productive work for all, including women. The EU-East African Community EPA also contains explicit reference to gender equality in relation to key sectors. The focus on gender as a cross-cutting theme is also evidenced in EU agreements with other areas of the world. For example, the EU-Mexico Global Agreement (1997, revised in 2000) includes a commitment to giving attention to the role of women in the production process, with gender equality regarded as a cross-cutting issue to be mainstreamed in development cooperation. US trade agreements have also incorporated gender issues into their frameworks. For example, 2005 the Dominican Republic-Central America Free Trade Agreement (CAFTA-DR) includes gender as an annex to the labour cooperation and capacity building mechanism, while a side agreement to the North American Free Trade Agreement (NAFTA), the North American Agreement on Labour Cooperation, contains a commitment to promote cooperative activities with regard to gender equality.

The approaches exemplified in these agreements have however come under some critique. Within the EU itself, a study of the approach taken by the EU Directorate-General for Trade has characterized its commitment to gender equality objectives as 'lukewarm'.[12] The UN Conference on Trade and Development (UNCTAD) have also questioned the way in which gender has been addressed in these agreements, arguing that it is a partial approach based on the incorporation of gender into the preamble or addressed as cross-cutting themes. It argues that this is a light-touch approach and that in order to fully address gender inequality, gender-related considerations need to be firmly included into the body of trade agreements. This would require a substantive shift and the adoption of the kinds of models exemplified in more recent trade agreements in which gender equality is addressed in specific chapters. UNCTAD argues that the inclusion of gender-related considerations into the body of trade agreements as specific chapters makes these more visible and prominent. For example, the Chile-Uruguay FTA (2016) includes a chapter on gender and trade and highlights the need for gender mainstreaming for inclusive economic growth and the key role of gender equality policies. Importantly, it recognizes commitments in multilateral conventions to equal pay for equal work, maternity protection, protection for domestic workers and the reconciliation of professional and family life.

Recent developments in the Canada-Chile agreement, amending the 1997 Canada-Chile FTA, similarly includes a specific chapter on gender and trade and affirms the recognition of multilateral commitments, both within CEDAW and others, to adopt, maintain and implement gender equality rights, laws and policies. In both of these agreements there is an emphasis on enhanced cooperation and capacity building, and greater participation of civil society and the private sector in the implementation of the agreement.

Despite the inclusion of the trade and gender chapters in the Chile-Uruguay and Canada-Chile FTAs these both remain somewhat limited. For example, the chapters do not include specific gender-related standards, preferring instead just to reference the implementation of multilateral commitments to gender equality commitments. Additionally, milestones or specific goals are not included and dispute settlement mechanisms do not apply to the trade and gender chapters. Finally, there is no mandated harmonization of gender-related legislation, and the potential impact of trade liberalization on women's well-being and economic empowerment is not addressed. Thus, both agreements pave the way for future inclusion of gender rights in trade agreements but neither fully respond to the critical issues raised by feminist economists and activist groups in relation to the gendered impact of trade liberalization nor fulfil expectations of deep regulatory change to address these.

Future directions in gender-aware trade policies

In recognition of the lack of a substantive and generalized regulatory framework within international trade policies aimed at delivering gender equality and enhancing women's livelihoods, and of the limitations of current approaches, a number of recommendations have been put forward by various advocates for change. The Women and Development Network has emphasized the role of individual states in building national capacity in relation to gender and trade, and ensuring that it is consistent with international commitments to human rights and gender equality. This would provide traction for trade partners to request that gender-related standards and enforcement or dispute resolution mechanism be included in trade agreements, or more expansively that gender-related legislation is harmonized between the signatories.

Other recommendations focus on the possibilities of positive discrimination, for example in supporting women to enter global markets such as the 'She Trades' initiative.[13] This online platform facilitates trade with women-owned businesses with the aim of connecting one million women entrepreneurs to the global economy by 2020. Trommer and Hannah argue that national regulations based on positive gender discrimination are the most effective gender equality policies, although this is an approach that is at odds with the WTO's anti-discrimination stance. However, they also note that the WTO's position on non-discrimination has been most forcefully pursued in relation to good and services rather than labour and gender rights.[14] This was an issue addressed by Canada in the negotiations for the Trade in Services Agreement when it proposed its gender-sensitive domestic services initiative which included measures to ensure that licensing and qualification requirements and procedures do not discriminate on the basis of gender.

There is a common consensus by a variety of actors on recommendations for the inclusion of gender and human rights impact assessments in trade agreements, and that trade negotiations should be transparent and participatory. The inclusion of ex ante gender-related assessments of trade and the measuring of gender impacts of trade policies would highlight the differential impacts of trade agreements on women before the conclusion of negotiations and could identify areas of possible reform and/or accompanying measures. For example, UNCTAD has developed the Trade and Gender Toolbox as an approach for undertaking gender-related assessments of trade reforms.[15] Advocates of the inclusion of impact assessments highlight that the commitments to gender mainstreaming via the Beijing Platform require that WTO trade policies be reviewed for their gender impacts. The WTO Marrakesh Agreement includes a Trade Policy Review Mechanism, which could be a tool for such monitoring, although not as an enforcement or dispute settlement mechanism. In making trade negotiations transparent and participatory a range of civil society actors and activists would be able to monitor commitments to gender rights and equality and ensure that these remain a focus of future agreements. However, Women Watch, the UN Inter-Agency Network on Women and Gender Equality, warn against two common shortcomings in mainstreaming gender in trade policy in this way. The first is the 'adding on' shortcoming, whereby gender issues are an afterthought and impact assessments are conducted after the most crucial phases of trade policy are formulated and negotiated. The second is the 'evaporation' shortcoming, whereby gender issues discussed and assessed during trade policy formulation and negotiation are not translated into concrete measures.[16]

A more expansive approach is advocated by the ILO. It calls for more fundamental, integrated and transformative measures and policy interventions, based on ILO international labour standards, which seek to eliminate discrimination and the achieve gender equality at home and at work:

> [F]or substantive gender equality to be achieved, it is essential that societies recognize that both women and men have a right to work and care. In particular, failures to address workers' family responsibilities underlie sectoral and occupational segregation, gaps in wages, working hours and access to social protection. Thus, gender inequalities at work can be eliminated only by neutralizing the disadvantages stemming from women's reproductive function and promoting the equal sharing of unpaid care work between women and men, and between the family and society at large.[17]

Conclusion

In light of the debates about the gendered impact of trade liberalization, there has been recognition by the WTO itself of the need to develop gender-aware and gender-sensitive trade policies. While the approach taken at global level and within some bilateral relations has thus far had a relatively light touch, there have been a variety of initiatives within recent trade agreements that have sought to pursue a more expansive agenda. These, however, still fall short of measures to enshrine and enforce gender rights, to include specific gender-related standards or to mandate the harmonization of gender-related legislation. Moreover, there is a preference for supporting female entrepreneurialism rather than introducing concrete measures to ensure women's equality in the workplace and in society more broadly. While efforts to press these reforms are still ongoing and face considerable opposition, there are recommendations for future trade agreements, such as the inclusion of ex ante gender impact assessments, that have garnered increasing support. This marks a recognition that trade liberalization has particular effects on gender relations and inequality and that trade agreements can be effective and appropriate mechanisms through which to address these.

Notes

1 WTO (2016) *Gender Aware Trade Policy: A Springboard for Women's Economic Empowerment*, Geneva: WTO.
2 cf. Irene van Staveren, Diane Elson, Caren Grown and Nilufer Catagy (eds) (2007) *The Feminist Economics of Trade*, London: Routledge.

Gender rights and trade agreements

3 See the Gender and Development Network (2017) 'Making Trade Work for Gender Equality', *Briefings*, July, London: Gender and Development Network.
4 E. Papyrakis, A, Cocarrubias and A. Verschoor (2012) 'Gender and Trade Aspects of Labour Markets', *Journal of Development Studies*, 48(1): 81–98.
5 WTO, *Gender Aware Trade Policy*.
6 See WTO (n.d.) *Labour Standards: Consensus, Coherence and Controversy* Geneva: WTO. Available at www.wto.org/english/thewto_e/whatis_e/tif_e/bey5_e.html.
7 For a full outline of the WTO position on labour standards, see WTO, *Labour Standards*.
8 See V. Balcuinaite (2008) 'The WTO and Female Labor Rights in Developing Countries', The Institute for European Studies Working Paper 3/2008, Brussels: Institute for European Studies.
9 WTO (2017) *Women and the WTO Gender Statistics (1995–2016)*, Geneva: WTO. Available at www. wto.org/english/news_e/news17_e/gender_stats_march2017_e.pdf.
10 The WTO Trade Facilitation Agreement is regarded as being particularly beneficial for SMEs. These are in turn viewed as a mechanism to support women, both as entrepreneurs and as employees. The Standards and Trade Development Facility provides support to help build capacity in developing countries to implement sanitary and phytosanitary standards, which the WTO argues helps women as they are major players in the agricultural sector of developing countries. The Enhanced Integrated Framework promotes gender balance and inclusiveness in least developed countries by running trade capacity programmes to support women's empowerment in certain developing countries, for example.
11 See UNCTAD (2017) 'The New Way of Addressing Gender Equality Issues in Trade Agreements: Is It A True Revolution', *Policy Briefing* no. 53, October, Geneva: UNCTAD.
12 See Directorate-General for Internal Policies, Policy Department C (2016) 'Gender Equality in Trade Agreements', *Study for the FEMM Committee*, Brussels: European Parliament.
13 V. Erogbogbo (2016) 'She Trades, because She Can', *International Trade Forum*. Available at http://dx. doi.org/10.18356/3374e34b-en.
14 See S. Trommer and and E. Hannah (2017) *What Does Gender Mean at the WTO and Who Benefits?* Available at http://blog.policy.manchester.ac.uk/posts/2017/10/gender-trade-wto-who-benefits/.
15 UNCTAD (2017) *Policy Brief* no. 53.
16 Women Watch, The United Nations Inter-Agency Network on Women and Gender Equality (2011) 'Gender Equality and Trade Policy', Resource Paper, available at www.un.org/womenwatch/feature/trade/gender_equality_and_trade_policy.pdf.
17 ILO (2016) *Women at Work: Trends 2016*, Geneva: ILO.

12

Trade agreements and the environment

Inkyoung Kim

Introduction

The Marrakesh Agreement,[1] the birthplace of the World Trade Organization (WTO), begins with a clear message on the environment. The very first paragraph in the Preamble of this agreement lists its objectives, including 'raising standards of living, ensuring full employment and a large and steadily growing volume of real income and effective demand, and expanding the production of and trade in goods and services'.[2] This paragraph continues with how to achieve these goals by 'allowing for the optimal use of the world's resources in accordance with the objective of sustainable development, seeking both to protect and preserve the environment and to enhance the means for doing so in a manner consistent with their respective needs and concerns at different levels of economic development'.[3] Thus, the WTO highlights that the aims of upholding an open trading system and acting to protect the environment should be mutually supportive rather than contradictory.

The WTO's logic behind the need to pay attention to the environment is clear. The form of furthering trade openings in goods and services promotes economic development and in turn provides stable conditions for innovation, and this whole process will eventually, according to the WTO, promote the 'efficient allocation of resources, economic growth and increased income levels that in turn provide additional possibilities for protecting the environment'.[4] Some WTO rules were designed to provide a balance between the basic open trade disciplines and regulatory measures on the environment and health issues. For example, the Agreement on Technical Barriers to Trade deals with production regulations, recognizing that countries can take necessary measures for 'the protection of human health or safety, animal or plant life or health, or the environment' as long as member countries do not discriminate against or use the measures as disguised protectionism.[5]

There exist concerns about the growing number of regulations and measures against free trade. As the European Commission acknowledges, 'the most significant trade barrier is not the tariff paid at the customs, but so-called 'behind-the-border' obstacles to trade, such as different safety or environmental standards for cars'.[6] This chapter examines the tensions between environmental regulations and free trade. In doing so, it focuses on the evolution of the precautionary principle,[7] its implementation and its limitations. This study questions whether the

Trade agreements and the environment

application of the precautionary principle will form the basis for balanced policy between promotion of sustainability and facilitation of the growth of trade and investment.

Precautionary principle

The precautionary principle can be defined as 'the philosophical authority in a rational yet chaotic age to take public policy or regulatory decisions about the protection of the environment or human health in the face of scientific uncertainty, or worse, ignorance'.[8] The precautionary principle advocates the need for precaution even if some scientific uncertainty exists. Although preventive action involves state intervention 'in relation to known risks,' precaution against suspected risk 'involves a preparedness by public authorities to intervene in advance in relation to potential, uncertain or hypothetical threats'.[9] The precautionary principle obligates consultation and information sharing between member countries as well as environmental impact assessments.[10] Even though it is not a simple binary question of where the burden of proof should be allocated,[11] for some, the precautionary principle 'shifts the burden of scientific proof from those who would like to prohibit or slow down a potentially dangerous activity to those who conduct the activity'.[12]

Environmental impact assessments can be one prominent example of this principle.[13] Since the USA required environmental impact assessments in its 1969 National Environmental Policy Act, many countries in Europe and Asia have adopted environmental impact assessments at domestic level, such as Australia in 1974, Thailand in 1975, France in 1976, the Philippines in 1978, Israel in 1981, and Pakistan in 1983 despite variation among countries concerning the scope of procedures for assessments.[14] According to the Food and Agriculture Organization of the United Nations (FAO), 89 countries out of the 166 aquaculture producing countries in the world have some kind of environmental impact assessments in place.[15]

The international community has increasingly dealt with 'the need to mitigate risks and prevent environmental harm through a sophisticated network of international procedural obligations'.[16] The UN Conference on Environment and Development (also known as the Rio Summit) adopted the Rio Declaration on Environment and Development which raised awareness of the need to create a more integrated approach to environment and development in 1992. Principle 15 of the Rio Declaration states:

> In order to protect the environment, the precautionary approach shall be widely applied by States according to their capabilities. Where there are threats of serious or irreversible damage, lack of full scientific certainty shall not be used as a reason for postponing cost-effective measures to prevent environmental degradation.[17]

Agenda 21 of the Rio Summit's Plan of Action also described the need for a precautionary approach to protect the marine environment. The Convention on Biological Diversity and the UN Framework Convention on Climate Change, both adopted at the summit, also reflected the precautionary principle. The 1987 Montreal Protocol on Substances that Deplete the Ozone Layer and the 1995 UN Agreement on Straddling Fish Stocks and Highly Migratory Fish Stocks explicitly state that states need to be more cautious in the face of scientific uncertainty, and that the absence of reliable and adequate scientific information does not excuse states from postponing or failing to take measures in favour of conservation and management of the environment.[18] The Cartagena Protocol on Biosafety was adopted in 2000 and came into effect in 2003. It also allows states to ban imports of modified organisms when there is lack of scientific certainty to avoid their potential adverse effects.[19]

123

We can observe these environmental efforts in the international trade agreements. The General Agreements on Tariffs and Trade (GATT), signed in 1947 by 23 member countries, contained Article XX, offering general exceptions from international trade obligations for sovereign and unilateral trade measures to pursue specified purposes such as the protection of human health or safety, animal or plant life or health, or the environment.

> Subject to the requirement that such measures are not applied in a manner which would constitute a means of arbitrary or unjustifiable discrimination between countries where the same conditions prevail, or a disguised restriction on international trade, noting in this Agreement shall be construed to prevent the adoption or enforcement by any contracting party of measures:
> (b)   necessary to protect human, animal or plant life or health; ...
> (g)   relating to the conservation of exhaustible natural resources if such measures are made effective in conjunction with restrictions on domestic production or consumption.[20]

Article XX poses an important question for trade-environment policy, 'within the economic framework of multilateral trade, under what conditions should national governments have policy space to pursue ecological goals by restricting international trade in certain goods in order to promote the conservation of environmental resources harmed by production of those goods?'[21] Article XX is an important component of a balanced approach to trade interests and environmental objectives.

In particular, the Agreement on Sanitary and Phytosanitary Measures (SPS Agreement) exemplifies the growing focus of international trade law on the precautionary principle. The SPS Agreement concerns food safety and animal and plant health to ensure that a country's consumers are supplied with food that is safe to eat.[22] The SPS Agreement recognizes the 'limitations of scientific prediction' and the need to 'act first and then set about ascertaining the facts more closely'.[23] Member states are required to assess 'the risks to human, animal or plant life or health', based on the available 'risk assessment techniques developed by the relevant international organizations' (Article 5.1). It also identifies specific procedures that member states can take in case sufficient relevant scientific evidence does not exist, stating that a member may adopt provisional measures 'on the basis of available pertinent information' from sanitary or phytosanitary measures applied by other Members as well as the relevant international organizations, and 'Members shall seek to obtain the additional information necessary for a more objective assessment of risk and review the sanitary or phytosanitary measure accordingly within a reasonable period of time' (Article 5.7).

The SPS Agreement also emphasizes an economic assessment of provisional measures to prevent sanitary and phytosanitary measures from being 'applied in a manner which would constitute a disguised restriction on international trade' (Article 2.3). Member states are required to 'take into account as relevant economic factors' including 'the potential damage in terms of loss of production or sales in the event of the entry, establishment or spread of a pest or disease; the costs of control or eradication in the territory of the importing Member; and the relative cost-effectiveness of alternative approaches to limiting risks' (Article 5.3).

This precautionary principle responds to the critique of globalization by promising more democratic decision-making in relation to issues of sustainability and risks associated with both economic and technological development. The principle ensures that policymaking procedures are open to 'wider participation and greater transparency and democratic accountability.'[24]

There has been considerable criticism about this precautionary principle in regard to its obscure definition and its adverse effects such as 'don't do anything'.[25] It is also still debatable whether or not this principle meets the level of customary international law.[26] However, it seems evident that the precautionary principle is 'an evolving, culturally framed concept "that takes its cue from changing conceptions about the appropriate roles of science, economics, ethics, politics and the law in pro-active environmental protection and management"'.[27]

Regional trade agreements and the environment

The WTO defines regional trade agreements (RTAs) as 'reciprocal trade agreements between two or more partners' including free trade agreements (FTAs)/mechanisms and customs unions.[28] It is notable that all WTO members now have RTAs in force as of June 2016 when Mongolia and Japan signed their RTA. Even though non-discrimination among members is the core principle of the WTO, RTAs are exempted by the WTO for special treatments of their partners, subject to a set of rules.[29]

While the purpose of an RTA is to reduce tariffs, an increasing number of these agreements deal with trade-related issues including labour and the environment. Most RTAs allow states parties some regulatory leeway over certain goods for the sake of the environment, based on Article XX of the GATT.[30] Since the North American Free Trade Agreement (NAFTA) established major environmental provisions in the 1990s, countries have adopted provisions dealing with environmental issues. Environmental provisions within RTAs vary from as little as a line or two in the preamble, one or more chapters or sections in the agreement, or a separate environmental chapter, to a separate environmental agreement accompanying the trade agreement.[31]

How have countries enacted the precautionary principle in RTAs? Have countries incorporated this principle when they reach agreements for regional free trade? These questions will be discussed below.

Europe

Since the precautionary principle was first articulated in 1968 in the *Bundes-Immissionsschutzgesetz* (Air Pollution Act) of the Federal Republic of Germany,[32] it has guided European Union (EU) environmental policy particularly since it was adopted in the 1992 Maastricht Treaty.[33] The 1979 Directive on the testing of new chemicals was the first piece of EU legislation adopting the precautionary principle, and followed the model of US legislation. Paradoxically, the EU exceeded the USA in its application of the precautionary principle by the 1990s.[34] Since then, the EU has emerged as the main proponent of the precautionary principle in European regulatory policy and international agreements.[35]

> The Community policy on the environment ... shall be based on the precautionary principle and on the principles that preventive action should be taken, that environmental damage should as a priority be rectified at source and that the polluter should pay. Environmental protection requirements must be integrated into the definition and implementation of other Community policies.[36]

The EU has extended the use of the principle from the environment into other policy domains including human, animal, and plant health, which has led to a convergence of environmental regulation and other areas including trade policy. The EU has sought to apply the precautionary principle in all instances, unlike some other governments such as the US administration, which seems to aim to tailor the use of this principle to the specific policy area. With regard to the link with food safety and trade, the EU's bans on certain hormones in beef in 1988 and four anti-biotics[37] in animal feed in 1998 are the two of the most significant examples of the enactment of the precautionary principle, along with the two Directives of the European Commission on genetically modified crops in 2001.[38]

The principle is firmly anchored in the jurisprudence of the European Court of Justice. Furthermore, the EU member states and European institutions, including the European Parliament, have endorsed its clear and consistent approach to the principle.[39] For example, the judgment of the Court in case C-157/96 relating to agriculture animal health emergency measures against transmission of bovine spongiform encephalopathy (BSE), commonly known as 'mad cow disease', confirmed in 1998 that the precautionary principle can be used to ban the sale of a certain product:

> Whereas, under current circumstances, a definitive stance on the transmissibility of BSE to humans is not possible; whereas a risk of transmission cannot be excluded; whereas the resulting uncertainty has created serious concern among consumers; whereas under the circumstances and as an emergency measure, the transport of all bovine animals and all beef and veal or derived products from the United Kingdom to the other Member States should be temporarily banned.[40]

However, Asian and Latin American governments have expressed concern about the EU's regulations particularly with regard to 'disguised protectionism'.[41] Most of the concern is based on several trade disputes involving the USA. For instance, the US beef exporters responded to the European Community's ban on imports of meat and meat products from the USA and other WTO members that the ban was 'arbitrary and had protectionist intent, because US beef had been found to be safe in the US, on the basis of a sound science test'.[42] In fact, the USA requested consultations with the European Community under the Dispute Settlement Body of the WTO in 1996. The Panel and Appellate Body concluded that the EC's ban on imports was inconsistent with the SPS Agreement as the EC had not conducted a complementary risk assessment of potential risks to human health from hormone residues in bovine meat and meat products before imposing the import ban.[43]

However, for some observers, this concern about the precautionary principle is 'inaccurate and superficial'.[44] Stephen Woolcock contends that the precautionary principle has been driven by political pressure from domestic constituents such as consumers, and that voters are not confident in the existing regulatory regimes and are sceptical of the scientific certainty. However, he also argues that the EU's practices, based on the precautionary principle, are not a rejection of sound science as the EU's approach to risk assessment is science-based. However, the EU recognizes scientific uncertainty in risk assessment and management, and places 'scientific risk assessment within a broader framework which also includes non-scientific value judgements of what is an acceptable risk for society'.[45]

Even in Europe, there is concern about the chilling effect that an excessive degree of precaution will have on investment in new technologies, particularly in the biotechnology field.[46] Moreover, the EU has concerns about trade barriers in its relations with strategic trade partners who use SPS restrictions to protect domestic producers of agricultural products from free trade. In particular, the EU has found that the Russian and Indian governments frequently go beyond international standards and what is required for protecting the health of their consumers without scientific justification.[47]

North America

NAFTA was a landmark RTA due to its positive achievements on linking trade and the environment. According to Kevin P. Gallagher, 'NAFTA was the first significant trade agreement that included environmental provisions through a side agreement, and established parallel institutions for monitoring and finance'.[48] As we can see in a major speech by the US Democratic presidential candidate, Bill Clinton, on 4 October 1992, there were concerns about NAFTA's deficiencies, particularly regarding different environmental and labour standards among parties as well as import surges.[49] When President Clinton took office, the states parties to NAFTA, the US, Canadian and Mexican governments, initiated side agreement negotiations to deal with these issues, and finally reached an agreement on 13 August 1993 which subsequently came into effect on 1 January 1994.

An unprecedented level of environmental diplomacy and cooperation among the three states parties to NAFTA has been visualized by its environmental side agreement, the North American Agreement on Environmental Cooperation, adopted in 1993.[50] It created a North American Commission for Environmental Cooperation (CEC) that a transparent and representative public advisory committee partially oversees. There have been several concrete results of these efforts. First, a 'Pollutant Release and Transfer Registry' law in Mexico was established to secure environmental protection under NAFTA even though it is 'broader in scope than similar laws'[51] in the other two parties.[52] Second, the CEC has a unique citizen submissions process whereby third parties can file violations of environmental laws in the three member countries. This process has made it possible for the public to take part in fact-finding missions through a new international forum and engage with domestic government officials and discuss concerns about domestic governance.[53] Finally, the CEC has created an institutional mechanism that provides funding for local communities and small businesses to assist them in complying with environmental law and for the creation of the North American Development Bank and the Border Environmental Cooperation Commission to run water and sanitation projects along the border between the US and Mexico.

Despite the fears of many environmentalists, 'NAFTA did not result in Mexico becoming a "pollution haven" for dirty U.S. firms seeking weaker environmental regulations'.[54] In fact, following the establishment of NAFTA, Mexico recorded a larger decrease in the amount of dirty industry than the USA.[55] Kevin P. Gallagher contends that Mexico's abundance of unskilled labour attracts jobs primarily in manufacturing assembly plants that are 'less pollution-intensive than more capital-laden manufacturing activities such as cement, pulp and paper, and base metals production' which 'has actually fallen off in Mexico during the NAFTA period'.[56]

However, these achievements are exceptional rather than usual. According to Mexico's National Institute for Statistics, Geography, and Information Systems, the financial cost of environmental degradation such as soil erosion, waste, air and water pollution were estimated about 10 per cent of GDP from 1988 to 1999, thereby overwhelming the country's annual economic growth, which stood at just 2.5 per cent.[57]

This limited achievement can be explained by the lack of endorsement of the precautionary principle under NAFTA and its side agreements. NAFTA's Chapter 11 and its investor-state dispute settlement has impinged on sovereign regulatory authority to protect their environment and natural resources.

Chapter 11 indicates that member countries can take environmental measures 'to ensure that investment activity in its territory is undertaken in a manner sensitive to environmental concerns' (Article 1114.1).[58] It adds:

> The Parties recognize that it is inappropriate to encourage investment by relaxing domestic health, safety or environmental measures. Accordingly, a Party should not waive or

otherwise derogate from, or offer to waive or otherwise derogate from, such measures as an encouragement for the establishment, acquisition, expansion or retention in its territory of an investment of an investor. If a Party considers that another Party has offered such an encouragement, it may request consultations with the other Party and the two Parties shall consult with a view to avoiding any such encouragement.

(Article 1114.2)

These environmental measures have been debunked by NAFTA's dispute settlement processes between a state party and an investor belonging to another state party, and numerous dispute settlements in favour of investors. In terms of processes, investors have significant advantages over the states. Foreign investors from the member countries can launch a claim and invoke arbitration unilaterally without seeking consent from their home governments and trying to resolve a complaint through their domestic court system. Chapter 11 has led three states parties to give their 'unconditional, prior consent' to submit investor claims to arbitration. Tribunal decisions, made by three members (one selected by the investor, one by the challenged government, and a third appointed by mutual agreement), are binding and final.[59] Even though tribunals have no power to force the challenged government to change its NAFTA-inconsistent measures, they can award fully enforceable monetary damages to investors in the domestic courts.

In addition to processes favouring private investors, cases that have been decided pose a significant threat to the regulatory authority of states parties which use the precautionary principle. Of cases decided by the tribunal or a negotiated settlement, governments have won 69 per cent (24 cases) and lost 31 per cent (11 cases).[60] These numbers can be elusive as the USA has lost none and won all 11 cases. Looking at the decided cases for Canada and Mexico, the threat becomes more prominent. Canada has won six and lost five of decided cases. Mexico has won six and lost five, but has incurred the highest monetary damages valued at more than US $204 million to foreign investors.[61]

Claimants can challenge governments' regulatory measures that are allegedly unfair or inequitable (Article 1105), discriminatory (Articles 1102 and 1103), constitute in/direct expropriation (Article 1110) or apply performance requirements (Article 1106). In fact, more than 40 per cent of claims are associated with environmental protection and resource management.[62]

For example, in the 1997 ethyl case, a US chemical company filed a complaint against the Canadian government, challenging a Canadian import and interprovincial trade ban on the gasoline additive MMT, which was a 'suspected' neurotoxin. The company was awarded monetary damages valued at US $13 million, and, furthermore, the Canadian government was compelled to overturn the ban and issue a formal apology.

Thus, NAFTA's investor-state mechanism has given multinational corporations too much power and constrained the governmental role in enforcing regulations. NAFTA's Chapter 11 has resulted in 'a massive restriction on the ability of governments to legislate in ways that protect human health and ensure environmental vitality and sustainability' as government action that can infringe on 'the rights of private investors to receive returns on their investment is deemed expropriatory and therefore illegal under the agreement'.[63]

Asia

Many RTAs typically feature environmental cooperation and consultation mechanisms that range from broad arrangements to a specific area of special interest, as well as environmental standards to enforce environmental laws. Asian countries have relied heavily on environmental cooperation and information-sharing mechanisms, rather than actually adopting the precautionary principle.

The People's Republic of China included few environmental provisions in its earlier RTAs with Macau (2003), Hong Kong (2003), ASEAN (2004), Pakistan (2005), Chile (2005), New Zealand (2008), Singapore (2008), Peru (2009), Costa Rica (2010), Iceland (2013), Switzerland (2013), the Republic of Korea (2015), Australia (2015), and Georgia (2017).[64] The environmental provisions in these agreements are at most limited to the inclusion of the principle of sustainable development, environmental measures as exceptions to trade obligations, environmental cooperation, and market access commitments on environmental goods and services.[65]

This 'cautious approach' by China to environmental provisions in regional environmental agreements has changed into a more engaging approach to environmental provisions.[66] Henry Gao's examples of this change are notable. China's FTA with Singapore presented a new model for environmental cooperation as the first inter-governmental eco-city in the world, referring to the Sino-Singapore Tianjin Eco-city project. More recent trade agreements with Switzerland and the Republic of Korea include chapters on environmental concerns.

Article 12.16 of the Free Trade Agreement Between the Government of the People's Republic of China and the Government of the Republic of Korea indicates environmental measures as follows:

> Each Party recognizes that it is inappropriate to encourage investment by investors of the other Party by relaxing its environmental measures. To this effect each Party should not waive or otherwise derogate from such environmental measures as an encouragement for the establishment, acquisition or expansion of investments in its territory.[67]

Besides this brief statement on the environmental measures, the Agreement has an entire chapter on 'Environment and Trade' (Chapter 16). However, the chapter is fairly general and lacks specific components. Article 16.3 outlines the level of environmental protection required to secure interdependent and mutually supportive components of sustainable economic and social development:

1 The parties reaffirm each Party's sovereign right to establish its own levels of environmental protection and its own environmental development priorities, and to adopt or modify its environmental laws and policies.
2 Each Party shall seek to ensure that those laws and policies provide for and encourage high levels of environmental protection, and shall strive to continue to improve its respective levels of environmental protection.[68]

Unlike the general statement about sustainable development, this chapter puts considerable emphasis on bilateral cooperation with an indicative list of areas of cooperation (Article 16.7). The list includes the promotion of environmental goods, technology and industry along with an exchange of information on policies and environmental measures and capacity building through knowledge exchanges.

It is worthwhile highlighting a provision in an environmental impact assessment of the FTA as well as addressing the enforcement problem and requiring both parties to 'effectively enforce its environmental measures including laws and regulations, through a sustained or recurring course of action or inaction, in a manner affecting trade or investment between the Parties.'[69]

It should, however, be noted that this change still has a long way to go, because none of these trade agreements have created a dispute settlement mechanism within the environmental chapter. For example, Article 16.9 on non-application of dispute settlement of the Free Trade Agreement Between the Government of the People's Republic of China and the Government

Inkyoung Kim

of the Republic of Korea states that states parties shall not have recourse to dispute settlement for any matter arising under the 'Environment and Trade' chapter. This suggests that although environmental provisions by China are evolving, Asian countries are still reluctant to accept such environmental commitments as binding, legally enforceable obligations, which is far from the application of the precautionary principle.[70]

Conclusion

This chapter has examined the evolution of the precautionary principle in international trade agreements and its application to the relationship between trade and the environment. The precautionary principle can be traced back to the 1970s in Europe and particularly the German philosopher Hans Jonas who discussed an ethics for the technological civilization.[71] Since 1971, the word *Vorsorge* (precaution) has appeared in the environmental policy of the Federal Republic of Germany. From the GATT's Article XX on general exceptions from trade obligations to ensure a state's sovereign right to protect its environment and people to the SPS Agreement under the WTO for food safety and animal and plant health for its consumers, the international community has become more inclusive of environmentally preventive and precautionary measures.

International scholars have been debating whether or not this principle has reached the status of a rule of customary international law. As shown above, its application to different RTAs shows a lack of unity because its application remains diverse depending on their own interpretations of this concept. Furthermore, unlike the widely accepted stereotypes and generalizations of Europe as being more precautionary than the USA, in reality the precautionary practices are occasional and selective.[72] It has been found that the EU has adopted the principle in its treaty but its adoption of this principle has been sporadic rather than consistent, while although the USA does not formally endorse this principle, its adoption of it is rather consistent.[73] In reality, the precautionary principle is more complex than a simple scenario of policy convergence or divergence, but even so, the precautionary principle is rapidly shifting from soft law to hard law through the active legal orders and authentic recommendations of international organizations including the EU, the WTO, and the World Health Organization who all aim to create a balance between trade interests and environmental protection.[74] This shift will be intensified by the increasing role for science in environmental regulation.

Notes

1 The Marrakesh Agreement was adopted in 1994 by 124 countries. It was the culmination of the 12-year-long Uruguay Round, establishing the WTO in 1995, the successor of the GATT that took effect in 1948.
2 WTO (n.d.) 'Marrakesh Agreement Establishing the World Trade Organization', Geneva: WTO, available at www.wto.org/English/docs_e/legal_e/04–wto_e.htm.
3 Ibid.
4 WTO (n.d.) 'An Introduction to Trade and Environment in the WTO', Geneva: WTO, available at www.wto.org/english/tratop_e/envir_e/envt_intro_e.htm.
5 WTO (n.d.) 'Agreement on Technical Barriers to Trade', available at www.wto.org/english/docs_e/legal_e/17-tbt_e.htm.
6 Lucas Bergkamp and Lawrence Kogan (2013) 'Trade, the Precautionary Principle, and Post-Modern Regulatory Process', *European Journal of Risk Regulation*, 4: 493–507.
7 A 'precautionary approach' is different from 'precautionary principle' largely applied to jurisprudence and history in the environmental field in the sense that a precautionary approach considers that these precedents would not be applicable to other fields. See Stephen Woolcock (2002) 'The Precautionary

130

Principle in the European Union and Its Impact on International Trade Relations', Center for European Policy Studies Working Document No. 186, Brussels: Center for European Policy Studies, p. i, available at www.ceps.eu/system/files/book/96.pdf.

8 James Cameron (2001), 'The Precautionary Principle in International Law', in Timothy O'Riorden, James Cameron, and Andrew Jordon (eds) *Reinterpreting the Precautionary Principle*, London: Cameron May, p. 113.

9 Caroline E. Foster (2011) *Science and the Precautionary Principle in International Courts and Tribunals: Expert Evidence, Burden of Proof and Finality*, New York: Cambridge University Press, p. 18.

10 Gunter Handl (1991) 'Environmental Security and Global Change: The Challenge to International Law', in W. Lang, H. Neuhold and K. Zemanek (eds) *Environmental Protection and International Law*, London: Dordrecht and Boston, MA: Graham and Trotman/Martinus Nijhoff.

11 Annecoos Wiersema (2016) 'The Precautionary Principle in Environmental Governance', in Douglas Fisher (ed.) *Research Handbook on Fundamental Concepts of Environmental Law*, Cheltenham and Northampton, MA: Edward Elgar, pp. 449–74.

12 Mary Stevens (2002) 'The Precautionary Principle in the International Arena', *Sustainable Development Law & Policy*, 2(2): 13–15.

13 James Cameron (1999) 'The Precautionary Principle: Core Meaning, Constitutional Framework and Procedures for Implementation', in Ronnie Harding and Elizabeth Fisher (eds) *Perspectives on the Precautionary Principle*, Annadale: The Federation Press, pp. 29–58.

14 Japanese Ministry of Environment, 'History of EIA Systems and Measures Taken Around the World', available at www.env.go.jp/earth/coop/coop/document/10-eiae/10-eiae-2.pdf.

15 Doris Soto, José Aguilar-Manjarrez and Elena Irde (2009) 'Countries Implementation of Environmental Impact Assessment in Aquaculture According to Information Reported to and Collected by FAO', in FAO Fisheries and Aquaculture Technical Paper No. 527, Rome: FAO, pp. 553–62, available at www.fao.org/3/a-i0970e/i0970e01i.pdf.

16 Foster, *Science and the Precautionary Principle in International Courts and Tribunals*, p. 7.

17 UN General Assembly (1992) 'Annex I of the Report of the United Nations Conference on Environment and Development', available at www.un.org/documents/ga/conf151/aconf15126-1annex1.htm.

18 See Article 6 of the UN Agreement on Straddling Fish Stocks and Highly Migratory Fish Stocks, which was adopted in 1995 and came into force in 2001.

19 Foster, p. 7.

20 WTO, 'Article XX General Exceptions', available at www.wto.org/english/res_e/booksp_e/gatt_ai_e/art20_e.pdf.

21 Sanford Gaines (2001) 'The WTO's Reading of the GATT Article XX Chapeau: A Disguised Restriction on Environmental Measures', *U. Pa. J. Int'l Econ. L.* 22(4): 739–862.

22 WTO (n.d.) 'Sanitary and Phytosanitary Measures', available at www.wto.org/english/tratop_e/sps_e/sps_e.htm.

23 Foster, p. 18.

24 Woolcock, 'Precautionary Principle in the European Union and Its Impact on International Trade Relations', p. i.

25 Bergkamp and Kogan, 'Trade, the Precautionary Principle, and Post-Modern Regulatory Process'.

26 For legal commentators who argue it has achieved its status as the customary international law, see Cameron, 'The Precautionary Principle'. For commentators who argue that it has not yet achieved, see Catherine Tinker (1996) 'State Responsibility and the Precautionary Principle', in David Freestone and Ellen Hay (eds) *The Precautionary Principle and International Law: The Challenge of Implementation*, The Hague, London and Boston, MA: Kluwer Law International, pp. 53–72.

27 Mary Stevens, 'The Precautionary Principle in the International Arena', p. 15.

28 WTO (n.d.) 'Regional Trade Agreements and Preferential Trade Agreements', available at www.wto.org/english/tratop_e/region_e/rta_pta_e.htm.

29 WTO (n.d.) 'Regional Trade Agreements', available at www.wto.org/english/tratop_e/region_e/region_e.htm.

30 OECD (2007) *Environment and Regional Trade Agreements*, Paris: OECD Publishing, available at www.keepeek.com/Digital-Asset-Management/oecd/environment/environment-and-regional-trade-agreements_9789264006805-en#.WjqRtmahzow#page1.

31 Dale Colyer (2011) *Green Trade Agreements*, New York: Palgrave Macmillan.

32 Paul Guy (2004) 'Throwing Caution to the Wind: The Precautionary Principle, NAFTA and Environmental Protection in Canada', *Dalhousie Journal of Legal Studies*, 13: 187–209. The Federal German government indicated in 1984 in its report on environmental policy that the 'principle of precaution

(*Vorsorge*) commands that damages done to the natural world ... should be avoided in advance and in accordance with opportunity and possibility. Precaution further means the early detection of dangers to health and the environment by comprehensive, synchronized ... research ... [It] also means acting when conclusively ascertained understandings by science is not yet available'. Woolcock, p. 3.

33 Stevens.
34 Ibid.
35 Ibid.
36 Article 130r, para. 2, Treaty establishing the European Community – Title XVI – Environment – Article 130R /★Codified Version of the Treaty Establishing the European Community★/, available at http://eur-lex.europa.eu/legal-content/GA/TXT/?uri=CELEX:11992E130R.
37 Four antibiotics found in animal feed (virginiamycin, bacitracin zinc, tylosin phosphate and spiramycin) were banned on the grounds that use of these antibiotics can promote human resistance to antibiotics and reduce their effectiveness for human treatment. The ban on certain beef hormones was based on their carcinogenic risks.
38 Woolcock.
39 Ibid.
40 The Court of Justice of the European Communities (1998) 'Judgement of the Court', available at http://curia.europa.eu/juris/document/document.jsf?text=&docid=43817&doclang=EN.
41 Renee Johnson (2015) 'The U.S.-EU Beef Hormone Dispute', *Congressional Research Service,* available at https://fas.org/sgp/crs/row/R40449.pdf.
42 Woolcock, p. 13.
43 WTO, 'DS26: European Communities – Measures Concerning Meat and Meat Products (Hormones)', available at www.wto.org/english/tratop_e/dispu_e/cases_e/ds26_e.htm.
44 Woolcock, p. ii.
45 Woolcock, p. iii.
46 Woolcock.
47 European Commission Trade (2011) 'Trade and Investment Barriers Report 2011: Engaging Our Strategic Economic Partners on Improved Market Access: Priorities for Action on Breaking Down Barriers to Trade', available at http://trade.ec.europa.eu/doclib/docs/2011/march/tradoc_147629.pdf.
48 Kevin P. Gallagher (2009) 'NAFTA and the Environment: Lessons from Mexico and Beyond', in Kevin P. Gallagher, Enrique Dussel Peters and Timothy A. Wise (eds) *The Future of North American Trade Policy: Lessons from NAFTA*, Pardee Center Task Force Report, Boston University, November, p. 61, available at www.bu.edu/pardee/files/2009/11/Pardee-Report-NAFTA.pdf.
49 Steve Charnovitz (1996) 'The NAFTA Environmental Side Agreement: Implications for Environmental Cooperation, Trade Policy, and American Treatymaking', in Seymour J. Rubin and Dean C. Alexander (eds) NAFTA and the Environment, Boston, MA: Kluwer Law International.
50 Commission for Environmental Cooperation, available at www.cec.org/about-us/NAAEC.
51 Gallagher, 'NAFTA and the Environment', p. 62.
52 Mark Winfield (2003) 'North American Pollutant Release and Transfer Registries', in David Markell and John Knox (eds) *Greening NAFTA: The North American Commission for Environmental Cooperation*, Stanford, CA: Stanford University Press.
53 David L. Markell (2003) 'The CEC Citizen Submissions Process: On or Off Course?', in David L. Markell and John H. Knox (eds) *Greening NAFTA: The North American Commission for Environmental Cooperation*, Stanford, CA: Stanford University Press.
54 Gallagher, p. 62.
55 Kevin P. Gallagher (2004) 'Free Trade and the Environment: Mexico, NAFTA, and Beyond', Americas Program, Silver City, NM: Interhemispheric Resource Center.
56 Ibid, p. 2.
57 Ibid.
58 NAFTA Secretariat (2014), 'North American Free Trade Agreement', available at www.nafta-sec-a lena.org/Home/Texts-of-the-Agreement/North-American-Free-Trade-Agreement?mvid=1&secid=5 39c50ef-51c1-489b-808b-9e20c9872d25#A1114.
59 Scott Sinclair (2015) 'Democracy under Challenge: Canada and Two Decades of NAFTA's Investor-State Dispute Settlement Mechanism', Ottawa, ON: Canadian Center for Policy Alternative, available at www.policyalternatives.ca/sites/default/files/uploads/publications/National%20Office/2015/01/ NAFTA_Chapter11_Investor_State_Disputes_2015.pdf.
60 Sinclair, 'Democracy under Challenge'.

61 Ibid., p. 31.
62 Ibid.
63 Guy, 'Throwing Caution to the Wind', p. 204.
64 Ministry of Commerce, PRC (2017) 'China's Free Trade Agreements', available at http://fta.mofcom.gov.cn/english/fta_qianshu.shtml.
65 Henry Gao (2017) 'China's Evolving Approach to Environmental and Labour Provisions in Regional Trade Agreements', available at www.ictsd.org/opinion/china-3.
66 Ibid.
67 Free Trade Agreement Between the Government of the People's Republic of China and the Government of the Republic of Korea, available at http://fta.mofcom.gov.cn/korea/annex/xdzw_en.pdf.
68 Ibid.
69 Ibid.
70 Ibid.
71 Djibril Moudachirou and Hamid Mukhtar (2016) 'Precautionary Principle in International Environmental Law: Rule of Customary International Law', *International Journal of Management Sciences*, 6(12): 564–71.
72 Jonathan B. Wiener, Michael D. Rogers, James K. Hammitt and Peter H. Sand (eds) (2011) *The Reality of Precaution: Comparing Risk Regulation in the United States and Europe*, London and New York: RFF (Resources for the Future) Press.
73 Ibid.
74 Moudachirou and Mukhtar, 'Precautionary Principle in International Environmental Law'.

13

Neoliberal globalization and its opponents

Anne L. Clunan

Resisting neoliberal globalization: from Heiligendamm to crisis to Trump

In June 2007 tens of thousands of protesters gathered in the small German town of Heiligendamm. Under the slogan of 'make capitalism history: shut down the G-8', 'broad networks of direct actionists, anti-racist groups, anti-border groups, anti-fascist militants, queer activists, squatters, debt-relief groups, trade unions, environmental organizations and many others' protested against globalization during the meeting of the leaders of the G8 economies; a couple of thousand anarchist and left- and right-wing militants turned what had been a peaceful protest into a violent melee.[1]

Six months later, the global neoliberal capitalist system collapsed, not through the efforts of those who opposed it in Heiligendamm, but from its own internal workings. Global credit vanished, and stock markets around the world crashed. Everywhere, governments took on huge public debts in order to save bankers, and thereby, global capitalism.[2] Despite the injection of public funds, world trade declined by 10 per cent, as global demand evaporated along with investment and the global supply chain broke apart. Global capital flows and cross-border bank lending collapsed. Unemployment soared. Global finance and trade would remain flat for a decade. In 2010, just three years after it began, the Bank of England estimated that the crisis had already cost the world between US $60–$200 trillion dollars.[3] Within the European Union (EU), people in Central Eastern Europe flooded west in search of jobs. Migration from the global south increased to levels not seen since the late 19th century, as people in developing countries fled poverty and war to find opportunities in the developed world, particularly Europe.[4]

The cost of rescuing the global financial system was by and large to be paid not by the financiers who endangered the entire global economy, but the average taxpayer, the '99%' of the global workforce that had not reaped a proportionate share of the gains from global liberalization. The USA alone saw a loss in production worth US $6–$14 trillion, or 40–90 per cent of US pre-crisis gross domestic product (GDP). The household wealth of Americans dropped by $16 trillion, and the loss in human capital was estimated at 90 per cent of pre-crisis GDP. Government estimates of US Administration liabilities in bailing out the financial sector were feared to be as high as $24 trillion.[5] In late 2017 US output was 13 per cent below its pre-crisis trend. According to Andy Haldane, chief economist of the Bank of England, in Europe the lost output costs 'have been the highest they have been for a century'. Globally, he notes, the costs to governments and their publics of saving the financial system are greater than those of the Great Depression.[6]

It is no surprise therefore that the greatest global economic collapse since the Great Depression galvanized popular outcry in a manner not seen since the 1930s. In 2011 popular protests about the lack of economic opportunity and equity swept across the globe, from the 'Arab spring' to the Occupy movement, causing regimes to topple, governments to fall and far too much blood to be shed. Five years on, popular anger produced the British vote to leave the EU (known as Brexit), the electoral success of a far-right party in Germany and a nationalist presidential candidate Donald Trump in the USA.

There is a long history of public anger at liberal capitalism producing political movements that threaten to sweep the global economic system away, including populism, socialism, nationalism and fascism. Karl Polyani details the manner in which these forces mobilized to resist the first era of globalization, that of laissez-faire liberalism prior to the First World War.[7] The People's Party, the first populist political party, appeared in late 19th-century USA in direct response to the effect that international trade and the Gold Standard were having on farmers and workers. Populist and feminist Mary Elisabeth Lease relayed in 1890 sentiments that resonate today, railing that,

> We wiped out slavery and our tariff laws and national banks began a system of white wage slavery worse than the first. Wall Street owns the country. It is no longer a government of the people, by the people, and for the people, but a government of Wall Street, by Wall Street, and for Wall Street. The great common people of this country are slaves, and monopoly is the master ... Money rules, and our Vice-President is a London banker. Our laws are the output of a system, which clothes rascals in robes and honesty in rags.[8]

Such populism has little political agenda other than giving more power to the people, and it is usually paired with a left- or right-wing ideology that may be more or less antagonist to neoliberal capitalism. Populists consider 'the people' to be noble and pure and 'the elite' to be corrupt and/or undemocratic. Right-wing populism attacks both the political, technocratic and business establishment but also excludes many groups and minorities from its narrow conception of 'the people'. Left-wing populism also targets the corporate and political elite, the technocracy, as well as political and economic imperialism and hierarchy, and usually offers a more inclusive view of 'the people'. Populism offered a base of appeal for the fascist and socialist political parties of the 1930s in Europe and is equally instrumental to leftists and rightist authoritarian regimes in Latin America, Turkey, the Russian Federation and Asia today. So, it is worth unpacking which critiques bring those on the right and the left to respond to appeals to alter or end neoliberal globalization.

The many challengers today to neoliberal globalization are almost too numerous to number. They include, among others, anarchists; socialists; social democrats; environmentalists; left- and right-libertarians; labour, democracy, animal and human rights activists; feminists; chauvinists; racists; anti-racists; anti-imperialists; nativists; communitarians; religious fundamentalists; Pope Francis; liberation theologists; and militant Islamists.[9] There is not, therefore, a single 'anti-globalization movement', so much as networks of networks connecting disparate movements at local, national and transnational level. Most scholars studying anti-globalization movements restrict themselves to left-oriented activists, leaving right-oriented groups understudied.[10] Even within the left, scholars disagree as to whether there is a coherent overarching network or movement, which scholars such as Peter Evans call a 'progressive counter-hegemonic movement' against globalization.[11] Historically and today, the voices of the left compete and occasionally collaborate with potent populist, nationalist and racist forces against neoliberal globalization, which Evans calls 'regressive forces for social protection'.

This chapter first gives a brief history of neoliberal globalization as its opponents might see it. It next identifies three core concerns – popular self-determination, collective cultural autonomy, and global social justice – that motivate this diverse set of actors and how these concerns have been put into practice in the 21st century.

Neoliberal globalization: a brief critical history

Neoliberal globalization is defined in this chapter as the increasing economic and technological integration across national boundaries that began in the 1970s, guided by the ideological strictures of neoliberal economic theories and market capitalism. Neoliberalism's contemporary hegemony, like that of laissez-faire liberalism prior to the First World War, is the deliberate outcome of state policy, rather than a natural result of human nature. Karl Polyani observed in 1944 that the long process that produced the globalization of laissez-faire liberalism in the 19th century was historically unprecedented, and resulted in markets being disembedded from society.[12] In turn, he argued, the dominance of laissez-faire begat a 'spontaneous' countervailing movement to re-embed the market and 'to resist the pernicious effects of a market-controlled economy' through the creation of systems of social protection.[13] That countervailing movement, taking place at national level in the Western states, produced what would be known as the social democratic welfare state and the Bretton Woods international economic system.

Following the Second World War, facing an encroaching communist ideology and with the dangers of fascism fresh in leaders' minds, the USA and Great Britain led the way in establishing the political foundations for building another liberal international economic order. This new order, however, would secure the right of all populaces to state-provided social welfare, especially full employment, while at the same time promoting a more open international trading system.[14] The shift in the governance of the global economy, from laissez-faire liberalism prior to the First World War to 'embedded' liberalism after the Second World War, created new expectations of what governance and statehood entailed: state-provision of social welfare, ranging from domestic economic growth and employment to education, environmental protection, and health care.

The embedded form of liberalism tolerated significant state intervention in the economy in an effort to prevent instability domestically and internationally. This held true in the developed and the developing world, where, Thomas Biersteker recounts, the 1960s and 1970s witnessed an 'ever increased role for state economic intervention in the economy'.[15] Internationally, embedded liberalism promoted multilateralism and created the International Monetary Fund (IMF), the World Bank, and the General Agreement on Tariffs and Trade to govern and protect the global trade and monetary systems and to ensure reconstruction and development.

By the 1990s a more reflexively capitalistic neoliberal economic ideology had largely replaced 'embedded' or social democratic liberalism. The global diffusion of neoliberalism – which John Ruggie called the 'resurgent ethos of liberal capitalism' – began in the 1960s in the West and took hold in the late 1970s with the elections of Margaret Thatcher and Ronald Reagan. The neoliberal movement sought to rejuvenate capitalism through a 'supply-side' economics revolution, reversing the Keynesian orthodoxy that state protections of society, labour and the environment were necessary. Instead, the mantra was 'privatize, liberalize and deregulate' the economy, bringing more and more public goods under the aegis of the market.[16]

Neoliberal globalization and its opponents

One of the most consequential neoliberal reforms that began in the 1970s was the removal of capital controls. This freed up capital to move globally, significantly reducing state sovereignty over macroeconomic policy.[17] Also beginning in the 1970s, technological advancements revolutionized global systems of production, finance, transportation and communications to create globally distributed supply and value chains. Multinational corporations and transnational financial markets have used technological advances to create a new form of global economy that is far more interdependent and complex than the golden age of pre-1914 capitalism.[18]

The dominance of neoliberalism led to demands from Western and international donors and creditors that economic aid and development assistance be conditioned on increasing private control of the market, liberalization of trade and finance, and decreasing state regulation. What became known as the Washington Consensus effectively globalized neoliberalism over the course of three decades. In Biersteker's words, neoliberalism led to the 'sudden and dramatic transformation of economic policy throughout the developing world between the 1970s and 1980s', a transformation that went truly global following the collapse of communist regimes in 1989–91.[19] Western states, along with the IMF and the World Bank, exhorted states to give way to private actors in governing the economy.[20] In trade, the creation of the World Trade Organization (WTO) included a new, supranational dispute settlement mechanism that allowed an independent board of experts to determine the outcome of disputes between member states. In addition, new multilateral agreements on intellectual property (the Agreement on Trade-Related Aspects of Intellectual Property Rights – TRIPs), services (the General Agreement on Trade in Services – GATS) and investment (the Agreement on Trade-Related Investment Measures – TRIMs) meant deeper intrusion on national economic sovereignty.

This wave of neoliberal globalization led to the deregulation of trade and financial markets, the increased porousness of national borders to economic actors, and changes in national-level institutions throughout the world. The shift to a neoliberal global economy in the second half of the 20th century compromised countries' 'interdependence sovereignty', or the ability of the state to regulate cross-border flows of goods, services, information, technology, people and environmental harm.[21] Indeed, the meteoric rise of global financial markets prompted scholars to warn that the state was in retreat, and that the power to set the rules of the game now lay in the boardrooms of transnational corporations.[22]

Neoliberalism therefore created a contest of authorities between states, their polities and economic actors, in which the state retreated in the face of economic pressure from multinational and private entities, shrinking its social welfare functions and loosening its control of national resources.[23] The extraordinary growth of the global financial markets began to pose ever greater threats to states' abilities to manage their economies. Market forces punished those states that were thought to disregard this template with capital flight and currency speculation.[24]

The 1997 Asian financial crisis that also engulfed Brazil and Russia led to widespread criticism of the Washington Consensus and demands for a new international financial order.[25] The biggest demonstration against neoliberal globalization the world had seen occurred in 1999 under the slogan 'The World Is Not for Sale', and successfully shut down the WTO's launch of a new round of trade negotiations. That protest became known as the Battle in Seattle, and activists' demanded that trade governance must promote social protection, justice and environmental sustainability, among many other things.

Many countries and their populations, including Brazil, the People's Republic of China and India, prospered enormously through their partial conformity to the neoliberal economic order.[26] When these newly powerful economies in the global south tried to flex their economic muscle in the WTO in 2001, however, their Development Agenda was blocked first by Western governments, and ultimately by disagreements between their own agricultural interests.

Anne L. Clunan

That same year, the first World Social Forum was convened in Porto Alegro, Brazil, as a counter-action to the Davos World Economic Forum, and a space for activists to model and develop alternative forms of global governance.

No new global trade or financial order appeared, however, even after the 2007–09 global financial crisis shattered the Washington Consensus. The West, meanwhile, began to pursue 'open' economic regionalism in the form of mega-regional trade agreements such as the Comprehensive and Progressive Agreement for Trans-Pacific Partnership (CPTPP) and the Trans-Atlantic Trade and Investment Partnership (TTIP). These negotiations represent efforts to create an economic order premised on deeper behind the border neoliberal integration, rather than to cooperate on an equal footing in the WTO with newly strong southern economies to alter existing neoliberal global trade and investment rules.

Resisting neoliberal globalization: three critiques

There is to date no single 'anti-globalization' movement. The label itself was in fact first used by *advocates* of neoliberal globalization in the mid-1990s. They applied it to anyone who opposed neoliberalism, the Washington Consensus, and/or the North American Free Trade Agreement (NAFTA).[27] Today, the term applies as much to Al Qaeda as to Greenpeace. Left-oriented opponents prefer to call themselves the alter-globalization or global social justice movement. Four different forms have evolved to resist and alter the neoliberal economic order.[28] The oldest method of mobilizing opposition to globalization is through national political parties and domestic class and interest group politics, with some diffusion of rhetoric and methods to similar organized groups across borders.[29] A second method is the transnational activist network that brings local non-governmental organizations (NGOs), usually in the global south, together with northern international non-governmental organizations (INGOs) to pressure governments and intergovernmental organizations (IGOs) on discrete issues.[30] A third form of mobilizing opposition to neoliberal globalization uses market forces to change consumption patterns in the global north. These include efforts such as boycotts and disinvestment campaigns, branding products as environmentally sound or made without child or forced labour, and the 'buy local' and 'slow food' campaigns to support local farmers, artisans and producers.[31] The fourth and final form is also the most recent, a network of networks and movements that creates a flexible and horizontal structure for people to oppose globalization and simultaneously enact its alternative in physical and virtual spaces, peacefully or violently.[32] This form is most closely associated with the left-oriented opponents of globalization, but is also the basis for global radical Islamist networks and, increasingly, far-right movements.[33] Given the diversity of actors and causes, what animates them to resist or destroy neoliberal globalization and the trading system? The remainder of this chapter lays out the central themes that galvanize globalization's opponents.

Three broad critiques animate opponents of neoliberal globalization, although they are only analytically distinct and often melded in practice. The first critique might be termed populist, in that it centres on popular representation and political self-determination. Opponents argue that the global neoliberal economic order is undemocratic and unaccountable. In this view, the global economy is run by technocrats in the service of self-serving elites who are unaccountable to citizens yet impose neoliberalism and its consequences on the rest of society.[34] The second critique centres on collective cultural autonomy and appears as something of an analogue to the first, claiming that globalization endangers national and local identities and lifestyles, not just livelihoods. The third, 'global justice' critique charges that neoliberal globalization is inequitable and destructive, as it places profit and efficiency ahead of the need for social justice, collective well-being, and environmental sustainability. Out of these critiques, activists on the left and the right have woven a set of narratives to mobilize action against those they believe to be the representatives and beneficiaries of neoliberalism locally, nationally and globally. Many of these narratives combine elements of all three critiques, giving a broadly populist cast to diverse actors who can be radically cosmopolitan or exclusionary and racist in their views and aims.

The demand for popular representation

The first critique of globalization deals with the proper site for authoritative decision-making to ensure popular representation. Opponents believe that international and supranational institutions, including the World Bank, the IMF, the WTO, the G8, the G20 and the EU, are undemocratic and non-transparent. These institutions suffer from a 'democratic deficit', in that they are unelected and unaccountable to the citizens whose lives and livelihoods they affect, and are often said to serve the interests of a transnational capitalist elite.[35] This view is shared by international economists, such as Nobel Prize laureate Joseph Stiglitz and Dani Rodrik, who have become prominent and important critics of neoliberal globalization.[36]

The remedies for the democratic deficit in global and European institutions, in the view of critics, range from returning trade and economic decision-making to the national or subnational level, reforming these institutions to make them more representative of and open to civil society, empowering civil society to directly decide global economic governance issues, to creating a world democratic government with globally representative legislative bodies.[37] Right-wing groups favour national, religious and/or ethnic forms of popular sovereignty over capitalism and the economy. Left-oriented NGOs and INGOs have worked for the systematic incorporation of social, economic and environmental protection in the economic decision-making and operations of IGOs and the EU. Radical leftist (left-libertarian) groups argue for direct democracy to replace what they view as corrupt national, international and supranational governance. Neo-mercantilists favour measures to ensure national security and technological independence.

The demand for cultural autonomy

The second core critique of neoliberal globalization is its effects on collective cultural autonomy, as it erodes and obliterates communities, cultures and ways of life through the market mechanism.[38] An onslaught of foreign brands, merchandise and media introduce new ideas, values, ethics and merchandise that compete with local counterparts. Multinational companies demand raw materials ranging from lithium to timber to diamonds, displacing local economies. Neoliberal globalization is thus seen to take control of livelihoods and to remove ways of life from of the hands of communities and make them subject to faceless market forces. Similar in some respects to the concern about neoliberalism's 'democratic deficit', this concern for maintaining national, religious and local identities free from the homogenizing and liberal aspects of global capitalism animates leftist groups such as the World Social Forum as well as right-wing groups such as Islamic State, although they clearly have widely different views on what properly constitutes the communities and ways of life that need protection and deserve autonomy.

The most familiar neoliberal culprit in this vein is corporate offshoring – the movement of jobs from developed to developing economies and the subsequent loss of local and municipal income that 'hollows out' communities and begets dynamics of urbanization, rural decline and poverty. This is not merely a protectionist economic critique about foreign competition, but one that very much links national and local economies with society and culture. It emphasizes that national and local communities, enterprises and identities are forged around their relationships to people, land and landscape.

Globalization, by changing local enterprise, pulls a thread that can unravel the cultural tapestry. In economic thought, when an industry declines, the cost of adjustment is simply that of retraining workers. For proponents of cultural autonomy, such thinking ignores the intimate connection between community, identity and culture that is destroyed alongside jobs. Right-wing movements from Al Qaeda and Islamic State to the US Tea Party to Alternative für Deutschland draw on this critique to promote what they argue to be the proper cultural identity and ways of life that are endangered by neoliberal capitalism. These movements combine the populist critique against the elitism of global capitalism with its destruction of conservative, religious and/or ethno-racial values and communities.

Sometimes the cultural destruction is argued to be literal and physical. Multinational companies have been sued for colluding with governments in Nigeria and Myanmar (formerly Burma) to destroy or repress local communities in pursuit of resource extraction and profits. In the Amazon and the far north, the global forces of neoliberal capitalism are said to produce deforestation of ancestral rain forests and expropriation of tribal lands for beef farming or oil and gas drilling, driving Amazonian and northern indigenous tribes off their lands and threatening the extinction of their traditions, languages and identity.

The cultural autonomy critique plays out in the developed world as well. Jose Bové, a French farmer, became a symbol of this concern when he destroyed a McDonald's fast-food restaurant. His protest against imports of genetically modified organisms (GMOs), including beef and dairy products, was not only an expression of concern about farmers' livelihoods but also about the cultural associations made by French people with their land, their agricultural methods and their cuisine. Concern within Europe over GMOs became so widespread that the EU banned imports containing them, only to have this ban overturned by the WTO. As a result, French farmers, regardless of political ideology, continue to protest against the consequences of trade liberalization on their livelihoods and culture by dumping milk, vegetables and manure over public spaces and in front of administrative offices associated with the government agencies that are not able to protect France from these supranational organizations.

The demand for global social justice

Finally, the third, more complex, critique is largely premised on the notion of 'global social justice'. It holds that equity, solidarity, social justice and environmental stewardship should dictate the workings of the economy rather than the other way around. Three sets of ideas motivate this critique, all of which echo Karl Polyani's early 20th-century insights about the ill effects of free-market globalization. First is the rejection of the notion that humans and nature are market commodities. Market liberalism's 'fictitious' commodification of human beings and the natural environment, what Polyani called the great transformation, is central to this critique of neoliberalism today. It exposes and rejects the 'commodity fiction' that acts as the central organizing principle of market capitalism, as it is essential for the supposed 'self-regulation' of markets. 'The idea of a self-adjusting market implied a stark utopia', in Polyani's view. 'Such an institution could not exist for any length of time without annihilating the human and natural substance of society; it would have physically destroyed man and transformed his surroundings into a wilderness.'[39] The outcome of such commodification, in Polyani's words, was a 'satanic mill', a term that resonates with contemporary opponents of global neoliberalism and corporate capitalism.[40]

The social justice critique is based, second, on the idea that a spontaneously occurring market is a myth. Neoliberal capitalism, in this view, is the deliberate product of states and IGOs who serve the interests of corporations and financers. It is only through state patronage and intervention that the supposedly laissez-faire fiction can reorganize society as a whole to make it subject to the market mechanism.[41] Today, this critique targets states, the WTO, the IMF, the World Bank and the EU as the handmaidens of corporate and financial forces who benefit from neoliberal globalization. It contends that neoliberals have created a global order in which 'the rights of capital are the most important foundation of economic and political power', and the 'superiority of the market allocation is ideologically dominant'.[42]

The third animating idea in the social justice critique is that neoliberal globalization harms the collective well-being of humankind and the planet in the pursuit of wealth.[43] In the language of economics, these harms are the market's negative externalities, or social costs, and its inability to provide collective goods, such as a clean environment, infrastructure and healthcare. Climate change is the paradigmatic case of market failure to mitigate and prevent negative effects of the globalization of industrial capitalism, one that puts the entire planet at risk. Neoliberalism, this critique argues, is 'congenitally blind' to the market's failings, principally the need for social protection, collective good provision and risk mitigation. These concerns, in the eyes of critics, are much more consequential and urgent today than they were in the pre-1914 era of globalization.[44] As Peter Evans puts it, 'inability to provide collective goods to Nigerian agriculturalists in 1900 unquestionably diminished well-being, but the misery and social dislocation generated by the inability to provide basic collective services to the 15 million citizens of Lagos have global implications of an entirely different order of magnitude. The evolution of the global economy and society has made the collective goods that markets fail to deliver more central to human well-being. The same process of socio-economic change has made more dangerous the kinds of "negative externalities" that only social regulation can prevent markets from generating. In short, the untrammeled reign of the self-regulated market has become significantly more threatening.'[45]

Conclusion: three critiques of 21st-century globalization in action

The Great Recession unleashed a global wave of popular anger at governments seen as corrupt or beholden to international economic institutions and corporate elites. *Time* magazine named 'The Protester' as person of the year for 2011. In April 2011 Mohamed Bouazizi, a poor Tunisian fruit vendor, burned himself alive to protest against the corrupt crony capitalism that enriched the few and that were depriving Arab youth of dignity and life chances.[46] His death triggered the 'Arab spring' across the Middle East and North Africa, with governments falling to or repressing sustained street protests demanding the dignity of economic opportunity and transparency in political and economic life. In Europe, mass protests took place across the continent against the European Central Bank and its policy of austerity. All three critiques of globalization have led to the concept of 'glocalization', that the global and local levels are intimately connected. According to James C. Scott, submerged networks of people resist neoliberal globalization in their everyday lives through their consumption choices and daily actions.[47]

In the wake of the Great Recession, right-wing populism took hold in Central Eastern Europe, with populists winning a parliamentary supermajority in Hungary in 2010 and an absolute majority in Poland in 2015. These governments soon began a concerted campaign to reorder their countries' political system in an authoritarian manner, a pattern that was playing out all over Latin America during the 2000s.[48] In mid-2011 the epicentre of neoliberal globalization, the USA, saw its credit rating downgraded for the first time ever. Later that year the Occupy Wall Street movement began in New York City and spread worldwide, voicing outrage over rising income and wealth inequalities generated over the preceding 30 years that had allowed the '1%' to capture the halls of government and enrich themselves while the '99%' struggled to hold onto their homes and their quality of life.

In 2016, what had seemed unthinkable happened, when Britons voted in June to leave the EU and Donald Trump campaigned as a Republican against free trade agreements, immigration and globalization, winning not only the party's nomination, but the US presidency. Breaking the long-standing free trade and pro-globalization stance of the Republican Party, Trump ran his electoral campaign on a national-populist platform that explicitly targeted globalization, saying in June 2016 that, 'Our politicians have aggressively followed a policy of globalization, moving our jobs and our factories to Mexico and overseas ... Globalization has made the financial elite who donate to politicians very, very wealthy ... but it has left millions of our workers with nothing but poverty and heartache'. Many credit the global financial crisis of 2007–09 and the Great Recession that followed as facilitating Trump's electoral victory.[49] Anger about the neoliberal policies of the EU meant that a far-right candidate nearly became president in Austria. Street protests against elite corruption ousted the South Korean president and gave a left-populist mayor a place among 'the Big 3' in the subsequent presidential run-off. A right-wing populist 'death squad mayor' became president of the Philippines and blamed globalization for hurting that country.[50] In France later that year, only the late emergence of an independent centrist campaign prevented France from having its first far-right president, Marie Le Pen of the National Front. In 2017 the establishment German political parties faced their new anti-EU and anti-immigrant far-right rival, Alternative für Deutschland, which gained an shocking 94 seats in parliament. Four days after taking office in January 2017, US President Donald Trump fulfilled one of his anti-globalization campaign promises, and withdrew the USA from negotiations on the TPP trade agreement. Several months later, he officially opened NAFTA for renegotiation. In 2018, the anti-EU populist Five-Star Party and the proto-fascist Liga party formed the new government of one of the EU's founding members, Italy.

At the time of writing, populist and autonomy movements appear far more of a danger to neoliberal globalization that the leftist 'global social justice' or 'alter-globalization' network. Yet the global social justice critique has altered neoliberal globalization and global governance in meaningful ways. None of them have fundamentally reformed neoliberal capitalism or ended the 'democratic deficit' of the IGOs, but they have modified the normative environment in which global corporations and states operate to one that includes societal and environmental impacts.

Under the banner 'a better world is possible', the network of movements for social justice, environmental conservation and human rights have altered the terms under which the World Bank and the IMF assess loans and projects, and they have critically shaped states' awareness and response to climate change, sustainable development and inequality.[51] They have prevented multinational pharmaceuticals from profiting from the TRIPS accord at the expense of HIV/AIDS victims in the developing world.[52] They have shamed corporations into adopting codes of corporate responsibility and prompted the United Nations to undertake first the Millennium Development Goals and now the Sustainable Development Goals. In trade, these critiques have helped to champion the development agenda that many developing countries and the sustainability goals environmentalists and human rights activists have long advocated.[53] They have also successfully stymied US participation in the Trans-Pacific Partnership, making what was once a non-issue so central to the US presidential election of 2016 that candidates of both parties swore to pull out of it.

The three critiques of neoliberal capitalism have galvanized resistance to globalization from across the political spectrum for half a century. That opposition has evolved over time, with significant changes in organizational methodologies arising from the radically reduced costs of communicating and traveling globally. Yet the core messages and methods have changed little except in their urgency.

Notes

1 Rob Augman (2012) 'G-8 Summit Protests in Germany: Against Globalization and its Non-emancipatory Responses', *libcom.org* 12 December, available at https://libcom.org/library/g8-summit-protests-germany-against-globalisatin-its-non-emancipatory-responses-rob-augm.

2 Mark Blyth (2013) *Austerity: The History of Dangerous Idea*, New York: Oxford University Press, ch. 3.

3 Ben Chu (2013) 'Donald Trump's First Gift to the World Will Be Another Financial Crisis', *The Independent*, 20 January, available at www.independent.co.uk/voices/donald-trump-inauguration-first-thing-to-do-gift-to-world-republican-financial-crisis-recession-a7536706.html.

4 Michael D. Bordo (2017) 'The Second Era of Globalization Is Not Yet Over: An Historical Perpsective', Dallas Federal Reserve Bank Globalization and Monetary Institute Working Paper No. 319, July, pp. 8–9.

5 Tyler Atkinson, David Luttrell and Harvey Rosenblum (2013) 'How Bad Was It? The Costs and Consequences of the 2007–2009 Financial Crisis', Dallas Federal Reserve *Staff Paper* No. 20, July.

6 Andy Haldane, David Aikman, Sujit Kapadia and Marc Hinterschweiger (2013) 'Rethinking Financial Stability', Paper prepared for delivery at the 'Rethinking Macroeconomic Policy IV' Conference, Peterson Institute for Economics, Washington, DC, 12 October, pp. 2–3, available at www.bankofengland.co.uk/-/media/boe/files/speech/2017/rethinking-financial-stability.pdf.

7 Karl Polyani (2012) The Great Transformation: The Political and Economic Origins of Our Time, Mattituck, NY: Amereon.

8 W. E. Connelley (ed.) (1928) *History of Kansas, State and People* 2, Washington, DC: American Historical Society, p. 1167.

9 Owen Worth (2013) *Resistance in the Age of Austerity: Nationalism, the Failure of the Left and the Return of God*, London: Zed Books.

10 Ruth Reitan (2012) 'Theorizing and Engaging the Global Movement: From Anti-Globalization to Global Democratization,' *Globalizations*, 9(3): 323–35, DOI: 10.1080/14747731.2012.682364.

11 Peter Evans (2008) 'Is an Alternative Globalization Possible', *Politics and Society*, 36(2), June: 271–305.

12 Karl Polyani ([1944] 1957) *The Great Transformation*, Boston, MA: Beacon Press, p. 141.

13 Ibid., p. 76.

14 John Gerard Ruggie (1982) 'International Regimes, Transactions, and Change: Embedded Liberalism in the Postwar Economic Order', *International Organization*, 36(2).

15 Thomas Biersteker (1992) 'The 'Triumph of Neoclassical Economics in the Developing World: Policy Convergence and Bases of Governance in the International Economic Order', in James Rosenau and Ernst-Otto Czempiel (eds) *Governance without Government: Order and Change in World Politics*, Cambridge: Cambridge University Press, p. 105.

16 Mark Blyth (2002) *Great Transformation: Economic Ideas and Institutional Change in the Twentieth Century*, Cambridge: Cambridge University Press.

17 Mark Blyth (2013) *Austerity*, New York: Oxford University Press.

18 Michael D. Bordo, Barry Eichengreen and Douglas A. Irwin (1999) 'Is Globalization Today Really Different than Globalization a Hundred Years Ago?', in Susan Collins and Robert Lawrence (eds) *Brookings Trade Policy Forum*, Washington, DC: Brookings Institution, pp. 1–72.

19 Ruggie, 'International Regimes', p. 413; Biersteker, 'Triumph', p. 105.

20 Blyth, *Great Transformations*.

21 Stephen D. Krasner (1999) *Sovereignty: Organized Hypocrisy*, Princeton, NJ: Princeton University Press, p. 4.

22 Susan Strange (1996) *Retreat of the State: The Diffusion of Power in the World Economy*, Cambridge: Cambridge University Press.

23 Blyth, *Great Transformations*; Ruggie, 'International Regimes'.

24 Blyth, *Austerity*, and Blyth, *Great Transformations*.

25 Kishore Mahbubani (2008) 'The Case against the West', *Foreign Affairs*, (May/June): 111–24.

26 Branko Milonvic (2016) *Global Inequality*, Cambridge, MA: Belknap Press.

27 Evans, 'Is an Alternative Globalization Possible'.

28 Michael Mousseau (2002/03) 'Market Civilization and Its Clash with Terror', *International Security*, 27 (3): 5–29.

29 Sidney Tarrow (2005) *The New Transnational Activism*, Cambridge: Cambridge University Press.

30 Margaret Keck and Kathryn Sikkink (1998) *Activists across Borders: Advocacy Networks in International Politics*, Ithaca, NY: Cornell University Press; Robert O'Brien, Anne Marie Goetz, Jan Aart Scholte and Marc Williams (2000) *Contesting Global Governance*, Cambridge: Cambridge University Press; James H. Mittleman (2000) *Globalization Syndrome*, Princeton, NJ: Princeton University Press.

31 Audie Klotz (1995) 'Norms Reconstituting Interests: Global Racial Equality and US Sanctions against South Africa', *International Organization*, 49(3): 451–78; Benjamin Cashore (2002) 'Legitimacy and the Privatization of Environmental Governance: How Non-State Market-Driven (NSMD) Systems Gain Rule–Making Authority', *Governance*, 15(4) October: 503–29; Kelly Kollman and Aseem Prakash (2001) 'Green by Choice?: Cross-National Variations in Firms' Responses to EMS-Based Environmental Regimes', *World Politics*, 53(3) April: 399–430; Nicola Phillips and Fabiola Mieres (2014) 'The Governance of Forced Labour in the Global Economy', *Globalizations*, pp. 1–17, DOI: 10.1080/14747731.2014.932507.

32 Ronald Deibert (2000) 'International Plug 'n Play? Citizen Activism, the Internet, and Global Public Policy', *International Studies Perspectives*, 1(3) December: 255–72; Jeffrey S. Juris (2005) 'The New Digital Media and Activist Networking within Anti–Corporate Globalization Movements', *The ANNALS of the American Academy of Political and Social Science*, 597(1): 189–208.

33 Donatella della Porta (2006) *Globalization from Below: Transnational Activists and Protest Networks*, Minneapolis, MN: University of Minnesota Press; Juris, 'New Digital Media'.

34 Louis Pauly (1997) *Who Elected the Bankers?* Ithaca, NY: Cornell University Press; Ngaire Woods (2006) *The Globalizers: The IMF, the World Bank, and their Borrowers*, Ithaca, NY: Cornell University Press.

35 Dani Rodrik (2011) *The Globalization Paradox: Why Global Markets, States, and Democracy Can't Coexist*, Oxford: Oxford University Press; Michael Greven and Louis Pauly (2000) *Democracy beyond the State? The European Dilemma and the Emerging Global Order*, Lanham, MD: Rowman and Littlefield.

36 Joseph Stiglitz (2002) *Globalization and its Discontents*, New York: W.W. Norton; Joseph Stiglitz (2012) *The Price of Inequality*, New York: W.W. Norton; Dani Rodrik (2007) *One Economics, Many Recipes*, Princeton, NJ: Princeton University Press; Rodrik, *Globalization Paradox*.

37 David Held (1995) *Democracy and the Global Order*, Stanford, CA: Stanford University Press; Ann Florini (ed.) (2000) *The Third Force: The Rise of Transnational Civil Society*, Washington, DC: Carnegie Endowment for International Peace; Juris, 'New Digital Media'; Rodrik, *Globalization Paradox*.

38 Yale H. Ferguson and Richard W. Mansbach (1999) 'Global Politics at the Turn of the Millennium: Changing Bases of "Us" and "Them"', *International Studies Review*, 1(2) Summer: 77–107.

39 Polyani, p. 3.

40 Ibid., p. 73.

41 Ibid., p. 72–73.

42 Ibid., p. 72.

43 Amatrya Sen (1999) *Development as Freedom*, New York: Alfred Knopf.

44 Evans, p. 276.

45 Ibid., p. 278.

46 Raymond Hinnebusch (2015) 'Globalization, Democratization, and the Arab Uprising: The International Factor in MENA's Failed Democratization', *Democratization*, 22(2): 335–57.

47 James H. Mittelman (2000) *The Globalization Syndrome*, Princeton, NJ: Princeton University Press, pp. 170–72; James C. Scott (1990) *Domination and the Arts of Resistance*, New Haven, CT: Yale University Press.

48 Anna Gryzmala-Busse (2017) 'Populism and the Erosion of Democracy in Poland and Hungary', Memo presented at Global Populisms as a Threat to Democracy Conference, Stanford University, Stanford, CA, November 3–4, available at http://fsi.stanford.edu/sites/default/files/grzymala-busse_memo_1_0.pdf; Steven Levitsky (2017) 'Populism and Competitive Authoritarianism', Memo presented at Global Populisms as a Threat to Democracy Conference, Stanford University, Stanford, CA, November 3–4; Dani Rodrik (2017) *Populism and the Economics of Globalization*, No. w23559, Washington, DC: National Bureau of Economic Research.

49 Mark Whitehouse (2016) 'Trump's Debt to the Financial Crisis', *Bloomberg View*, 21 November, available at www.bloomberg.com/view/articles/2016-11-21/why-trump-should-love-financial-crises.

50 Adam Taylor (2016) 'The Global Wave of Populism that Turned 2016 Upside Down', *Washington Post*, 19 December, www.washingtonpost.com/news/worldviews/wp/2016/12/19/the-global-wave-of-populism-that-turned-2016-upside-down/?utm_term=.c89047e3d07b; 'Duterte on Inclusive Growth, Globalization', *Manila Bulletin*, 16 November 2017, available at https://news.mb.com.ph/2017/11/16/duterte-on-inclusive-growth-globalization/.

51 O'Brien *et al., Contesting Global Governance*; Keck and Sikkink, *Activists across Borders*.

52 Susan K. Sell and Aseem Prakash (2004) 'Using Ideas Strategically: The Contest between Business and NGO Networks in Intellectual Property Rights', *International Studies Quarterly*, 48(1) March: 143–75.

53 Sanjeev Khagram (2004) *Dams and Development: Transnational Struggles for Water and Power*, Ithaca, NY: Cornell University Press.

Part II
Regional/Country Analysis

146

14

NAFTA

Robert A. Blecker

Introduction

The North American Free Trade Agreement (NAFTA) created one of the world's two largest regional trading blocs, along with the European Union (EU), when it came into effect in 1994.[1] By combining a leading emerging market nation (Mexico) with two major industrialized nations (Canada and the USA), NAFTA constituted a pioneering effort at north-south integration on a regional scale. For Mexico, NAFTA represented a continuation and extension of the country's market opening and liberalization policies, which were instituted in the late 1980s in the aftermath of the debt crisis earlier in that decade. For Canada, NAFTA built upon the previous bilateral Canada-US free trade agreement (CUSFTA) of 1989. For the USA, NAFTA was part of a strategy to open up foreign economies to US exports and investment, and to condition preferential access to the US market on other countries' adoption of rules and procedures favourable to US investors and corporations. After more than two decades of bipartisan support for NAFTA by US presidents, however, Donald Trump (2017–present) has taken a distinctly hostile position, calling it one of 'the worst trade deals ever' and threatening to withdraw the USA from it unless it is renegotiated to his satisfaction.[2]

In fact, NAFTA has been the subject of much controversy along multiple dimensions ever since it was proposed. In the USA, the agreement sparked fears of job losses in manufacturing due to increased imports from Mexico, where wages were (and remain) much lower than US wages.[3] For Mexico, critics worried that the government's abandonment of developmental state policies would undermine the country's long-term growth, while even some supporters expressed concern about the potential impact of agricultural liberalization on employment and migration.[4] In Canada, NAFTA generated less controversy than the earlier CUSFTA, but was still feared to accelerate the country's deindustrialization, undermine its social welfare state and increase inequality.[5]

Even NAFTA's supporters were divided in their motives and visions for the agreement. On the one hand, enthusiasts of industrial policy saw NAFTA as potentially creating a competitive trading bloc, which, by combining US capital and technology with Mexican labour and Canadian resources, would strengthen the North American economies relative to their European and East Asian rivals.[6] On the other hand, free traders emphasized the trade-creating as opposed to the trade-diverting effects of NAFTA, and hoped that it would accelerate the process of multilateral

147

trade liberalization and serve as a role model for future trade agreements.[7] On all sides, there was deep ambiguity about whether NAFTA represented an initial step towards deeper regional integration in North America, perhaps using the European Union (EU) as a model,[8] or if it was simply a one-off trade agreement that would remain limited in scope and create only a 'shallow' form of integration.

Origins, negotiation, debate and enactment

In some respects, NAFTA deepened and codified a process of trade liberalization and regional integration that was already occurring in North America. US-Canadian integration efforts dated back to the Auto Pact (officially known as the Automotive Products Agreement) of 1965, which lowered or removed tariffs on bilateral trade in cars and auto parts, and culminated in the formation of CUSFTA in 1989.[9] Mexico created the *maquiladora* programme, under which imports of inputs for assembly were exempted from tariffs if they were used to produce finished or semi-finished goods for export, in 1965. These export-processing activities expanded rapidly between the late 1970s and early 1990s as Mexico sought to diversify its exports away from oil and other primary products. Mexico joined the General Agreement on Tariffs and Trade (GATT), the predecessor to the World Trade Organization (WTO), in 1986, which required the country to drastically lower its formerly high tariffs and to abandon other protectionist measures (such as import-licensing requirements).[10] The USA had previously focused mainly on multilateral trade liberalization through the GATT, but had signed an FTA with Israel in 1985 as well as CUSFTA with Canada in 1989. Before NAFTA, US tariff policies encouraged the development of the *maquiladora* industries by allowing a deduction for the value of US-produced inputs from the value of imports from Mexico subject to US duties – and some Mexican exports also qualified for lower US tariffs under the General System of Preferences (GSP) for developing countries.

The primary impetus to move beyond these earlier measures and form NAFTA came about as a result of the disappointing outcome of Mexico's unilateral liberalization efforts in the late 1980s. Despite joining GATT, lowering its trade barriers and liberalizing foreign direct investment (FDI), Mexico achieved only modest increases in exports and FDI inflows and faced rising trade deficits during the period 1987–93 (due in part to monetary policies that led to overvaluation of the peso and the peso crisis of 1994–95). As Europe was focused on its own internal integration process via the EU, European leaders rebuffed the Mexican government's overtures for enhanced trade and investment ties. In response, Mexican President Carlos Salinas de Gortari announced the idea of negotiating a Mexico-US free trade agreement (FTA) in 1990 and the Administration of President George H. W. Bush rapidly agreed.[11] According to Nora Lustig, the Salinas administration thought that it was necessary to 'increase the expected rate of return on investment and boost private sector confidence' in order 'to entice the capital inflows required for economic recovery and sustained growth', and that the best way to achieve this was to 'ensure future access to the US market, and ensure the durability of Mexico's open economy strategy' through an FTA.[12] In short, NAFTA was seen as a means of 'locking in' the country's neoliberal reforms and a key lever for attracting inflows of foreign investment.

Given that Canada had already entered CUSFTA and did not want to see its preferences in the US market undermined, the government of Prime Minister Brian Mulroney decided that it wanted to be part of any negotiations for a Mexico-US agreement, and hence the idea of a trinational NAFTA was born early in 1991. On the US side, the NAFTA negotiations enabled the Bush Administration to further its agenda of making Mexico more open to foreign trade and investment.[13] The USA also saw the NAFTA initiative as a means of pressuring countries outside North America to reach an agreement in the GATT Uruguay Round negotiations. Furthermore, US trade officials realized that they could achieve certain objectives – particularly in regard to intellectual property rights (IPRs), property rights of foreign investors, investor-state dispute resolution and liberalization of services (especially financial services) – more easily in the trinational forum of NAFTA, where the USA had more leverage, than in the multilateral setting of GATT/WTO, where US influence was more diluted. Negotiations for NAFTA began in June 1991 and concluded with the signing of the negotiated agreement by Bush, Mulroney and Salinas in December 1992.[14] However, the agreement still needed to be ratified, and in the USA this responsibility fell to the newly elected administration of President Bill Clinton, who took office in January 1993.

In the ensuing debate, some supporters and opponents of the agreement made claims that, in retrospect, were clearly exaggerated.[15] In Mexico, Salinas made a trio of promises that NAFTA would enable Mexico to develop via 'trade not aid', promote the 'export of goods not people', and raise the country's living standards to 'first-world' levels. The Clinton Administration claimed that NAFTA would relieve immigration pressures and create a vast market for US exports by enriching the Mexican economy. In the USA, the debate over NAFTA polarized the country, as labour and environmental activists were largely opposed while business and financial interests were generally supportive. US critics predicted not only that NAFTA would lead to large losses of manufacturing jobs, but also that it would unleash a 'race to the bottom' in which industries would move (or threaten to move) to Mexico in pursuit of weaker (or less enforced) environmental regulations and lower labour standards. Nationalists worried that NAFTA's dispute resolution mechanisms would undermine US sovereignty.

The ratification of NAFTA was never in doubt in Canada or Mexico, as Mulroney enjoyed a conservative majority in the parliament of the former while Salinas presided over what was still a one-party system in the latter. In the USA, however, both major political parties were split over NAFTA. On the whole, Republicans were more in favour while Democrats were more sceptical or opposed. Clinton brought Canada and Mexico back to the negotiating table in 1993 to reach 'side agreements' on labour and environmental issues in an effort to win more Democratic votes in Congress. Although NAFTA opponents argued that the side agreements lacked any effective enforcement provisions, these agreements nevertheless gave some Democrats cover to support the overall package. An extension of Trade Adjustment Assistance (TAA) for cases of NAFTA-related job losses and a North American Development Bank (NADB, which had an extremely limited scope and budget) were included to entice more support. Massive lobbying by US corporations and the Mexican government, in conjunction with the Clinton Administration's efforts, were just sufficient to win passage of NAFTA in the US Congress in November 1993.

Content of the agreement

Despite its label as a 'free trade agreement', NAFTA contains many exceptions to free trade and also covers many areas beyond trade policy narrowly defined. On the trade side, NAFTA did lower tariffs and other trade barriers for most goods, to zero in most cases, but with extended phase-in periods that varied by product and country and numerous exceptions or exclusions. In return for preferential access to the Canadian and US markets, Mexico ceased to qualify for GSP and other pre-existing tariff preferences, which became moot when US tariffs on most imports from Mexico were eliminated anyway. For bilateral US-Canadian trade, NAFTA superseded CUSFTA and the latter ceased to exist after 1 January 1994.

NAFTA granted especially strong rules of origin in certain key sectors. For most textile and apparel products, NAFTA imposed the 'triple transformation test', which can be summarized as requiring 'that finished products be cut and sewn from fabric spun from North American fibers in order to qualify for NAFTA preferences'.[16] This provision stimulated a brief boom in Mexican exports of textile and apparel products in the mid- to late 1990s, building upon the earlier expansion of such exports under the *maquiladora* programme. However, the triple transformation test eventually became largely a moot issue, as the entire textile and apparel complex in North America shrank drastically after the People's Republic of China joined the WTO in 2001 and the global quota scheme known as the Multi-Fibre Arrangement (MFA) was abolished in 2005 (as mandated in the Uruguay Round GATT agreement that established the WTO, which took effect in 1995).[17]

In contrast, NAFTA's rules of origin have had a more lasting impact in sustaining the North American automotive industry. NAFTA mandated that (after phase-in periods) finished automobiles and certain types of parts (e.g. engines, transmissions) would have to contain 62.5 per cent North American content, while other auto parts would need 60 per cent content, in order to qualify for NAFTA tariff preferences.[18] Moreover, North American content would be measured by tracing back the national origin of the value added in all parts and components. Combined with provisions to phase out Mexico's domestic content rules and the elimination of all intra-NAFTA automotive tariffs, these rules of origin helped to foster what is perhaps the most successfully integrated, most competitive and best rationalized industry in North America.[19] NAFTA and its rules of origin helped not only to preserve the US auto companies, but also to attract foreign investment by European, Japanese and later Korean auto companies in North America. By the second decade of the 21st century, production of auto parts (especially those embodying less advanced technology) and smaller cars had largely become concentrated in Mexico, while most production of luxury cars and larger vehicles (including SUVs, minivans and light trucks) took place in the USA or Canada.

As a result, transportation equipment (which in Mexico consists mainly of automotive products) is the only branch of Mexican manufacturing that has experienced a significant increase in employment in the past decade. As shown in Figure 14.1, employment in Mexican transportation equipment rose by 290,700 or 55.5 per cent from 2007–16, while employment in all other manufacturing sectors together fell by 6,700 (with small increases in some sectors, large losses in textiles, apparel and leather goods, and smaller losses in computers and electronic equipment). In the USA and Canada, although automotive employment fell sharply during those years, some jobs were preserved through the rationalization of the industry and the continued production of larger vehicles.

For agriculture, NAFTA contained three separate bilateral agreements. For US-Canadian agricultural trade, NAFTA largely extended the previously adopted provisions of CUSFTA (with some alterations to the rules of origin). For Mexican-Canadian agricultural trade, a new agreement was adopted that reduced many tariffs but also allowed quotas to stay in place for various sensitive products. The US-Mexican agreement on agriculture was very complicated and left some issues unresolved (or subject to secretive letters of understanding, which were not part of the official text of NAFTA and were often disputed in later years). Mexico agreed to phase out most of its restrictions (tariffs and quotas) on agricultural products, but with transition periods that lasted from five to 15 years and sometimes involved the temporary adoption of tariff-rate quotas (TRQs) that could later be phased out. Some US agricultural products continued to receive protection from Mexican exports for up to ten years, and US agricultural interests won the right for special safeguard tariffs in cases of sudden 'surges' of agricultural imports from Mexico. Overall, NAFTA encouraged the USA and Canada to specialize in grains, soybeans and other field crops, and Mexico to specialize in fruits, vegetables and other horticultural products (especially on a seasonal basis). However, many Mexican–US trade disputes since

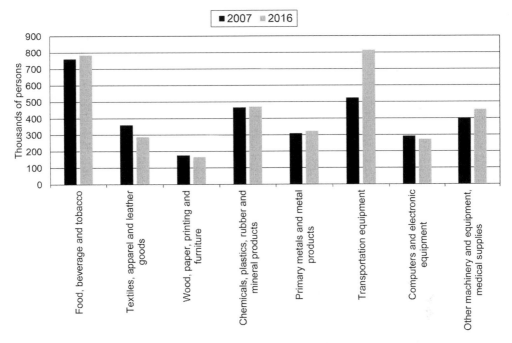

Figure 14.1 Total employment in Mexican manufacturing by industry, 2007 and 2016
Source: Author's calculations based on data from Instituto Nacional de Estadística y Geografía (INEGI), Encuesta mensual de industria manufacturera (EMIM), available at hwww.inegi.org.mx/ (accessed 22 June 2017). Monthly data for 'total de personal ocupado' were averaged for each year; data for August–December 2016 are preliminary. Industries are defined by the following three-digit NAICS (North American Industrial Classification System) codes: Food, beverage, and tobacco, 311–312; Textiles, apparel, and leather goods, 313-314-315-316; Wood, paper, printing, and furniture, 321-322-323, 337; Chemicals, plastics, rubber, and mineral products, 324-325-326-327; Primary metals and metal products, 331–332; Transportation equipment, 336; Computers and electronic equipment, 334; Other machinery and equipment including medical supplies, 333, 335, 339.

NAFTA have focused on agricultural goods, such as tomatoes and sugar. Across the northern border, the USA has had running trade disputes with Canada over various agricultural goods, especially dairy products which it accuses Canada of protecting or subsidizing.

Some sectors received more blanket exclusions from the trade and investment liberalizing provisions of NAFTA. The Mexican energy sector, which had been state-managed since the nationalization of the oil industry in 1938, remained largely untouched in NAFTA. Foreign investment was not allowed in oil exploration and drilling, and foreign companies were not permitted to participate in the domestic refining, distribution or marketing of petroleum products in Mexico. However, there was a limited opening to foreign contracting for procurement in the oil sector, as well as a more extensive opening of cross-border trade in natural gas and foreign investment in coal mining. Much later, Mexico opened up its oil sector to foreign participation in oil drilling and gasoline retailing in the energy sector reforms of 2014, but the state-owed oil company (Petróleos Mexicanos, or Pemex) has never been privatized.[20] NAFTA did not allow US consumers to purchase cheaper prescription medications from Canadian suppliers, and it did allow Canada to continue to support its cultural industries (news media and entertainment).

Aside from its trade provisions, NAFTA broke new ground in its provisions for foreign investment, intellectual property and government procurement.[21] NAFTA required Canada and Mexico to follow US practice in adopting stronger IPRs, especially longer (20-year) patent protection. NAFTA guaranteed national treatment and most-favoured-nation (MFN) status for foreign investment (as well as for foreign goods, for which these were already guaranteed by GATT). NAFTA prohibited governments from imposing performance requirements on foreign firms or limiting foreign ownership (again, with some exceptions such as Mexican oil and Canadian media). NAFTA also included an 'expropriation' clause, which was ostensibly intended to prohibit nationalizations of private, foreign-owned enterprises, but was later interpreted broadly to apply to any government regulations or policies that could be seen as reducing the potential profits of a foreign firm. In this last respect, NAFTA went far beyond the property rights that are recognized in the domestic laws of any of the member countries. In regard to public sector procurement, NAFTA required federal governments to open up many types of contracts to bids by foreign companies (with a ten-year phase-in for Mexico), but with numerous exceptions (including defence and security); such requirements were not established for subnational units, and federal governments could still favour national suppliers under various circumstances.

Last but not least, NAFTA created two types of dispute settlement mechanisms. First, Chapter 11 allowed for investor-state dispute settlement (ISDS), in which foreign firms can sue governments (national, state, provincial or local) for alleged infringements of their property rights under NAFTA, broadly defined to include losses of potential profits that were never actually received. This has allowed many companies to file claims that could not be sustained in the national courts of any of the member countries, because national laws do not recognize all of the 'property rights' established in NAFTA. Occasionally, complainants have won cases and government units have been forced to pay large settlements; more often, even if the complainants eventually lose, they impose steep legal costs on the defending government units and can intimidate the latter from adopting various kinds of regulations and policies. Similar types of ISDS provisions have been incorporated in later US FTAs and were included (with some modifications) in the Trans-Pacific Partnership (TPP) agreement, which the USA (under Trump) has now abandoned.

Second, NAFTA's Chapter 19 created a dispute settlement mechanism for trade issues between the member countries. These could involve alleged NAFTA violations, such as when Mexico claimed that the USA was failing to honour its commitment to allow Mexican trucks to operate in the USA. NAFTA trade dispute settlement could also be invoked in response to the use of other trade policies, such as safeguard tariffs, anti-dumping duties and countervailing duties: for example, when Canada appealed the US imposition of countervailing duties on imports of Canadian softwood lumber that the USA claimed were illegally subsidized. Many of these trade disputes have dragged on for years, and governments have sometimes failed to implement (or have delayed implementing) decisions reached by NAFTA panels. Critics have complained that the 'experts' who are appointed to the ISDS and other dispute settlement panels by the three countries are unelected and unaccountable to any democratic authority, that they are usually corporate lawyers or former trade officials who are predisposed to favour business interests, and that their decisions cannot be appealed against in national courts.[22]

NAFTA is just as notable for what it did not include as for what it did. NAFTA did not establish a customs union, so it did not create common external tariffs. The member countries could (and did subsequently) separately negotiate other FTAs with other nations. NAFTA did not eliminate the use of safeguards, anti-dumping duties and countervailing duties between the member countries, and even created some special safeguards (such as for US agricultural products), but it did allow the Chapter 19 dispute settlement panels to hear complaints against such measures. NAFTA did not attempt to address the contentious issue of labour migration, except in a very limited way by creating special visas for highly educated professional workers from the member countries. Unlike the EU, NAFTA did not consider that free movement of goods should be accompanied by free movement of people. Also unlike the EU, NAFTA contained no provisions for development assistance to the poorer regions of the less developed members; this was based on the ideology that Mexico only required 'trade not aid'. The only exception was that the NAFTA implementing legislation created the small and underfunded NADB, which was mainly limited to financing small infrastructure projects in border areas.

NAFTA did nothing to harmonize social, labour or environmental regulations; the labour and environmental side agreements set up commissions that could study the issues and exhort each country to enforce its own laws, but did not create dispute settlement panels with enforcement powers of the type created for trade and investment disputes. The major exception in regard to harmonization was in agricultural trade, in which Mexico was required to meet Canadian and US levels of phytosanitary standards for exported produce. NAFTA contained no provisions to deal with the adjustment costs of regional integration; any such efforts were left up to the member countries. In the USA, the implementing legislation for NAFTA included an extension of TAA, known as NAFTA-TAA, which provided for supplemental unemployment benefits, conditional upon enrolment in retraining programmes, for workers whose jobs were displaced by imports from (or a shift in production to) Canada or Mexico.[23] NAFTA includes a vague and untested accession clause, and contains no process for amendment or updating.

Economic impact of NAFTA

Trade and investment effects

The first and foremost thing that one would expect a trade agreement to do is to promote trade among the member countries. Based on the raw data, NAFTA appears to be a stunning success in this regard. Between 1993 and 2016 the value of Mexico's exports to Canada and the USA combined increased seven-fold from US $45 billion to $313 billion, while US exports to Canada and Mexico increased by a factor of almost 3.5 (from $141 billion to $497 billion) and Canadian exports to Mexico and the USA increased by a factor of almost 2.5 (from $115 billion to $303 billion) during the same period.[24] Even if we discount for the well-known measurement problems with these bilateral trade data,[25] there is no question that intra-North American trade has mushroomed since the passage of NAFTA.

However, estimates of the causal effects of NAFTA's tariff reductions on the trade of the member nations suggest a more modest impact. According to one recent study, NAFTA's tariff reductions increased US-Mexican trade by 23.2 per cent and Canadian-Mexican trade by 27.5 per cent.[26] This same study finds that NAFTA's tariff reductions actually reduced US-Canadian trade by 0.3 per cent, after the tariff reductions in CUSFTA had previously increased it by 4.1 per cent, and that NAFTA reduced Mexico's trade with non-member countries by 9.5 per cent. A newer study, which places more emphasis on trade in intermediate goods and inter-sectoral linkages, finds that NAFTA tariff reductions boosted intra-North American trade by 118 per cent for Mexico, 11 per cent for Canada and 41 per cent for the USA (this study did not address CUSFTA).[27]

Furthermore, if we examine the NAFTA trade statistics in the broader context of the expansion of the member countries' global trade since the 1990s, the record of encouraging intraregional trade looks distinctly less impressive. Figure 14.2 shows each member country's exports to its two NAFTA partners as a percentage of its total global exports. For all three countries these percentages trended slightly upwards in the late 1990s, but then declined

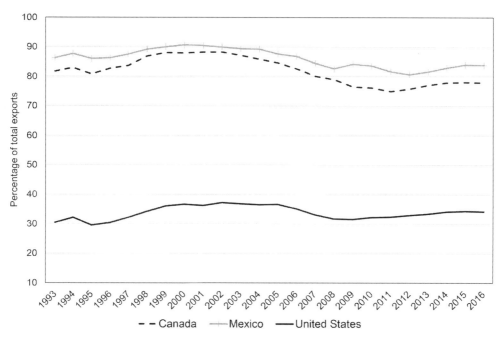

Figure 14.2 Exports of goods to the other NAFTA members as a percentage of each country's total exports of goods, 1993–2016
Source: Author's calculations based on data from the IMF, *Direction of Trade Statistics*, available at www.imf.org/en/Data (accessed 29 May 2017).

gradually after about 2000. Only in the US case is the percentage of exports going to NAFTA partners higher in 2016 than in 1993 (34 per cent compared with 30 per cent); for both Canada and Mexico, the percentages are slightly lower in 2016 than in 1993 (78 per cent compared with 82 per cent, and 84 per cent compared with 86 per cent, respectively). Turning to imports, the long-term trends are even more dramatic. As shown in Figure 14.3, the percentage of Mexico's imports coming from Canada and the USA plummeted from a peak of 78 per cent of its total imports in 1996 to only 49 per cent in 2016. Canada's intra-NAFTA imports peaked at 71 per cent of total Canadian imports in 1998 and declined to 58 per cent in 2016, while US intra-NAFTA imports decreased more modestly from a peak of 30 per cent of total US imports in 2001 to 26 per cent in 2016. Thus, after a brief period of more intensive intraregional trade in North America in the late 1990s, the entire region experienced a de-regionalization of its trade in the first two decades of the 21st century.

What can account for this de-regionalization of North American trade, which began less than a decade after NAFTA was created? One factor is that the tariff preferences granted in NAFTA soon became less significant than they originally appeared, not only because of the reductions in MFN tariffs under the WTO starting in 1995, but also because of the many other preferential trade agreements that the member countries entered into after joining NAFTA.[28] A second factor was changes in exchange rates: each of the NAFTA currencies went through a period of being overvalued at some point during the late 1990s and/or early 2000s, resulting in a loss of competitiveness relative to non-NAFTA countries.[29] A third factor was the entry of China into the WTO in 2001, which gave China access to all North American markets at MFN tariff rates at a time when the Chinese currency was undervalued.[30] A fourth factor was a structural

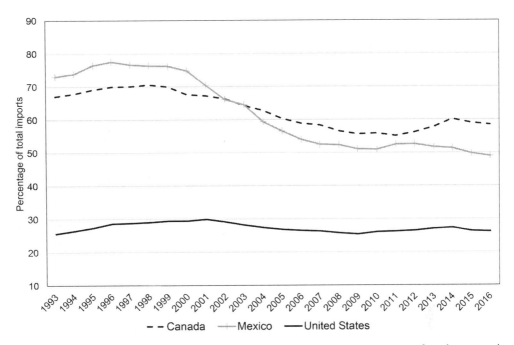

Figure 14.3 Imports of goods from other NAFTA members as a percentage of each country's total imports of goods, 1993–2016
Source: Author's calculations based on data from the IMF, *Direction of Trade Statistics*, available at www.imf.org/en/Data (accessed 29 May 2017).

transformation in the sourcing pattern of Mexican export industries, which went from primarily processing US inputs into exports in the 1980s and 1990s to primarily processing inputs imported from non-NAFTA countries (chiefly in Asia) after 2000.

In fact, the three NAFTA countries together have accounted for a declining share of total world trade since the agreement came into effect. Including their intraregional trade, total NAFTA exports (Canada + Mexico + USA) decreased from 17.7 per cent of total world exports in 1993 to 14.0 per cent in 2016; excluding intraregional trade, total exports of the three NAFTA countries to non-member countries fell from 9.6 per cent of total world exports in 1993 to 7.0 per cent in 2016. Furthermore, the three NAFTA countries have all exhibited increasing trade deficits with their non-NAFTA trading partners during this same period. As Figure 14.4 shows, the total trade deficit of all three NAFTA countries with non-member countries reached US $900 billion in 2016, including $660 billion for the USA, $149 billion for Mexico and $91 billion for Canada. Despite the frequent focus on the bilateral US trade deficit with Mexico, in recent years Mexico has had trade deficits with all other countries (principally in Asia, secondarily in Europe) that are larger than its surplus with the USA, resulting in an overall deficit for Mexico. Of course, global market shares and trade deficits are at best crude measures of competitiveness, but NAFTA clearly did not transform North America into a region that would account for a larger share of world trade or one that would achieve surpluses with other regions.

One way in which NAFTA does appear to have lived up to its promises is in regard to FDI inflows into Mexico. As shown in Figure 14.5, Mexican FDI inflows (from all countries and in all sectors), after averaging only 1.2 per cent of Mexico's GDP in the pre-NAFTA years shown (1980–93), have fluctuated around a notably higher mean of 2.7 per cent of GDP since

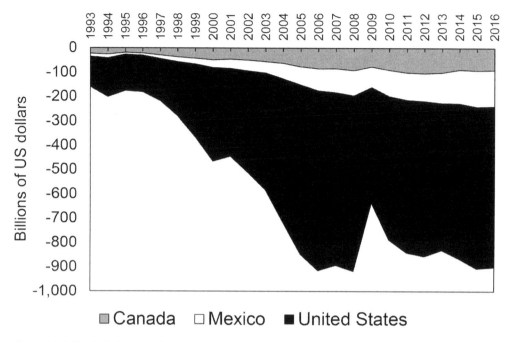

Figure 14.4 Trade balances of NAFTA members with non-NAFTA countries, 1993–2016
Source: Author's calculations based on data from the IMF, *Direction of Trade Statistics*, available at www.imf.org/en/Data (accessed 29 May 2017).

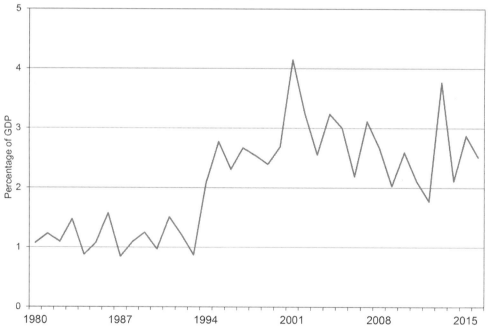

Figure 14.5 Mexican foreign direct investment inflows as a percentage of GDP, 1980–2016
Source: World Bank, *World Development Indicators* (WDI), available at http://data.worldbank.org/data-catalog/world-development-indicators (accessed 16 June 2017). (The figure for 2016 is the author's estimate based on INEGI data for FDI and IMF/WEO data for Mexican GDP in US dollars, accessed 7 April 2017).

NAFTA (1994–2016). Given the timing of how this percentage jumped in the mid-1990s and has remained at a higher level ever since, it seems likely that the increased average level can be attributed to the effect of NAFTA – not only the trade liberalization aspects, but also the protections for property rights of foreign investors and the 'lock-in' of Mexico's neoliberal policy regime. For Canada, however, there was a net outflow of FDI during most of the period from the formation of CUSFTA in 1989 through the early years of NAFTA.[31]

Employment effects

Given the emphasis on employment effects in US debates about NAFTA, it should come as no surprise that various analysts have attempted to estimate the net impact of North American trade on US jobs. For example, Robert E. Scott estimated that increased US trade deficits with Mexico and Canada caused a loss of 879,000 US jobs over the nine-year period 1994–2002, or 98,000 per year (mostly, but not entirely, in manufacturing).[32] In response, Gary C. Hufbauer and Jeffrey J. Schott claimed that increased US exports to Canada and Mexico had expanded US manufacturing employment by more than the number of job losses certified under the NAFTA-TAA programme for that period, implying a net gain of 42,000 jobs per year (or about 378,000 total).[33] However, none of these estimates is based on a methodology that could credibly identify the causal effects of NAFTA compared with other factors that may have increased intraregional trade flows, and Hufbauer and Schott conceded that 'Eligibility for NAFTA-TAA did not depend on a demonstrated link to NAFTA trade concessions'.[34]

Although the numbers of jobs 'created' or 'destroyed' in these estimates may sound large when cited in public debates, they appear minuscule in the context of the entire US economy, in which total non-farm payroll employment averaged about 114 million in 1994 and 131 million in 2002,[35] and where the monthly variations in employment are often larger than these average annual net changes. Nevertheless, Scott's estimated loss of 686,700 manufacturing jobs due to increased US trade deficits with Canada and Mexico between 1993 and 2002 corresponds to 4 per cent of the 17 million manufacturing jobs in the USA at the outset of NAFTA in 1994.[36] Even so, this is only true in an accounting sense; it does not prove that the jobs would not have been 'lost' to some other country if not to Mexico or Canada, and it does not prove that the job losses were caused by NAFTA as opposed to other factors.

On the Mexican side, manufacturing employment increased after NAFTA, but not by enough to address most of the country's long-term employment needs, and not all of the increase can be attributed to the trade agreement. Total payroll employment in Mexican manufacturing rose from 2.9 million in 1993 to 3.8 million in 1998 (at a time when the peso had depreciated), and then dipped to 3.4 million in 2013 (the year of the most recent quinquennial economic census), before rising slightly to 3.6 million in 2016.[37] Thus, Mexican manufacturing employment exhibited a net increase of roughly 700,000 from 1993 to 2016 – which, perhaps not coincidentally, is close to Scott's more recent estimate of 650,000 US manufacturing jobs lost due to increased US trade deficits with Mexico between 1993 and 2013.[38] While 700,000 is not a negligible increase in employment, it is relatively small in a country where the labour force grew by an average of 1 million *per year* during the 23-year period from 1993 to 2016.[39]

A few studies have applied more rigorous econometric methods to identify the employment impact of the tariff reductions in CUSFTA or NAFTA. Daniel Trefler found that the CUSFTA reductions in Canadian tariffs lowered Canadian manufacturing employment by about 5 per cent overall, and by about 12 per cent in the most affected, import-competing industries (where tariffs were cut the most).[40] A recent study of the local US labour market impact of NAFTA by Shushanik Hakobyan and John McLaren finds evidence of significantly greater outmigration (within the USA) of workers from the local communities most affected by NAFTA tariff reductions, but only for workers with less than a high school level of education.[41] Both of these studies suggest that preferential trade liberalization in North America has created significant adjustment costs, but ones that are concentrated in particular industries, local communities and segments of the labour force.

Net welfare effects and productivity gains

In terms of the conventional efficiency gains from trade, the aggregate impact of NAFTA appears to be very small or negligible for the USA and Canada, and only slightly different from zero (and not necessarily positive) for Mexico. John Romalis estimated that the combined impact of the CUSFTA and NAFTA tariff reductions on US and Canadian welfare was very close to zero, while the NAFTA tariff reductions actually decreased Mexican welfare by 0.3 per cent of GDP.[42] According to Romalis, strong trade diversion effects offset the efficiency gains from trade creation because the largest tariff preferences under both CUSFTA and NAFTA were granted for goods in which the three member countries lacked comparative cost advantages. Using a model that emphasizes the role of trade in intermediate goods, input–output relationships and effects on non-traded goods sectors, Lorenzo Caliendo and Fernando Parro estimated that NAFTA's tariff reductions led to a minuscule welfare gain of 0.08 per cent of GDP for the USA, a larger (but still relatively small) gain of 1.31 per cent of GDP for Mexico, and a slight net loss (driven by trade diversion) of 0.06 per cent of GDP for Canada (none of these authors studied the impact of CUSFTA).[43] Both of these studies focus only on the impact of preferential tariff reductions; they do not attempt to analyse the effects of other aspects of CUSFTA or NAFTA.

Another type of gain from trade liberalization can be increased productivity. Trefler estimated that the Canadian tariff reductions in CUSFTA raised labour productivity at industry level in the most affected, import-competing Canadian industries by 15 per cent, mostly because of diminished market shares of lower productivity plants, while the US tariff reductions in CUSFTA raised labour productivity at plant level in the most affected, export-oriented Canadian industries by about 14 per cent.[44] We are not aware of a similar study of the impact of NAFTA tariff reductions on productivity in any of the member countries. However, James R. Tybout and M. Daniel Westbrook researched the efficiency impact of Mexico's earlier trade liberalization after it joined GATT in the late 1980s – an episode of liberalization that reduced tariffs by much more than NAFTA did.[45] Using plant-level data for 1984–90, Tybout and Westbrook found that productivity growth in Mexican industries was positively related to their degree of openness, but for different reasons in different industries: in import-competing sectors (similar to that which Trefler later found for Canada in CUSFTA), 'market shares apparently shifted toward firms with relatively high productivity', while for export-oriented industries 'their relatively large average cost reductions were mainly due to favourable changes in input prices relative to output prices' that in turn could be partly attributed to reduced costs of imported inputs.[46]

Distributional and developmental impact

Given that the impact of NAFTA on aggregate welfare was in all probability very small to negligible, attention naturally shifts to the distributional impact. Ex ante, many economists worried that greater US integration with a lower-wage country that was relatively more abundant in less-skilled labour would depress wages of less-skilled workers and exacerbate inequality.[47] On the assumption that Mexico would export goods intensive in less-skilled labour, most economists expected that NAFTA would reduce wage inequality in Mexico and probably raise Mexican wages overall.[48]

For the USA, the expectations of depressed wages for less-skilled workers have been confirmed by recent research. Using econometric methods that can identify the local labour market impact of trade policy shocks, Hakobyan and McLaren find significant, albeit highly localized, negative effects of NAFTA tariff reductions on US wages, especially for workers with less education. According to the authors, these negative effects are felt not only by blue-collar workers in the industries that had the largest tariff reductions and in which the tariff reductions were most rapidly phased in, but also by services sector workers in the local communities where the industrial impact was greatest. They also find 'an even larger industry effect, with wage growth in the most protected industries that lose their protection quickly falling 17 percentage points relative to industries that were unprotected to begin with'.[49] Hakobyan and McLaren conclude that 'the distributional effects of NAFTA are large for a highly affected minority of workers'.[50]

For Mexico, the evidence quickly began to contradict the ex ante expectation of reduced wage inequality: the wage premium for skilled labour (variously measured by education levels, white-collar vs blue-collar, or non-production vs production workers) increased steadily from the mid-1980s until the late 1990s, precisely when Mexico first opened its economy by joining GATT followed by NAFTA.[51] Ana L. Revenga and Claudio E. Montenegro explained this increased wage inequality by observing that Mexico's tariff reductions were greatest in the least skill-intensive industries, whereas Gerardo Esquivel and José Antonio Rodríguez-López attributed it to skill-biased technological change.[52] Using data for 1975–88, Robert C. Feenstra and Gordon H. Hanson found that FDI inflows were positively correlated with the relative demand for skilled labour at regional level in Mexico, and that 'growth in FDI can account for over 50 percent of the increased in the skilled labor wage share that occurred in the late 1980s'.[53] However, Fernando Borraz and José Ernesto López-Córdova later found that wage inequality increased less in the Mexican states that were most connected to the global economy by trade and investment linkages (mainly the northern and border states) than in the less connected regions (centre and south), using data for 1994–2002.[54] Eric Verhoogen found that the currency devaluation shocks of 1985–87 and 1994–95 were more important than the (relatively smaller) tariff reductions in NAFTA in causing 'quality upgrading' in Mexico's export industries, which in turn fostered greater wage inequality.[55]

Alessandro Nicita analysed how Mexico's tariff reductions (as a result of NAFTA and other policy changes) affected household welfare through their impact on prices and wages between 1989 and 2000.[56] Overall, he found that household welfare increased by an average of 1.8 per cent nationwide as a net result of the changes in consumer and producer prices and wages, but the welfare gains were concentrated in the northern and border states and in urban areas, as well as among upper-income households. Nicita also found that tariff reductions caused a small increase in the average real wage while contributing slightly to the wage gap between more and less skilled workers, and that 'households that were net suppliers of agricultural goods were hurt by lower agricultural income' although the net losses to such household were very small.[57] Overall, Nicita's results suggest that Mexico's trade liberalization created a very unequal pattern of gains.

In terms of Mexico's economic development and convergence with the USA and Canada, NAFTA and related liberalization policies were not sufficient to achieve the lofty objectives expressed by the Salinas government at the time of the agreement's adoption. Figure 14.6 shows three alternative measures of Mexico's per capita income or labour productivity measured as percentages of US levels from 1950–2014. All three measures rose steadily from the 1950s through the 1970s, then collapsed during the debt crisis of the 1980s, and have failed to show any long-term increases since the early 1990s (although they exhibit short-term recoveries in

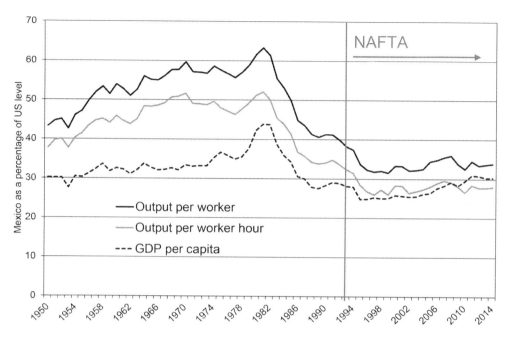

Figure 14.6 Mexico's labour productivity and per capita GDP as percentages of US levels, 1950–2014
Source: Author's calculations based on data from Penn World Tables, version 9.0, available at www.ggdc.net/pwt (accessed 4 April 2017). See Robert C. Feenstra, Robert Inklaar and Marcel P. Timmer (2015) 'The Next Generation of the Penn World Table', *American Economic Review*, 105(10): 3150–82.

the late 1990s from the negative impact of the 1994–95 peso crisis). Mexico's labour productivity was a lower percentage of the US level in 2014 than in 1950, while its GDP per capita was only marginally above the levels (again relative to the US) of 1950 and 1993.

With regard to wages, hopes that NAFTA would raise average Mexican wages sufficiently to lessen incentives for migration to the USA and Canada have also not been realized. Both legal and illegal migration of Mexicans to the USA continued at a rapid pace in the first decade of NAFTA (late 1990s–early 2000s), and while estimates of the 'illegal' or 'undocumented' sort vary widely, numbers on the order of 2–3 million seem reasonable for that period.[58] As shown in Figure 14.7, the real hourly compensation of production workers in Mexican manufacturing was still slightly lower in 2016 than in 1994, in spite of a recovery in the late 1990s from the depressing effects of the peso crisis in 1994–95. Similarly, the hourly compensation of Mexican production workers as a percentage of US production workers in manufacturing (with Mexican compensation converted to US dollars at current exchange rates) fell in the early years of NAFTA, mainly as a result of the peso depreciation of 1994–95, and recovered thereafter, but as of 2015 (the last year for which such comparative data are available) remained only about 14 per cent of the US level (compared with 18 per cent in 1994). Clearly, there has been no convergence in wages, productivity or per capita income during the NAFTA era.

The reasons why Mexico has failed to grow rapidly enough to raise real wages or achieve convergence with the USA have been hotly debated ever since the adoption of the trade liberalization policies of the late 1980s and early 1990s (including but not limited to NAFTA). In general, the explanations suggest that policy failures in other areas besides trade prevented

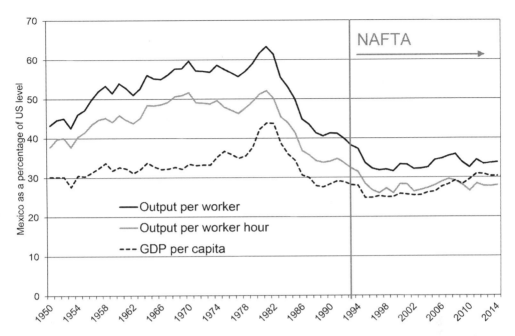

Figure 14.7 Hourly compensation of Mexican production workers, in real terms and as a percentage of the US level, 1994–2016

Note: The BLS international comparisons series have been discontinued, but are now provided by the Conference Board's International Labor Comparisons programme. These series were last updated for production workers (up to 2009) in March 2011 and for all employees (to 2015) in April 2016; the latter series (obtained from the Conference Board) was used to extrapolate the former for 2010–15. The Mexican real hourly compensation data prior to 2007 do not include *maquiladora* workers.

Source: Author's calculations based on data from Banco de México, available at www.banxico.org.mx; INEGI, EMIM, www.inegi.org.mx/; US Bureau of Labor Statistics (BLS), International Labor Comparisons, www.bls.gov (accessed 26 June 2017 and earlier); and Conference Board, available at www.conference-board.org/ilcprogram/ (accessed 9 August 2017).

Mexico from reaping more dynamic gains from its international opening and regional integration. Some of the leading explanations include: the rise of domestic monopolies in privatized sectors, such as telecommunications; uncompetitive exchange rates (especially in the early 2000s); a financial system that does not channel enough finance into industry; the rise of Chinese competition in North American markets; growing informalization and continued dualism between modern and informal firms; rising inequality that impedes the growth of the domestic market; institutional failures including corruption, insecurity and generally inadequate 'rule of law'; inadequate rates of both public and private investment; and the lack of a fiscal reform that would allow the government to adequately finance necessary public expenditures.[59] On the whole, these explanations suggest that it was never realistic to expect an international trade agreement to achieve the kinds of developmental gains that were promised by the Salinas administration in the early 1990s, in the absence of a host of complementary policies and reforms. In addition, critics have argued that NAFTA narrowed the policy space available to the Mexican government to promote long-term national industrial development, and that the focus on assembly of imported intermediate goods in Mexico's exports of manufactures has limited the value-added content and employment gains from those exports.[60]

Robert A. Blecker

The future of NAFTA post-Trump

The renegotiation of NAFTA at the behest of the US Trump Administration will move the North American countries into uncharted territory. As of mid-2018 the Trump Administration's negotiating agenda was focused on strengthening NAFTA's rules of origin to encourage greater North American content, encouraging greater US production within NAFTA and requiring a 'sunset' review of NAFTA (and its possible termination) every five years. The Trump negotiating team had also announced a target of balancing bilateral trade with Mexico and was seeking to abolish the Chapter 19 trade dispute settlement mechanism while allowing an 'opt-in' or 'opt-out' choice for ISDS in each country.[61] The Canadian and Mexican governments were opposed to most of these proposals (except possibly the higher region-wide rules of origin) and had to contemplate the possibility of a US withdrawal from NAFTA if the negotiations did not reach an agreement acceptable to Trump.

In some areas, all three countries have agreed to modernize NAFTA, for example by introducing regulations for e-commerce and digital trade. But if negotiations break down and Trump makes good on his threat to pull the USA out of the agreement, US-Mexican and US-Canadian trade would revert to MFN tariffs (and other multilateral rules) under the WTO.[62] Canada and Mexico would have the option of maintaining a bilateral FTA with each other or relying on their membership in the revised TPP along with other Pacific Rim countries (without the USA). Nevertheless, the loss of preferential access to the US market could disrupt global supply chains that now pass through Mexico en route to US and Canadian markets and could be devastating for the Mexican economy in general. A US withdrawal from NAFTA would also hurt many US export interests, such as corn farmers and producers of agricultural equipment and supplies.

The most positive possible outcome of a NAFTA renegotiation is that it could potentially strengthen North America as a more competitive region, in line with the intentions of the industrial policy camp of the 1990s (albeit at the possible cost of greater trade diversion). Weakening or eliminating the ISDS provisions could arguably empower national and local governments to adopt more beneficial social and environmental regulations. It seems quite unlikely, however, that a mercantilist rewrite of NAFTA based on the Trump Administration's demands would restore the US industrial structure of 1993 or bring back millions of US manufacturing jobs. Furthermore, some of the Trump initiatives could backfire, for example, because firms could evade stronger rules of origin by ignoring NAFTA tariff preferences and bringing in cheaper goods with less North American content from other parts of the world under other tariff provisions. Future competitiveness in North America will depend more on investments in areas such as infrastructure, education, science and technology, as well as on macroeconomic and monetary policies that maintain competitive exchange rates, rather than a renegotiation of NAFTA.

Notes

1 Measured at current US dollar prices using market exchange rates, the total GDP of the NAFTA countries has exceeded that of the EU (including all 28 member countries of the latter as of 2017) in all but five of the years from 1994 through 2016, according to data from the IMF, *World Economic Outlook Database*, April 2017, available at www.imf.org/external/pubs/ft/weo/2017/01/weodata/index.aspx (accessed 28 June 2017).

2 See Julie Hirschfield Davis (2017) 'Trump Sends Nafta Renegotiation Notice to Congress', *New York Times*, 18 May, available at www.nytimes.com/2017/05/18/us/politics/nafta-renegotiation-trump.html, and Ashley Parker, Phillip Rucker, Damian Paletta and Karen DeYoung (2017) "'I Was All Set to Terminate": Inside Trump's Sudden Shift on NAFTA', *Washington Post*, 27 April, available at www.

washingtonpost.com/politics/i-was-all-set-to-terminate-inside-trumps-sudden-shift-on-nafta/2017/04/27/0452a3fa-2b65-11e7-b605-33413c691853_story.html (both accessed 28 May 2017).

3 See Robert A. Blecker (1996) 'The Political Economy of the North American Free Trade Agreement', in Robert A. Blecker (ed.) *U.S. Trade Policy and Global Growth: New Directions in the International Economy*, Armonk, NY: M. E. Sharpe, pp. 136–76.

4 See Adolfo Aguilar Zinser (1993) 'A Critical View of a NAFTA Including Mexico', in Richard S. Belous and Jonathan Lemco (eds) *NAFTA as a Model of Development: The Benefits and Costs of Merging High and Low Wage Areas*, Washington, DC: National Planning Association, pp. 96–101; Sherman Robinson, Mary Burfisher, Raúl Hinojosa-Ojeda and Karen Thierfelder (1993) 'Agricultural Policies and Migration in a U.S.-Mexico Free Trade Area: A Computable General Equilibrium Analysis', *Journal of Policy Modeling*, 15(5–6), October–December: 673–701.

5 See Ricardo Grinspun and Maxwell A. Cameron (eds) (1993) *The Political Economy of North American Free Trade*, New York: St. Martins; Andrew Jackson (2007) 'From Leaps of Faith to Hard Landings: Fifteen Years of "Free Trade"', in Ricardo Grinspun and Yasmine Shamsie (eds) *Whose Canada? Continental Integration, Fortress North America, and the Corporate Agenda*, Montréal: McGill-Queen's University Press and Canadian Centre for Policy Alternatives, pp. 211–33.

6 See Lawrence Chimerine and Robert Cohen (1992) *NAFTA: Making It Better*, Washington, DC: Economic Strategy Institute.

7 See Gary C. Hufbauer and Jeffrey J. Schott (1993) *NAFTA: An Assessment*, Washington, DC: Institute for International Economics, 1993.

8 See Robert A. Pastor (2001) *Toward a North American Community: Lessons from the Old World for the New*, Washington, DC: Institute for International Economics, 2001.

9 See Michael Howlett, Alex Netherton and M. Ramesh (1999) *The Political Economy of Canada: An Introduction*, 2nd edn, Don Mills, ON: Oxford University Press, pp. 120–56.

10 See Nora Lustig (1998) *Mexico: The Remaking of an Economy*, 2nd edn, Washington, DC: Brookings Institution, pp. 114–40; Gary C. Hufbauer and Jeffrey J. Schott (1992) *North American Free Trade: Issues and Recommendations*, Washington, DC: Institute for International Economics, pp. 91–105; and Juan Carlos Moreno-Brid and Jaime Ros (2009) *Development and Growth in the Mexican Economy: A Historical Perspective*, New York: Oxford University Press, pp. 176–205.

11 See Hufbauer and Schott, *North American Free Trade*, p. 24, for precise dates of the various decisions that led up to the negotiation of NAFTA.

12 Lustig, *Mexico*, p. 134.

13 According to Sweder van Wijnbergen (1991) 'Mexico and the Brady Plan', *Economic Policy*, 6(12), April: 13–56, the USA had required Mexico to commit to market-opening 'structural reforms' as a condition for receiving debt restructuring under the US-sponsored Baker Plan of 1986 and Brady Plan of 1989.

14 See Hufbauer and Schott, *North American Free Trade*, p. 24, and *NAFTA: An Assessment*, p. 1.

15 For more details about the NAFTA debate and ratification process in the US, see Stephen D. Cohen, Robert A. Blecker and Peter D. Whitney (2003) *Fundamentals of U.S. Foreign Trade Policy, Economics, Politics, Laws, and Issues*, 2nd edn, Boulder, CO: Westview, pp. 286–301.

16 Hufbauer and Schott, *NAFTA: An Assessment*, p. 44.

17 Enrique Dussel Peters and Kevin P. Gallagher (2013) 'NAFTA's Uninvited Guest: China and the Disintegration of North American Trade', *CEPAL Review*, no. 110, August: 83–108.

18 Hufbauer and Schott, *NAFTA: An Assessment*, pp. 40–41.

19 Dussel Peters and Gallagher, 'NAFTA's Uninvited Guest'.

20 See 'Build Pipelines, Not Walls: American Energy Firms Enjoy a Bonanza South of the Border', *The Economist*, (17 June 2017): 62.

21 Hufbauer and Schott, *NAFTA: An Assessment*, pp. 79–90, 141.

22 See Public Citizen, 'Investor-State Dispute Settlement (ISDS): Extraordinary Corporate Powers in "Trade" Deals', available at www.citizen.org/our-work/globalization-and-trade/investor-state-system (accessed 27 June 2017).

23 See Gary C. Hufbauer and Jeffrey J. Schott (2005) *NAFTA Revisited: Achievements and Challenges*, Washington, DC: Peterson Institute for International Economics, pp. 129–30.

24 All trade data in this section are from the IMF, *Direction of Trade Statistics* (DOTS), available at www.imf.org/en/Data (accessed 29 May 2017), and author's calculations, except as otherwise noted.

25 First, these data are expressed in current dollars and not adjusted for inflation. Also, reported bilateral exports and imports measure the gross values of the goods shipped, which includes the value of raw

materials, parts and components imported from third countries. Furthermore, the USA includes 're-exports' in its total export statistics, which tends to exaggerate bilateral exports to its neighbours Canada and Mexico. Nevertheless, we use the conventionally reported data here for consistency with most other literature, and because the broad trends we identify are not qualitatively affected by these anomalies.

26 John Romalis (2007) 'NAFTA's and CUSFTA's Impact on International Trade', *Review of Economics and Statistics*, 89(3): 416–35.

27 Lorenzo Caliendo and Fernando Parro (2015) 'Estimates of the Trade and Welfare Effects of NAFTA', *Review of Economic Studies*, 82(1): 1–44.

28 As of June 2017, Mexico had nine other FTAs with a total of 43 countries, not including the USA and Canada, while the USA had 13 other FTAs with 18 countries other than Canada and Mexico, and Canada had ten other FTAs in force with 13 countries outside North America. See ProMéxico, 'Trade Agreements', available at www.promexico.gob.mx/en/mx/tratados-comerciales; Office of the United States Trade Representative, 'Free Trade Agreements', available at https://ustr.gov/trade-agreements/free-trade-agreements; and Global Affairs Canada, available at www.international.gc.ca/trade-comm erce/trade-agreements-accords-commerciaux/agr-acc/index.aspx?lang=eng (all accessed 27 June 2017).

29 See Robert A. Blecker and Mario Seccareccia (2014) 'Would a North American Monetary Union Protect Canada and Mexico against the Ravages of "Dutch Disease"? A Post-Financial Crisis Perspective, in Gerald A. Epstein, Tom Schlesinger and Matías Vernengo (eds) *Banking, Monetary Policy and the Political Economy of Financial Regulation*, Cheltenham: Edward Elgar, pp. 171–202; and Robert A. Blecker (2014) 'The Mexican and U.S. Economies after Twenty Years of NAFTA', *International Journal of Political Economy*, 43(2), Summer: 5–26.

30 See Kevin P. Gallagher, Juan Carlos Moreno-Brid and Roberto Porzecanski (2008) 'The Dynamism of Mexican Exports: Lost in (Chinese) Translation?', *World Development*, 36(8): 1365–80; Robert C. Feenstra and Hiao Looi Kee (2009) 'Trade Liberalization and Export Variety: A Comparison of Mexico and China', Washington, DC: World Bank © World Bank, available at https://openknow ledge.worldbank.org/handle/10986/27107 License: CC BY 3.0 IGO; and Gordon H. Hanson and Raymond Robertson (2009) 'China and the Recent Evolution of Latin America's Manufacturing Exports', in Daniel Lederman, Marcelo Olarreaga and Guillermo E. Perry (eds) *China's and India's Challenge to Latin America: Opportunity or Threat?* Washington, DC: World Bank, pp. 145–78, 245–63.

31 Jim Stanford (2003) 'Economic Models and Economic Reality: North American Free Trade and the Predictions of Economists', *International Journal of Political Economy*, 33(3), Fall: 28–49.

32 Robert E. Scott (2003) 'The High Price of "Free Trade": NAFTA's Failure Has Cost the United States Jobs across the Nation', Economic Policy Institute, Briefing Paper No. 147, November. All numbers are rounded to the nearest thousand.

33 Hufbauer and Schott, *NAFTA Revisited*, pp. 39–41.

34 Ibid., p. 129.

35 Data from US Bureau of Labor Statistics, Employment, Hours, and Earnings from the Current Employment Statistics survey (National), available at www.bls.gov (accessed 15 June 2017).

36 Ibid. and Scott, 'The High Price', p. 8.

37 Author's calculations (rounded to the nearest 100,000) based on data from INEGI, Censos Económicos 2014 and earlier, and Encuesta mensual de la industria manufacturera (EMIM), available at www. inegi.org.mx/ (accessed 22 June 2017 and earlier). Each economic census provides data collected in the previous year, so for example the 2014 census reports data for 2013. The number given here for 2016 is the monthly average from EMIM, which was not available before 2007.

38 Robert E. Scott (2014) 'The Effects of NAFTA on US Trade, Jobs, and Investment, 1993–2013', *Review of Keynesian Economics*, 2(4), Winter: 429–41 (the 650,000 number is given on p. 438).

39 Author's calculation based on data from the World Bank, *World Development Indicators*, available at http://data.worldbank.org/data-catalog/world-development-indicators (accessed 24 June 2017).

40 Daniel Trefler (2004) 'The Long and Short of the Canada-U.S. Free Trade Agreement', *American Economic Review*, 94(4), September: 870–95.

41 Shushanik Hakobyan and John McLaren (2016) 'Looking for Local Labor Market Effects of NAFTA', *Review of Economics and Statistics*, 98(4), October: 728–41.

42 Romalis, 'NAFTA's and CUSFTA's Impact', p. 429. His estimates show that CUSFTA caused slight net welfare losses of −0.01 per cent of GDP for the USA and −0.02 per cent of GDP for Canada, while NAFTA led to an exactly offsetting net gain of 0.01 per cent for the USA and no offset for Canada. The sum for each country is very close to zero.

43 Caliendo and Parro, 'Estimates of the Trade and Welfare Effects', p. 20.

44 Trefler, 'The Long and Short', pp. 880–81.

45 James R. Tybout and M. Daniel Westbrook (1995) 'Trade Liberalization and the Dimensions of Efficiency Change in Mexican Manufacturing Industries', *Journal of International Economics*, 39(1–2), August: 53–78.

46 Ibid., p. 76.

47 See Clark W. Reynolds (1993) 'The NAFTA and Wage Convergence: A Case of Winners and Losers', in Belous and Lemco (eds), *NAFTA as a Model*, pp. 18–22; Edward E. Leamer (1993) 'Wage Effects of a U.S.-Mexican Free Trade Agreement', in Peter M. Garber (ed.) *The Mexico-U.S. Free Trade Agreement*, Cambridge, MA: MIT Press, pp. 57–125.

48 See, for example, the studies cited in Hufbauer and Schott, *North American Free Trade*, Table 3.4, p. 58.

49 Hakobyan and McLaren, 'Looking for Local Labor Market Effects', p. 729.

50 Ibid., p. 741.

51 See, for example, Gordon H. Hanson, 'What Has Happened to Wages in Mexico since NAFTA? Implications for Hemispheric Free Trade,' in Antoni Estevadeordal, Dani Rodrik, Alan M. Taylor and Andrés Velasco (eds) (2004) *Integrating the Americas: FTAA and Beyond*, Cambridge, MA: Harvard University Press, pp. 505–37.

52 Ana L. Revenga and Claudio E. Montenegro (1998) 'North American Integration and Factor Price Equalization: Is There Evidence of Wage Convergence between Mexico and the United States?', in Susan M. Collins (ed.) *Imports, Exports, and the American Worker*, Washington, DC: Brookings Institution, pp. 305–47; Gerardo Esquivel and José Antonio Rodríguez-López (2003) 'Technology, Trade, and Wage Inequality in Mexico Before and After NAFTA', *Journal of Development Economics*, 72(2), 543–65.

53 Robert C. Feenstra and Gordon H. Hanson (1997) 'Foreign Direct Investment and Relative Wages: Evidence from Mexico's Maquiladoras', *Journal of International Economics*, 42(3–4): 371–94.

54 See Fernando Borraz and José Ernesto López-Córdova (2007) 'Has Globalization Deepened Income Inequality in Mexico?', *Global Economy Journal*, 7(1), Article 6 (online).

55 Eric A. Verhoogen (2008) 'Trade, Quality Upgrading, and Wage Inequality in the Mexican Manufacturing Sector', *Quarterly Journal of Economics*, 123(2): 489–530.

56 Alessandro Nicita (2009) 'The Price Effect of Tariff Liberalization: Measuring the Impact on Household Welfare', *Journal of Development Economics*, 89(1), May: 19–27.

57 Ibid., p. 20.

58 Based on data cited in Gordon H. Hanson (2006) 'Illegal Migration from Mexico to the United States', *Journal of Economic Literature*, 44(4), December: 869–924 (Table 1, p. 875).

59 See Gordon H. Hanson (2010) 'Why Isn't Mexico Rich?', *Journal of Economic Literature*, 48(4), December: 987–1004; Jaime Ros Bosch (2013) *Algunas Tesis Equivocadas Sobre el Estancamiento Económico de México*, Mexico City: El Colegio de México; E. Bolio, J. Remes, T. Lajous, J. Manyika, E. Ramirez and M. Rossé (2014) *A Tale of Two Mexicos: Growth and Prosperity in a Two-speed Economy*, San Francisco, CA: McKinsey Global Institute; Isabel Guerrero, Luis Felipe Lopez-Calva and Michael Walton (2009) 'The Inequality Trap and Its Links to Low Growth in Mexico', in Santiago Levy and Michael Walton (eds) *No Growth Without Equity? Inequality, Interests, and Competition in Mexico*, Washington, DC: World Bank, and Basingstoke: Palgrave Macmillan, pp. 111–56; Francisco E. González (2014) 'Mexico: Emerging Economy Kept on a Leash by Mismatched Monopolies', in Robert E. Looney (ed.) *Handbook of Emerging Economies*, London: Routledge, pp. 287–305; and Robert A. Blecker (2016) 'Integration, Productivity, and Inclusion in Mexico: A Macro Perspective', in Alejandro Foxley and Barbara Stallings (eds) *Innovation and Inclusion in Latin America: Strategies to Avoid the Middle Income Trap*, New York: Palgrave Macmillan, pp. 175–204.

60 See Eduardo Zepeda, Timothy A. Wise and Kevin P. Gallagher (2009) 'Rethinking Trade Policy for Development: Lessons From Mexico Under NAFTA', Washington, DC: Carnegie Policy Outlook, December; Moreno-Brid and Ros, *Development and Growth*, pp. 222–51; Juan Carlos Moreno-Brid, Jesús Santamaría and Juan Carlos Rivas Valdivia (2005) 'Industrialization and Economic Growth in Mexico after NAFTA: The Road Travelled', *Development and Change*, 36(6): 1095–119.

61 See Office of the United States Trade Representative (2017) 'Summary of Objectives for the NAFTA Renegotiation', 17 July. Available at https://ustr.gov/sites/default/files/files/Press/Releases/NAFTAObjectives.pdf (accessed 17 July 2017).

62 It is possible that CUSFTA could come back into effect between Canada and the USA, but whether this would happen automatically or a new bilateral free trade agreement would have to be negotiated is uncertain.

15

CAFTA-DR: diverging trajectories and uneven development

Mary Finley-Brook

Introduction

This chapter addresses the first decade of the implementation of the Dominican Republic–Central American Free Trade Agreement (CAFTA-DR) between the USA, five Central American countries (Costa Rica, El Salvador, Guatemala, Honduras and Nicaragua, referred to hereafter as the CA-5), and the Dominican Republic. The free trade agreement (FTA) builds on historical integration and regional exchange within the CA-5 as well as on strong economic ties between the USA and the countries of Central America and the Caribbean (referred to hereafter as the CAC). CAFTA-DR is the first FTA to comprise a superpower and a series of small low-income nations. Preliminary impacts after the initial decade of the FTA demonstrate unevenness between and within countries as some peoples and places experience harm while others benefit.[1]

Central American regional integration, defined as transborder cooperation through shared institutions and rules, extends into nearly all aspects of governance; however, free trade is the most contested element. Despite significant public protest during negotiations, there remains little direct opposition to the FTA, although critics denounce trends they perceive as tied to the expansion of neoliberal reforms and economic liberalization, such as dispossession (i.e. land grabbing), environmental destruction, and insecurity of food and nutrition.[2]

Background and motivations

Two important precursors to CAFTA-DR were (1) prior regional integration; and (2) US economic and political dominance in CAC.

Regional integration

The Central American nations have attempted to cooperate for a long time.[3] Following independence, the CA-5 formed a Central American Federation in 1823; it disbanded within two decades. A Greater Republic of Central America lasted from 1895 to 1898. Following the emergence of the Organization of Central American States in 1951, cooperation intensified. In

1960 a Central American Common Market (CACM) was established in order to develop economies of scale and improve terms of trade.[4] Although the region's economy developed under CACM, more industrialized countries, particularly El Salvador and Guatemala, proved better able to take advantage of intraregional trade.[5] CACM disintegrated after 1969 for various reasons, including political instabilities. By the 1980s civil wars had destabilized Central America. In 1991, following the signing of peace accords, the CA-5 and Panama formed the Central American Integration System (Sistema de la Integración Centroamericana (SICA)) to help to consolidate a Central American community through the creation of regional institutions, such as a court and central bank.[6]

The US relationship with the five Central American countries

Following independence from Spain, US imperialism in the CAC countries flourished. 'Gunboat diplomacy' involved the use of the US military to defend interests.[7] Political support for authoritarian regimes, such as the Somoza family in Nicaragua, benefited US corporations.[8] In the 1980s socialism in El Salvador, Guatemala and Nicaragua became part of the Cold War as Russia supported their revolutionary movements and the USA backed the political elite with weapons and financial support. Dozens of Central American military leaders trained at the School for the Americas (SOA), now called the Western Hemisphere Institute for Security Cooperation, in Georgia. SOA graduates were allegedly responsible for assassinations and torture in their home countries.[9] Central America has not recovered from civil wars: current leaders often have ties to historical atrocities and state institutions remain weak.

In recent decades, the USA has assumed the role of regional development financier and sponsor. In 1983 the US Congress enacted the Caribbean Basin Initiative (CBI), a preferential trading agreement for the islands and surrounding countries, including the CA-5. Over the next 30 years, the CBI oriented trade toward the USA and entrenched dependence. For example, CBI tax exemptions favoured situations whereby US components were assembled in the Caribbean and exported back to the USA.[10] Thus, new export processing zones (EPZ) created few forward or backward linkages.

Negotiations

At the time of negotiation, in 2000, the USA accounted for 73 per cent of combined CAFTA-DR member exports and 55 per cent of imports.[11] Central American officials approached the USA to create the FTA due to concern about possible deleterious impacts from the North American Free Trade Agreement (NAFTA) and the potential phasing out of the CBI.[12] They believed that together they would have the power to insist on favourable terms, but with different national strengths and weaknesses their trade interests diverged.

The USA had several geopolitical and economic objectives with CAFTA-DR, including counteracting the trading competition from the People's Republic of China and undermining the expansion of Latin American socialism, not least because Venezuela's aid to Central America worried US policymakers. US trade representatives also wanted to cement advantageous trade terms with Central America to set the stage for favourable negotiation of a Free Trade Area of the Americas (FTAA) among 34 countries, although FTAA talks disintegrated soon afterwards.[13]

US President George W. Bush suggested that reducing trade barriers would support political freedom and democracy.[14] Ironically, CAFTA-DR negotiations took place behind closed doors and in secret. Trade representatives signed an agreement prohibiting discussion of details, meaning the public remained uninformed and could not provide any input.[15] The pace of

CAFTA-DR talks was aggressive, some of the fastest ever. In the space of a year, the states parties produced and agreed upon more than 500 pages of text. The Dominican Republic joined after the CA-5 had concluded negotiations and integrated into the FTA in four months.[16] The rapid pace restricted analysis of how trade policies would influence different sectors and groups. Meanwhile, trade talks skirted discussions about social vulnerability; for example, when covering policies that would restrict access to affordable medicines, US representatives insisted on discussing trade and took health impacts off the table.[17]

Opposition and ratification

CAFTA-DR faced significant opposition from Central American civil society, including advocacy organizations focusing on labour rights, gender equality, the environment and food sovereignty. For the most part, these activist networks existed prior to the emergence of CAFTA-DR, although opposition to the FTA created opportunities for new collaboration between movements.[18] While the public did not have access to specific CAFTA-DR terms prior to approval of the FTA, they assumed that NAFTA-type language would prioritize corporate rights above citizen protections. Both NAFTA and CAFTA-DR contain investor rights provisions allowing firms to sue countries for enforcing environmental or health regulations that diminish actual or expected corporate profit.[19] Opponents worried that labour and environmental standards would be weak; in fact, CAFTA-DR only required compliance with national laws that were widely known to be inadequate.[20] Moreover, it seemed unlikely that five Central American countries would have the capacity or power to monitor and hold international firms accountable.

El Salvador ratified CAFTA-DR in a vote held before dawn in December 2004 to avoid demonstrations, but protesters still broke into the legislative chambers and temporarily stalled proceedings before riot police removed them by force.[21] The Guatemalan state used bullets, tear gas and arrests to deter protestors while journalists received death threats to discourage public criticism. Guatemalan leaders violated a national law to read a bill out loud three times before voting. In other countries, armed forces dissipated public opposition by blocking roads and cutting off crowd formation when protests were staged against the FTA.[22]

In 2007 Costa Rica held a public referendum, the first time ever that a national electorate was given the opportunity to vote for or against joining a FTA.[23] Nonetheless, analysts suggest that this was not a democratic process owing to the misuse of state power and resources to manipulate public opinion.[24] State officials threatened subordinates with retribution if they failed to vote for the FTA.[25] The 'yes' movement financed an aggressive media campaign drawing on fear tactics such as the threat of expanding socialism or the total withdrawal of US trade and aid.[26] In the end, Costa Ricans narrowly voted to pass CAFTA-DR and the National Assembly subsequently approved the trade bill 51 to 48.

The first decade of consequences

For most of the parties to the agreement the CAFTA-DR became effective in 2006, and thus there has been more than a decade under new trade rules.[27] There is evidence of advancement of economic freedom in two countries, the Dominican Republic and Honduras, since CAFTA-DR (Table 15.1).[28] An annual index from the Heritage Foundation systematically tracks business freedom, trade freedom, fiscal freedom, government spending, monetary freedom, investment freedom, financial freedom, property rights, freedom from corruption, and labour freedom. Economic freedom improved in Nicaragua from 2000 onwards, but declined overall from a high score prior to CAFTA-DR. Between 2000 and 2017 economic freedom scores slipped

Table 15.1 Economic Freedom Index

Country	2000	2005	2010	2015	2017
Costa Rica	68.4	66.1	65.9	67.2	65.0
Dominican Republic	59.0	55.1	60.3	61.0	63.0
El Salvador	76.3	71.5	69.9	65.7	64.1
Guatemala	64.3	59.5	61.0	60.4	60.3
Honduras	57.6	55.3	58.3	57.4	58.8
Nicaragua	56.9	62.5	58.3	57.6	59.2
USA	76.4	79.9	78.0	76.2	75.1

Source: Data available at http://thf_media.s3.amazonaws.com/2017/2017_IndexOfEconomicFreedom.pdf.

overall in the remaining four countries, although there was some movement upwards at certain points in all the states parties except El Salvador.

CAFTA-DR countries have relatively open economies as defined by the percentage of gross domestic product (GDP) from trade, which is necessary in small countries that need to trade for the goods and services they cannot produce. Trade balances worsened from 2005 to 2015 in all CAFTA-DR countries except the USA (Table 15.2).

Table 15.3 shows continued reliance on the USA in most countries, although US portions of import and exports have come down, in part due to increases in exchanges with Mexico and China.[29] The top three countries often account for 60 per cent or more of the total. Frequently, the USA holds around 40 per cent of the total and significantly more than the next largest partner.

In El Salvador and Guatemala, the gap between imports from the USA and exports to the USA has progressively widened, although Nicaragua's trade balance improved (Table 15.4).

Although there are significant demographic differences between countries, urbanization is ubiquitous (Table 15.5). Rural production among smallholders became less viable following CAFTA-DR.[30] Meanwhile, EPZs attracted workers to cities. Urban infrastructure was inadequate and newcomers settled into precarious housing with limited services. Struggling to meet basic needs, parents often worked long hours and were unable to monitor youth behaviour, instil positive values, or create healthy emotional bonds with children, a situation that was made worse for single mothers. Rapid urbanization is known to contribute to gang expansion due to

Table 15.2 Foreign balance of goods and services

Country	2005 (US $ millions)*	2015 (US $ millions)[†]
Costa Rica	−486.53	−809.53
Dominican Republic	−37.50	−140.0
El Salvador	−3.08	−4.15
Guatemala	−34.89	−42.74
Honduras	−77.36	−80.07
Nicaragua	−24.33	−62.07
USA	−713.60	−521.97

Sources: * Data available at https://data.oecd.org/trade/trade-in-goods-and-services.htm.† Data available at https://www.census.gov/foreign-trade/balance.

Mary Finley-Brook

Table 15.3 Top trade partners, 2015

Country	% of exports	% of imports
Costa Rica	USA (40.8)	USA (39.8)
	Panama (5.8)	China (12.6)
	Guatemala (5.5)	Mexico (7.4)
Dominican Republic	USA (53.6)	USA (41.3)
	Haiti (12.1)	China (13.4)
	Canada (8.4)	Mexico (4.6)
El Salvador	USA (47.0)	USA (39.4)
	Honduras (13.9)	Guatemala (9.6)
	Guatemala (13.5)	China (8.1)
Guatemala	USA (38.8)	USA (37.1)
	El Salvador (11.5)	Mexico (11.6)
	Honduras (8.4)	China (10.6)
Honduras (2014)	USA (44.3)	USA (40.8)
	Germany (7.2)	China (11.3)
	El Salvador (6.1)	Guatemala (7.5)
Nicaragua (2014)	USA (48.4)	USA (16.3)
	Mexico (12.4)	China (14.9)
	Venezuela (7.8)	Mexico (9.5)
USA	Canada (18.6)	China (21.8)
	Mexico (15.7)	Canada (13.1)
	China (7.7)	Mexico (12.9)

Source: Data available at http://data.un.org/CountryProfile.aspx.

Table 15.4 Trade balance with the USA (US $ millions)

Country	2000	2005	2010	2015
Costa Rica	1,078.3	−183.3	3,519.0	−1,556.0
Dominican Republic	−89.5	−115.0	−2,907.5	−2,449.5
El Salvador	152.8	134.5	−228.1	−717.0
Guatemala	706.8	302.0	−954.2	−1,700.4
Honduras	506.1	495.4	−673.5	−456.4
Nicaragua	208.3	555.3	1,026.2	1,921.4

Source: Data available at www.census.gov/foreign-trade/balance.

social exclusion, weak social capital and overcrowding.[31] Violence and crime encourage emigration, which is found everywhere but the USA and Costa Rica, although the rates of departure have generally come down, except in the Dominican Republic.

Lower national fertility rates shown in Table 15.5 mask class divisions as wealthier families have fewer children while low-income families remain large.[32] While many families living in CAC countries continue to struggle to meet basic needs, overall GDP growth occurred in most countries (Figure 15.6). Nonetheless, GDP growth rates have decreased from 2005 levels in all countries except Nicaragua. Male labour force participation dropped in half of the countries and female labour force participation increased in most countries. Women are over-represented in low-skilled, low-paid sectors.[33]

170

Table 15.5 Demographic characteristics, 2005–15

Country	Population	Population density (per km^2)	Urban population (%)	Migration (net)	Fertility rate
Costa Rica 2005	4,247,843	83	66.8	8,400	2.17
2010	4,454,273	89	73.7	6,100	2.01
2015	4,807,850	94	79.9	3,900	1.85
Dominican Republic 2005	9,237,565	191	68.1	−30,500	2.83
2010	9,897,983	205	74.6	−30,800	2.67
2015	10,528,391	218	79.9	−30,600	2.53
El Salvador 2005	5,947,206	287	62.9	−62,600	2.62
2010	6,038,306	291	66.2	−57,100	2.23
2015	6,216,583	296	70.0	−48,100	1.97
Guatemala 2005	13,183,505	123	45.4	−40,000	4.16
2010	14,732,261	138	48.0	−26,400	3.61
2015	16,342,897	153	51.3	−24,000	3.30
Honduras 2005	6,880,181	62	48.6	−30,000	3.63
2010	7,503,875	67	52.5	−20,000	2.99
2015	8,075,060	72	57.1	−16,000	2.47
Nicaragua 2005	5,379,327	45	56.7	−34,800	2.84
2010	5,737,722	48	58.1	−31,000	2.56
2015	6,082,032	51	60.5	−27,000	2.32
USA 2005	296,139,635	32	80.5	1,029,800	2.04
2010	309,876,170	34	81.4	1,014,100	2.06
2015	321,773,631	35	82.5	1,001,600	1.89

Source: Data available at www.worldometers.info.

In all countries, industry declined as measured by percentage of employment and gross value added (Table 15.7), perhaps due to growing trade with Asia. Services increased in all countries except Nicaragua, but the rise in unemployment is a concern in the Dominican Republic, where services add value but employ fewer people.[34] There were slight increases in agriculture in El Salvador and the USA but declines elsewhere. US agricultural exports to Central America more than doubled following the passage of CAFTA-DR.[35] During the CAFTA-DR negotiations the USA insisted on keeping domestic agricultural subsidies while forcing small CAC states to eliminate their protections.[36] The CAC countries underwent incremental reductions of subsidies to sensitive goods, such as staple foods like corn, so as to reduce the shock of implementation.[37]

Historically, CAC countries exhibited high social and economic inequality, a situation that persists in member countries following the signing of CAFTA-DR. As shown in the quintile ratio, the wealthiest 20 per cent% earn at least ten times as much as the poorest 20 per cent% in all but two CAFTA-DR countries (Figure 15.8). Notably, the USA's Gini co-efficient (a measure of the concentration of income), in which a low number demonstrates equality, is only slightly lower than El Salvador's. However, the Human Development Index (HDI), which records health and education rates alongside income, shows that inequality does not cause as severe an adverse fall in the index in the USA, suggesting that it has broader access to social services. There is significant HDI decline due to inequality in the already low HDI scores of Guatemala, Honduras and

Mary Finley-Brook

Table 15.6 Economic indicators by country, 2005–14

Country	GDP million current US $	GDP per caput US $	GDP growth rate (annual %)	Labour force participation women (%)	Labour force participation men (%)
Costa Rica 2005	19,965	4,700.0	5.9	43.6	80.2
2010	36,298	7,986.0	5.0	44.1	77.1
2014	49,553	10,415.4	3.5	46.7	76.6
Dominican Republic 2005	35,662	3,860.6	9.3	48.8	80.7
2010	53,043	5,359.0	8.3	49.3	78.7
2014	63,969	6,147.4	7.3	52.2	78.7
El Salvador 2005	17,094	2,874.3	3.6	45.2	78.5
2010	21,418	3,547.1	1.4	46.4	78.9
2014	25,164	4,120.2	2.0	49.0	79.1
Guatemala 2005	27,211	3,673.1	6.1	36.3	83.1
2010	41,338	2,806.0	3.7	44.2	84.6
2014	58,827	3,673.1	3.1	47.0	84.4
Honduras 2005	9,757	1,418.1	6.1	36.3	83.1
2010	15,839	2,110.8	3.7	44.2	84.6
2014	19,497	2,448.9	3.1	36.3	83.1
Nicaragua 2005	6,321	1,175.1	4.3	43.7	80.4
2010	8,741	1,523.5	3.2	46.8	80.6
2014	11,806	1,963.1	4.7	48.9	80.2
USA 2005	130,937.20	44,214.7	3.4	58.3	72.2
2010	149,643.80	48,291.5	2.5	57.6	70.0
2014	173,480.72	54,306.3	2.4	56.1	68.5

Source: Data available at http://data.un.org/CountryProfile.aspx.

Nicaragua. Employment in the informal sector remains high, more than half of total Honduran employment, but exploitative or dangerous conditions remain unregulated.

Statistics on sanitation facilities in Table 16.8 draw attention to urban-rural disparities, although improved sanitation facilities range from flush toilets to open-pit latrines. Regional and local differences are generally not apparent in national data, which fail to show differences based on factors like class, gender or race. We often find a pattern of poverty and insecurity among indigenous and Afro-descendant populations across CAC countries,[38] but marginalization of low-income women of colour demonstrates the need to pay greater attention to inter-sectionalities.[39] Table 15.9 suggests that CAFTA-DR countries are breaching environmental limits, although carbon emissions are low except in the USA. Overall, statistics imply loss of forest, natural resource depletion, and that rates of water withdrawal are not sustainable; all these harm national earnings. Yet many environmental indicators are not measured. For example, CAC countries lack consistent documentation of the six basic pollutants regulated in the USA, such as sulphur dioxide and nitrous oxide. Hazardous waste data and records of public health impacts from pollution (i.e. pesticide poisoning, lead and mercury exposure, etc.) are frequently missing.

CAFTA-DR

Table 15.7 Employment indicators by country, 2005–14

Country	Agriculture (% of gross value added)	Agriculture (% employed)	Industry (% of gross value added)	Industry (% employed)	Services (% of gross value added)	Service (% employed)
Costa Rica 2005	8.6	15.2	27.8	21.5	63.6	62.9
2010	6.8	15.0	24.9	19.5	68.2	64.7
2014	5.2	12.7	23.2	19.0	71.6	68.2
Dominican Republic 2005	8.1	14.6	32.7	22.3	59.2	58.8
2010	6.5	12.0	30.1	14.9	63.4	52.4
2014	6.2	14.5	28.7	17.4	65.1	41.9
El Salvador 2005	10.2	20.0	28.7	22.2	61.1	54.8
2010	12.1	20.8	25.9	21.4	62.1	57.8
2014	11.0	19.6	25.8	20.4	63.3	60.1
Guatemala 2005	13.1	38.3	28.6	19.5	58.3	42.2
2010	11.4	33.2	28.0	22.8	60.6	44.0
2014	11.2	32.7	28.1	17.1 (2013)	60.8	50.2
Honduras 2005	13.1	39.2	27.6	20.9	59.3	45.4
2010	11.9	37.5	26.2	18.5	62.0	43.3
2014	13.0	35.8	24.8	18.8	62.2	39.7
Nicaragua 2005	17.7	28.9	23.0	19.7	59.3	51.4
2010	18.8	32.2	24.3	16.5	57.0	51.3
2014	20.5	–	25.7	–	53.8	–
USA 2005	1.0	1.6	21.5	20.6	77.5	77.8
2010	1.1	1.6	20.2	17.2	78.8	81.2
2014	1.2	–	20.4	–	78.4	–

Source: Data available at http://data.un.org/CountryProfile.aspx.

Diverging national trajectories

States parties register heterogeneous CAFTA-DR consequences: the USA, Costa Rica and Nicaragua benefit most while the Northern Triangle countries (Guatemala, Honduras and El Salvador) typically experience political and economic crises.[40] A positive gain in one area may bring a corresponding negative impact in another.

The USA

CAFTA-DR has been a major success for US agricultural exports and ongoing expansion is predicted.[41] Domestic subsidies and genetic modification increased grain yields, out-performing competitors lacking these same inputs. There was also an uptick in exports of processed food

173

Mary Finley-Brook

Table 15.8 Inequality and vulnerability, 2015

Country	Income inequality, quintile ratio	Income inequality, Gini-coefficient	Human Development Index (HDI)	Loss in HDI due to inequality (%)	Employment in the infor-mal sector (%)*	Rural population with improved sanitation facilities (%)	Urban population with improved sanitation facilities (%)
Costa Rica	12.8	48.5	0.776	19.1	20.7	92.3	95.2
Dominican Republic	10.8	47.1 (2010)	0.722	21.8	41.7	75.7	86.2
El Salvador	8.4	41.8	0.680	22.2	37.6	60.0	82.5
Guatemala	12.1	48.7	0.640	29.6	44.5	49.3	77.5
Honduras	15.8	50.6	0.625	29.2	53.3	77.7	86.7
Nicaragua	10.9	47.0	0.645	25.8	47.1	55.7	76.5
USA	9.1	41.1	0.920	13.5	n/a	100.0	100.0

Source: Data available at http://data.un.org/CountryProfile.aspx.

Note: * Defined specifically as the percentage of employed people engaged as unpaid family workers and own-account workers.

Table 15.9 Environmental indicators, 2015

Country	Forest change 1990–2015 (%)	Natural resource deple-tion (% of GNI)	Water withdrawal (% of total renewable water resources)	Threatened species	Carbon diox-ide emissions (metric tons per caput)
Costa Rica	7.5	1.2	2.1	323	1.6 (2013)
Dominican Republic	79.5	1.4	30.4	153	2.2
El Salvador	−29.7	2.1	8.5	83	1.0
Guatemala	−25.4	4.6	2.6	282	0.9
Honduras	−43.6	4.4	no data	294	1.1
Nicaragua	−31.0	7.4	0.9	141	0.8
USA	2.7	0.7	13.6	1,299	16.1 (2013)

Source: Data available at http://data.un.org/CountryProfile.aspx.

and meat, indicators used to demonstrate rising incomes as well as opportunities for future trade profit. Increased consumption of processed foods and meat has contributed to new health pro-blems in CAC countries, including diabetes, heart disease and obesity.[42] Dietary transition cre-ates the need for expensive health care surpassing the capacity of inadequate medical and pharmaceutical systems. CAFTA-DR's investor protections assert the intellectual property rights of drug companies and lay the groundwork for higher cost and lower availability of essential medication.[43] Few CAC countries produce their own medicines and thus remain dependent on foreign supplies.

Costa Rica

Costa Rica has largely transitioned from traditional agriculture to higher-profit advanced manufacturing, a process which began prior to CAFTA-DR. Costa Rica's economic growth was dubbed an 'Intel effect' due to the establishment of semi-conductor and microchip processing facilities.[44] However, Intel closed its largest operation in Costa Rica in 2014. Costa Rica could be a victim of its own success.[45] The country's high-technology sector was based on a free trade zone model, which means that foreign firms import inputs and export products without paying taxes. One implication is the scarcity of state funds to invest in infrastructure. Costa Rica's poor road conditions and inadequate transportation systems create inefficiencies and discourage foreign investment. Costa Rica is also experiencing a 'green gap': although known for its biodiversity and forest conservation, human and industrial waste are dangerously contaminating the air and water.[46] Although Costa Ricans have greater technological training and education than many CAC inhabitants, they are insufficiently skilled to take on the most profitable parts of the supply chain, such as research and development.

Dominican Republic

The Dominican Republic has the largest stock of foreign direct investment and the most diversified exports of the CAC nations.[47] The country moved away from tropical commodities (i.e. sugar, cacao, coffee) towards manufacturing and services;[48] however, gains were poorly distributed and unemployment persists.[49] The economy is reliant on tourism and incentives to attract foreign investment included import and income tax reductions.[50] While some service sector jobs emerged, multiplier effects were minimal and linkages between tourism and other sectors did not occur.

Nicaragua

Nicaragua received advantageous tariff preference levels owing to the fact that it was the poorest member of CAFTA-DR, but these advantages were phased out after a decade.[51] Nicaragua's greatest competitor is Haiti, which received tariff preference level status as part of a CAFTA-DR side agreement.[52] Haitian tariff preference levels are larger and extend longer. Nicaragua's strongest sector, apparel manufacturing, remains vulnerable to the exodus of firms from the country because only a few are Nicaraguan-owned and there has been scant investment of domestic capital. Apparel firms in Nicaragua depend on foreign supplies of inputs like yarn due to low levels of industrialization and technical expertise within the country. Some firms came to Nicaragua because it had the lowest wages in CAFTA-DR countries.[53] The quality of life for low-skilled workers can be precarious. For example, the diet of assembly workers consists of poor-quality foods such as white bread and carbonated soft drinks.[54] Single mothers often leave their children unattended during their working hours, since they cannot afford childcare and schools are too far away.

Northern Triangle

The Northern Triangle has the highest rate of non-political violence in the world.[55] Human rights violations have worsened in recent years.[56] State agents have murdered dozens of human rights defenders.[57] These countries continue to export low-profit raw materials, tropical agricultural commodities, and simple manufactured goods, meaning that they are vulnerable to

Mary Finley-Brook

volatility in terms of trade. Illegal dismissals, health and safety violations, and violence against union members and labour organizers remain widespread, particularly in Guatemala. There was a rise in the number of murders of Guatemalan union organizers following CAFTA-DR, but US pressure for reform was slow and limited.[58] Even after US-Guatemala meetings on labour rights from 2011 to 2014, Guatemala refused to adhere to an enforcement plan. CAFTA-DR failed to inspire improved worker protection, as supporters suggested would occur.[59]

Prospects for deeper integration

There are three areas of expanding transboundary collaboration: securitization, infrastructure integration and environmental oversight.

Securitization

The USA has committed US $2.5 billion to Mexico and Northern Triangle countries for securitization. These securitization efforts (i.e. anti-gang and drug war) allow unscrupulous state actors to use excessive force against civilians.[60] In the absence of effective judicial systems, securitization efforts involve broad sweeps that gather up innocent people or those guilty of minor infractions while ignoring violent criminal networks with links to high levels of government.[61] The US government financially supports Central American militaries in regional securitization efforts even though officials commit atrocities against their own people.[62]

Following CAFTA-DR, the USA experienced the greatest increase in its exports to Guatemala.[63] Narco-money suffuses the entire Guatemalan economy and corrupt leaders across the private and public sectors engage in illicit activities.[64] Expanding trade with Guatemala appears counterproductive to the goal of eradicating drug and criminal syndicates, as profits from US-Guatemala trade bleed into underground economies, including those run by Mexican mafia working in Guatemala. Compromised executives and companies launder money from illicit activities through front operations engaged in CAFTA-DR trade.

A justification for US leadership in securitization is immigration as gang violence and criminal networks increase rates of departure from CAC countries. However, violence and insecurity also contribute to migration as assassinations of environmental activists and of active land defenders are numerous and increasing.[65] In the agricultural sector, the growth of monocrop plantations contributes to high water and agrichemical use, restricts land access, and leads to dispossessions, whereby farmers are evicted using intimidation or murder, rape, kidnapping and torture.[66] Following earlier reforms to improve land distribution, a reconcentration of land holdings is occurring as producers with more political influence, money and weapons displace the poor and powerless.[67]

Infrastructure expansion

International finance institutions promote regional integration of economic infrastructure (i.e. transport, energy, telecommunications) as a base for CAC growth.[68] Central American transboundary projects have developed slowly. Poor-quality road and rail networks and inefficient airports and ports discourage prospective investors.[69] Likewise, limitations to social infrastructure (i.e. water and sewage systems, schools and health care centres) are widespread.[70] In Central America there is a large gap between the current supply of infrastructure and demand, requiring major investments to compete economically and improve standards of living.

Cross-border economic infrastructure could increase efficiency, but project implementation is proving to be challenging. In 2004 regional state utility companies confirmed their plans to build the Central American Electrical Interconnection System (known as SIEPAC), an integrated regional grid of towers and electrical lines covering approximately 2,000 km. Countries with lower production costs can export excess energy and thus create more affordable regional supply. The long-term goal is to connect through Colombia to the Andes and across Mexico to the USA.[71] However, a decade later, several countries have yet to complete their portion of SIEPAC due to property disputes and regulatory delays. For now, low-quality, highly contaminated petroleum is the main source of energy and imported fuel prices are high. New natural gas terminals and pipelines may bring down electricity costs and reduce air pollution, but after a decade of delays to SIEPAC investors remain cautious.[72]

Environmental oversight

Unsustainable extraction and use of natural resources occurred prior to CAFTA-DR and is continuing. There is toxic contamination from mining and industry as well as desertification, deforestation, over-fishing and other ecological problems that are expensive to remedy.[73] Recognizing the threats to the environment, the USA invested millions of dollars in capacity building and transboundary resource oversight. Short-sighted resource use and degradation continues.[74] Even Costa Rica, widely recognized as the region's greenest country, has calamitous waste management systems and dangerously polluted water.[75]

Some experts argue that CAFTA-DR can help to diffuse environmental norms and suggest that US mentoring has contributed to the introduction of new laws and training workshops.[76] Evidence of effective implementation of recent laws or improved capacity is limited, but norm diffusion can be a lengthy process and more time may be necessary for results to appear. However, although CAFTA-DR theoretically created participatory environmental governance, the processes for receiving and utilizing citizen input is flawed and ineffective. Weight of proof is on concerned citizens, who need to have technical knowledge of the FTA's procedures and operations as well as ecological information and investigative skills because cases with partial information are dismissed.[77] By 2017 only 6 per cent of citizen submissions had led to a factual record. There are additional limitations to the process: (1) findings from this process are not legally binding; (2) it excludes laws related to worker safety or health; and (3) it excludes commercial harvest of a natural resource (e.g. mining, logging and fishing), which is widespread and inadequately regulated.

Conclusion

CAFTA-DR has created mixed impacts within and among member countries. Subsistence agriculturalists are particularly vulnerable during trade liberalization, a pattern that is evident after a decade under CAFTA-DR.[78] While trade shifts generally benefit the USA, marginalized CAC populations face economic insecurity exacerbated by violence and human rights violations. Pollution and resource over-extraction intensify vulnerability.[79] At the start of the FTA, trade experts highlighted the need for supplementary social programmes and economic policies to avoid exacerbating inequality and to reduce harm to rural areas, but measures to improve transition or create social safeguards seldom emerged.[80] Investments in social programmes for education and health care are necessary so that economic disparities do not continue to widen.[81] Policy transfers and other initiatives to improve labour rights or environmental

Mary Finley-Brook

protection appear to be mainly symbolic rather than dealing with inadequacies or bringing about substantive change.[82]

Notes

1 Mary Finley-Brook (2012a) 'El Tratado de Libre Comercio entre Centroamérica, República Dominicana y Estados Unidos (CAFTA-DR) y el Desarrollo Desigual', *Mesoamérica*, 54: 54–93; Stacey Frederick, Jennifer Bair and Gary Gereffi (2015) 'Regional Trade Agreements and Export Competitiveness: The Uncertain Path of Nicaragua's Apparel Exports under CAFTA', *Cambridge Journal of Region, Economy, and Society*, 8: 403–20; Danielle M. Perry and Kate A. Berry (2016) 'Central American Integration through Infrastructure Development: A Case Study of Costa Rican Hydropower', *Regions & Cohesion*, 6(1): 96–115.

2 Mary Finley-Brook and Katherine Hoyt (2009) 'CAFTA Opposition: Divergent Networks, Uneasy Solidarities', *Latin American Perspectives*, 36(6): 27–45; Arantxa Guereña (2016) *Unearthed: Land, Power, and Inequality in Latin America*, Oxford: Oxfam.

3 Victor Bulmer-Thomas (1998) 'The Central American Common Market: From Closed to Open Regionalism', *World Development*, 26(2): 313–22; F. Rueda-Junquera (2005) 'Prospects for the Central American Customs Union', *The European Union and Regional Integration:A Comparative Perspective and Lessons for the Americas*, Coral Gables, FL: European Union Center/Jean Monnet Chair, University of Miami, pp. 113–34.

4 CACM members are the CA-5, Belize and Panama. The Dominican Republic is an associate member. Rueda-Junquera, 'Prospects for the Central American Customs Union'.

5 Victor Bulmer-Thomas (1998) 'The Central American Common Market: From Closed to Open Regionalism', *World Development*, 26(2): 313–22.

6 Belize joined SICA in 2000. The Dominican Republic became an associated state in 2004 and a full member in 2013.

7 William M. Leogrande (2007) 'A Poverty of Imagination: George W. Bush's Policy in Latin America', *Journal of Latin American Studies*, 39: 355–85.

8 Marcelo Bucheli (2008) 'Multinational Corporations, Totalitarian Regimes and Economic Nationalism: United Fruit Company in Central America, 1899–1975', *Business History*, 50(4): 433–54.

9 Ginger Williams and Jennifer Disney (2015) 'Militarism and Its Discontents: Neoliberalism, Repression, and Resistance in Twenty-First-Century US-Latin American Relations', *Social Justice*, 41(3): 1–28.

10 Tony Heron (2006) 'An Unraveling Development Strategy? Garment Assembly in the Caribbean Basin after the MultiFibre Arrangement', *Bulletin of Latin American Research*, 25(2): 264–81.

11 J. F. Hornbeck (2012) *The Dominican Republic-Central America-United States Free Trade Agreement (CAFTA-DR): Developments in Trade and Investment*, Washington, DC: Congressional Research Service.

12 Arturo Condo, Forrest Colburn and Luis Rivera (2005) *The United States Central America Free Trade (CAFTA) Agreement: Negotiations and Expected Outcome*, Alajeula: Latin American Center for Competitiveness and Sustainable Development.

13 Mary Finley-Brook (2012b) 'Geoeconomic Assumptions, Insecurity and 'Free' Trade in Central America, *Geopolitics*, 17(3): 629–57.

14 Leogrande, 'A Poverty of Imagination'; Finley-Brook, 'Geoeconomic Assumptions'.

15 Condo *et al.*, '*The United States Central America Free Trade (CAFTA) Agreement*'.

16 Chad P. Bown and Mark Wu (2014) 'Safeguards and the Perils of Preferential Trade Agreements: Dominican Republic Safeguard Measures', *World Trade Review*, 13(2): 179–227.

17 Simon Walker (2011) 'The United States-Dominican Republic-Central America Free Trade Agreement and Access to Medicines in Costa Rica: A Human Rights Impact Assessment', *Journal of Human Rights Practice*, 3(2): 188–213.

18 Finley-Brook and Hoyt, 'CAFTA Opposition'.

19 Finley-Brook, 'El Tratado de Libre Comercio'.

20 Gerda Van Roozendaal (2015) 'The Diffusion of Labour Standards: The Case of US and Guatemala', *Politics and Governance*, 2(2): 18–33.

21 Clare Ribano (2005) *CAFTA: Regional Issues*, Washington, DC: Congressional Research Service.

22 Finley-Brook and Hoyt, 'CAFTA Opposition'.

23 Anita Breuer (2009) 'Costa Rica's 2007 Referendum on the Dominican Republic-Central America Free Trade Agreement (DR-CAFTA): Citizen Participation or Citizen Manipulation?' *Representation*, 45(4): 455–69.

24 Alberto Cortés Ramos (2008) 'Los Límites del Referendo sobre el TLC como instrumento de participación política en Costa Rica', *Revista de Ciencias Sociales*, 3(121): 31–47; Breuer, 'Costa Rica's 2007 Referendum'.

25 Finley-Brook, 'El Tratado de Libre Comercio'.

26 Cortés Ramos, 'Los Límites del Referendo'; Finley-Brook, 'El Tratado de Libre Comercio'.

27 CAFTA-DR entered into force in 2007 in the Dominican Republic and in 2009 for Costa Rica.

28 Heritage Foundation (2017), Index of Economic Freedom, available at www.heritage.org/index/about (accessed 14 October 2017).

29 Hornbeck, *The Dominican Republic-Central America-United States Free Trade Agreement*.

30 Ibid.

31 Orlando J. Peréz, Orlando (2013) 'Gang Violence and Insecurity in Contemporary Central America', *Bulletin of Latin American Research*, 32: 217–34.

32 Whitney Eulich and Catherine Osborne (2015) 'In Latin America, an Exception to Falling Birth Rates Draws New Scrutiny', *Christian Science Monitor*. Available at www.csmonitor.com/World/Americas/2015/1221/In-Latin-America-an-exception-to-falling-birthrates-draws-new-scrutiny (accessed 15 September 2017).

33 Maurizio Bussolo, Samuel Freije, Calvin Z. Djiofack and Melissa Rodríguez (2011) 'Trade Openness and Labor Gender Gaps', in J. Humberto López and Rashmi Shankar (eds) *Making the Most Out of Free Trade Agreements in Central America*, Washington, DC: World Bank, pp. 309–44; Cruz Caridad Bueno (2015) 'Stratification Economics and Grassroots Development: The Case of Low-Income Black Women Workers in Santo Domingo, Dominican Republic', *Review of Black Political Economy*, 42: 35–55.

34 J. Caraballo-Cueto (2016) Free Trade Zones, Liberalization, Remittances, and Tourism, For What? Jobless Growth in the Dominican Republic', *International Journal of Development Issues*, 15(2): 181–200.

35 US Grains Council (2016) 'CAFTA-DR Boosts U.S. Ag. Trade with Central America', available at www.grains.org/news/20160901/shareables-cafta-dr-boosts-us-ag-trade-central-america (accessed 25 September 2017).

36 Finley-Brook, 'Geoeconomic Assumptions'.

37 Hornbeck, *The Dominican Republic-Central America-United States Free Trade Agreement*.

38 Finley-Brook, 'El Tratado de Libre Comercio'.

39 Bueno, 'Stratification Economics'.

40 Hornbeck, *The Dominican Republic-Central America-United States Free Trade Agreement*.

41 USDA (United States Department of Agriculture) (2016) *Spotlight on Guatemala as Trade Flourishes under CAFTA-DR*, Washington, DC: Foreign Agriculture Service.

42 Anne Marie Thow and Corinna Hawkes (2009) The Implications of Trade Liberalization for Diet and Health: A Case Study from Central America', *Globalization and Health*, 5(5): 1–15.

43 Pierguiseppe Pusceddu (2014) 'Access to Medicines in Developing Countries and Free Trade Agreements: The Case of US-DR-CAFTA with Focus on Costa Rica', *Journal of Intellectual Property Rights*, 19: 104–12.

44 Hornbeck, *The Dominican Republic-Central America-United States Free Trade Agreement*.

45 Ilmi Granoff, Monica Araya, Philip Ulbrich, Sam Pickard and Caroline Hayward (2015) *Bridging Costa Rica's Green Growth Gap*, Eschborn, Germany: GIZ.

46 Granoff *et al.*, 'Bridging Costa Rica's Green Growth Gap'; Laura Alvaro (2016) 'Costa Rica Has the Most Contaminated River in Central America', *The Costa Rican Star*, available at http://news.co.cr/costa-rica-contaminated-river-central-america/51577/ (accessed 25 September 2017).

47 Ribano, *CAFTA: Regional Issues*.

48 Leticia Arroyo Abad and Amelia U. Santos-Paulino (2013) 'Trading Development or Developing Trade? The Dominican Republic's Trade, Policies, and Effects in Historical Perspective', *Historia Caribe*, VIII(23): 209–39.

49 Mateusz, J. Filipski, Edward Taylor and Siwa Msangi (2011) 'Effects of Free Trade on Women and Immigrants: CAFTA and the Rural Dominican Republic', *World Development*, 39(10): 1862–77; Bueno, 'Stratification Economics'.

50 Arroyo Abad and Santos-Paulino, 'Trading Development or Developing Trade?'.

51 Jennifer Bair and Gary Gereffi (2014) 'Toward Better Work in Central America: Nicaragua and the CAFTA Context', in Arianna Rossi, Amy Luinstra and John Pickles (eds) *Towards Better Work:*

Understanding Labour in the Apparel Global Value Chains., Basingstoke: Palgrave Macmillan, 251–75; Frederick *et al.*, 'Regional Trade Agreements'.

52 Bair and Gereffi, 'Toward Better Work'.

53 Wendy Sellers Campbell, Idania Lisette Lainez Hernández, Jessica Ceremuga and Hallie Farmer (2010) 'Globalization and Free Trade Agreements: A Profile of a Nicaraguan Factory Community', *Journal of Community Practice*, 18: 440–57; Finley-Brook, 'El Tratado de Libre Comercio'.

54 Campbell *et al.*, 'Globalization and Free Trade Agreements'.

55 WOLA (Washington Office on Latin America) (2017) In Their Own Words: Central Americans Face Violence, Corruption, and Impunity, available at www.wola.org/analysis/central-america-needs-smart-u-s-investments-video/ (accessed 24 September 2017).

56 Jo Tuckman (2014) 'Central American Women Put Their Lives on the Line for Human Rights', *The Guardian*, available at www.theguardian.com/global-development/2014/feb/25/central-america-women-human-rights-initiative (accessed 15 September 2017); Global Witness (2017) 'Defenders of the Earth', available at www.globalwitness.org/en/campaigns/environmental-activists/defenders-earth/ (accessed 24 September 2017); WOLA, 'In Their Own Words'.

57 Tuckman, 'Central American Women Put Their Lives on the Line'; WOLA, 'In Their Own Words'.

58 Finley-Brook, 'Geoeconomic Assumptions'; Finley-Brook, 'El Tratado de Libre Comercio'.

59 Van Roozendal, 'The Diffusion of Labour Standards'.

60 Hal Brands (2011) 'Crime, Irregular Warfare, and Institutional Failure in Latin America: Guatemala as a Case Study', *Studies in Conflict and Terrorism*, 34: 228–47; Peréz, 'Gang Violence and Insecurity'.

61 Brands, 'Crime, Irregular Warfare, and Institutional Failure'.

62 Williams and Disney, 'Militarism and Its Discontents'.

63 USDA, 'Spotlight on Guatemala'.

64 Brands, 'Crime, Irregular Warfare, and Institutional Failure'.

65 Global Witness, 'Defenders of the Earth'.

66 Finley-Brook, 'El Tratado de Libre Comercio'; Mariel Aguilar-Støen (2016) 'Beyond Transnational Corporations, Food and Biofuels: The Role of Extractivism and Agribusiness in Land Grabbing in Latin America', *Forum for Development Studies* 43(1): 155–75; Sara Mingorría (2017) 'Violence and Visibility in Palm Oil and Sugarcane Conflicts: The Case of Polochic Valley, Guatemala', *Journal of Peasant Studies*, available at http://dx.doi.org/10.1080/03066150.2017.1293046 (accessed 5 July 2017).

67 Aguilar-Støen, 'Beyond Transnational Corporations'.

68 Jeannette Lardé and Ricardo J. Sánchez (2014) *The Economic Infrastructure Gap and Investment in Latin America*, Santiago: Economic Commission for Latin America and the Caribbean (CEPAL); Perry and Berry, 'Central American Integration'.

69 Granoff *et al.*, *Bridging Costa Rica's Green Growth Gap'*.

70 Lardé and Sánchez, *The Economic Infrastructure Gap*.

71 Perry and Berry, 'Central American Integration'.

72 Paul Shortell, Kathryn Baragwanath and Carlos Sucre (2014) *Natural Gas in Central America*, Washington, DC: Inter-American Dialogue.

73 J. Timmons Roberts (2013) *Trouble in Paradise: Globalization and Economic Crises in Latin America*, 2nd edn, New York: Routledge.

74 Mingorría, Violence and Visibility in Palm Oil.

75 Granoff *et al.*, *Bridging Costa Rica's Green Growth Gap*; Alvaro, 'Costa Rica Has the Most Contaminated River'.

76 Sikina Jinnah and Abby Lindsay (2016) 'Diffusion through Issue Linkage: Environmental Norms in US Trade Agreements', *Global Environmental Politics*, 16(3): 41–61.

77 J. C. Upton, C. M. Tucker and S. Sanchez (2017) 'The Dominican Republic-Central American Free Trade Agreement's Symbolic Nod to Environmental Protection: Legal Perspectives on the Citizen Submission Process', *Society & Natural Resources*, pp. 1–11.

78 Hornbeck, *The Dominican Republic-Central America-United States Free Trade Agreement*.

79 Finley-Brook, 'El Tratado de Libre Comercio'; Mingorría, 'Violence and Visibility In Palm Oil'.

80 Carlos Felipe Jaramillo and Daniel Lederman (2006) *Challenges of DR-CAFTA: Maximizing the Benefits for Central America*, Washington, DC: World Bank.

81 Hornbeck, *The Dominican Republic-Central America-United States Free Trade Agreement*.

82 Van Roozendaal, 'The Diffusion of Labour Standards'; Upton *et al.*, 'The Dominican Republic-Central American Free Trade Agreement's Symbolic Nod'.

16

CARICOM

Lester Henry

Introduction

The very small, open economies of the largely English-speaking Caribbean, which came together to establish the Caribbean Common Market (CARICOM), have had a fairly long history of involvement in free trade agreements (FTAs). The Treaty of Chaguaramas established CARICOM on 4 July 1973 and was signed by Barbados, Guyana, Jamaica, and Trinidad and Tobago, the four largest English-speaking countries in the region. It was later expanded to include most of the smaller territories, including the Cayman Islands, the British Virgin Islands, Haiti, Suriname and the Bahamas. Unsurprisingly, there exists a wide variety of legal and political differentiation between the nations. Most are independent while some remain colonies, or quasi-colonies, with questionable degrees of control over their own affairs. This makes for a fascinating, or painstaking, approach to external trade agreements because it is often very difficult to obtain consensus within the group and in negotiations with external parties. Nevertheless, the region has successfully concluded a modest number of agreements. Questions remain, however, about their utility due to scant evidence of accrued benefits to the region, past or present.

This chapter presents a brief history and analysis of CARICOM's involvement in external trade agreements. Section two provides a brief description of the region and some basic data. Section three discusses CARICOM's almost involuntary participation in non-reciprocal agreements such as the Caribbean Basin Initiative (CBI), the Caribbean-Canada Trade Agreement (CARIBCAN) and the Lomé Convention. It also focuses on more recent reciprocal agreements with the European Union (EU) and several Latin American countries. Section four assesses the impact of these agreements. Section five concludes with a brief summary of the key issues.

The CARICOM region: a brief description

As noted above, CARICOM is an amalgamation of very small, open economies. No individual member has enough trade in any single commodity to impact world prices. Therefore, individually or as a group they are all price-takers. Despite various attempts at diversification, they have all remained primary producers of commodities, tourism, and to some extent, financial services. Traditionally, export goods comprised mainly sugar cane, bauxite, bananas and oil.

Almost all members were exporters of sugar cane, with Guyana and Jamaica also becoming well known for their exports of bauxite, the raw material in aluminium production. Trinidad and Tobago developed a vibrant oil sector in the early 20th century and later diversified into exporting various energy products such as methanol, urea and liquefied natural gas. The country has also established a successful, but subsidized, light manufacturing sector which exports mainly within the protected CARICOM market.

The islands, with few exceptions, have per capita incomes that are on par or better than most developing countries, and most rank very well in terms of the United Nations Development Programme (UNDP)'s Human Development Index. However, they remain quite vulnerable, especially to climate change and frequent extreme weather patterns, as witnessed by the destructive hurricanes that caused widespread damage in many of the islands in 2017.

The USA remains the major trading partner for most of these islands. As a group, they receive roughly 29 per cent of their imports from the USA and a similar share of their exports goes to the USA. The second largest export partner, Canada, receives around 3 per cent of their total exports. Brazil, Puerto Rico, the United Arab Emirates and three other EU countries account for the other main extraregional export markets for CARICOM goods. The source of regional imports is moderately concentrated in the USA. Gabon, the People's Republic of China, the Russian Federation and Columbia are the other main extraregional suppliers of imports. Brazil, Japan, Venezuela and the United Kingdom are small, but significant, sources of CARICOM imports.

In terms of intraregional trade, the market is dominated by Trinidad and Tobago, which accounts for around 74 per cent of all exports. These are largely made up of petroleum products and light manufacturing goods. Jamaica and Guyana are the main destinations for intraregional exports. Clearly, Trinidad and Tobago with its petroleum sector and manufacturing base has been the major beneficiary of the CARICOM integration movement thus far.

The formulation of the Caribbean Single Market and Economy and complementary trade policy facilitated greater trade within the region and increased access to international markets. New trade agreements were meant to expand the scope of products and services exported by the region and to improve trade and economic relations with other countries. Agreements can foster partnerships with other nations that encourage innovative production methods among exporters, new and competitive products along global value chains and favourable trade pricing.

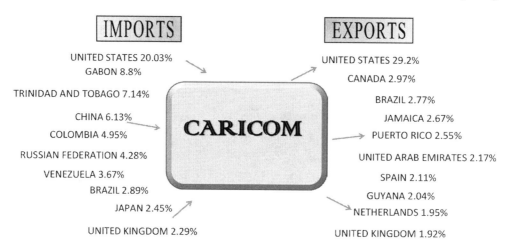

Figure 16.1 CARICOM's main trade partners, 2014 (%)
Sources: www.caricomstats.info/tradsysonline/; www.caricom.org.

CARICOM trade agreements were not only intended to increase ties and cooperation between regional states, but also to enable them to overcome their small size constraints. Furthermore, these agreements were meant to provide a safe and sustainable environment for export firms which would shield them from unfair practices or unlawful competition. Also, information-sharing and mechanisms to promote investment among countries can be helpful in achieving development goals.

It was hoped that trade agreements would promote better policy implementation and sustainable policies, particularly so in the case of the smaller economies in CARICOM. For instance, the policy regime may be quite weak in certain countries, but membership of a trade agreement carries inescapable obligations. Agreements are beneficial because it assists governments by 'locking-in' certain development policies that they would otherwise be tempted to change for political reasons. As Schott states,[1] policymakers want to avoid changing policies that may inadvertently break the rules of a trade agreement. In doing so, these agreements make trade policies and regulations more stable and create a more welcoming environment for investors. The punishment for non-cooperation usually aligns the interests of both parties and ensures that both parties gain by opening their markets to each other. Also, Grossman argued that treaties act as policy tools that help governments to address market failures that constrain exporters in the domestic market.[2]

If an agreement is reached with more powerful countries, the benefits can be one-sided. The weaker group of countries can benefit from aid and institutional investment which would help them to become more developed (this was the intention of the CBI and CARIBCAN). Aid for trade or for infrastructure can provide the necessary funds to make policy goals a reality. Donors can hold countries accountable for the implementation of projects which encourages states to perform efficiently.

As a group, Caribbean nations clearly have a better chance at negotiating with more powerful nations. However, this requires differences to be put aside and common interests to come to the forefront. Although CARICOM member countries differ in size and states of development, the formation of a common market allowed the more developed states (MDCs) such as Barbados, Guyana, Jamaica, and Trinidad and Tobago to cooperate with, and provide support for, the less developed countries.

As a unified regional body, CARICOM has been able to negotiate better terms with outside parties, e.g. the World Trade Organization (WTO). In fact, 'CARICOM has been a very effective political instrument for winning trade and financial concessions with the United States, Canada (CBI and CARIBCAN) and the European Union (Lomé Convention). In addition, favourable non-reciprocal trade agreements with Venezuela and Columbia have been negotiated in 1992 and 1993 respectively'.[3]

This has become important for maintaining the reputation and viability of the future Caribbean Single Market and Economy (CSME). Countries with similar backgrounds and interests can work together to motivate WTO reforms in their favour. CARICOM has been involved with other large organizations and trading blocs such as the African, Caribbean and Pacific (ACP) and EU countries (ACP-EU), the General Agreement on Tariffs and Trade (GATT)/ WTO, UN Conference on Trade and Development (UNCTAD), the Free Trade Area of the Americas (FTAA), the G8, the Organization of American States (OAS) and the Latin American Economic System (Sistema Económico Latinoamericano) (SELA). Being members of GATT/ WTO has allowed most CARICOM countries to enjoy most-favoured-nation (MFN) status with other members of this organization[4]. CARICOM has had a stronger voice in the international arena with greater recognition than any one country would have attained on its own. It has been able to successfully maintain its presence internationally, with influential posts being filled by Caribbean nationals including the Commonwealth Secretary-General and the ACP

Secretary-General.[5] On behalf of developing countries, CARICOM had sought to formally request special treatment and concessions for countries based on their size and level of development in the ongoing Doha Round of trade negotiations.

CARICOM's involvements in trade agreements

Caribbean Basin Initiative

CARICOM's first involvement in a major extraregional trade arrangement was with the Caribbean Basin Initiative (CBI) also known as the Caribbean Basin Economic Recovery Act (CBERA) which was passed by the US Congress in 1983. The CBI was a preferential trade agreement involving several Caribbean countries and the USA. The main aim was to encourage economic expansion and export diversification in the region with most goods securing duty-free access to the US market. It encompassed the CBERA which was implemented in 1984 and the Caribbean Basin Trade Partnership Act (CBTPA) which was launched in 2000. The CBI was expanded to include more goods via the Caribbean Basin Economic Recovery Expansion Act of 1990 (CBI II). CBERA will continue indefinitely, but CBTPA is expected to conclude in 2020.

A total of 17 countries fall under CBERA: Antigua and Barbuda, Aruba, the Bahamas, Barbados, Belize, the British Virgin Islands, Curaçao, Dominica, Grenada, Guyana, Haiti, Jamaica, Montserrat, Saint Kitts (Christopher) and Nevis, Saint Lucia, Saint Vincent and the Grenadines, and Trinidad and Tobago. In addition, eight countries receive benefits (mainly relating to textiles and petroleum) under the CBTPA. These countries are Barbados, Belize, Curaçao, Guyana, Haiti, Jamaica, St Lucia, and Trinidad and Tobago. Finally, Haiti-only textile benefits are provided under the Haitian Hemispheric Opportunity through Partnership Encouragement Act (HOPE), HOPE II and the Haiti Economic Lift Program (HELP). Each of the additional programmes was created by amending the base CBERA law, with HOPE being launched in 2006, followed by HOPE II in 2008, and HELP in 2010.

Although the CBI has managed to expand trade between the Caribbean and the USA, many of the benefits seem to be limited to certain countries. Also, the agreements focus on particular export products which undermine diversification efforts.[6] While the preferences offered under CBTPA and HOPE have been fruitful, there is concern that services and energy-based exports are not being adequately addressed. The presence of other trade agreements, such as the Dominican Republic-Central America-United States Free Trade Agreement (CAFTA-DR), leaves members of the CBI struggling for a share of the US apparel market owing to the flexibility and coverage of those programmes.

The Caribbean-Canada Trade Agreement

Similar to the CBI, Canada offered to CARICOM members a unilateral preferential trade agreement known as CARIBCAN which entered into force on 15 June 1986. It offered eligible Caribbean countries (18 countries receive duty-free benefits: Anguilla, Antigua and Barbuda, Bahamas, Barbados, Belize, Bermuda, the British Virgin Islands, the Cayman Islands, Dominica, Grenada, Guyana, Jamaica, Montserrat, St Kitts and Nevis, St Lucia, St Vincent and the Grenadines, Trinidad and Tobago, and the Turks and Caicos Islands) non-reciprocal duty-free benefits on most goods exported to Canada. A WTO waiver which was extended until 2011 allowed Canada to offer these preferences without being expected to extend the same treatment to other parties.[7] It was accompanied by the Commonwealth Caribbean Countries Tariff which was applied to

Canadian goods entering the Caribbean. In order for Caribbean exports to enjoy preferential access, rules of origin require at least 60 per cent of the inputs of the good to be derived from member countries or Canada, with final production occurring in Caribbean countries.[8] However, some of the goods excluded from these benefits included textiles, apparel, handbags and methanol.[9]

As with the CBI, the arrangement was meant to foster both economic development and deeper cooperation between Caribbean countries and Canada. The programme benefits were designed to aid Commonwealth Caribbean countries by providing development assistance. However, not all observers are convinced of the true benefits of the agreement to CARICOM members. For example, one of the most famous products from the region is rum. In spite of CARICAN, Caribbean rum still faces stiff obstacles in the Canadian market. As Chaitoo[10] asserts, 'Apart from the highly controlled and inefficient system of provincial liquor board monopolies on the sale of alcohol, Caribbean rum faces two other obstacles. Under Bill S-38 (2005) rum may only be sold under the name "Caribbean" if it has been made from sugarcane products of a Commonwealth Caribbean country, or if it has been imported in bulk from such a country and subjected to blending either with other Caribbean rum or with Canadian rum 'in proportions that result in 1 to 1.5% Canadian rum by volume in the final product'. It is perhaps, not surprising then, that after many years of the promised concessions of CARIBCAN, in 2014 Canada only accounted for roughly 3 per cent of the region's exports.

It is important to note that Canada plays a much bigger role in the Caribbean due to its long and well-established presence in the financial services sector. For over a century, Canadian banks and insurance companies have dominated regional markets. Canadian financial institutions have enjoyed unfettered and non-reciprocal access to CARICOM's markets. This need to address issues of trade in financial services along with the general trend towards more WTO-compliant FTAs is what prompted Canada to engage the region in negotiations for the establishment of a CARICOM-Canada FTA.

Negotiations started in 2007. However, after seven attempts at formal negotiations, to date no agreement has been reached. According to a Canadian Ministry of Trade website,[11] 'Unfortunately, despite Canada's extensive accommodation and negotiating flexibility during this period, Canada and CARICOM were not able to reach an agreement. Given the lengthy negotiations and that Canada and CARICOM continue to have different objectives for a Canada-CARICOM trade agreement, no additional negotiations are planned at this date.' Given this predicament, the CARIBCAN arrangement has been extended another waiver by the WTO until 2023.

From the Lomé Convention to EU-EPA

Initially, the Lomé Convention governed the trade relationships with the ACP and Europe. It facilitated extensive preferential treatment (duty-free access with no quantity limits) for exports entering the EU. It came into force in 1975 and became embroiled in controversy because the USA challenged that it was inconsistent with WTO rules. Lomé II was signed in 1979, Lomé III in 1984 and Lomé IV in 1989, and was extended to more member countries in 1995.[12] In 2000 it was replaced by the ACP-EU Partnership Agreement (known as the Cotonou Agreement).[13] The duration of the agreement was to be 20 years with revisions to be made every five years. This agreement was meant to enhance the economic, cultural, social and political development of these countries. It upholds the importance of sustainable development and the integration of members into the global environment. A long-term goal of the EU was to transform previously non-reciprocal arrangements into reciprocal Economic Partnership Agreements (EPAs) with the ACP countries. However, the Dominican Republic was included in the negotiations with CARICOM and hence the new grouping became known as CARIFORUM by the ACP Caribbean signatory countries.[14]

By far the most intensive trade agreement ever engaged in by CARICOM was this agreement with the EU. The negotiations for the EU and Caribbean EPA began in 2004 in Jamaica. The CARIFORUM-EU EPA was signed in 2008 and approved by Parliament in 2009,[15] a free trade and economic integration agreement with 15 Caribbean states: CARICOM: (Antigua and Barbuda, the Bahamas, Barbados, Belize, Dominica, Grenada, Guyana, Haiti (signed in 2009), Jamaica, St Kitts and Nevis, St Lucia, St Vincent and the Grenadines, Suriname, and Trinidad and Tobago) and the Dominican Republic. This EPA was the first of its kind between the EU and one of the member blocs of the ACP states. The agreement combined trade objectives with development and cooperation goals. The tariff liberalization schedule is shown in Table 16.1. A generous phase-in period of 20 years for almost full liberalization was one of the hallmarks of the agreement.

It promoted reciprocal preferential access (51 per cent of goods imported from the EU are tariff-free) which expands the markets available for Caribbean exports and the options available to consumers. The agreement was supported by aid targeted at improving trade and the export competitiveness of the region. Some of main exports to the EU are resource-based (petroleum and minerals) and primary commodities (bananas and sugar). There was concern that the agreement might not be sufficient to promote more value-added products. The agreement has a broader scope compared to other agreements because it covers both trade in goods and services.[16] By facilitating investment within the region and improving trade relations between CARIFORUM member countries, the EPA was also regarded as having a strong development component. It was supported by investment in institutions such as implementation units throughout the CARIFORUM countries to assist in capacity building and to facilitate better dialogue between the two parties. However, the intended benefits of the EPA may be short-lived if constraints such as high input and transaction costs and private sector problems continue to prevent countries from exploiting new export opportunities (especially in services).[17]

Table 16.1 CARIFORUM tariff liberalization schedule

CARIFORUM-EC Trade			
CARIFORUM Exports to the EU	US $1.38 billion		
CARIFORUM Imports from the EU	US $2.45 billion		
of which:			
	% Imports from EU	*% Total trade*	*% Tariff lines*
Liberalized at application (2008)	52.8%	70.0%	3.0%
Liberalized within 5 yrs (1.1.2013)	56.0%	72.0%	17.1%
Liberalized within 10 yrs (1.1.2018)	61.1%	75.3%	63.4%
Liberalized within 15 yrs (1.1.2023)	82.7%	89.3%	84.7%
Liberalized within 20 yrs (1.1.2028)	84.6%	90.5%	88.4%
Liberalized within EPA (1.1.2033)	86.9%	92.0%	90.2%
Excluded from EPA	13.1%	8%	9.8%

Source: CARICOM Secretariat (2008). Available at www.caricom.org.

CARICOM bilateral agreements: Venezuela, Columbia, Dominican Republic, Costa Rica, and Cuba

The CARICOM-Venezuela partial scope agreement was signed in 1992 and is non-reciprocal in nature. Imports from Venezuela are subject to duties in CARICOM member states of the MFN type (Common External Tariff), but Venezuela offers free access to CARICOM products entering its market. The arrangement sought to confer mutual benefits to both parties in the areas of trade, investment and development. Some products gained immediate duty-free access while others experienced a phased reduction in tariff rates from 1993 to 1996. There may be revisions to the non-reciprocal arrangement for MDC members of CARICOM, but negotiations are forthcoming.

The agreement sought to promote trade financing where necessary and cooperation in the services sector. The rules of origin had to be met in order to be eligible for benefits. Certain products such as fresh fruit, live animals, fish, live plants, and spices such as curry, saffron and bay leaf are considered as Caribbean in origin. Products that use inputs from countries outside the region will be considered eligible if the cost, insurance and freight of the inputs from extraregional countries is not greater than 40 per cent of the free on board export value. The agreement includes safeguard mechanisms that may be implemented to protect the external position of the country or to prevent any deterioration in the production of domestic goods.

The CARICOM-Colombia partial scope agreement began in 1994 and again sought to improve the integration movement within the region by fostering greater economic and technical cooperation between both parties. It was meant to promote greater exports and investment in the region while encouraging private sector involvement in the process. In terms of trade liberalization, CARICOM states were granted tariff-free access (milk, cement, pitch and other chemicals like sulphuric acid) and gradually reduced tariffs on other products originating from member states. Some imports from Colombia were duty-free (butter, garlic, seeds, medicines, tobacco, etc.) and others are subject to the MFN tariff /non-preferential duty, but for least developed countries (LDCs) such measures were not necessary. There were also temporary precautionary measures such as tariff rates which can be implemented to protect the local industry and the economic position of the country in the event of a serious threat. Cooperation is a key objective of this arrangement. The agreement fosters the sharing of information between both parties that would allow for the exploitation of joint investment opportunities. Another key aspect was deepening cooperation in research ventures, human resource and environmental management, tourism, energy and educational opportunities such as graduate studies and institutional exchanges.[18]

The CARICOM-Dominican Republic free trade agreement was entered into on 22 August 1998, but excluded Haiti and the Bahamas. The protocol to enact the agreement was signed in 2000. It was the first FTA negotiated by the Caribbean region and enhanced the strength of both parties in trade negotiations. However, the member countries applied the protocol at different times: Suriname in 2005, Guyana in 2004, the Dominican Republic in 2002 and Barbados, Jamaica, and Trinidad and Tobago in 2001.[19] The agreement aimed to achieve barrier-free trade between the two parties with initially only a few goods being excluded until 2005. For goods such as pasta, sausages and biscuits the reduction of the tariff would be gradual. For certain meats, fish and milk, the MFN duty would be applied (every country was subject to the same duty regardless of origin). There were also special trade arrangements for certain agricultural products, with MFN duties being applied in particular seasons and CARICOM's oil and fat arrangement covering certain products that would not be subject to free trade.[20]

The MDCs of the region (Jamaica, Trinidad and Tobago, Barbados, Guyana, and Suriname) are subject to reciprocity with the Dominican Republic. Once again, the agreement was non-reciprocal for the LDCs of CARICOM given their existing conditions, but this was not a permanent measure and was to be reviewed in 2005.[21] The intention was not only to liberalize trade in goods, but to include free capital movement and the liberalization of the services sector. There are hopes of establishing similar sanitary and phytosanitary mechanisms in line with WTO standards, cooperating in key sectors (agriculture, finance, mining, tourism, tele-communications, etc.), deepening investment opportunities and strengthening ties with the active involvement of the private sector in joint investment ventures. The agreement seeks to discourage practices that can disadvantage participants in either market, such as unfair competi-tion via export subsidies, low quality imports (dumping) and other distortionary factors.[22] There are mechanisms that automatically come into effect to protect local industries if there are concerns that producers may suffer due to excessive imports of similar products.[23]

The CARICOM-Cuba Trade and Economic Cooperation Agreement became official in 2000. This partial scope agreement aimed to enhance integration within the Latin American and Caribbean region. It was intended to expand trade in goods and services, strengthen financial relationships, increase cooperation and investment and promote healthy competition. As the agreement outlined, a free trade area will facilitate 'more dynamic and balanced economic and trade relations based on mutual benefits and a gradual reduction in customs tariffs and trade obstacles'.[24] Several goods are expected to enter the Cuban market freely such as beer, fish and agricultural products. This will be reciprocated by allowing Cuban imports such as pharma-ceuticals, and duty-free access to CARICOM markets with the MDC states being able to charge duties on other goods.[25] The proposed advantages of this arrangement are increased market size beyond the region, enhanced options for consumers and greater possibilities for investment.

The CARICOM-Costa Rica free trade agreement was negotiated successfully in 2003 and officially signed in 2004. It entered into force with CARICOM members at different times: Barbados in 2006, Belize in 2011, Guyana in 2006 and Trinidad and Tobago in 2005.[26] In line with other agreements, some products were traded freely while others were subjected to duties which were to be gradually phased out by 2007 (starting in 2005) and certain products (under the oils and fats agreement) are protected. Also, the region's MDCs each experienced different levels of 'access' for 'special' traded products with Costa Rica.[27] Not only did the agreement hope to promote trade by the region having access to a market of four million, but it is expected to have economic, political and cultural benefits.

The MDCs of CARICOM offer duty-free access to Costa Rican products while the LDCs (the Organisation of Eastern Caribbean States (OECS) and Belize) of the region enjoyed a non-reciprocal arrangement that gave them free access to that market. In order to benefit from preferential rates, products must meet certain rules of origin.[28]

Assessing CARICOM's involvement in trade agreements

Taking into consideration the CBI, the EU EPA, as well as FTAs with assorted Latin American countries, there is not much evidence to support the view that the CARICOM region has gained significant benefits from any of them. Several studies have confirmed this assessment across all the agreements. Beginning with the CBI, Whittingham, after expressing disappoint-ment at the observed data, noted that 'Given the fact that the Caribbean Basin Economic Recovery Act covered mainly trade in goods, the appropriate sectors on which to focus atten-tion are agriculture and manufacturing. Here, too, the impact has not been visibly significant to date'.[29] Evidence suggested that Costa Rica and the Dominican Republic appeared to have benefited from the American initiative, but CARICOM members did not share in these gains.

In the case of the CARIBCAN, again there is no clear evidence that CARICOM has received any major boost in exports stemming from the initiative. Many of the goods included were already entering Canada duty-free under the Generalized System of Preferences (the so-called enabling clause) or via MFN clauses. In 2007 for example, 86.5 per cent of CARICOM duty-free imports into Canada entered under MFN conditions. This fact perhaps dampened the appetite for the proposed CARICOM-Canada FTA. Also, Canada was seeking parity with the CARIFORUM-EU EPA and this seemed to present a critical challenge.

Almost ten years after the signing of the EPA with the EU, the CARICOM region has again only seen very meagre returns. McLean *et al.* concluded that 'for the majority of CARICOM countries the Agreement has yet to deliver the broad-based welfare and trade gains expected'.[30] They went on to argue that 'the Dominican Republic has largely benefitted because of its capacity to implement the Agreement and its trade preparedness'. Furthermore, in a specific case study of Barbados, Lorde and Alleyne[31] found the trade and revenue impact on the country to be 'relatively small' with estimated changes to be of the order of 1 per cent. In fact, one of the major concerns prior to the signing of the agreement was the potential loss of tariff revenue, especially among the smaller islands, since they rely more heavily on this as a source of government revenue. Indeed, subsequent findings suggest that this was a legitimate concern as McLean *et al.* asserted that all of the CARICOM countries examined in detail were expected to show 'a loss in tariff revenues'.[32]

Given the above, one may question why CARICOM pursued the EPA. One simple answer is that the members had no choice as they were caught up in the drift away from non-reciprocal trade agreements. Perhaps another explanation can be found in the non-trade aspects of the agreement. More specifically, the quantum of promised developmental assistance may have been the perfect carrot. According to European Commission briefing documents on the EPA, the EU is funding implementation structures throughout the Caribbean, including a €47 millon programme for governments and businesses, and investing €59 million to help governments with various integration efforts in the region.[33] Therefore, the real benefits to the CARICOM members may lie in these outlays on the part of the EU and not in any gains from trade.

With respect to CARICOM agreements with Latin American countries, the limited empirical studies point in a similar direction to those already discussed. For example, Felix *et al.* [34] found that 'CARICOM did not benefit from the agreements signed with Dominican Republic and Costa Rica' and that 'trade potential remained high throughout the period 2001/ 2010, thus showing that CARICOM's exports in the selected groups did not capture any significant market shares in either the Dominican Republic or Costa Rica'. Therefore, the inability of the region to capitalize on trade agreements stands out even with neighbouring Latin America countries that are much closer in geographical distance than the EU.

The overall poor performance of CARICOM in trade agreements reflects a low utilization rate of these agreements by its members. As Table 16.2 suggests, while fluctuating at times, CARICOM's exports to trading partners that it shares agreements with, has been declining in many cases. However, trading with more developed countries has been relatively stable. A combination of factors has led to less than satisfactory results. These outcomes can be attributed to, 'poor economic infrastructure, low and declining competitiveness, weak institutions, fragmented production systems and limited productive capacity'.[35]

Summary and conclusion

The CARICOM region has engaged in a number of trade agreements with larger and more sophisticated trading partners, all with the promise of improved opportunities for greater exports

Lester Henry

Table 16.2 Shares of exports to various CARICOM trading partners, 2007–16

Years	Columbia	Costa Rica	Venezuela	Dominican Republic	Cuba	European Union (EU 27)	USA
2007	1.42	0.48	0.08	2.07	0.12	15.30	49.28
2008	1.15	0.57	0.10	2.43	0.19	18.60	45.59
2009	0.81	0.42	0.08	1.01	0.04	16.74	47.72
2010	1.81	0.83	0.49	0.92	0.14	11.79	43.32
2011	1.16	0.39	1.08	1.20	0.11	15.37	45.12
2012	1.30	0.05	0.79	0.78	0.08	13.71	44.63
2013	3.78	1.12	1.01	1.26	0.21	11.93	39.50
2014	2.00	0.38	0.75	0.89	0.04	11.41	43.89
2015	2.45	0.43	0.60	1.19	0.05	13.42	39.91
2016	0.87	0.19	0.03	0.06	0.04	13.21	36.44

Source: International Trade Centre (ITC) Trade Map, available at www.trademap.org/.

Note: Based on both mirror and reporter data.

and diversification of their economies. While the CBI and CARIBCAN were imposed unilaterally by the USA and Canada, respectively, and not 'true' trade agreements, they were important forerunners to the problems that the regions would face when participating in actual agreements. The EPA with the EU was negotiated within a context of great turmoil among many regional actors. Perhaps if it were not for the threats of possible sanctions, the agreement might have never been signed. Generally, the main benefit to CARICOM of the EPA has been the development and technical assistance provided through its support programmes and not via gains from trade. The region's failure to capitalize on the opportunities offered by trade agreements is perhaps the most glaring issue of all.

On a broader level, the islands often lack cohesion in trade policy and hence some of the larger countries like Jamaica and Trinidad and Tobago often negotiate their own bilateral agreements. The collapse of the possible Canada–CARICOM FTA is a reminder of the difficulty in obtaining consensus among such a varied group of small states. However, the success they have had in negotiating and maintaining special or differential treatment and extracting development assistance from larger partners has been very reassuring.

Notes

1 J. J. Schott (ed.) (2004) Free Trade Agreements: US Strategies and Priorities, New York: Columbia University Press.
2 G. M. Grossman (2016) 'The Purpose of Trade Agreements', Handbook of Commercial Policy, 1, Amsterdam: North Holland, pp. 379–434.
3 Uziel Nogueira (1997) 'The Integration Movement in the Caribbean at a Crossroads: Towards a New Approach to Integration', Intal (Institute for the Integration of Latin America and the Caribbean) Working Paper Series, Paper No 1, April, p. 11.
4 A. Jessen (2005) 'CARICOM Report Number 2' (Subregional Integration Report Series CARICOM/Informes Subregionales de Integración CARICOM; n. 2) (No. 2), BID-INTAL, Turkeyen, Greater Georgetown: CARICOM Secretariat.
5 M. Schiff (2002) Regional Integration and Development in Small States, Washington, DC: World Bank, available at https://elibrary.worldbank.org/doi/pdf/10.1596/1813-9450-2797.
6 J. F. Hornbeck (2011) 'U.S. Trade Policy and the Caribbean: From Trade Preferences to Free Trade Agreements', Washington, DC: Congressional Research Service.

7 http://ctrc.sice.oas.org/Trade/caribcan/Caribcan_e.asp.

8 http://ctrc.sice.oas.org/Trade/caribcan/741.pdf.

9 www.bidc.org/documentation-handbook/section-ii/caribcan.

10 Ramesh Chaitoo (2013) 'Time to Rethink and Re-energize Canada-CARICOM Relations', *Caribbean Journal of International Relations & Diplomacy*, 1(1), February: 39–67.

11 http://international.gc.ca/trade-commerce/trade-agreements-accords-commerciaux/agr-acc/caricom/fta-ale/background-contexte.aspx?lang=eng.

12 www.sice.oas.org/TPD/CAR_EU/CAR_EU_e.asp.

13 http://caricom.org/the-cariforum-eu-epa-in-context.

14 www.cepal.org/publicaciones/xml/1/23581/L.66.pdf.

15 http://trade.ec.europa.eu/doclib/docs/2009/september/tradoc_144912.pdf.

16 http://ec.europa.eu/trade/policy/countries-and-regions/regions/caribbean/.

17 www.swp-berlin.org/fileadmin/contents/products/research_papers/2015_RP06_scm.pdf.

18 www.sice.oas.org/Trade/CARICOME_1.ASP.

19 www.sice.oas.org/Trade/Ccdr/English/Ccdr_in.asp.

20 www.tradeboard.gov.jm/tblweb/mid_Article2.php?id=135&menuID=.

21 http://caricom.org/media-center/communications/press-releases/caricom-dominican-republic-free-trade-agreement.

22 http://caricom.org/media-center/communications/press-releases/basic-information-on-free-trade-agreement-between-caricom-and-the-dominican.

23 www.carib-export.com/login/wp-content/uploads/2009/08/CARICOM%20DR%20FTA.pdf.

24 CARICOM-CUBA Trade Agreement, available at http://cms2.caricom.org/documents/15338-caricom-cuba_trade_and_economic_cooperation_agreement.pdf.

25 http://caricom.org/media-center/communications/news-from-the-community/cuba-agrees-to-extension-on-trade-agreement-with-caricom.

26 www.sice.oas.org/Trade/crcrcom_e/crcrcomind_e.asp.

27 http://caricom.org/media-center/communications/press-releases/caricom-and-costa-rica-initial-free-trade-agreement.

28 http://caricom.org/communications/view/caricom-and-costa-rica-sign-free-trade-agreement.

29 Wilfred Whittingham (1989) 'The United States Government's Caribbean Basin Initiative', *CEPAL Review*, 39, December: 73–92.

30 Sheldon McLean, Errol Humphrey and Jeetendra Khadan (2014) 'Trade and Development Nexus: Reflections on the Performance of Trade in Goods under the CARIFORUM-European Union Partnership Agreement: A CARIFORUM Perspective', LC/CAR/L.448. ECLAC Regional Sub-Headquarters for the Caribbean, Port-of-Spain, p. 7. Available at https://www.cepal.org/en/publications/38275-trade-and-development-nexus-reflections-performance-trade-goods-under-cariforum.

31 T. Lorde and A. Alleyne (2016) 'Estimating the Trade and Revenue Impacts of the European Union-CARIFORUM Economic Partnership Agreement: A Case Study of Barbados', Cave Hill Department of Economics, Working Paper Series, 1–16, June.

32 Ibid., p. 22.

33 European Commission (2012) 'How the EU Is Putting the EPA into Practice', Brussels: European Commission.

34 See Nkosi Felix, Govind Seepersad, Randel Esnard and Ranjit H. Singh (2012) 'An Evaluation of the Impact of Free Trade Agreements on the Competitiveness of the CARICOM Region', 48th Annual Meeting, 20–26 May, Playa del Carmen, Mexico 253708, Caribbean Food Crops Society.

35 See McClean, 'Trade and Development Nexus', p. 22.

17

Mexico's approach to preferential agreements[1]

Luz Maria de la Mora Sanchez

Introduction

Trade policy has been the cornerstone of Mexico's economic growth since the early 1990s. Mexico has built a strategy of integration into the world economy through its membership of the World Trade Organization (WTO) and an open regionalism strategy that has resulted in the creation of a network of 12 free trade agreements (FTAs) with 46 countries, eight economic complementation agreements with Latin American partners, and 32 bilateral investment treaties (BITs) with 33 countries in Latin America, the Asia-Pacific region, Europe and the Middle East.[2]

In this chapter, I explain how Mexico's open regionalism has made it a key player in international trade. I look at the motivations behind its decision to go beyond multilateral liberalization commitments and to seek to establish numerous bilateral and regional trade agreements (RTAs) with trading partners in North, Central and South America as well as with European countries, the Middle East and Asia. Since the 1990s this regionalism has enabled Mexico to integrate into global value chains consistent with its export-oriented development model. The creation of a network of FTAs has been decisive for the dynamism that Mexican trade and investment flows have experienced. In 2016 Mexico was the eighth largest trading nation globally, the largest in Latin America,[3] the 15th largest recipient of foreign direct investment (FDI) worldwide,[4] and international trade accounted for 78 per cent of its gross domestic product (GDP).[5]

Mexico's strategy of creating a network of RTAs was designed with the USA at the core based on three 'pillars'. The first is ensuring preferential access for its exports, mainly but not exclusively to the US market, consistent with an export-oriented model of development. The second pillar relates to opening up the Mexican market to imports of inputs, machinery and equipment that are vital to maintaining a competitive export platform. The third involves using RTAs to attract FDI to support Mexico's manufacturing export-oriented sector.

In this chapter I analyse the way in which Mexico's RTAs have been developed by forging relationships with North America, Europe, Latin America, Asia and the Middle East. I also elaborate on the challenges that Mexico's regional trade strategy faces as a result of the election of Donald Trump to the US presidency and the impact that a more protectionist US trade policy might have on Mexico.

I conclude that Mexico's open regionalism will continue to exist, even if the North American Free Trade Agreement (NAFTA) is renegotiated, since the Mexican economy is highly dependent on the global marketplace. I address the perceived need to diversify export markets and create new FTAs with new partners.

Mexico's FTA network

Since the mid-1980s Mexico's economy has opened up considerably having shifted from an inward-looking development model to an export-oriented one. As part of the structural adjustment programmes negotiated with the World Bank and the International Monetary Fund to address the 1982 debt crisis, Mexico opened its economy. It eliminated almost all of its import permits, reduced average import duties from 100 per cent to 10 per cent and established a 20 per cent tariff ceiling across the board.[6] Since then, trade liberalization has been central to Mexico's economic policy and has also been used as an instrument of macroeconomic stability and competitiveness. Since the mid-1980s Mexico has showed consistency in its pursuit of trade liberalization even in the face of transition to multi-party democracy and changes in partisan control of the federal government.

On 24 August 1986, at the start of the Uruguay Round negotiations, Mexico became the 92nd member of the General Agreement on Tariffs and Trade (GATT). Consistent with its export-led growth strategy, it made sense to ensure that Mexican exports were eligible for most-favoured-nation and national treatment.[7] Given Mexico's dependence on international trade, the smooth operation of an international rules-based trading system has been a priority of its trade policy agenda. Since the WTO Doha Round of trade negotiations was launched in 2001, Mexico has remained an active supporter.[8]

In the early 1990s Mexico launched a very aggressive strategy of open regionalism and reached out to partners in North America, Europe, Latin America, the Middle East and Asia. After over two decades of negotiations, Mexico has created a network of 12 FTAs with 46 countries (see Table 17.1).

Through these bilateral and regional trade negotiations, Mexico deepened its multilateral liberalization commitments in trade in goods and services as well as in investment protection thus giving a boost to its trade and investment flows. Today, almost 80 per cent of Mexico's total trade is done with its trading partners under preferential conditions offered by its 12 RTAs (see Table 17.2).

In addition to its network of 12 FTAs of which nine include an Investment Chapter,[9] Mexico has negotiated BITs in order to attract foreign capital. BITs help to address political risk and offer protection guarantees to investors and their investments. Mexico has negotiated 32 BITs with 33 countries as a means of making the country a more attractive investment location (see Table 17.3).

In what follows, I analyse Mexico's region-wide FTAs as well as their scope and results in terms of trade and investment.

The North American Free Trade Agreement

The North American Free Trade Agreement (NAFTA) came into effect on 1 January 1994 and was the first FTA to be signed between a developing and two developed economies.[10] NAFTA heralded the beginning of a new era of regional and bilateral FTAs and set a new standard for those negotiated by its three members. It became the model for other FTAs including the failed Free Trade Area of the Americas (FTAA).[11]

Luz Maria de la Mora Sanchez

Table 17.1 Mexico's network of RTAs

Agreement/partner(s)	Date of signature	Entry into force
1. NAFTA (Canada–Mexico–USA)	17 December 1992	1 January 1994
2. Colombia	13 June 1994	1 January 1995
3. European Union	8 December 1997	1 October 2000
4. Chile	17 April 1998	1 August 1999
5. Israel	10 April 2000	1 July 2001
6. European Free Trade Association (EFTA)	27 November 2000	1 July 2001
7. Uruguay	15 November 2003	15 July 2004
8. Japan	17 September 2004	1 April 2005
9. Peru	06 April 2011	1 February 2012
10. Central America (Costa Rica, El Salvador, Guatemala, Honduras and Nicaragua)	22 November 2011	Costa Rica: 1 July 2013 El Salvador and Nicaragua: 1 September 2012 Guatemala: 1 September 2013 Honduras: 1 January 2013
11. Pacific Alliance	10 February 2014	1 May 2016
12. Panama	3 April 2014	1 July 2015

Source: OAS, Foreign Trade Information System (Mexico; Trade Agreements). Available at http://sice.oas.org/ctyindex/MEX/MEXagreements_e.asp (accessed 1 May 2017).

Table 17.2 Mexico's trade with RTA partners, 2016 (US $, billions)

RTAs	Total trade	Share in Mexico's total trade
1. NAFTA (Canada–USA)	502.3	66.00%
2. European Union	61.8	8.11%
3. Japan	21.5	2.83%
4. Central America (Costa Rica, El Salvador, Guatemala, Honduras and Nicaragua)	6.8	0.90%
5. Colombia	4.2	0.55%
6. Chile	3.0	0.40%
7. European Free Trade Association (EFTA)	2.6	0.34%
8. Peru	1.9	0.26%
9. Israel	0.9	0.12%
10. Panama	0.9	0.12%
11. Uruguay	0.5	0.07%
12. Pacific Alliance (see Chile, Colombia and Peru)	–	–
Total	606.4	79.7%

Mexico's approach to PTAs

Table 17.3 Mexico's network of BITs

Agreement/partner(s)	Date of signature	Entry into force
1. Argentina	13 November 1996	22 July 1998
2. Australia	23 August 2005	21 July 2007
3. Austria	29 June 1998	26 March 2001
4. Bahrain	29 November 2012	30 July 2014
5. Belarus	4 September 2008	27 August 2009
6. BLEU (Belgium-Luxembourg Economic Union)	27 August 1998	18 March 2003
7. China	11 July 2008	6 June 2009
8. Cuba	30 May 2001	29 March 2002
9. Czech Republic	4 April 2002	13 March 2004
10. Denmark	13 April 2000	24 September 2000
11. Finland	22 February 1999	20 August 2000
12. France	12 November 1998	11 October 2000
13. Germany	29 August 1998	23 February 2001
14. Greece	30 November 2000	27 September 2002
15. Haiti	7 May 2015	Pending
16. India	21 May 2007	23 February 2008
17. Iceland	24 June 2005	27 April 2006
18. Italy	24 November 1999	4 December 2002
19. Kuwait	22 February 2013	28 April 2016
20. The Netherlands	13 May 1998	1 October 1999
21. Panama	11 October 2005	14 December 2006
22. Portugal	11 November 1999	4 September 2000
23. Singapore	12 November 2009	3 April 2011
24. Slovakia	26 November 2007	8 April 2009
25. Republic of Korea	14 November 2000	6 July 2002
26. Spain	10 November 2006	3 April 2008
27. Sweden	3 October 2000	1 July 2001
28. Switzerland	10 July 1995	14 March 1996
29. Trinidad and Tobago	3 October 2006	16 September 2007
30. Turkey	17 December 2013	Pending
31. United Kingdom	12 May 2006	25 July 2007
32. Uruguay	30 June 1999	1 July 2002

Source: Mexico, Secretaría de Economía. Available at www.gob.mx/se/acciones-y-programas/comercio-exterior-paises-con-tratados-y-acuerdos-firmados-con-mexico (accessed 1 May 2017).

When NAFTA came into effect in 1994, Mexico was the only developing country to enjoy preferential access to the US and Canadian markets, and this allowed it to become an export platform from which any investor established in Mexico could sell to the US market under preferential conditions. Mexico sought to become the ideal location from which to export manufactured products, especially to the US market, given that it could offer to investors its proximity, the preferential access under NAFTA and access to a skilled and cheap labour force.

195

NAFTA allowed Mexico to integrate into regional value chains. Consequently, Mexico has become the USA's second largest source of imports and second largest export market. US-Mexico trade increased roughly by a factor of six, increasing from US $88 billion in 1993 to $482 billion in 2016.[12] For Mexico, the USA represents its top export market with 80 per cent of its total foreign sales. NAFTA also created a market for Mexico in Canada with which the country so far had carried out very little trade, making it Mexico's third largest export destination and accounting for 2.79 per cent of its exports in 2016. At the same time, Mexico became Canada's fourth largest export market and third largest source of imports. In terms of FDI, between 1999 and the first half of 2017, US and Canadian capital inflows into Mexico reached close to $256.4 billion (roughly 20 per cent of Mexico's GDP), which amounted to 52.7 per cent of its FDI stock.[13]

Despite being in place for more than 24 years, some NAFTA provisions have yet to be fully implemented. For example, the US government deliberately decided to violate the agreement in the case of land transportation services.[14] In the case of the temporary entry of people into the country, there has been little interest in implementing NAFTA provisions which allow for the liberalization of 60 different professions (Appendix 1603.D.1) that could provide services in North America. After more than 20 years, only a few Mutual Recognition Agreements – for engineers, accountants and architects – have been negotiated and implemented. Another area in which the Mexican private sector has yet to tap NAFTA opportunities has to do with the US and Canadian governments' procurement markets as provided for in the agreement; Mexican companies have not taken advantage of the public procurement provisions.[15]

While NAFTA pioneered provisions for the liberalization of trade in services, Mexico's participation is still poor and it ranks 23th as a services exporter and 22nd as an importer of services worldwide. Mexico's share in world services exports represented 0.5 per cent and 0.63 per cent of world services imports.[16]

This dynamic trade and investment growth notwithstanding, few disputes in Mexico-US trade have taken place. The NAFTA Secretariat reports only two disputes between Mexico and the USA at government level (Chapter 20 of NAFTA). The first one dates from 1998 and concerned the US Safeguard Action Taken on Broom Corn Brooms from Mexico[17] and in 2001 in the matter of Cross-Border Trucking Services.[18] At the WTO, the USA has brought five cases against Mexico[19] while the latter has brought eight cases against the former in areas relating to NAFTA commitments.[20] In the case of NAFTA's Chapter 19 (Review and Dispute Settlement in Antidumping and Countervailing Duty Matters), 14 cases have been brought against Mexico; two by Canada and 12 by the USA. Mexico has initiated 22 cases against the USA and one against Canada.[21]

The election of President Trump has put NAFTA in jeopardy since he promised to renegotiate or repeal the agreement. Trump categorized NAFTA as 'one of the great economic disasters' that has 'destroyed' the country. His evidence is the US $64.3 billion trade deficit with Mexico and the manufacturing jobs lost as part of the relocation process of production facilities that took place under NAFTA.[22]

The NAFTA renegotiations started on 16 August 2017. While the USA seeks to achieve a fair and balanced trading relationship, Mexico and Canada are looking to modernize the agreement. Given these clashing points of view it is likely that negotiations will be very difficult and it will be extremely challenging to reach a common consensus.

In the early 1990s the disciplines negotiated in NAFTA became the state-of-the-art trade rules in the so-called new areas including agriculture, trade in services, investment, and intellectual property. NAFTA became the laboratory in which new rules were developed and later placed on the negotiation agenda of the Uruguay Round and the WTO. Once again, other countries will closely follow the rules and disciplines that the three countries in North America negotiate since these will offer a very clear guide to the direction that global trade may take in the future.

Europe: the EU and the EFTA

In the first years of NAFTA's implementation starting in 1994, Mexico's international trade suffered a deviation from traditional trading partners, mainly the European Union (EU). Although in 1982 Mexico's EU imports represented 19 per cent of its global purchases, by 1998 these declined to 9 per cent. Likewise, on the export side, Mexican sales to the EU also suffered a dramatic reduction from 8.9 per cent in 1990 to 3.9 per cent in 1999. In 1999 Mexico-EU trade accounted for 6.5 per cent of Mexico's world trade compared to 11.4 per cent in 1990.[23] In order to reverse this situation and revamp bilateral trade and investment flows both parties agreed that the best option was to negotiate an RTA. While the EU sought to obtain NAFTA-parity (i.e. that it should receive the same preferential treatment as Canada and the USA in the Mexican market since 1994), Mexico's goals were to diversify its export markets, attract FDI from EU sources, ensure preferential access to inputs and machinery for its manufacturing export platform and reduce its dependence on the US market.[24]

In May 1995 Mexico and the EU signed the Joint Solemn Declaration that established both parties' commitment to create a framework conducive to 'developing trade in goods, services, and investments, including their progressive and reciprocal liberalization'.[25] In December 1997 Mexico and the EU signed three documents. The first was the Economic Partnership Agreement (EPA) which contains a political pillar, a cooperation pillar, and a third pillar that established the objectives for the negotiation of an FTA. The second one was the Interim Agreement on Trade and Trade Relations and it established the principles for trade negotiation in the areas of competence of the European Commission (trade in goods, public procurement and competition policy). The third was the Joint Declaration on Trade between the European Community and its 15 member states on one hand, and Mexico on the other, and it laid down the principles of negotiation on trade issues that were of mixed competence, since both the European Commission and the 15 member states took part in the negotiations (trade in services, capital movements and payments, some elements of intellectual property and investment). The Mexico-EU FTA negotiations were launched in July 1998 and concluded in November 1999.[26]

The Mexico-EU FTA in the areas related to trade in goods, public procurement and competition policy were incorporated into Decision 2/2000 of the EU-Mexico Joint Council, and entered into force on 1 July 2000. Liberalization commitments in trade in services and investment as well as cooperation in intellectual property were established in Decision 2/2001 of EU-Mexico Joint Council, which entered into force on 1 March 2001. Both Decisions constitute the Mexico-EU FTA. Together they include provisions on market access, rules of origin, technical standards, sanitary and phytosanitary standards, safeguards, investment and related payments, trade in services, government procurement, competition policy, intellectual property and dispute settlement.

Both Decisions also incorporated built-in provisions (known as review clauses) to continue negotiations in order to deepen trade liberalization in agriculture (Article 10 – review on a case by case basis of customs duties and tariff quota quantities), services (Article 17 – elimination of substantially all remaining discrimination) and investment (Article 35 – progressive liberalization of investment) three years after the date of the entry into force of each Decision (2/2000 and 2/2001). In the specific case of trade in agriculture, special conditions applied since trade in a group of products (mainly those that received substantive support under the EU's Common Agriculture Policy such as cereals, meat, dairy products and sugar) could not be liberalized and they remained on a waiting list. This meant that no liberalization schedule was allocated to such products. Despite several attempts at addressing these review clauses, negotiations were never concluded.

The EU enlargements allowed Mexico to increase its number of trading partners in 2004 when ten new member states (Cyprus, the Czech Republic, Estonia, Hungary, Latvia, Lithuania, Malta, Poland, Slovakia and Slovenia) were incorporated into the EU, in 2007 with the accession of Bulgaria and Romania and, in 2013, with Croatia. The British decision to leave the EU (known as Brexit) will also have implications for the Mexico-EU FTA as the UK will no longer be a member of the EU and modifications will need to be made to the agreement. Mexico will then have to seek a bilateral trade negotiation with the UK once its EU exit process concludes since this country is its fifth largest EU trade partner.

In addition to the Mexico-EU FTA, in 2001, Mexico and the European Free Trade Area (the EFTA, formed by Iceland, Lichtenstein, Norway and Switzerland) also entered into an FTA. The Mexico-EFTA FTA looks very much like the Mexico-EU FTA and covers trade in goods and services, investment and public procurement. On the EFTA side, this was logical after the EU implemented its agreement with Mexico since the EFTA countries are part of the European Economic Area (EEA). The EEA Agreement provides for the free movement of people, goods, services and capital within the European Single Market, which operates as 'one territory without any internal borders or other regulatory obstacles to the free movement of goods and services'.[27]

As a result of the FTAs with the EU and the EFTA, bilateral regional trade received a strong boost. Currently, the EU is Mexico's third largest trading partner, while for the EU, Mexico ranks 13th. Mexico-EU28 trade more than tripled between 1999 and 2016, while Mexican exports to the EU increased by more than 240 per cent from US $5.7 billion to $19.4 billion and imports grew by 225 per cent from $13 billion to $42.3 billion. Mexico's main EU trading partners are Germany, Spain, Italy, France and the UK, which account for 70 per cent of Mexico-EU trade. The Mexico-EU FTA does not regulate FDI flows from EU sources into Mexico since these fall under the scope of BITs. EU28 investment into Mexico has also increased substantially; currently, it accounts for almost 35.9 per cent of all FDI in Mexico with a stock of $174.8 billion in 2016, up from $3.8 billion in 1999. Although EFTA-Mexico trade is far more modest it also experienced growth of 214 per cent ,from $586 million in 2000 to $1.8 billion in 2016, when Switzerland accounted for 89 per cent of total trade.[28]

Attempts to revise the Mexico-EU FTA chapters on agriculture, services and investment based on the review clauses in the agreement have been unsuccessful on multiple occasions since 2004.[29] In order to update it, both parties agreed to undertake a modernization of the Global Agreement at the 2013 Santiago summit of the Community of Latin American and Caribbean States (Comunidad de Estados de América Latina y el Caribe – CELAC).[30] In May 2016 Mexico and the EU launched negotiations to update rules and disciplines on market access for goods, rules of origin, trade facilitation, competition, technical barriers to trade, sanitary and phytosanitary measures, intellectual property, public procurement, trade in services (including telecommunications, e-commerce), investment, regulatory improvements, trade and sustainable development, energy and raw materials, cooperation on small and medium-sized enterprises (SMEs), and improvements in trade dispute procedures. The negotiation and modernization of the Mexico-EU FTA will help to reinforce Mexico's regional FTAs protectionist forces.

Latin America

In Latin America, Mexico has followed both the RTA route and the less ambitious liberalization scheme under the Latin America Integration Association (Asociación Latinoamericana de Integración – ALADI)[31] which intends to gradually establish a common Latin American market under the 'enabling clause' that allows countries to offer trade concessions only among themselves.[32] ALADI has enabled Mexico to negotiate Economic Complementation Agreements

(ECA or Acuerdos de Complementación Económica – ACE) that can accommodate sensitivities that otherwise may impede any kind of trade liberalization (see Table 17.4). ECA are less ambitious to the extent that they only cover trade in goods and include related disciplines regarding rules of origin, technical standards, sanitary and phytosanitary measures, and safeguards. While this may be considered the second-best option since the coverage of such agreements is not as ambitious as a fully fledged FTA, it has allowed Mexico to deepen liberalization and obtain preferential access for its exports, mostly manufactures, to countries in South America. Preferential trade with Argentina, Bolivia, Brazil, Cuba, Ecuador, Mercosur (Mercado Común del Sur – Southern Common Market) and Paraguay has been conducted under ALADI agreements. Specifically, the ACE 55 provides for the establishment of free trade in the automotive sector and the integration and productive complementation of the automotive sectors between Mexico and its Mercosur partners (Argentina, Brazil, Paraguay and Uruguay). In 2011 provisions were modified and tariff-rate quotas were introduced. These quotas were renegotiated in 2015 for four years until 2019.

Mexico has also signed FTAs with the five Central American nations (Costa Rica, El Salvador, Guatemala, Honduras and Nicaragua), Panama and five countries in South America (Colombia, Chile, Peru and Uruguay). In 2016 the Framework Agreement of the Pacific Alliance that Mexico established with Colombia, Chile and Peru came into effect. This network has mainly sought to improve access to Mexico's exports in the region, especially of manufactured goods and at creating the best conditions for Mexican FDI in those countries.

Closer trade and investment ties between Mexico and its Latin American partners also have had an important political component. In the specific case of Central America, trade negotiations in the 1990s were initially conceived as an essential part of the region's peace process. The January 1991 Tuxtla Heads of State Declaration[33] confirmed the countries' interest in creating a free trade zone by the end of 1996, which resulted in three FTAs; one with Costa Rica (1995); another one with Nicaragua (1998) and a third one with Guatemala, Honduras and El Salvador (2001). In 2011 a single FTA between Mexico and the five Central American countries was

Table 17.4 Mexico's network of ECAs under ALADI

Partner/ ECA	Date of signature	Date of entry into force
1. Argentina (ACE 6)	24 October 1986	1 January 1987
2. Bolivia (ACE 66)	17 May 2010	7 June 2010
3. Brazil (ACE 53)	3 July 2002	2 May 2003
4. Cuba (ACE 51)	17 October 2000	28 February 2001
5. Ecuador (ACE-AAP 29)	Not available	1 May 1983
6. Mercosur Framework (ACE 54)	5 July 2002	5 January 2006
7. Mercosur Automotive (ACE 55)	27 September 2002	Argentina-Mexico: 1 January 2003 Brazil-Mexico: 1 January 2003 for Mexico and 15 January 2003 for Brazil Paraguay-Mexico: 1 February 2011 Uruguay-Mexico: 1 January 2003
8. Paraguay (ACE-AAP 38)	Not available	1 July 1984

Source: ALADI. Acuerdos Actuales. Mexico. Available at www.aladi.org/nsfaladi/textacdos.nsf/vpaisesR/mexico (accessed 31 August 2017).

finally established; this was facilitiated by Central America's own integration process and the FTA that these countries had negotiated as a region with the USA (Dominican Republic-Central America FTA – CAFTA-DR).

Mexico's FTA network in Latin America has not escaped challenges since its free trade orientation has clashed with the visions of countries like Venezuela under President Hugo Chávez and Bolivia under President Evo Morales. In the first case, Mexico lost a trading partner in November 2006 when Venezuela denounced the G3 FTA (Colombia, Mexico and Venezuela) that had been in place since 1995.[34] President Chávez's economic policy orientation detached itself from that pursued by previous Venezuelan governments and decided to denounce the agreement. Therefore, the Mexico-Venezuela trade and investment relation lost its preferential framework. As a result, Mexican investments were left without protection and Mexican companies suffered expropriation with limited compensation.[35] In addition, trade plummeted as preferences disappeared. While Mexico-Venezuela trade reached its peak in 2007, at US $3.3 billion, following Venezuela's withdrawal it declined dramatically to close to $773 million in 2016, roughly a quarter of its maximum levels. When preferences were eliminated Mexican exports suffered a sharp decline, falling from $2.3 billion in 2008 to $600 million in 2016. Mexican exports were replaced by products from other trading partners such as Brazil which enjoys preferential treatment under ALADI agreements in the Venezuelan market.[36]

Another country over which Mexico has had to downgrade its level of ambition in an FTA was Bolivia. In 2010 President Evo Morales followed suit after Venezuela renounced its FTA with Mexico. Instead of completely eliminating the 16-year-old FTA, Bolivia asked to reduce its scope and keep only the provisions related to market access for trade in goods as provided under the ALADI agreement. On 7 June 2010 the Mexico-Bolivia FTA was replaced by ACE 66 under ALADI, which nonetheless kept in place tariff preferences for originating products (i.e. products that comply with the rules of origin and thus can enjoy preferential access). Unlike the case of Venezuela, bilateral trade flows were not affected and even showed an increase, from US $142 million in 2010 to $765 million in 2016, since tariff preferences remained untouched.[37]

In 2010 Peru's President Alan Garcia invited Chile, Colombia and Mexico to deepen their integration and define joint actions in order to build trade links with the Asia-Pacific region.[38] The Pacific Alliance was built on the existing bilateral trade agreements among the states parties and was formally launched on 28 April 2011, during the Lima Summit. The Pacific Alliance seeks to consolidate a deep integration project through the establishment of a free trade zone in goods, services, investments, free movement of people and stock markets. It seeks to promote the four economies' growth, development and competitiveness to increase well-being, overcome socio-economic inequality and improve the social inclusion of its inhabitants.

On 6 June 2012 the presidents of Chile, Colombia, Mexico and Peru signed the Framework Agreement of the Pacific Alliance that established the vision, objectives and structure, as well as the basis for its external relationship. Four years later, on 1 May 2016, the Additional Protocol to the Pacific Alliance Framework Agreement entered into force. This Additional Protocol constitutes the trade component and provides for the free movement of goods, services, capital and persons among the four countries. It has 19 chapters that include rules for the liberalization of trade in goods, services (professional, financial, maritime, telecommunications and cross-border services), investment and people. It provides immediate duty-free access for 92 per cent of the products included in the agreement, while the other 8 per cent are expected to be liberalized in the short to medium term so that by 2030 all originating products should be able to circulate freely in the free trade zone.[39]

The four Pacific Alliance countries share a common vision with respect to the value of an open regime for trade in goods and services as well as investment as a way to promote their integration with the world. They exercise an open regionalism which gives each member country the possibility of developing their own extensive networks of trade agreements. The Pacific Alliance has made substantive progress since it was conceived because it has been placed at the top of its members' foreign policy agendas and has been considered a political priority for all heads of state to promote the project. In addition, each country has been able to consistently defend market-friendly approaches despite changes in government.[40]

Mexico's FTAs and ECAs with its Latin American partners have mostly been a way of promoting its manufacturing exports. However, these markets still represent a very small share of Mexico's exports and trade with the world. In 1993 Mexico's exports to its 12 Latin American Integration Association (LAIA) partners amounted to US $3.7 billion, while by 2016 exports totalled $13.3 billion, a 259 per cent increase.[41] In that year Mexico's trade with LAIA partners accounted for 2.99 per cent of its global trade, while Mexican exports to the region amounted to 3.58 per cent of its global sales.[42]

Meanwhile, Mexico's exports to Central America also expanded, from US $621 million in 2000 to $6.9 billion in 2016, a ten-fold increase. However, despite preferential trade conditions, in that year Mexico's trade with its Central American neighbours accounted for 0.91 per cent of its global trade and represented 1.3 per cent of Mexican exports worldwide.[43] In spite of these small numbers relative to global trade, these are key markets for SMEs in Mexico's manufacturing sector.

Asia-Pacific

Asia has become a key trading partner for Mexico, accounting for 35 per cent its imports and 5 per cent of its exports.[44] This region has become key as a source of inputs, parts and components that allow Mexico to maintain a competitive export platform, particularly in the US market, while Asian markets remain fundamentally unexplored. Mexico has only established one RTA in the region – with Japan. Its most recent efforts to expand its presence in the region were through the Trans-Pacific Partnership Agreement (TPP), however, this agreement's future is uncertain.

It is worth noting that in spite of the fact that eight of Mexico's 15 leading trading partners are Asian (the People's Republic of China, Japan, the Republic of Korea (South Korea), Malaysia, Taiwan, India, Thailand and Viet Nam),[45] Mexico has negotiated just one FTA – again, with Japan.

Mexico approached Japan to establish an FTA mainly with the purpose of promoting Japanese investment in Mexico. Before establishing a bilateral agreement, experts undertook some exploratory work to determine the convenience of the agreement, especially for Japan since negotiating RTAs was new to its trade policy agenda. In 1999 Japan created a Committee for Closer Economic Relations between Japan and Mexico under the surveillance of the Japan External Trade Organization (JETRO). In 2000 the Committee released a report recommending the negotiation of a bilateral FTA as a means of strengthening economic ties. The NAFTA and the Mexico-EU negotiations had placed Japan at a disadvantage in the Mexican market. In June 2001 Vicente Fox Quezada, President of Mexico and Junichirō Koizumi, Japan's Prime Minister, established the Mexico-Japan Bilateral Commission integrated by academics and members of the public and private sectors as well as the Japan-Mexico Joint Study Group on the Strengthening of Bilateral Economic Relations to explore measures to further advance bilateral trade and investment relations and to examine the desirability and feasibility of negotiating an FTA. In July 2002 the Joint Study Group released its final report, which put forward recommendations towards the liberalization of trade in goods and services, government procurement, and investment. Based on those recommendations, in November 2002 Mexico and Japan launched FTA negotiations that lasted for 16 months and concluded in March 2004; the agreement was signed on 17 September 2004.[46]

The Mexico-Japan FTA or EPA contains 18 chapters that establish rules and disciplines on bilateral trade in goods including national treatment principles, sanitary and phytosanitary measures and technical barriers to trade. Japan gave its first step in the partial liberalization of trade in agriculture (300 products or 43 per cent of tariff lines), a highly sensitive area for both sides. As a result, Mexico got preferential access for key export products such as pork (80,000 metric tons on an annual basis) and orange juice (6,500 tons on an annual basis).[47] Also for Mexico, trade liberalization in the auto sector was a sensitive issue so Mexico offered Japanese auto producers a duty-free quota equivalent to 5 per cent of its local market, above which a 25 per cent import duty would apply. The EPA also includes regulations on rules of origin, certification of origin and customs procedures, bilateral safeguard measures, investment, cross-border trade in services, financial services, entry and temporary stay of nationals for business purposes, government procurement, competition, improvement of the business environment and bilateral cooperation. It also included a dispute settlement mechanism but to date no disputes have arisen.

In April 2005 the Mexico-Japan Agreement for the Strengthening of the EPA entered into effect. This agreement constitutes Mexico's cornerstone in its Asia trade agenda. With this EPA, Mexico sought to open new export markets, diversify imports of high-technology inputs to strengthen production in Mexico, attract FDI, support production in high added-value sectors, and increase technical cooperation on vocational education, and training and support for SMEs to be able to take advantage of the benefits of liberalization. For Japan, this was its second FTA after the one it had signed with Singapore but the first one with a developing country. This was also its opportunity to 'regain competitiveness in Mexico, where [it] had faced competition from US and European producers, which had been in a stronger position due to Mexico's existing FTAs with these countries'.[48] The EPA made Japan Mexico's third largest trading partner (after the USA and China) and the second most important Asian partner. Japan is Mexico's third largest supplier after the USA and China and its fifth largest export destination. In 2016 bilateral trade reached US $21.5 billion with a deficit for Mexico of $13.9 billion. Between 2004, the year prior to the implementation of the EPA, and 2016 Mexican exports increased 217 per cent to reach $3.7billion, while bilateral trade grew by 73 per cent.[49] Nonetheless, Mexican exports to Japan represent only 1 per cent of its world exports. The EPA has also achieved one of its main goals: to increase Japanese FDI in Mexico. Currently, Japan ranks seventh as a source of FDI, accounting for 2.9 per cent of total foreign capital received between 1999 and September 2016. Japanese investments in Mexico have allowed the development of high value-added sectors such as the production of flat screen TVs where Mexico has become the leader in the Americas and one of the most important in the world.

Mexico still needs to build bridges with key trading partners in Asia. In the past, Mexico has made several attempts at negotiating an FTA with South Korea, its sixth largest trading partner and the third most important among Asian countries after China and Japan, but its efforts have been unsuccessful. In 2005 South Korea and Mexico established the 'Strategic Partnership for Common Prosperity in the 21st Century'. Talks towards an FTA were launched on 9 December 2007, but negotiations did not make any progress after the second round in 2008 due to sensitivities of the Mexican manufacturing sector, especially the automotive sector and agriculture producers in South Korea. The stalled talks were relaunched in 2016 during the meeting in Mexico City between South Korean President Park Geun-hye and Mexico's President Enrique Peña Nieto. Both leaders mandated the creation of a working-level team to discuss the resumption of FTA negotiations. Even without an FTA in place, bilateral trade increased from US $954 million to $16.1 billion between 1993 and 2016 (17 times its size in 1993). South Korea is the second most important source of Asian FDI in Mexico after Japan, with stock worth $3.8 billion. An FTA could boost trade and investment even more in key Mexican sectors such as energy and infrastructure and this would help to leverage Mexico's presence in Asia.[50]

One of Mexico's recent attempts at building trade and investment bridges with Asia included the TPP. When the USA made its participation in the TPP official in 2009, it was important that Mexico took part in these negotiations. This amounted to a defensive move on Mexico's part to safeguard its position in the North American production chain. If Mexico had been absent from these negotiations it would have meant losing market share to third parties in its main export market, the USA. It would also have resulted in exclusion from US exports to Asian countries since its inputs would not have been considered as originating in order to comply with origin requirements. Not being part of the negotiations would have meant paying a higher cost for Mexico than sitting at the table and offering concessions to partners with whom Mexico previously had not shown any interest in negotiating an FTA such as Malaysia, Brunei Darussalam or Viet Nam.

The TPP also gave Mexico an opportunity to update NAFTA without having to renegotiate it since the former incorporated new disciplines in topics such as e-commerce or state-owned enterprises while there was an improvement in the quality of the regulations; this would have been enough to take NAFTA to another level of sophistication in the rules that regulate North American integration.

Being part of the TPP would have helped Mexico to diversify its export markets and build bridges in a region that hosts economies that offer great growth potential. The TPP offered Mexico preferential access to six new partners (Australia, Brunei, Malaysia, New Zealand, Singapore and Viet Nam) that in 2016 accounted for almost 2.3 per cent of Mexico's total trade. Mexican imports from these countries accounted for 3.71 per cent of total trade, while exports were only 0.86 per cent. Preferential access to these new markets may have prompted Mexico's efforts to diversify exports to the Asia-Pacific region. However, following President Trump's decision to withdraw from the TPP, Mexico has been forced to look for new alternatives in the Asia-Pacific region by relaunching bilateral talks with TPP partners such as Australia or New Zealand, new partners such as South Korea, as well as seeking new opportunities with China, its second largest trading partner.

Last but not least, Mexico's interest in participating in the agreement was also systemic since it was crucial to ensure participation in the drafting of international trade rules that allow for unrestricted participation. Mexico is highly dependent on international trade and FDI flows that are comparable to the remittances that it receives annually (on average US $25 billion). Joining the TPP negotiations was an opportunity to become one of the countries attempting to design the new rules of international trade given the stagnation in the WTO Doha Round negotiations.

Challenges to Mexico's open regionalism

The new Trump Administration has jeopardized Mexico's regional trade strategy since it has given rise to doubts about the operation of NAFTA as well as about the rules that govern world trade. This shift in US trade policy has reinforced Mexico's regionalism by revealing its need to negotiate new regional trade agreements rather than being driven into a protectionist direction away from international trade.

In Asia, Mexico has reached out to South Korea (see above) in order to explore the possibilities of establishing an FTA. In the Middle East, Mexico has also rekindled trade talks with Turkey. In December 2013 Mexico and Turkey signed a Joint Declaration for the establishment of a Framework of Strategic Cooperation and Partnership.[51] Negotiations were launched in 2014 and in February 2017 the ministers of foreign affairs of both countries met in Mexico City and committed to concluding negotiations at the earliest possible date. For its part, negotiations with Jordan for an FTA started in 2014 and two rounds of negotiations took place in that same year. [52]

In Latin America, Mexico has tried to deepen its trade links with Argentina and Brazil, whose presidents Macri and Temer, respectively, expressed their interest in pursuing closer ties with Mexico 'alarmed by US President Donald Trump's promises to tear apart trade deals and build a wall to protect American jobs'.[53] Mexico and Argentina have in place the ACE 6, which offers preferential treatment to around 40 per cent of all tariff items. For their part, Mexico and Brazil offer preferences to 10 per cent of all tariff items so there is plenty of room to increase coverage and promote trade.

While it is key that Mexico tries to meet the Trump challenge by reaching out to new trade partners, market diversification will not be achieved in a day. In addition, even if Mexico was able to negotiate FTAs with many new markets, its regionalism strategy would still need to be adjusted to divert the emphasis from the US market to others in Europe, Latin America and Asia. Last, but not least, Mexico's export platform has concentrated on manufactured goods and on a few industries such as automobile and auto parts, electronics, and aircraft where trade flows respond to intra-firm and intra-industry decisions that consider the US market as their main target. Thus, for Mexico to take advantage of its network of FTAs and to reduce its export dependence on one market, it will be compelled to develop an alternative export strategy that diversifies markets and products.

Conclusion

The export-led growth development model that Mexico has followed for decades triggered its strategy to create a network of FTAs that were intended not only to promote exports and competitive imports, but also to attract FDI in order to turn Mexico into an export platform for industrial products. Open regionalism has given Mexico wide preferential access to 46 countries in North, Central and South America, Europe, the Middle East and Asia, and partial preferential access to six countries in Latin America. As a result of these RTAs, Mexican exports experienced significant increases while the country has become an attractive destination for FDI. The downside of Mexico's regionalism strategy has been the increased dependence on the US market while also making the country extremely vulnerable to economic and political cycles abroad over which Mexico has little or no control at all. Mexico faces a very serious challenge from the Trump Administration. It is unclear what the renegotiated NAFTA will look like but it is clear that it may have serious implications for Mexico's trade and investment relations with the USA and for its own economic growth.

This renegotiation may have systemic implications for world trade. What happens with the agreement may well have an impact on the way in which the USA will try to shape international trade policy and the international trading system in the years to come. In the early 1990s the Uruguay Round negotiations and te NAFTA were both in the making. The NAFTA negotiations, concluded in August 1992, proved to be the laboratory for trade policy since many provisions were tested in the regional forum and once the wording had been drafted it was taken to the multilateral forum. This was particularly the case for the new issues on the

Mexico's approach to PTAs

agenda such as intellectual property, trade-related investment provisions, and dispute settlement mechanisms.

In the face of Trump's protectionism, Mexico has stated its commitment to an open trading system and has revamped bilateral and regional trade negotiations with current and new trading partners in order to strengthen its network of FTAs. Market expansion and product diversification may well be important one possibility; however, Mexico would also need to redefine its strategy where the US market has been central. The current RTA strategy has given Mexico a place in international trade but has also made the country highly vulnerable to decisions taken beyond its borders.

Notes

1 I am grateful to Kent Eaton for his generous and insightful comments about this work.
2 México, Secretaria de Economía, Comercio Exterior/Países con Tratados y Acuerdos firmados con México. Available at www.gob.mx/se/acciones-y-programas/comercio-exterior-paises-con-tratados-y-acuerdos-firmados-con-mexico?state=published (accessed 1 May 2017).
3 World Trade Organization, Statistics Database, Trade Profiles, Mexico. Available at http://stat.wto.org/CountryProfile/WSDBCountryPFView.aspx?Language=E&Country=MXX (accessed 21 September 2017). In 2016 Mexico was the eighth largest importer and exporter worldwide, if we consider the EU-28 as one player in international trade. If it is considered on a one-on-one basis then it would be the 13th exporter and 12th importer.
4 UNCTAD (2016) *World Investment Report*, Geneva: United Nations, p. 5.
5 WTO, Statistics Database.
6 F. De Mateo (1998) 'Chapter 42: Mexico's Free Trade Agreement with the European Union', in J. A. Vargas (ed.) *4 Mexican Law: A Treatise for Legal Practitioners and International Investors*, Eagan, MN: West Group. p. 139. Lee Axelrad (1993) 'NAFTA in the Context of Mexican Economic Liberalization', *Berkeley J. Int'l L.*,11: 201–22. Available at http://scholarship.law.berkeley.edu/bjil/vol11/iss2/4 (accessed 1 May 2017).
7 Mexico twice attempted to become a member of GATT. The first time was in 1947. Then Mexico participated in the drafting of the original GATT. However, it did not become part since the liberalization commitments were in contradiction with an import substitution model adopted at the time. In 1979 Mexico attempted membership again but the oil boom derailed it. See P. S. Falk and B. Torres (eds) (1989) *La Adhesión de México al GATT: Repercusiones internas e impacto sobre las relaciones México-Estados Unidos*, Mexico City: Centro de Estudios Internacionales, El Colegio de México, p. 423.
8 Mexico hosted the fifth Cancún Ministerial meeting in 2003. In 2012, when Pascal Lamy's tenure as WTO Director-General expired, Mexico expressed an interest in leading the organization by presenting the candidacy of former Trade Minister and Chief NAFTA Negotiator, Herminio Blanco. In 2015 Ambassador Fernando de Mateo, Permanent Representative of Mexico to the WTO, acted as President of the WTO's General Council. See Luz Maria de la Mora (2010) 'México en el Sistema de Comercio Internacional', in B. Torres and G. Vega (eds) *Los Grandes Problemas de México*, vol XII: *Relaciones Internacionales,* Mexico City: Centro de Estudios Internacionales, El Colegio de México, pp. 676–713.
9 The Mexico-EU FTA, the Mexico-EFTA FTA and the Mexico-Uruguay FTA do not incorporate a chapter on investment.
10 M. Irish (2008) 'Regional Trade, the WTO and the NAFTA Model', in R. Buckley, Vai lo Lo and L. Boulle (eds) *Challenges to Multilateral Trade*, Austin, TX:. Kluwer International Law, p. 103.
11 The FTAA was launched by President Clinton in December 1994 during the Summit of the Americas in Miami. The proposed FTAA was intended to create a free trade area among 34 countries in the Western Hemisphere (North America, Central America, South America and the Caribbean, except Cuba). Negotiations were supposed to conclude by 1 January 2005, but the process remained unfinished. J. Gershman and K. Hansen-Kuhn (2005) 'FTAA Fails to Gain Support from Citizens and Governments Across the Region', *Institute for Policy Studies*. Available at www.ips-dc.org/ftaa_fails_to_gain_support_from_citizens_and_governments_across_the_region/ (accessed 1 May 2017).
12 Mexico, Secretaría de Economia, Comercio Exterior/Información Estadística y Arancelaria/Importaciones y exportaciones por país 1993–2016/Por socios. Available at www.gob.mx/se/documentos/

205

comercio-exterior-informacion-estadistica-y-arancelaria-importaciones-y-exportaciones-por-pais-1993-2016-por-socios (accessed 1 May 2018).

13 Mexico (Jan.–June 2017) 'Comisión Nacional de Inversiones Extranjeras', *Informe Estadístico sobre el Comportamiento de la Inversión Extranjera Directa en México*: 5.

14 P. Blustein (1995) 'Mexican Truck Delay Draws NAFTA Protest', *Washington Post*, 20 December. Available at www.washingtonpost.com/archive/business/1995/12/20/mexican-truck-delay-draws-nafta-protest/2421f52a-4736-48e6-9efb-a3ea2ffc7755/?utm_term=.b1f8fa3f571e (accessed 1 May 2018).

15 L. de la Mora (2010) 'NAFTA at 30: A Mexican Perspective', *Perspectives on the Americas 4*, Miami: University of Miami, Center for Hemispheric Policy. Available at https://umshare.miami.edu/…/…/De%20La%20Mora%20-%20Final.pdf (accessed 1 May 2018).

16 Trade Profiles (Mexico). In 2016 Mexico was the 34th largest importer and the 38th biggest exporter worldwide, if we consider it on a one-on-one basis.

17 US Safeguard Action Taken on Broomcorn Brooms from Mexico, case no. USA-97-2008-01 (30 January 1998).

18 In the Matter of Cross-Border Trucking Services, case no. USA-MEX-1998-2008-01 (6 February 2001).

19 These include Mexico: Anti-Dumping Investigation of High-Fructose Corn Syrup (HFCS) from the United States DS 101, Mexico: Anti-Dumping Investigation of High-Fructose Corn Syrup (HFCS) from the United States DS 132, Mexico: Measures Affecting Trade in Live Swine Mexico – Measures Affecting Trade in Live Swine DS 203, Mexico: Definitive Anti-Dumping Measures on Beef and Rice DS 295, and Mexico: Tax Measures on Soft Drinks and Other Beverages DS 308. Available at www.wto.org/english/tratop_e/dispu_e/dispu_status_e.htm (accessed 15 August 2017).

20 These include United States: Anti-Dumping Investigation Regarding Imports of Fresh or Chilled Tomatoes from Mexico DS 49; United States: Continued Dumping and Subsidy Offset Act of 2000 DS 234: United States: Countervailing Duties on Steel Plate from Mexico DS 280: United States: Anti-Dumping Measures on Cement from Mexico DS 281: United States: Anti-Dumping Measures on Oil Country Tubular Goods (OCTG) from Mexico DS 282; United States: Anti-Dumping Determinations regarding Stainless Steel from Mexico DS 325: United States: Final Anti-Dumping Measures on Stainless Steel from Mexico DS 344: United States: Certain Country of Origin Labelling Requirements DS 386. Available at www.wto.org/english/tratop_e/dispu_e/dispu_status_e.htm (accessed 15 August 2017).

21 NAFTA Secretariat, *NAFTA Dispute Settlement: Decisions and Reports*. Available at www.nafta-sec-alena.org/Home/Dispute-Settlement/Decisions-and-Reports (accessed 15 August 2017).

22 Lien Yeun (2016) *Donald Trump Says NAFTA 'Destroyed' U.S. at Rally Near Canadian Border,* CBC News, 7 May. Available at www.cbc.ca/news/canada/british-columbia/donald-trump-calls-nafta-disaster-at-rally-15-min-south-of-b-c-border-1.3572100 (accessed 31 May 2017). John F. MacManus (2016) 'Industries Still Heading for Mexico', *The New American*, 23 April. Available at www.thenewamerican.com/reviews/opinion/item/23035-industries-still-heading-for-mexico (accessed 31 May 2017). United States Census Bureau, Foreign Trade, *Trade in Goods with Mexico*. Available at www.census.gov/foreign-trade/balance/c2010.html (accessed 31 May 2017).

23 De Mateo, 'Chapter 42: Mexico's Free Trade Agreement with the European Union', p. 147.

24 Cámara de Diputados, Unidad de Estudios de las Finanzas Públicas (2000) *Tratado de Libre Comercio México-Unión Europea*, p. 55.

25 Mexico, SECOFI (Nov. 1999) *Tratado de Libre Comercio México-Unión Europea*. Available at http://zedillo.presidencia.gob.mx/pages/pub/publics/tlcue99/tlcue99.html(accessed 15 August 2017).

26 Organization of American States (OAS), Trade Policy Developments, *Mexico-European Union*. Available at www.sice.oas.org/TPD/MEX_EU/MEX_EU_e.asp (accessed 15 September 2017).

27 *The European Single Market*, European Commission. Available at http://ec.europa.eu/growth/single-market_en (last updated 1 June 2017). EFTA states that are part of the EEA Agreement participate in the EU's internal market without having to become EU members. Switzerland is not part of the EEA Agreement, instead it has negotiated bilateral agreements.

28 Mexico, Secretaría de Economia, Comercio Exterior/Información Estadística y Arancelaria/Importaciones y exportaciones por país 1993–2016/Por socios.

29 Review clauses were part of the assessments undertaken by the Joint Council and the Joint Committee Declarations from 2004, 2006, 2007, 2008, 2010 and 2011. ECORYS (February 2017) *Ex post Evaluation of the Implementation of the EU-Mexico Free Trade Agreement, Final Report,* European Commission, Directorate-General for Trade Directorate C – Asia and Latin America Unit C3 – Latin America. pp. 64–65.

Mexico's approach to PTAs

30 European Commission, Modernisation of the Trade Pillar of the EU-Mexico Global Agreement. Available at http://ec.europa.eu/smart-regulation/roadmaps/docs/2015_trade_001_modernisation_eu_mexico_agreement_en.pdf (accessed 31 August 2017).

31 ALADI has its origins in the early 1960s when Mexico participated in the creation of the Latin American Free Trade Association (Asociación Latinoamericana de Libre Comercio, ALALC) the first regional attempt at creating a regional free trade zone. In 1980 this mechanism evolved into ALADI. Its 13 members are Argentina, Bolivia, Brazil, Chile, Colombia, Cuba, Ecuador, Mexico, Panama, Paraguay, Peru, Uruguay and Venezuela. Nicaragua is in the process of accession.

32 World Trade Organization, *Enabling Clause: Main Legal Provisions*. Available at www.wto.org/english/tratop_e/devel_e/d2legl_e.htm (accessed 31 August 2017). The 'enabling clause' is an exception to GATT's most-favoured-nation clause as it allows developed members to afford differential and more favourable treatment to developing countries. It is officially known as the 'Decision on Differential and More Favourable Treatment, Reciprocity and Fuller Participation of Developing Countries' adopted under GATT in 1979. The Enabling Clause is the legal basis for ALADI countries to offer tariff reductions only to other ALADI members without violating GATT commitments.

33 Tuxtla Gutiérrez Statement (11 January 1991). Available at www.revistas.una.ac.cr/index.php/ri/article/view/8841/10143) (accessed 10 September 2017).

34 EFE (2006) 'Chávez confirma la retirada del G3, que integra con México y Colombia', *El País*, 22 May. Available at https://elpais.com/internacional/2006/05/22/actualidad/1148248802_850215.html (accessed 1 May 2017).

35 Press release, CEMEX Media Centre (13 December 2011). Available at www.cemex.com/Media Center/PressReleases/PressRelease20111213.aspx (accessed 31 May 2017). Mexican cement firm CEMEX was expropriated in 2008. In 2011 CEMEX settled for US $600 million, below the $ 1.3 billion CEMEX had initially sought in compensation. Mexican investment was left without any legal protection when Venezuela denounced the G3 FTA.

36 Mexico, Secretaría de Economia, Comercio Exterior/Información Estadística y Arancelaria/Importaciones y exportaciones por país 1993–2016/Por socios.

37 'Bolivia elimina TLC con México', 4 June 2010, *EXPANSION*. Available at http://expansion.mx/economia/2010/06/04/tlc-mexico-bolivia-comercio-cnnexpansion (accessed 1 May 2017).

38 Perú, Ministerio de Comercio Exterior y Turismo, Acuerdos Comerciales del Perú, Alianza del Pacífico. Available at www.acuerdoscomerciales.gob.pe/index.php?option=com_content&view=category&layout=blog&id=166&Itemid=185 (accessed 1 May 2018).

39 OAS, Foreign Trade Information System, Pacific Alliance. Available at www.sice.oas.org/Trade/PAC_ALL/Framework_Agreement_Pacific_Alliance_s.pdf (accessed 31 May 2017).

40 Ibid. Available at http://sice.oas.org/TPD/Pacific_Alliance/Pacific_Alliance_s.asp (accessed 31 May 2017). Between 2011 and 2016 the Pacific Alliance held 11 summits to revise progress and offer new mandates to deepen integration.

41 The figures for 1993 do not consider trade with Cuba since it became a member of LAIA in 1999 or Panama that acceded membership in 2012. Data for 1993 from Mexico, Secretaria de Economia. Data for 2016 obtained from ITC, Trade Map.

42 International Trade Center, Trade Map. Last revised on 20 September 2017.

43 Ibid.

44 The Asia definition is broad and includes 49 countries in Asia and the Middle East. ITC, Trade Map. Available at www.trademap.org/Country_SelProductCountry_TS.aspx?nvpm=1|484|||20|TOTAL|||2|1|1|1|2|1|2|1|1 (accessed 31 August 2017).

45 Ibid.

46 OAS, Foreign Trade Information System, Trade Policy Developments, Mexico-Japan. Available at www.sice.oas.org/TPD/MEX_JPN/MEX_JPN_e.ASP (accessed 31 August 2017).

47 Mireya Solis (2005) *The Political Economy of the Japan-Mexico EPA: How Does a Cross-Regional Initiative Affect the Future of Japan's Regional Integration Efforts?* Research Institute of Economy, Trade and Industry, 4 July. Available at www.rieti.go.jp/en/events/bbl/05070401.html (accessed 31 August 2017).

48 Japan, Mexico Reach Free Trade Agreement,8 Bridges, no. 1,2004. Available at www.ictsd.org/bridges-news/bridges/news/japan-mexico-reach-free-trade-agreement (accessed 31 July 2017).

49 Mexico, Secretaría de Economía, Comercio Exterior/Información Estadística y Arancelaria/Importaciones y exportaciones por país 1993–2016/Por socios.

Luz Maria de la Mora Sanchez

50 M. Herh (2016) 'Korea-Mexico Summit. Korea, Mexico Open New Chapter for Mutual Growth', *BusinessKorea*, 7 April. Available at www.businesskorea.co.kr/english/news/politics/14342-korea-mexico-summit-korea-mexico-open-new-chapter-mutual-growth (accessed 31 August 2017).

51 OAS, Foreign Trade Information System, Trade Policy Developments, Mexico-Turkey. Available at www.sice.oas.org/TPD/MEX_TUR/MEX_TUR_e.ASP (accessed 3 September 2017).

52 OAS, Foreign Trade Information System, Trade Policy Developments, Mexico-Jordan. Available at www.sice.oas.org/TPD/MEX_JOR/MEX_JOR_e.ASP (accessed 3 September 2017).

53 Alonso Soto (2017) *Brazil, Argentina Push for Closer Trade with Mexico in Trump Era*, Business News: Reuters, 7 February. Available at www.reuters.com/article/us-brazil-argentina-mexico-idUSKBN15M2BK (accessed 31 May 2017).

18

CETA

Kurt Hübner

Introduction

The Comprehensive Economic and Trade Agreement (CETA) between Canada and the European Union (EU) came into provisional effect on 21 September 2017. However, critical parts of the agreement in the area of foreign direct investment (FDI) and the so-called investor-state dispute mechanism were excluded as they were seen as contractual elements outside the negotiation discretion of the European Commission. As a result, all EU member states need to ratify CETA according to their respective constitutional rulers, and this includes in some cases provincial/regional parliaments in addition to the federal parliament. Whether the whole agreement will pass this test will be only decided years from now. This is not a new situation for the EU. The trade agreement with the Republic of Korea (South Korea), for example, also only provisionally came into effect and ratification happened afterwards. CETA is a different beast, however, as it includes new and potentially ground-breaking mechanisms when it comes to disputes about FDI. This mechanism entered the agreement at a very late stage and only after it turned out that the political resistance to the traditional treatment of FDI issues threatened the overall agreement. CETA still needs to be ratified throughout the EU if it does not want to end up as an incomplete agreement. Even if this worst-case scenario were to become a reality, CETA goes beyond cherry-picking low-hanging fruit as it comprises new elements that so far have not been part of any existing EU trade agreements.

Pre-history

CETA is the culmination of a longer history of agreements between the two entities. In 1959 the Canadian government and the European Atomic Energy Community (Euratom) agreed to cooperate on the peaceful uses of atomic energy. More general agreements regarding trade and economic cooperation date back to 1976, with the bilateral 'Framework Agreement for Commercial and Economic Cooperation'. This agreement is the EU's first economic agreement with another industrialized country. A key outcome of this framework was the creation of the Joint Cooperation Committee (JCC). The JCC's main role, which persists to this day, is to provide a forum for structured dialogue between Canada and the EU. Building upon the wider 1976

209

agreement, Canada and the EU have conducted multiple sectorial agreements. These include agreements on Science and Technology (1996), Higher Education and Training (1995, 2000), Customs Cooperation (1998), Mutual Recognition (1998), Veterinary Equivalency (1998), Competition Cooperation Agreement (1999) and a Wine and Spirits Agreement (2004). Beyond these sectorial agreements, there are a variety of agreements in existence that were created to settle specific issues. Examples include the World Trade Organization (WTO) dispute about scallops (1996) and the Bilateral Framework on Regulatory Cooperation and Transparency (2004). Since April 2017 the Strategic Partnership Agreement came (provisionally) into effect which provides opportunities for cooperation in areas such as climate and foreign and security policies.

In the early 2000s both Canada and the EU began to consider the potential benefits of closer economic cooperation. Canada was interested in a bilateral trade agreement with the EU because of the potential markets offered by the EU as well as a way of lessening its heavy export dependence on the USA. While Canada's interest in a bilateral agreement with the EU is obvious, the EU's interest in Canada is less evident, as Canada is only the EU's 12th largest trading partner. The main reason why the EU was interested in opening CETA negotiations may have been the chance to 'test' one of the pillars of its 2006 Global Europe Strategy, in particular, the goal to include public procurement in new trade agreements and to build on its regulatory capacity. Moreover, as a member of the North America Free Trade Agreement (NAFTA) Canada was viewed as a promising partner regarding a potential backdoor route to the USA. Furthermore, as the Joint Study (see below) argued, Canada and the EU had not made the best use of their trade potential in the past, and were actually in a situation of 'under-trading': The total trade between Canada and the EU is almost the same size as the total trade between India and the EU, yet the Canadian economy is one and a half times larger than the Indian economy. Similarly, Canada's gross domestic product (GDP) is one and a half times larger than South Korea's, yet EU trade with Canada is 25 per cent less than it is with South Korea. CETA is seen by both sides as an agreement that would exploit the unused potential and provide an impetus for more dynamic exchanges in the future. In 2016 bilateral trade volumes in goods and services amounted to close to €100 billion. At least as relevant is the mutual relationship regarding FDI with about €250 billion outward investment from the EU and €230 billion inward investment from Canada. Both entities are heavily invested in each other, and CETA was widely seen to give this relationship a further push.

As both parties identified economic potential in a more comprehensive economic cooperation, the EU and Canada discussed possibilities further during the Canada-EU summit in Berlin in 2007. During the summit the EU and Canada decided to conduct a joint study examining the cost and benefits of pursuing a closer economic partnership. Besides drastically reducing tariffs, both sides focused particularly on the potential impact of eliminating existing barriers to trade. The 'Joint Study on Assessing the Cost and Benefits of a Closer EU-Canada Economic Partnership' was released on 16 October 2008. It suggests that cooperation could be enhanced in areas relating to energy, the environment as well as science and technology. The study hypothesizes that Canadian industrial and export sectors, such as metal, transportation and electronic equipment would benefit most from increased cooperation. As for the EU, the machinery, chemical and transportation sectors are projected to benefit most from CETA. As a consequence, both parties decided to pursue closer economic cooperation during the 2008 Canada-EU summit in Québec. This meeting focused on the analysis and identification of specific subjects that could be covered in the negotiations; at the 2009 Canada-EU summit in Prague, both parties eventually announced the formal start of negotiations.

What is CETA all about?

The EU praised CETA as the most far-reaching bilateral agreement that it has negotiated with any non-EU nation due to its comprehensive scope. Across a broad range of sectors, CETA eliminates 98 per cent of customs duties and import tariffs as soon as it is ratified and 100 per cent of tariffs within the next seven years. Still, the abolition of tariffs does not mean frictionless trade as quotas in some areas continue to exist. While this trade liberalization is a key feature of CETA, it needs to be stressed that it is not the abolishment of tariffs that makes CETA so important, given that Canada and the EU already had relatively low tariffs for industrial products. This new-era agreement between Canada and the EU is comprehensive for three main reasons: public procurement, FDI and regulatory cooperation.

The access to public procurement for the private sectors of both entities opens up two large and to date externally closed markets. Public procurement already exists within the EU, and the emphasis placed by the EU on gaining access to provincial service and procurement was a test run to draw public procurement into other bilateral or multilateral agreements that the EU is negotiating. In CETA both parties agreed to open up these markets and to allow competitive offers above certain threshold values. The agreement includes exceptions in Canada for public transport tenders in Ontario and Québec, cultural industries, Aboriginal businesses, defence, research and development, financial services and services in the fields of recreation, sport and education, as well as social and health care services. Canadian companies will now have opportunities to compete at all levels of the EU government procurement market with exemptions in security-related sectors. It is not by chance that European Trade Commissioner Cecilia Malmström – addressing the European Parliament on 9 December 2015 – referred to procurement as the second major success of the EU in the CETA negotiations (after the elimination of 98 per cent of duties on exports), stating that 'Canada opens up procurement more in CETA than in the WTO's Government Procurement Agreement, NAFTA, and the Transpacific Partnership'.

The third component that makes CETA a comprehensive agreement beyond a pure trade agreement is the chapter on regulatory cooperation. One element of regulatory cooperation is the mutual acceptance mechanism, which can take form through approximation, negotiation of mutual recognition (NMR) or mutual recognition agreements (MRAs). An approximation is the most serious form of regulatory cooperation as it attempts to align national legislations. NMRs are more bilateral as two parties are agreeing that specific regulations, while different in form, are equivalent in effect. MRAs are the least ambitious form of regulatory cooperation as they accept differences in national standards and mainly focus on labelling for exports. The CETA prefers mutual recognition as a means to save exporting companies the need to gain double acceptance, at home and abroad. The EU and Canada also agreed to set up a voluntary Regulatory Cooperation Forum which is supposed to enable regulators to exchange experiences and information and to identify areas of deeper regulatory cooperation. This forum will have no power to make any binding suggestions. The second element of regulatory cooperation is CETA's negative list approach, which states that all goods and services, except for the ones listed, are subject to liberalization. This is a large expansion in scope for an economic trade agreement, as both sides are agreeing to liberalize sectors that so far have showed various forms of restrictions.

That CETA was running into serious political problems has less to do with the success stories regarding public procurement, tariff reduction and regulatory issues than with the initial plan for the FDI regime in general and the investor-state dispute settlement (ISDS) in particular. The initial version of ISDS was modelled along the version that has been used in over 3,000 existing trade agreements that deal with conflicts by decisions of a non-public dispute 'court' mechanism. Because this system is the international norm, neither Canada or the EU foresaw that ISDS would be met with strong political resistance by civil society organizations as well as by political parties (see in detail below). When it became obvious that a number of EU member states were concerned about the initial ISDS version due to strong political opposition by civil society organizations, both sides – encouraged also by the change in federal government in Canada – decided to use the 'legal scrubbing' phase for a far-reaching reform of the ISDS mechanism (see below).

Even though CETA is characterized as a comprehensive agreement, it needs to be noted that its provisions and rules are a far cry from the level of economic liberalization that member states of the EU enjoy between each other. This is obvious in the service chapters of CETA, in particular in the agreement on financial services, whereby CETA mainly confirms given practices and does not add any additional relevant liberalization measures. Rather than giving financial institutions so-called passporting rights that would allow them to offer services in the respective economic spaces without actually hosting physical institutions, CETA only allows activities that are covered by WTO rules. In a world, though, in which the making of trade agreements has become difficult, CETA can be seen as a lighthouse that has the potential to become a model for other negotiations. However, this only holds if CETA ever comes fully into effect.

Canadian interests in CETA

Historically, Canada can be seen as a trading nation that relies on open markets abroad, in particular with its largest and dominant trading partner in the south. As a small economy, measured in economic size, the country can benefit from cross-border exchanges. And yet, the attitude of citizens towards trade is not overwhelmingly positive as the conflicts over the North American Free Trade Agreement (NAFTA) demonstrated. When it came to trade, Canada was for a long time a policy-taker that responded to the actions of others. This has changed over the past few decades, also due to overall changes in the global economy. The General Agreement on Trade and Tariffs (GATT) and then the WTO were for some time successful multilateral institutions that paved the way for trade liberalization. When the low-hanging fruit was cherry-picked, national governments turned increasingly to bilateral and regional trade agreements. The initiative for CETA was at least partially driven by the insight that Canada needs to diversify its trading portfolio and deepen its economic relations with important regional centres of the global economy.

When it comes to trade policy, Canada is a complex federal case: the federal government has the right to negotiate international agreements and treaties but needs the active support of the provinces and territories to eventually enact an agreement. This dual structure has created problems in the past as provinces and territories made use of their veto power and thus prevented far-reaching trade policy initiatives from reaching fruition. Three main actors can be identified that pushed negotiations forwards. These are the Canadian government, spearheaded by then Prime Minister Harper and swiftly followed by the incoming liberal Trudeau government; some provinces, particularly Québec and Ontario; and business lobby groups. Due to the pro-liberalization agenda of the Progressive Conservative Party, the Harper government repeatedly pushed for the CETA negotiations, as it believed that CETA's success would help the Harper government not only in electoral strongholds but also would help to create a true single market at home. When the Liberal government came into office, CETA was pushed further forwards and was very much driven by the interest in widening and deepening market access for Canadian business. Including provinces and territories in negotiations was a natural part of the strategy of both governments to form a strong coalition. As a result, the CETA negotiations represent the first time that Canadian provinces were fully involved in negotiating an FTA. Québec and Ontario, in particular, were key initiators throughout the negotiation process, due to their prioritization of an open market economy and the relatively strong orientation of businesses towards EU markets. The export-oriented businesses were traditionally eager to reach out to new markets, and Europe was long seen as a preferred trading partner. It turned out that this open trade coalition was highly resilient against opposing voices, which mainly came from civil society organizations.

Motivation of the EU

The key players on the European side that pushed for an agreement with Canada were the European Commission, specific member states (France, the United Kingdom and Germany), as well as business lobby groups. The way in which this open trade coalition was set up looks very similar to its Canadian counterpart. Unlike in Canada, though, civil society organizations emerged as relevant actors in the process of trade policymaking which had the power to change the trade agenda. Moreover, the legal situation for the Commission to negotiate a truly comprehensive trade agreement turned out to be rather complex, even compared to the position of the Canadian federal government about the provinces and territories. The Treaty of Lisbon, which was concluded in 2007 and entered into force in 2009, conferred to the EU exclusive competence over trade in goods and services, commercial aspects of intellectual property and FDI. Article 207 (1) of the Lisbon Treaty granted the European Commission these powers and replaced the former agreement concerning trade, Article 133 of the 1957 Treaty of the European Community. During the negotiations this broad mandate was questioned (see below). Rather than being a fully mandated negotiating party, the Commission's mandate was curtailed.

While the Commission took the lead in the negotiations, France, the UK and Germany were particularly interested in forging a closer relationship with Canada. France's historical connection with Canada and its ongoing extensive economic partnership are the two key reasons why the nation supports CETA. France's historical connection with French-speaking provinces and regions of Canada has created an ongoing cultural exchange between the francophone entities. French people represent the second largest group of people travelling to Canada and France is the third most popular travel destination for Canadians, after the USA and the UK. This shared cultural heritage translates into strong economic ties. France is Canada's ninth largest trading partner and the fourth largest within the EU. In 2014 Canada-France trade amounted to C $9.2 billion. France is also Canada's third largest partner in the world for services, and the second largest in Europe. There are 550 French companies in Canada which provide around 96,000 jobs and 220 Canadian companies in France which provide 21,000 jobs.

Similarly to France, the UK has strong historical and indeed economic ties with Canada. Canada is a member of the Commonwealth, and its system of parliamentary democracy is heavily influenced by the British system. Cultural exchange through travel fosters an ongoing connection. The UK is the primary travel destination for Canadians within the EU and the second globally after the USA. As was the case in France, this connection translates into economics. The UK is Canada's most important commercial partner in Europe and the second biggest trading partner in the world after the USA. Particularly strong bilateral relations exist in science, technology and innovation; furthermore, the UK is a major recipient of Canadian oil imports. Most importantly, the UK has always positioned itself as a free trade advocate, and thus it was a 'natural' attitude to strongly press in favour of CETA. Besides France and the UK, Germany's role in CETA cannot be overlooked. It is difficult to pinpoint Germany's role throughout the CETA negotiation process, as publicly Germany remained relatively quiet about

CETA for a long time. There is evidence, though, that the German governments of the day were strong supporters of CETA negotiations from the very start.

As was the case in Canada, European business organizations were strong supporters of a comprehensive liberalization of economic relations with Canada, and the European Commission involved them in the early stages of negotiation talks to help to identify trade barriers. From the many active lobby groups, three specifically were important in the context of CETA: the European Round Table of Industrialists (ERT); BusinessEurope; and the European Services Forum (ESF).

The ERT is a forum that brings together 50 chief executives and chairs from major multinational companies across a variety of European industrial and technical sectors. ERT was one of the main lobby groups that advocated for the completion of the single market project and published *Europe 1990: An Agenda for Action*, which became the basis for the Commission's White Paper that provided arguments for a business-driven liberalization of markets. BusinessEurope, recognized as having 'privileged access' to European political leaders, acted as a powerful lobby group in Brussels when it came to CETA. The third key group, ESF, represents more than 30 major service companies across a variety of sectors. These include services such as audio-visual (European Broadcasting Union), water and power (Veolia Environment), finance and insurance (Deutsch Bank AG, Lloyd's of London), postal services, engineering and architecture, and shipping and telecommunications (France Telecom, Vodafone). ESF was established in the late 1990s by the chairman of Barclays Bank at the request of Leon Brittan, EU Trade Commissioner at the time, so that the group could help the EU with the General Agreement on Trade and Services (GATS) negotiations at the WTO in 2000. ESF supported CETA in general, even though it was clear from the outset that the sectors it represents may not figure prominently in a final agreement.

Just as with the member states, it is challenging to highlight specific examples of these groups' involvement throughout the CETA process. Their long history of collaboration with the EU, and the way in which they have influenced EU trade policy over time, is evidence of a sturdy relationship. A November 2015 report released by a multitude of non-governmental organizations on the Corporate Europe Platform notes that CETA and the Transatlantic Trade and Investment Partnership (TTIP) are heavily influenced by the 'reverse lobbying' that goes on between the EU and BusinessEurope and ESF.

This open trade coalition dominated for a long time the agenda as well as the negotiations strategy of the Commission. Trade Commissioner Karel de Gucht acted as the lead proponent for a CETA that would be as liberal as possible as, in his view, barrier- and tariff-free trade would have a huge impact on economic growth. The emphasis on opening markets and tearing down non-tariff barriers was the political denominator of the open trade coalition. The coalition was successful in dealing with the concerns of civil society organizations, as long as the latter intervened with 'traditional' anti-trade arguments. This changed when the EU and the USA decided to start talks about a TTIP.

Cracks in the European trade coalition

Until the start of TTIP talks, European civil society organizations showed only modest interest in CETA. In Europe, TTIP and CETA became increasingly interconnected, and the public discourse treated both as more or less identical agreements. This shift in political attention created a paradox situation. At the request of the EU, Canada made sure that its provinces and territories were closely involved in the negotiations, partly because the EU anticipated that the public procurement clause would not be viewed positively by the Canadian provinces and as a result this critical pillar of CETA would not come into effect. The Canadian side did not harbour similar sentiments towards the Commission and its relation to the member states, as it was assumed that trade policy would be mainly in the hands of the Directorate-General for Trade (DG Trade) and the Council. As it turned out, DG Trade came under intense pressure from civil society organizations and consequently from some member states that had to deal with massive protests against CETA. Some EU member states, such as Germany, Austria and France, vocally proclaimed that they would reject an agreement that included the traditional form of ISDS as this would strengthen corporate power yet further. Although these concerns were raised before CETA negotiations closed in October 2014, the Commission did not incorporate these concerns into their final negotiations, not least because the traditional form of ISDS was seen as being well tested and as an elementary part of any liberalization strategy. Moreover, DG Trade was confident in its ability to push through the agreement. In hindsight, this turned out to be a gross miscalculation. First, it underestimated the influence of the European Parliament which won significant power in trade policy following the 2009 ratification of the Lisbon Treaty. Additionally, since some European citizens and EU member states had a negative view of the agreement, the Commission would have been well advised to involve them better in the negotiations, particularly when it became obvious that some national governments came under immense pressure from civil society organizations as well as from trade unions and political parties. While the EU was concerned about Canada's strong federalism and its implications for the CETA negotiations, it arguably overestimated the power that it wielded over the member states. Second, the Commission was insensitive towards those governments that were coming under pressure from mostly centre-left political parties, trade unions and civil society organizations in their own countries. Rather than dealing with the emerging concerns, the Commission and in particular DG Trade clung to their deep-seated convictions that liberal trade benefits everyone. Third, the Commission was not willing to positively deal with the rising public doubts about globalization and the effects thereof. When the Commission decided to open negotiations with the USA about a TTIP it would have been necessary to communicate the strategy of such an agreement. Instead, the EU kept quiet and relied on its supposedly positive globalization policy.

The political miscalculation had negative effects on CETA as civil society organizations widened the political protest against TTIP to include the agreement with Canada. The ISDS clause in CETA quickly became the point of attack, which was not surprising given that it encapsulated critics concerns about the negative aspects of unfettered liberalization. However, rather than giving thought to these criticisms, the EU ignored them. Only when key actors like the German government signalled that it would not be willing to support the ISDS version included in CETA, the situation began to change. The Canadian government saw no reason to push its negotiation counterpart in a different direction. Until the legal scrubbing of the CETA text was finalized on 29 February 2016, the Canadian government continued to push for keeping the initial ISDS clause in the text. Canada's adherence to the ISDS system was mainly driven by the fact that it was involved in a variety of multilateral trade agreements with developing countries that included the regular clause, and thus it was keen to prevent the adoption of a different contractual model that might have been seen by third parties as an invitation to negotiate a new ISDS clause. Yet in February 2016 it was announced that CETA would have a new ISDS mechanism with a new investment court system. This change was accepted by the new Canadian government not so much because it felt that the new regime would be a huge improvement but because it became obvious that CETA could only be changed if the old ISDS clause was replaced by a new mechanism. The suggested investment court system was expected to have independent, fully qualified judges who would hold transparent proceedings. Also, the investment court system would have a Tribunal of First Instance and an Appeal Tribunal. This volte face was a result of the political pressure felt by the Commission, and when the new clause was debated in late 2015, the new situation came as a surprise to the Canadian government. The new clause was accepted by the Canadians as this was seen as the best way to accelerate the final ratification.

On 28 June 2016 European Commission President Juncker declared publicly that CETA would be ready for ratification as it would be an EU-only agreement. The Commission again miscalculated the political sentiment in critical member states of the EU, and as a result of open opposition by key governments, the Commission had to perform an astounding turnaround by declaring CETA to a mixed agreement. This amounted to no less than a political defeat for the Commission as under the new circumstances it was now up to member state governments and in some cases to provincial governments to determine CETA's fate.

Conclusion

The final text of CETA can be seen as a success for civil society organizations as it no longer includes the controversial investor-state dispute mechanism that is an integral part of traditional EU trade agreements. Instead, CETA includes an innovative new regime that differs from regular practices, which can be regarded as being superior to the previous mechanism in terms of transparency and democratic control. Paradoxically, it is exactly this regime that may never come into effect as it is possible that it will fall victim to the ratification processes throughout the EU member states. The decision to declare CETA to be a mixed agreement opened the door for national actors and their specific interests. It may well be that as a result CETA will only be a provisional agreement for quite a time. And yet CETA still will be a successful test case for the EU as it entails the opening of public procurement markets, and this was one of the key elements of the EU's global trade strategy. In times when trade agreements come under pressure by mercantilistic political interests, the Canada-EU agreement goes far regarding mutual liberalization. It would be a baseless exaggeration, though, to expect that increased trade between both entities would generate significant macroeconomic growth effects, in terms of GDP as well as jobs. Figures presented by Canadian Prime Minister Trudeau at the time of the signing of CETA were part of political rhetoric as they were taken from the 2008 Joint Study, and were therefore outdated and probably inclined towards the upper side of modelling estimates.

Economic globalization, including cross-border trade, has scaled down over the last few years, not least as an implication of the global financial crisis. In Europe, the eurozone crises urged member states to turn towards export-enhancing policies as a way of compensating for the effects of domestic austerity policies. Moreover, since the start of CETA negotiations ten years ago, the economic world has changed. Future trade will be much more driven by services and forms of digital exchanges – all elements that do not figure prominently in CETA.

From the outset, CETA was seen as an enormously ambitious agreement in terms of its scope and also in setting new norms and rules for EU and Canadian trade policy. As things have turned out, if followed by a successful ratification process, CETA will be seen as an agreement that has quite substantially changed the way in which trade policymaking will be conducted. This holds from the very start for Canada given that for the first time ever provinces and territories have been included in trade policy affairs. It also holds for the EU where civil society organizations have triggered a reshaping of the way in which trade agreements are negotiated as well as the way in which trade policy elements are defined. In this sense, CETA provided the European Commission as well as national governments with lessons and insights that will have implications for future trade policies.

Time will tell whether CETA will come into full effect. In terms of economic effects, it seems fair to say that expectations may have to be reduced due to the decision of the UK to leave the EU as well as the single market and the customs union. Given that the UK is Canada's second largest global export destination and its sixth largest source of imports, it will be necessary for Canada to negotiate a bilateral agreement with the UK. Depending on the terms of such an agreement, it may be well the case that the UK may even increase its exports to Canada by substituting some exports from other EU countries. On the other hand, the UK and Canadian exporters might have to deal with less attractive conditions, in particular when it comes to regulatory issues and public procurement, with the result that the level of exchange will become smaller. What holds for the fate of CETA also holds for UK–Canada relations: uncertainty reigns.

19

Mercosur

Walter Antonio Desiderá Neto

The foundation of Mercosur and the economic-commercial phase (1991–2002)

In the mid-1980s the continuing democratization of Argentina and Brazil led to a growing rapprochement between them. Following mutual requests, they embarked on a process of integration in a changing international context due to the end of the Cold War and the consequent surge in economic globalization. The resolution of the Itaipu-Corpus Issue,[1] and the easing of the nationalist suspicions present on both sides during the preceding military dictatorships, especially in respect of their nuclear programmes, created space for embarking on common development projects.

From the politico-strategic point of view, it was important for both nations to regain their credibility with the major Western powers by jointly guaranteeing their renewed commitment to peace, democracy and market economy. Given the external debt crises experienced by Latin American countries, it was also necessary to act in concert in order to restructure their debt agreements with private creditors.

Following Fernando Collor de Mello's rise to power in 1990 to become Brazil's first popularly elected president in nearly 30 years, Brazilian foreign policy underwent a considerable change in its priorities. With respect to the economy, the new government was imbued with the idea that a series of modernizing and pro-market reforms – including the liberalization of trade and investment flows and privatization of public enterprises – were an inevitable path to pursue in order to solve the problems of external debt (access to finance) and the low competitiveness of domestic industry.

In terms of regional integration, the Presidents of Brazil and Argentina (Carlos Saúl Menem was elected to the presidency in 1989) released the Act of Buenos Aires in which they anticipated the deadline for the definitive confirmation of the bilateral common market for 1994,[2] signifying an acceleration of the process that had begun in the 1980s as well as a significant softening in the principle of gradualism in the integrationist project. According to the terms of the act, special emphasis would be given to generalized, linear and automatic tariff reductions, being this the main methodology for establishing the common market – revealing the abandonment of the developmentalist perspective and the adoption of the new vision for regional integration promoted by the United Nations Economic Commission for Latin America and the Caribbean[3] making it compatible with the phenomenon of globalization and multilateral liberalization: open regionalism.

The new liberalization process between the two largest countries of the Southern Cone was registered on the Latin American Integration Association (Asociación Latinoamericana de Integración – ALADI)[4] as the Economic Complementation Agreement No. 14 (ACE-14). From the perspective of open regionalism and the strategic view that regional integration in small blocks would be important for the productive sectors to have time to adjust to global competition. Paraguay and Uruguay, which had already participated in the process in different ways, were invited to join the Southern Common Market (Mercado Común del Sur – Mercosur) when the Treaty of Asunción, its founding agreement, was signed in 1991.

Regarding the incorporation of the two minor partners, the fact that the deadline for consolidating the common market and the philosophy of open regionalism that were present in ACE-14 remained intact deserves attention. In other words, the two countries simply adhered to the process initiated by the major partners, without making additions or changes or receiving relevant differentiated treatment.[5] The Treaty of Asunción did not provide for any mechanism for development cooperation.

The deadline to consolidate the common market (1994) was called 'transitional period' by the Treaty of Asunción. The exhaustive detail of the procedure to be followed in order to consolidate this objective was set out in the Las Leñas Timetable (1992), in which it was made clear that in fact, by December 1994, it would only be possible to conclude the Common External Tariff (TEC) or, in other words, a customs union with limitations.[6]

In 1993 the Brazilian President Collor de Mello resigned in a failed attempt to stop his impeachment trial for corruption by the Brazilian Senate, leaving the country in a very weak political and economic condition. The presidency was assumed by Vice-President Itamar Franco. With regard to regional integration, during his brief tenure Franco continued to pursue the actions that had been agreed by the previous incumbent. However, some adaptations were necessary in order to pursue more modest goals. It is worth highlighting two turns of events: the promotion of Decision 13/93 by the Common Market Council (CMC), taken in Colonia del Sacramento, Uruguay, formally postponing the consolidation of the common market after the transition period; and the result obtained for the institutional structure of Mercosur in the Protocol of Ouro Preto in 1994, without any organism with supranational prerogatives. On this occasion, the TEC was established, formalizing the customs union.

In early 1995 Fernando Henrique Cardoso was elected to the Brazilian presidency and the inauguration of his first government marked a period of democratic consolidation as well as economic stabilization brought about by the 'Plano Real'. The idea that the new international order would be characterized by the low importance of security issues and the stratification of international politics in multilateral and thematic international regimes was legitimated. From an economic point of view, in addition to the globalization of economic flows, one could perceive an international tendency of being organized in regional blocs, as a way of being prepared for a later scheduled multilateral trade opening. At this point, Mercosur, which had been arranged before this global trend emerged, had a patrimonial value to Brazil.

In what is called the 'Mercosur model promoted by the Brazilian foreign policy' that was mainly developed during Fernando Henrique Cardoso's government, 'the characteristics of the bloc must agree with the principles of autonomy and development which are expressed in

Mercosur by two main characteristics of the South Cone integration process: inter-governmentalism and the difficulty in dealing with existing asymmetries.[7]

Concerning trade negotiations, the signing of the 1995 Interregional Cooperation Framework Agreement between Mercosur and the European Union (EU) initiated a process of instrumentalizing the bloc as an international coalition for negotiating on two separate circumstances (the EU and the Free Trade Area of the Americas – FTAA), and using the offers made by one or the other to present as alternatives side by side. In addition, Brazil prioritized multilateral negotiations in the recently created World Trade Organization (WTO), to obtain advantages through the use of the Dispute Settlement Mechanism, mainly in the commercial areas in which Brazil is highly competitive.[8]

From an economic point of view, the period comprising the signature of the Treaty of Asunción in 1991, the Brazilian economic stabilization brought about by the 'Plano Real' in 1994, until the 1997 Asian financial crisis, corresponds to the best economic and commercial phase of Mercosur. The trade flows among members of the bloc grew at an annual average of more than 25 per cent. The relative importance of intra-bloc transactions increased from 8.9 per cent in 1990 to 22.4 per cent in 1997. Brazilian foreign direct investment (FDI) in Argentina increased five-fold between 1993 and 1997.

However, the financial crisis contaminated global market liquidity and it became increasingly difficult for Brazil to maintain the regime of exchange rate bands that was supporting economic stability in the country, along with other measures. Following the decline in international liquidity due to the Russian crisis,[9] the Brazilian government would not have sufficient resources to sustain the appreciation of the Brazilian currency for a long time. Thus, following the general election in 1998, the floating exchange rate regime was adopted and the currency soon suffered a strong devaluation. Automatically, relative prices within Mercosur changed in favour of Brazil.

Argentina, which was also following an economic model based on the artificial parity of its currency, the peso, with the US dollar, suffered the effects of the same international financial crisis in an even tougher way. The devaluation of the real only aggravated Argentina's situation. According to Ferrer, not only did the central bank of the country maintain the parity with the dollar by emptying its reserves, but also the following errors contributed to the accumulation of an unpayable debt by the Argentine government: (1) the opening of its internal market with an overvalued exchange rate that destroyed their domestic industry; (2) the setting up of foreign subsidiaries with deficits in transactions abroad; and (3) the reform of the social security sector which reduced public resources.[10]

President Fernando de la Rúa governed Argentina from 1999 to 2001. After decreeing the *corralito*,[11] which sparked national unrest, he had no choice other than to resign. The economic crisis turned into a political one and after many candidates were nominated for the presidency, Eduardo Alberto Duhalde Maldonado took over and ruled the country during 2002. Although efforts were made, the Argentine risk premium reached the highest peak ever seen in economic history and the partial default on external debt was inevitable, causing difficulties in finding finance for the nation that endure to the present day.

The social, political, participatory and distributive phase (2003–10)

The election, in 2003, of Néstor Carlos Kirchner in Argentina and Luiz Inácio Lula da Silva in Brazil, therefore occurred in a post-crisis context. At that time, the trend in thinking was to enhance the bilateral partnership and question the free trade model on which Mercosur had been based up until then. The two presidents met in the Argentine capital in October. 'Consensus of Buenos Aires', the document resulting from the meeting, proposed that Mercosur should be revived, but that its objectives must be reprioritized to give more attention to the social, political, participatory and distributive dimensions of regional integration. Although trade liberalization was not abandoned, the new slogans guiding the process were social justice (the fight against poverty, inequality, hunger and illiteracy); joint action in multilateral arenas; the participation of civil society; and the reduction of regional imbalances.

In December 2003, at the biannual summit in Montevideo, the four member states approved a work programme for 2004–06 that incorporated this new perspective. The tasks identified included:

i   Economy and trade: consolidate the common external tariff, formulate the Common Customs Code, promote productive integration, achieve macroeconomic co-ordination, and evaluate external negotiations;
ii Social: broaden mechanisms for the participation of civil society, and research social issues such as work, education, and human rights;
iii Institutional: establish the Mercosur parliament, and strengthen existing institutions;
iv 'New agenda': promote cooperation in science and technology, and the integration of energy supply systems.

Progress towards meeting these objectives was uneven, with both successes and failures recorded. According to Vázquez and Ruiz, this was the result of the first part of the programme:

> the consolidation of the customs union has stalled because of the difficulties in adopting a Common Customs Code, currently under negotiation, and in finding joint mechanisms for the distribution of customs revenue. Productive integration projects are modest, especially given the large asymmetries among member states, particularly in terms of resources earmarked and the scope of national competitiveness programs.[12]

Indeed, this analysis is confirmed by the fact that in 2010 the CMC issued Decision no. 56/10, the 'Customs Union Consolidation Programme', in which many of the commitments that remained open since the launch of the Mercosur Work Programme 2004–06 were extended. The main challenges that had yet to be faced included economic incentives (use of special customs regimes in intra-bloc trade relations, such as drawback); the failures of the rules of origin, which give rise to the problem of infiltration of Asian competition through triangulation; and the end of the exceptions and the double collection of the TEC, with the proper redistribution of the customs income.[13] Regarding the Common Customs Code, even though it has been approved, it still needs to be ratified by national legislations.

Steps were duly taken to improve the economy. In addition to the approval of the Mercosur Productive Integration Programme in 2008, the creation of the Mercosur Structural Convergence Fund in 2004 proved to be the main example of change. Since then, it has become a reality in the structure of the bloc, not only a mechanism of development cooperation, but also aimed to face the structural asymmetries among the members. Even though it took four years for it to begin operating, since 2007 many projects have been approved annually.

With regard to the second part of the programme, Social Mercosur, although the advances were slow and gradual, it is possible to state that, at a certain level, it could reflect the demands made by social movements that were supportive of the domestic action against poverty and social inequality led by each government of the member states. Thus, as Martins points out, the efforts are certain due to the establishment of the Mercosur Coordination Commission for Social Affairs Ministers (CCMASM), the creation of the Mercosur Social Institute (ISM), the approval of the Strategic Plan for Social Action (PEAS), the institutionalization of the Mercosur Social Summits (CSM) and the adoption of the [Action Plan for Conforming] the Citizenship Statute.[14]

In this sense, we can add to this list the creation of the Mercosur Institute of Public Policies on Human Rights (IPPDH) in 2009. In terms of including the civil society in the decision-making processes related to the directions the bloc would go, there has been the Mercosur Social Summits, held regularly since 2006, prior to the semi-annual summit meetings that occur at the end of each *pro tempore* presidency. As there are numerous and diversified institutions of organized civil society, the Social Summits hold debates and discussions so that a final document containing the agreed demands is submitted for the appreciation of the heads of state. Although this document has no binding force, a formal channel of dialogue has been opened between societies and governments ever since. In the same vein, the Social Accountability Office was created in 2013 to act as a formal mechanism that allows organizations and social movements to request information for the organs of Mercosur.[15]

As for the third area of the programme, Institutional Mercosur, the approval of the Constitutive Protocol of the Mercosur Parliament in 2005 and its entry into force in 2006 should be analysed as a considerably rapid process for the complexity of this task. In any case, due to the maintenance of the intergovernmental institutional framework of Mercosur, it is necessary to consider that Parlasur has many limitations in its attributions, since it does not have legislative competence.

> The main funcionality of Parlasur was inherited from JPC [Joint Parliamentary Commission], which was responsible for assisting Mercosur's rules incorporation and harmonization in national legislatures. The drafts aiming to integrate the norms also aim to guarantee the coherence and adaptation of the laws of each State to the decisions of Mercosur regional organs. In short, Parlasur presents: (i) an advisory role in the legislative sphere; (ii) a controlling role of other Mercosur spheres; (iii) the role of defending human rights and democracy in the bloc; and (iv) the function of harmonizing regional and national standards, in close cooperation with national legislatures.[16]

Another significant advance, from the institutional point of view, was the creation of the office of Mercosur's High Representative-General (MHR) in 2010. The Representative-General fulfils several functions relating to motivating the development of cooperation among members, as well as representing the bloc to other countries and third parties under the express mandate of the CMC. Curiously, even though it is not its specific function, the Representative-General proved to be quite active and effective in negotiating for the enlargement of the bloc.

Still in the political context, it is worth pointing out that the content of positions taken on global issues in the joint biannual communiqués has broadened, along with the growth of the convergence of votes in international organizations such as the United Nations General Assembly. It shows clear success in the objective of promoting the functioning of Mercosur as an international coalition.[17]

Finally, the fourth point of the programme, the New Agenda for Integration, regarding cooperation in science and technology, was developed mainly through bilateral cooperation between states parties. In the case of physical and energy integration, the theme remained under the auspices of the South American Regional Infrastructure Integration Initiative (IIRSA), as it will be discussed later.

For the purposes of this chapter, we need to note that the participants succeeded in extending the agenda of regional integration, giving Mercosur a political and strategic direction in addition to its economic and commercial aspects. This, in turn, led to the increased coordination of the foreign policy positions of the member states. In fact, the revival of Mercosur along these lines formed part of, and contributed to, a broader thrust towards South American unity. Led by Brazil, this initiative started with the First South American Summit held in Brasília in 2000, when its main goals were defined as:

i   bolstering the physical integration of the continent, including the establishment of the IIRSA;
ii initiating a process of convergence between Mercosur and the Andean Community of Nations (Comunidad Andina de Naciones – CAN), with a view to forming a free trade area between the two blocs;
iii coordinating negotiating positions in respect of the FTAA in order to ensure access to international markets; and
iv confirming the status of the region as a zone of peace, and affirming a commitment to democracy.

These goals were reaffirmed at the Second South American Summit, held in Guayaquil, Ecuador, in 2002. It adopted a Declaration on the South American Zone of Peace and celebrated the significance of the First Meeting of the Ministers of Foreign Affairs of Mercosur, Chile and the CAN, which had occurred the previous year. In addition, it established the Mechanism of Dialogue and Political Coordination to encourage the convergence of views on issues of common interest.

The Third South American Summit, which formally created the South American Community of Nations (CASA), was held in Cusco, Peru, in 2004. Political and diplomatic co-ordination, understood as a means of strengthening the continent's negotiating capability and international stature, was named as a major goal. In 2008 all countries on the continent signed the Constitutive Treaty of the Union of South American Nations (Unión de Naciones Suramericanas – Unasur). Its goals included the 'strengthening of political dialogue between the Member States to ensure a forum for coordination and to reinforce South-American integration and the participation of Unasur in the international arena'.[18]

This broader coordination and integration process was largely driven by the Lula government in Brazil, which adopted a more proactive foreign policy posture, based on a revised understanding of the international context.[19] The previous administration sought to gain credibility in the eyes of the great powers by adopting Western standards, in the belief that it would benefit from being considered a globalizing and modernizing country. By contrast, the Lula government sought to retain Brazil's autonomy by forming alternative political fora that signalled a rejection of a unipolar world order, as well as a devolution of global power. It did so in the belief that an unfettered process of globalization tended to generate inequalities, and that Brazil (and other South American countries) would need to develop the requisite skills and capabilities to become effective global players.

This also happened within a changing international context. The global 'war on terror' promoted by the US Administration of George W. Bush from 2001 onwards, involving some unilateral initiatives such as the invasion of Afghanistan and Iraq, had a major impact on US global leadership.[20] It also resulted in the USA giving less attention to Latin America, and focusing on the Middle East and Asia instead. Thus, the circumstances in the early 2000s were conducive to the launch of developing country initiatives that challenged US hegemony and sought allies in the defence of multilateralism. This trend gained strength towards the end of the decade following the 2008 financial crisis, the Chinese economic advance, and the euro crisis.

In this context, Brazil started to advocate for a multipolar global order based on the principles of multilateralism. South-south cooperation was the key element of the new project. Regional integration was meant to fit into this broader strategy. Thus, the government 'Balance Sheet for 2003–2010', posted on the presidency website, stated that

> the consolidation of political and economic relations between the South American countries will contribute to the socioeconomic development of South America and to the preservation of peace in the region; to the development of the South American internal market and the increasing competitiveness of countries in the international market; and to the strengthening of Brazil's capacity to act in other international fora. South American integration is based on two pillars: Unasur and Mercosur.[21].

In keeping with this strategy, Mercosur countries were inserted into three of the five new international south-south coalition initiatives promoted by Brazil: the G20, formed within the framework of the Doha Round of negotiations in support of the elimination of barriers to trade in agricultural goods; the Summits of the South American-Arab Countries; and the Summits of South America-Africa.[22]

This makes it easier to understand why in 2004 Mercosur and the CAN signed a trade agreement, and Colombia, Ecuador, Peru and Venezuela joined the Southern Cone bloc as associates,[23] participating in its biannual summits since then. In 2012 Guyana and Suriname also joined Mercosur as associates, giving it the same membership as Unasur. In the process, at long last, Mercosur and Unasur became complementary elements of the same project, aimed at increasing the participation of South American states in global affairs, bolstering development and creating regional governance institutions.

On the other hand, when it comes to Mercosur agreements with third markets,[24] this period was marked by the slow pace of negotiations in most initiatives, including those with the EU, because of both the difficulties to close common liberalization packages between the bloc's states parties, and the possible counterpart initiatives. Therefore, little of what was put under evaluation was effectively consolidated.

Besides the signing of trade agreements with India, Israel, the Southern African Customs Union, Egypt, the Palestinian (National) Authority and Lebanon, the aforementioned conclusion of the negotiations for the Mercosur free trade agreement with the CAN in 2004 must be highlighted. Although presenting a limited initial scope when it comes to the breadth of tariff lines, and the postponed deadlines for its effective realization, it had an important political significance for the Brazilian objective of, on the one hand, extending the geographical scope of regional integration to South America, and on the other hand, clearly demonstrating its preference for a free trade area of a narrower scope than the one proposed by the USA, the FTAA.

The uncertainty phase (2011–)

The achievement of good economic fundamentals for Brazil up to 2011 coincided with a very favourable international scenario for the primary exporting countries. At first they provided resources for the country to cope with the difficulties imposed by the external environment during the economic crisis of 2008. However, over the years and the dragging on of the crisis, which was intensified in Europe in 2011 and forcefully reached the People's Republic of China a little later, the countercyclical measures adopted in Brazil progressively lost their effectiveness – in addition to producing a growing fiscal cost.

Regarding the external sector, the development model that had been adopted was becoming increasingly dependent on exports of primary goods, as well as on the financing of the capital account through FDI.[25] Between April 2011 and 2015 Bloomberg's commodity price index decreased by 42 per cent, nearly uninterrupted, mostly because of the maintenance of an accelerated growth of supply at a point when a slowdown in (mainly) Chinese demand for these products could be observed. The inflow of FDI, for its part, also decreased, but in a smoother way. Thus, the model crashed and difficulties were imposed on the balance of payments not only in Brazil, but also in the other Mercosur countries whose export patterns are even more concentrated in raw materials. The end of the super-cycle of commodities put in question the countercyclical policies based on stimulating domestic consumption.

Argentina, having experienced difficulties in accessing the international financial system since 2001, was hit even more severely by this situation, which exerted strong pressure on its international reserves. On the trade side, one of the main sources of its deficit was held with Brazil. For these reasons, in 2012 the country started to control imports through the introduction of the Anticipated Declaration of Imports and through the suspension of automatic licenses for several imported products. Since then, Argentine importers have been required to make a commitment to compensating for their foreign purchases with equivalent exports, in order to avoid foreign currencies evasion.

Brazil was the country most affected by these measures. In the context of Mercosur, Argentina's protectionism not only impacted the bloc's commercial network, but also contaminated the integration agenda in a general way. In other words, the commercial disputes between the two biggest partners and the deceleration of economic growth within the bloc meant that there were no conditions to somehow advance with the initiatives for the new dimensions of integration. In the economic and commercial field, in which Paraguay and Uruguay had been demanding more openness for years, the change of position of the Federation of Industries of the State of São Paulo, Brazil (which became more willing to yield, with the idea of integrating itself within the global value chains) enabled the Dilma Rousseff government to reactivate negotiations with the EU. However, the reluctance of agriculture and livestock sectors in France, Ireland and Poland to reach an agreement, on the one hand, and Argentina's slowness to submit proposals for tariff cuts, on the other, prevented the signing of the agreement once again. In 2014 the Argentine debt crisis with the so-called vulture funds only aggravated the difficulties of the country's external accounts, reducing even more the space for Mercosur partners to demand the suspension of intra-bloc import control measures.

Still in relation to the commercial theme, it is important to point out that the period was marked by the progressive growth of the Chinese presence in the total trade of all countries of South America, becoming the main commercial partner of the subcontinent and source of financing and loans. The growth of Chinese investments in productive sectors and in infrastructure projects related to the market of commodities exports was also a common feature in the region. It was also characterized as the most important outlet for the external financing crisis in the case of Argentina, as well as in Ecuador, Guyana, Suriname and Venezuela. In view of this, Benatti[26] calls attention to the dilemmas of this relationship, based essentially on the export of primary goods and the import of industrialized products by the South American countries: price volatility of the commodities; dependence on the Chinese growth rate; low employment in the primary export sector; external financial vulnerability; the possibility of generating conflicts domestically owing to income redistribution (with the increase of exporters' wealth).

In fact, in recent years virtually all of these risks have become reality. Currently, South America is characterized by its participation in global value chains via the most elementary stages of the production processes. Regarding the relations established with China, the regional integration institutions should develop a common strategy for receiving Chinese credit and investment, so as to optimize them in favour of the region. Arranging their positions, the main concern should be to envisage ways in which these investments could contribute to the integration of infrastructure, to regional productive complementarity and to the increase of the value added of South American exports.

The Brazilian discourse in defence of the association of its economic, social and political development with that of its neighbours was more present in the second half of the 2000s and at the beginning of Dilma government, notably in her inauguration. Since the worsening of the economic and political crisis in Brazil at the beginning of her second mandate, the country turned to its domestic problems and did not present significant proposals at a regional level.

Beyond these structural economic difficulties, some political disruptions in the region have also recently impacted the regional integration processes. The resignation of Paraguay's President Fernando Lugo in 2012, a result of a violent episode originated from the confluence of conflicting interests between peasant social movements and Brazilian businessmen of soybean agribusiness, revealed dilemmas of the growing international projection of Brazil in the region.[27] Paraguay was promptly suspended from the institutions of Mercosur and Unasur, which led to the definitive incorporation of Venezuela into the bloc, which had been delayed because it did not receive the consent of the Paraguayan parliament. This tense climate would only cool down following the conclusion of the Paraguayan elections in 2013 and the readmission of the country to the bloc.

In addition, during the last decade Latin America and the Caribbean have been trying to fill the political space opened up by the reduction in US hemispheric influence and have been exposing a collective identity in a variety of ways and at various opportunities – particularly creating institutions that attempt to progressively organize the international relations of the region over the heads of the old hemispheric mechanisms, essentially the Organization of American States (OAS). With this in mind, the constitution of the Community of Latin American and Caribbean States (CELAC) in 2011, which started bringing together at summits all the countries of the Americas, excluding Canada and the USA, was the main symbol of these new hemispheric dynamics.[28]

In terms of hemispheric relations, CELAC's main motto was the pressure to reintroduce Cuba to the OAS and the demand for an end to the economic blockade of the country. This demand has repeatedly materialized through joint declarations by Mercosur, Unasur and CELAC, and was echoed at the 2009 and 2012 Summits of the Americas. The region demonstrated cohesion and conviction, with these attitudes, in the objective of achieving the emancipation of its international insertion.

Indeed, China's growing political and economic presence in the traditional zone of influence of the global hegemon – definitely attested by the periodic completion of the CELAC-China Summits – has been a key additional factor in leading the USA to rethink its regional approach. Thus, at the end of 2014 the USA began a process of rapprochement with Cuba, which included the release of political prisoners by both countries, the end of some consular restrictions and the reopening of embassies, as well as the potential cessation of the economic embargo.

On the other hand, the uncertainties of the period continued to accumulate because of the unfolding of two other fundamental political issues in the region. First, the death of Hugo Chávez in 2013 created a crisis of succession in Venezuela. Nicolas Maduro, the ruling candidate, was eventually elected, but with a very narrow advantage (50.6 per cent). In the following years, the fall in the price of oil and the reduction of government income caused the twin deficits, increasing the opposition voices. The situation has led to the scarcity of even some basic hygiene products imported by the country. Since then, Venezuela has immersed itself in a political crisis that has hit the streets, leading to violence. Ideological polarization and intolerance on the political scenario turned out to be a trend in the region and in the world.

Second, Brazil has been struggling since 2012 against the most severe effects of the international crisis that began in 2008 and the Argentine protectionism. With the change of the national productive structure during the boom period (increase of the share of primary goods in the composition of the gross domestic product), the industrial sector faced difficulties caused by the appreciated exchange rate and the increase of the external competition, especially China. This new scenario had a negative impact on the indicators that have been showing good results. Among other factors, the pace of economic growth slowed to a recession, unemployment grew steadily, the improvement in social indicators stagnated and inflation spiralled out of control (especially from the last quarter of 2014 onwards).

At that juncture there had been a political crisis that began with the narrow victory of the coalition led by the government against the opposition in the second round of the 2014 elections,[29] and passed through the widespread corruption scandal exposed by the federal police Operation Car Wash. The corruption scandals led to a crisis within the government's ruling coalition in the national congress and caused the impeachment of President Dilma in 2016 – a parliamentary-judicial coup very similar to the one that took place in Paraguay years before.

The rise to power of Vice-President Michel Temer led to a new party coalition that gave representation to the opposition campaign project. The election to the presidency of Horacio Cartes in Paraguay in 2013 and Mauricio Macri in Argentina in 2015 led to a favouring of the right wing in Mercosur. The Venezuelan government lost support from Brazil, and the division in the bloc forced Uruguay, under pressure, to concede and agree with the suspension of Venezuela at the end of 2016, due to its humanitarian crisis.[30]

Having the country out, the idea of the new rulers was to retake Mercosur's initial economic trade agenda and increase its integration into global value chains, based on two alternatives: signing preferential agreements as a bloc with as many countries as possible; or bringing an end to the customs union, freeing members to sign trade agreements with third countries individually. In any case, this agenda has been put on hold since the election of Donald Trump to the US presidency in 2016, followed by the denunciation of the Trans-Pacific Partnership agreement and his growing nationalistic and protectionist government agenda. All these factors have provoked a radical change in the global context of international trade and the negotiation of preferential agreements. Very recently, this situation opened space for Mercosur to advance the negotiations with the EU. However, the same European countries – France, Ireland and Poland – are still blocking the main parts of the agreement.

Conclusion

This chapter aimed both to expose the strategic sense given to Mercosur by its member countries since its inception and to indicate which factors best explained the changes observed along the three phases distinguished here for analytical purposes. The review carried out in the text leads to three fundamental conclusions about the development of the Mercosur regional integration process. First, the directions taken by Brazilian foreign policy and the decisions derived from it are decisive for the strategic sense given to the bloc. Second, the intergovernmental format and the consensus rule for decisions have remained intact over the years precisely to meet Brazil's desire not to cede parcels of sovereignty to the regional project, which ultimately is one of the main sources of the frequent and abrupt changes in the directions taken by the bloc. Finally, the current conjuncture, coupled with the economic and political crises that have been observed in almost all South American countries since the beginning of the decade of 2010, indicates the beginning of a new and fourth phase in which the economic agenda will be brought back to the centre of the process. However, it seems that the political weakness of the coalitions ruling each one of the countries will contribute to slowing the pace of this change.

Notes

1 The issue was solved by the ratification of the Tripartite Agreement on Technical-Operational Coordination for the Hydroelectric Use of Itaipu and Corpus, signed by Argentina, Brazil and Paraguay in 1979, by which the three neighbouring countries have set the conditions to peacefully share the resources of the hydrographic basin of the River Plate.

2 Under the 1988 Agreement on Integration, Cooperation and Development between Brazil and Argentina, the deadline for the consolidation of the free trade area was set to the year of 1998.

3 Known as ECLAC, or in Spanish CEPAL, which is a UN regional commission created in 1948 that undertakes studies, research and other support activities to promote economic and social development through regional and subregional cooperation and integration.

4 ALADI is the successor to the Latin American Free Trade Association (Asociación Latinoamericana de Libre Comercio – ALALC), which was abandoned mainly due to the inflexibility of its mechanisms and the unwillingness of the participating countries at the time (1960–80) to make tariff concessions on items that were subject to the import substitution process. See P. R. Almeida (2008) 'Evolução histórica do regionalismo econômico e político na América do Sul: um balanço das experiências realizadas', *Cena internacional*, 10(2): 72– 97; R. Teixeira and W. Desiderá (2012) 'A recuperação do desenvolvimentismo no regionalismo latino-americano', *Texto para Discussão*, n. 1790, Brasília: IPEA, p. 18).

5 There were only some specific differences predicted in the pace of the trade liberalization programme, with a deadline to 1995. A.Vaz and C. Cooperação (2002) *Integração e processo negociador: A construção do Mercosul*, Brasília: FUNAG, IPRI.

6 R. Baumann (2001) 'Mercosul: origens, ganhos, desencontros e perspectivas', in R. Baumann (ed.) *Mercosul, Avanços e desafios da integração*, Brasília: IPEA, p. 26.

7 M. Mariano and H. Ramanzini, Jr. (2012) 'Uma análise das limitações estruturais do Mercosul a partir das posições da política externa brasileira', *Revista de Sociologia e Política*, 20(43): 23.

8 T. Vigevani, M. F. Oliveira and R. Cintra (2003) 'Política externa no período FHC: a busca de autonomia pela integração', *Tempo Social Revista de Sociologia da USP*, p. 49.

9 The financial crisis that hit the Russian Federation on 17 August 1998 resulted in the Russian government and the Russian Central Bank devaluing the ruble and defaulting on its debt.

10 A. Ferrer, (2006) *A economia argentina: De suas origens ao início do século XXI*, Rio de Janeiro: Elsevier, pp. 299–302.

11 The informal name given to the economic measures taken in Argentina at the end of 2001 by Minister of Economy Domingo Cavallo in order to stop a bank run, and which were fully in force for one year.

12 Vigevanti, Oliveria and Cintra, 'Política externa no período FHC', p. 39.

13 A. Calixtre and W. Desidera (2011) 'Desafios para a consolidação da união aduaneira no Mercosul', *Boletim de Economia e Política Internacional*, IPEA 8 (Oct./Dec.).

14 J. R. V. Martins (2014) 'Mercosul: a dimensão social e participativa da integração regional', in W. Desidera (ed.) *O Brasil e novas dimensões da integração regional*, Brasília: IPEA, p. 107.

15 It is worth remembering that, since 1994 (Protocol of Ouro Preto), regarding the participation of civil society, there was only the Economic and Social Consultative Forum in the institutional structure of Mercosur.

16 B. T. Luciano (2012) 'A inclusão da representatividade direta no Parlamento do Mercosul', *Boletim de Economia e Política Internacional*, 11, IPEA (July/Sept.): 52.

17 W. Desidera (2016) 'The Evolution of Mercosur Behaving as an International Coalition, 1991–2012', *Contexto Internacional*, 38(2), May/Aug.

18 Unasur Constitutive Treaty, Article 3, section a.

19 M. R. S. Lima (2005) 'A política externa brasileira e os desafios da cooperação Sul-Sul', *Revista Brasileira de Política Internacional*, 48(1): 11–13; C. Amorim (2010) 'Brazilian Foreign Policy under President Lula (2003–2010): An Overview', *Revista Brasileira de Política Internacional*, 53, special edn, p. 215.

20 B. Buzan (2007) 'A Leader without Followers? The United States in World Politics after Bush', Policy Paper no. 2, The Global Policy Institute.

21 Balanço de governo 2003–10 (2010). Available at www.balancodegoverno.presidencia.gov.br/ (accessed 18 September 2013).

22 The other two initiatives are the IBSA Dialogue Forum (India, Brazil and South Africa), and the annual BRIC summits (Brazil, Russia, India and China), to which South Africa was added in 2011.

23 Venezuela, particularly, ended up in 2006 by starting a process to achieve full membership, which eventually happened in 2012 at the time of the temporary suspension of Paraguay.

24 Negotiations in progress, in chronological order: Association of Southeast Asian Nations (ASEAN), Canada, the Republic of Korea (South Korea), Cuba, Caribbean Community (CARICOM), Gulf Cooperation Council (GCC), Jordan, Morocco, Pakistan, Russia (after Eurasian Customs Union), Syria, Central American Integration System (SICA), Turkey, European Free Trade Area (EFTA), Japan, Mexico, China, Australia, New Zealand and Tunisia.

25 A. B. Calixtre, A. M. Biancarelli and M. A. M. Cintra (eds) (2014) *Presente e futuro do desenvolvimento brasileiro*, Brasília: IPEA.

26 A. S. Benatti (2011) A presença da China no Mercosul: implicações sobre o processo de integração regional, *Oikos*, 10(2): 229–30.

27 F. L. B. Santos (2014) 'A problemática brasiguaia e os dilemas da influência regional brasileira', in W. Desidera (ed.) *O Brasil e novas dimensões da integração regional*, Brasília: IPEA p. 447–78.

28 C. S. Pecequilo (2013) 'A América do Sul como espaço geopolítico e geoeconômico: O Brasil, os Estados Unidos e a China', *Carta Internacional*, 8(2), July-Dec.: 100–15.

29 Although the massive street protests that occurred in June 2013 had been initiated due to increases in transportation tickets prices, they ended up being co-opted in general by movements opposed to the government. They announced the crisis that was about to come, since the same groups called for impeachment in 2015.

30 The suspension was formalized in other terms, pointing out a lack of required progresses for the country to incorporate the block. However, political leaders made it clear, in their statements to the press, that the real reason was the Venezuelan domestic conjuncture.

20

The Pacific Alliance

Gian Luca Gardini

In April 2011 the presidents of Chile, Colombia, Mexico and Peru issued the Lima Declaration, which set out the vision for the creation of the Pacific Alliance (Alianza del Pacífico). The Declaration was notable for its conciseness unlike many Latin American political statements. Its clarity and restraint in terms of objectives and ambitions were remarkable too. The vision enshrined in the Declaration went against the prevailing zeitgeist. It emphasized the economic character of the undertaking, the commitment to free trade and entrepreneurship as well as the belief in investment and competitiveness as the best way to pursue societal development and international insertion. In particular, the initiative intended to reach out to the Asia-Pacific region, a novel approach to integration in Latin America.[1]

The mood dominating Latin America at that time was quite different. The 'pink tide', the wave of left-leaning governments that characterized the first decade of the 21st century in Latin America, was solidly in power and gaining consensus domestically and internationally. Blaming neoliberal policies for most of Latin America's problems was very fashionable.[2] Criticism of free trade and its proponents, that was on occasion quite harsh, was widely accepted in the political discourse, although less so in practice.[3] The alternative versions of the pink tide, ranging from state-supported capitalism to soft protectionism and even utopian barter-based exchanges, seemed to work quite well, and so also did the high international prices of major commodities, still the crucial export sector for most of the region.

This political and economic climate prompted a rethinking of regional trade and integration in Latin America. A proliferation of new proposals that were critical of global capitalism, the existing international order, and intended to increase Latin American influence internationally, ensued. In 2004 the Bolivarian Alliance for the Peoples of Our America (Alianza Bolivariana para los Pueblos de Nuestra América – ALBA) was created to unite Latin America in the resistance against free markets and the perceived evil side of US-sponsored international capitalism. In 2008 the Union of South American Nations (Unión de Naciones Suramericanas – UNASUR) marked the emergence of Brazilian regional and global status directing regional policy along the lines desired by Brasília, including a soft criticism of the USA, and its interference in Latin America. In 2011 all 33 Latin American and Caribbean states created the Community of Latin American and Caribbean States (Comunidad de Estados de América Latina y el Caribe – CELAC), a platform for the continent to speak with one voice at major international venues.

By the end of the first decade of the new millennium, the signs of a counter-reaction to this wave of ideologically charged regionalism were palpable. The search began for pragmatic, less rigid and more results-oriented forms of cooperation rather than deep, ambitious and almost all-encompassing, but hardly consequential, economic integration. Latin America had reached the peak of traditional regionalism and now sought geographically diffused, multilateral rather than regional, development and insertion strategies.[4] The peak of regionalism as economic integration did not exclude but on the contrary envisaged other forms of cooperation. This became increasingly visible in the so-called third-generation regionalism, which stresses the need for increased international projection of regional groupings and their insertion into global networks.[5]

The Pacific Alliance was a symptom of, and a first response to, these dynamics and needs. The 2012 Pacific Alliance constitutive treaty may well signal a fourth wave of Latin American regionalism. The closed regionalism of the 1960s and 1970s was followed by the open regionalism of the 1990s, and the post-neoliberal and post-hegemonic wave of the 2000s. This new phase of 'modular regionalism'[6] is characterized by the coexistence of several modes of regional cooperation. The distinctive features of the Pacific Alliance are a preference for free trade as an instrument to pursue inclusive economic and social development, and a projection towards the Asia-Pacific. The regional level thus becomes primarily a platform from which to reach extra-regional trade partners and markets, while the intraregional dimension is essentially devoted to societal improvement.

Consequently, the Pacific Alliance is a *sui generis* project of both regional integration and trade agreement. The following sections address the nature, functioning and main achievements of the Pacific Alliance; its use as a tool for national strategies of development and international insertion; and the most topical challenges faced by and initiatives of the organization.

Nature, functioning and achievements of the Pacific Alliance

The Pacific Alliance is 'an area of regional integration' between Chile, Colombia, Mexico and Peru.[7] This formulation is quite vague. While Article 1A points to the direction of a 'deep integration', this definition does not match scholarly understandings or actual policy. The Pacific Alliance was established in order to create a free circulation area for goods, services, capital and people with the aim of improving the well-being of its citizens, overcome social inequalities, and project its members to the world, with emphasis on the Asia-Pacific. Deep integration does not mean the creation of a customs union or a common market, according to the Latin American tradition of regional integration, e.g. the Andean Community of Nations (Comunidad Andina de Naciones) or the Southern Common Market (Mercado Común del Sur – Mercosur). Furthermore, it does not imply any cession of national sovereignty or the creation of supranational institutions, as is the case in the European tradition of integration.

The Pacific Alliance is a no-frills integration model. It aims to constitute an effective free trade area among members and to articulate a political and economic platform to facilitate its members' insertion in international markets and global value chains. It emphasizes trade facilitation and simplification of export and customs procedures. This 'minimalism' appears to be the key to its early success.[8] This approach is evident in the pragmatic modus operandi of the organization. On the one hand, the Alliance works according to the logic of piecemeal agreements, namely that members agree upon and proceed with specific and well-defined measures, thus avoiding the strenuous negotiations and/or stalemates associated with grand packages. On the other hand, an 'early harvest approach' means that relatively uncontroversial issues are tackled first to generate a chain of successful deals.[9] This strengthens trust among members and reinforces the confidence of external partners in the ability of the organization to deliver.

Minimalism characterizes the slim institutional structure of the organization too. The highest decision-making body of the Alliance is composed of the four presidents. They decide the key orientations, generally during Presidential Summits. Some of these have been held via video conference in order to save time and resources. The organization has no permanent secretariat. The *pro tempore* presidency has these functions. It hosts and organizes the presidential meetings, coordinates the sessions of the other bodies, keeps documents and archives, and represents the organization with international partners and forums.[10] Each member state holds the *pro tempore* presidency for one calendar year in rotating alphabetical order.

The main executive bodies are the Council of Ministers and the High Level Group. The former is composed of the Ministers of Foreign Affairs and the Ministers of Foreign Trade. The Council adopts decisions about the implement the presidents' key indications and the provisions in the framework agreement. It also monitors compliance with and implementation of its decisions, and it evaluates the results achieved by the Pacific Alliance. The Council also has the power to define the external projection of the Alliance.[11] The Council adopts decisions by consensus. The High Level Group, which comprises the Deputy Ministers of Foreign Affairs and Trade, supervises the work of the technical groups and proposes new areas of cooperation. The technical groups bring together government officials specializing in specific fields under discussion by the Alliance.[12] The institutional architecture is not only highly intergovernmental, but inter-presidentialism is a major feature of the Alliance's dynamics and motives.

Two other bodies are attached to the Pacific Alliance: the Business Council and the Integrated Latin American Market (Mercado Integrado Latinoamericano – MILA). The former is a consultative body in which business representatives from the four member states have a dual role. On the one hand, they can make recommendations to improve the integration process and to undertake initiatives geared at third markets. On the other, and quite interestingly, they act as 'ambassadors' of the Alliance vis-à-vis the entrepreneurial community.[13] Far from being a dormant mechanism, the Business Council has so far taken an 'active, assertive role',[14] prioritizing issues such as financial integration, equivalence of technical standards and tax harmonization. This suggests quite extensive support for the Alliance from the business sector. Looking at the positive experience of the European Union (EU)[15] and the less positive one of Mercosur,[16] a proactive business sector is indispensable for the success of economic integration projects.

MILA was launched in 2011 as an independent initiative on the part of the private sector. It was later incorporated into the Pacific Alliance. The Stock Exchanges in Lima, Santiago, Bogotá and Mexico City have integrated their equity markets to provide investors with the largest possible choice and issuers with more sources of financing. Using registered brokers in each member state, MILA allows transactions to be made in local currency in each of the four markets. This saves stock operators the cost of currency conversion and the taxes associated with the transfers.[17] This generates more business in and around MILA, as shown for instance by the purchase of the Chilean brokerage and asset manager Celfin Capital by the Brazilian investment bank BTG Pactual. In 2016 there were already over 770 companies listed with MILA and a stock capitalization of over US $744 billion, the first and second largest figures, respectively, of all capital markets in Latin America.

The early achievements of the Pacific Alliance are impressive. In addition to the creation of MILA, the Alliance has plenty to show.[18] The Additional Protocol establishing the Pacific Alliance free trade area entered into force in 2016. It eliminates tariffs on 92 per cent of goods between the member states with the expectation of freeing the remaining 8 per cent, including the most sensitive sectors, within seven years. The system for the interoperability of Foreign Trade Windows has been implemented, thus allowing the online exchange of documents. An Entrepreneurs Capital Fund was created in collaboration with the Inter-American Development

Bank (IDB). A Pacific Alliance Investment Facilitation Initiative was launched and a procedure to simplify and speed up the obtaining of patents in the four countries is in place. The homologation of digital certificates of origins is a reality. The Regional Observatory on small and medium-sized enterprises (SMEs) provides a virtual space to share information with the goal of strengthening SMEs.

Achievements are not limited to finance and trade.[19] Tourist and business visas are no longer required for citizens belonging to member states of the Pacific Alliance and for foreign residents. The agreement on a common platform of information on migration, for the exchange of data on human mobility, offers interesting opportunities for the future. Among these is the potential diversion of air routes to Asia from the USA and Canada towards Pacific Alliance airports, which would enjoy a less restrictive and quicker entrance and transit policy.[20] A new regional digital agenda was devised. In the area of education, a common Platform for Academic and Student Mobility has already made nine calls, created a single channel of application, and delivered over 1,400 scholarships. In the area of external projection, the Alliance has been particularly active, especially towards Asia. It opened seven shared embassies and two joint trade offices. It counts on 52 observer members including the USA, the People's Republic of China, the Republic of Korea (South Korea), India, Japan, Indonesia, Thailand, 25 European countries and Turkey, and most Latin American countries. It has held two Dialogues with the presidents of the Asia-Pacific Economic Cooperation (APEC) and three ministerial meetings with its Association of Southeast Asian Nations (ASEAN) counterparts.

The results are very positive and the potential of the Alliance is promising. It has a cumulative gross domestic product (GDP) that accounts for 38 per cent of the total GDP of Latin America and the Caribbean. It constitutes a very attractive market with a largely young population of over 217 million inhabitants and a GDP at purchasing power parity of over US $17,500 per caput. It received 41 per cent of the total foreign investments directed towards Latin America in 2016. The estimated growth rate for 2017 was 2.3 per cent compared with the average forecast of 1.1 per cent for the region.[21] Yet challenges do exist. The following two sections discuss some of them.

Regional integration as a national strategy

Chile, Colombia, Mexico and Peru share a Pacific shore and a Pacific vocation, a preference for open economies and free trade, and close relations with the USA. In recent years, they have achieved consistent growth and stable political environments, and they have reduced poverty and inequality. They all feature as high performers for ease of doing business in the World Bank index.[22] They also share some ideological affinities. That said, the four countries also have different political interests and employ different strategies to pursue them. Regional integration is only one of these strategies, within a more complex plan for development and international insertion. The Pacific Alliance currently lies right at the intersection of these national interests and strategies.

The four members of the Pacific Alliance are not as cohesive as it may at first appear. Mexico plays a dominant role in demographic and economic terms, to the point that the Alliance can be seen as Mexico plus the others.[23] This is not dissimilar from Mercosur, where Brazil holds a vastly preponderant position and where, after the initial enthusiasm, advances were hampered by asymmetries between members, among other factors. Mexico alone accounts for 57 per cent of the Pacific Alliance population, 61 per cent of its GDP, and over 70 per cent of its exports.[24] Mexican exports to the USA alone account for over 50 per cent of the total exports of the bloc.[25] In addition, Mexico is territorially disconnected from the other members, occupying an area that is not renowned for the quality and quantity of its infrastructure. Mexico is also the only member of the Alliance whose exports largely comprise manufactured goods (machines and electrical material, terrestrial vehicles and parts). The other members are predominantly commodities exporters (copper, petroleum, gold and silver). This influences each member's national and international insertion strategy and its interest in the Pacific Alliance.

Mexico stands out also for its specific interest in and understanding of the Pacific Alliance. It is the only member for which the bloc has perhaps more political-strategic than economic value. Mexico's proximity to the USA has led to tight political and trade links with its northern neighbour. These resulted in the conclusion of the North American Free Trade Agreement (NAFTA) in 1994, which codified the integration of Mexico into the US economic sphere. The Fox presidency (2000–06) amplified this trend.[26] Latin American countries perceived this choice as Mexico distancing itself from the continent and Mexico lost ground in the rest of Latin America, especially South America, in the new millennium. A parallel rise of Brazil and its soft resistance to US influence in Latin America, of which Mexico was seen as a proxy, accompanied this development.

President Calderón (2006–12) instigated the reinsertion of Mexico into Latin America and sought special relationships with the continent.[27] President Peña Nieto (2012–18) strengthened this strategy, which culminated with Mexico's participation in CELAC in 2011, and most of all in the Pacific Alliance. The Alliance has a dual strategic advantage for Mexico. It has facilitated a Mexican foothold in South America and it rebalances power relations with Brazil. Geopolitically, the Alliance also allows Mexico to act as a bridge between the USA and the most dynamic part of South America. The foreign policy of Peña Nieto prioritized the diversification of Mexican foreign political and trade links, especially towards the Asia-Pacific.[28] Support for the Alliance, APEC and the Trans-Pacific Partnership fit this strategy perfectly. The economic advantages may be all but negligible too. Mexico expects the Pacific Alliance to back its Asian strategy, increase business deals, attract more investments, also through MILA, and boost tourism.

Colombia is relatively new to APEC. The Pacific Alliance is a tool both to make up for this lag and to operationalize Colombia's economic potential in Latin America.[29] Internal problems with guerrillas and narco-traffic have traditionally hampered Colombia's development. In order to overcome these problems the government has allied itself quite closely with the USA and has established close military and trade links with Washington. While this has gained good results in the fight and helped stabilize the country under President Uribe (2002–10), Bogotá has found itself relatively isolated in the region, especially at the height of the pink tide.[30] The realization of the potential that the Pacific shore has for trade diversification, and that other countries relatively peripheral to the big economies of Brazil and Argentina shared Colombia's economic aims, led to Bogotá's enthusiasm for participation in the Pacific Alliance.

Colombia's President Santos (2010–18) has sought a realistic and balanced foreign policy. The Pacific Alliance has turned into an effective instrument for this purpose. Colombia expects the Alliance to reinforce its business sector and to facilitate its adaptation to a non-US-centric multipolar world. With the languishing of the CAN, the difficulties of Mercosur (of which Colombia is an associate member) and UNASUR, and the Brazilian recession, the Alliance is the best trade option for Colombia in Latin America. It not only links Colombia to the most dynamic economies in the continent but to those in the Asia-Pacific too. The Alliance shares the burden of branding costs in new markets and multiplies potential benefits. These can be substantial for Colombia's farming and manufacturing sectors.[31]

Peru, like Colombia, sees the Pacific Alliance as a preferential tool to operationalize its considerable economic potential. Unlike Colombia, though, Peru has a consolidated Pacific vocation. As early as the Fujimori government (1990–2000), 'one can begin to see glimpses of a clear economic identity', based on neoliberal principles and the search for opportunities in Asia and Oceania while continuing to invest in the traditional partners of the CAN.[32] During the presidency of Alejandro Toledo (2001–06) Peru consolidated its foreign policy axis around the CAN and the strengthened its relations with the industrialized countries of the Asia-Pacific.[33]

President Alan García (2006–11) can to be credited with originating the idea of the Pacific Alliance. This was outlined at the 2010 Ibero-American Summit and was officially launched in Lima the following year. By then Peru had to face the irreversible decline of the CAN and also acknowledge the split between Peru and Colombia on the one hand, and between Bolivia and Ecuador on the other, tantamount to a division between outward- and inward-looking economies. While Colombia was an obvious partner, Chile had increasingly become a role model for Peruvian elites and their international strategies. The leftist President Ollanta Humala (2011–16) maintained the same economic stance and committed himself to the Alliance in his wish to internationalize Peru's economy and the need to attract foreign direct investment. The Peruvian government perceives the Alliance as a tool to increase its negotiating power in Asia, to enter regional value chains to diversify export, and to improve its trade balance with the Asia-Pacific. For Lima, the Alliance is essentially an unprecedented opportunity for national rebranding and increasing its status.[34]

Chile has an established Asia-Pacific orientation based on free trade. The Pacific Alliance is therefore a logical consequence, and an integral part, of the country's identity and external strategy. Chile's first overtures towards Asia date back to the 1970s and the Pinochet dictatorship. The military regime was committed to extensive economic and trade liberalization but was often ostracized internationally by traditional partners, sometimes the same ones that had praised its economic reforms.[35] Authoritarian regimes in South-East Asia instead welcomed its opening as well as its combination of authoritarianism and capitalism, quite similar to their own. From 1990 onwards the democratic governments maintained and strengthened their focus on the Pacific Basin and Chile joined APEC in 1994. By then, Chile was already sending 50 per cent of its exports to APEC member countries and this share increased to nearly 80 per cent by 2003.[36] The Pacific Alliance has also presented Chile with an opportunity to re-engage with Latin America. Initially isolated owing to the dictatorship, Chile has subsequently chosen not to integrate fully in any Latin American regional project, maintaining associate membership of the CAN and Mercosur, and participating only in undertakings of a political rather than an economic nature, such as CELAC or UNASUR.

Chile has its own reasons for favouring the Pacific Alliance. Members are likeminded in their unequivocal support of free trade and the elimination of tariffs, and convincingly share the drive to the Pacific. The Alliance has the potential to generate value chains, which would significantly boost Chile's non-traditional exports, and this is a key objective for Santiago. This would help Chile to reduce the risk of reprimarization. The Alliance also helps to share and reduce the costs of penetration in Asia, a strategy that Chile would pursue anyway. Due to its long-standing experience in Asia, Chile has a comparative advantage in the organization. It can teach the others important lessons, lead the Alliance agenda and negotiations in a discreet, non-threatening way, and assume a behind-the-curtains leadership. At present, the Pacific Alliance is a successful and advantageous minimum common denominator for Chile, Colombia, Mexico and Peru's national strategies. However, challenges to the long-term cohesion and sustainability of the project exist too. The next section tackles some of them.

Challenges and new initiatives

One can read the statistics underpinning the success and potential of the Pacific Alliance, like all figures, in different ways. The Alliance prides itself in being the eighth largest economy in the world in terms of aggregated GDP.[37] However, one can make three observations. First, on what basis are the four economies counted together? After all, the Pacific Alliance is neither a common market, nor a customs union (and does not aspire to become one), and its free trade area is still incomplete. There are no supranational bodies. Scandinavian countries or NAFTA members could also improve their global rankings by piling up national data. Is there any substance beyond marketing? Second, Mexico accounts for about 60 per cent of the Alliance's GDP. Why should Mexico be counted in the Alliance and not in NAFTA? The latter is far more consolidated despite President Trump's proposals for reform. Third, in global terms the Alliance's impressive figures tend to become less stunning: the combined GDP, the total population and the total share of global trade all amount to approximately 3 per cent of the world total.[38] The aggressive marketing strategy of the Pacific Alliance is not to be criticized nor its achievements belittled. Yet unpacking arguments and putting them into perspective may highlight challenges that marketing campaigns and political declarations might miss.

Challenge one: grab the added value of the free trade area. The Pacific Alliance boasts that it has made major advances in the bloc's free trade area. Thus, 92 per cent of goods are free of duty and there is a schedule in place to phase out the remaining barriers. However, what is the real impact? First, one of the requirements for membership of the Alliance is to have a free trade agreement (FTA) with each and all of the other members already in place at the time of accession. One may wonder what is the added value of the Alliance FTA when all members already had bilateral ones with all the others beforehand. One plausible explanation is that 'many of the free trade agreements negotiated by Latin American countries are not as comprehensive as those negotiated with the United States'.[39] This is to say that the bilateral FTAs contain so many loopholes and exceptions that the bloc's FTA can only offer significant improvements. That said, the remaining 8 per cent comprise sensitive sectors, such as agriculture and textiles. This is only a hint of the politically delicate negotiations that lie ahead. Furthermore, the real added value of the Alliance's FTA lies in the liberalization of capital and services. While MILA is a promising step, services have yet to be tackled substantially. Second, the relevance of intraregional trade to members is limited. Trade between them varies between 4 per cent and 12 per cent.[40] A fully functioning FTA may increase these figures but it can hardly have a major impact on the members' economies.

Challenge two: grab the advantages of a joint strategy in Asia and tame the negative effects of trade patterns in the Pacific Basin. One of the declared aims of the Pacific Alliance is to strengthen commercial relations with the Asia-Pacific. Chile already has over 20 FTAs linking it with some 60 countries, including China, Japan and South Korea. Colombia has a dozen FTAs in place but only with South Korea in Asia. Mexico has 11 FTAs involving 46 countries but only with Japan in Asia. Peru has 17 FTAs in place including China, Japan, South Korea, Singapore and Thailand. Chile and Peru are way ahead of the others. The latter may benefit substantially more from further joint actions by the Alliance. It is also encouraging, to note that there is a lot of room to manoeuvre. The four countries together can certainly increase their negotiating power. Yet the Alliance has no juridical powers, which means that it cannot conclude international treaties on behalf of its members. They will have to negotiate and sign agreements themselves.

Joint negotiations are potentially invaluable but they will also pose a serious test of political commitment and unity. What will happen in the event that Asian partners offer bilateral deals with different treatments? Deep commercial ties with Asia, especially China, pose a major risk of deindustralization. China, South Korea, India and Japan have displayed the same trade patterns towards Latin America as have the USA and European countries. They are interested in the import of commodities and the export of manufactured goods.[41] Most industrial sectors in

Latin America may not survive competition from more advanced Asian competitors with a serious risk of deindustrialization and job losses. The commitment of each and all members to the Pacific Alliance will determine its real added value in Asia.[42]

Challenge three: capitalize on the international attention and do not lose momentum. The Pacific Alliance has attracted widespread interest and support internationally. It has 52 observer members and counts on the institutional and financial support of the IBD, the Andean Development Corporation (CAF), the UN Economic Commission for Latin America and the Caribbean (ECLAC), the World Bank, the EU, and the Organisation for Economic Co-operation and Development (OECD). How to capitalize on this extensive network? Observer states have a limited role and they are generally, and vaguely, interested in the Alliance's activities related to market access in Asia. Some of Asian observers see the Alliance as an opportunity to compete with China in Latin America.[43] Yet it is not clear what many observers expect from their status nor what the Alliance's expectations are. There is no clear agenda or framework for cooperation between the Alliance and its observers. Most of the admittedly quite limited activity is carried out bilaterally following the Alliance's declared priorities without a coordinated agenda or framework.[44]

New initiatives have recently been undertaken. In addition to its traditional policy advice, the OECD, together with three academic institutions in three of the potentially most interested observer countries on this agenda,[45] is supporting the discussion and drafting of specific policy proposals for cooperation with the observers to be delivered at the 2018 Pacific Alliance summit in Mexico. This is a commendable joint public-private undertaking to advance the international agenda. Another recent development is the creation by the Pacific Alliance Council of Ministers of the category of 'partner states'. These put into force a binding agreement with all Alliance members on high standards in economic and trade matters. While the definition remains generic, the Alliance already opened negotiations with Australia, New Zealand, Canada and Singapore. Overall, observer status may help countries to understand better the Alliance prospects and to profit from some of its Asian programmes. Yet the point is to find ways to avoid the view that 'observer status will become merely symbolic'.[46]

Challenge four: operationalize the societal objectives to deliver inclusive development. A compelling task is to link economic and social advances. One of the novelties of the Pacific Alliance is the use of extraregional economic integration to pursue intraregional social improvements. The two aspects are mutually reinforcing. The Alliance has set in motion actions to improve the standards of living in areas other than economic prosperity. The first part of this chapter discussed progress made in education. Digitalization plays an important role on the Alliance agenda and has already led to a regional digitalization agenda and a roadmap to improve competitiveness through information technology and communication. Gender equality is a centrepiece to growth and development in the Alliance,[47] and OECD formulated policy recommendations that are now under consideration by the Alliance technical group on gender.[48] These actions are subservient to economic performance, which in turn will generate resources to foster social policies. People (the 'ordinary people') must be empowered so that they can grab the opportunities that trade connections and regional and global value chains can offer. Education, especially vocational training and technical skills, in the languages too, as well as proactive policies of inclusiveness, are essential to this goal. Only by tackling these issues effectively will the Pacific Alliance meet its greatest challenge: to live up to the high expectations that it has generated.

Conclusion

When Chile, Colombia, Mexico and Peru launched the Pacific Alliance in 2011, the project stood out for its minimalism and pragmatism, its emphasis on open economies and free trade, and its explicit engagement with the Pacific Basin. At that time, the pink tide administrations and their different levels of criticism of neoliberal policies and free trade dictated the prevailing political mood in Latin America. Today the winds have changed course. The integration schemes underpinning the pink tide stance on regional affairs, such as ALBA, UNASUR and even Mercosur are languishing. Many of the left-leaning leaders have lost office and/or credibility. In turn, more moderate figures are in office. The Pacific Alliance is widely praised and it has turned into a model. It can boast of significant achievements, such as the launch of the bloc's free trade area, MILA, a dense network of institutionalized relations in Asia and internationally, and a credible common promotion strategy, including in areas other than trade.

Still, the Alliance faces considerable challenges. So far, the organization has tackled relatively easy issues and the difficult part is probably yet to come. The lack of institutionalization allows flexibility and rapid reaction but there is a risk of quickly ending up in 'low cap' regionalism wherein the room for consensus may be rapidly exhausted.[49] Close links with advanced Asian economies may generate value-added chains but they may also result in deindustrialization in the weaker economies. The temptation to cash in on initial success and bring in new politically relevant members or indulge in grand strategies may lead the Alliance to enlarge its membership to include countries whose commitment is less than proven. The record of Latin American regionalism and the experience of Mercosur with Venezuela should be a warning.

The achievement of the ultimate goal of economic and social inclusive development is perhaps that which will determine the fate of the Pacific Alliance. One should not forget that the Alliance has been in place for only six years. Consequently, perhaps one should also not give in to the temptation of applying grand theories to understand the Alliance but should accept its essentially pragmatic nature. After all, the Pacific 'Alliance, quite simply, is four countries whose temperaments, priorities, desires, and capacity to work together have uniquely positioned them to integrate and achieve their common goals'.[50]

Notes

1 Presidential Declaration on the Pacific Alliance (Lima Declaration) (2011). Available at www.sice.oas.org/TPD/Pacific_Alliance/Presidential_Declarations/I_Summit_Lima_Declaration_s.pdf (accessed 11 November 2017).
2 M. Reid (2007) *Forgotten Continent: The Battle for Latin America's Soul*, New Haven, CT and London: Yale University Press.
3 G. L. Gardini and P. W. Lambert (2011) *Latin American Foreign Policies between Ideology and Pragmatism*, New York and Basingstoke: Palgrave Macmillan.
4 A. Malamud and G. L. Gardini (2012) 'Has Regionalism Peaked? The Latin American Quagmire and its Lessons', *International Spectator*, 47(1) March: 116–33.
5 F. Soderbaum and L. Van Langenhove (eds) (2006) *The EU as a Global Player: The Politics of Interregionalism*, London: Routledge.
6 G. L. Gardini (2015) 'Towards Modular Regionalism: The Proliferation of Latin American Cooperation', *Revista Brasileira de Política Internacional*, 58(1): 210–29.
7 Framework Agreement of the Pacific Alliance, 6 June 2012. Available at www20.iadb.org/intal/catalogo/PE/2013/11593.pdf (accessed 11 November 2017).
8 E. Pastrana Buelvas (2016) *The Pacific Alliance: Facing Regional Projects and Global Transformations*, Mexico City: Konrad Adenauer Foundation, p. 13.
9 D. Dade and C. Meacham (2013) *The Pacific Alliance: An Example of Lessons Learned*, Washington, DC: Center for Strategic and International Studies, p. 6.
10 Framework Agreement of the Pacific Alliance, Art. 7.
11 Ibid., Art. 4.
12 At present, there are 20 technical groups and six sub-groups.

13 Constitutive Act of the Business Council of the Pacific Alliance, Objective Two. Available at https://alianzapacifico.net/wp-content/uploads/2015/08/constitucion-del-Consejo-Empresarial.pdf (accessed 3 December 2017).

14 J. Varillas Velasquez (2017) 'A Word from the Chairman of the Pacific Alliance Business Council: Peruvian Chapter', in EY, *Pacific Alliance Business and Investment Guide 2017/18*. Lima: EY, p. 13.

15 E. B. Haas (1958) *The Uniting of Europe: Political, Social, and Economical Forces 1950–1957*, Notre Dame, IN: Notre Dame University Press.

16 G. L. Gardini (2006) 'Government-Business Relations in the Construction of Mercosur', *Business and Politics*, 8(1): article 3, pp. 1–28.

17 C. Vasquez (2014) 'Is the Pacific Alliance the Next Big Thing?', *World Policy Blog*, 4 November. Available at www.worldpolicy.org/blog/2014/11/04/pacific-alliance-next-big-thing (accessed 3 December 2017).

18 See EY, *Pacific Alliance Business and Investment Guide*; A. Soler (2015) 'The Pacific Alliance: Creating Opportunities for Investors', *TMF Group Briefing*, July. Available at www.tmf-group.com/en/news-insights/publications/2015/pacific-alliance/ (accessed 3 December 2017); Pacific Alliance (2017) 'Declaration of Cali', 30 June. Available at: https://alianzapacifico.net/en/declaracion-de-cali/ (accessed 3 December 2017).

19 Pacific Alliance (2016) 'Declaration of Puerto Varas', 1 July. Available at https://alianzapacifico.net/en/?wpdmdl=7888 (accessed 3 December 2017); Pacific Alliance, 'Declaration of Cali'; Embassy of Colombia to Stockholm (2017) 'Alianza del Pacífico', document distributed at the conference 'The Pacific Alliance: An Emerging Region in a Global World', Stockholm, 5 December.

20 Dade and Meacham, *Pacific Alliance*.

21 EY, *Pacific Alliance Business and Investment Guide*, p. 17.

22 World Bank (2017) Ease of Doing Business Index. Available at https://data.worldbank.org/indicator/IC.BUS.EASE.XQ?view=map (accessed 4 January 2018).

23 D. Nolte (2016) *The Pacific Alliance: Nation-Branding through Regional Organisations*, GIGA Focus/Latin America, no. 4 August, Hamburg: GIGA, p. 2.

24 M. Villareal (2016) 'The Pacific Alliance: A Trade Integration Initiative in Latin America'. US Congressional Research Service, 29 May, p. 9.

25 Nolte, *The Pacific Alliance*, p. 2.

26 A. Covarrubias (2011) 'Mexico's Foreign Policy under the Partido Acción Nacional: Promoting Democracy, Human Rights and Interests', in G. L. Gardini and P. W. Lambert, *Latin American Foreign Policies: Between Ideology and Pragmatism*, New York and Basingstoke: Palgrave Macmillan, pp. 213–33.

27 Ibid.

28 Z. Villamar (2013) 'La política exterior mexicana tras el regreso del PRI: Una visión para los próximos seis años', *Nueva Sociedad*, 247, Sept.-Oct.: 16–26.

29 Pastrana Buelvas, *The Pacific Alliance*.

30 S. Randall (2011) 'The Continuing Pull of the Polar Star: Colombian Foreign Policy in the Post-Cold War Era', in G. L. Gardini and P. W. Lambert, *Latin American Foreign Policies: Between Ideology and Pragmatism*, New York and Basingstoke: Palgrave Macmillan, pp. 139–57.

31 *The Economist* (2015) 'How Deep Is Their Love? The Pacific Alliance Is a Great Brand in Search of a Shared Product, 12 May. Available at www.economist.com/news/americas/21646273-pacific-alliance-great-brand-search-shared-product-how-deep-their-love (accessed 4 April 2018).

32 Pastrana Buelvas, p. 46.

33 B. St John (2011) 'Ideology and Pragmatism in the Foreign Policy of Peru', in G. L. Gardini and P. W. Lambert, *Latin American Foreign Policies: Between Ideology and Pragmatism*, New York and Basingstoke: Palgrave Macmillan, pp. 119–37.

34 Nolte, p. 8.

35 J. Fermandois (2005) *Mundo y fin de mundo: Chile en la política mundial 1900–2004*, Santiago: Ediciones Universidad Católica de Chile.

36 Pastrana Buelvas, p. 39.

37 The Pacific Alliance (2017) *Pacific Alliance ABC Book*, p. 5. Available at https://alianzapacifico.net/wp-content/uploads/2017/07/CARTILLA-ALIANZA.pdf (accessed 18 January 2018).

38 R. Aichele (2015) 'Dimensions and Economic Effects of the Pacific Alliance', IFO Center for International Economics, presentation at KAS-SOPLA Lateinamerika, San José, 5 March.

39 Villareal, The Pacific Alliance, p. 2.

40 Aichele, 'Dimensions and Economic Effects of the Pacific Alliance', p. 5.

Gian Luca Gardini

41 See ECLAC (2015) *Latin America and the Caribbean and China: Towards a New Era in Economic Cooperation*, Santiago: ECLAC; ECLAC (2011) *India and Latin America and the Caribbean: Opportunities and Challenges in Trade and Investment Relations*. Available at www.cepal.org/en/publications/3021-india -and-latin-america-and-caribbean-opportunities-and-challenges-trade-and (accessed 19 January 2018); M. Mesquita Moreira (ed.) (2011) *Korea: Breaking the Mold of the Asia-Latin America Relationship*, Washington DC: Inter-American Development Bank; ECLAC (2015) *Economic Relations between Latin America and the Caribbean and the Republic of Korea: Advances and Opportunities*, Santiago: ECLAC.

42 G. L. Gardini (2013) 'The Added Value of the Pacific Alliance and "Modular Regionalism" in Latin America, *LSE Ideas Blog*, 25 May. Available at http://blogs.lse.ac.uk/ideas/2013/06/the-added-va lue-of-the-pacific-alliance-and-modular-regionalism-in-latin-america/ (accessed 19 January 2018).

43 *The Economist*, 'How Deep Is Their Love?'.

44 The Declaration of Puerto Varas (2016) Art. 7 set four priorities for relations between the Pacific Alliance and observer countries: education; science, technology and innovation; internationalization of SMEs; and trade facilitation. The Declaration of Cali (2017), Art. 11, added the movement of people.

45 The European Institute of International Studies in Sweden, the Copenhagen Business School in Denmark, and the Friedrich Alexander University Erlangen-Nuremberg in Germany.

46 Nolte, p. 4.

47 Declaration of Cali (2013), art. 6.

48 OECD (2016) *Gender Equality in the Pacific Alliance: Promoting Women's Economic Empowerment*, Paris: OECD Publishing.

49 F. Peña (2003) Interview with the author, Buenos Aires, 25 February. F. Peña was Argentina's Undersecretary of Economic Integration (1991–92) and is a highly respected analyst of Latin American integration.

50 Dade and Meacham, *The Pacific Alliance*, p. 5.

21

ALBA

Asa Cusack

Introduction

The Bolivarian Alliance for the Peoples of Our America (Alianza Bolivariana para los Pueblos de Nuestra América – ALBA) differs markedly from many of the trade agreements analyzed in this volume in that it was created to oppose the inherently liberalizing model of open regionalism that dominated trade policymaking in the 1980s and 1990s. Officially launched in December 2004 by Hugo Chávez, President of Venezuela, and Fidel Castro, President of Cuba, it emerged as an explicit alternative to the hemispheric Free Trade Area of the Americas (FTAA),[1] which was at that time supported by much of the region and crucially by the USA under Bill Clinton and George W. Bush. ALBA went beyond debates about whether regionalism represented a stepping stone or a stumbling block to multilateral trade liberalization, challenging instead the nature and desirability of that very process by proposing a comprehensive form of counter-globalization premised upon cooperation, complementarity and solidarity.[2]

Following the derailment of the FTAA in 2005, ALBA became more proactive, launching initiatives across every level of governance – local, state, national, regional, global – in an attempt to bolster the pro-social, autonomist, state-led development models of its core Latin American member states and to counter the influence of neoliberal globalization in the wider region. Innovative solutions to long-standing economic and social problems – particularly the well-known 'oil for doctors' arrangement between Venezuela and Cuba – initially produced impressive results and brought many new members into the bloc, not least Bolivia under Evo Morales and Ecuador under Rafael Correa (as well as Nicaragua, Dominica, Saint Vincent and the Grenadines, Antigua and Barbuda, Saint Lucia, Grenada, and Saint Kitts and Nevis). ALBA quickly became the most prominent region-level expression of the Latin American 'pink turn' during the 2000s.

Yet by the end of the decade, the global financial crisis of 2008, severe oil price fluctuations, and the bloc's inability to reverse the withdrawal of Honduras (2008–09) following a US-condoned coup had also revealed ALBA's vulnerability to economic and political upheaval. More specifically, it became clear that when Venezuela sneezes, ALBA catches a cold, and at this point the situation in Venezuela was already taking a turn for the worse. Serious economic distortions were going unchecked, development planning and governance were slipshod, and deficient accountability allowed corruption to prosper while at the same time militating against efforts towards its elimination. These problems inevitably spilled over into ALBA, with the early success of some initiatives undermined by the revelation of serious failings – and outright malfeasance – in the implementation of others. The collapse of oil prices in 2014 and the authoritarian drift of the Venezuelan government further delegitimized ALBA, yet its de facto leader Nicolás Maduro continued to press for a grand but extremely improbable convergence between ALBA and other prominent Latin American and Caribbean trade agreements. By 2018 the once inaccurate depiction of ALBA as an insignificant talking shop had begun to ring true.

The emergence of ALBA

ALBA's gestation began with Hugo Chávez's spontaneous proposal for a counter-FTAA regional scheme during the 2001 summit of the Association of Caribbean States, but its roots lie in the wider counter-neoliberal processes that brought about the 'Left Turn' or 'pink tide' of the 2000s. This trend dates back to 1988 and General Pinochet's lost referendum in Chile, which was quickly followed by the rioting and repression in Venezuela in 1989 – known as the Caracazo – following the unexpected implementation of neoliberal reforms. Opposition soon moved to the regional level via the São Paolo Forum meetings, where social movements and left-of-centre parties formulated joint demands for a novel form of bottom-up integration prioritizing sovereignty over demands for deregulation from multinational corporations.[3] By the turn of the century this amorphous discontent was being channelled into political movements, with the victory of Venezuela's Hugo Chávez in 1998 demonstrating the electoral potential of focusing on the needs of the marginalized majority. Left-of-centre wins for Lula da Silva in Brazil and Nestor Kirchner in Argentina began to herald a wider 'Left Turn' that ultimately swept through Uruguay, Bolivia, Ecuador, Chile, Paraguay and a number of Central American countries.

Between the first mention of ALBA in 2001 and its launch in 2004, it was Venezuela's Chávez and Cuba's Castro who laid the enduring foundations of the scheme. The two key influences were anti-FTAA social movements (particularly the Hemispheric Social Alliance) and the Venezuela-Cuba Integral Cooperation Convention signed in 2000.[4] From these sources ALBA's founding agreement borrowed and extended central principles of solidarity, cooperation and fairness, as well as its rejection of the narrow trade and investment focus typical of contemporary preferential trading arrangements (PTAs). 'Mutual benefit' trumped competition; benefits could be economic, political, social or cultural; and legally binding treaties were but one form that initiatives could take. This flexible approach produced an agreement containing everything from programmes for reinforcing Latin American identity and sharing sports facilities to exemptions from local taxes for state investments and a multi-billion-dollar exchange of Venezuelan oil for the services of Cuban health professionals. Tariffs were also reduced to their minimum level by both parties: this meant zero for all Venezuelan exports to Cuba, but importantly Venezuela could not reciprocate due to prior obligations within the Andean Community of Nations (Comunidad Andina de Naciones –CAN).

But ALBA also served the more immediate political and economic needs of its founders. Hugo Chávez had already survived a coup (2002) and a crippling, elite-led oil strike (2002–03) when the opposition invoked a recall referendum on his presidency in 2004. Domestically, middle-class voters had already begun to desert Chávez, and victory was far from assured, leading to a renewed focus on delivering immediate yet substantive benefits to the poor majority that had always backed him. Internationally, Chávez sought to forge supportive relationships with partners of any ideological stripe, conscious that regional support could temper the threat of external sanctions and interventions. Cuba, meanwhile, faced new restrictions on

US travel and remittances, a faltering economy, and the relative political and economic isolation enforced by US diplomacy and the long-standing embargo. ALBA emerged out of this combination of high ideals and pressing needs, providing regional reinforcement of its member states' foreign policy, domestic development and political legitimacy.

From Alternative to Alliance, contestation to content

The first and foremost means of making this regional link was the 'mission' format of internationalized social programmes. The aforementioned 'oil for doctors' exchange (Misión Barrio Adentro) saw Cuban doctors staffing new clinics in poor areas that had never known local, free health care, while Cuba's receipt of subsidized Venezuelan oil meant less of its precious foreign exchange would go towards energy imports. The success of the Barrio Adentro program led to further missions in other high-impact areas, including eye surgery (Milagro), literacy (Robinson), and assessment of disability needs (José Gregorio Hernández). The rapid and massive roll-out of these programmes was enabled by assigning responsibility for their implementation to the state oil company Petróleos de Venezuela, SA (PDVSA). Not only was it flush with ready resources due to rising oil prices, much internal opposition had been removed by mass sackings during the earlier oil strike, and furthermore the head of PDVSA was politically appointed. This gave the Venezuelan presidency effective control over a newly pliable and massively powerful institution, but it also began to incubate deficiencies in governance, planning and accountability that would later prove highly damaging. The innovative nature and early success of the missions gave concrete form to the ideal of complementarity and established the perception of ALBA as Latin America's specialist in socially focused regional integration. But aside from that fact that the missions themselves are a form of barter trade – worth as much as US \$5.4 billion annually[5] – this has distracted from the clear economic focus of ALBA's initiatives from 2005 onwards.

Petrocaribe, a scheme to buffer skyrocketing energy prices by converting much of Central America and the Caribbean's oil import bill into concessionary loans was launched in 2005; 17 countries signed up to the scheme during its first decade. Then came the People's Trade Treaty (Tratado de Comercio de los Pueblos – TCP) in 2006 and 2009, which aimed to establish a framework for negotiating cooperative trade agreements compatible with ALBA principles. International joint ventures between state companies, known as 'grandnational' enterprises (2007), would boost trade and investment in strategic areas. The Unified Regional Compensation System (Sistema Único de Compensación Regional – SUCRE) virtual currency would also incentivize intra-ALBA trade by reducing transaction costs, as well as saving member states' foreign exchange. Reserves themselves would be held by the ALBA Bank (2008) and invested in productive or social projects. There were scores of other initiatives in other policy areas and involving many other actors, often beyond ALBA's geographical limits, but these few were key in terms of resources, discourse and participation of full member states. The overarching aim was to use regional governance to enable state-guided, cooperative, complementary development, thereby creating an 'economic zone of shared development'.

Implementing innovative ideas

However, ALBA's approach to participation and institutionalization is avowedly flexible: one initiative might involve a local social movement in a non-member country, a given ministry of a member state, and a regulated channel of regional interaction that trades a social benefit for a more explicitly economic one. As such, neither ALBA's limits nor its effects are easily identified. This is because in many ways ALBA acts as a brand rather than a formally structured integration scheme.[6] Thus, the social 'missions' predate ALBA, overstep its formal bounds by servicing non-member countries, and receive little attention or oversight from its small secretariat, yet they are consistently promoted as ALBA's most significant achievement. Likewise, politically negotiated bilateral trade and investment agreements between ALBA member states may be ascribed to ALBA even if they differ little from deals done prior to its invention or from those agreed with ideologically aligned non-members. Thus, when Bolivia's textile exports were damaged by the politically motivated withdrawal of US preferences (under the Andean Trade Promotion and Drug Eradication Act), Venezuela stepped in to provide a market, with the deal providing the basis for a network of ALBA Shops selling clothing at subsidized prices. But beyond this initial agreement between a Bolivian export promotion agency and a state enterprise linked to Venezuela's Ministry of Trade, there is little to suggest that products were not imported from the open market based on availability and price, robbing the initiative of its supposed 'ALBA' character. As such interactions are often irregular and short term, this chapter focuses on those economic initiatives that are best placed to provoke substantive and durable changes in economic relations across the formal ALBA space.

The People's Trade Treaty

Aside from across-the-board and 'immediate' tariff elimination agreed by Cuba towards Venezuela in 2004 and extended to Bolivia in 2006 – the former only entering into force in 2009 and the latter only partially in 2011[7] – the most important ALBA initiative in the area of trade has been its People's Trade Treaty.

Just as ALBA was a reaction to the FTAA, the TCP was a reaction to its aftermath, when the USA attempted to create a patchwork FTAA by negotiating bilateral FTAs with individual states. The signing of such agreements by Peru and Colombia in 2006 effectively eliminated the possibility of the customs union to which they were committed – along with Venezuela, Bolivia and Ecuador – within the CAN. Venezuela reacted by abandoning the CAN altogether, invoking a five-year withdrawal period, meaning that as of 2011 a new trade regime would be required with fellow ALBA members Bolivia and Ecuador, and the expiry of the CAN rules would provide an unusually propitious opportunity to create it.

To this end, ALBA's members established a framework of principles in 2009 that would guide negotiations towards a comprehensive multilateral agreement covering both trade and also related areas such as investment, intellectual property and public procurement. These principles inverted many neoliberal orthodoxies of the time: social impact trumped economic impact as the ultimate arbiter of desirability; social protection and sovereignty were prioritized over boosting firms' cost competitiveness via deregulation; poorer states would receive special and differential treatment rather than the expectation of reciprocal liberalization; tariff protections were permitted to protect social welfare; nationalization was endorsed; arbitration of conflicts would be national rather than international; procurement would serve developmental ends; and small and associative actors (cooperatives, small and medium-sized enterprises) would be prioritized.

Vis-à-vis the rest of the world, the aim was to boost the autonomy of ALBA states by reasserting a degree of regulatory control at national and intraregional level which had earlier been lost in the rush towards globalization. Domestically, the TCP would also reinforce the endogenous development strategies of major Latin American members, which aimed to diversify towards exports with higher value added by creating regional value chains, thereby generating more employment at improved skill and wage levels. Production from prioritized associative organizations like cooperatives could also be used to provide inputs for social programmes in other member states. Thus, development would become regionally cooperative, benefiting the poorest at both ends of these chains of interdependence, with an associated political dividend from catering for these core constituencies.

In practice, however, the TCP has not been implemented in multilateral or even bilateral form, though both were attempted. The most basic issue was that shared political will and common development strategies were far from sufficient conditions to overcome deeper structural and institutional legacies. Not only are ALBA's major economies the least diverse in Latin America, meaning less chance for complementarity, their common commitments to protecting national industry also led to the exclusion of product categories in which members competed, leaving virtually nothing left to trade. Apart from Cuba, members also had more valuable pre-existing commitments at subregional (the CAN, the Caribbean Community) and global level (especially the World Trade Organization), and concern about their possible contravention militated against the TCP.

The bilateral process between ALBA's largest trade partners Ecuador and Venezuela, meanwhile, was undone, first, by officials' inability to operationalize TCP principles in which many did not believe and for which their experience and education provided no template. The TCP was also thwarted by a rancorous split in Ecuadorian development policymaking between pro-TCP and pro-FTA (with the USA and European Union – EU) factions. The latter won out partly because of Venezuela's dysfunctional foreign exchange regime – designed to enable state-guided prioritization of certain industries, organizational forms and labour practices – became so arbitrary and bureaucratic as to represent an insurmountable non-tariff barrier to any trade, whether under TCP rules or otherwise. Ultimately, the two parties were forced simply to renew pre-existing CAN rules, with Bolivia and Venezuela following suit soon after. Not only had this uniquely favourable opportunity to reshape trade and investment within ALBA been lost, it also demonstrated to regional policymakers, officials and firms that ALBA could raise transaction costs even through its attempts to reduce them.

The Unified Regional Compensation System

A second major initiative in the area of trade was the SUCRE virtual currency, which was designed to incentivize intra-ALBA trade, allow smaller actors to reach international markets, and alleviate foreign exchange pressures for participating states.

The system functions by allocating to each participating state based on their economic size and predicted levels of trade (Venezuela, Cuba, Bolivia, Ecuador, Nicaragua) a certain number of sucres, whose value in each member's currency is weighted with reference to a 'basket' of hard currencies. Intra-zone trade can then be carried out using these sucres in place of US dollars, with only the balance being cleared in US dollars every six months. If trade were perfectly balanced between participants, no foreign exchange would be required. The initiative also boasts a fund designed to finance production-for-export projects in order to achieve a better balance.

For small actors in particular, the use of local currency circumvents the prohibitive cost and intimidating bureaucracy of maintaining dollar-denominated accounts. For firms more generally, transaction costs are reduced as currency conversion fees are eliminated, various margin-skimming middlemen are circumvented, and payments are almost immediate, making delayed payment or later default less likely. This can reduce transaction costs by as much as 90 per cent, which can significantly improve cost competitiveness within the SUCRE area, thereby promoting intra- over extra-ALBA trade (non-participating Eastern Caribbean member states notwithstanding).

For states, less hard currency goes on the import bill, the risk of balance of payments issues is lowered, and reserves are potentially boosted. This increased intraregional trade corresponds to their push for autonomy, multipolarity and shared development, particularly as it robs the USA of seigniorage, promotes a trend towards de-dollarization of international trade, favours ALBA producers, and keys into a political and developmental preference for boosting small and cooperative producers in order to create employment, improve material conditions for the worst off and foster collectivist values.

These benefits, however, are achieved only to the extent that firms and states opt to utilize the system. Since all of ALBA's Latin American members did ratify the SUCRE treaty (Nicaragua only in 2013), 99 per cent of ALBA trade was available to be channelled by the system. Uptake from firms was initially impressive growing to a value of over US $1 billion within two years (Figure 21.1) at a time when normal ALBA trade was plateauing. The fact that 92 per cent of SUCRE trade in 2012 involved private firms also suggests generalized recognition of its benefits.

Yet closer analysis tells a different story, as statistics by partner states reveal that Venezuela was involved in 98 per cent of ALBA trade, and its relationship with Ecuador alone accounted for 89 per cent. Crucially, the latter was far from balanced, with Ecuador doing virtually all of the exporting and Venezuela the importing. Since Venezuela's sucre deficit must ultimately be cancelled out in dollars, many of the system's benefits are cancelled out with it. The size of transactions and the limited use of cooperative agent banks also implies that there was little engagement from small and cooperative actors despite their prioritization. The fund designed to redress SUCRE trade imbalances through developing new export projects had received only US $5.2 million in contributions by 2014, far below the stipulated 5 per cent of sucre allocations, and even this paltry sum had not been invested.

Most gravely of all, however, the fact of Ecuador's dollarized economy combined with Venezuela's overvalued currency, capital controls and parallel currency market provided a massive incentive for inflating or inventing transactions in order to gain access to subsidized dollars in Venezuela. With demand for dollars far outstripping official supply, by 2016 the black market rate was 142 times the official one, making arbitrage almost irresistibly profitable. When the problem began to be tackled in 2012, Ecuadorian officials estimated that one-third of SUCRE trade was fictitious, amounting to an astonishing $277 million.

The loss of this fictitious trade, and the declining Venezuelan imports as its economy faltered, together with the caution bred by association with these two issues all combined to undermine

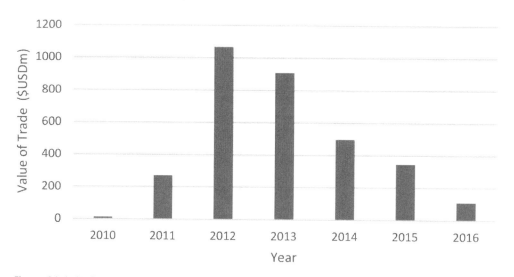

Figure 21.1 SUCRE trade volumes (US $) 2010–16

SUCRE trade after 2012. By 2016 trade volumes had fallen to one-tenth of their 2012 peak, and the system into relative obscurity. Again, ALBA's push to create an 'economic zone of shared development' had been undermined by Venezuela's overwhelming preponderance and dysfunctional aspects of its political economy, particularly its currency regime and its failure to curb widespread corruption. Indeed, the SUCRE actually provided a new channel for parasitic currency arbitrage, which – aside from draining state resources – reinforced hyper-individualist mindsets and practices to the point of criminality. This is the very opposite of the socially minded collectivism sought by ALBA and its members.

Petrocaribe

The third important trade initiative within ALBA is Petrocaribe, which allows Venezuela to offer the 18 other signatories a means of buffering rising oil prices, a source of development finance and a barter trade facility. Its central function is to supply Venezuelan oil with ever larger portions of the bill being converted into concessionary loans as prices rise (60 per cent when over US \$100, for example), which effectively caps the upfront cost. Discounts on shipping, free infrastructure upgrades, and below-inflation interest rates also help to shrink the debt over long payment schedules. Recipient governments then put aside funds for repayment and invest them in socially important development projects in the meantime, although they can also apply to a second development fund fed irregularly by Venezuelan donations. Alternatively, the debt can be paid in kind with national produce at 'fair trade' prices.

The main aim is to insulate energy-dependent Caribbean states from oil supply and oil price shocks, as these could cripple entire economies, cause significant political upheaval, and constrain governments' already limited policy space. The social purpose conditionality of development funding, meanwhile, is designed to benefit especially the poorest members of ALBA societies, even when ideologically disparate governments might have other priorities. And the barter facility provides a new channel for intraregional trade, again outside of the usual dollar-denominated system (like the SUCRE).

With oil prices skyrocketing from 2005 when Petrocaribe was launched, the scheme had many adherents, with 19 by 2014. Yet, of those, Venezuela and Cuba's relationship was in reality managed bilaterally, Guatemala has never taken up its quota, Honduras has been suspended since 2010 following a coup, and the Bahamas has since claimed never to have signed up despite appearing in official reports until 2014. But for the remainder that did utilize Petrocaribe's facilities, the impact has been enormous, as it effectively capped upfront oil prices at less than half of their real value from 2005 to 2015. With many signatories running persistent current account deficits, this extra pressure could have been catastrophic.

Investment in local oil infrastructure created temporary and permanent employment in small economies, as well as ensuring state-led provision, sometimes subsidized, of vital energy sources such as liquefied petroleum gas for cooking. Development finance allowed for a variety of social programmes in education, housing and infrastructure, and even new transfer benefits in some cases.

The scheme's barter trade aspect, however, has failed to flourish, with only four signatories taking part. Although barter valued at US \$2.7 billion was conducted up until 2014, Nicaragua (80 per cent) and Guyana (15 per cent) accounted for nearly all of it. Opaque management of associated funds and favouritism towards state-linked elites in Nicaragua, as well as deliberate obfuscation of 'fair' (above market) prices, also made Petrocaribe controversial and politically damaging in Venezuela, where the accusation of 'giving away the oil' is a staple of political discourse. This has only increased as domestic problems have worsened, especially as

Venezuela's distress has led it to accept debt buybacks from wealthier members Jamaica and the Dominican Republic at half of their face value.

As with the TCP and SUCRE, Venezuela's overwhelming centrality to Petrocaribe is highly problematic. Although domestic opposition is fragmented, tone deaf, and consistent only in its inconsistency, popular discontent is such that it is only question of when rather than if it will be harnessed to defeat the Maduro government. But because Petrocaribe is renewed annually and operated via PDSVA, itself subject to presidential control, when eventually there is a change of government, the scheme could easily be wound down. Since Venezuela's deterioration relates not only to falling oil prices, which naturally stiffen financing conditions via Petrocaribe's sliding scale, but also to falling production, the economic rationale for cutting back on the scheme is also growing stronger.

The impact of irregular implementation

Overall, ALBA's impact on trade and investment has been both significant and short-lived, with important interventions and innovations but little structural change.

In the most basic sense of trade in goods, ALBA's record is ultimately poor. The year of highest intra-ALBA trade (2011) between 2005 and 2016 did represent a 40 per cent increase on its first year (2005). But by 2016 ALBA trade was less than one-quarter of what it had been 11 years previously. Likewise, ALBA's share of intraregional trade – generally low at around 3 per cent, compared to 62 per cent for the EU, say – had also fallen to below 1 per cent by 2016.

The ultimate cause and significance of this is clear when we compare the trajectories of intra-ALBA trade, intra-ALBA trade share, Venezuelan imports and oil prices. With only minor and temporary deviations, these four indicators track very similar paths across ALBA's lifetime (as shown for ALBA trade and oil prices in Figure 21.2). In essence, Venezuela's economy is hyper-dependant on oil revenues, meaning that imports rise and fall with oil prices, and Venezuelan imports represent the vast bulk of trade within ALBA. This dependence on

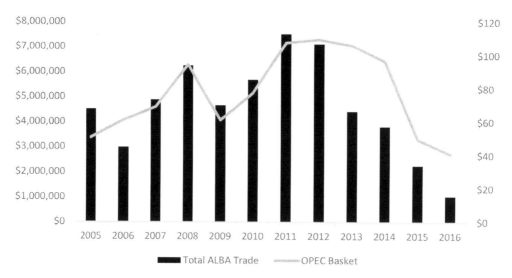

Figure 21.2 Total ALBA trade (US $000) and Organization of the Petroleum Exporting Countries (OPEC) basket price ($) 2005–16.
Sources: trademap.org; opec.org.

intraregional demand from one member state based on external appetites for one volatile primary commodity is a far cry from the regionally reinforced sustainable development and autonomy envisioned by ALBA's leaders, officials and agreements.

Likewise, in terms of changes to the landscape of PTAs in the region, ALBA has had little lasting impact. The TCP's failure to provide a viable alternative to expiring CAN rules in 2011 means that all ALBA trade has continued to be regulated via the same free trade inflected agreements in place when Chávez took office. Only Venezuela's full entry into Mercosur in 2012 represented a significant change, but this too went with the grain of the international trade system that ALBA had originally set out to challenge – this was in any case undone in late 2016 by Venezuela's (ongoing) suspension from the bloc.

More significant has been ALBA's role in creating and shaping the more politically focused institutions the Community of Latin American and Caribbean States (Comunidad de Estados de América Latina y el Caribe – CELAC) and the Union of South American Nations (Unión de Naciones Suramericanas – UNASUR). By excluding the USA and Canada, CELAC has provided an alternative to the Organization of American States that is free of overpowering external influences. But while this political forum can focus regional minds on regional problems, its remit remains narrow and its meetings infrequent. UNASUR, however, has already successfully handled various regional conflicts (especially Bolivia's political crisis of 2008 and the Venezuela-Colombia stand-off in 2010), hopes eventually to expand its coverage even into the economic domain, and has established permanent institutions with dedicated staff. In the same way that Venezuela created policy space for other left-wing governments at the national level, ALBA's perceived radicalism helped to create and normalize the ideological space into which these regional institutions emerged.

But just as the rise of these autonomist institutions was related to the rise of the left, their recent stagnation has been related to the 'return of the right' epitomized by the presidencies of Mauricio Macri in Argentina and Michel Temer in Brazil. At the regional level, a number of countries that had repeatedly clashed with Venezuela over their signing of FTAs with the USA and supposed Venezuelan interference in elections – Peru, Colombia, Mexico and Chile – ultimately formed a competing alliance, the Pacific Alliance, based on the inherently liberalizing open regionalism model that ALBA was created to resist. This has essentially entrenched divisions that have existed since the decline of the FTAA and US attempts to create a patchwork replacement via bilateral FTAs. Nowhere is this clearer than in UNASUR's failure to appoint a new Secretary-General, with the post left vacant throughout 2017 and into 2018 following the departure of Colombian Ernesto Samper.

ALBA's prospects for future integration

Sadly, ALBA's leaders, particularly its two de facto heads Hugo Chávez and Nicolás Maduro, opted to ignore and obscure the scheme's many failings, even though this would be the first step in correcting them. Instead, Maduro has followed in his predecessor's footsteps by launching new initiatives whose ambition ironically rises in inverse relation to their real viability.

The clearest example of this is the announcement in 2013 of a grand regional convergence between ALBA, Petrocaribe, the Caribbean Community (CARICOM) and Mercosur to establish an economic zone of shared development akin to the one proposed but unachieved within ALBA. The fact that even a bilateral version of the TCP could not be realized, let alone an ALBA-wide agreement, is enough to undermine any notion of this idea's feasibility. But the Ecuadorian technocrats tasked internally with assessing the initiative also rightly found Brazil in particular 'unlikely to subordinate its economic trade agenda to a Venezuela-dominated space and a political line of Bolivarian progressiveness',[8] whereas even ideologically aligned Cuba and the smaller Caribbean states of the Organisation of Eastern Caribbean States considered it highly unlikely and potentially fruitless.[9]

Indeed, ALBA's fundamental Venezuela-centrism makes stagnation a far more likely outcome.[10] The 2014 plunge in oil prices cut the flow of off-budget resources usually used for ALBA projects, and even existing funds had to be redirected to the domestic arena, particularly to pay for vital imports of food and medicines. Unchecked inflation, a wildly dysfunctional currency regime, rampant corruption, haphazard planning and the Maduro government's impotent (or collusive) response to these issues have also made Venezuela an extremely unattractive partner in any economic initiative, even where states have comparable development priorities and strategies. Worse yet, the drift towards anti-democratic practices under Maduro – blocking a recall referendum, installing an illegitimate constitutional assembly, arbitrarily rescheduling presidential elections – renders ALBA guilty by association, creating political disincentives on top of economic ones. Even a sharp jump in oil prices, itself unlikely given the resilience of US shale output, would only provide temporary respite from this inexorable deterioration.

Thus, deeper integration in ALBA's alternative terms is highly improbable. Conversely, in fact, the erosion of ALBA's credibility due to ineffective implementation illustrates instead the 'threat of a bad example', as even well-designed, beneficial initiatives such as the SUCRE and Petrocaribe have been undermined by their association with the wider project. This decline has robbed alternative 'post-(neo)liberal' forms of regional integration of the impetus that they enjoyed in the 2000s, with the unintended and undesired consequence of affording the previous model of open regionalism a sense of relative solidity or even resurgence in the 2010s. Where ALBA once made important and innovative contributions to regional political economy, its present of political posturing suggests a future of increasing irrelevance.

Notes

1 Originally called the Bolivarian Alternative for the Americas, ALBA has been formally known as ALBA-TCP since 2008. The TCP element refers to the People's Trade Agreement (Tratado de Comercio de los Pueblos) adopted with Bolivia's accession in 2006 and developed further in 2009.

2 See, among many others by the same author, Thomas Muhr (ed.) (2013) *Counter-Globalization and Socialism in the 21st Century: The Bolivarian Alliance for the Peoples of Our America*, London: Routledge.

3 Olivier Dabène (2018) 'ALBA and the Fourth Wave of Regionalism in Latin America', in Asa K. Cusack (ed.) *Understanding ALBA: Progress, Problems, and Prospects of Alternative Regionalism in Latin America and the Caribbean*, London: Institute of Latin American Studies, pp. 39–50.

4 Marcelo I. Saguier (2007) 'The Hemispheric Social Alliance and the Free Trade Area of the Americas Process: The Challenges and Opportunities of Transnational Coalitions against Neo-Liberalism', *Globalizations*, 4(2): 251–65.

5 Elizabeth Gonzalez (2016) 'Weekly Chart: The Cuba-Venezuela Oil Relationship', AS/COA, 8 April. Available at www.as-coa.org/articles/weekly-chart-cuba-venezuela-oil-relationship.

6 Asa K. Cusack (2018) *Venezuela, ALBA, and the Limits of Postneoliberal Regionalism in Latin America and the Caribbean*, New York: Palgrave Macmillan.

7 ALADI (2009) 'AAP.CE No. 40 Acuerdo Acuerdos de Alcance Parcial'. Available at www.aladi.org/nsfaladi/textacdos.nsf/0f226c9002f6aebf03257491004226fe/642e78a0e1503c5803256c9400570557?OpenDocument; ALADI (2011) 'AAP.CE No. 47 Acuerdo Acuerdos de Alcance Parcial'. Available at www.aladi.org/nsfaladi/textacdos.nsf/0f226c9002f6aebf03257491004226fe/bb6c8740bbc992900325750f00621b4e?OpenDocument.

8 Ministerio de Comercio Exterior (2014) 'Convergencias Ideológicas Entre ALBA-TCP, PETROCARIBE y MERCOSUR', 17 January.

9 Cusack, *Venezuela, ALBA, and the Limits of Postneoliberal Regionalism in Latin America and the Caribbean*.

10 Dabène, 'ALBA and the Fourth Wave of Regionalism in Latin America'.

22

The European Union

Christian Schweiger

Introduction

The European Union (EU) has undergone several profound crises during the past decade but nevertheless remains the prime global trading power and still surpasses both the USA and the People's Republic of China. Currently, there are 28 member states (EU-28) which exported goods worth approximately €1,702 billion and services worth over €700 billion to economies around the world in 2013–14. This amounted to a global share of trade in goods and services of around 16 per cent, compared with around 13 per cent for the USA, 12.9 per cent for China, 4.9 per cent for Japan, 1.6 per cent for the Russian Federation and 1.1 per cent for India.[1] The EU's trade is equally dependent on imports and exports but overall has strengthened its exports in recent years. This is reflected in the latest figures which show that global exports from the EU-28 increased to €156.8 billion in September 2017, which equals growth of 9 per cent in the total number of exports in the first half of 2017. During 2017 the EU member states also collectively managed to reverse the negative global trade balance which the single market had suffered in 2016. While it still stood at −1.6 per cent in September 2016, with the total level of imports outweighing exports by €149 billion to €147.4 billion, a total export volume of €156.8 billion exceeded the total import volume of €153.7 billion. The EU's export volume in 2016 was particularly boosted by growth in trade with Russia (21.4 per cent), China (18.8 per cent), the Republic of Korea (South Korea) (16.9 per cent) and Switzerland (11.5 per cent).[2] Moreover, the EU retains the largest share of global trade in services, where it even surpasses the USA.[3]

The USA and China remain the EU's most important partners in global trade, followed by Switzerland, Russia and Turkey. As political relations with the latter two have been increasingly strained over recent years the focus has shifted in particular to China, where substantial further growth potential lies. The same applies to the USA, in which case the EU Commission has tried to implement the Transatlantic Trade and Investment Partnership (TTIP) despite growing resistance from member states. Ironically, opposition towards the TTIP agreement has most noticeably grown in Germany, the EU's most export-orientated member state, which has a substantial trade surplus with the USA. Owing to the adverse conditions which have continued to affect EU member states following the 2008 global financial crisis and the subsequent triple economic, banking and sovereign debt crisis in the eurozone, protectionist sentiments are on the increase in many member states. As the EU Commissioner for Trade Cecilia Malmström emphasized in her speech in Karlsruhe in January 2006:

251

> More than at any time in decades, the value of open markets is being questioned and discussed … Sadly, all too often, we see extreme views, opposed to open societies and economies, dominating discussions and suggesting answers that would lead to an inward-looking, intolerant decline.[4]

The EU hence faces the ever greater challenge of maintaining unity in its external trade strategy and will have to reconfigure it at a time when the United Kingdom as the third largest member state and the second biggest economy of the single market is preparing to exit the EU in 2019 (known as Brexit).[5]

The challenges to the EU's global trade position

Even under intensifying global competition and multiple challenges the EU managed to maintain its status as the leading global trade power.[6] Just like the USA the EU has seen a significant decline in its global share of world trade during the past decade. The EU's share of world trade fell from 17.9 per cent in 2004 to 14.8 per cent in 2014, while China's share rose from 8.4 per cent to 14.2 per cent. In the case of the USA and the EU the decline can partially be explained by the economic slowdown brought about by the financial crisis. In China's case its growing importance as a low-cost production hub for Western, especially European, products, also plays a significant part.

The EU's share of global gross domestic product (GDP) has declined continuously over the past decade.[7] Between 2004 and 2014 it decreased by almost 10 per cent, while the share of competitors in Asia and the rest of the world grew substantially. In particular, China's contribution to global GDP tripled during the same period, which illustrates the strategic future challenge facing the EU. European economies have been significantly weakened as a result of the financial crisis and are struggling to recover significant growth rates.

The main challenge for the EU's standing as a global trading power will therefore be to overcome the persistently low growth rates in the member states, which were already sluggish prior to the 2008 financial crisis and have been dampened further ever since. The late 2017 growth forecast provided by the European Commission shows that on average the single market grew by only 2.4 per cent in 2017 and is predicted to continue with growth at or just above 2 per cent in 2018 and 2019. The same applies to the eurozone. Of the 28 member states only eight were forecast to have grown by more than 4 per cent in 2017 (Estonia, the Czech Republic, Ireland, Latvia, Malta, Poland, Slovenia and Romania).[8] It is noticeable that six of those are Central Eastern European countries, a region which has witnessed substantially higher growth rates than in the rest of the EU since their accession in 2004 and 2007. In comparison, China is forecast to have annual growth rates of more than 6 per cent in the period between 2017 and 2019. Trade Commissioner Cecilia Malmström emphasizes in this respect that the EU member states have to acknowledge the fact that in future 90 per cent of global growth will occur outside the borders of the single market and that trade provides the link 'to be connected to it' to ensure that jobs in the member states can be secured for the long term.[9]

The challenge of coordinating trade policy in the diverse European single market

Trade remains a controversial issue in the European single market which is characterized by a variety of diverse economies. The EU member states' distinctive trade interests stem from the fact that the so-called single market consists of a wide variety of diverse economies. These range from Anglo-Saxon liberal models (the UK, Ireland, the Baltic States) to Central European continental (Germany, France, Austria, the Benelux countries), Southern European and the post-communist transition models in Central Eastern Europe.[10] Although the 28 member states of the EU have agreed on collective trading standards and policies and above all also granted the European Commission the mandate to negotiate international trade agreements on their behalf, national governments remain protective towards maintain national sovereignty in this crucial policy area. This explains why recent joint initiatives to implement bilateral free trade agreements (FTAs) between the EU and major partners remain controversial.

Germany stands out in the single market as the only member state with a substantial external trade balance, which amounted to €134 billion in the period between January and September 2017. Germany hence remains the EU's export locomotive which surpasses all the other member states in terms of global export performance outside of the single market. Many of the other EU member states had a negative external trade balance, most noticeably the UK (–€52.5 billion), the Netherlands (–€94.2) and Spain (–€23.7). During the same period only ten other EU member states had a positive external trade balance: Ireland (€26 billion), Italy, (€24.1 billion), France (€16.4 billion), Sweden (€11.4 billion), Denmark (€7.6 billion), Austria (€5.3 billion), Finland (€4.8 billion), Lithuania (€1.5 billion), Estonia (€0.5 billion) and Latvia (€0.4 billion).

This leaves Germany in a rather isolated position when it comes to its own economic interests. No other member state is as export-orientated as Germany. Between January and September 2017 Germany had an export volume of €397.2 billion outside the single market and a staggering €559.8 billion when it comes to export trade with other EU member states.[11] The rest of the EU consequently is strongly dependent on German trade and particularly its export volume. Germany is the main exporter within the eurozone. The Central Eastern European region is particularly heavily dependent on the German 'export machine'.[12]

Based on the importance of exports for its economy Germany positions itself principally as a promoter of free trade. At the same time, based on Germany's economic culture of ordoliberalism,[13] which favours state-driven rules for economic interaction and shows an inherent scepticism towards the general confidence in market forces displayed in liberal market economies, public scepticism in Germany towards an unlimited global free trade agenda has grown.[14]

This explains why German Chancellor Angela Merkel's strong support for the EU's free trade agenda, especially the Transatlantic Trade and Investment Partnership (TTIP), has met mounting opposition at home. The USA remain particularly Germany's most important trading partner when it comes to the export of goods. German's total exports to the USA amounted to €107 billion in 2016.[15] The German so-called grand coalition between the conservative Christian Democrat Union/Christian Social Union and the centre-left Social Democrats under Merkel had made substantial efforts to implement the TTIP agreement despite growing domestic opposition. Opinion polls conducted on attitudes towards the TTIP in the EU in late 2016 still showed slight overall support of 53 per cent for the TTIP among the EU-28. The UK is a strong supporters of the TTIP (64 per cent) along with other liberal market economies such as Ireland (75 per cent), Lithuania (78 per cent) and Estonia (64 per cent). In contrast, however, 52 per cent of Germans and 72 per cent Austrians were opposed to the TTIP. In France, opponents and supporters of the agreement were almost evenly split.[16]

The Special Eurobarometer report on the future of Europe and social issues published in November 2017 illustrates that the majority of citizens in the EU (45 per cent) prioritize 'social equality and solidarity' over free trade and the market economy (23 per cent). Individual country results show that in ten EU member states, including Germany and France, more than half of all citizens favour social equality over free trade.[17] An overwhelming 83 per cent of all citizens in the EU-28 think that a free market economy needs to be accompanied by a high level of social protection.[18] As one of the core projects of the European Commission in the area of trade, the TTIP agreement therefore came under increasing public scrutiny. Following the unexpected election of billionaire businessman Donald Trump as the new US president in November 2016, the TTIP agreement essentially was put on ice. Trump openly advocated protectionist policies during his election campaign and his Administration has essentially terminated negotiations on the TTIP. Moreover, the Trump presidency also poses fundamental questions about the important future US trade relations with Europe. Trump has repeatedly singled out the German trade surplus with the USA as 'very, very bad'.[19] This reflects his overall scepticism towards free trade with the European partners. Trump has given the EU mixed signals about the TTIP. More recently the president indicated that he might be willing to revive negotiations on the deal. During a speech in Berlin in June 2017 US Secretary of Commerce Wilbur Ross offered the EU the possibility to reopen negotiations,[20] but progress to date has been limited. Currently, the prospects for the TTIP are bleak, mostly because of the political uncertainty surrounding the impact of the UK's exit from the EU (known as Brexit) and the policy shifts in Germany following the creation of a grand coalition government in early March 2018. As long as signals from Washington on the TTIP remain mixed and Germany continues to be governed by an administrative coalition progress is unlikely to occur. Moreover, with the UK now moving towards a departure from the EU in March 2019 the EU will lose its major advocate for the transatlantic trade deal.

The assessment of EU Council President Donald Tusk at the EU Council summit on 20 October 2016, at which the EU-Canada Comprehensive and Economic Trade Agreement (CETA) was adopted, that 'CETA could be our last free trade agreement if we are not able to convince people that we negotiate to protect their interests'[21] currently seems to be most accurate. CETA has been less controversial than the TTIP as the EU's trade volume with Canada amounts to €8.3 billion per year, which places Canada in 10th position in the ranking of the most important global trading partners for the EU, with a 1.9 per cent of the Union's total global trade. In contrast, the USA and China have a combined share of 32.7 per cent of the EU's total global trade activities (17.8 and 14.9 per cent each respectively). The removal of trade barriers on goods and services with both countries is therefore substantially more controversial among the EU-28. Concerns about maintaining EU standards on consumer protection rank high on the list of critics of the TTIP as do any attempts to liberalize trade with China. Moreover, echoing the sentiments which the EU Commissioner for Trade Cecilia Malmström expressed in her Karlsruhe speech in January 2016, the growing scepticism towards open markets across the EU also substantially stems from general disbelief in the political promise that open markets will result in employment growth. Instead, the 'Stop TTIP' initiative, which calls on the European institutions and the EU member states to stop their negotiations with the USA on the TTIP and not to ratify CETA with Canada, emphasizes that there is a risk that jobs will be lost, especially in the area of services. This is because under both CETA and the TTIP 'public contracts would therefore be even more subject to the logic of competition and the market. Encouragement of the local economy or of socio-ecological procurement would be made more difficult, and partially forbidden'.[22]

In spite of these public concerns the European Commission is proposing the initiation of two new bilateral trade agreements with Australia and New Zealand by 2019 with the aim of 'moving forward quickly in view of the political imperative of strengthening the EU's trading position in the world' and to create a value-based trade policy that 'preserves the right of governments to regulate in the public interest'.[23] In addition, the Commission is working towards the establishment of further FTAs with Mexico and Japan.[24]

The impact of the global financial crisis

The growing public scepticism towards FTAs stems to a large extent from the negative social effects of the 2008 global financial crisis that was experienced by many member states. The obvious regulatory failures in the financial industry have substantially contributed to the credibility crisis of the EU's governance. Prior to the onset of the crisis the EU had advocated an approach which allowed member states a wide scope to maintain national regulatory standards. The severe banking crisis in some member states, most noticeably in the liberal economies of Ireland, the UK and the Baltic states but also in France and the Southern European economies, revealed the lack of an effective single rulebook with binding regulatory standards. This reflected the overall EU approach towards financial sector regulation, which in essence left the regulation of banks and other financial service providers in the hands of national regulators.

This minimal and disjointed regulatory approach resembled the culture that prevailed in the USA. Prior to the crisis the European Commission had openly promoted US regulatory practices as an example of effective practice to national governments in the EU. In preparation for the revision of the Lisbon Strategy in 2014 the High Level Group chaired by Wim Kok had promoted the Commission's Financial Services Action Plan as the way forward towards what it called 'unleashing the dynamism of financial markets'. The report emphasized that 'dynamic and highly competitive financial markets are not only desirable themselves – they are an essential driver of growth in all other sectors of the economy'.[25] The Financial Services Action Plan was based on the work of another High Level Group of Experts, the Lamfalussy Committee, which had determined the strategy of the EU in the area of financial services as one which would prioritize the removal of 'administrative, regulatory or other types of obstacles which in practice impede cross-border securities'.[26] In practice, the Lamfalussy Committee recommended that financial sector regulation should be oriented 'so as to meet the expectations of dealers and brokers, issuers and investors who wish to be able to deal with one another throughout the European Union in an effective, entirely secure and informed manner'.[27] This meant that the legal implementation of regulatory powers should rest with national regulators on the basis of core principles determined by national parliaments, a model that was also common practice in the USA.[28]

With hindsight, however, it is obvious that the EU's promotion of minimal regulation on the basis of trust in the capacity of the financial industry to exercise responsible self-regulation at national level was completely at odds with the reality of increasingly globally interconnected banks and financial institutions.[29] In countries where the US financial crisis spilled over into their own banking sectors bringing the threat of the insolvencies of individual banks taxpayers discovered that they were obliged involuntarily to bail these out. The resulting adverse effect on the budgetary situation in the affected countries led to the imposition of severe austerity policies. These were most noticeable in Southern European member states such as Greece, Spain and Portugal. However, they also occurred in liberal economies such as Ireland and the UK, where governments had to cover substantial banking liabilities to avoid the total collapse of individual institutions and the loss of private assets deposited in them. The Irish government faced financial liabilities of between €46 billion and €72 billion each year during the period 2010–13 to avoid the almost complete collapse of the domestic banking sector. Ireland also received a total of €75.5 billion in joint support from the EU and the International Monetary Fund to cover these liabilities on the condition that it would reduce spending by about 9 per cent of its GDP per year until it resolved its liquidity problems.[30] The UK faced liabilities of between €127 and €205 billion per year during the period 2009–13. These were resolved by the British government through the introduction of an unprecedented prolonged austerity programme which reduced government spending by 40 per cent between 2010 and 2015.[31]

Under the conditions of financial crisis and the subsequent eurozone crisis public trust in the EU's institutions declined markedly. Between 2009 and 2012 trust in the EU fell by 26 percentage points from 57 per cent to 31 per cent and recovered slightly in 2017 (42 per cent).[32] Currently, a majority of citizens in nine of the 28 member states do not trust the EU. Support

Christian Schweiger

for globalization is also on the wane. Polls show that on average 51 per cent of citizens in the EU consider globalization to be a good opportunity for national companies, while 38 per cent consider it to be a 'threat to employment and companies' in their own country. In five countries (Belgium, Cyprus, Latvia, France and Greece) more than 50 per cent of citizens express the latter view.[33] Furthermore, 63 per cent of citizens in the EU-28 think that globalization increases social inequality. Only in one member state (Malta) less than half of the population agrees with this view (43 per cent), while in all other member states the majority supports it.[34]

The EU's perception as a safeguard against the negative effects of globalization is equally weak. Only 45 per cent of all citizens in the EU think that the EU is protecting them from the negative effects of globalization, while 43 per cent disagree. In four member states (Slovakia, the Czech Republic, France and Greece) a clear majority of citizens (between 54 per cent and 65 per cent do not consider the EU to be a safeguard against globalization.[35] The growing scepticism towards market-based solutions has its roots in the decline of the post-war democratic consensus, under which the public put its trust in free market solutions based on the expectation that they would deliver sustainable economic growth and tangible positive social effects. In this context the EU has been accused of having advocated a 'neoliberal turn' under which the traditional Keynesian welfare state has been dismantled in favour of 'maximizing competitiveness in terms that favour the market over other social goals'.[36]

Perspectives for the EU after Brexit

Since the narrow decision of the 51.9 per cent of the British electorate to opt for exit from the EU at the public referendum held in the UK on 23 June 2016 the EU has entered a new phase of potentially wider disintegration of its membership. The UK's long-standing reputation as an awkward partner in the EU, which has never been able to come to terms with integration into the EU's complex system of multi-level governance, has been widely documented. Based on the UK's former status as global colonial empire and its supposed special transatlantic relationship with the USA, British foreign policy has never considered political engagement in Europe as a major priority. The UK had belatedly joined the European Economic Community (EEC) in 1973 predominantly on economic grounds. The main motive for British EEC membership was the aspiration to be able to enjoy the benefits of tariff-free trade with the European continent. This reflected the UK's preference for free trade and its perception of the European project's purpose as predominantly that of a free trade area. The UK has hence been the strongest advocate of the swift liberalization of the European market. This was most obviously shown by Prime Minister Margaret Thatcher's support for the 1987 Single European Act and the subsequent creation of the European single market as the core project of the EU.[37] The rising level of Euroscepticism in the UK had its origins in the disappointment about the lack of progress in market liberalization and the tendency of other EU member states, particularly France and Germany, to combine the process with demands for deeper political integration. The recalibration of the eurozone governance framework under Germany's leadership in the aftermath of the financial crisis re-emphasized British concerns about the increasing loss of political sovereignty. Concerns concentrated on the potential for the spill-over of political integration from the eurozone core into the wider single market.[38]

The UK government has determined 29 March 2019 as the official date for the UK's exit from the EU. This means that the EU is likely to lose the second biggest economy in the single market with GDP per caput of 108 purchasing power standards (PPS) in relation to the EU-28 100 index[39] and a current trading volume of €293 billion[40] by that date. The impact on the trading power of the UK is currently the subject of a contested British domestic debate between those who consider the complete detachment from the single market as an opportunity and those who warn of fundamental negative consequences for the British economy. The final report of the London-based Centre for European Reform commission on Brexit highlights that the UK services and manufacturing sectors are strongly dependent on exports to other EU member states. The commission therefore estimates the impact of trade with the EU to be around 10 per cent of the UK's total GDP, which would manifest itself in a loss of around 1.3 per cent of annual GDP growth, if tariff-free access to the single market could at least partially be maintained, and 2.7 per cent if a hard Brexit forces the UK to revert to World Trade Organization rules when trading with the EU. Estimates deteriorate further if the loss of productivity is taken into account.[41] For the Union itself the actual impact of Brexit on the level of economic growth in the remaining 27 EU member states is considerably smaller. According to the economic impact scenarios developed by the European Parliament, Brexit will result in a reduction of between 0.11 per cent and 0.52 per cent of the average GDP growth across the EU-27. Individual member states are, however, likely be affected more profoundly, depending on the intensity of their trade relations with the UK.[42]

The most affected states are likely to be Ireland, Belgium and the Netherlands, whose export volumes to the UK make up between 6 per cent and 7 per cent of their GDP. Germany, Hungary and Slovakia export between 2 per cent and 4 per cent of their GDP to the UK and therefore face at least a moderate impact on their overall economic performance. Malta is also likely to be significantly affected as it is heavily dependent on imports from the UK, which make up almost 6 per cent of its GDP.[43] More profoundly, Brexit poses a substantial risk in terms of the adverse impact the loss of the UK is likely to have on the standing of the EU as a global trading power. At the same time, the exit of the member state which is the most dedicated promoter of internal and external free trade poses the risk that protectionist sentiments will increase among the remaining member states. These are already visible, particularly in the formerly liberal economies of Central Eastern Europe, most noticeably in Hungary and Poland,[44] but also in France and partially in Germany, where unlimited free trade and open markets are regarded with considerable scepticism. On the other hand, Brexit offers the opportunity for the remaining 27 member states to regroup and to revitalize their cooperation on external trade.

This will not be easy given the persistent disparities in the structure of individual economies and the resulting diverging interests in terms of trade. The biggest risk emerging from Brexit lies less in its potential negative economic impact but in the danger of the emergence of a wider trend towards the political and ultimately also the economic disintegration of the EU. The failure to effectively address both the growing economic and social divisions in the EU and the mounting public concerns about the lack of democratic accountability in the multi-level decision-making processes of the EU is likely to further increase support for populist Eurosceptic forces.[45] There has been a growing core-periphery cleavage in the EU in the aftermath of the financial and eurozone crises, which has augmented the already existing economic peripheralization of regions in the EU.[46] The economic core in terms of GDP per inhabitant in PPS above the EU average is now obviously limited to the Central European regions, such as the western parts of Germany, the Benelux states, Austria, the Nordic countries (Denmark, Sweden and Finland) and the south-eastern region of the UK. The rest of the EU is drifting ever further below the EU average, which includes large parts of France but significantly also Eastern Germany.

The further expansion of the already substantial social periphery in large parts of the Central Eastern and the south-eastern region of the EU[47] would further undermine the already substantially weakened consensus on pursuing an agenda of open markets and free trade. On trade, as on many other crucial policy issues, the EU faces the fundamental choice between a new isolationism or a new phase of effective cooperation. This was the core of the message delivered

Christian Schweiger

to member states by Commission President Jean-Claude Juncker in his 2017 State of the Union address: 'Either come together around a positive European agenda or each retreat into our own corners'.[48]

Notes

1 European Commission (2016) *DG Trade Statistical Guide*. Available at http://trade.ec.europa.eu/doclib/docs/2013/may/tradoc_151348.pdf (accessed 28 November 2017).
2 Eurostat (2017) *Euro Indicators*, 15 November. Available at http://trade.ec.europa.eu/doclib/docs/2013/december/tradoc_151969.pdf (accessed 28 November 2017).
3 European Commission, *DG Trade Statistical Guide*, p. 20.
4 Cecilia Malmström (2016) *Dealing with Challenges through Global Trade*, 11 January. Available at http://trade.ec.europa.eu/doclib/docs/2016/january/tradoc_154155.pdf (accessed 28 November 2017).
5 Valentina Romei (2017) 'UK Economy Is the EU's second-largest', *Financial Times*, 14 March. Available at www.ft.com/content/9c154df4-08c5-11e7-ac5a-903b21361b43 (accessed 28 November 2017).
6 See European Commission, *DG Trade Statistical Guide*, p. 23. Available at http://trade.ec.europa.eu/doclib/docs/2013/may/tradoc_151348.pdf.
7 See Eurostat (2016) *The EU in the World, 2016 Edition*, the European Union, Brussels: Eurostat, p. 79. Available at http://ec.europa.eu/eurostat/documents/3217494/7589036/KS-EX-16-001-EN-N.pdf/bcacb30c-0be9-4c2e-a06d-4b1daead493e (accessed 28 November 2017).
8 European Commission (2017) European Economic Forecast, Autumn 2017, p. 1. Available at https://ec.europa.eu/info/sites/info/files/economy-finance/upd_ip063_en.pdf (accessed 28 November 2017).
9 Cecilia Malmström (2015) *Trade and Global Challenges*, 30 November. Available at http://trade.ec.europa.eu/doclib/docs/2015/november/tradoc_154009.pdf (accessed 28 November 2017).
10 Christian Schweiger (2014) *The EU and The Global Financial Crisis: New Varieties of Capitalism*, Cheltenham: Edward Elgar.
11 European Commission, *Euro Indicators*.
12 Bela Galgoczi (2014) 'The Tale of Two Peripheries in a Divided Europe', *Perspectives on European Politics and Society*, 15(3): 367.
13 Ordoliberalism is the belief that capitalism needs a strong government to create order in markets.
14 V. Berghahn and Brigitte Young (2013) 'Reflections on Werner Bonefeld's "Freedom and the Strong State: On German Ordoliberalism" and the Continuing Importance of the Ideas of Ordoliberalism to Understand Germany's (Contested) Role in Resolving the Eurozone Crisis', *New Political Economy*, 18 (5): 775; Lothar Funk (2015) 'Essentials of the British Economic Debate on German Ordoliberalism', in Christian Schweiger (ed.) *Drifting Towards the Exit? Taking Stock of Britain's EU Membership after 40 Years*, Augsburg: Wißner Verlag, pp. 102–25.
15 German Federal Statistical Office (2016) *Germany's Major Trading Partners*.
16 European Commission (2016) *Standard Eurobarometer Autumn*. November, p. 19. Available at http://ec.europa.eu/commfrontoffice/publicopinion/index.cfm/ResultDoc/download/DocumentKy/79402 (accessed 28 November 2017).
17 European Commission (2017) *Special Eurobarometer 467: Future of Europe and Social Issues*. November, p. 15. Available at http://ec.europa.eu/commfrontoffice/publicopinion//includes/images/mimetype/pdf1.gif (accessed 28 November 2017).
18 European Commission, *Trade Indicators*, p. 39.
19 Anthony Faiola (2017) '"The Germans Are Bad, Very Bad": Trump's Alleged Slight Generates Confusion, Backlash', *Washington Post*, 26 May. Available at www.washingtonpost.com/world/trumps-alleged-slight-against-germans-generates-confusion-backlash/2017/05/26/0325255a-4219-11e7-b29f- (accessed 28 November 2017).
20 *Deutsche Welle News* (2017) 'Angela Merkel Welcomes US Offer to Resume TTIP Talks', 27 June.
21 *Daily Express* (2016) 'CETA Could Be EU's Last: Donald Tusk Admits the Great Brussels Plan Is Falling Apart', 20 October.
22 European Initiative Against TTIP and CETA (2017) 'TTIP & CETA in Detail'. Available at https://stop-ttip.org/what-is-the-problem-ttip-ceta/faqs/ (accessed 28 November 2017).
23 European Commission (2017) *Communication to the European Parliament, the Council, the European Economic and Social Committee and the Committee of the Regions: A Balanced and Progressive Trade Policy to*

Harness Globalisation, 13 September, pp. 6 and 8. Available at http://trade.ec.europa.eu/doclib/docs/2017/september/tradoc_156038.pdf.

24 Press Conference by Commissioner Malström on the 'Report on Trade and Investment Barriers', 26 June 2017. Available at http://europa.eu/rapid/press-release_SPEECH-17-1799_en.htm (accessed 28 November 2017).

25 High Level Group Chaired by Wim Kok (2004) *The Lisbon Strategy for Growth and Employment*. November, p. 26. Available at https://ec.europa.eu/research/evaluations/pdf/archive/fp6-evidence-base/evaluation_studies_and_reports/evaluation_studies_and_reports_2004/the_lisbon_strategy_for_growth_and_employment__report_from_the_high_level_group.pdf (accessed 28 November 2017).

26 Final Report of the Committee of Wise Men on the Regulation of European Securities Markets, 15 February 2001, p. 98. Available at http://ec.europa.eu/internal_market/securities/docs/lamfalussy/wisemen/final-report-wise-men_en.pdf (accessed 28 November 2017).

27 Ibid., p. 99.

28 Ibid., p. 93.

29 David Mayes (2015) 'The European Union after the Global Financial Crisis: Consequences and Reactions', in Normann Witzleb, Alfonso Arranz and Pascaline Winand (eds) *The European Union and Global Engagement: Institutions, Policies and Challenges*, Cheltenham: Edward Elgar, p. 65.

30 Eurostat (2017) *Summary Table for Government Interventions to Support Financial Institutions*. October. Available at http://ec.europa.eu/eurostat/documents/1015035/8338723/Summary-table-gov-interventions-Oct2017.xlsx (accessed 28 November 2017).

31 HM Treasury (2015) *2010 to 2015 Government Policy: Deficit Reduction*, 8 May. Available at www.gov.uk/government/publications/2010-to-2015-government-policy-deficit-reduction (accessed 28 November 2017).

32 European Commission (2017) *Standard Eurobarometer 87: Key Trends*, 23 June, p. 5. Available at http://ec.europa.eu/commfrontoffice/publicopinion/index.cfm/ResultDoc/download/DocumentKy/79590 (accessed 28 November 2017).

33 Eurobarometer (2017) *Designing Europe's Future: Trust in Institutions, Globalisation, Support for the Euro, Opinions about Free Trade and Solidarity*, June. Available at http://ec.europa.eu/commfrontoffice/publicopinion/index.cfm/ResultDoc/download/DocumentKy/78720 (accessed 28 November 2017), pp. 6 and 33.

34 Ibid., p. 38.

35 Ibid., p. 42.

36 Kenneth Dyson (2017) 'The Political Economy Context of EU Crises', in Desmond Dinan, Neill Nugent and William E. Paterson (eds) *The European Union in Crisis*, London: Palgrave Macmillan, p. 43.

37 Christian Schweiger (2015) 'The British Liberal Market Economy after the Global Financial Crisis', in Christian Schweiger (ed.) *Drifting Towards the Exit: Taking Stock of Britain's EU Membership after 40 Years*, Schriftenreihe des Arbeitskreises Deutsche England Forschung (ADEF) 70, Augsburg: Wißner, pp 126–50.

38 Lee McGowan and David Phinnemore (2017) 'The UK: Membership in Crisis', in Desmond Dinan, Neill Nugetna and William E. Paterson (eds) *The European Union in Crisis*, London: Palgrave Macmillan, p. 82.

39 Eurostat GDP per caput in PPS. Available at http://ec.europa.eu/eurostat/data/database# (accessed 28 November 2017).

40 Eurostat (2017) *Euro Indicators*.

41 John Springford, Simon Tilford, Christian Odendahl and Philip McCann (2016) *The Economic Consequences of Leaving the EU: The Final Report of the CER Commission on Brexit 2016*, 21 April, pp. 30 and 38. Available at www.cer.eu/publications/archive/report/2016/economic-consequences-leaving-eu-final-report-cer-commission-brexit (accessed 28 November 2017).

42 European Parliament (2017) *An Assessment of the Economic Impact of Brexit on the EU 27*, March, pp. 28 and 33. Available at www.europarl.europa.eu/RegData/etudes/STUD/2017/595374/IPOL_STU(2017)595374_EN.pdf (accessed 28 November 2017).

43 Ibid., p. 11.

44 Tim Haughton (2017) 'Central and Eastern Europe: The Sacrifices of Solidarity, the Discomforts of Diversity, and the Vexations of Vulnerabilities', in Desmond Dinan, Neill Nugetna and William E. Paterson (eds) *The European Union in Crisis*, London: Palgrave Macmillan, p. 257; Oliver Kovács (2016) 'The Hungarian Agony over Eurozone Accession', in José M. Magone, Brigid Laffan and Christian

Schweiger (eds) *Core-Periphery Relations in the European Union: Power and Conflict in a Dualist Political Economy*, Abingdon: Routledge, pp. 243–44.

45 Douglas Webber (2017) 'Can the EU Survive?', in Desmond Dinan, Neill Nugetna and William E. Paterson (eds) *The European Union in Crisis*, London: Palgrave Macmillan, p. 350.

46 See Eurostat (2017) Regional Yearbook, p. 120. Available at http://ec.europa.eu/eurostat/documents/3217494/8222062/KS-HA-17-001-EN-N.pdf/eaebe7fa-0c80-45af-ab41-0f806c433763 (accessed 28 November 2017).

47 Béla Galgóczi (2016) 'The Southern and Eastern Peripheries of Europe: Is Convergence a Lost Cause?', in José M. Magone, Brigid Laffan and Christian Schweigr (eds) Core-Periphery Relations in the European Union: Power and Conflict in a Dualist Political Economy, Abingdon: Routledge, pp. 130–47.

48 European Commission (2017) President Jean-Claude Juncker's State of the Union Address, 13 September. Available at http://europa.eu/rapid/press-release_SPEECH-17-3165_en.htm (accessed 28 November 2017).

23
TTIP

Christoph Scherrer

Introduction

In 2013 the European Commission and the government of the USA began to negotiate a Transatlantic Trade and Investment Partnership (TTIP). As its name suggests, the accord would not only eliminate remaining tariffs on trade in goods but also facilitate investments among the trading partners. It would lead to an even deeper integration of the already intensely enmeshed economies on both sides of the Atlantic which account for roughly 47 per cent of global gross domestic product (GDP), one-third of world trade flows and more than half of foreign direct investment.[1]

After 15 rounds of negotiations, the TTIP project became embroiled in the US presidential elections of 2016. During the presidential campaign all the main candidates distanced themselves from the Trans-Pacific Partnership (TPP) which, negotiated in parallel to TTIP, had already been concluded and awaited ratification. On his first day as President, Donald Trump withdrew the USA from the TPP. While attracting much less contentious attention in the USA, Trump's decision led to an indefinite suspension of the USA from the TTIP negotiations. Given the continued interest of US corporations in a comprehensive trade agreement with the European Union (EU), the resumption of negotiations cannot be ruled out for the coming years. It therefore remains of interest to take a closer look at the genesis and objectives of the TTIP negotiations, the areas of consent and dissent, as well as the critics' arguments against TTIP.

TTIP: long in the making[2]

The current negotiations on a trade and investment agreement between the USA and the EU continue a transatlantic dialogue of many years' standing, as well as many initiatives to institutionalize cooperation on regulation issues.[3] Back in 1990, just after the ending of the Cold War, the EU and the USA had already agreed in the Transatlantic Declaration that representatives of the US government, the European Commission and the European Council would meet regularly to discuss the aim of economic liberalization. In 1995 they launched the New Transatlantic Agenda, which aimed notably to help to promote trade and investment relations and improve exchanges at non-governmental level, for example through recognition of the role of the

Transatlantic Business Dialogue (TABD) among major corporations on both sides of the Atlantic. Later renamed the Trans-Atlantic Business Council (TABC), the TABD's mission became the achievement of a transatlantic free trade agreement. Alongside individual sector-specific firms, the TABC had a major influence on the negotiations. In the consultations held by the European Commission for drafting a negotiation agenda, 92 per cent of all encounters were with business associations and only 4 per cent with public interest groups.[4]

In 1998 the governments established a Transatlantic Economic Partnership which led to the Roadmap for EU-US Regulatory Cooperation and Transparency (2004 and 2005), which embodied 15 sector-specific projects, and various other dialogue forums followed. However, despite all these initiatives, success on regulatory issues remained limited. For instance, various agreements on mutual recognition were never implemented, due to a lack of reciprocal trust. Against this backdrop, German Federal Chancellor Angela Merkel, who was also President of the EU Council at that time, US President George W. Bush and EU Commission President José Manuel Barroso set up the Transatlantic Economic Council (TEC). The TEC is designed to provide stronger political support, at ministerial level, for cooperation initiatives. It is advised by the Transatlantic Legislators' Dialogue (European Parliament and US Congress), the Transatlantic Consumer Dialogue and the TABC. And it was the TEC that, at the behest of the EU-US summit, set up the High Level Working Group on Jobs and Growth in November 2011. That working group prepared the TTIP negotiations.

With the 'Global Europe' and 'Trade Growth and World Affairs' strategies, presented in 2006 and 2010 respectively, the European Commission explicitly espoused the link between external market opening and the European internal market reforms – i.e. in both cases the dismantling of 'unnecessary' regulations, as part of the overarching aim of competitiveness. Thus, the liberalizing trade policy is not only motivated by boosting exports, but also serves as a justification for structural reforms of the internal market and the neoliberal disciplining of the less 'deregulation-happy' actors within the EU.[5]

Neither the US negotiators nor the European Commission have made any secret of the fact that the trade policy aims involved go beyond purely bilateral relations. In particular, both parties sought to set new standards for world trade in those critical fields where progress at multilateral level would be significantly more difficult to achieve – or would entail more extensive concessions, for example to the late industrializing countries. In particular, these critical fields include the so-called Singapore issues (investment protection, state-supported companies, and transparency in government procurement) and stronger protection for intellectual property rights (IPRs) – for instance, stronger patent protection for medicines in relation to the development and sale of generics, as well as further liberalization (i.e. market opening) of services. The EU and the USA intended not only to provide templates for future World Trade Organization (WTO) negotiating rounds on these issues, but also at the same time to use their joint political and economic sway to open up third country markets for their firms, through direct pressure for adjustment, and to push back the regulations that these countries have adopted, often for development policy reasons – for instance, rules about local content. After all, for both parties, this was about halting their loss of trade policy clout, particularly vis-à-vis the Asian region.

The EU negotiation mandate

Recognizing that the corporate agenda for greater protection of investments and IPRs as well as less protection for public services might not be popular with significant parts of the electorates, the negotiating partners tried to keep their mandates and proposals secret. Corporate

Observatory Europe had to appeal to the information disclosure regulation before the European Commission revealed the composition of the advisory groups that informed the bargaining agenda.[6] Even after sustained civil society protests and complaints by parliamentarians, access to the content of the negotiated TTIP proposals remained restricted to a small group of ministerial bureaucrats. Parliamentarians were given only limited time to look at the long legal documents and were forbidden to take notes.[7] An assessment of the negotiations' progress has therefore to rely on rather vague statements by the negotiating partners and some leaked documents.

The High Level Working Group on Jobs and Growth that informed the EU mandate called for the liberalization of the service sector, the dismantling of 'domestic' non-tariff trade barriers such as state regulations, the adaptation or harmonization of regulatory standards (e.g. technical ones), complete protection of investments including IPRs, the opening up of state procurement systems, and competition policy measures such as the limitation of state support for state-owned companies and the abolition of local content clauses. Finally, environmental and social protection criteria were to be documented in a separate sustainable development chapter. Due to space limitations, I will present the negotiating mandate of the EU Council for the EU Commission's Directorate-General for Trade[8] but not the US mandate.[9] Instead, I highlight the areas of consent and dissent between the EU and the USA.

Improved Market Access

For trade in goods, tariffs, quantitative restrictions, fees, etc. are to be abolished or phased out as completely as possible – save for any exceptions that may be made. While the average rate of customs is just 5 per cent *ad valorem* for EU duties and 3.5 per cent *ad valorem* for US duties, in some product categories customs duties are significantly higher. Sectors that are explicitly under negotiation include, in particular, agriculture, automobiles, chemicals, pharmaceuticals and medical technology, energy and raw materials. This means not only scrapping the remaining tariffs, which are still quite substantial in some sectors, but also harmonizing rules of origin, for example.[10] In the energy and raw materials sector, export restrictions are also to be abolished, price regulation is to be reduced and negotiations are to take place on issues concerning access to infrastructure networks. Moreover, in line with WTO rules, the agreement is to include clauses on anti-dumping and compensatory measures. But at the same time, a safeguard clause is to be put in place in case of serious damage due to an over-rapid increase in imports and exceptions are to be decided under Articles XX and XXI of the General Agreement on Tariffs and Trade (GATT).

As for services, in accordance with Article V of the General Agreement on Trade in Services (GATS), regardless of the sectors and modes of delivery concerned, the highest degree of liberalization in each respect is to be adopted and remaining barriers are to be dismantled. In addition, the parties are to commit to transparency, impartiality, lawful authorization procedures and the national treatment principle and are to facilitate mutual recognition of professional qualifications. Up for negotiation are not only sectors such as communications and transport, but also, for instance, financial, health and care services. Although exemption provisions in line with Articles XIV and XIV of the GATS have not been ruled out, uncertainties about terms or definitions and competing interests mean that the possible negotiating outcomes are difficult to predict. For example, national entry and residence regulations are supposed to remain applicable, provided that they do not run counter to the aims of the agreement, and regulations by the EU and its member states on conditions of work and employment are also to stay in force. But just how reliably or consistently such reservations will ultimately be pursued or applied is still an open question. The same goes for the definition of services supplied in the exercise of

Christoph Scherrer

governmental authority, under GATS Art. I.3, or the provisional exemption of audiovisual services. In this respect, the Commission emphasizes that, in principle, no field is to be treated a priori as an exception, and the explicit swing towards a negative list approach (a list of explicitly exempted fields), at least in the case of public services, highlights the Commission's preference for liberalization.

As regards public procurement, in line with the WTO's revised Government Procurement Agreement (GPA), mutual market access to public provision is to be expanded at all levels. Foreign bidders are to be put on an equal footing with local ones and barriers to access, such as local content clauses, production requirements or exemption rules, are to be dismantled.

Regulations and non-tariff barriers

If economic estimates are to be believed, the non-tariff trade barriers and regulations are equivalent to tariff rates of 10 per cent to 70 per cent.[11] In principle, i.e. 'horizontally' across all sectors, the agreement is therefore supposed to dismantle 'unnecessary' regulations and barriers to trade and investment, and/or to achieve efficient regulation through greater compatibility, harmonization or mutual recognition, and where necessary to deepen this by means of sector-specific provisions. However, according to the Commission, the right to regulate on health care, public safety, social and environmental standards and cultural diversity is to remain, provided that the aims and measures are regarded as 'appropriate' or 'legitimate'.

Particularly for sanitary and phytosanitary measures and technical regulations, the line of the relevant WTO agreements is to be followed with regard to greater transparency and convergence, forms of cooperation and possibilities for the recognition of equivalent or compliant procedures. The right to take unilateral protective measures is, particularly in the absence of sufficient scientific evidence, to be restricted to the protection of life and health.

Rules and investment protection

On investment protection, for which the EU Commission has had sole competence since the 2009 Lisbon Treaty took effect, the mandate goes beyond the report of the High Level Working Group on Jobs and Growth. The maximum amount of liberalization and protection achieved so far is also to be laid down for fields in which competence is shared between the EU Commission and the member states, such as portfolio investments. Standards for the treatment of foreign bidders are, in particular, to abide by the principles of national and most-favoured-nation treatment and are to rule out 'unreasonable', arbitrary or discriminatory types of treatment. In addition to issues of security, investment protection is to extend to forms of direct and indirect expropriation, for which it should include 'adequate' compensation rights, as well as to unimpeded flows of capital. Investment protection, which would be binding at all levels of state governance, is be ensured through an independent, comprehensive investor to state dispute settlement (ISDS) system, as well as state-to-state arbitration and an umbrella clause. The ISDS system, in particular, is to protect enterprises against 'unjustified' claims.

In response to widespread criticism, the EU Commission publicized its proposal for an ISDS process for TTIP. It invited civil society to comment on its proposal in mid-2014 and 150,000 Europeans responded, of which 97 per cent rejected the ISDS. A year later the Commission revealed its modified, allegedly independent version of the ISDS, now called the Investment Court System. It now contains a provision that safeguards the government's right to regulate in the public interest; exempts EU rules on state aid; and replaces the present system of ad hoc arbitration with an Investment Tribunal and an Appeal Tribunal.[12]

264

In addition, the agreement is to contain competition policy provisions on state aid, monopolies, state enterprises and other exclusive benefits, liberalization in the field of raw materials and energy, trade-related aspects of small and medium-sized enterprises (SMEs), transparency rules and full-scale liberalization (including a standstill clause – i.e. a ban on any further regulation) of payments and capital movements, except in case of grave monetary or currency policy dangers or tax-relevant aspects. To minimize state influence on competition, the forms of state influence or of favourable treatment of individual firms, sectors or regions are to be broadly defined. It will be difficult to evade such categorization – or else the legitimate exceptions will be tightly defined. State enterprises or those granted favourable treatment are to be obliged, beyond the tasks concerned here, to adopt a commercial orientation, and cross-financing in non-monopolistic markets is to be prohibited (similarly to GATS Art. VIII). Finally, transparency rules for subsidies, going beyond the existing WTO regulations, are intended to have a demonstration effect on other countries and speed up progress on equivalent global regulations.

Environmental and social standards

Social and environmental standards are to be promoted through the application of internationally recognized norms, including the core International Labour Organization (ILO) labour standards, an accompanying Sustainability Impact Assessment, and provisions for monitoring the implementation of these standards. Civil society actors are to be involved in this, and complaints procedures are to be established. For inclusion in the chapter on sustainable development, the Commission proposes the 1998 ILO Declaration on Fundamental Rights and Principles at Work, as well as the 2006 Declaration on Social Justice for a Fair Globalization and trade-related elements of the Decent Work Agenda. But apart from references to internationally recognized standards, voluntary initiatives or corporate social responsibility practices, the proposals on implementation and monitoring are still not very concrete. The involvement of those concerned and of civil society actors is mostly restricted to the right to be informed and to be heard. There is no mention of any clearly defined scope for influence or sanctions.

Areas of consent and dissent between the EU and the USA[13]

In March 2017 the EU Commission informed its Transatlantic Trade and Investment Partnership Advisory Group about the progress achieved in the negotiations. Among the areas of consent the Commission mentioned the recognition of good manufacturing practices in the pharmaceutical sector, rules of origin, and rules for SMEs. Furthermore, both parties seem to have recognized that the differences concerning regulatory practices need to be respected.

The list of remaining differences between the EU and US proposals appears to be longer. In addition to important chapters such as sustainable development and energy and raw materials, the key areas which require considerable further work include the following:

Agricultural market access: The agricultural sector is one of the manifestly contentious issues. Not only have the tariffs in this sector remained above average, the 'production models' are also very different on either side, and each has its own practices and regulations. US agriculture is characterized by big farms with an average usable area of 447 ha, whereas the average holding in Germany is about 56 ha. The production methods are correspondingly different, and include the widespread use of genetically modified organisms (GMOs) in the US. Behind such hotly debated items as 'gene food' and 'chlorine chickens', there are indeed fundamental differences of conception about approval or labelling requirements for certain processes or products. While the European side prefers to apply the precautionary principle in cases where the scientific evidence for health safety is deemed insufficient, the US side insists on precedence for scientifically supported risk assessments. This is, for example, the basis of the 'substantial equivalence' principle applied to genetically manipulated food in the USA, where there is no GM labelling requirement. Therefore, the negotiations showed little progress in the areas of sanitary and phytosanitary rules.

Sea and land transport: Both of these transport modes are relatively closed markets in the USA, due to national regulation (e.g. the Jones Act). While the EU would like to negotiate on these sectors within the framework of TTIP, the US side points explicitly to the Air Transport Agreement that already exists between the EU and the USA.

Government procurement: Estimates assume that the US government procurement market, particularly due to 'Buy American' and similar provisions, is significantly more 'closed' than the European one, and that, for example, only one-third of American procurement, compared with 90 per cent of that in the EU, is covered by the plurilateral GPA. Consequently, opening up procurement is a high priority for European firms and also for the Commission. In addition, they aim to reduce the thresholds for public tenders – towards EU standards – as was the case in the negotiations with Canada.[14] However, the regulatory means and competences in this field are spread across different levels of American government (federal and subfederal) and have not been fully clarified. Thus, individual US states, such as Maine, frequently insist on exceptional provisions in bilateral and multilateral trade agreements. Thus, the US negotiators, contrary to practice in other fields, have expressed scepticism about the negative list (a list of explicitly exempted fields) approach that the Commission has been taking on this issue. Not least because of the considerable asymmetry and the different distribution of potential gains and losses in case of deregulation, there is also considerable resistance to this within US civil society. However, US negotiators would like to subject the European Structural and Investment Funds to closer examination, and this could also provoke stronger resistance at regional and local level in the EU.

Geographical indications: The EU is particularly interested in protecting the geographic indications for agricultural products such as spirits from Cognac, specific sorts of cheese (e.g. Gouda), or 'Schwarzwälder Schinken' (Black Forest ham). It tabled a shortlist of 223 geographical indications covering food and spirit names. It requested the USA to provide a 'level of protection that prohibits the use of a GI name even when the consumer is not misled, i.e. when the true origin of the product is indicated or in translation or accompanied with expressions such as "kind", "type", "style", "imitation" or the like'.[15] The USA is reluctant to accede to these requests as a number of European geographical indications have acquired generic nature in the USA.

Investment protection: Ever since the signing of the North American Free Trade Agreement (NAFTA), US corporations and trade negotiators have pushed for the inclusion of ISDS mechanisms. As explained above, under pressure from civil society and some member state governments, the European Commission revised its original proposal for the investment chapter. While the original proposal was much in line with US demands (except for the issue of investment protection in the pre-establishment phase), the newly proposed Investment Court System was rejected by the US trade negotiators.

Social and labour standards: Some of these standards are certainly higher in Europe, which is why US trade unions are hoping or even insisting that any agreement should foster improvements in these standards. However, experience with trade agreements so far does not exactly encourage hopes that they can be used as a lever for raising standards. True, the USA did build dispute arbitration mechanisms, including on social standards, into past agreements (e.g. the US-Korea FTA – KORUS), whereas the EU did not (e.g. the EU-South Korea FTA – KOREU). However, these mechanisms are generally aimed at breaches of standards by the trading partner, not in the homeland.

Academic and societal critique of TTIP

TTIP has been promoted by pointing to the significant gains in welfare that would be realized through additional exports and employment growth. Critics, however, cite the dangers it would pose to democracy, consumer protection and working conditions. Some of the arguments are listed below:

Biased studies on employment impact

The promoters of TTIP point to significant welfare gains due to additional exports, higher growth, and increases in efficiency, income and employment. In doing so, they draw on various economic studies. Based on complex modelling, these studies all come to the conclusion that a TTIP would increase prosperity in all member states of the trade and investment agreements.[16] However, a closer look at these studies reveals surprisingly small gains. The most optimistic study for Germany calculated an increase of 181,000 jobs for its 'comprehensive scenario', i.e. in the unlikely event that the level of liberalization between the USA and the EU reaches the level of the EU single market. That amounts to less than one per mille of the 41.8 million people gainfully employed in 2012, the base year of the study. The period for when these gains will be realized is not explicitly made clear. The study is targeted on long-term effects without a clearly specified time frame.[17]

In the interim, jobs will be lost. The studies do not deny this fact; they just do not emphasize it. These losses will follow from their main argument. More trade-enforced specialization will lead to the elimination of less productive jobs. Those who have lost their jobs will move to the more productive jobs. While in many export-oriented nations more productive, better paying jobs were created over time, those who have actually lost their jobs in the trade-induced restructuring of the economy, however, had on average a long search for re-employment which usually paid significantly less than their old occupations.[18]

The ex ante assessments of NAFTA were equally optimistic as the current studies supporting the 'mega-regionals'. The comparison with the ex post experiences of NAFTA reveals that the ex ante projections substantially overestimated the economic effects. For Mexico, NAFTA even diminished GDP growth, cut into real wages, and increased income inequality.[19] A careful analysis of the commonly used computable general equilibrium models for assessing the impact of trade liberalization points to their systematic bias in favour of free trade. Their core assumptions turn out to be unrealistic. These econometric studies generally neglect the potential macroeconomic adjustment costs as well as the social costs of regulatory change. Attention should be paid to the likely occurrence of balance of payments problems for individual EU member states, to losses for the public budgets of the EU and its member states owing to the elimination of the remaining tariffs, and to the difficulties of re-employing less-skilled workers in import-competing sectors who lose their jobs owing to increased competition. As social costs, they identify threats to consumer safety, public health and the environment.[20]

In contrast to the aforementioned studies informed by the insights of neoclassical supply-side economics, Jeronim Capaldo developed a Keynesian demand-side model based on the United Nations Global Policy Model. His calculations for TTIP turned out to be quite the opposite from the mainstay studies. TTIP would lead to losses in terms of net exports and of GDP after a decade. Job losses would amount to approximately 583,000 in the EU.[21] While some of the assumptions of Capaldo's model appear to be more realistic, predicting the job gains or losses remains a daunting task for the comprehensive TTIP that hardly leave any economic practice untouched.

Christoph Scherrer

Encroachment on public services

A mega-regional trade agreement such as TTIP is about anti-discrimination. Foreigners are not to be discriminated against. National laws and regulations concerning the supply of services shall not favour domestic suppliers over foreign ones. In the case of trade in goods, some state rules traditionally aimed at discriminating against foreign providers, in particular through the imposition of duties. By contrast, state rules for the supply of services are based on a quite different set of motives. These are intended to ensure that basic services are provided nationwide and are universally accessible, that quality standards are maintained and, particularly in the case of education, that democratic participation and control are assured. Since TTIP comprises the application of the simple anti-discrimination rule developed for trade in goods to the supply of services (as had already happened in the 1995 GATS), it encroaches deeply into a body of rules that was and still is committed to goals other than hindering or facilitating cross-border economic activities.

Education is a good example for demonstrating the effects of the anti-discrimination rule on public services. Education is predominantly organized by the state (on different levels) around the world and in particular in continental Europe. Non-profit providers such as churches usually operate under very similar rules and state oversight. For foreign providers little space is left. Access to state funding is in most places non-existent. If they are allowed to operate at all, they compete head-on with institutions supported by the taxpayers, unless they occupy a very special niche. In other words, they are discriminated against if not by intent then by the very structure of the education system. Creating a so-called level playing field for those providers would necessitate a major overhaul of the education systems.[22]

Therefore, the application of the anti-discrimination rule would not only influence the relationship between foreign and domestic suppliers, but would have wide-reaching implications also for domestic providers vis-à-vis governments. By limiting the power of the nation state to discriminate against foreign service suppliers, the anti-discrimination rule restricts the scope for public and democratic choice in matters of basic services. Since suppliers are predominantly corporations, trade agreements on services concern the rights of capital vis-à-vis governments or, more precisely, the definition of rights for holders of property. These rights include guarantees against expropriation, but also safeguards for management prerogatives concerning investment and employment.

TTIP, therefore, fits nicely into a political strategy that Stephen Gill has termed 'new constitutionalism'.[23] While the 'old' constitutionalism defined the rights and freedoms of citizens through the king cum autocratic state, the new constitutionalism protects property holders against the modern state. The democratic as well as the developmental state have taken an expansive view of property rights: they include obligations towards the common good, for instance universal service, accountability, or the protection of workers' health. In contrast, new constitutionalism takes a narrower view of property rights: the interests of stakeholders other than owners, such as workers, consumers or citizens, are excluded. It aims not only at committing present governments to its definition of property rights but, furthermore, tries to prevent future governments from undoing liberal governmental and market reforms. New constitutionalism, therefore, amounts to 'the politico-juridical locking in of commitments to a disciplinary neo-liberal framework of accumulation on the world scale'.[24] TTIP is a form of constitutionalism because the rights of governments vis-à-vis property holders are circumscribed and cannot easily be changed. Comparable to constitutional rights in the national arena, a simple majority is not sufficient for withdrawal from or revision of the once agreed upon rights of capital.

Investment rules: protection of corporate power[25]

TTIP foresees an additional specific privilege for corporations: the right of foreign investors to sue the governments of the participating countries before private international tribunals. An investor-state settlement process provides corporations with the possibility of suing states for compensation, before an allegedly independent arbitration tribunal, if they think that state measures or regulations run counter to the investment protection enshrined in the agreement. However, such dispute settlement procedures not only give foreign investors extensive protection, they also restrict states' regulatory possibilities, unless the states want to run the risk of having to pay out large amounts of compensation.

The danger lies in the vagueness about what constitutes a 'legitimate' public interest and what may be regarded as 'indirect' expropriation. The greater the room for interpretation, the more important is the quality of the process – such as the basis of its legitimation, its transparency and its independence. Currently, firms' complaints are handled by arbitration bodies. The proceedings are not held in public, they are often not transparent, and the arbitrators and lawyers concerned have no sovereign or democratic credentials. For the great majority of these proceedings, the arbitrators and lawyers are recruited from only about 20 big, internationally active practices, which more or less take it all in turns and swap roles. Not only do these practices maintain close relations with the big corporations, they also more or less proactively 'scan' national policies and regulation plans in search of promising complaint opportunities, they circulate proposals on that basis, and they fund complaints via the financial markets.

These dispute settlement processes can be criticized on two counts. First, due not only to the damages payable in case of losing an arbitration case but also to the high legal bills that have to be footed by the taxpayer come what may, states are deprived of means that could otherwise be put into useful community projects such as investments or social compensation. Second, the more frequently these complaints are brought, with high damages at stake and high costs, the more likely it is that even the threat of such action will have a deterrent effect on political representatives. Thus, regulations or policy measures that are democratic but are rejected by business are not only potentially expensive, they are prevented from the outset.

The EU Commission's proposal for an Investment Court System features an improved selection process for arbitrators, enhanced ethics rules, and the establishment of an appellate body. While these features are certainly an improvement, they fall short of addressing the substantial democratic deficit of such private tribunals.[26] The German association of judges (Deutscher Richterbund) wrote in a public statement: 'Neither the proposed procedure for the appointment of judges of the ICS nor their position meets the international requirements for the independence of courts'.[27]

Notes

1 Memorandum of the European Commission, European Union and United States to Launch Negotiations for a Transatlantic Trade and Investment Partnership, 13 February 2013. Available at http://ec. europa.eu/trade/policy/in-focus/ttip/documents-and-events/index_en.htm#_documents [hereinafter European Commission's Memorandum (13 Feb. 2013)].

2 Here I rely on S. Beck (2014) 'TTIP: Possible Negotiating Outcomes and Consequences', in C. Scherrer (ed.) *The Transatlantic Trade and Investment Partnership: Implications for Labor*, Rainer Hampp Verlag. Munich: Mering. pp. 10–40; Christian Pitschas (2016) 'Transatlantic Trade and Investment Partnership (TTIP): The Devil in Disguise or a Golden Opportunity to Build a Transatlantic Marketplace?' in *Br. J. Am. Leg. Studies*, 5, DOI: 10.1515/bjals-2016–0011.

3 Mark A. Pollack (2003) *The Engines of European Integration: Delegation, Agency, and Agenda Setting in the EU*, Oxford: Oxford University Press.

4 See https://corporateeurope.org/international-trade/2014/07/who-lobbies-most-ttip.

5 Ferdie De Ville (2013) 'EU Trade Policy as the Continuation of Internal Market Policy by Other Means', in Tamara Takács, Andrea Ott and Angelos Dimopoulos (eds) *Linking Trade and Non-Commercial Interests: The EU as a Global Role Model?* CLEER Working Papers 2013/4, Center for the Law of EU External Relations, pp. 93–103.

6 See https://corporateeurope.org/international-trade/2015/07/ttip-corporate-lobbying-paradise (accessed 21 November 2017).

7 See www.independent.co.uk/news/world/europe/ttip-controversy-secret-trade-deal-can-only-be-read-secure-in-reading-room-in-brussels-10456206.html (accessed 21 November 2017).

8 See the European Commission's Memorandum (13 Feb. 2013).

9 The latest legislative delegation occurred with the Trade Promotion Authority from 2015 (TPA-2015), which is valid until 1 July 2018. Available at www.congress.gov/114/plaws/publ26/PLAW-114publ26.pdf.

10 Rules of origin are employed to determine a product's national source. In a bilateral free trade zone, they are used to exclude producers in countries outside the zone from the trade preferences within the zone.

11 Lonel Fontagné, Julien Gourdon and Sébastien Jean (2013) 'Transatlantic Trade: Whither Partnership, Which Economic Consequences?' CEPII Policy Brief No.1, Centre d'Études Prospectives et d'Informations Internationales, Paris. p. 8.

12 See http://trade.ec.europa.eu/doclib/docs/2015/november/tradoc_153955.pdf.

13 Here I rely on European Commission (2017) 'U.S.-EU Joint Report on TTIP Progress to Date', 17 January, Brussels: European Commission, as well as on Beck, 'TTIP: Possible Negotiating Outcomes and Consequences'.

14 See https://trade.ec.europa.eu/doclib/docs/2014/december/tradoc_152982.pdf, p. 12.

15 See http://trade.ec.europa.eu/doclib/docs/2016/march/tradoc_154372.pdf.

16 e.g. K. Berden, J. Francois, M. Thelle, P. Wymenga and S. Tamminen (2009) 'Non-Tariff Measures in EU-US Trade and Investment: An Economic Analysis', in: ECORYS, Study for the European Commission, Directorate-General for Trade. Available at http://trade.ec.europa.eu/doclib/docs/2009/december/tradoc_145613.pdf; and CEPR (2013) 'Reducing Transatlantic Barriers to Trade and Investment: An Economic Assessment', London: Final Project Report, Centre for Economic Policy Research. Available at http://trade.ec.europa.eu/doclib/docs/2013/march/tradoc_150737.pdf.

17 G. J. Felbermayr, B. Heid and S. Lehwald (2013) 'Transatlantic Trade and Investment Partnership (TTIP): Who Benefits from a Free Trade Deal?' Part 1: Macroeconomic Effects, Gütersloh: Bertelsmann Foundation. Available at www.bfna.org/sites/default/files/TTIP-GED %20study %2017June %202013.pdf, pp. 41 and 14, n. 13, 69, 111.

18 R. E. Scott (2012) 'The China Toll: Economic Policy Institute', Washington DC: EPI Briefing Paper, p. 345.

19 W. Raza, J. Grumiller, L. Taylor, B. Tröster and R. Von Arnim (2014) 'An Economic Assessment of the Claimed Benefits of the Transatlantic Trade and Investment Partnership (TTIP)', in C. Scherrer (ed.) *The Transatlantic Trade and Investment Partnership: Implications for Labor*, Munich: Rainer Hampp Verlag, pp. 62–66.

20 Ibid.

21 J. Capaldo (2014) 'TTIP: European Disintegration, Unemployment and Instability', GDAE Working Paper no. 14–03, Tufts University, p. 14.

22 C. Scherrer (2005) 'GATS: Long-term Strategy for the Commodification of Education', *Review of International Political Economy*, 12(3): 484–510.

23 S. Gill (2002) 'Privatization of the State and Social Reproduction? GATS and New Constitutionalism', Paper prepared for International Workshop GATS: Trading Development? Center for the Study of Globalisation and Regionalization, University of Warwick, Coventry, 20–21 September.

24 See Gill, 'Privatization of the State and Social Reproduction?'.

25 Here I benefit from P. Eberhardt (2014) 'Investment Protection at a Crossroads', in C. Scherrer (ed.) *The Transatlantic Trade and Investment Partnership: Implications for Labor*, Munich Rainer Hampp Verlag, pp. 100–19.

26 P. Eberhardt (2016) *The Zombie ISDS Rebranded as ICS, Rights for Corporations to Sue States Refuse to Die,* Brussels: Corporate Europe Observatory.

27 Deutscher Richterbund (2016) Stellungnahme zur Errichtung eines Investitionsgerichts für TTIP – Vorschlag der Europäischen Kommission vom 16.09.2015 und 12.11.2015. Nr. 04/16, 4 February 2016, unofficial translation available at www.foeeurope.org/sites/default/files/eu-us_trade_deal/2016/english_version_deutsche_ richter-bund_opinion_ics_feb2016.pdf.

24

EFTA

Marius Vahl and Aslak Berg[1]

Introduction

The European Free Trade Association (EFTA) was set up in 1960 to promote free trade and closer economic cooperation among its members. Since its establishment, EFTA has changed considerably, both in terms of its membership and with regard to the main tasks it performs for its member states.

Originally comprising seven countries, EFTA currently has four member states: Iceland, Liechtenstein, Norway and Switzerland. All are relatively small, advanced and open economies that are dependent on trade for their prosperity. They share generally liberal approaches to trade, while being highly protective of their agricultural sectors. In comparison with other regional trade associations, EFTA is unusual in that its four member states do relatively little trade with each other. Thus, in 2016 intra-EFTA trade only constituted 0.55 per cent of EFTA's global trade in goods. The rationale for EFTA can therefore not be found in the depth of trade ties between its member states, but rather in historical developments and the continued utility of EFTA for managing their trade relations.

Although intra-EFTA trade remains important in absolute terms, in practice EFTA's main purpose today is to facilitate joint cooperation with third countries. While intra-EFTA relations used to dominate its agenda at the outset, now EFTA's principal activities are to manage trade and economic relations with the European Union (EU) through the Agreement on the European Economic Area (EEA), and the negotiation and management of free trade agreements (FTAs) with partners across the globe.

EFTA has a dual structure. The EFTA Convention, which regulates trade and the free movement of persons between the member states, and negotiations and trade relations with non-EU countries, are managed from EFTA's headquarters in Geneva on behalf of all EFTA states (referred to as 'EFTA at four'). The EEA Agreement, through which three EFTA states – Iceland, Liechtenstein and Norway (the EEA EFTA states[2]) – participate in the EU's single market, is managed jointly with the EU in Brussels.

The establishment of EFTA[3]

EFTA traces its roots to the post-Second World War era, when European leaders saw the need for enhanced economic integration in Western Europe. The European Coal and Steel

Community was formed in 1951, and its six member states rapidly started discussions on establishing the European Economic Community (EEC), which came into being with the Treaty of Rome in 1958. At the same time, there were discussions on establishing a broader free trade area covering all of Western Europe, but these plans never came to fruition. This was largely due to divergences between the countries prioritizing tighter integration through the EEC, and those preferring a looser relationship that focused more on free trade. As a result, negotiations ended in 1958.

Based on the discussions that had taken place about the broader Western European-wide trade area, officials from seven countries – Austria, Denmark, Norway, Portugal, Sweden, Switzerland and the United Kingdom – started exploratory discussions among themselves in February 1959, and by summer had agreed in principle to create a free trade association. Discussions progressed quickly, and the Stockholm Convention establishing EFTA was signed on 4 January 1960 and entered into force on 3 May 1960 after rapid ratification in all countries. The Convention provided detailed provisions for rules of origin, tariff reductions and the elimination of quantitative restrictions, but otherwise provided a basic framework with guiding principles instead of detailed rules.

Development of relations with the EU

The relationship with the EU and its predecessors – the EEC and the European Community (EC) – has been a central issue for EFTA and its member states since the beginning. While the founding EFTA states agreed on the importance of free trade to promote prosperity, these were countries that, at that time, did not share the political goal of an 'ever closer union' and were not willing to 'pool' their sovereignty or accept supranational institutions managing their economic cooperation.

This fundamental reluctance to commit to supranationality remains a defining characteristic of the EFTA states. However, there have been significant changes in the relationship between the EFTA states and the EU over the last six decades, as the EFTA states have grappled with the challenges posed by the process of ever closer European economic and political integration.

Arguably, the most significant development in EFTA-EU relations has been that a number of EFTA states have left EFTA to join the EC (which later became the EU). Indeed, most EFTA states have at one stage or another applied to join the EC/EU. So far, six states have left EFTA to join the EC/EU,[4] while three of the current EFTA states have, at one stage or another, applied for EC and/or EU membership, but without actually joining.[5]

As for the states that have remained in EFTA, over time they have concluded successive agreements on closer economic and trade cooperation with the EU. Various efforts had already been made by the EFTA states in the 1960s towards greater economic cooperation with the EC, culminating in the conclusion of bilateral FTAs between six EFTA states and the EC during 1972 and 1973. These FTAs provided for the gradual removal of import duties on most products by 1977.[6]

EFTA-EC relations were further intensified following the adoption of the joint EFTA-EC Luxembourg Declaration in 1984, which called for the creation of a 'dynamic European economic space'. The aim was to remove technical and other non-tariff barriers, and extend cooperation to other areas, such as research and development and the telecommunications sector. However, soon after, the EC embarked upon a process of renewed economic integration, which was to culminate in a single European market with the free movement of goods, services, capital and persons by the end of 1992. This '1992 project' created a new challenge for EFTA-EC relations, and in January 1989 the European Commission proposed a new structured relationship between the EC and EFTA. Negotiations on what became known as the EEA were formally launched the following year.

The EEA Agreement: EFTA-EU relations beyond free trade

Signed in May 1992 the EEA Agreement entered into force on 1 January 1994. Although trade is a key rationale, the EEA Agreement provides for far-reaching economic integration and political cooperation, which (with the exception of the treaties on the EU itself) goes much further than most other international agreements on economic cooperation. The uniqueness of the EEA Agreement is reflected in its substantive and geographical scope, its institutional structures and its decision-making procedures.[7]

The EEA Agreement provides for the participation of three EFTA states – Iceland, Liechtenstein and Norway[8] – in the European single market. By establishing a legally homogenous area, the so-called four freedoms (the free movement of goods, services, capital and persons) are extended to the EEA EFTA states, including common policies on competition and state aid. The EEA Agreement further provides for the participation of the EEA EFTA states in EU programmes and agencies covering a broad range of areas, including research, innovation, education, transport, telecommunications, environment and energy, to mention a few. The EEA EFTA states also make significant financial contributions to reducing social and economic inequalities in Europe through dedicated financial mechanisms. These mechanisms provide funding for programmes and projects that promote social and economic development in the less affluent parts of the EU.

The EEA Agreement does not entail the participation of the EEA EFTA states in the EU's customs union, nor in its Common Agricultural and Fisheries Policies (CAP and CFP, respectively).[9] However, there are numerous important provisions regarding agriculture and fisheries in the EEA Agreement, which are quite politically sensitive areas for some of the EEA EFTA states. Sanitary and phytosanitary rules and standards form a numerically large part of the EEA rules and regulations, and the EEA Agreement also contains provisions on trade in agricultural products and a protocol on trade in fishery products. While tariffs for processed agricultural products and certain fishery products are regulated in the EEA Agreement itself, tariffs for basic agricultural products and the remaining fishery products are regulated in separate bilateral agreements. The EEA Agreement obliges parties to carry out reviews of the conditions of trade in agricultural products, and to decide on any further liberalization every second year, although in practice these reviews have been conducted less frequently.

The EEA Agreement is a dynamic agreement. In order to ensure legal homogeneity throughout the entire EEA, new or revised single market legal acts adopted by the EU are incorporated into the EEA Agreement[10] and are made part of the national legal orders of the EEA EFTA states. In order to manage this dynamic development of legislation, and to monitor compliance in the EEA EFTA states and provide enforcement at judicial level – a rather complex institutional structure has been established, known as the 'two-pillar structure' (see Figure 24.1).

Notably, and in addition to the more traditional joint bodies tasked with its management, the EEA Agreement calls for two additional bodies to be established on the EFTA side. Mirroring the surveillance tasks of the European Commission vis-à-vis the EU member states, the EFTA Surveillance Authority monitors compliance with the EEA Agreement by and in the three EEA EFTA states. The EFTA Court is responsible for the enforcement of the EEA Agreement in the EEA EFTA states, in a role corresponding to that of the EU Court of Justice with regard to the EU member states.

Compared with other agreements between the EU and non-member states, the EEA Agreement accords the EEA EFTA states an unprecedented level of participation in the

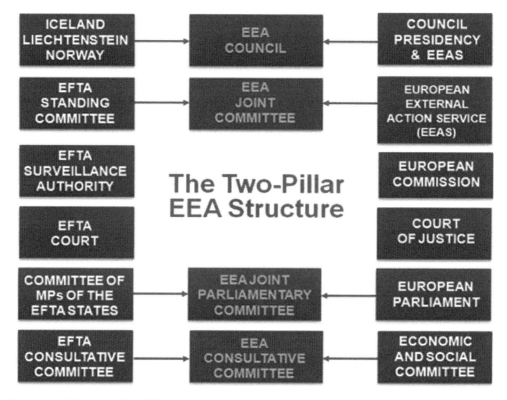

Figure 24.1 The two-pillar EEA structure
Source: EFTA Secretariat.

institutions of the EU, such as the various committees assisting the Commission in drawing up new legislation and in managing EU programmes, and in the growing number of EU agencies. However, and crucially, the EEA EFTA states do not participate in the decision-making bodies of the EU: the Council of the EU and the European Parliament. In practice, this means that a significant amount of what eventually becomes the national laws, rules and standards in the EEA EFTA states have been adopted without their participation. This 'democratic deficit' was – and remains – a major point of criticism of the EEA Agreement.

The creation of EFTA's third-country policy

As mentioned, EFTA was originally set up to manage trade within Europe – first and foremost among its members as an alternative to the supranational EC. However, there were also early attempts to establish relations between EFTA as a group and other parties beyond the EC. In as early as 1967, a joint working group was established with Yugoslavia, which, by the early 1980s, had evolved into a formal Joint EFTA-Yugoslavia Committee. But EFTA's very first trade agreement was negotiated with Madrid as Spain transitioned into a democracy. The short-lived EFTA-Spain Trade Agreement entered into force in 1980 and expired when Spain joined the EC in 1985. The purpose of this agreement was, on the one hand, to give EFTA countries a similar level of market access to that achieved by the EC in its agreement with Spain and, on the other hand, to give Spain a similar level of access granted by the EFTA states to the EC in their respective FTAs. As Spain had already applied for EC membership along with Portugal, it was always intended to be a transitional arrangement, but it set an early example for later agreements.

At the EFTA ministerial meeting in June 1990 in Gothenburg, ministers formally decided to establish a network of FTAs in parallel with the development of the EC network. As had been the case with Spain, the impetus behind the decision was to secure equal terms and avoid discrimination compared to European competitors. With the ending of the Cold War, the EC at the time had decided to develop trade relations with the former Communist countries in Central and Eastern Europe as a first step towards closer integration. The EFTA states wanted to contribute to this process, as they feared being left behind. No effort seems to have been made to offer EFTA membership to the newly democratic countries as an alternative to the EC, perhaps primarily because at the time virtually all the EFTA states were in discussions with the EU about possible membership, and the future of EFTA itself was therefore in doubt. As was the case with Spain, many of the initial trade agreements were therefore intended to be transitional in nature, bridging the gap until EC membership for one or more of the parties had been agreed.

Having followed the EC in negotiating trade agreements with Turkey and Israel from 1991 to 1992, the EFTA states concluded agreements in rapid succession with Bulgaria, Czechoslovakia, Hungary, Poland and Romania from 1992 to 1993. By 1995 it was clear that neither Norway nor Switzerland would join the EU following Norway's rejection of EU membership in 1994 and Switzerland's earlier rejection of the EEA in 1992. Iceland and Liechtenstein had not started an accession process at all. With several trade agreements already in place or under negotiation, it was a natural decision to continue negotiating together when feasible. EFTA continued to negotiate agreements with Central and East European states pending their eventual EU membership, such as Slovenia and the Baltic states (1995). In addition, EFTA also continued to negotiate with partners in the larger Euro-Mediterranean area, establishing EFTA as a permanent tool for free trade relations with third countries outside the EU. Facing a multiplication of bilateral and regional preferential trade agreements following the conclusion of the multilateral Uruguay Round and the establishment of the World Trade Organization (WTO) in 1994, the decision was later made to negotiate with countries outside the Euro-Mediterranean region.

Development of intra-EFTA relations

The EFTA Convention itself has been updated on several occasions since its initial signing. The liberalization of industrial products achieved in the 1960s was coupled with the liberalization of trade in seafood in 1987. A larger revision and modernization of the EFTA Convention was signed in 2001 in Vaduz, mainly in order to accommodate the EEA Agreement and the bilateral agreements that had been negotiated between Switzerland and the EU following Swiss rejection of the EEA, as well as reflecting commitments made to third countries in FTAs.

The 2001 revision extended the content of the Convention to include services, investment, sanitary and phytosanitary measures, technical barriers to trade and other areas. In a number of areas, the revision extended within EFTA treatment that was already granted to the EU through the EEA Agreement and the Swiss-EU bilateral agreements, such as sanitary and phytosanitary measures and the free movement of persons. Notably in services, the three EEA EFTA states are actually more closely integrated with each other through the EEA Agreement than they are with Switzerland through the EFTA Convention. For trade between the EEA EFTA states, in practice the EFTA Convention only comes into effect in areas excluded from the EEA Agreement, i.e. trade in fish and other marine products and agricultural goods. The

EFTA Convention thus largely regulates trade between the EEA EFTA states on the one hand and Switzerland on the other, in addition to the relatively minor concessions for agricultural goods given in the EFTA Convention.

The functioning of the EEA

The EEA Agreement is now well into its third decade of operation and has successfully fulfilled its primary objectives. The envisaged homogenous legal area covering the EU and the EEA EFTA states is well established and continuously updated with new and revised rules and regulations, allowing for the free movement of goods, services, capital and labour among all parties to the EEA Agreement. The EFTA institutions that were created to ensure compliance by and in the EEA EFTA states perform their tasks as set out in the EEA Agreement.

The key task in the running management of the EEA Agreement is to maintain legal homogeneity by incorporating new or revised EU single market legislation into the EEA Agreement. Approximately 400 to 500 new or revised single market legal acts (directives, regulations and decisions) that have been adopted by the EU are incorporated into the EEA Agreement every year. Since its entry into force in 1994, more than 11,000 legal acts have been incorporated into the EEA Agreement. At the time of writing, the total body of EEA law consisted of more than 5,500 legal acts. However, for formal procedural reasons, this incorporation process can only take place after these legal acts have been formally adopted by the EU. It is therefore inevitable that there will be a certain backlog of legal acts that have been adopted in the EU, but that have not yet been incorporated into the EEA Agreement. Reducing and minimizing this backlog of pending acts is a key and ongoing challenge in the EEA, the success of which is a *sine qua non* for the EEA Agreement.

The 25 years that have passed since the EEA Agreement was signed has been a period of profound transformation for the European integration process. Through four enlargements and four rounds of treaty reform, the erstwhile Western European Community of 12 member states has become a pan-European Union comprising 28 countries. These changes have also had a significant impact on the EEA.[11]

The enlargements of the EU have entailed a significant geographical expansion of the EEA, as all EU member states are obliged to become parties to the EEA Agreement.[12] Upon its entry into force in January 1994, the EEA comprised 17 states (five EFTA states[13] and 12 EU member states). Following the accession of Croatia to the EU and the EEA in 2013, the EEA now comprises 31 countries, with a combined population of more than 500 million. In addition to creating new economic opportunities associated with a significantly expanded market, these EU and EEA enlargements have also led to significant movements of labour from the 'new' EU and EEA countries in Central and Eastern Europe to Western Europe, with a proportionately large influx into the EFTA states. This has given rise to concerns, as seen throughout Europe in recent years, about 'social dumping' and immigration more generally. The accession of less affluent countries to the EU and the EEA has also led to a significant increase in the amount of financial contributions of the EEA EFTA states, with a particularly large increase in connection with the 2004 enlargement. The contributions for the three EEA EFTA states through the EEA financial mechanisms are thus expected to increase from between €20 million and €25 million annually which they were in the late 1990s, to approximately €400 million annually in the period 2014–21.

Since the early 1990s the four EU treaty reforms have transformed the structure and governance of the EU. A key feature of these reforms has been to increase the power of the European Parliament. At the time of the negotiation of the EEA Agreement, the European

Parliament was, with some exceptions, a consultative body. Since the entry into force of the Lisbon Treaty in 2009, the European Parliament has been co-legislator with the Council on all policy issues of relevance to the single market of the EU, and thus of the EEA. Commission legislative proposals are now often substantially altered by the Council or the European Parliament. As a consequence, the effectiveness of the 'decision-shaping' mechanisms available to the EEA EFTA states through the EEA Agreement, which largely relate to the work of the Commission, is reduced.

When the EEA Agreement was negotiated, the EU's single market was very much a work in progress. Since then, the EU has moved closer towards the goal of completing the single market. In addition to the large amounts of new legislation this process has produced, there have also been important changes in how the single market is governed in the EU, with important ramifications for the EEA and the EEA EFTA states. A key issue in this respect has been the establishment of numerous regulatory agencies and authorities in the EU, with decision-making powers in various sectors of the single market, such as financial services, energy and telecommunications. Finding solutions for these new structures that respect the constitutional limits of the EEA EFTA states while at the same time ensuring legal homogeneity has been a key and challenging task in recent years.

Another key aspect of the EU treaty changes has been the streamlining of the decision-making process in the EU, which has facilitated cross-sectoral legislation. This can be problematic in an EEA context, as one is increasingly confronted with legislation that falls simultaneously inside and outside the material scope of the EEA Agreement. The question of whether or not new EU legislation should be considered *EEA relevant* has thus climbed higher on the agenda. The negotiation of the necessary adaptations has proven to be a difficult and time-consuming affair, although so far, the question of EEA relevance has been unproblematic in a large majority of cases, and is mostly a technical rather than political issue.

Overall, the combination of a bigger and more heterogeneous EU with the shifting of power between EU institutions has made it more difficult to achieve substantive changes to single market policies and legislation that take into account specificities in the EEA EFTA states. From an EFTA perspective, developments in the EU since the early 1990s have thus further accentuated the democratic deficit of the EEA Agreement.

EFTA's third-country policy: developing relations beyond the EU

As of 2017 EFTA's free trade network covered almost 14 per cent of EFTA's global trade in goods and 38 countries and territories through 27 different agreements (see Table 24.1).[14] Geographically, it covered most of Europe west of the Russian Federation, most Mediterranean countries, most of the Americas except Mercosur[15] and the USA, and four partners in Asia: Hong Kong, the Republic of Korea (South Korea), the Philippines and Singapore. EFTA also has a very active negotiating agenda, with talks on new agreements ongoing with Ecuador, India, Indonesia, Malaysia and Viet Nam. Negotiations with Algeria, the Russian Federation, Belarus, Kazakhstan, Thailand and Honduras have been initiated, but are on hold for various reasons. The network is complemented by five joint declarations on cooperation with Mauritius, Moldova, Mongolia, Myanmar and Pakistan.

The EU remains the pre-eminent partner of EFTA, with over 55 per cent of imports and exports going to the EU-28. Over time, the share of trade with non-EU FTA partners has risen, as a result of both the expansion of the EFTA FTA network and a faster rate of growth with FTA partners. This has been due in part to the aftermath of the financial crisis and, in the case of Norwegian exports, to lower hydrocarbon prices since 2014. Among the EFTA countries, Switzerland has the highest share of exports to the FTA network with 16 per cent,

Table 24.1 EFTA trade in goods, 2016 (value in US $ billion)

Partner	Total trade		Exports		Imports	
	Value	% of global trade	Value	% of global exports	Value	% of EFTA global imports
Intra-EFTA trade	4.1	0.55	2.1	0.53	1.9	0.56
EU-28	418.4	56.15	219.7	55.38	198.7	57.01
FTA network	106.8	14.33	56.9	14.33	50.0	14.35
Non-EFTA bilateral FTAs (People's Republic of China, Japan)	65.4	8.78	38.6	9.72	26.9	7.71
FTA negotiating partners (including negotiations on hold)	47.5	6.37	27.2	6.85	20.3	5.83
Joint Declaration on Cooperation partners	1.6	0.21	0.5	0.12	1.1	0.32
Rest of the world	101.4	13.61	51.8	13.07	49.5	14.22
Total trade	745.2	100.00	396.7	100.00	348.4	100.00

Source: EFTA Secretariat.

compared to 4 per cent for Iceland and 6 per cent for Norway. This discrepancy is explained by the significance of commodity exports that largely go to neighbouring countries (aluminium, fish, oil and natural gas) for the two Nordic countries, while Swiss exports are dominated by trademarked or patent-protected products such as pharmaceuticals and luxury goods.

The first agreements concluded by EFTA primarily covered trade in goods, including intellectual property rights (IPRs). These 'first-generation agreements' include all the early agreements with countries such as Turkey and Israel, but also some of the later agreements with Eastern European countries, such as Serbia in 2009 and Bosnia and Herzegovina in 2013, with the latter also including a chapter on sustainable development.

In general, however, EFTA now tries to conclude so-called second-generation agreements including commitments that go beyond the WTO General Agreement on Trade in Services (GATS) in the areas of trade in services and investment and government procurement. The first such agreement was the FTA with Mexico in 2001, with substantial commitments in services and government procurement. This was in large part possible due to Mexico having already concluded an agreement with the EU with similar provisions. Since then, EFTA has generally tried to include substantial commitments in these areas, although in practice this has not always been possible. Other areas, such as technical cooperation and trade facilitation, have also gradually been added.

Since 2010 EFTA has consistently included a separate chapter on trade and sustainable development in all FTAs signed. The chapter typically focuses on labour and environmental issues and reaffirms existing commitments in other international treaties and conventions.

EFTA has also undertaken to modernize older FTAs. Chapters on sustainable development have been added to earlier agreements with Serbia and Albania, but efforts have also been made to substantially revise and expand pre-existing agreements. Negotiations have been launched with Turkey and Mexico and, in November 2017, the first significant success was marked with the announcement of the conclusion in principle of the modernisation of the FTA with Turkey.

In terms of trade in goods, all EFTA states are highly protective of their agricultural sectors, while being free traders for all non-agricultural goods. Despite this apparent tension, EFTA has largely succeeded in achieving similar market access for industrial goods and seafood as competitors, while not giving substantial concessions for agriculture. Since a primary driver from the beginning has been to secure equal terms for economic operators in the EFTA states vis-à-vis their competitors in the EU, EFTA's free trade policy has largely been a success. The EFTA states retain the capacity to negotiate bilateral FTAs outside the EFTA framework, but the fact that so far they have only done this when the counterpart insists (China and Japan)[16] shows that the member states continue to value EFTA as a mechanism that allows them to punch above their weight and be more attractive as a partner than they would be individually.

Future challenges for the EEA

Considering the transformation of the EU over the last decades, the EEA Agreement has proven to be remarkably robust. Essentially, the economic benefits of being part of the single market of its most important trading partner by far, have been perceived to outweigh the political costs of the close association with the EU. For the time being, there is a broad and stable consensus in the EEA EFTA states in favour of EEA Agreement. However, the changes taking place within the EU and the broader European integration process are likely to lead to new challenges for the EFTA states, which could in turn have an impact on the domestic support and legitimacy of the EEA in the EFTA states.

With regard to the EEA, the continued evolution of the single market through further changes in governance, with additional powers devolved to supranational authorities, could require further adaptations in order to ensure the continued functioning of the EEA Agreement. More broadly, the issue of EEA relevance could become a more frequent and challenging issue, if plans for deeper integration in the EU in other, yet EEA-related, policy fields, such as the economic and monetary union and justice and home affairs, are further developed and implemented.

The further deepening of EU relations with other non-member states is another emerging challenge. In recent years, the EU has concluded agreements on closer cooperation and integration with a number of other partners. Increasingly, these go beyond traditional trade policy towards partial and gradual integration with the EU's single market, as well as cooperation in other areas.[17] In addition to the impact that such agreements, when fully implemented, will have on the competitive position of the EEA EFTA states, they will also give rise to a number of legal and institutional issues related to the free movement of goods, services, capital and persons between the EEA EFTA states on the one hand and these third countries on the other, which will, eventually, have to be addressed.

These issues are likely to be particularly acute with regard to Brexit. The United Kingdom is one of the most important trading partners of the EFTA states, and its withdrawal from the EU raises several challenges for EFTA. At the time of writing, it is very unclear what the outcome of the EU27-UK negotiations will be, both with regard to the terms of the UK's withdrawal from the EU, including possible transitional arrangements, and to the future relationship between the UK and the EU. It is, however, clear that this will dominate EFTA's agenda in the coming years, both in Brussels due to its impact on the EEA Agreement, and in Geneva with regard to the relationship between the post-Brexit UK and the EFTA states.

Future challenges for EFTA's third-country policy

While the fact that the four member states of EFTA are a trade bloc is a product of historical accident as much as intent, EFTA has thus on the whole been successful in establishing one of the world's most comprehensive free trade networks. The EFTA states negotiate together, with the assistance of the EFTA Secretariat in a coordinating role. They are all relatively small but extremely prosperous economies that are highly dependent on trade. They share the same, broadly liberal outlook on trade, and have found ways to accommodate each other's specific interests in free trade negotiations, e.g. market access for seafood and maritime services for Norway and Iceland, and IPRs and financial services for Switzerland and Liechtenstein. Although individual countries' priorities may be different during negotiations, they are on the whole differences in emphasis rather than in kind, and have generally proven not to be significant barriers to cooperation.

There are, however, also challenges for EFTA's third-country policy in the future. The four EFTA countries, even combined, still struggle to convince partners to effect the desired political change through FTAs in areas such as government procurement, IPRs and services and investment. In many cases, this is less of a problem than it might seem, since these are changes that larger partners such as the EU or the USA will also seek in their agreements. Once concessions have been made to other partners, it is comparatively easier for EFTA to obtain similar terms. However, when no such other agreements are in place, EFTA has sometimes had to lower its level of ambition in certain areas to secure an agreement.

Furthermore, while EFTA has so far been able to conclude agreements without opening up its agricultural sector to trade, it remains to be seen whether it can continue to do so in the future. In 2017 EFTA opened negotiations with the Southern Common Market (Mercado Común del Sur – Mercosur), which is expected to put forward important demands in that area. There are also other potential partners, such as the USA or Australia, which would expect more substantial commitments in this field than the EFTA states are currently in a position to grant. This has been compounded by the increased competitiveness of EU agriculture, which has put the EU in a position to grant much deeper liberalization of agricultural trade than in the past. This increased level of ambition for liberalization poses a problem for EFTA in that the gap between what the EU and EFTA can offer on agriculture has increased dramatically, which again renders the task of obtaining similar market access for EFTA exports more challenging. If the Transatlantic Trade and Investment Partnership between the EU and the USA is ever concluded, this may force the EFTA states to choose between being at a disadvantage compared to EU competitors in one of the world's most important markets and allowing for politically painful concessions on agriculture.

These challenges are, however, not due to the nature of EFTA or the cooperation among its member states. Instead, they are due to the nature of the member states themselves, and would be harder to overcome outside of EFTA. By negotiating together, the EFTA states are able to present a package deal that is more attractive to its partners than its parts would be by themselves. EFTA is therefore likely to continue developing its trade relations as a bloc, and none of the EFTA states have shown any interest in a radical change to its trade policy since Iceland suspended its accession process to the EU.

Notes

1 The views and opinions expressed in this chapter are those of the authors, and do not necessarily reflect the official position or policy of EFTA or its member states.
2 Switzerland withdrew from the EEA Agreement following its rejection in a referendum in December 1992.
3 A more detailed historical analysis can be found in Kåre Bryn and Guðmundur Einarsson (eds) (2010) 'EFTA 1960–2010: Elements of 50 Years of European History', Geneva: EFTA.

4 Denmark and the UK joined the EC in 1973, Portugal in 1986, and Austria, Finland (which had become a full member of EFTA in 1986, having joined as an associate member in 1961) and Sweden became members of the EU in 1995.

5 Norway applied for EC membership four times – in 1962, 1967, 1972 and 1992. Switzerland applied for EC membership in 1992, but the application was suspended later the same year and formally withdrawn in 2016. Iceland, which had joined EFTA in 1970, applied for EU membership in 2009, but withdrew its application in 2013 before the accession negotiations were concluded.

6 The exceptions were for duties of certain 'sensitive' products, which were only removed in the early 1980s.

7 For a more detailed analysis, see the contributions in Carl Baudenbacher (ed.) (2016) 'The Handbook of EEA Law', New York: Springer.

8 Switzerland, which was one of the signatories of the EEA Agreement, withdrew its participation in the EEA following its rejection in a referendum in December 1992.

9 Beyond the scope of this chapter, it should also be mentioned that all of the EFTA states have numerous agreements on cooperation with the EU in other policy areas such as justice and home affairs and foreign, security and defence policy. All four EFTA states are, for instance, part of the Schengen system with regard to the free movement of persons and external borders.

10 This is done by amendments to the 22 annexes to the EEA Agreement, covering the various policy areas of the internal market, and/or (some of) its 49 protocols.

11 For a more detailed analysis, see Jacqueline Breidlid and Marius Vahl (2015) 'Current and Future Challenges for the EEA', *The European Economic Area: Past, Present and Future*, Geneva: EFTA.

12 According to Article 128 of the EEA Agreement.

13 These were Austria, Finland and Sweden, which joined the EU in 1995, and current EFTA states Iceland and Norway. Liechtenstein joined the EEA in May 1995.

14 Albania, Bosnia and Herzegovina, Canada, Central American States (Costa Rica, Guatemala and Panama) Chile, Colombia, Egypt, Georgia, the Gulf Cooperation Council, Hong Kong, Israel, Jordan, Lebanon, Macedonia, Mexico, Montenegro, Morocco, Palestinian Authority, Peru, the Philippines, Singapore, the Southern African Customs Union, South Korea, Serbia, Tunisia, Turkey and Ukraine.

15 Argentina, Brazil, Paraguay and Uruguay.

16 Switzerland has a bilateral FTA with Japan and China. Iceland also has a bilateral FTA with China, while Norway and China are in negotiations. The older FTAs with Greenland and the Faroe Islands are further exceptions.

17 In addition to its numerous agreements with Switzerland, the EU has negotiated 'deep and comprehensive free trade agreements' with several Eastern European partners. It is negotiating agreements with very small European states on their internal market participation, and is in the process of modernizing its customs union agreement with Turkey. Last but not least, it is expected to conclude, eventually, an ambitious FTA with the UK after the latter's withdrawal from the EU.

25

Eastern Partnership countries

Inmaculada Martínez-Zarzoso

Introduction

The Eastern Partnership initiative (EaP) was launched by the European Union (EU) in 2009 at the Prague Summit as a means of providing a forum in which the EU could discuss with the post-Soviet states of Armenia, Azerbaijan, Belarus, Georgia, Moldova and Ukraine issues related to trade agreements and economic collaboration between the EaP and the EU. The EU is committed to building bilateral relations with each of the six partners offering a differential and inclusive framework that involves all of them. The policy developments during the period 2015–20 are guided by the 2015 review of the European Neighbourhood Policy and by the 2016 EU Global Strategy. The main policy goals are related to achieving good governance, economic development, wider connectivity and a stronger society. The European Neighbourhood Instrument is used to ensure the implementation of these financial goals; between 2014 and 2017 the EaP countries had already received €2.8 billion of EU funds.

This chapter presents the main developments that the EaP countries have made in terms of quality of institutions, trade and economic integration in the last decade and evaluates the main effects of these agreements in terms of increasing trade.

The rest of the chapter is organized as follows. Section 2 describes the process of negotiating trade agreements between the EU and the EaP countries. Section 3 reviews the quality of institutions in the EaP countries. Section 4 presents the evolution of trade over time and across trading partners and the composition of trade. Section 5 presents the main results in terms of trade gains from recently signed Deep and Comprehensive Free Trade Areas (DCFTAs) and from improvements in institutional quality. Section 6 discusses the main trade policy alternatives for EaP countries and concludes the chapter.

Trade negotiations between the EU and the EaP countries

One of the EaP goals is to foster economic cooperation and deepen economic integration between the EU and the interested partner countries. In the case of three out of the six countries, namely Georgia, Moldova and Ukraine, the implementation of DCFTAs was part of the specific policy goals.

The EU announced in July 2013 that the negotiations that started early in 2012 on Association Agreements had been completed, including DCFTAs with Armenia, Georgia and Moldova. These agreements were to be initialled at the EaP Summit in Vilnius on 28–29 November 2013 and the DCFTA agreement with Ukraine was to be signed at the same time, subject to prior fulfilment by Ukraine of certain conditions related to the judicial system.

The successful negotiation of DCFTAs with these three states in only one and a half years was surprising,[1] as was the announcement made by Armenia in September 2013 that it would join the Eurasian Customs Union proposed by the Russian Federation instead of initiating its Association Agreement with the EU. Armenia's decision was influenced by Russia's threat to withdraw its troops, which protected the region of Nagorno Karabahk, largely populated by Armenians, in Azerbaijan. Georgia and Moldova also reported measures and threats by Russia to restrict their exports to Russia in an effort to persuade them to join the Eurasian Customs Union. A few days before the Summit, following threats by Russia to disrupt trade and oil and gas supplies as well as offers of significant loans, Ukraine announced that it too would not sign the Association Agreement with the EU.

Ukraine's decision not to sign the Association Agreement had undesirable consequences. Massive and sustained demonstrations in Maidan Square in Kiev, displaying the EU flag, bore witness to widespread popular support in Western Ukraine for signing the Association Agreement[2] (Campos, 2013). After several months of demonstrations, President Viktor Yanukovych ordered military troops to open fire causing over 100 deaths. This evoked sufficient rage to compel the President to flee the country on 21 February 2014. The next day Parliament elected a provisional President and installed a new government. In early March Russia deployed anonymous troops in Crimea, which it called self-defence groups, to protect Russian citizens.[3] A referendum held on 16 March in the Autonomous Republic of Crimea and the self-governing district of Sevastopol voted to accede to Russia. On 21 March President Putin signed the documents admitting Crimea and Sevastopol into the Russian Federation. Moscow time and the Russian ruble were introduced soon afterwards throughout the Crimea. This must certainly be one of the most unintended consequences of a proposed trade agreement ever and further consequences are likely. This chapter will assess the potential benefits of FTAs signed by Georgia, Moldova and Ukraine with the EU in June 2014.

The results suggest that the EaP countries, of which Ukraine is by far the largest in the group, benefit significantly from FTAs with the EU, but gain little if anything from FTAs with Russia. The quality of institutions in the EaP countries has also played an important role in fostering trade.

Quality of institutions in the EaP countries

When the Iron Curtain fell in 1991, the six EaP countries were unprepared for economic integration with Western market economies. All countries except Moldova had been integral parts of the Soviet Union from its foundation and thus were subject to its system of central planning and state ownership of the means of production. They lacked national institutions and experience of running market economies. In contrast, the countries of Central and Eastern Europe, despite being satellites of the Soviet Union, had retained their national institutions during the Cold War.[4]

Following the dissolution of the Soviet Union, each of the newly sovereign states faced the difficult task of establishing and running a market economy. The three Baltic states, which had been sovereign states during the interwar period, made the transition from Soviet republics to functioning democracies and market economies faster than the six other former Soviet republics.[5] They acceded to the EU in 2004 together with the countries of Central Europe and joined the North Atlantic Treaty Organization (NATO) that year, along with Bulgaria, Romania, Slovakia and Slovenia. By contrast, only two of the six EaP states had started to establish functioning democracies by 2004. Georgia's progress was hampered by the internal turmoil associated with the Rose Revolution in November 2003 and Ukraine by the Orange Revolution in December 2004. This section illustrates how slow and imperfect were the transitions to democracy and market economies in most of the six EaP states.

Democracy and the free press

The Polity IV Project run by the Center for Systemic Peace, provides ratings of various aspects of democracy in countries around the world, including the EaP countries under review. A commonly used measure of democracy is the Polity2 variable that is designed to reflect 'the characteristics of democratic and autocratic authority' in governing institutions rather than discrete and mutually exclusive forms of governance. The Polity2 variable spans a range of governing authority from 'fully institutionalized autocracies through mixed authority regimes to fully institutionalized democracies'. The range is a 21-point scale ranging from −10 (hereditary monarchy) to +10 (consolidated democracy). Countries are classified as democratic if their Polity2 score is larger than or equal to +6, as neither democratic nor autocratic if the score lies between +5 and −5, and as autocratic if their score is smaller than or equal to −6.

Three of the six former republics had consistently high and stable scores of 6 or more during the period 1994–2012 (see Figure 25.1). These were Moldova and Ukraine, and Georgia from 2004 onwards. By comparison, Russia scored 6 from 2000 to 2006 and 4 since then. Ukraine vacillates between 5 and 7, dropping to 6 in 2010, the year in which Yanukovich was elected President. Since 1998 Armenia has been stable at 5 and, like Russia, is classified as neither democratic nor autocratic. Azerbaijan and Belarus scored −7 from the late 1990s onwards and are classified as autocratic.

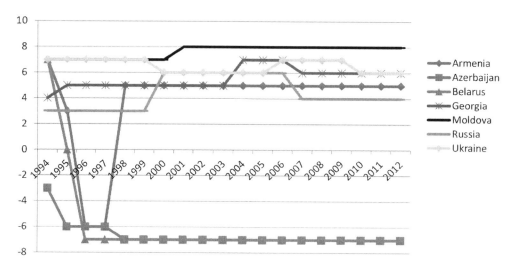

Figure 25.1 Democracy, 1994–2012
Source: Polity IV project, Center for Systemic Peace website. Note: Democratic >/= 6. Autocratic </= −6.

Eastern Partnership countries

The freedom that these countries accord their press is closely correlated with their scores for democracy. Freedom House's classification of countries by freedom of the press divides the former Soviet republics and Russia into two distinct groups (see Figure 25.2). The press is not free in Belarus, Russia, Azerbaijan and Armenia. Furthermore, the rankings of all these countries but Armenia have declined since 2005. Ukraine, Moldova and Georgia have had a partly free press during most of this period (ranking between 31 and 60). Moldova and Georgia have consistently improved their rankings during this period, albeit modestly. In short, none of the six EaP states qualify as having had a free press since 1995.

Among the six EaP states, Georgia and Moldova qualify as democracies with a partly free press. Armenia and Ukraine are borderline cases, moving slowly and uncertainly towards functioning democracies with a barely free press. Azerbaijan and Belarus are in a class of their own, being neither democratic nor having even a partly free press.

An examination of these statistics suggests that a democratic regime and a free press are interdependent institutions, and that together their existence can influence the speed of transition to a market economy. The next section considers how the six former Soviet republics have made this transition.

Transition to market economy

The transition to a functioning market economy has been slow in most of these countries relative to the progress made by countries in Central Europe. For some time now the European Bank for Reconstruction and Development (EBRD) has measured the progress made by the formerly centrally planned economies towards a market economy. The current status of their progress is summarized in Figure 25.3.

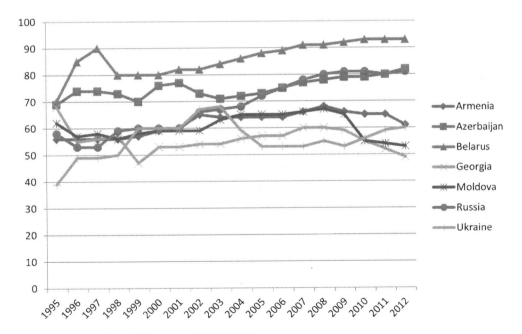

Figure 25.2 Freedom of the press, 1995–2012
Note: a ranking above 60 denotes that there is no free press in that country.
Source: Freedom of the Press. Available at www.freedomhouse.org.

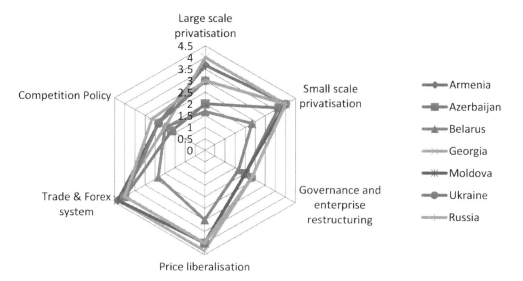

Figure 25.3 Key determinants of transition to market economy, 2012
Note: According to the bank, transition indicators range from 1 to +4 with 1 representing little or no change to a rigid centrally planned economy and +4 the standards of an industrialized market economy. Here, the + sign and the − sign have been replaced by adding or subtracting 0.25.
Source: EBRD, *Transition Report 2013*, London: EBRD, p. 112.

Belarus remains a centrally planned economy on almost all counts. All the other EaP countries have liberalized domestic prices, foreign exchange and foreign trade dealings – the easy variables through which to achieve liberalization. By contrast, none of the EaP countries have made much progress in their transition from planned to market economies with regards to competition policy and governance and enterprise restructuring, both of which are key variables for a DCFTA.

Georgia and Moldova have made slightly more progress than the others. A comparison with other countries shows that as a group the EaP countries lie below the Western Balkans and on par with Bosnia and Herzegovina, the most reluctant reformer in that group. Thus, even the most advanced EaP countries lag significantly behind the Central European countries that acceded to the EU in 2004 and behind the Western Balkan countries that seek accession but remain far from it.[6] The ability to implement a DCFTA appears limited in Ukraine and Armenia. It appears to be a challenging task in Georgia and Moldova in the absence of significant foreign aid and technical assistance.

Two additional variables confirm the picture given here concerning the quality of institutions, namely ease of doing business and the level of corruption. These indicators give additional hints of why Georgia and Moldova lead the four EaP countries that have negotiated DCFTAs.[7] Unfortunately, as will be shown, a deterioration of the indicators is observed for some countries after 2012.

Ease of doing business

Since the mid-2000s the World Bank has carried out an annual assessment of the ease of doing business in some 180 countries. According to its assessments, between 2007 and 2017 the six EaP states ranked between 42nd and 120th place (a first-place ranking indicates the greatest ease of doing business). Azerbaijan and Georgia made dramatic improvements until 2012 when they ranked 50th in the world (see Figure 25.4). However, after 2012–13 both countries moved

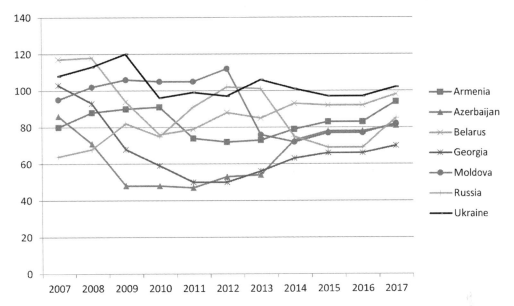

Figure 25.4 Ease of doing business, 2007–17
Note: The greater the ease of doing business, the lower the index.
Source: World Bank (2017) *Ease of Doing Business*, Washington, DC: World Bank.

back to 82nd and 70th place, respectively. Moldova is the only other EaP state to register a consistent improvement after 2012. The other countries retained their poor rankings or even dropped further down in the index.

Companies in Ukraine, as in Russia, have experienced increasing difficulties in doing business since 2011 and were no better off in 2017 than in 2007. The business environment in these two countries remained a bureaucratic nightmare. Armenia and Belarus occupied an intermediate position, with Belarus showing a modest improvement over the whole period.

Corruption

Since the EaP states achieved independence in the 1990s, corruption has been rampant as a result of poor governance and bad habits. Corruption distorts investment and production decisions. Belarus, Azerbaijan and Ukraine, like Russia, ranked consistently between a poor 100th and 140th place among the 180 or so countries examined by Transparency International (see Figure 25.5). Georgia, as well as the Baltic states (not shown), has made significant progress in combating corruption since 2000 as did Armenia in 2012–13.[8] The decrease in corruption in Georgia places it close to Latvia (55th place) and Lithuania (49th place) although it still lags far behind Estonia (28th place). Thus, the EaP states, with the exception of Georgia, have failed to reduce corruption markedly since 2007. Further progress is essential because pervasive corruption can be a serious impediment to rapid long-term economic growth. Strong and consistent political will is required to implement necessary and far-reaching changes in the judiciary to curb corruption. Developments not only in Ukraine but also in Bulgaria and Romania have demonstrated both the importance of this task and the difficulty of achieving it.

Here, as was the case in terms of ease of doing business, Georgia was the only country among the EaP states to have moved from a group of countries with rampant corruption to a group with little corruption. This demonstrates that persistent political will can dramatically improve

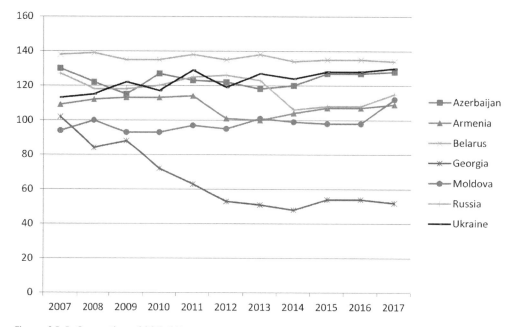

Figure 25.5 Corruption, 2007–17
Note: The less corrupt a country is perceived to be, the lower its position in the rankings.
Source: Transparency International. Available at www.transparency.org.

the economic environment. The combined effect of greater ease of doing business and less corruption is essential for increasing investment over time, especially foreign direct investment. Other states must imitate Georgia in making make the extensive changes required to improve this indicator.

Transparency International measures business corruption, bribes, etc.; the less corrupt the country is perceived to be, the higher the index. A recent Gallup poll asked a large sample of voters in 129 countries the following question: 'Is corruption widespread throughout the government of [your country], or not?' Only one-quarter of the Georgian respondents considered their government corrupt compared with three-quarters or more in Armenia, Azerbaijan, Ukraine, Russia, Moldova and Lithuania.

Trust

Other sources report similar findings for corruption in business and government. The Legatum Institute reports a variety of survey results covering many different aspects of economic and institutional foundations, including aspects related to economic quality, business environment, governance, personal freedom and social capital.[9]

Another asset that produces economic returns and contributes to improved well-being is social capital. Figure 25.6 shows the evolution of 'social capital' or 'trust' indicating whether citizens believe they can rely on others and on institutions such as the police and whether they believe they have a say in the political process. The low level of interpersonal trust in the six countries under review is striking, as is the lack of improvement in this area. The EaP countries's positions in the rankings have slipped to between 115th and 140th place in 2017. By comparison, according to the Legatum Institute, crisis-stricken Greece was in 89th place in 2017, while the Scandinavian countries occupied between 12th and 18th place.

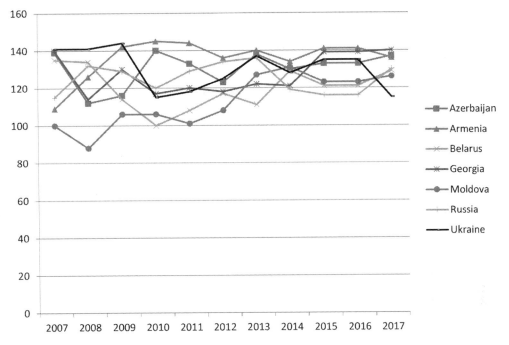

Figure 25.6 Trust, 2007–17
Source: Legatum Institute. Available at www.prosperity.com.

In sum, this section shows that the transition to democracy and market economy has been slow in most of the EaP states and lags far behind the progress made by other former Soviet republics, such the Baltic states. Georgia and Moldova are ahead of the other EaP states in terms of democracy and having a free press, and score slightly better in terms of ease of doing business. Meanwhile, Georgia has relatively low levels of corruption. Even so, the picture is a mixed one with low levels of interpersonal trust recorded in Georgia and Moldova. Armenia and Ukraine are borderline cases with regard to the transition to democracy and to a market economy. Both countries score poorly in terms of corruption and trust. Belarus and Azerbaijan do not qualify for a DCFTA; both must first accede to the WTO in order to be considered. Overall, these indices suggest that it is perhaps not surprising that Georgia and Moldova initialled their Association Agreements in Vilnius while Ukraine and Armenia did not. It took a popular revolt against an autocratic and corrupt government for Ukraine to reverse course and sign the DCFTA in June 2014.

Actual trade patterns

This section briefly reviews the pattern of trade in the six EaP countries in terms of openness to trade, the types of traded products and their geographical origins and destinations.

Level and commodity composition of exports

Since the mid-1990s Estonia has been one of Europe's most open economies as measured by the share of exports of goods and services in gross domestic product (GDP), while Lithuania is not far behind (see Figure 25.7). Russia, on the other hand, saw its share of exports in GDP decline to about 25 per cent in 2016. Since 1999 exports have risen relative to GDP in Georgia

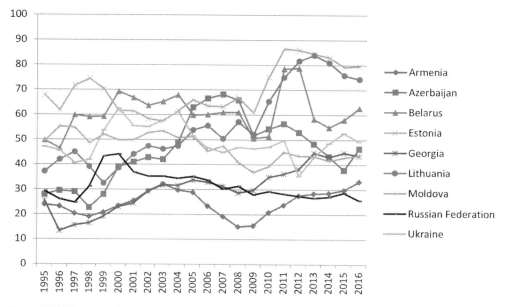

Figure 25.7 Exports of goods and services, 1995–2016 (% of GDP)
Source: World Bank, *World Development Indicators*, Washington, DC: World Bank.

and in the Baltics states, but not in Moldova, while they have fluctuated at similar levels elsewhere in the EaP region. The ability to produce goods and services that households and firms in other countries want to buy is key to economic growth. While exports of natural resource intensive products are dictated by a country's resource endowments, exports of manufactures are largely determined by the industry and skills set of its population. Since the 1990s the share of manufactures in total exports increased in Georgia and Moldova but only until 2012, while elsewhere in the EaP region, and in Russia, it declined (see Figure 25.8).

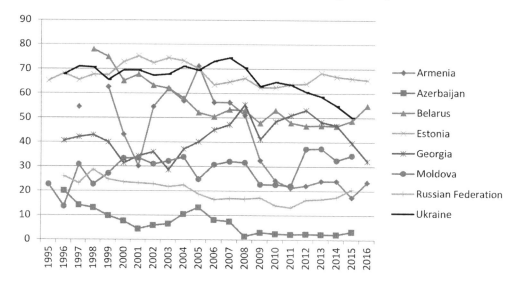

Figure 25.8 Exports of manufactures, 1995–2016 (% of total merchandise exports)
Source: World Bank, *World Development Indicators*.

Eastern Partnership countries

Directions of trade

Since independence, most of the EaP states have increased their share of trade with the EU, while reducing it with Russia. All EaP states except Belarus are now more dependent on trade with the EU than on trade with Russia (see Figure 25.9). Moldova conducts more than half of its trade with the EU and Ukraine about one-third, while Armenia, Belarus and Georgia each conduct less than one-third of their trade with the EU. Georgia and Moldova conduct only about 10 per cent of their trade with Russia, while Armenia, Azerbaijan, Belarus and Ukraine conduct about 20 per cent of their trade with Russia. It is clear that the trade of Armenia, Georgia, Moldova and Ukraine with one another and with the EU is significantly more

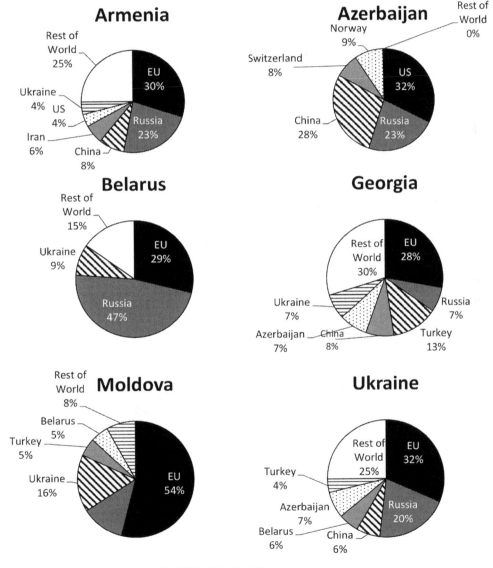

Figure 25.9 Direction of trade in 2012 (% of total)
Source: European Commission.

important for them than trade with Russia. The failure of the export ratio to rise in all the EaP states except Georgia and Moldova suggests that the expansion of trade with the West in these countries is largely the result of a replacement of trade with Russia rather than an addition to it.

Finally, Figure 25.10 shows the evolution over time of exports and imports with the EU-28 of Georgia and Moldova in comparison with Armenia, a country of similar size in terms of population, but one that did not sign a DCFTA with the EU. Both the left- and right-handside of the figure show that after 2009 Georgia and Moldova experienced a sharp increase in nominal exports (left) and imports (right) to the EU, whereas the figures for Armenia remained stable or even decreased after 2012 in the case of exports. Interestingly, before 2009 the three countries recorded a similar evolution over time of their trade figures. It is a statistical question whether the differential increase observed after 2009 in Georgia and Moldova can be attributed to their association with the EU. This issue is addressed below.

Trade negotiations

The EaP countries focused on concluding bilateral DCFTAs between the EU and each partner country but did not call for DCFTAs between the partner countries themselves. This approach avoided the inter-state conflicts. Had the EU required the EaP states to conclude DCFTAs with each other, the conflicts would immediately have come to the forefront and their solution would have required Russian participation. The most difficult conflicts to solve in the EU's neighbourhood are those where participants lack a membership perspective and where a third country is party to the conflict.[10] Now that Russia is in direct conflict with the EU over Ukraine, regional conflict resolution is unavoidable. The key question is whether potential trade between the EaP states is sufficient to entice them to normalize their relations with each other and whether normalization of Russia's trade relations with the EU is sufficiently beneficial for it to find conflict resolution worthwhile.

In summary, the trade policy implications are clear. The six EaP states are located between two major economic powers – the EU to the west and Russia to the east. While the EU's combined purchasing power parity-adjusted GDP is more than five times as large as that of Russia, the six countries have well-established traditional export markets in the east. Although the EU has steadily increased in importance as a market for most EaP states in the last two decades, Russia remains an important market for all of them.

The best trade policy for the six EaP states is, therefore, to have FTAs with both the EU and Russia.[11] Russia's proposed Eurasian Customs Union excludes that option. As a member of the Eurasian Customs Union an EaP country cannot also have an FTA with the EU. While the Eurasian Customs Union can negotiate an FTA with the EU in the future, it is likely to be inferior to the DCFTA already negotiated by Ukraine and Armenia with the EU and would take significantly

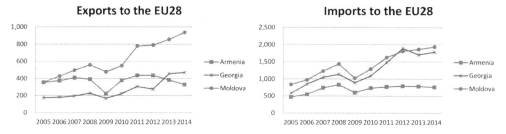

Figure 25.10 Exports and imports to EU-28, 2005–14
Source: Eurostat.

longer to enter into force. From a strictly economic viewpoint having FTAs with both the EU and with Russia is a superior solution for the EaP states. The next section examines what part of the trade increase between EaPs and the EU can be attributed to the DCFTAs.

The effects on trade of the DCFTAs

Gylfason *et al.*[12] estimated econometric models to quantify the trade effects of the different FTAs on bilateral exports. They rely on the gravity model of trade, a widely used theoretical apparatus underpinning estimates of the effects of trade agreements.[13] Specifically, the authors' main aim is to assess how the trade relations of the EaP states will be affected by signing a DCFTA (or a shallow FTA) with the EU or a customs union with Russia. The authors also evaluate an intermediate case, which is likely to be the outcome for the next few years if Georgia, Moldova and perhaps Ukraine as well turn west while Azerbaijan, Armenia and Belarus turn east.

The main results suggest that entering into trade agreements with the EU provides a greater stimulus to trade than joining the agreements promoted by Russia. In particular, full accession to the EU (in this case the enlargements in 2004 and 2007) increased export shares by 317 per cent. However, as stated above, this is not an explicit option for EaP countries. When evaluating the effect of deep trade agreements with the EU and with Russia, the results indicate that a DCFTA with the EU will increase export shares less than full membership, or by 86 per cent, whereas a DCFTA with Russia will not result in any significant increase in export shares for the EaP countries under review. This result might reflect the fact that FTAs with Russia are less deep and less strictly implemented.

With regard to the shallow FTAs, the results are less stable and vary widely across specifications, thus making them less robust. On the one hand, a shallow FTA with Russia will have no positive effects on trade; in fact, the results suggest that trade will even be reduced. On the other hand, a shallow FTA among EaP states will result in export shares almost trebling. These results are probably overestimated in this case because the data sample for these countries starts only in 1995/96 and trade among these countries has expanded rapidly in recent years.

Kohl[14] also used the gravity model of trade and econometric techniques to estimate the effect of 166 single European Integration Agreementss with data from 1950 to 2010 for 150 countries. According to his results, none of the estimates for Russia's agreements with Armenia, the Kyrgyz Republic and Ukraine is statistically significant. The same applies to the Eurasian Economic Community and the Commonwealth of Independent States estimates; the latter is even negative ($-1.55\star$) and significant at the 10 per cent level. In contrast, he finds a number of positive effects on trade for EU single agreements with some Baltic states (Latvia: $0.74^\star$) and among pairs of former Soviet Republics (e.g. Georgia-Kazakhstan: $0.88\star\star$; Georgia-Turkmenistan: $0.01\star$).

Gylfason *et al.*[15] also assess whether the quality of institutions has affected trade in EaP states. Mansfield *et al.*[16] suggest that a democratic society is more likely to liberalize foreign trade than an autocratic one since trade barriers create rents which benefit a small minority and encourage the emergence of oligarchs who veto tariff reductions. The results suggest that a one point increase in the Polity2 score will increase exports by about 12 per cent. For example, in Azerbaijan and Belarus, which had democracy scores of -7 from the late 1990s onwards, the potential for increasing trade is huge if they move towards more democratic institutions. Most of the EaP states could benefit from additional exports by improving their democracy scores. Mansfield *et al.*[17] show that an effective democracy provides an incentive for politicians to enter FTAs with other countries. Such agreements provide a 'surveillance mechanism' that assures voters that politicians prevent special interests from enjoying rents provided by protection.[18]

When using a proxy for corruption as a regressor Gylfason *et al.*[19] find a weak negative correlation between corruption and exports. The causality between corruption and exports

Inmaculada Martínez-Zarzoso

seems to be bidirectional. Indeed, a positive effect of corruption on exports could be expected in the short term if trade barriers are evaded through bribes.[20] For the same reason, trade could encourage corruption. However, equally valid is the expectation of a negative long-term effect of trade on corruption and vice versa. The authors cannot disentangle these effects, possibly due to the short time span for which data are available.

Conclusion

The evidence suggests that the EU overestimated the economic and political readiness of the EaP states to sign DCFTAs. One key factor that characterizes the EaP countries is the slow progress made concerning their institutional quality. Only Georgia and to a lesser extent Moldova made significant progress after 2005 in reducing corruption and increasing the ease of doing business. Ukraine and Armenia were little different from Russia in this respect. Similarly, the functioning of the market economy in the EaP states was uniformly poor, much poorer than in the Central and Eastern European states at an earlier stage of their development and even poorer than in the Balkan states. The Commission's requirement that EaP states should focus on institution building in order to qualify for a DCFTAs proved correct.

Another key factor is the importance of democracy and a free press as instruments for institutional change and for providing a solid political base for international agreements. It has been shown that in this respect Georgia and Moldova were ahead of the other EaP states, which were remarkably similar to Russia. Ukraine encountered such significant problems prior to initialling and signing its DCFTA probably due to its weak initial conditions as concerns democracy, free press and the functioning of a market economy. As a result of the experience with Ukraine, the Commission was required to evaluate the preparedness of a country to negotiate a DCFTA prior to a decision to open negotiations with it.

Russia underestimated the strong popular support that existed in the former Soviet countries for the democratic values that the EU represents, while the EU, in turn, underestimated the opposition of Russia to such agreements with the countries in its neighbourhood.

The EU needs to review the EaP in order to prevent future failed agreements. An agreement negotiated with a government that lacks widespread popular support is an uncertain agreement. Measures that reduce this uncertainty and thereby the risk of sudden policy reversals are necessary. The EU not necessarily has to require as precondition for starting negotiations on a DCFTA that the trading partner has a functioning democracy with a free press. In the end, the difference between negotiating membership and a DCFTA is significant. The EU should focus its EaP partners' attention on measures that are necessary to improve the functioning of their market economies in the course of negotiations, in particular, on eliminating corruption and in improving the ease of doing business. The significant progress made by Georgia in this critical respect has facilitated its progress, while the poor record of Ukraine has contributed to its problems.

Empirical analysis shows that the EaP partners stand to gain significantly from trade agreements with the EU, whether deep or shallow, while the customs union proposed by Russia produces negligible or even negative benefits. It also shows that the EaP countries gain significantly from FTAs with each other. While further research is necessary to ascertain more precisely the size of these benefits, their rough relative magnitude is supported by other studies. Despite these gains, only Georgia and Moldova initialled Association Agreements at the Vilnius Summit in November 2013. It can be concluded that the prospects for the EaP are complex. The EU should continue to dedicate the entire resources of the Comprehensive Institution Building facility to fill the 'institutional vacuum' in Georgia, Moldova and Ukraine and focus on the fundamentals of commercial politics.

Notes

1 Negotiating the DCFTA with Ukraine had taken five years and negotiations with Georgia to start negotiations on a DCFTA had taken almost four years. Armenia was a latecomer to this project and had worse initial conditions than Georgia. Hence, both the decision to start negotiations in 2012 and their rapid conclusion were surprising. Compared with these countries, Moldova had a headstart through its negotiation of a regional FTA with the Western Balkans and its Stability and Association Agreement with the EU.

2 N. Campos (2013) 'What Drives Protests in the Ukraine? This Time It Is Institutions', *VoxEU.org*, 22 December.

3 President Putin later referred to these anonymous troops as Russian.

4 Some 15 years after independence the EaP countries continued to languish in an institutional vaccum that had far-reaching consequences for the individual states.

5 In this chapter the term 'the former Soviet republics' refers to the countries on Russia's western border. These are, from north to south, Estonia, Latvia and Lithuania and the six EaP states Belarus, Ukraine, Moldova, Georgia, Armenia and Azerbaijan.

6 Croatia acceded to the EU in 2013.

7 Belarus and Azerbaijan are disqualified from a DCFTA since they are neither members of the WTO nor democracies.

8 The improvement in the corruption perceptions index in Armenia, denoting less corruption, in 2012 and 2013 can be ascribed to the then ongoing negotiations for a DCFTA and has been reversed after Vilnius.

9 The International Country Risk Guide (ICRG) survey also offers an index of corruption. It codes corruption in different countries on a scale from 0 to 6, with high scores indicating low levels of corruption. The ICRG measure has an extensive coverage and uses a single survey methodology for all countries, which permits comparisons across countries and over time. This index is highly correlated with the corruption measures described in the text.

10 See T. Gylfason, I. Martínez Zarzoso and P. M. Wijkman (2015) 'Free Trade Agreements, Institutions and Exports of Eastern Partnership Countries', *Journal of Common Market Studies*, 53(6): 1214–29.

11 See T. Gylfason and P. M. Wijkman (2017) 'Which Conflicts Can the European Neighborhood Policy Help to Resolve?' in B. J. Christensen and C. Kowalzyck (eds.) *Globalization: Strategies and Effects*, New York: Springer Verlag.

12 Gylfason *et al.*, 'Free Trade Agreements, Institutions and Exports of Eastern Partnership Countries'.

13 See R. Feenstra (2004) *Advanced International Trade*, Princeton. NJ: Princeton University Press; and I. Martínez-Zarzoso (2013) 'The Log of Gravity Revisited', *Applied Economics* 45(3): 311–27.

14 T. Kohl (2014) 'Do We Really Know that Trade Agreements Increase Trade?' *Review of World Economics* 150(3): 443–69.

15 Gylfason *et al.*

16 See E. D. Mansfield, H. V. Milner and J. C. Pevehouse (2007) 'Vetoing Cooperation: The Impact of Veto Players on Preferential Trading Arrangements', *British Journal of Political Science*, 37(3): 403–32; and E. D. Mansfield, H. V. Milner and B. P. Rosendorff (2002) 'Why Democracies Cooperate More: Electoral Control and International Trade Agreements', *International Organization*, 56(3): 477–513.

17 Mansfield *et al.*, 'Why Democracies Cooperate More'.

18 Mansfield *et al.* conclude that during the post-war period pairs of democracies are twice as likely to enter a PTA as are a democracy and an autocracy and that the latter pair is twice as likely to enter a PTA as a pair of autocratic countries. Furthermore, the likelihood of a given country entering into a PTA increases with both the size and the proximity of its partner country.

19 Gylfason *et al.*

20 See P. Dutt and D. Traca (2010) 'Corruption and Bilateral Trade Flows: Extortion or Evasion?' *Review of Economics and Statistics* 92(4): 843–60; and E. De Jong and C. Bogmans (2011) 'Does Corruption Discourage International Trade?' *European Journal of Political Economy*, 27: 385–98.

26

Trade agreements and regional integration

The European Union after Brexit

Annette Bongardt and Francisco Torres

EU trade dynamics: towards comprehensive FTAs and unaffected by Brexit

The European Union (EU) has greatly benefited from multilateral trade liberalization in the past. As an open economy, the Union naturally continues to take a strong interest in furthering free trade also after the demise in 2005 of the World Trade Organization's (WTO) Doha Round. Since then the world has experienced a shift from multilateral trade agreements towards bilateral and regional arrangements. The EU, too, which has traditionally championed multilateral trade agreements in global trade, negotiated through the WTO and its predecessor, the General Agreement on Tariffs and Trade (GATT), has, initially reluctantly, come to embrace an increasing number of bilateral and regional trade agreements. It has come to adopt a more active policy of negotiating bilateral trade deals, guided by economic objectives rather than by political affinities and objectives,[1] and, with tariff barriers already relatively low among WTO members, embarked on a new generation of international agreements. In most cases, and given the absence of any one-size-fits-all trade agreement, the EU negotiates comprehensive (i.e. deep) free trade agreements (FTAs) with third countries.

The Union now counts well over 50 FTAs and is negotiating about 20 trade agreements with 60 countries.[2] Various factors have contributed to EU trade dynamics, which are characterized both by an increase in and an acceleration of bilateral trade agreements but also, and perhaps more importantly, by a change in their nature, as comprehensive trade agreements touch upon regulatory preferences and EU member state competences.

International trade agreements offered the EU a way to exit from the cumulative effects of the global economic and financial (2008/09) cum sovereign debt (2010/14) crises, to the extent that they foster growth and employment. Promoting trade is rather attractive among the options to promote recovery from the crises and growth. Not only are trade arrangements a priori relatively easy to implement provided that they fall within the area of exclusive competencies of the EU (trade in goods) but they also come relatively cheap in terms of resource requirements. Recent political developments, above all the current US Administration's more protectionist trade stance (manifested for instance by the rejection of multilateral commercial agreements and border tax threats), have·

296

strengthened the EU's push for free trade or investment agreements by raising the importance of ensuring free trade for the Union, but likewise also for many other countries. That shared concern has predictably promoted and accelerated new trade deals with existing and prospective trading partners. Last but not least, US protectionism has opened up a strategic space for the EU to further and try to condition global trade on its preferred terms.

The conclusion, after a long drawn-out process, and entering into force in 2017 of the EU-Canada Comprehensive Economic and Trade Agreement (CETA) has further contributed to dynamics towards new EU trade agreements.[3] The prospective Trans-Pacific Partnership (TPP) countries, which have turned to the EU to make (or accelerate or deepen) free trade and investment deals, are a case in point.[4] There has been a fresh impetus for a number of free trade negotiations that were previously slow-moving or had stalled (among others with Japan, the Republic of Korea (South Korea) and the Southern Common Market (Mercado Común del Sur – Mercosur) and to upgrading existing ones (such as with Mexico). Being regarded as the EU's most progressive trade agreement, CETA assumes a particular significance and hence a natural blueprint for other, deeper EU free trade agreements, including as an option for a possible future free trade relationship between the EU and the United Kingdom. The UK's prospective exit from the Union in 2019 has not dented EU trade dynamism.

Brexit is a peculiar case in an international trade context

International trade agreements tend to aim at freer trade and are motivated by mutual gains from trade. In the event that no agreement is reached among the states parties, it is the status quo that represents the fallback position. In other words, should countries not manage to agree they forego potential gains from trade but do not endanger their well-being. The fact that the UK's exit from the Union arguably owes more to political preferences and choices – an estrangement from the political integration objectives of the club and regulatory sovereignty considerations led to the decision to leave it altogether, rather than any economic rationale and evaluation of economic costs and benefits[5] – does not make the UK's case less peculiar in an international trade context. In exiting the EU, the UK will become an EU outsider and pass from membership of the Union, with full rights and obligations, to third-country status.

From an international trade point of view, Brexit is bound to be a lose-lose situation, above all for the UK but, albeit to a lesser extent, also for the EU.[6] The objective is not to abolish any barriers to trade, rather it is to produce the opposite effect. As an EU member, the UK had the deepest possible and most comprehensive relationship with the Union; the UK and the EU start out being fully integrated and with regulatory alignment.

Due to its smaller market size the UK is bound to be significantly more affected by leaving the EU's single market than the EU is by impaired access to the UK market. And while the EU continues to benefit from its plethora of international trade agreements, the UK, if it leaves the customs union, needs to negotiate its own agreements and even WTO schedules, without, however, being able to draw on the bargaining power of the EU trading bloc. On leaving the EU, both market access to the EU and to other countries will probably be inferior to the present situation. The UK's fallback position as a non-EU member is trade on WTO terms.[7] More favourable terms depend on the successful conclusion of trade arrangements with the EU and the rest of the world.

Brexit and the EU

After an in-out referendum on its membership of the EU in June 2016, the UK invoked the exit clause contained in the Treaty on European Union (Article 50 of the Treaty on European

Union –TEU) on 29 March 2017. The UK's notification to the EU means that the clock starts ticking for achieving an orderly withdrawal agreement from the Union within the two-year time limit established for exit negotiations. The challenge is no less than to disentangle and sever the UK's manifold ties with the highly integrated Union. Prime Minister Theresa May made clear in the notification letter that leaving the EU the UK was to leave the single market and the EU customs union.

The other 27 member states of the Union (EU-27) gave their chief negotiator (former Commissioner Michel Barnier) an agenda and public and detailed guidelines for negotiating the UK's orderly withdrawal from the EU. On the UK's part, negotiation objectives have remained nebulous until well into the withdrawal negotiations, apart from repeated commitments to 'Brexit means Brexit' coupled with expectations that the UK could simultaneously 'have its cake and eat it' (that is, keep the benefits of membership without incurring the perceived sovereignty costs) with regard to a future relationship.

The EU made any talks on the post-exit relationship conditional on progress on withdrawal. At its December 2017 summit the European Council acknowledged that the UK had made sufficient progress on the chief withdrawal issues, set in motion the preparations of binding negotiating guidelines on trade and again called on the UK to spell out what bilateral trade relationship it envisages entering into with the EU after its withdrawal from the Union. The fact that the UK made progress on the preconditions for the withdrawal agreement makes a cliff-edge scenario – whereupon the UK crashes out of the Union without a withdrawal agreement – more unlikely; so does the fact that the UK has done almost nothing to prepare for such a scenario. Still, in the impossibility of reaching agreement on how to unwind more than 40 years of UK-EU relations and consecutively on the end state of the future bilateral relationship, the UK would find itself out of the EU on 30 March 2019 and, by default, back to trade with the EU on WTO terms.[8]

Post-Brexit, the UK claims to seek a new, deep and special partnership with the EU (objective enshrined in the Queen's speech in June 2017 and in the Prime Minister's Florence speech of 22 September 2017). Yet the UK has not further fleshed out its meaning nor has it been willing or able to specify its desired end state of the future bilateral EU-UK trade relationship. Instead, it has asked for an 'implementation' (that is, transition) agreement that would prolong the preferences it had as a member of the single market and customs union for around two years after Brexit.

The EU's negotiator signalled the possibility of the EU granting the UK a time-limited (21-month) standstill transition which could cover the single market and the customs union, with the UK, by then an EU outsider, having no voting rights on EU legislation and no say on EU policies. Details of the transition will form part of the withdrawal treaty, which would need to be agreed around October 2018 in order to be ratified by the Council of the EU (by qualified majority) and the European Parliament (consent) on time for taking effect on Brexit day (30 March 2019).[9]

For the EU, Brexit brings to the fore the issue that a higher level of economic integration (associated with higher benefits) requires sovereignty sharing or pooling and also political commitment. Countries whose electorate is deeply divided on the issue of EU membership and on the objective of an ever-closer union should not, then, remain in the EU. In the light of their different preferences (or red lines) it is preferable that they come to establish more or less deep trade agreements with the EU (like the ones the EU has with Norway, Switzerland, Turkey or Canada). In the UK's case, long-standing divisions have led to the country ending up being a member of the EU without participating in two of its most important areas of integration: the euro and the Schengen Agreement. The UK's participation in the European project became essentially limited to the single market but even there it dislikes being subject to EU regulations, which ensure that the internal market works in the first place. However, open borders and economic integration in the EU require common rules cum enforcement. Arguably, in such conditions there is no point remaining a member of the Union or even of the single market, neither from the UK's nor from the EU's point of view.

As for the EU, it faces a credibility (and indeed sustainability) issue with regard to the exact terms that it grants the UK post-Brexit: it cannot simply accept whatever member states or third countries want to do based on their national interests, at the expense of the Union and of the European project.[10]

Prospective arrangements for a post-Brexit EU-UK trade relationship

On leaving the EU, the UK will pass from EU membership, with full regulatory alignment with the single market (the world's second largest market with more than 500 million consumers), to some form of preferential trade agreement (PTA) or, in its absence, to trade on WTO terms. In order to trade on something better than the multilateral WTO terms post-Brexit, the EU and the UK need to conclude some kind of PTA.

While the UK is still a member the EU can discuss its withdrawal from the Union but cannot, by definition, conclude trade deals before it becomes a third country. The UK's future bilateral trading relationship with the Union is to be detailed in negotiations post-exit, but for self-evident reasons will be inferior to the status quo provided by EU membership. To be approved by the two parties, any agreement needs of course to be mutually beneficial, although bargaining power shifted to the EU trading bloc, with its significantly larger market size, upon the UK's Brexit notification.

Existing EU trade agreements give an idea of the potentially available and relevant arrangements for a future EU-UK trade relationship. They are something in between European Economic Area (EEA) membership and trade on multilateral WTO terms and stretch from EEA membership (like Norway), a Switzerland-type agreement (shadowing EEA membership), membership of the EU customs union (like Turkey) to (comprehensive) FTAs. Only membership of the single market and the customs union would provide for trade that is frictionless.

Suffice it here to draw attention to some main features of existing EU trade agreements and their relevance to the UK's case and to how they perform with regard to the UK's major Brexit concerns (controlling the movement of persons, ending jurisdiction of the Court of Justice of the EU (CJEU) over the UK, having regulatory autonomy, ending large financial contributions to the EU budget, and having an independent trade policy).

If the UK wanted to leave the EU's political integration project but stay in the internal market, it could apply to join the EEA. EEA membership grants countries (currently the members of the European Free Trade Association (EFTA), Norway, Liechtenstein and Iceland) participation in the EU's single market (free of tariffs and doing away with non-tariff barriers, although rules of origin apply).[11] The single market being inseparable from its constituent freedoms (the free movement of goods, services, capital and persons), the UK would have to respect all of those (that means also the free movement of persons) and follow EU rules and regulations subject to the jurisdiction of the CJEU. No longer being an EU member would make the UK a rule-taker. Access to the EEA also requires a significant contribution to the EU budget.

As an alternative, the UK could aim at a Swiss-style agreement, which, however, grants more restricted access to the single market. In reality, the agreement in question consists of some 120 agreements that emulate EEA membership, and where the violation of one single agreement triggers the termination by the EU of all the others, and also comprises a significant financial contribution to the EU. Although it requires the free movement of labour it does not extend to financial services. With a view to obtaining regulatory equivalence, Switzerland anticipates and emulates EU rules. It is doubtful that the EU would wish to replicate Swiss-type agreements in the future. Not only because the agreement is static in nature (as opposed to the EEA that is dynamic) so that updating it in accordance with EU legislation is burdensome, requiring renegotiations, but also because it was intended as a stepping stone towards full EU membership, whereas the UK is to exit the Union.

If the UK opted to stay in the EU customs union (like Turkey), it would have tariff-free single market access, but for goods only. Not being subject to the free movement of persons would allow the UK to control immigration from the EU. As a member of the customs union the UK would, however, not be free to pursue its own commercial policy and strike trade deals with third countries.

Last but not least, the UK could aim at a comprehensive FTA with the EU (along the lines of the one concluded with Canada) so as to be free of single market and customs obligations. It would mean limited market access (CETA most notably does not include financial services and regulatory equivalence is not automatic). On the other hand, the UK would be free to control immigration from the Union (no free movement of persons) and to make trade deals with other countries.[12]

In her notification letter of March 2017 Prime Minister Theresa May stated that the country was well aware of the implications for bilateral trade of leaving the single market and the EU customs union. The discourse was that no trade agreement with the Union – the UK's largest trading partner – was preferable to a bad deal. The UK thereby threatened the EU (to no avail) with the possibility of a cliff edge; as the negative economic consequences of Brexit started to sink in and businesses became more wary, the discourse changed somewhat over time. And while the no-deal WTO scenario appears a lot less likely after the UK fell into line with EU demands on the preconditions for a withdrawal agreement by December 2017, the European Commission is also preparing for this scenario, as it cannot be excluded.

By late 2017 the Prime Minister's Florence speech highlighted the need for a deep and special relationship with the EU that, in light of the existing ties and deep integration, the UK would not want to be of the existing ('off-the-shelf') EU arrangements but a bespoke agreement. UK Secretary of State for Exiting the European Union David Davis described it as a 'Canada +++' FTA. The idea would be to pick the best features from a UK perspective from the Canada, Japan and South Korea deals and add single market access for the UK's service sector, above all for financial services (given their large weight in the UK's economy), coupled with regulatory autonomy.

Challenges facing the UK as an EU outsider

Brexit presents a two-fold challenge, namely for the UK as 'global Britain', a 'global trading nation', to operate simultaneously in a newly designed relationship with its trading partner and closest neighbour, the EU.

On the day of Brexit, the UK ceases to be part of the EU and with it of the Union's trade agreements. The UK has already asked for a transition period that would go beyond the two-years granted by Article 50 TEU for an orderly withdrawal, so as to preclude a cliff-edge scenario whereby EU laws and regulations would cease to apply but new dispositions with regard to the future trade relationship had not (yet) been agreed. At this point it seems likely that the EU will grant a transitional period until the end of 2020. A standstill agreement (granting continued access to the single market and customs union, without EU membership rights[13]) would spare UK and European businesses a wasteful duplicated adaptation to whatever new regime (end state of the trading relationship) will be agreed in principle as part of the withdrawal agreement.[14] There are also indications that the UK might wish to continue to be covered also by EU trade agreements while being free to negotiate new ones.

As a consequence of the UK becoming an EU outsider, EU trade agreements will no longer apply to the UK as of Brexit day. Before that, while still being an EU member the UK is not allowed to negotiate and even less sign its own trade agreements. Nor does it appear realistic to simply roll over existing EU trade agreements by means of a 'copy and paste' exercise, not least because the EU and its trading partners would need to give their agreement to such an undertaking. The EU will defend its member states' commercial interests against the UK. Trading partners are also likely to heed their own commercial interests and to want to take advantage of the UK's urgency in striking PTAs and its lesser bargaining power (compared to the EU) to negotiate more favourable terms than they had managed with the EU. Nor do agreements between the EU and the UK on to how to split WTO import quotas suffice since these require unanimous agreement by WTO members.[15]

What the UK fails to accept is that there is a trade-off between the economic benefits that can be had and the degree of sovereignty loss/regulatory autonomy in each of the alternative arrangements for a post-Brexit preferential EU-UK trade relationship. All the abovementioned off-the-shelf agreements imply a trade-off between economic gains from trade and sovereignty but, importantly, they do so to different degrees. As a rule, higher economic benefits require higher integration, which can only be had with sovereignty sharing or pooling. Put differently, the UK's preference for regaining sovereignty and national control and for regulatory autonomy implies lower potential economic benefits from future EU trade.

The position of the EU

From the EU's point of view, the UK's red lines will determine which of the existing types of EU trade agreements are a priori applicable.

Given UK objections to CJEU jurisdiction, the free movement of persons and substantial financial contributions, and insistence on regulatory autonomy, the option of the closest association next to EU membership, which is participation in the single market through membership of the EEA (the Norway option), is a priori excluded. The Switzerland option, which does not feature CJEU jurisdiction, is not applicable either if the UK objects to the other three preconditions.[16] Any pretension of an independent trade policy, on the other hand, renders the Turkey option of membership of the EU customs union unviable.

The fact that the UK presents all of the above five issues as red lines means that the country auto-excludes itself from a future trade relationship that features staying in the single market and the customs union. As the EU's Brexit negotiator Michel Barnier has made clear, a comprehensive trade agreement along the lines of the one with Canada, not Norway, is the only alternative left if the UK sticks to its red lines.

The UK demands a bespoke comprehensive FTA from the Union. Each EU FTA is to a certain extent tailor-made to the state party in question, but the Union sets clear limits. The EU has been consistent in its affirmation (reiterated in the directives that set out the EU's position on the Brexit transition) that there can be no cherry-picking and that the prerogative of any future trade deal with the UK is to preserve the correct functioning and integrity of the single market. For the EU, the integrity of the single market and the four freedoms as well as safeguarding the autonomy of EU decision-making and of the single market's dynamic system of rule-making are non-negotiable. By the same token, any transition agreement that envisages time-limited continued participation in the single market and the EU customs union post-Brexit would also come with all the inherent obligations and constraints. EU key principles are incompatible with UK demands such as for sector-based participation in the single market (to obtain passporting rights for the UK's financial sector in the EU) or automatic regulatory conformity.

Deep FTAs prompt a qualitative change in EU trade

The EU trade dynamics lead it towards deepening globalization through bilateral trade deals, although abandoning multilateralism tends to distort global trade and harm third countries and has disadvantages for the EU, too. Pursuing FTAs like TTIP or CETA rather than trying to revive the multilateral Doha Round locks the Union into a less dynamic geographical area and also has the effect of excluding other countries and regions, most notably the People's Republic of China.[17] With tariffs already low in international trade, it seemed nevertheless a logical step for the EU to embark on an ever increasing number and geographical spread of deep FTAs that seek to abolish also non-tariff barriers to trade.

The economic case for EU comprehensive trade agreements rests on realizing hitherto largely untapped benefits from abolishing non-tariff barriers to trade. However, not only are those benefits more difficult to quantify but trade and welfare effects are complex and may even be ambiguous.[18] While conditioned by the scope of the agreements in question (e.g. covering (public or regulated) services, intellectual property rights (IPRs), investment protection), they tend to have broader implications for society and impact its model of development.[19] For instance, the CETA treaty exemplifies the far-reaching rules that govern issues as diverse and broad as access to goods and services markets, investments and public procurement; IPRs; sanitary and phytosanitary measures; sustainable development, regulatory cooperation; mutual recognition; trade facilitation; cooperation on primary materials; and the resolution of disputes and of technical barriers to trade.

Bilateral rules established to govern a trade relationship not only influence global norms and standards but also come to feed back into and interact with the EU's economic order in a way that traditional trade agreements have not. Comprehensive economic and trade agreements thereby trigger a qualitative change in EU trade. They could thereby reinforce the European model or in case of weakening it, risk eroding the trust of European citizens and economic agents in the Union.[20] The matter is economically and politically sensitive at a time when the European model, as a result of the limited progress to date with respect to the EU's economic and institutional modernization agenda and on the belated implementation of the social pillar has yet to be consolidated. To complicate matters further, deep FTAs imply higher coordination needs and raise issues of preferences and sovereignty when invading the competences of EU member states.[21]

The new generation of EU trade agreements is likely to affect the European model given that addressing non-tariff barriers to trade and other issues such as investment protection interferes with political preferences regarding the role of the state in the economy and highlights the role of regulation, which is also intrinsically political given that it is based on values and beliefs. Deep FTAs will promote market-making but may well come to constrain market correction. Rather predictably, this creates friction within the EU, also because as in many policy areas now included in those agreements it is the EU member states that have retained competences for market correction.

In this light, public contestation of the EU's new generation of comprehensive trade agreements sits uneasily with EU trade dynamics. TTIP and CETA in particular crystallized popular concern with the effects of globalization on European society and the environment. The EU's new trade policy that vowed to protect EU values in external trade showed little calming effect.[22] More preoccupying from an EU point of view, the backlash against the effects of globalization became directed against the Union, perceived as prioritizing economic (commercial) interests over making sure that its economic goals were compatible with societal (social and environmental) concerns.[23]

Of course, bilateral deeper FTAs in principle also offer the EU an easier and speedier way to advance European goals and project its values onto the global stage in comparison with multilateral forums. Still, critiques persist and centre on fears that they could lower environmental and labour standards and give multinational firms the power to challenge national laws and limit the EU and its member states' regulatory space. The concern that the European model is losing out to globalization and to being sacrificed in order to harness global trade for EU post-crises growth emerged as a common trait in reaction of populist, anti-EU movements against comprehensive EU trade agreements.

A trade focus in comprehensive agreements may easily lead the EU to overlook the complex and potentially broad consequences for society of economic and trade agreements, as the Belgian region of Wallonia has reminded the EU in the case of the CETA agreement.[24] The European Commission has subsequently modified the principles that guide its trade talks, emphasizing that EU trade policy is to become more effective with respect to delivering economic results, more transparent and also to not only to protect EU interests but further European values.[25]

The issue of regulation in internal and external trade

The regulation pinpoints the complexity of European internal trade and the EU's new generation of deep FTAs magnifies this issue. The market-making versus market-correcting – or negative versus positive integration[26] – issue gives a foretaste of the issues (of a much larger scale) at stake in deep FTAs. The CETA case illustrated that rules on regulation in comprehensive trade agreements, such as through regulatory cooperation, mutual recognition or investment court arbitration, may come to limit the European and national policy space.

Most EU-level rules currently refer to risk regulation, which pursues safety, health, environmental and consumer protection objectives. This risk regulation concerns mostly goods and services markets – for example financial market regulation and supervision, and network industry aspects – and only sporadically labour and capital markets. At a more horizontal level, it includes environmental regulation and consumer protection and rights.[27] The precautionary principle, enshrined in the treaties, is an important EU principle in this context. What made regulation-based integration possible in the EU, economically and politically speaking, was a sufficient similarity of preferences.[28] Heterogeneity of preferences leads to and requires societal acceptability of competition between regulatory systems.[29]

Mutual recognition is an essential principle for the functioning of the single market in European varieties of capitalism. It presupposes a degree of trust that rules will be similar in their effect as well as enforcement capacity. As a principle it has at times proven problematic even in a European context since it allows for regulatory arbitrage (competition between regulatory systems) in an EU that has become more heterogeneous after successive enlargements; the issue of harmonized standards for financial services is a case in point. Crucially, the case of CETA has shown that trust is already limited in a fellow G7 country. Certainly, in many respects (but not all) the UK's preferences are similar to Canada's (such as labour or product market regulation) whereas they do not seem representative of EU's preferences. That may partly explain why the UK is leaving the EU.

As an EU outsider, the UK cannot expect to have regulatory autonomy cum mutual recognition. Equivalence presupposes correspondence with conformity assessment rules. The Union also has to heed Economic and Monetary Union requirements, above all regulation that safeguards the common goods of financial market stability.

To the extent that they come to constrain market correction, comprehensive agreements could reinforce negative integration tendencies in the EU by putting downward pressure on standards through trade. To hope otherwise would require a notion of similarity with regard to third countries that is already stretched even within the EU. After the contestation of TTIP on the basis of the recognition of US regulation, the EU heeded lessons with regard to the reach of the third country regulatory autonomy on its territory, which are relevant also for the future EU–UK relationship.[30]

The EU's furthermost integration with EU outsiders is with the three EFTA countries that form part of the EEA. Those countries need to implement all the relevant EU legislation and abide by regulation without having a voice. It would be counterproductive for the EU to let other countries shape European rules and norms while countries that are more deeply integrated with the EU and are arguably more similar cannot.

With Brexit, the UK's participation in the EU's many regulatory agencies ends, among which the European Medical Agency and the European Banking Authority that are being relocated from London to Amsterdam and Paris, respectively. This fact will have consequences for the UK's access to the single market in areas as diverse as medicines, fishing, haulage, aviation, or agriculture, food and drink, to name but a few.

The UK starts out with full regulatory alignment. If the UK's commitment to avoiding a hard border between the Republic of Ireland and its province of Northern Ireland is to be taken at face value, regulatory divergence may turn out to be limited. As a non-EU member and with regulatory autonomy it is free to diverge. It is in the EU's interest to avoid a next-door competitor that undermines its standards in health, safety, the environment or taxation.

Last but not least, any future comprehensive trade agreement with the UK is further constrained by the EU's need to avoid upsetting existing trade relations with third countries. The EU cannot grant to the UK what it did not grant to countries like Norway or Canada without risking having to renegotiate existing agreements.

In conclusion, the EU's trade dynamics have been unaffected by Brexit. They increasingly comprise comprehensive trade and economic agreements, of which the UK may become part when it concludes a future bilateral trade deal with the EU. Given the UK's red lines and the importance for the EU to flesh out and implement the European model, a comprehensive trade agreement may suit both parties best.

Notes

1 See Gabriel Felbermayr (2016) 'The EU and the US: TTIP', in Harald Badinger and Volker Nitsch (eds) *Routledge Handbook of the Economics of European Integration*, Abingdon: Routledge, pp. 220–37. The 2006 Global Europe Strategy stipulates that trade should serve as the external dimension to the EU's growth and jobs agenda. See European Commission (2006) *Global Europe: Competing in the World*, Brussels: European Commission, External Trade.
2 Of the latter, the Transatlantic Trade and Investment Partnership (TTIP), which the EU and the USA started to negotiate in 2013 in order to create a transatlantic marketplace with low barriers to trade and investment and aspirations to shape the world trade order, is currently on ice.
3 CETA entered into force provisionally in 2017. As a comprehensive trade agreement, CETA qualifies as a mixed agreement, which does not only require EU-level but also ratification at the EU member state, and in some cases regional, level.
4 Prospective TPP members, left 'orphans' by US desistence from an already signed agreement, decided to pursue with regional integration on their own and have embarked on reinforcing ties with the EU (like Japan or Latin American countries).
5 See Annette Bongardt and Francisco Torres (2017) 'A Qualitative Change in the Process of European Integration', in N. Costa Cabral, J. R. Gonçalves and N. C. Rodrigues (eds) *After Brexit: Consequences for the European Union*, Basingstoke: Palgrave Macmillan.
6 For geographical and historical reasons Britain never really felt at home the EU and with sovereignty pooling, as UK Prime Minister Theresa May pointed out in her speech in Florence of 22 September 2017. On the other hand, Brexit could be beneficial for the European integration project. For a

The European Union after Brexit

discussion, see Annette Bongardt and Francisco Torres (2016) 'The Political Economy of Brexit: Why Making It Easier to Leave the Club Could Improve the EU', *Intereconomics: Review of European Economic Policy*, 51(4): 214–19.

7 Although a founder of the multilateral trading system, the UK now belongs to it as an member of the EU. The UK will have to negotiate the resumption of full independent WTO membership in an international organization that proceeds by consensus of its 164 members. An acrimonious split with the EU would hence be counterproductive. But even if the EU and the UK agreed, for instance on the division of EU import quotas, other WTO members can object if they see their commercial interests affected. The case of agricultural import quotas, on whose division the EU and UK had agreed, has already given a foretaste of the kind of hard-nosed bargaining that awaits 'Global Britain' once it is out of the EU.

8 To avoid the so-called cliff-edge outcome, the UK would need to ask for a prolongation or interruption of the withdrawal process, which would require the unanimous approval of the EU-27 and would almost certainly come with new conditions attached. This would constitute a rather humiliating situation for the UK and would only further erode its credibility and bargaining power.

9 The supplementary directives for the negotiation of an agreement with the UK setting out the arrangements for its EU withdrawal, have confirmed this. See Council of the European Union (2018) 'Annex to the Council decision supplementing the Council Decision of 22 May 2017 authorizing the opening of the negotiations with the UK for an agreement setting out the arrangements for its withdrawal from the EU', XT 21004/18, ADD 1 REV 2, Brussels, 29 January.

10 More fundamentally, the UK's stance towards the EU sits uncomfortably with the political European integration project. Each time there is a treaty revision in the EU the solution turns out to be suboptimal, not least because of the UK's particular red lines. This has resulted in insufficient integration and a popular backlash against the Union in many EU countries and also in the UK. The situation is clearly not sustainable. The EU needs to move forward with increased political integration to deal with a host of urgent transnational issues from which Brexit is little more than a distraction. The UK may want to take a distinct approach to problems and should be free to try it out.

11 It is not clear whether countries like Norway, Iceland and Liechtenstein would welcome the UK's application as a new member in light of its disparate size.

12 Any comprehensive agreement would be complicated to negotiate and ratify in light of the multiple interests involved. Going beyond EU trade competences, it would require the unanimous ratification by 30 parliaments (EU, EU member states and some regions). For a critical appraisal and criticism of the EU's current strategy of pursuing comprehensive bilateral trade agreements underpinned by far-reaching bilateral rules that govern the relationship, see Annette Bongardt and Francisco Torres (2017) 'Comprehensive Trade Agreements: Conditioning Globalization or Eroding the European Model?', *Review of European Economic Policy*, 52(3), May/June: 165–70.

13 Such as without voting rights on EU legislation, seats on technical committees or the freedom to implement trade deals, all issues that the UK is likely to contest.

14 In technical terms, the transition agreement and the political declaration on the future relationship are part of Article 50 TEU.

15 An EU-UK agreement to split agricultural import quotas was opposed even by some of the UK's long-standing friends like New Zealand, Canada, and the USA.

16 An objection to CJEU jurisdiction and the insistence on regulatory autonomy would make an Association Agreement like the one with Ukraine, which does not stipulate the free movement of persons nor any significant financial contribution, unviable. UK talk about an Association Agreement rather focuses on preserving political cooperation in areas like foreign and security policy, on the fight against crime and, given that the country is also to exit Euratom, nuclear materials.

17 Alan Winters (2014) 'The Problem with TTIP', *VoxEU*, 24 May.

18 A review of studies on the economic effects of TTIP can be found in Felbermayr, 'The EU and the US: TTIP'. Overall, it yields that a tariffs-only agreement would have only a small effect on trade flows with very low welfare gains. For a comprehensive TTIP the increase in bilateral trade flows would be sizeable but studies differ substantially with respect to welfare effects. A comprehensive TTIP could harm third countries.

19 See for instance Dani Rodrik (2016) 'Straight Talk on Trade', Project Syndicate, 15 November.

20 On the European model see Annette Bongardt and Francisco Torres (2009) 'Is the EU Model Viable in a Globalized World?', in P. Della Posta, A. Verdun and M. Uvalic (eds) *Globalization, Development and Integration: A European Perspective*, Basingstoke: Palgrave Macmillan, pp. 215–31.

305

21 The incompleteness of the European model has fuelled fears of the potential impact of comprehensive agreements on policy domains beside narrow trade in goods, many of which have remained in the EU member state sphere. They regard the fleshing out of a European model in line with European citizens' present or evolving preferences.

22 European Commission (2015) *Trade for All: Towards a More Responsible Trade and Investment Policy*, Brussels: European Commission.

23 It is aggravated by the difficulty to distinguish between single market liberalization and reform and modernization needs at national level in the face of globalization.

24 See Paul Magnette (2016) 'Wallonia Blocked a Harmful EU Trade Deal – But We Are Not Isolationists', *The Guardian*, 14 November. It was due to contestation by civil society and especially the refusal of the Belgian region of Wallonia to sign the original agreement, which resulted in some amendments before CETA could be signed by at the EU-Canada summit in late October 2016. Wallonia obtained a number of assurances, among others on investor-state dispute settlement (which was initially not even to be replaced by the investment court system), regulatory cooperation (requiring common agreement by member states), safeguards with respect to genetically modified organisms, a guarantee of the precautionary principle.

25 European Commission, *Trade for All*.

26 In the terminology of Jan Tinbergen (1954) *International Economic Integration*, Amsterdam: North Holland.

27 On EU regulatory thinking, see Jacques Pelkmans (2013) 'The Economics of Single Market Regulation', in Amy Verdun and Alfred Tovias (eds) *Mapping European Economic Integration*, Basingstoke: Palgrave Macmillan, pp. 79–104. He argues that there is a general acceptance of an economic evidence-based regulatory logic at EU level.

28 The issue of regulation for single market integrity and growth is discussed further in Annette Bongardt (2016) 'Growth: The Possibility of a Truly Single Market', *EU Essays*, London: IPPR, pp. 68–90.

29 The rejection of the original services directive, based on the home country principle, illustrated clearly the political difficulties even within the (with increasing membership ever more heterogeneous) EU club.

30 TTIP was heavily contested in the EU. The EU had been prepared to go further under TTIP with the USA than the USA had been under TPP, with deeper agreement on regulatory issues, covering three broad areas, namely market access, regulatory issues and non-tariff barriers, and rules.

27

The GCC trade agreements: regional integration challenges and opportunities

Joseph A. Kéchichian

Introduction

When the six monarchies nestled on the Arabian Peninsula – Bahrain, Kuwait, Oman, Qatar, Saudi Arabia and the United Arab Emirates (UAE) – joined together in early 1981 to create the Cooperation Council of the Arab States of the Gulf, better known as the Gulf Cooperation Council (GCC), few observers believed that the promise for close trade relationships would bind conservative rulers and their societies together. At the time, and ever since, the priority was security to ensure regional peace and, as far as that objective was concerned, inevitable compromises were found even if the founding fathers camouflaged their goals behind economic integration. Ironically, and although a painful political divorce within the GCC family was seldom contemplated, the crisis that enveloped Qatar in 2017 threatened to unravel much of the progress made during the past few decades, while a new generation of *Khalijis* (Arab Gulf citizens) grew into full interdependence. To be sure, and beyond critical security ties, effective economic relationships have fostered greater intimacy as GCC officials developed and adopted mutually beneficial policies. Moreover, and while the economic benefits of the GCC's 1981 Unified Economic Agreement remained far less impressive than the architects of the deal promised – since all six member states conducted most of their trade with foreign powers instead of with each other – non-negligible geostrategic benefits of integration occurred even if few anticipated the latest crisis with Doha. Remarkably, the GCC states opted to deal with bilateral free trade agreements (FTAs) at various levels, which aimed to lessen tensions, although the opposite occurred after two members favoured individual bilateral treaties with the USA that, inevitably, sparked a major row between Saudi Arabia and Bahrain when Manama signed with Washington, and between Saudi Arabia and Oman when Muscat approved its own FTA with the USA.

Notwithstanding these two separate accords, the GCC as a regional organization coordinated its trade activities to establish multilateral FTAs with other economic entities, including Australia, the People's Republic of China, Japan, Jordan, the Republic of Korea (South Korea), Turkey, New Zealand, India, Iran, as well as the Southern Common Market (Mercado Común del Sur – Mercosur), the Association of Southeast Asian Nations (ASEAN) and the European Union (EU). Not all of these efforts produced effective results – although the regional

Joseph A. Kéchichian

organization hoped for the best. It even signed an FTA with Syria (2005), a broken society with few prospects for immediate affluence, and more recently with Singapore (2008) as well as the European Free Trade Association (EFTA) states (Iceland, Lichtenstein, Norway and Switzerland) in 2009, all of which illustrated specific preferences that presumably better served economic goals.

What were the GCC states' economic regional integration challenges, and did member states benefit from the opportunities that arose to achieve their aims through trade agreements? How were the two odd cases of bilateral FTAs between the USA with Bahrain and Oman perceived, and were these an attempt to bypass the GCC to strengthen bilateralism at the expense of multilateralism? What about the GCC's recently approved FTAs with several other countries? Have they led to positive prognoses that may be identified through brief examinations of three accords (EFTA, Singapore and India) for example? Was it possible to decipher clues regarding trade agreement challenges and opportunities? Finally, what were the GCC states' plans to alleviate future economic woes through FTAs, and could one assess whether these would succeed?

GCC economic integration goals

Although the GCC states sought to achieve greater regional integration, and significant strides were made with the removal of nominal trade barriers that encouraged cross-border investments, success has been rather limited. In fact, and ever since its inception in 1981, the GCC Charter emphasized the role of 'coordination, integration and inter-connection between member states in all fields', which, in practice, translated into greater political cooperation in the face of emerging security threats.[1] Still, the establishment of a customs union as well as the adoption of a common market failed to usher in the kind of regional integration officials contemplated, because of important structural obstacles. Equally important was the dearth of robust economic policy coordination that many observers talked about but few implemented. It is critical to recall that when the GCC was established in 1981, member countries agreed on specific objectives, rules and functions. They also settled on implementing a unified economic agreement that, in time, would result in an economic union. Towards that end, the six founder monarchs established a free trade area in 1983, under which tariffs on goods of national origins were entirely eliminated, while each country retained external tariffs on specific items. This modest integration effort encouraged trade and investment among member states, although no agreement could be reached on economic harmonization, allegedly because such privileges protected economic independence.[2] While this phenomenon mimicked EFTA and many of the current multinational economic associations, including the North American Free Trade Agreement (NAFTA), the Australia-New Zealand Closer Economic Relations and Trade Agreement (ANZCERTA), or the Latin American Integration Association (Asociación Latinoamericana de Integración—ALADI), the GCC *intended* to quickly move towards a full-scale economic integration scheme through a common external tariff (CET) – 5 per cent on all foreign imported goods except for exempted commodities – that, miraculously, entered into force in January 2003 when the GCC customs union was approved. A second step towards integration was the adoption of a single market, which encouraged the free movement of goods produced within the GCC arena. Interestingly, and even if the establishment of a single market in the Gulf dated back to 1983 – when the GCC countries finally agreed on the implementation of their unified economic agreement – conditions were still not ripe to allow for the free movement of capital. Over time, however, GCC regulators developed intricate details that encouraged both the private and public sectors to flourish, adopted joint social insurance and pension schemes, agreed to similar education, health and social services, and ushered in common tax laws.

Consequently, a relatively solid record of development was established, in part because of somewhat favourable oil prices, but also because of steady GCC policies that promoted economic growth. According to World Bank data, the GCC states' gross domestic product (GDP) doubled to US $1.6 trillion between 2004 and 2014, as financial services, tourism and manufacturing added to the grand total. Indeed, this boom led the Kingdom of Saudi Arabia, a nascent economic power in its own right, to join the G20 in 1999.

That is not to say that GCC vulnerabilities to swings in international energy markets had disappeared but that lower oil prices during most of the 1980s persuaded all six states to look at their interests through economic integration plans. There were a number of obstacles that the 2001 updated Economic Agreement was supposed to address, including the adoption of a fully fledged monetary union, although that initiative remained in abeyance. As stated above, a customs union was announced in 2003, but implementation lagged behind as conflicts in revenue sharing emerged and, far more importantly, integration suffered a blow after Bahrain and Oman signed separate bilateral FTAs with the USA in 2004 and 2006, respectively. In the event, a key step was taken in 2008 when the GCC common market was launched, which granted economic equality across borders and it was announced that a single currency would be adopted by 2010. Regrettably, that effort was stymied by the emergent eurozone crisis at the international level, and because of various doubts raised by Oman as well as sharp disagreements by the UAE regarding the physical location of a future central bank.[3] Seven years later, the future of the common currency, the *Khaliji*, remained in doubt even before the 2017 crisis with Qatar because the commitment of the remaining states faded away despite the fact that Riyadh predicted a more positive outcome should union be eventually achieved.

Astonishingly, and inasmuch as the GCC states were driven by oil-based production, most experienced several years of negative growth during the 1980s, a period that saw declining oil prices, which contributed to a widening of aggregate budget deficits to 4 per cent of GDP as well as slow economic growth throughout the region. In the early 1990s, and despite the Gulf War, GCC economies recorded strong growth rates, the result of increasing oil prices, which dramatically transformed these traditional societies. GDP growth performances improved with Saudi Arabia, for example, recording average annual growth of 4.5 per cent growth between 1990 and 1995. Others fared well too.

Bilateral FTAs

Notwithstanding these figures, bilateral as well as multilateral economic performances were subjected to serious swings between 1981 and 2016, the first being a sharp drop during the period that followed the events of 11 September 2001, when GDP growth rates declined and the price of oil scraped the lower US $ 20 per barrel margin, before beginning a steady recovery starting in 2005. Riyadh saw a light at the end of the tunnel and hoped that its integration initiatives would bear fruit as dramatic improvements emerged. Yet what dismayed Saudi Arabia was the Bahraini and Omani conclusion of FTAs with the USA, which Riyadh perceived as attempts to bypass the GCC as an effective regional economic organization. Moreover, Riyadh assumed that the real intention of the FTAs was to strengthen bilateral ties at the expense of multilateral ones. Of course, other countries opted for bilateral FTAs too, but that was before the GCC was taken more seriously from 2003 onwards. What were the conditions that led the Kingdom of Bahrain and the Sultanate of Oman to welcome their respective FTAs, and how have they fared since?

Joseph A. Kéchichian

Table 27.1 GCC countries' economic growth rates (GDP)

Year	Bahrain	Kuwait	Oman	Qatar	Saudi Arabia	United Arab Emirates	Oil prices US$
1980s	0.03	−0.87	8.26	1.75	−0.61	1.62	−
1990	4.40	−	−0.13	−	15.19	18.32	22.26
1991	11.20	−	6.07	−	15.00	0.86	18.62
1992	6.68	−	8.41	−	3.98	3.34	18.44
1993	12.87	33.99	6.04	−	−1.36	1.26	16.33
1994	−0.25	8.43	3.87	−	0.55	6.89	15.53
1995	3.92	4.85	4.99	−	0.21	6.68	16.86
1996	4.11	0.60	3.94	−	2.63	5.79	20.29
1997	3.09	2.47	6.03	−	1.10	8.19	18.86
1998	4.79	3.66	2.64	−	2.89	0.29	12.28
1999	4.29	−1.78	−0.12	−	−3.76	2.90	17.44
2000	5.29	4.69	5.40	−	5.62	10.85	27.60
2001	2.49	0.72	4.48	3.89	−1.21	1.39	23.12
2002	3.61	3.00	−1.10	7.18	−2.81	2.43	24.36
2003	6.02	17.32	−2.66	3.71	11.24	8.80	28.10
2004	6.98	10.76	1.29	19.21	7.95	9.56	36.05
2005	6.76	10.07	2.49	7.49	5.57	4.85	50.59
2006	6.46	7.52	5.37	26.17	2.78	9.83	61.00
2007	8.29	5.99	4.45	17.98	1.84	3.18	69.04
2008	6.24	2.47	8.19	17.66	6.24	3.19	94.10
2009	2.53	−7.07	6.11	11.95	−2.05	−5.24	60.86
2010	4.33	−2.36	4.80	19.59	5.03	1.63	77.38
2011	1.98	9.62	−1.10	13.37	9.99	6.35	107.46
2012	3.73	6.62	9.33	4.68	5.41	5.10	109.45
2013	5.41	1.14	4.37	4.41	2.69	5.78	105.87
2014	4.34	0.50	2.54	3.97	3.65	3.28	96.29
2015	2.86	1.84	5.65	3.55	4.10	3.82	49.49
2016	−	−	−	2.23	1.74	3.03	40.6

Sources: The World Bank (2017) World Development Indicators, 2 August. Available at https://data.worldbank.org/data-catalog/world-development-indicators. For the average annual Organization of the Petroleum Exporting Countries (OPEC) crude oil price (in US$ per barrel) see www.statista.com/statistics/262858/change-in-opec-crude-oil-prices-since-1960/.

Note: Annual percentage growth rate of GDP at market prices based on constant local currency. Aggregates are based on constant 2010 rate for US dollars. GDP is the sum of gross value added by all resident producers in the economy plus any product taxes and minus any subsidies not included in the value of the products. It is calculated without making deductions for the depreciation of fabricated assets or for the depletion and degradation of natural resources.

The case of Bahrain

The USA first expressed an interest in an FTA with Bahrain in 1999 when the two countries signed a bilateral investment treaty (BIT), which entered into force on 31 May 2001. At the time, this was the first economic treaty signed between the USA and a GCC member state and presumably aimed at stimulating the flow of private investment between the signatories. Within a year, and based on relatively positive American investments, the USA and Bahrain initialled a trade and investment framework agreement (TIFA) on 18 June 2002, which hinted that fully fledged negotiations for an FTA would follow. In fact, the TIFA was specifically designed to thrash out differences over trade liberalization and, presumably, sorely needed economic reforms within the island kingdom. Within two years, the USA and Bahrain had signed an epochal agreement (14 September 2004), which was first ratified by the House of Representatives on 7 December 2005, and approved by the Senate on 13 December 2005. President George W. Bush signed the Implementation Act into law on 11 January 2006, which entered into force on 1 August 2006, and thereby removed all trade barriers.[4]

According to the Office of the US Trade Representative (USTR), this FTA generated 'export opportunities for the United States, creating jobs for U.S. farmers and workers' while it further supported 'Bahrain's economic and political reforms, and enhance[d] commercial relations with an economic leader in the Arabian Gulf'.[5] Of course, given Bahrain's small size – less than 1.3 million inhabitants in 2017 – the USTR's claims that 'U.S. farmers have significantly increased their agricultural exports to Bahrain' sounded more clear celebration than concrete economic progress. To be sure, Manama opened up its services market, which helped US financial service providers and companies that offer telecommunications, express delivery, distribution, health care, architecture, and engineering services, and others, to gain unique footholds in the heart of the Arabian Gulf. This was confirmed by later developments as Washington secured fresh concessions on customs-related concerns, which was a net gain for the USA as it increasingly relied on Manama to channel goods and services throughout the GCC economic zone. As the FTA specified that signatories must also comply with labour and environmental obligations, Bahrain's Ministry of Labour and Social Affairs, along with other government officials, pledged to update the Kingdom's labour laws. Although guided by International Labour Organization (ILO) regulations, what the FTA actually did was to increase controls over labour and environmental inspections, which compelled Manama to make key decisions that had not originally been on its own agenda. In other words, while Bahrain was a willing participant in numerous socio-economic reform programmes, the US FTA was, in reality, a vehicle to further accelerate the economic liberalization of a critical Arab country.

One source provided a fairly complete and largely positive assessment a decade after the FTA entered into force, further confirming that the real intention was to push for bilateral contacts and, perhaps far more importantly, to accelerate the reformist agenda. Robert J. Castro – who served as the legislative director and trade policy adviser for the US House of Representative Ways and Means Trade Subcommittee member, Representative Clay Shaw (Republican, Florida) between 2000 and 2002 – acknowledged that bilateral trade agreements in the early 2000s 'were very often aspirational, hopeful efforts to build bridges economically, diplomatically and technically to benefit both sides', although he added: 'By helping create technical capacity and adherence to common rules and best practices – and favoring U.S.-based rules over counterparts that often competed for primacy, such as EU standards – the U.S. hoped not to dominate smaller economies, but instead lift them to the level of equal partners in negotiation to provide sustainable, long-term, win–win agreements.'[6] To be sure, Washington intended to mix economic priorities with larger security objectives in the Gulf region, although any FTA between a hyper-power and a minuscule economic entity could not possibly benefit the smaller party as 'an equal partner'. Be that as it may, the FTA with Bahrain added to the Kingdom's overall stability even if, in reality, it benefited the USA much more.

According to Castro, Washington emphasized bilateral trade and investment agreements with several countries 'to create bottom-up trade deals while also pursuing top-down global, comprehensive agreements like the so-called "Uruguay Round", which had created the World

Trade Organization (WTO) out of its predecessor, the General Agreement on Tariffs and Trade'.[7] There was truth in that assessment but also disappointment in the Doha Round of WTO negotiations launched in 2001, presumably because those discussions did not produce tangible results. At the time and since, the so-called Free Trade Area of the Americas (FTAA) as well as the Trans-Pacific Partnership (TPP), which were conceived as ideal multilateral mechanisms to enhance regional integration goals, fell by the wayside. Inasmuch as protectionist policies dominated increasingly fragile societies, neither the FTAA nor the TPP stood a chance. Likewise, and while Washington meant to display full security and economic backing to a GCC member country, the commitment was heavily tilted towards defence concerns. The so-called partnership in the mislabelled but politically correct global 'war on terror' gained momentum, which the opportunistic FTA with Bahrain sealed, given that the two economies were not similarly situated in size and scale. In this instance, trade was used as a positive tool in diplomacy and national security, although the impression was that FTA-imposed reforms in the rule of law — along various specific labour-related, environmentally driven, and commercially defined regulations — would protect Bahraini and GCC interests. Of course, the strength of the FTA was and remains in its bilateral commitments that will further enhance collaboration in many fields, including education, culture, arts and sports, as well as super-sensitive regional threats and human rights concerns.

Despite the fact that discussions on such thorny issues cannot be underestimated, Bahrain is a conservative Arab Gulf monarchy, situated next to similarly inclined societies, and while Manama stood to gain added US military assistance — something that it enjoyed for decades — the bilateral FTA created a serious wedge with its GCC partners, especially the Kingdom of Saudi Arabia. Of course, there were marginal economic benefits too, including the establishment of the US food manufacturing giant Mondelez to improve its presence in Bahrain to manufacture and distribute signature American food brands throughout the region, or the investment by BFG International — a Bahraini fibreglass and composites manufacturer — in Nashville, Tennessee. Moreover, several smaller American enterprises embarked on local manufacturing projects, which the FTA encouraged, but the real markets were in the GCC economic zone that, once again, caused raised eyebrows in Riyadh. Put simply, and correctly, Saudi Arabia perceived the Bahrain-US FTA as an intrusion in the area, at a time when there was a preference for regional integration at the multilateral level.

The case of Oman

The US-Sultanate of Oman FTA, which entered into force on 1 January 2009, resembled its Bahraini counterpart and aimed to promote economic reform and openness as the two sides hoped for fresh export opportunities. In reality, the advantage was clearly in favour of the USA, as American goods and service providers entered Omani markets in far greater numbers than their Omani counterparts could match in the vast North American country. While Muscat wished to enhance its investment contacts, Washington insisted on commitments to economic liberalization, along with pledges to strengthen intellectual property rights (IPRs) protection and enforcement. Towards that end, the USA applauded the Sultanate's promises, and worked closely with local officials to implement FTA regulations.[8]

In early December 2008 Washington and Muscat authorized companies based in the USA to open branch offices in Oman to provide goods or services on par with Omani commercial institutions. The purpose of this unprecedented initiative was to encourage foreign direct investment (FDI) and to eliminate as much bureaucracy as possible and to issue licenses to US companies that wished to establish themselves in the Sultanate. By having a local branch, US

The GCC trade agreements

companies/individuals avoided the burdensome requirement to have an Omani shareholder to establish a limited liability company, something that was the norm throughout the area. There were a few minor conditions, including a minimum capital of OMR 20,000 (USD 52,000) – a significant reduction when compared to other foreign nationals' minimum capital of RO 150,000 (US $390,000) – and certain residency requirements, but these were inconsequential as American businesses and nationals were permitted to invest in every sector at full (100 per cent) ownership. Even the documentation certification process was simplified, which was taken as a good omen, because it eliminated excessive paperwork. In fact, these first steps proved so successful that American and Omani officials opened fresh discussions in February 2010 over a broad range of trade issues, including implementation of Oman's obligations under the labour and environment chapters of the FTA, ostensibly to abide by ILO regulations. According to the USTR, and in order to advance common goals under the Labour Chapter of the FTA, US officials agreed with Oman's Ministry of Manpower, along with other representatives from labour and business groups that all differences could be resolved through dialogue on key concerns. To that end, the US Department of Labor funded a project implemented by the ILO to increase the effectiveness of labour inspections by Oman's Ministry of Manpower, which highlighted the growing dependence on Washington on this question simply because of limited Omani resources. Muscat aimed to encourage high levels of US FDI in the Sultanate, if for no other reason than to ensure that trade and environmental goals would be mutually supportive and sustainable, although it also conceded that far larger benefits would accrue to US companies. The effort was deliberate as the perception in Oman hovered around secure American commitments to the Sultanate's economic and security needs. Inasmuch as these bilateral agreements satisfied Omani requirements, they overtook precedence over GCC multilateral FTAs, something that Riyadh was determined to encourage precisely to empower the alliance with the economic wherewithal to negotiate from a position of relative strength rather than to enter into separate bilateral deals that denied the GCC the power of regional integration in the full meaning of the word.

The case for free trade in the GCC

Whether these two bilateral trade agreements hindered or substantially delayed a fully fledged GCC-US FTA will long be debated, although both Bahrain and Oman could have secured far better deals had they not pursued unilateral agreements. Be that as it may, and while there is genuine power in numbers, both Manama and Muscat sought to leverage their FTAs with Washington's security pledges. Moreover, and as highlighted in the statistical data for 2015, both the Kingdom of Bahrain and the Sultanate of Oman initialled their FTAs with the USA on much more than economic grounds, since the USA was not their primary trading partner.

Nevertheless, and as the data confirms, the leading Arab countries preferred to trade with European or Asian powers rather than among themselves even though the GCC would very much like to enhance regional economic integration. Despite their proximity, however, and for protectionist as well as long-established tribal reasons that continued to hamper fully fledged cooperation, intra-GCC trade remained minuscule. According to an Omani scholar, 'the intra-GCC trade has now grown nearly forty-fold since its establishment and has reached more than 90 billion U.S. dollars in 2013', although it 'made up about 8% of the GCC total trade in 2014'.[9] In 2014 total GCC trade stood at around US $1 trillion, a figure that rose to around $1.022 trillion in 2015.[10] Interestingly, these figures were expected to change dramatically after the GCC customs union entered into effect, presumably because tariffs between the six states were eliminated and a common 5 per cent tariff on imported goods across the region was

313

Joseph A. Kéchichian

Table 27.2a Bahrain's trade partners, 2015

Top 10 export partners	Export volume (US $)
Saudi Arabia	4,193,648,812
UAE	$961,129,540
USA	$710,760,371
Kuwait	$393,772,016
Egypt	$330,073,480
Qatar	$265,101,253
Algeria	$174,804,006
India	$137,433,580
Oman	$137,426,562
Morocco	$131,585,752

Table 27.2b

Top 10 import partners	Import volume (US $)
China	$1,571,374,908
UAE	$1,169,611,719
USA	$1,151,535,729
Japan	$1,119,006,822
Australia	$785,081,309
Saudi Arabia	$773,525,998
Germany	$544,138,199
India	$507,388,734
United Kingdom	$420,177,445
Brazil	$414,298,654

Source: globalEDGE™, International Business Center at Michigan State University. Available at https://globaledge.msu.edu/countries/bahrain/tradestats.

adopted. To date, however, the results have been less than stellar, and although GCC citizens could move freely across borders, invest as they wished, and accept employment in any member state at will, barriers inhibited closer trade. Even the much discussed and theoretically agreed upon combined value-added tax (VAT) was put on ice after oil prices crashed. Of course, the proposed monetary union was placed in abeyance too, after Abu Dhabi objected to Riyadh hosting the contemplated GCC central bank. Despite the goodwill displayed by the member states, extraordinary roadblocks prevented closer integration, something that the latest crisis with Qatar was bound to complicate further. Political disagreements among the member states lingered, which two scholars foresaw as a harbinger for a 'weak integrated regional organization', presciently concluding that the GCC confronted 'serious obstacles [that] have hampered closer integration, including bureaucratic and administrative inefficiencies, as well as old rivalries and a desire among smaller Gulf states to retain their autonomy'.[11] When oil prices were relatively high, few bothered with the calls for union, as most ruling family members believed that they could ride the tide without making the necessary sacrifices. Yet when oil prices collapsed, the *need* to make radical changes grew, something that the latest crisis with Qatar confirmed. In fact,

The GCC trade agreements

Table 27.3a Oman's trade partners, 2015

Top 10 export partners	Export volume (US $)
China	$14,070,668,729
UAE	$2,050,237,332
India	$1,088,233,602
Saudi Arabia	$1,014,278,200
Japan	$635,023,908
Singapore	$626,624,642
Thailand	$594,127,413
South Korea	$565,664,714
Yemen	$562,983,022
USA	$514,600,941

Table 27.3b

Top 10 import partners	Import volume (US $)
UAE	$10,159,603,199
India	$1,564,069,133
China	$1,456,449,360
Saudi Arabia	$1,173,374,720
USA	$1,051,492,683
Netherlands	$672,222,089
Brazil	$623,004,904
South Korea	$529,478,419
Qatar	$528,168,779
Italy	$526,821,234

Source: globalEDGE™, International Business Center at Michigan State University. Available at https://globaledge.msu.edu/countries/oman/tradestats.

concrete tensions were palpable between Qatar and Saudi Arabia, the UAE and Bahrain, when the latter three first withdrew their ambassadors from Doha in March 2014 over complaints that the Emir of Qatar, Sheikh Tamim Al Thani, interfered in Arab internal affairs. Naturally, this dispute was political and was temporarily solved in late 2014 when the Qatari ruler travelled to Riyadh and was reconciled with the late King Abdullah bin Abdul al-Aziz. Nevertheless, underlying tensions hovered around the Saudi desire for closer GCC union, not only to present a unified posture against genuine regional threats, but also, and presumably, to coordinate economic efforts to recover billions of dollars in lost revenue.

In an increasingly globalized environment, GCC governments foresaw the need to intensify export programmes, both to diversify income sources and, whenever possible, enter into agreements with countries that extended mutually beneficial terms. That was the chief reason why the GCC, as a regional alliance, entered into trade talks with the EU, Japan, China, India, Pakistan, Turkey, Australia, New Zealand, South Korea, Brazil, Argentina, Uruguay and Paraguay, among others, with which they either established, or wished to pursue, free trade zones. As discussed below, they also focused on key Asian countries with whom they actually signed multilateral FTAs, which eliminated or significantly reduced import tariffs. Interestingly, the FTA trend was set by Singapore, India and South Korea, even if negotiations with the latter were still under way in mid-2018.

GCC FTA accords with three partners

To mitigate globalization concerns and, naturally, to prepare for the decades to come, the GCC either established FTAs or contemplated serious negotiations with Australia, China, India, Iran, Japan, Jordan, South Korea, Turkey, New Zealand, as well as the ASEAN, Mercosur and EU blocs, though its most successful accord was with Singapore. An equally positive experience was recorded with the EFTA states, while talks with India were ongoing at the time of writing. What have been the results of these efforts and how useful were these multilateral FTA schemes? Was the GCC inclined to forego any of its economic partners owing to interminable negotiations? Were there realistic alternatives to consider?

The case of Singapore

One of the richest countries in the world per capita, Singapore successfully 'positioned itself as a gateway to Asia and [enjoyed] one of the most open markets globally'. Except for a mild duty on agricultural products, Singapore opted for an 'almost-blanket zero tariff policy', which stood the test of time and transformed the small country into an economic powerhouse.[12]

The GCC-Singapore FTA (GSFTA), which came into effect in September 2013, lowered tariffs on Singapore-made goods and refined oil products, and granted GCC nationals preferential treatment in several sectors, including the legal field and engineering projects. Faisal Tabbaa, the deputy managing partner of the Saudi-based law firm Dhabaan & Partners, was quoted in press reports as saying that the pact had brought about 'some very interesting numbers'.[13] According to Tabbaa, 'more than QR900m [US \$247 million] from Singaporean businesses [were invested] in Qatar [and] there was \$9.2bn in trade with the UAE in the first three quarters of 2013', which led him to conclude that the GSFTA proved to be 'a good one, and it's a win-win'.[14] In fact, 99 per cent of all tariffs were eliminated as a result of the GSFTA, in what turned out to be a 'genuinely comprehensive accord that covered goods and services, investments, rules of origin, customs procedures, government procurement, electronic commerce and economic cooperation'.[15] Interestingly, the GSFTA was signed in Doha between Singapore Prime Minister Lee Hsien Loong, GCC Secretary-General Abdul Rahman bin Hamad Al-Attiyah and, representing the GCC Ministerial Council, the then Prime Minister of Qatar Sheikh Hamad bin Jassim Al Thani. It immediately granted tariff-free access for most of Singapore's domestic exports to the GCC states, worth about S\$5.34 billion in 2016.[16] Reciprocally, the GSFTA granted tariff-free access to all GCC goods entering Singapore, which were estimated at around S\$68.6 billion in 2012, an increase of 62 per cent since 2007, and mostly accounting for Singapore's oil imports. In fact, the GCC states provided 35 per cent of Singapore's oil needs, which made the small Asian country the GCC's fifth largest trading partner.[17]

If the GSFTA proved to be successful, it was in some measure because of the steps taken by all concerned to accept halal standards in the six-member Arab trade group.[18] Remarkably, the GCC as a bloc recognized the Singapore Muis Halal Standards (SMHS) as being consistent and compliant with similar standards in their countries that, naturally, facilitated trade in halal product exports to the GCC. Moreover, and because a growing number of GCC inhabitants visited Singapore, knowing that the country was SMHS-compatible, this amenability gave greater assurance to those anxious to follow specific dietary requirements. Although this was a tangential issue, the mere fact that it could be addressed created noticeable goodwill, something that surely facilitated specific GSFTA negotiation planks. In fact, and rather than cover every aspect of the accord, suffice it to illustrate this point with reference to the service sector, which permitted Singapore-based companies and Singapore Permanent Residents to hold majority stakes in key sectors within GCC markets. Consequently, Singaporean companies gained greater access in the UAE, Saudi Arabia and Qatar in the construction field as well as in most professional areas, including legal and engineering areas. Many other issues were settled as well, including Information Technology and business investments. By any standards, the GSFTA expanded economic ties at a time when protectionism gained momentum in leading Western powers that, according to Premier Lee Hsien Loong, was short-sighted. Lee confirmed that the GSFTA recorded a 127 per cent increase between 2002 and 2010.[19] Expectations were high that more recent data would further corroborate the pattern.

The case of EFTA

Successfully but also very discreetly, the four European countries that comprise EFTA – Iceland, Liechtenstein, Norway and Switzerland – have signed about 25 FTAs with the EU as well as with at least 35 global partners in recent years. In 2014 an FTA entered into force with the GCC, which covered most goods, trade in services and government procurement projects. According to press reports, 'two-way merchandise trade between the EFTA and the GCC countries … increased by an annual average of 9%, reaching a value of USD 9.2 billion in 2013, [and, interestingly, the GCC economic zone represented] EFTA's fifth most important partner worldwide as an export destination'.[20] Iceland and Norway concentrated on fisheries while Liechtenstein and Switzerland focused on industrial products, all of which benefited from duty-free access to GCC markets. Bilateral agreements between the GCC and individual EFTA states provided for preferential trading conditions for a number of products too. Importantly, the EFTA states build on the WTO framework to secure solid deals on the service sector, while they signed fresh instruments over IPRs and investments, two critical areas that were placed on two-year review tracks. The sophisticated approach proved to be relatively successful with no major complaints recorded in the years following implementation.

Negotiations with India

If Singapore and the EFTA countries managed to conclude effective agreements over a short period of time, negotiations with the EU on the one hand and India on the other entered into interminable cycles that stretched every imagination. The case with India, which is addressed here, is the more valuable to draw lessons from, because the world's second-most populated country is a neighbour of the GCC states. Equally important, the presence of over 6.7 million Indian nationals within GCC countries presented unusual problems, although it also could be viewed as a testament of unprecedented loyalty and impeccable security. Herein lies a solid lesson for challenged negotiators: what not to do when faced with FTA hurdles.

Remarkably, the GCC signed a Framework Agreement on Economic Cooperation with India on 25 August 2004, which compelled both parties to consider ways and means to liberalize trade relations in order to enter into serious discussions that would, within a short period of time, result in a workable FTA. A first round of negotiations was held in Riyadh in March 2006, when the conservative Arab Gulf monarchies agreed to include services as well as investment and general economic cooperation in the proposed GCC-India FTA. An agreement on the modalities for negotiations was also finalized, although no progress was made until

September 2008, when representatives returned to the GCC headquarters. The best that could be done at that juncture was the establishment of Working Groups even if substantive conversations were held on proposed tariff liberalization concerns. Both sides agreed to reconvene in Delhi, without setting a date, which was strange to say the least. What prevented officials from addressing vital questions in a timely fashion remained a mystery. Even more perplexing was the overall acknowledgment that an FTA between Delhi and Riyadh was critical given the enormous stakes. In fact, the Indian Minister of Commerce and Industry, Kamal Nath, revealed that his country's total trade with the GCC countries had risen more than four-fold from US $5.55 billion in 2000–01 to $23.42 billion in 2005–06, that reached even greater heights since then, despite a slight dip in 2015–16.[21]

The figures rose steadily as the GCC economic zone became India's largest trading partner with US $138 billion worth of trade in 2014–15, up from only $5.5 billion in 2001, having been boosted by significant oil purchases. Indeed, more than 50 per cent of India's oil and gas came from the GCC countries that, it is worth repeating, hosted over 6.7 million Indian expatriate workers, ranging the gamut from low-skilled construction workers to highly skilled professionals, including physicians and engineers. Everything pointed to the desirability of an FTA between the two partners, which is why difficulties in negotiations were nearly impossible to comprehend. Both sides acknowledged the value that the other held, with the Indian embassy in Riyadh affirming in a 2017 report that the GCC states held tremendous significance for India, and constituted 'the immediate neighborhood of India separated only by the Arabian Sea'. 'India, therefore', the report continued, 'has a vital stake in the stability, security and economic well-being of the Gulf', which was a sublime affirmation if any.[22] 'As a group,' the document elaborated, the 'GCC has been increasingly determining the economic, political, and security policies of its member States … moving ahead rapidly with their economic integration efforts'. Moreover, India recognized that the GCC had emerged as a major trading partner and could present significant investment potentials not only because of the GCC states' 'substantial oil and gas reserves [that were of] vital importance for India's energy needs', but also because of the large Indian expatriate community, estimated at 'more than 6.5 million Indian workers in the region' who were of 'vital interest to India'.[23] For their part, GCC societies valued India as well, leading one commentator to conclude that 'this substantial interaction has ensured that now every GCC country has committed itself to setting up a "strategic partnership" with India, founded on cooperation in political, security, defense, economic and cultural areas'.[24] For

Table 27.4 India's trade with GCC countries (in US $ million)

Country	2014–15			2015–16		
	Imports	Exports	Total	Imports	Exports	Total
Bahrain	446	473	919	357	654	1,011
Kuwait	13,382	1,999	14,581	4,968	1,246	6,214
Oman	1,752	2,379	4,131	1,673	2,191	3,864
Qatar	14,605	1,055	15,660	9,019	903	9,922
Saudi Arabia	28,108	11,163	39,271	20,315	6,396	26,711
UAE	26, 140	33,029	59,169	19,425	30,321	49,746
Total	84,433	49,293	133,730	55,756	41,712	97,468

Source: Government of India Ministry of Commerce and Industry, Directorate General of Foreign Trade. Available at www.indianembassy.org.sa/india-saudi-arabia/india-gcc-relations, 'India-GCC Relations,' Riyadh: Embassy of India, 2 July 2017.

another, the 'Indian presence in the Gulf region is civilizational and has developed into a vibrant relationship over the years' and has taken on strategic dimensions.[25] In short, Delhi was deemed a vital partner, which was why an incomplete FTA stood as a major anomaly.

Conclusion

If the GCC-EU FTA, under negotiation since 1988, or its counterpart, the India-GCC FTA remained in abeyance, it is nevertheless critical to point out that the GCC-Singapore model was truly successful, and this raises a fundamental question: can the GCC states alleviate their future economic woes through FTAs and, should this prove the case, is it possible to speculate whether they will succeed with some partners and not with others?

Owing to the ongoing crisis within the GCC, which has its basis in the decision of Saudi Arabia, Bahrain and the UAE (along with Egypt) to boycott Qatar for security reasons, it might be useful to quote the Qatari representative at the GCC-Singapore FTA signing ceremony in January 2009 when he criticized EU negotiators, stating that the 'Gulf states should take a decision soon to suspend talks until the EU works out this issue', presumably 'because such talks could not and ought not last forever'.[26] In the event, the GCC suspended negotiations with the EU shortly afterwards because negotiators believed that the leading powers routinely mixed politics with economic reform, which presumably preoccupied GCC leaders and envoys who expressed reservations about making further 'political concessions' to secure FTAs with any country at any price. This was the gist of what the GCC, as a regional economic/military alliance, remained focused on as the member states aimed to reduce their dependence on Western economies, even if this was easier said than done. For GCC governments, the future clearly lay in Asia; several new FTAs were under consideration with China, Pakistan, Japan, Malaysia, Viet Nam and South Korea. Of course, negotiators were optimistic, although many were stunned by the Bahrain-US FTA and the Oman-US FTA deals, which suggested – at least to some officials – that bilateral and multilateral agreements could co-exist, even if the preference was for the collective variety. In fact, and long before the most recent crisis that divided the GCC into two camps (GCC3 vs Qatar), it was important to remember that the GCC-Singapore pact was first started at a bilateral level with Qatar which, wisely, converted its negotiations into a more comprehensive multilateral deal. In Singapore's case, however, there was a clear desire on the part of the Asian powerhouse to build on previous BITs with Bahrain (2003), Saudi Arabia (2006), Oman (2007), Kuwait (2009), and the UAE (2011), though it was the Qatari effort that elevated the accords to a multilateral level that benefited the entire economic zone. Few missed the irony of this development in the light of the most recent and ongoing crisis that isolated Doha from the economic zone. With Gulf economies losing precious oil revenues and export diversification becoming ever more essential, trade agreements will undoubtedly require greater emphasis, something that all GCC states, including Qatar, cannot overlook. What these efforts illustrated, nevertheless, was crystal clear: despite challenges, the best opportunities for the GCC remained in multilateral FTAs, which would succeed when the alliance stood united and forged its common destiny.

Notes

1 For the Charter of the Gulf Cooperation Council, see www.gcc-sg.org/eng/indexfc7a.html.
2 For essential background, see Belaid Rettab and Abdulaziz Istaitieh (2007) *GCC Economic Integration in Focus with Special Reference to the UAE*, Dubai: Chamber of Commerce and Industry. Available at http://web.dubaichamber.ae/LibPublic/GCC%20Economic%20Integration%20in%20Focus%20with%

20Special%20Reference%20to%20the%20UAE.pdf; and Steffen Hertog (2007) 'The GCC and Arab Economic Integration: A New Paradigm', *Middle East Policy*, 14(1), spring: 52–68. Available at www.mepc.org/journal/gcc-and-arab-economic-integration-new-paradigm.

3 Robin Wigglesworth (2009) 'UAE Quits Gulf Monetary Union', *Financial Times*, 20 May. Available at www.ft.com/content/822cab2e-4534-11de-b6c8-00144feabdc0.

4 The chronological details for these negotiations and agreements are available in Elizabeth Becker (2004) 'U.S. and Bahrain Reach a Free Trade Agreement', *New York Times*, 28 May. Available at www.nytimes.com/2004/05/28/business/us-and-bahrain-reach-a-free-trade-agreement.html. See also Reuters (2006) *'Bahrain Pact Signed by Bush', New York Times*, 12 January. Available at www.nytimes.com/2006/01/12/business/bahrain-pact-signed-by-bush.html.

5 Executive Office of the President (n.d) 'Bahrain Free Trade Agreement', Washington, DC: Office of the United States Trade Representative. Available at https://ustr.gov/trade-agreements/free-trade-agreements/bahrain-fta. For the text of the accord, see https://ustr.gov/trade-agreements/free-trade-agreements/bahrain-fta/final-text.

6 Robert J. Castro (2016) '10 years of the US-Bahrain Free Trade Agreement', *The Hill*, 20 April. Available at http://thehill.com/blogs/pundits-blog/international/276946-10-years-of-the-us-bahrain-free-trade-agreement.

7 Ibid.

8 Executive Office of the President (n.d.) 'Oman Free Trade Agreement', Washington, DC: Office of the United States Trade Representative. Available at https://ustr.gov/trade-agreements/free-trade-agreements/oman-fta. For the text of the accord, see https://ustr.gov/trade-agreements/free-trade-agreements/oman-fta/final-text.

9 Nasser Al-Mawali (2015) 'Intra-Gulf Cooperation Council: Saudi Arabia Effect', *Journal of Economic Integration*, 30(3), September: 532–52, 38.

10 'World Ranking of GCC in Total Trade Exchange – 2015', in *GCC Annual Statistical Year Book 2015*, Riyadh: Gulf Cooperation Council Statistical Division, June 2017, p. 27.

11 Silvia Colombo and Camilla Committeri (2013) *Need to Rethink the EU-GCC Strategic Relations*, Rome: Sharaka [Istituto Affari Internazionali], 1: 4, 11. Available at www.iai.it/sites/default/files/Sharaka_RP_01.pdf.

12 Courtney Trenwith (2015) 'An Unprecedented Number of Free Trade Agreements Are Being Signed Globally, but the GCC Remains Far Behind', *Arabian Business*, 28 August. Available at www.arabianbusiness.com/the-case-for-free-trade-in-gcc-604126.html.

13 N. Janardhan (2013) 'Gulf Cooperation Council-Singapore Free Trade Agreement Comes into Force on September 1', *The Straits Times*, 1 September. Available at www.straitstimes.com/business/gulf-cooperation-council-singapore-free-trade-agreement-comes-into-force-on-sept-1.

14 Ibid.

15 For details on the actual terms of the GSFTA, see Singapore Government, International Enterprise Singapore, 'GCC – Singapore Free Trade Agreement (GSFTA)',. Available at www.iesingapore.gov.sg/Trade-From-Singapore/International-Agreements/free-trade-agreements/GSFTA.

16 'Singapore Exports by Country', in Trading Economics. Available at https://tradingeconomics.com/singapore/exports-by-country.

17 'Gulf Cooperation Council-Singapore Free Trade Agreement Enters into Force' (2013) Singapore: Ministry of Trade and Industry, 1 September. Available at www.mti.gov.sg/NewsRoom/Pages/GULF-COOPERATION-COUNCIL-SINGAPORE-FREE-TRADE-AGREEMENT-ENTERS-INTO-FORCE.aspx.

18 Halal food standards refer to products that are prepared according to Muslim dietary laws and regulations that determine what is permissible, lawful and clean. The word halal literally means 'permissible'.

19 National Archives of Singapore (2008) 'Free Trade Agreement between the Cooperation Council for the Arab States of the Gulf and the Republic of Singapore (GSFTA)', 15 December. Available at www.nas.gov.sg/archivesonline/data/pdfdoc/20081222005/mti+pr+(15+dec)+gsfta+info+kit.pdf.

20 Ögmundur Magnússon (2014) 'EFTA-GCC Free Trade Agreement Enters into Force on 1 July 2014', Geneva: European Free Trade Association, 18 June. Available at www.efta.int/free-trade/news/efta-gcc-free-trade-agreement-enters-force-1-july-2014-2836.

21 'India-GCC FTA Soon', *The Hindu*, 28 September 2016. Available at www.thehindu.com/todays-paper/tp-business/India-GCC-FTA-soon/article14770599.ece.

22 'India-GCC Relations', Riyadh: Embassy of India, 2 July 2017. Available at www.indianembassy.org.sa/india-saudi-arabia/india-gcc-relations.

23 Ibid.

24 Talmiz Ahmad (2013) 'Widening Horizons of GCC–India Trade & Investment', Abu Dhabi: Emirates Center for Strategic Studies and Research, 8 April. Available at http://ecssr.com/ECSSR/print/ft.jsp?lang=en&ftId=/FeatureTopic/Talmiz_Ahmad/FeatureTopic_1662.xml.

25 Samir Pradhan (2010) 'India and the Gulf Cooperation Council (GCC): An Economic and Political Perspective', *Strategic Analysis*, 34(1), February: 93–103.

26 Quoted in N. Janardhan (2009) 'GCC-Singapore FTA Offers Hope amid Crisis', *Khaleej Times*, 4 January. Available at www.khaleejtimes.com/article/20090103/ARTICLE/301039998/1036.

28

Liberalization without integration
Egypt and PTAs (1990–2010)

Amr Adly

The curious case of liberalization-cum-PTAs

The 1990s marked a major transformation in Egypt's economic policies towards greater liberalization of trade and capital movement and a decisive shift towards a private sector-dominated economy. In 1991 the Egyptian government adopted a Structural Adjustment Programme (SAP) under the auspices of the International Monetary Fund (IMF) and the World Bank. The SAP entailed the reorientation of the Egyptian economy towards exports and the creation of a business environment conducive for foreign direct investment (FDI). Since that time, some significant trade liberalization has taken place on a unilateral, multilateral and preferential basis. The latter was particularly central to Egypt's path towards integration into the global economy.

Since the mid-1990s the Egyptian government has negotiated preferential trade agreements (PTAs) with its major trade partners and neighbours. This ranged from the European Union with which an association agreement was signed in 2001, to the Common Market for Eastern and Southern Africa (COMESA) in 1998. It also included multiple preferential trade agreements (PTAs) with Arab countries under the Agadir process (launched in 2001) and within the framework of the Greater Arab Free Trade Area (GAFTA) to which Egypt acceded in 1998. By 2012 'Egypt now has free trade areas (FTAs) with all its major trading partners with the exception of the USA, with whom Egypt has signed the Qualified Industrial Zones (QIZs) protocol which gives Egypt free access to the USA market for some of its major exports'.[1]

Despite the large number of PTAs to which Egypt has become party since the 1990s, the country's progress towards integration into global trade proved rather slow. Egypt's share of world trade stagnated or even declined throughout the period. The share of Egyptian exports in total world merchandise exports was 0.002 in 2005 and declined to 0.001 in 2015.[2] The ratio of goods and service exports to gross domestic product (GDP) in 2010 (21.4 per cent) was lower than that in 1991 (27.8 per cent). The overall average improved slightly between 21.8 per cent in the 1990s to 24.7 per cent in the period (2000–10).[3]

Moreover, there was a general failure to reorient the economy outwards towards more export activity. More importantly, Egypt remained reliant on exports of raw materials, namely oil and natural gas, and proved unable to upgrade its export structure into higher value-added manufactured products. According to World Trade Organization (WTO) statistics, during the period 1990–2010, exports of oil and natural gas constituted an average of 40 per cent of total exports. The share of manufactured exports stagnated at 37 per cent.

The principal questions that this chapter raises are: why has Egypt ended up with so many PTAs since the 1990s and why have they not produced the desired effects in terms of outwardly reorienting the Egyptian economy, thus allowing greater access to foreign markets and the upgrading of Egypt's exports?

I argue that in the case of Egypt, since the 1990s PTAs have been implemented by the Egyptian government to mitigate and to adapt to the intensifying pressures of trade liberalization. The primary goal, that was sometimes shared with Egypt's main trade partner (i.e. the EU), was to lower the adjustment cost and its sociopolitical repercussions on Egypt. Why PTAs failed to deliver on reorienting the Egyptian economy and allowing increases and upgrading in exports since the mid-1990s, can be explained by two principal factors. The first concerns weak external incentives and leverage as most PTAs were shallow and merely sought trade liberalization that was often piecemeal, gradual and partial. It seldom included deep integration measures that required changes in the legal or regulatory frameworks governing Egypt's economy.[4] Conversely, Egypt could use its geopolitical weight so as to modify the scope, scale and pace of liberalization under PTAs in order to avoid or at least lower the adjustment costs to be incurred by domestic economic activities. This often meant some feigned liberalization and continued protection for domestic producers, albeit increasingly on a non-tariff basis.

The second factor is a by-product of the first. Given weak incentives and leverage to alter Egypt's economic governance, PTAs were shaped by the interests and influences of an inward-oriented coalition of economic actors. The government prioritized lowering the adjustment costs of trade liberalization to accessing foreign markets but allowed a persistently inward orientation of Egyptian producers despite the increasing engagement with PTAs.

The two abovementioned political-economic factors contributed to perpetuating a certain mode of integration of the Egyptian economy into the global and regional division of labour that did not depend on merchandise trade. Instead, it depended on Egypt specializing in exporting traditional services (via tourism and the Suez Canal primarily) and receiving massive inflows of capital in the form of workers' remittances, aid, cheap credit and debt relief (with a minor role for FDIs, which are logically related to trade).

The end result was the failure of PTAs in altering the orientation of the Egyptian economy or its mode of insertion into the global and regional division of labour. With a weak goods export base, the Egyptian economy depended on generating surpluses in the capital and service accounts so as to fill the balance of payment gaps. This left the economy vulnerable to geopolitical fluctuations (including international oil prices) that determined its access to capital through remittances and intergovernmental aid and credit. It also left it dependent on traditional service sectors like the Suez Canal, which since 1990 has been stagnant as a percentage of GDP and government revenues in addition to a volatile sector like tourism that has been negatively affected many times by political and security instability.

The chapter will proceed by discussing some of the literature on the political economy of trade liberalization in terms of its relevance to the Egyptian case. The second section will provide some basic background information about Egypt's major PTAs in the period under study (1990–2010), which are the EU Association Agreement (AA henceforth) and its related PTAs (i. e. Agadir, the FTA with European Free Trade Association (EFTA) and Turkey), the Greater Arab Free Trade Area (GAFTA), the COMESA and finally the Qualified Industrial Zone (QIZ) Arrangement with the USA. It will show the proposed dynamic in each and every PTA under study. The third and final section offers a general conclusion which attempts to portray the wider picture.

Where does Egypt stand? A review of the literature

This section seeks to situate the Egyptian case within the broader literature on trade liberalization and PTAs. Based on the Ricardian assumption, neoclassical economics holds trade liberalization to be conducive for development as more competition would allow better specialization along lines of comparative advantage, more efficient allocation of resources and hence more welfare for all trade partners. However, as trade liberalization takes place in the context of heavy state regulation of the economy, it usually entails adjustment costs as some enterprises or even industries die out or at least contract and shed labour. Neoclassical economics makes the assumption that adjustment costs will be provisional or temporary and that overall welfare gains for the economy will eventually offset the initial cost.[5] Theoretically, adjustment will eventually prevent labour and capital losing out to competitive sectors. Overall, welfare gains will translate into greater access to export markets (where comparative advantages are enjoyed) and lower cost of imports and of domestic produce (which is good for final consumers but also for businesses seeking inputs at lower cost and of higher quality).

The literature invoked three – often parallel and simultaneous – paths towards trade liberalization. The first is multilateral, within the framework of the WTO/General Agreement on Tariffs and Trade (GATT) 1994. In this case trade liberalization happens along the four basic principles of national treatment, most-favoured-nation MFN) principle, transparency and the tariffication of trade barriers away from non-tariff barriers. Egypt has been a signatory of the GATT agreement since 1970. Its obligations came into effect in 1981. Egypt has been a founding member of the WTO since its inception and has accepted all of its obligations under the 'single undertaking' approach, adopted during the Uruguay Round in 1994.

The multilateral track, however, allowed for the signing of PTAs among WTO and (non-WTO) members. Despite the fact that PTAs are essentially in contradiction with the MFN principle, they are tolerated under the WTO agreements (Article 19). The neoclassical literature is split on the desirability and efficiency of PTAs. Some observers perceived them as distortionary and hence causing inefficiency and welfare losses for trade parties and for the world at large.[6] This trend has stressed the problem of trade diversion that may outstrip trade creation.[7] Conversely, others saw PTAs as a step towards further liberalization, albeit on non-multilateral basis. Overall, economists have had to tolerate the fact that PTAs are driven by non-economic factors including geopolitics, regional security arrangements and cultural ties. The EU (formerly the European Coal and Steel Community and the European Community – EC) being the pioneer and prototype since the signing of the Treaty of Rome in 1957 and the subsequent accession of European countries to the Community and later on to the Union in 1992.

The third and simplest path of trade liberalization is unilateral whereby a state lowers its trade barriers on a non–reciprocal MFN basis. Typical examples would be the small and open economies of Hong Kong, Dubai and Singapore. For a majority of developing countries, unilateral trade liberalization has often been part and parcel of economic restructuring. This has often happened under the auspices of the World Bank and the IMF conditionality. It was also associated with a broader transformation of developing economies through privatization, deregulation and the passage from inward-oriented import substitution industrialization programmes to export-led and FDI-driven growth models.

In the case of Egypt, the 1990s witnessed the coinciding of multilateral and unilateral trade liberalization. On the one hand, the WTO/GATT 1994 obligations came into effect following the Marrakesh conference. On the other hand, Egypt adopted a SAP in 1990/91 with the heavy and continuous involvement of international financial institutions. Overall, the Egyptian economy witnessed a considerable reduction in trade barriers. Non-tariff barriers were progressively eliminated with very few and economically negligible exceptions. Tariffs were bound by 99.3 per cent of the tariff lines (99.2 per cent for non-agricultural products), which was higher than the average of developing countries (73 per cent).[8]

In a similar vein, the average weighted tariff rate was significantly reduced.[9] According to Ghoneim, the maximum applied tariff rates in Egypt (excluding tobacco, alcoholic beverages and automobiles) decreased from 110 per cent in 1986 to 80 per cent in 1993 than to 40 per cent for the period between 1998 and 2007, and finally to 30 per cent in 2008.[10]

However, trade liberalization remained scarce and varied hugely from one sector or industry to another.[11] The levels of protection for existing manufacturing sectors remained relatively high compared to other developing nations in the same income bracket. The tariff structure also demonstrated unmistakable escalation, furnishing highly effective protection for sectors.

In general, trade liberalization on a PTA basis did not lead to massive structural change in Egypt. Many inward-oriented manufacturing and service activities could continue along their path unchanged by making use of some form of increasingly non-tariff protection and subsidization. Nor were there any dramatic changes in export volumes or structure. Egypt's share of global trade declined as a matter of fact. In the 1990s exports shrank in absolute as well as in relative terms. Many explanations were given for the inability to reorient or restructure Egypt's exports in the 1990s. These included currency appreciation, continued protection of uncompetitive sectors, institutional export biases (customs management for example) and the lack of channels of coordination between the state and the private sector.

Few changes took place in the period after 2004. A big devaluation, introduction of export subsidies and the resumption of customs reduction under a business-friendly cabinet removed many of the anti-export biases. However, little happened to Egypt's export structure. Egypt remained dependent on raw materials, namely fuels, which retained an average share of 40 per cent of total merchandise exports during the 2004–10 period, which is unchanged from the same ratio in the 1990s.

Contrary to neoclassical economics, critical accounts of free trade have focused on the unevenness of bargaining power that has engulfed rules-based trade liberalization on a multilateral or bilateral basis.[12] Inspired by earlier versions of dependency, world system and imperialism theories, the central notion of this critique is the integration of smaller, poorer and less developed political units into a global division of labour characterized by uneven exchange and exploitation. Typically, less developed and developing economies are rule-takers (as well as price-takers on the market). Conversely, developed economies impose the terms of integration that usually maximize the sectors in which they enjoy competitive advantages (including intellectual property rights for high-technology industries and the liberalization of trade in services) while keeping clear of those in which developing economies (and least developed countries) enjoy an advantage (e.g. agriculture, textiles and apparel, and restrictive movement of labour).

Being a poor, small country (in terms of its share of world trade), Egypt has indeed been a rule-taker. However, there is little indication that external factors, be they through conditionality or world market forces, overwhelmed the ability of the Egyptian government (and the domestic interests its stands for) to shape the scope, scale and pace of trade liberalization. PTAs are a very good example of geopolitical arrangements that created both constraints and opportunities for Egypt in pursuing trade liberalization. Egypt's entry into PTAs may have had economic purposes to serve such as lowering adjustment costs or accessing more markets. However, they were also driven by broader geopolitical and security concerns that manifested Egypt's continuing importance in the post-Cold War era.

This was the case with the launch of the Barcelona Process between the EU and a number of North African and Mediterranean countries in 1995. The Barcelona Process launched three parallel tracks that showed the priorities set by the EU: economic (with the final goal of the establishment of a Euro-Mediterranean free trade area); political and cultural cooperation. The idea was an extension of the original premise on which the EC/EU itself was established: regional peace and stability through economic integration. This made sense, of course, in the context of a then ongoing peace process in the Middle East and the rising concerns of curbing illegal migration from North Africa and containing sociopolitical tensions within these countries (e.g. the Algerian civil war and the rising tide of Islamist terrorism).

In this context, PTAs were the result of geopolitical constraints and opportunities that were supposed by the Egyptian government and other parties to smooth its broader economic transformation by bringing about access to markets and the lowering of adjustment costs. PTAs shaped Egypt's path to trade liberalization. They proved helpful in controlling the pace, scope and scale of liberalization so as to minimize the adjustment costs for many sectors and hence avoid economic instability (rising unemployment, dying uncompetitive industries, etc.) and subsequent sociopolitical instability and upheaval.

The Egyptian government could employ the country's geopolitical weight in order to get its partners to accommodate such concerns by harnessing leverage and even extending financial and technical support. This was particularly so because Egypt's importance remained mainly geopolitical rather than economic. The Egyptian market was never so big that tempted European or American businesses to open it up for them. The overall outcome of the establishment of PTAs was hence shielding the Egyptian economy from the major shocks and transformations that can result from liberalization. The economy subsequently remained heavily inward-oriented. Exports never picked up or diversified significantly. The role of Egypt in the global division of labour did not undergo any serious changes. PTAs did not facilitate the rise of a state-business coalition that would aggressively pursue export growth and diversification. Rather, the state-business coalition that remained was one that prioritized the reduction of adjustment costs of trade liberalization obligations and their subsequent sociopolitical adverse repercussions. Private businesses either kept enjoying their domestic market shares or moved steadily into the non-tradable sector, namely land speculation, construction and real estate. This may explain the puzzling co-existence between PTAs and the country's dismal international trade performance and the perpetuation of its non-trade-based integration into the global economy.

Egypt's many PTAs

Euro-Egyptian Association Agreement

One main defining feature of Egypt's external trade since the mid-1990s is its Association Agreement with the EU that was negotiated within the framework of the Barcelona Process. The Barcelona conference in 1995 took place within a specific international context. On the one hand, the EU had emerged following the Maastricht Treaty of 1992 as a major economic (and potentially political) bloc in the post-Cold War era. On the other hand, there was a new world order, dominated by the USA as the single superpower, that entailed a novel rearrangement of the Middle East, with the launch of the Arab-Israeli peace process in 1990. It was then that the EU sought the redefinition of its complex relations with its southern neighbours in the Middle East and North African (MENA) region.[13] The main idea behind the Barcelona Process was the creation of an area of shared security, stability and prosperity primarily through economic integration. This was of course replicating what happened with the EC/EU itself following the Second World War. The Barcelona Process included three rubrics: political and security, economic and cultural cooperation. The economic was by far the most well defined. It revolved around the main goal of creating a Euro-Mediterranean free trade zone by 2010 (postponed multiple times, and now set for 2020). The free trade zone was meant to integrate the southern neighbours of the EU into its markets. Given the development differential between the two regions, the Barcelona Process included financial and technical aid packages with the aim of supporting the ability of MENA economies to adjust and adapt in face of anticipated heightened competition with increasing liberalization.

The road to the Euro-Mediterranean FTA was initially pursued through establishing bilateral FTAs between the EU on the one hand and Egypt, Tunisia, Morocco and Jordan on the other. This took place through the signing of bilateral Associations Agreements establishing tracks for gradual trade liberalization. Tunisia was the first to sign an Association Agreement with the EU in 1995 (entering into force in 1998), followed by Morocco in 1996 (came into force in 2000). Egypt waited until 2001. The Association Agreement came into effect in 2004. Parallel to the EU track, there were attempts, initiated ironically from the European side, at liberalizing trade among the four signatory Arab countries themselves. This was launched under the name of the Arab Mediterranean Free Trade Agreement in May 2001 at a ministerial meeting held in Agadir, Morocco. This track became known henceforth as the Agadir Process. It aimed at gradual trade liberalization between the four Arab countries together with the harmonization of their rules of origin and standards along the EU lines. The agreement entered into force in 2003 with the agreed tables of tradable goods and a timetable for trade liberalization. The plan was to phase 65 per cent of customs duties in 2003, upon the entry into force of the agreement, followed by 80 per cent and 90 per cent in 2004 and 2005 with January 2006 marked as the moment for full trade liberalization between the four countries.[14] Egypt also signed FTA agreements with EU partners including Turkey and the EFTA countries.

The Association Agreement included annexes of tables of goods in which trade was to be liberalized either upon the entry into force of the agreement or at a later stage. The Egyptians were the last to sign the agreement due to concerns about intensifying competition from European products in domestic markets. For a heavily inward-oriented manufacturing sector in the 1990s, many saw themselves at a disadvantage. The head of the Federation of Egyptian Industries voiced such concerns in the Egyptian parliament calling for a refusal to sign the agreement at all. Ironically, the head himself being a major exporter of carpets, he stood for the interests of the majority of businesses who feared cheap European products swamping the Egyptian market.[15] The then Minister of Industry was also opposed to the Association Agreement. He shared the same fears of de-industrialization. It is said that his opposition was the reason why he was prematurely removed in 1999.[16] The Europeans attempted to soothe the concerns and opposition of Egyptian businesses (and hence the concerns garnered by the government) through promising technical and financial assistance to local business sectors and enterprises so as to build their capacity to compete in exporting and domestic markets. This came in addition to agreeing with relaxed adjustment periods with the Egyptian side, and which were sometimes postponed at later phases upon the Egyptians' request.

The Association Agreement was by no means the first attempt at framing trade relations between the EU and Egypt, or more generally its southern neighbours. Egypt signed a trade agreement with the EC back in 1977 according to which Egyptian manufactured products could enter into European markets free of tariffs. Of course, similarly to other 'preferential' arrangements given by developed countries to developing ones, privileged entry did not extend to agricultural products and textiles, in which Egypt had some comparative advantage.[17] Even though this preferential access to European markets had hardly impacted the orientation of the

Egyptian industrial sector, its unreciprocated nature made Egyptian producers indifferent towards it. Conversely, the Association Agreement was based on reciprocal liberalization, which was far from being uncontroversial among Egyptian businesses, policymakers and intellectuals concerned with de-industrialization, welfare losses, higher unemployment and of dependency.

Eventually, of course, the Egyptian government could not afford to be left behind with Tunisia and Morocco signing and ratifying their Association Agreements. This way, it was feared that Egypt would lose its market share in Europe to the two countries that produce and export almost the same bundle of goods to the EU.

From 2004 onwards the Association Agreement with Egypt made a considerable impact. It put more competitive pressure on Egyptian businesses in the domestic market. However, the impact on the Egyptian domestic market should not be exaggerated. Egypt witnessed neither de-industrialization nor mass lay-offs because of intensifying competition.[18] This can be explained in terms of a number of factors. Some of these were structural (the fact that the EU countries produce higher value-added and usually more technologically intensive products while Egypt does not), while others were policy-based as the two parties agreed on various tables of goods and put sectors deemed 'sensitive' with long adjustment periods. This leads us to the rationale behind the Euro-Egyptian Association Agreements.

The Association Agreements and the hoped-for Euro-Mediterranean FTA were driven by geopolitics more than economics.[19] The creation of shared prosperity through economic liberalization was meant to deliver stability and security that could address issues such as illegal migration, trafficking and terrorism, which already appeared high on the agenda as early as the mid-1990s. The four MENA countries had small economies (in terms of GDP) compared to the EU and hence represented a limited market potential for European producers and/or investors. The EU on the other hand did not have much to offer them in traditional areas in which these countries had comparative advantage, especially agriculture that remained restrained by the Common Agricultural Policy. Fuels, the other major import from North Africa, namely from Egypt (as Libya and Algeria remained out of any arrangement) was not covered by the Association Agreements or the future FTA anyway.

Overall, the MENA countries proved incapable of competing with the newly accessing Central and Eastern European economies that had better skilled labour (i.e. the Czech Republic and Hungary) leading to a massive inflow of European FDIs and growing trade as part of the integration process. Of course, none of this applied to the North African countries, which had no prospect at all for accession at any future point, not allowing them even the benefit of the doubt (as was the case with Turkey).

The primacy of the political rubric implied that a country like Egypt could convince the Europeans to avoid measures that could undermine social or political stability. This played well into the hands of the Egyptian government, which sought to lower the adjustment costs if not to evade them altogether in some sectors that lacked efficiency or the capacity to compete (e.g. automotive). It proved to be successful on this front. This again came to express a certain pattern of state-business relations in Egypt that prioritized access to the domestic market by lowering adjustment costs and continued protection over accessing external markets. Alternatively, the EU-Egyptian Association Agreement did not prove to be as much of a success on the trade front. The share of Egyptian exports to the EU declined so did imports originating in the EU. According to Ghoneim, the percentage of Egyptian exports to the EU declined from 47 per cent (of total Egyptian exports) in 1995 to 36 per cent in 2008. The same trend applied to imports which declined from 40 per cent in 1995 (of total Egyptian imports) to 32 per cent in 2008.[20]

Egypt's unexplored road to Africa: COMESA

Attempts by the Egyptian government to effect regional integration in the 1990s were not confined to the Euro-Mediterranean or Arab regions. Rather, they extended into Sub-Saharan Africa. In 1998 Egypt joined the Common Market for Eastern and Southern Africa (COMESA). Originally established in 1994 COMESA had 19 member states by 2014.[21] COMESA was one of several subregional integration programmes launched almost simultaneously in East, West, Central and Southern Africa in the hope of gradually achieving some African economic unity.

From the Egyptian perspective, joining COMESA served the economic purpose of accessing markets, especially with the hoped-for export reorientation of the Egyptian economy in the 1990s. Politically, it must have also served aims of bolstering Egypt's position in the continent especially with the Nile Basin countries where trade creation and economic inter-dependency were viewed as tools for Egyptian diplomacy.

COMESA however has had a rather humble impact on Egypt's external trade profile. According to Elmorsy, citing the COMESA database in 2011, 'Egypt exports to COMESA countries recorded 5% of its total exports, and Egypt's imports from COMESA countries recorded only 1.5% of its total imports, only 3% from Egypt trade occurs with COMESA'.[22] Egypt's record was by no means an exception. COMESA has had a weak impact on trade creation among its member countries. Intra-COMESA exports stood for 10.7 per cent of total exports with intra-imports representing only 5.8 per cent of total imports in 2011.[23] This could be interpreted in the light of the dependency of the member countries on the production of similar, low value-added primary commodities that oriented towards the EU and the People's Republic of China.

The fact that the gradual phasing out of trade barriers between Egypt and other COMESA members did not translate into greater market access is revealing. Not only did this have to do with restraints related to economic structure or dependency on extraregional trade, but it also showed an inability on the Egyptian side to introduce institutional changes in order to explore exporting opportunities in COMESA. Egypt is significantly more industrialized compared to other COMESA members, not to mention that its service sectors are more advanced that most others. COMESA could have created the incentive to redirect some manufacturing and service sectors towards Africa and could have shielded Egyptian goods and service exporters, partly at least, from extraregional competition. Yet none of this happened due to the absence of a functioning state-business alliance that could have pursued a sustained strategy for the accessing of external markets in Africa.

The role of the state was crucial at early stages so as to collect and process information and escort Egyptian businesses into new markets and hence sharing part of the cost and risk of exploring them. In the absence of strong trade links between Egypt and African countries, joining COMESA was motivated by strategic concerns harboured by the government of Egypt. However, the government never possessed the institutional channels with private businesses, mainly exporters, or the policy tools so as to coordinate an expansion of trade with member states henceforth.

The exception that proves the rule: Qualified Industrial Zones

'Qualified Industrial Zones (QIZ) are designated geographic areas, within Egypt, that enjoy a duty-free status with the United States. Companies located within such zones are granted duty free access to the US markets, provided that they satisfy the agreed upon Israeli component, as per the pre-defined rules of origin'.[24]

The QIZ agreement was signed as a last-minute attempt at saving the share of Egyptian textiles and ready-made clothes exports in the US market followed the anticipated abolition of the quota system in 2005 following the expiry of the multi-fibre agreement. Egyptian exporters, who enjoyed quotas since the 1970s, stood to lose a lot in the face of Asian competition. They hence sought the preservation of their privileged access to US markets under a new arrangement.

The US Administration had already used QIZs as a tool for the normalization of economic relations in the Middle East, between Jordan and Israel. It was seen as a geostrategic priority for the USA to do the same with Egypt, which has had a peace treaty with Israel since 1979 but with little actual normalization of economic relations. Egyptian-Israeli peace was described as 'cold' and the US conditioning effective business partnership between Egyptian and Israeli private businesses could do the job. The QIZ proved to be politically controversial as nationalist circles among the intelligentsia mobilized against it. This was especially in the context of heightened violence in the occupied areas and a collapse in the peace process. Business interests prevailed nevertheless. The Egyptian government feared the loss of the share of Egyptian ready-made clothes exports, at a time when Egypt's overall share of the world market had been consistently declining in the face of intensifying Asian competition.

QIZ are an example of the way in which PTAs proved to be a means of dealing with the consequences of multilateral trade liberalization. They served the interests of Egyptian exporters that could mobilize through informal networks in the ruling party as well as through business associations and private chambers of commerce (the American Chamber of Commerce notably). QIZ remained an exception nevertheless as it corresponded already to existing export interests and proved an intersection between geopolitics and economics. This has been hardly paralleled in other PTAs that were driven by political concerns and had little impact on reorienting business activity or effective trade creation as has been the case with COMESA and the Greater Arab Free Trade Area (GAFTA).

The QIZ agreement has been something of an exception on one particular issue. The private business interests of Egyptian exporters appeared at an early stage and played a significant role in bringing about the agreement. However, apart from this exception, QIZ was yet another instance where geopolitics overrode economics as Egypt used its geostrategic weight to retain its share in US markets. The issue is that in the absence of outward-oriented business interests in other PTA arrangements, the Egyptian government had usually prioritized lowering the adjustment costs of liberalization instead of creating new markets for Egyptian exports.

The GAFTA

The last important PTA that Egypt joined in the 1990s is the GAFTA, to which Egypt acceded in 1998 with the aim of creating an Arab FTA by 2008 through gradual tariff phasing. Arab economic integration has a long, albeit disappointing, history. Initiated as early as 1964 under Lt-Col Gamal Abd al-Nasir (Nasser), calls for the creation of a common market served as part of the Arab unity project and an economic expression of Arab nationalism and pan-Arabism. However, deep political divisions and a series of geopolitical upheavals, especially with the conflict with Israel (1967–73), the Lebanese civil war (1975–90) and the Iraqi invasion of Kuwait (1990/91) all precluded any serious prospect of achieving integration.

The impediments to Arab economic integration were not just political. Instead, there were many economic structural factors that hindered any meaningful integration. In the aftermath of the first oil shock of 1973, a new economic regional reality emerged. The Arab world became divided between usually small and sparsely populated oil-rich countries on the one hand (the current Gulf Cooperation Council (GCC) countries plus Libya, Iraq and Algeria) and another group of poor and more densely populated ones (namely Egypt, Syria, Morocco, Tunisia and Yemen).

This new reality created forms of interdependency between the two camps. However, these did not often take the form of merchandise trade flows but rather of labour and capital movement. The rent resulting from higher international oil prices became subject to complex regional mechanisms of recycling. Typically, transfers took place from oil-rich to oil-poor countries through workers' remittances, intergovernmental aid and credit in addition to private investment. However, deep economic integration was not pursued despite the intensifying flows of labour and capital. As a matter of fact, small oil-rich monarchies were the ones to form a regional bloc known as the Gulf Cooperation Council in 1981, which excluded all the non-oil and non-monarchical states.

Hence, there were non-trade-related dynamics of regional integration. These usually came in the context of geostrategic arrangements following the second Gulf War and the readmission of Egypt into the League of Arab States after almost a decade of freezing its membership in the Arab League following the signing of the Camp David Accords with Israel in 1978. From 1990 onwards Egypt was viewed as crucial for Persian Gulf security against Iraqi and Iranian threats. Rent recycling implied intensified intergovernmental aid, which came in the form of net transfers to the Egyptian government as well as debt forgiveness from the GCC countries. It is noteworthy that Egypt was rewarded through the cancellation of 50 per cent of its massive foreign debt and with the rescheduling of the other half.[25]

Improved macroeconomic performance through the direct engagement of the IMF and the World Bank in managing public finances and the economy facilitated an expanding portfolio of GCC investments in Egypt. Gulf investors sought investment in real estate, tourism and financial services.[26] Despite the fact that aid and investment did have a positive impact on Egypt's balance of payments, they hardly had an impact on merchandise trade, and especially on the prospect of raising Egyptian exports to the rich GCC markets. Most Gulf investments flowed into non-tradable sectors.

The oil-rich GCC countries (as well as Libya) depended on Egypt's large skilled and unskilled labour in the wake of the massive inflows of oil revenues in the 1970s. Hundreds of thousands of Egyptian workers and professionals ended up in these markets thus relieving the mounting pressure over the domestic labour in Egypt and contributing to the rise of a new middle class that depended on the stream of remittances. This has been no doubt a robust feature of regional complementarity and integration.[27] However, for a region (MENA) that was almost exclusively a supplier of raw materials in the global division of labour, there was little room for industrial integration. Most Arab countries had underdeveloped manufacturing sectors. Most relied on the exporting of raw material: oil, natural gas, phosphates, etc. Moreover, the significant jump in domestic consumption in oil-rich economies invited extraregional imports of goods and services. Furthermore, oil-rich countries had to invest their massive petro-dollar gains in the 1970s, the 1990s and especially after the 2008 surge in prices, in well-developed capital markets in the USA, Europe and East Asia. Thus, it makes more sense to perceive the dense economic ties between Egypt and the GCC countries as those of dependency rather than interdependency. In such a context, little space was given for a joint strategy of regional integration that depended on industrial and service upgrading into higher value-added sectors.

In the context of expanding PTAs, the GAFTA was launched within the boundaries of the Arab League. It achieved the goal of shallow integration through gradual tariff removal over ten years, ending in 2008. Egypt had almost removed all tariff barriers with GAFTA members by 2005. Yet the impact of GAFTA had very little effect in creating trade or raising the share of intra-GAFTA trade in the total trade of its members. This was interpreted in many ways, some of which were structural like the limited weight of industry in most GAFTA members' economies and the similarity in products. However, there were also other institutional factors such as the lack of precise definitions of which products were to be excluded from trade liberalization in a way that led to 16 members submitting a list of 600 commodities and goods to be

Amr Adly

exempted from free trade regulation.[28] The GAFTA also lacked clear mechanisms of monitoring and enforcement, thus providing the opportunity for some member states to delay trade liberalization beyond agreed deadlines.

Overall, the GAFTA did not differ in any substantial way from other PTAs that Egypt engaged. It was a shallow form of integration that comprised no institutional or regulatory component of integration. It was confined to only phasing out tariffs instead of including other non-tariff and technical barriers. Moreover, it did not extend to services or the regulation of labour and capital movement at regional level, where most of the action was in fact happening. Again, external factors here failed to provide the incentives or leverage to change the dynamics of the inward-oriented state-business coalition that prioritized the reduction of the costs of liberalization rather than coordinating an assault on foreign markets.

Conclusion: PTAs and feigned reorientation

What could explain the rather humble export performance throughout the same period and hence resolve the seeming puzzle of PTAs being signed without a successful outwardly reorientation of the Egyptian economy? Three major factors main explain this path of feigned integration: the first is Egypt's integration into the world economy on a non-trade basis; the second is the use of Egypt's geopolitical weight in order to effectively subject the scope, scale and pace of trade liberalization to priorities of internal social and political stability and hence avoiding any massive upsetting of existing inwardly-oriented economic activities and; third as a by-product of the previous two factors: the state-business coalition that influenced trade policy making and implementation was more focused on preserving access to domestic markets than accessing new ones abroad.

First, Egypt's attempts at reintegration into the world division of labour after almost two decades of import substitution industrialization in the 1957–74 period, targeted the securing of capital inflows in the form of FDIs, credit and aid in addition to workers' remittances. The critical link was the oil boom of 1973 and the insertion of the MENA as the world's major oil producer. Althoug not a big exporter, Egypt had to rely on intraregional rent recycling through aid, cheap loans, investments from the Gulf countries and transfers from Egyptian workers. This worked on many fronts. The Egyptian economy did receive large sums of dollars in many guises in the 1974–86 period that were almost all related directly or indirectly to oil. The problem of course is that it made Egypt too vulnerable to oil price fluctuations. Indeed, with the oil glut of 1986, the Egyptian government reached the brink of bankruptcy in 1989. Yet despite the fact that oil prices did not witness a major shock in the 1990s, it was still geopolitics assuming the form of capital inflows that saved Egypt's economy and government. In return for joining the coalition for the liberation of Kuwait in 1990/91, Egypt received a massive debt relief of almost 50 per cent of the huge external debts of around US $45 billion within the frame of the 'Paris Club'. The GCC countries poured money in the form of aid to the government in addition to debt forgiveness on their part.

The debt relief happened against a background of IMF and World Bank involvement for the restructuring of the Egyptian economy towards a more export-oriented, FDI-attractive and private sector dominated economy. However, all three components did prove to go side by side. Merchandise and service trade remained a weak link compared in how Egypt is reintegrated into the world economy. FDIs remained as humble and significantly concentrated in extractive industries that dominated Egypt's exports throughout the past three decades. Little FDIs went into other productive goods or service sectors.

Overall, Egypt's PTAs proved to shield the interests of an inward-oriented economy by reducing its adjustment cost and by allowing the rise of new non-tariff protection methods in addition to the relocation into non-tradable sectors altogether.

Notes

1 A. F. Ghoneim (2012) 'Investigating the Relationship between Trade and Poverty', *Economic and Trade Policies in the Arab World: Employment, Poverty Reduction and Integration*', 11: 35.

2 World Trade Organization (2016) World Trade Statistical Review, Geneva: WTO, p 135–36. Available at www.wto.org/english/res_e/statis_e/wts2016_e/wts2016_e.pdf.

3 World Bank (2017) World Bank Data: Exports of Goods and Services (% of GDP), Egypt. Available at https://data.worldbank.org/indicator/NE.EXP.GNFS.ZS?locations=EG.

4 For a more thorough discussion on deep integration and its impact on development and economic institutions see the following on the impact of EU enlargement on acceding Eastern and Central European countries: L. Bruszt and G. A. McDermott (eds) (2014) *Levelling the Playing Field: Transnational Regulatory Integration and Development*, Oxford: Oxford University Press; and U. Sedelmeier (2012) 'Is Europeanisation through Conditionality Sustainable? Lock-in of Institutional Change after EU Accession', *West European Politics, 35*(1): 20–38.

5 J. D. Sachs, A. Warner, A. Åslund and S. Fischer (1995) 'Economic Reform and the Process of Global Integration', *Brookings Papers on Economic Activity*, 1: 1–118.

6 J. N. Bhagwati and A. O. Krueger (1995) *The Dangerous Drift to Preferential Trade Agreements*, Washington, DC: American Enterprise Institute.

7 D. Medvedev (2010) 'Preferential Trade Agreements and their Role in World Trade', *Review of World Economics, 146*(2): 199–222.

8 WTO (2017) Egypt: Tariff Profile. Available at http://stat.wto.org/TariffProfile/WSDBTariffPFView.aspx?Language=E&Country=EG.

9 H. Kheir-El-Din and S. El-Shawarby (2000) 'Trade and Foreign Exchange Regime in Egypt', *Economic Research Forum Working Papers*, no. 2034, November.

10 Ghoneim, 'Investigating the Relationship between Trade and Poverty', p. 31.

11 A. Mishrif (2010) *Investing in the Middle East: The Political Economy of European Direct Investment in Egypt*, London: I. B. Tauris, p. 243.

12 C. Dowlah (2004) *Backwaters of Global Prosperity: How Forces of Globalization and GATT/WTO Trade Regimes Contribute to the Marginalization of the World's Poorest Nations*, University Park, PA: Penn State Press, p.116–20.

13 A. Galal and B. M. Hoekman (eds) (1997) *Regional Partners in Global Markets: Limits and Possibilities of the Euro-Med Agreements*, Washington, DC: Brookings Institution Press.

14 M. Tolba and E. M. Mohamed (2013) *A Study on the Agadir Agreement as the Gateway to Establish a Pan-Arab Free Trade Area: Assessment of Agadir's Trade Effects*, doctoral dissertation, KDI School of Public Policy and Management.

15 Sulaymān, S. (1999) *State and Industrial Capitalism in Egypt*, vol. 21, Cairo: American University in Cairo Press.

16 A. Adly (2012) *State Reform and Development in the Middle East: Turkey and Egypt in the Post-Liberalization Era*, London: Routledge.

17 Dowlah, *Backwaters of Global Prosperity*, p. 83.

18 M. Said and A. Elshennawy (2010) 'The Impact of Trade Liberalization on Manufacturing Employment and Wages in Egypt 1990–2007', *International Research Journal of Finance and Economics*, 46: 138–59.

19 M. Langan (2015) 'Budget Support and Africa-European Union Relations: Free Market Reform and Neo-colonialism?' *European Journal of International Relations, 21*(1): 101–21.

20 Ghoneim, p. 46.

21 S. S. Elmorsy (2015) 'Determinants of Trade Intensity of Egypt with COMESA Countries', *Bandung: Journal of the Global South*, 2(1): 5.

22 Ibid., p. 16.

23 Cited in Elmorsy 2015, p.15.

24 www.qizegypt.gov.eg/About_QIZ.aspx).

25 K. Ikram (2006) 'The Egyptian Economy, 1952–2000: Performance, Policies', *Issues*, p. 150.

Amr Adly

26 Ashraf Mishrif (2010) *Investing in the Middle East: The Political Economy of European Direct Investment in Egypt*, London: I.B. Tauris, London, p. 223.
27 A. Galal and B. M. Hoekman (eds) (2003) *Arab Economic Integration: Between Hope and Reality*, Washington, DC: Brookings Institution Press.
28 Mishrif, p. 222.

29

The African Union and the European Union

Trade reciprocity and/or economic development?

Mark Langan

Historically, the European Union's (EU) trade and development policy has dealt separately with North African countries (the Maghreb) and those of Sub-Saharan Africa (SSA). This state of affairs dates back to the post-colonial settlement when the then European Economic Community (EEC) dealt with the Associated African States and Madagascar (AASM) as an assemblage of SSA countries within the Yaoundé Accords (1963–75). This agreement was succeeded by the Lomé Conventions (1975–2000) which maintained the SSA character of 'Association', albeit as part of the creation of the wider African, Caribbean and Pacific (ACP) bloc. North African countries such as Tunisia and Egypt remained outside of this preferential trading system. Not only did they not enjoy the low-tariff and 'non-reciprocal' trade structures of Lomé, but they also did not qualify for the European Development Fund. The current ACP-EU Cotonou Agreement (2000–20) maintains this differentiated treatment of Maghreb and SSA nations both in terms of trade negotiations and aid links.

It should be noted, however, that in more recent times Maghreb nations have signed individual Association Agreements with the EU – for instance, Tunisia in 1998 and Morocco in 2000. This has paved the way for negotiation of Deep and Comprehensive Free Trade Agreements (DCFTAs) between North African parties and the EU. Meanwhile, SSA countries as part of regional blocs such as the Economic Community of West African States (ECOWAS) are negotiating Economic Partnership Agreements (EPAs) with the EU. Interestingly, there are major parallels between the DCFTAs and the EPAs in terms of their 'reciprocal' trade content. African nations – whether SSA or Maghreb – are expected to offer low-tariff access to Europe in exchange for low-tariff access into the EU marketplace. Both the DCFTAs and the EPAs, therefore, have raised concerns among local politicians and civil society organizations on the basis that they will engender deindustrialization and food insecurity, namely that premature tariff liberalization will lead to import-flooding of cheap European products at the expense of domestic producers and workers. Such fears are rooted in historical evidence regarding the impact of prior instances of tariff liberalization. Kenya, for instance, suffered greatly as it liberalized imports of textiles from the EEC in the early 1990s. As part of structural adjustment

335

Mark Langan

programmes, the Kenyan government allowed the importation of cheap second-hand clothing from the EEC, leading to the loss of around 70,000 jobs in the domestic cotton textiles chain.[1]

In the time frame of the DCFTA/EPA negotiations, the European Commission has also begun to focus more thoroughly on the African Union (AU)[2] as an institution with which to collaborate on matters concerning peace, security and trade and economic development. Notably, the Joint Africa-EU Joint Strategy signed in 2007 marked a discernible shift in the European Commission's approach.[3] Its political and economic focus on the AU marked a departure from its historical focus on the ACP Secretariat as the primary interlocutor for Africa-EU relations. This seeming volte-face is all too apparent in the context of negotiations for a successor to the Cotonou Agreement. Certain EU member states seem to be pushing for the abandonment of the ACP grouping altogether.[4] Indeed, some officials argue that the AU would appear a more natural partner in the post-2020 period. Moreover, they argue that in the timeframe of the universal UN Sustainable Development Goals (SDGs) that it would be more fitting for the EU to have a single approach to least developed countries within its trade outlook.[5] The AU, in this scenario, would be the chief collective interlocutor for African countries. It is in this context of the Joint Africa-EU Strategy and the post-Cotonou negotiations that this chapter examines the trading relationship between the EU and the AU. It does this via a parallel examination of both the DCFTA/EPA negotiations to examine the likely impact of 'reciprocal' trade structures in SSA and the Maghreb. Thereafter, the chapter considers the potential agency of AU officials to effectively resist reciprocal trade structures. In so doing, the chapter recalls the work of Kwame Nkrumah, the founding President of an independent Ghana, who predicted that only a pan-African response to European trade policy would augur effective change away from (neo)colonial patterns of exchange and production.

The moral economy of EU trade reciprocity as embodied within the EPA agenda

The European Commission strives to present EU trade policy as being fully commensurate with pro-poor development objectives. As part of sustaining Europe's apparent 'normative power', the EU institutions make clear that trade with developing countries is a means towards the desired ends of equitable growth and shared prosperity.[6] Europe, according to this 'development' discourse, is a benevolent partner driven by norms relating to the well-being of poorer peoples. This discursive marriage of trade and development within EU official text is especially pronounced in the case of African nations. The European Commission has made clear that its insistence on trade reciprocity is fully compatible with pro-poor economic development. In fact, the European Commission insists that its primary motivation is to stimulate African countries to become more competitive within globalised markets. The push for trade liberalization and 'reciprocity' is not a device through which to promote European producers' access to emerging new markets and to raw materials. Instead, it is a benevolent policy intervention aimed at helping poorer nations to realize their full economic potential within an increasingly interconnected global economy.

Notably, the European Commission has vigorously insisted that the EPAs in SSA contexts are in alignment with the Cotonou Agreement's vision of improving human development. An EPA 'factsheet' from February 2017, for example, insists that:

> the Economic Partnership Agreements between the EU and African, Caribbean and Pacific (ACP) countries aim at fostering the smooth and gradual integration of the ACP partners

into the world economy and ultimately contribute, through trade and investment, to sustainable development and poverty reduction.[7]

This discursive emphasis on ACP countries' smooth and development-friendly integration into a globalized (and liberalized) world market is repeated time and again. Another recent example, a leaflet published by the European Commission in November 2016, makes clear their view that 'the deals enable ACP countries to grow their economies in a sustainable way, and raise their citizens' standard of living'. Specifically, the leaflet states that 'EPAs help ACP countries to compete. That helps them expand their economies. New industries spring up, creating jobs'. This narrative of 'win-win' trade co-operation aimed at enhancing ACP competitiveness is cemented by a final quotation from EU Trade Commissioner, Cecilia Malmström, who remarks that 'trade helps to spur economic growth and development. By doing so it has already helped lift millions of people out of poverty. And with EPAs we're preparing the ground to continue that process'.[8]

Through such discursive practices, the European Commission has constructed what can be termed the 'moral economy' of trade reciprocity in relation to the EPAs.[9] Namely, it has embedded soon-to-be trade deals within moral and ethical norms pertaining to 'win-win' economic growth, industry expansion, job creation and poverty reduction through trickle-down free trade. Its pursuit of trade liberalization is therefore legitimized as a contribution to global development goals rather than as being seen as a neocolonial imposition on economies whose domestic enterprises are already struggling to compete with cheap imports from the EU member states. As Sayer reminds us, however, there can often be considerable ruptures between stated ethical intent within constituted 'moral economies' and their actual outcomes in terms of material impact on supposed beneficiaries.[10] Aware of this, the European Commission takes care to evidence the ostensible gains of the EPAs with reference to the 'voices' of ACP countries' citizenry themselves. Not only are the EPAs deemed to be pro-poor within the text of key EU officials such as Malmström, but voices from the subaltern are presented as further proof that the EU's trade policy is commensurate with moral goals pertaining to poverty alleviation. For example, a European Commission publication entitled *Economic Partnership Agreements: African, Caribbean and Pacific Voices Speak Up for Trade and Development* quotes a wide array of ACP business people and workers regarding their apparent support for the trade deals. A Mauritanian business leader, for example, is quoted in support of the argument that the EPAs stimulate ACP nations' competitiveness and standing within global markets. In this case the EPAs are deemed to be a tool for diversification and value addition:

> the EPA framework has provided Mauritius with the opportunity to develop from a mono-crop to an industry-based economy. Hopefully, the EPA will now give Mauritius the opportunity to develop its service sector as well. I believe the EPA will be a good tool for my country, as it will surely expand our trade with the EU. The new rules of origin for textile and apparel, that is, the single transformation, have helped to maintain our exports to the EU despite the financial crisis. Without the EPA the future might be quite bleak.[11]

The discursive purpose of such publications is readily discernible – responding to overt criticism of the EPAs levied by an array of ACP politicians, private sector agencies, trade unionists and workers. Moreover, in terms of an internal audience, such publications seek to mollify voices of dissent within the European Parliament, and among EU civil society. The statements from ACP business representatives seek to answer criticisms that the EPAs will lock ACP nations into asymmetrical trade patterns. The quoted narrative, for instance, emphasizes that value addition and diversification can take place even within reciprocal trading structures embodied by the EPAs. In other words, the legal status of the EPAs will give foreign investors the confidence to place capital into export-oriented sectors in ACP countries (such as banana production or textile manufacturing) secure in the knowledge that the EPA guarantees them low-tariff access to European consumers.

The counter-argument, however, voiced by a great many ACP institutions and policy actors is that this safeguarding of market access for export-oriented sectors will not compensate for the economic damage done to import-competing sectors in ACP countries, such as poultry or tomato production. The EPAs – even with the inclusion of a limited sensitive goods basket – will fail to safeguard ACP countries' need to levy restrictive tariffs against EU private sector production in vital areas.[12] Already the West African poultry sector, for example, is bracing itself for near collapse upon the regional enactment of a full EPA. Industry spokespeople lament the fact that their national parliaments will be unable to raise tariffs against European poultry production. They argue that their national economies require flexibility to be able to levy higher protectionist tariffs where necessary to safeguard the productive potential of domestic poultry farms.[13] Some in fact call for an outright ban on frozen chicken imports, given that they are often sold below production cost as EU industry seek to dispose of chicken parts (such as wings) which many European consumers spurn.[14] The lock-in of relatively low tariffs under an EPA will thus lead to industry retraction, job losses and loss of spill-over benefits for local communities, according to this 'EPA-sceptic' narrative. For example, a female poultry farm owner in Cameroon recounts the damage done to her business by the importation of cheap frozen chicken from the EU:

> My customers bought this cheap meat. I could no longer sell what I produced and lost everything. I miss the money that I earned. My children can no longer go to school regularly because we can't afford the school fees. I am hopeful again since ACDIC [a Cameroonian civil society coalition] has made the government reduce the import of frozen chickens. I am ready. I want to start up my poultry farm again and want to be able to pay back my loan. But it is hard to get together the start-up capital.[15]

The 'moral economy' of trade reciprocity embodied by EPAs is thereby contested in relation to the impact on domestic industry and upon poverty reduction. Indeed, the recent intervention of Cameroonian civil society to effect quantitative reductions upon imported chicken would not be possible within the strict legal confines of a regional EPA. The Cameroonian government would only be able to levy tariffs up to an agreed level under the ECOWAS Common External Tariff (CET) at around 35 per cent (well short of a possible 99 per cent tariff allowed under World Trade Organization regulations). This is despite the fact that poultry is included within the regional EPA's so-called sensitive goods basket in which certain vulnerable commodity lines are exempted from the deep tariff liberalization demanded by the EU across a majority of product lines.[16]

Unfortunately, this stark picture of deindustrialization and job losses is also underscored within the European Commission's own Sustainability Impact Assessments (SIAs). The SIAs point out that there is the potential for diversification among export-oriented sectors (for instance, the expansion of the floriculture industry). Nevertheless, they also indicate that ACP countries will experience economic hardship upon the implementation of the EU's free trade deals. In the context of aforementioned West Africa, for example, that region's SIA indicates that essential agricultural sectors including poultry, onions, beef and potatoes will suffer greatly upon import flooding of subsidized produce from the European member states.[17] This will lead to domestic industry retraction and subsequent job losses – combined with tax revenue decline within the West African countries themselves, quite contrary to the discourse espoused by EU negotiators. Moreover, Patel confirms that EU subsidies (under the Common Agricultural Policy) will continue to pose a challenge to otherwise competitive West African sectors such as dairy and millet rice.[18] Contrary to the theoretical ideals of 'comparative advantage' in free trade networks and 'win-win' trickle-down economic growth, the EPAs in such circumstances instead engender a period of economic stagnation, decreases in employment and lost tariff and tax returns for former colonies in SSA. Worryingly, this stark picture of poverty perpetuation is also seen in the case of the Maghreb and the DCFTA agenda.

DCFTAS and the moral economy of trade reciprocity in the Maghreb

The European Commission has similarly constructed a 'moral economy' of trade reciprocity in terms of DCFTAs. Again, the European Commission takes great pains to insulate itself from internal and external criticism. Notably, former European Commission President Barroso remarked in 2013 that the push for DCFTAs and a free trade zone in the case of Morocco would underpin a 'win-win' relationship that is conducive to both the social and economic needs of this former French and Spanish colony:

> The agreement will deepen our economic relations in the interests of our citizens, our businesses, our societies. We will all be direct beneficiaries of this new, more dynamic and competitive framework. It will provide better access to the market on both sides and improve the business environment so that it becomes more predictable and more stable. Together, we are laying the groundwork for a future common economic area between the EU and Morocco, and I am pleased that our partnership is being strengthened in such an important way.[19]

This development-oriented language has been repeated in the case of aforementioned Tunisia. The European Commission makes it clear that the talks are 'guided by the principles of asymmetry and progressiveness in favour of Tunisia'.[20] Moreover, it emphasizes that aid monies will be used to soften the potential blow of trade liberalization – 'the EU will support the negotiations and implementation of the future agreement with an important package of accompanying measures'.[21] This pro-development discourse is also underpinned within the joint EU-Tunisia Action Plan. The document, signed in the mid-2000s, firmly insists that EU trade and aid policies will be guided by the need to achieve sustainable development:

> The Action Plan, which by virtue of its flexibility can be adapted to Tunisia's needs and specificities, will also support the development and implementation of policies designed to promote economic growth, employment and social cohesion, reduce poverty and protect the environment, thereby contributing to the long-term objective of sustainable development.[22]

As with the EPAs in SSA, EU officials thereby make it clear that their trade outlook is guided by development norms, and not by a mercantilist desire to lock developing former colonies into (neo)colonial patterns of production and exchange. In alignment with the values of the Post-Washington Consensus and (now) the SDGs, the EU member states will ostensibly ensure that economic policy is married to the social needs of poorer citizens in Africa.

It is important to emphasize, however, that this pro-development and pro-poor discourse is contested by a great number of political actors and civil society bodies, whether in the Maghreb itself or within EU member states. With parallels to the EPAs in SSA – many are concerned about the potential impact of import flooding for predominantly agricultural economies, and for nascent industrialisation in sectors such as textiles. For instance, the anti-poverty charity War on Want explains that the EU's completion of DCFTAs with several Maghreb nations is aimed at an eventual Euro-Mediterranean Free Trade Area (EMFTA). They warn of the development consequences of DCFTAs and the EMFTA itself: 'the proposed creation of a Euro-Mediterranean Free Trade Area is predicted to cause the near collapse of the manufacturing sectors of Egypt, Morocco, Algeria and Tunisia and massive contractions in Syria, Jordan and Lebanon, with the loss of 3.4 million industrial jobs'.[23] Dimitrova and Novakova confirm that this concern about the impact of premature trade liberalization is mirrored by domestic civil society actors within Tunisia and Morocco:

> Local actors argue that the current circumstances are unfavourable for free trade because of the lack of subsidies for local producers and limited competitiveness on the international market. While increased trade volumes might be seen as an improved choice for consumers on both sides, the advantageous position of EU producers might be detrimental to local competition and hence indirectly curb creation of employment in given sectors. After a decade of progressive liberalisation of trade in goods, the EU continues to run a trade surplus both with Morocco and Tunisia.[24]

This sentiment is echoed within a report by the Rotterdam-based research and consultancy company Ecorys on its engagement with civil society, as part of a workshop held in Tunisia on the Euro-Mediterranean Partnership and trade ties. The report cites a concerned citizen who points to the rise of the informal economy as trade liberalization leads to job losses in more traditional sectors:

> Regarding [the] informal economy: what effects did the Association Agreement and neighbourhood policy produce in terms of creation/destruction of companies, jobs and informal economy growth? Did you take into account this expected growth of this precarious informal economy with its consequences on poverty and the economy? You spoke about jobs redistribution. The risk is that more jobs will fall into the informal economy, what are the measures to be taken to avoid an increasing informal sector? Moreover, the expected job redistribution would imply a restructuring of the labour market for which Tunisia is not yet ready.[25]

Such 'DCFTA-sceptic' discourse is repeated time and again with regard to concerns about the impact of premature trade liberalization for jobs in import-competing sectors, whether in agriculture or in nascent manufacturing in the Maghreb.

Furthermore, the European Commission's own sponsored SIAs indicate that North African signatories will experience retraction in key industries, including textiles, leather and carpets – as well as in agricultural sectors central to food security. For instance, the SIA on the likely impact of a DCFTA in the Moroccan situation finds that:

> In the agricultural segment of the economy, the grains and crops sector is expected to lose most due to the DCFTA (2.7 per cent reduction in output in the long run), which is largely triggered by the alignment of NTMs [non-tariff measures] between the EU and Morocco. Leather goods is the industrial sector in Morocco that is expected to be negatively affected by the DCFTA as output is estimated to contract by 3.6 per cent in the long run.[26]

The African Union and the European Union

This negative picture in the case of vital sectors such as leather is underscored within the SIA for the Tunisian DCFTA. The document finds that the Tunisian leather industry will contract by around 11 per cent due to competition from cheaper European competition.[27]

Interestingly, the SIA finds that vegetable exports from Tunisia to the EU marketplace will increase as a result of lower tariffs. Only indirectly, however, does the document note that non-tariff barriers (or what it terms technical barriers to trade) are likely to inhibit any major gains which might theoretically derive from lower tariffs in agricultural lines. In the case of West Africa, for instance, a wholesale ban has recently been enforced upon Ghanaian chilli due to allegations of pest infestation among such cargoes.[28] Ghanaian vegetable producers report that this ban has resulted in suicides among farmers who had sought to diversify into chilli farming in order to take advantage of some of the ostensible benefits of the interim EPA signed with the EU in 2008.[29] Given the challenges which inherently face small-scale farmers in meeting the EU's labyrinthine sanitary and phytosanitary standards, it is more than likely that Tunisian agriculturalists will not in truth reap the rewards promised within the SIA sponsored by the European Commission. The export of vegetables, meanwhile, does much to satiate food security requirements within the EU member states while doing little to improve the food security situation of poorer consumers in Tunisia itself. In this respect, the DCFTA would tend to perpetuate (neo)colonial patterns of trade whereby the EU exports value-added goods (such as leather) while importing raw materials or agricultural produce vital to European industry and to the food security of the EU citizenry. This would not appear to be a truly 'win-win' outcome for both parties.

Indeed DCFTAs would appear to lock Tunisia, Morocco and other DCFTA candidates in the Maghreb into asymmetric and (neo)colonial trade and aid relations. It is perhaps necessary to stress here that in both SSA and the Maghreb, the European Commission has furnished governments with aid money to ostensibly improve their trade capacities. In countries such as Uganda, Ghana and Tunisia, EU budget support has gone towards supporting governance capacity in vital ministries which simultaneously are engaged in highly controversial trade negotiations with the EU member states with regards to EPAs and DCFTAs. Moreover, the European Commission has promised that signatories of FTA deals will benefit from enhanced Aid for Trade to lubricate partners' transition into globalized free markets. In the West African context, for instance, EU officials have pledged €6.5 billion in aid money under the EPA Development Programme (EPADP) on the assumption that the West African nations fully implement the conditions of the free trade deal.[30] Such money will ostensibly assist signatories to upgrade existing industries and to diversify into new sectors in the aftermath of tariff dismantling. However, the lions' share of Aid for Trade money does not trickle down to the small and medium-sized enterprises (SMEs) who might genuinely constitute the 'engine of growth'. Instead, most of this money is spent on lucrative infrastructural projects, often fulfilled by European consortia, and enabling foreign investors to more easily extract value from the region via newer ports and roads. The ability of Aid for Trade to transform EPAs – or DCFTAs – into genuine vehicles for economic development and poverty reduction is thereby brought into critical light.[31] Meanwhile, the provision of budget support among other aid modalities is seen to sway elite African policy officials towards acquiescence in the case of free trade negotiations with the EU metropole.[32] In this situation it is now illustrative to consider the role of the AU in liaising with the EU for economic development and private sector growth strategies. Moreover, it is important to consider the potential agency of the AU and its member states to resist trade reciprocity in the light of growing concerns surrounding import flooding, deindustrialization and food insecurity both north and south of the Sahara.

Mark Langan

The AU-EU partnership and agency for progressive action to contest 'trade reciprocity'

As noted in the introduction, the EU is increasingly focusing on the AU as a locus for both political and economic interaction. The Joint Africa-EU Strategy, adopted at the Lisbon Summit in December 2007, identifies security, democracy, and economic growth combined with private sector development as vital sites for cross-party co-operation. Moreover, EU member state representatives have debated whether the AU Commission – rather than the ACP Secretariat – ought to be the focal point of future trade discussions between the European Commission and African developing countries. In the current timeframe of negotiations for a post-Cotonou framework, some EU representatives indicate a preference for retiring the ACP bloc and in focusing squarely on the AU – and on the universality of the SDGs. They believe that the ACP group is effectively moribund and a hangover from the colonial relationships of powers such as France, Portugal and – soon to be – Brexit Britain.

In this context, it is illustrative to consider how the statements of the AU-EU partnership reiterate the 'moral economy' of trade reciprocity. In keeping with bilateral negotiations for the EPAs in sub-regions of SSA and the DCFTAs in the Maghreb, the Joint Africa-EU Strategy notably reiterates the EU's commitment to 'win-win' economic co-operation as a means towards poverty eradication. More interestingly, it embraces a discourse of value addition and diversification away from dependence on (neo)colonial patterns of raw material exchange:

> One of the priorities of the Africa-EU partnership will be to help Africa improve its productive capacities, move up the value-added scale and become less dependent on raw materials and simple processed products, which in the long term is the best way to avoid a deterioration of the terms of trade and participate in, and benefit from, the global economy. Africa and the EU will also, together with other international partners, work to promote fair trade.[33]

Crucially, the document explicitly hails the EPAs and the DCFTAs as a means towards deeper trade integration between the blocs, which is conducive to African countries' attainment of prosperity within a globalized world market economy:

> Africa-EU cooperation will be underpinned by stronger bilateral development-oriented trading relationships between Africa and the EU: (i) through the implementation of Economic Partnership Agreements (EPAs) with African EPA regions (West Africa, Central Africa, Eastern and Southern Africa and the Southern African grouping), which involve the RECs and other African organisations, and the implementation of the EU Mediterranean Free Trade Agreement with the countries of North Africa.[34]

This key statement of intent to work towards a fairer trading system – built on EPAs and DCFTAs – is cemented in more recent publications. For instance, the most recent (fifth) AU-EU Summit, which took place in November 2017 in Abidjan, Côte d'Ivoire, focused on youth employment and sustainable business with an eye on the SDGs and the post-2015 consensus. Here, the EU pledges to assist African countries to achieve economic development that is conducive to the creation of jobs and the improvement of livelihoods for younger members of their growing populations. Specifically, the EU states that it will pay particular attention to the development of viable agro-processing value chains in Africa within the overarching EU trade agreements such as EPAs and DCFTAs:

342

The African Union and the European Union

> We will work together to seize market opportunities for African food production and sustainable social and ecological livelihoods, notably through development of sustainable and fair value chains, and through the applicable EU trade arrangements. To this end, we will build capacities to access to markets focusing on young farmers, small holders and family farmers, support partnership frameworks, strengthen AU-EU agriculture business relations through an AU-EU agribusiness platform and promote the full implementation of EPAs.[35]

As explored in the preceding sections, however, it is clear that the EPAs and the DCFTAs are not commensurate with poverty alleviation goals – whether those that are embedded in the Cotonou Agreement, the Maghreb Association Agreements, or within the AU-EU Joint Plan and subsequent summits. Nor are these agreements conducive to securing jobs and livelihoods within agricultural value chains or diversification into nascent manufacturing sectors. On the contrary, premature trade liberalization threatens existing economic success stories in sectors including (but not limited to) millet rice, poultry, textiles, leather production and tomato agro-processing. Even in the case of EPAs where a limited sensitive goods basket is permitted for certain vulnerable commodities, the maximum tariff level is not sufficient to meaningfully protect local producers. Meanwhile, ostensible gains to be made in vegetable exports fail to account for stringent non-tariff barriers which will effectively strangle the opportunities that might otherwise accrue to producers in sectors such as chilli farming (as per farmer suicides in the case of Ghana). Aid for Trade money – for instance those promised under the EPADP – also fail to marry trade liberalization to ostensible development norms within the 'moral economy' of trade reciprocity. Indeed, the lions' share of such money is directed towards large infrastructure programmes whose arteries do more to serve resource extraction from African recipients than to genuinely stimulate the SMEs that might constitute the 'engine of growth'.

In this context, it becomes imperative to consider potential strategies through which the AU – as a growing locus for Africa-EU co-operation – might galvanize resistance to premature trade liberalization and reciprocity on the grounds of its likely regressive impact on poorer peoples in the African continent. Moreover, action at the level of the AU is not only important given the shifting attentions of the European Commission (away from the ACP Secretariat). It also echoes historical calls from African leaders to mobilize a pan-African response to certain threats and challenges posed by neocolonial trade and aid interventions by former colonial powers (such as the EU member states). Notably, Kwame Nkrumah warned that subregional associations such as ECOWAS or the East African Community would fail in their attempts to challenge overt intrusions upon African state sovereignty by external powers.[36] Nor would these sub-regions have the clout to renegotiate asymmetric patterns of raw materials export and value-added importation. Only federal action via a Union of African States, for Nkrumah, would give African former colonies the political and economic capacity to deal as an equal with the then EEC.[37] Furthermore, African unity would ensure that the continent would not fall foul to the potential predations of superpowers or emerging economies (such as the People's Republic of China). In this vein, Nkrumah pointed to subregional entities as a stumbling block to continental unity, while also lambasting what he deemed the artificial distinction made between the Maghreb and countries of SSA. Notably, he condemned the 'tendency to divide Africa into fictitious zones north and south of the Sahara which emphasizes racial, religious and cultural differences'.[38]

Indeed, it is through a (re)discovery of the discourse and pan-African agenda of Nkrumahism that the AU can meaningfully act to galvanize resistance to the negative impact of premature liberalization, and to challenge the EU's construction of a 'moral economy' of pro-poor trade regimes. In other words, it would appear necessary for AU officials and member states to find a counter-hegemonic discourse through which to challenge the EU's prerogatives in the area of

343

the DCFTAs and the EPAs in Maghreb and SSA countries, respectively. Moreover, they need to find a counter-hegemonic discourse through which to challenge the EU's de facto tying of aid money (such as the EPADP or budget support) to African countries' acquiescence to detrimental trade patterns. Nkrumahism – understood in terms of a commitment both to pan-Africanism and to the construction of developmental states along East Asian models – would potentially be a potent discursive – and policy – vehicle with which AU officials could challenge the EU on its own rhetorical terrain of an 'equal partnership' geared towards 'poverty reduction' and 'sustainable development'. The European Commission, in particular, has left itself open to contestation on the normative grounds on which it itself promotes – and legitimizes – its trade policy agenda. An alternative, critical analytical lens – as offered by Nkrumahism – would likely yield results in uniting AU member states with the AU Commission to meaningfully draw international attention to the disjunctures between the EU's stated development intent and the actual material realities of job losses, deindustrialization and food insecurity wrought by trade reciprocity.

In fact, the AU could learn much here from the operation of non-governmental organizations (NGOs) and trade unions involved in the 'Stop EPA' campaigns which have flourished in SSA countries since the signing of the Cotonou Agreement in 2000. Hurt, for instance, has recently detailed the ways in which Southern African trade union groupings have mobilized – both discursively and materially – to raise public consciousness about the negative impacts of an EPA and trade reciprocity in the region.[39] In particular, they have drawn attention to the likely costs of the EPA in terms of job losses and reduced government tariff revenues. Hurt explains that trade union movements across a number of Southern African nations have worked together to produce a counter-discourse to the views that trade liberalization will result in 'win-win' collaboration with EU partners:

> The Botswana Federation of Trade Unions (BFTU) joined COSATU [the Congress of South African Trade Unions] in contributing to a statement by a network of African trade unions on EPAs, which argued that the 'rapid loss of government revenue will paralyse our governments' abilities to invest in education, health and decent jobs'. In responding to a Presidential State of the Nation address, BFTU were also critical of the long-term consequences of signing an EPA with the EU, suggesting that the government failed 'to place the link between diversification, economic strategy and trade policy'. Similar concerns were expressed by the National Union of Namibian Workers (NUNW) who, like COSATU in South Africa, supported their own government in refusing to sign.[40]

Crucially here – and with potential lessons for AU strategies – these trade union movements have embraced the language of neocolonialism to explain to their own domestic publics – and to wider international audiences – the ways in which EPAs lock African states into (neo)colonial patterns of production and exchange with erstwhile colonial centres. Notably, the International Trade Union Confederation (ITUC)'s General Secretary for Africa – Kwasi Adu-Amankwah – has said that 'the proposed Economic Partnership Agreements (EPAs) would allow the continued exploitation of the continent by European big business'.[41] Furthermore, he has drawn attention to how EPAs perpetuate exchange of raw materials for value added European manufactures and has stated that 'it is highly disingenuous to conceive of a free trade between the poorest continent on earth and the world's most powerful trading bloc as the solution [to poverty]'.[42] Trade unionists in this capacity have condemned a 'commercial colonialism', or in other terms the neocolonial economic penetration about which Nkrumah warned. Interestingly, this trade union activism in SSA has been noted by human rights activists in the Maghreb. 'Internationalist 360', for instance, a Libyan activist, notes that

The EPAs were widely opposed by the workers' movement in Africa and other ACP countries and by the TUC and other trade union centres in Europe, nevertheless they constitute the main basis for the economic relationship between the EU and the AU as well as other ACP countries. The relationship established between the EU, Africa and other ACP countries is one of neo-colonial domination and imperialist intervention and must be ended.[43]

This counter-discourse, meanwhile, is echoed by a Moroccan debt relief NGO which remarks that the DCFTAs themselves are a form of neocolonial incursion about African sovereignty:

The EU is working methodically to impose a new colonialism in a watered-down way. The DCFTA is the instrument allowing it to penetrate the local market. The harmonization of criteria, laws and standards is the way to achieve this colonization. The Moroccan economy will play the role of a complement to the European economy in the context of global competition.[44]

Perhaps most significantly there is already evidence that African political elites themselves are embracing the counter-hegemonic discourse of Nkrumah in their attempts to draw attention to the disjunctures between the EU's moral economy of trade reciprocity and its material consequences for the poor. Tanzania's President, John Magufuli, in February 2017 condemned the EPAs as a 'form of colonialism'.[45] In similar, although more measured terms, Ghana's President, Nana Akufo-Addo, remarked that African countries would have to move away from economic dependency upon the EU. Moreover, he alluded to African policymaking as being swayed by aid money from the EU, and the need to move towards greater policy sovereignty:

We can no longer continue to make policy for ourselves, in our country, in our region, in our continent on the basis of whatever support that the western world or France, or the European Union can give us. It will not work. It has not worked and it will not work.[46]

The transposition of this counter-discourse – from trade union movements, NGOs and individual African nations – to the forum of the AU would potentially mark a significant step forward in resisting the imposition of detrimental trade liberalization, whether in SSA or the Maghreb. Indeed, as Nkrumah noted, only collective agency on a continental scale would provide a feasible means of guarding against the 'collective colonialism' of the EEC (now EU). Utilizing the Joint Africa-EU Strategy of 2007 as a starting point for pointed debates about the impact of trade liberalization on ostensible goals of 'sustainable development' would be an important step in galvanizing African – and indeed European – opposition to the intentions of the European Commission in their ambition to impose DCFTAs and EPAs. Collective action in the AU – reinforced by the actions of bodies such as the ITUC – would bring EU trade policy agendas under much closer scrutiny, to the benefit of workers and emergent industries in both SSA and the Maghreb.

Conclusion

The European Commission's pursuit of far-reaching trade liberalization agreements in both the Maghreb and SSA poses severe challenges to economic growth and private sector development north and south of the Sahara. As discussed, the EPAs and the DCFTAs both threaten to bring about deindustrialization and food insecurity due to the import flooding of often subsidised

European commodities. This will, in effect, perpetuate (neo)colonial systems of production and exchange, whereby African countries continue to be effective sources of primary commodity extraction, as well as lucrative markets for European wares. Most significantly, this material impact of the EPAs and the DCFTAs is wholly refuted, and often hidden, through the European Commission's cultivation of a 'moral economy' of trade reciprocity. Through dissemination of strategic narratives about 'win-win' co-operation, trickle-down economic prosperity and African states' success in globalized (liberalized) markets through comparative advantage, EU officials maintain that the trade agreements are development friendly.

In response to this situation – and given the European Commission's own growing emphasis on the AU, rather than on the ACP bloc, as a forum for negotiation – it would appear imperative that pan-African responses to EU trade policies are found. Already civil society organizations and trade union bodies – as well as individual African governments such as that of Tanzania and Ghana – have signalled an unhappiness with economic dependency, and indeed with systems of neocolonial trade and aid linkages. Given the 'collective colonialism' of the EU-28 (and soon to be EU-27 following the United Kingdom's departure from the Union), a collective response from the AU – enabled by the development discourse of the Africa-EU Joint Plan – would seem to be a strategic necessity for challenging EU trade policy on the grounds that it is materially detrimental to the economic aspirations and social stability of former colonies in Africa. The cultivation of a counter-hegemonic discourse, espoused by AU officials, would do well to counteract the 'moral economy' of trade reciprocity. The (re)discovery of Nkrumahism and his pan-Africanist solutions to neo-colonial interference by the AU would in no small measure move the institution towards a progressive role in counteracting the likely impact of premature trade liberalization.

Notes

1 Kenyan Association of Manufacturers (2006) *Manufacturing in Kenya: A Survey of the Manufacturing Sector*, Nairobi: KAM.

2 The AU became fully operational In July 2002, replacing the Organization of African Unity (OAU), which had been founded in 1963.

3 European Commission (2007) *Joint Africa-EU Strategy*, Brussels: European Commission.

4 ECDPM (2017) *The Future of ACP-EU Relations*, Maastricht: ECDPM. Available at http://ecdpm.org/dossiers/dossier-future-acp-eu-relations-post-2020/.

5 Ibid.

6 M. Langan (2012) 'Normative Power Europe and the Moral Economy of Africa-EU Ties: A Conceptual Reorientation of "Normative Power"', *New Political Economy, 17*(3): 243–70.

7 European Commission (2017) *Economic Partnership Agreements*, Brussels: European Commission.

8 European Commission (2016) *EU Trade and Development Policy: 10 Benefits of Economic Partnership Agreements*, Brussels: European Commission.

9 M. Langan (2011) 'Private Sector Development as Poverty and Strategic Discourse: PSD in the Political Economy of EU-Africa Trade Relations', *Journal of Modern African Studies*, 49(1): 83–113.

10 A. Sayer (2007) 'Moral Economy as Critique', *New Political Economy*, 12(2): 261–70.

11 European Commission (2012) *Economic Partnership Agreements: African, Caribbean and Pacific Voices Speak Up for Development*, Brussels: European Commission.

12 ActionAid (2004) *Trade Traps: Why EU-ACP Economic Partnership Agreement (EPAs) Pose a Threat to Africa's Development*, London: ActionAid.

13 SOS Faim (2004) *Chicken Exports: Europe Plucks Africa! A Campaign for the Right to Protect Agricultural Markets*, Brussels: SOS Faim.

14 The Poultry Site, *Nigeria's Ban on Poultry Imports: Import Lessons for Ghana*. Available at http://www.thepoultrysite.com/poultrynews/37043/nigerias-ban-on-poultry-imports-important-lessons-for-ghana/ (accessed 31 December 2017).

15 SOS Faim, *Chicken Exports*.

16 European Commission (2014) *Economic Partnership Agreement with West Africa: Facts and Figures*, Brussels: European Commission.

17 Pricewaterhouse Coopers (2006) *Sustainability Impact Assessment of the ACP-EU Economic Partnership Agreement – West Africa – Agroindustry*, PwC: London.

18 M. Patel (2007) *Economic Partnership Agreements between the EU and African Countries: Potential Development Implications for Ghana*, Oxford: Realising Rights.

19 L'Usine Maroc (2013) *Accord Commerical Maroc-Union Europeene*, 5 March. Available at www.usine nouvelle.com/article/accord-commercial-maroc-union-europeenne-les-images-et-le-discours-de-la-vis ite-de-l-europeen-barroso-a-rabat.N192677 (accessed 31 December 2017).

20 European Commission (2017) *Relations between the EU and Tunisia*, Brussels: European Commission.

21 Ibid.

22 European External Action Service (2004) *EU Tunisia Action Plan*, Brussels: EEAS.

23 War on Want (2009) *Trading Away Our Jobs*, London: War on Want, p. 2.

24 B. Dimitrovova and Z. Novakova (2015) *Re-thinking the EU's Development Paradigm: Views from Morocco and Tunisia*, Brussels: European Policy Centre, p. 2.

25 Ecorys (2013) *TSIA of the DCFTA between the EU and Tunisia*, Rotterdam: Ecorys, p. 6.

26 Ecorys (2013) *Sustainability Impact Assessment in Support of Negotiations of a DCFTA between the EU and Morocco*, Rotterdam: Ecorys, p. 13.

27 Ecorys (2013) *Sustainability Impact Assessment in Support of Negotiations of a DCFTA between the EU and Tunisia*, Rotterdam: Ecorys, p. 16.

28 Joy Online (2017) *Ghana Loses $10 Million Following Ban on 5 Vegetable Exports*, 28 July. Available at www.myjoyonline.com/business/2017/june-28th/ghana-loses-10m-following-ban-on-five-vegetable-exports.php (accessed 31 December 2017).

29 Author interview, Accra, Ghana, May 2017.

30 M. Langan and S. Price (2015) 'Extraversion and the West African EPA Development Programme: Realising the Development Dimension of ACP-EU Trade?' *Journal of Modern African Studies*, 53(3): 263–87.

31 Ibid.

32 M. Langan (2014) 'Budget Support and Africa-European Union Relations: Free Market Reform and Neo-Colonialism?' *European Journal of International Relations*, 21(1): 101–21.

33 European Commission (2007) *Joint Africa-EU Strategy*, Brussels: European Commission, p. 9.

34 Ibid., p. 10.

35 African Union (2017) *Final Declaration: Investing in Youth for Accelerated Inclusive Growth and Sustainable Development*, AU: Addis Ababa.

36 Nkrumah cited in I. Wallerstein (1967) 'Implicit Ideology in Africa: A Review of Books by Kwame Nkrumah', *Conflict Resolution*, 11(4): 519–21.

37 K. Nkrumah (1966) *Neo-Colonialism: The Last Stage of Imperialism*, London: Thomas Nelson and Sons.

38 Nkrumah cited in I. Wallerstein, 'Implicit Ideology in Africa'.

39 S. Hurt (2016) 'The EU's Economic Partnership Agreements with Africa: "Decent Work" and the Challenge of Trade Union Solidarity', *Third World Thematics*, 1(4): 547–62.

40 Ibid., p. 553.

41 'Ex-Colonial Countries Use the European Union to Bleed Africa', *The Zimbabwean* 25 September 2017. Available at www.thezimbabwean.co/2017/09/ex-colonial-countries-use-european-union-bleed-africa/ (accessed 31 December 2017).

42 Ibid.

43 Internationalist 360 (2016) *The Neo-Colonialist Nature of the European Union and its Intervention in Africa*, 6 March. Available at https://libya360.wordpress.com/2016/03/06/the-neo-colonial-nature-of-the-europ ean-union-and-its-intervention-in-africa/ (accessed 31 December 2017).

44 CADTM (2015) *Free Trade Agreements: Colonial Agreements against the People – Analysis of the Free Trade Agreements between the EU and Morocco*, Marrakesh: CADTM, p. 28.

45 'EPA Trade Deal with Europe a Form of Colonialism Says Magufuli', *Daily Nation*, 30 February 2017.

46 'A Speech by Ghana's President Calling for Africa to End its Dependency on the West is a Viral Hit', Quartz Africa, 4 December 2017. Available at https://qz.com/1145953/ghanas-president-akufo-a ddo-shocks-frances-macron-with-africa-non-dependent-speech/ (accessed 31 December 2017).

30

ECOWAS

An economic commitment that needs political strengthening

Osaore Aideyan

Introduction

The signing of preferential trade agreements (PTAs) in Africa makes for good politics, but in order to become reality, they must extend beyond unfulfilled good intentions and have sufficiently sound institutional bases, and this is the focus of this chapter. In the case of the Economic Community of West African States (ECOWAS), the reluctance of political leaders in the region to encourage the seeming erosion of national sovereignty and the emergence of a supranational authority which would be necessary to co-ordinate and manage the affairs of economic integration constitute the greatest impediment to the goals of a common market and currency. Operationally defined, this means the adoption of a single currency to facilitate proper integration. While not conclusive, a single currency in this regard could help to address the challenges facing West Africa, such as the lack of independence of central banks and the non-convertibility of some currencies. Eventually, a common currency and other regional institutions associated with it could boost investor confidence in the region and promote trade that is currently at a very low level for a supposedly free trade zone. Put differently, West African leaders must move from making bold pronouncements to taking a cue from the one relatively successful integration efforts they have been trying to replicate, the European Union (EU) by creating a supranational institution as its primary decision-making body.

Since its establishment in 1975 ECOWAS has made several achievements in the various fields of economic and monetary union identified in the initial Treaty of 1975 as well as the revised 1993 Treaty. The United Nations Economic Commission for Africa (ECA) actually regards ECOWAS as the undisputed pillar on which the continental integration process, as advocated by the African Union, is based. At the same time, it has faced a number of constraints, which constitute severe obstacles and have hampered the implementation of its ultimate goal of a common market and currency. This chapter, which is an assessment of the sub-region's integration project, develops an argument on the relevance of a sufficiently sound political basis necessary for facilitating a common market and currency for West Africa. This assessment is imperative because among other setbacks ECOWAS has witnessed a ten-year delay at regional level in achieving its planned customs union, whose initial target date was set for 2005 and subsequently moved to start in 2015 and most recently to 2017. The customs union is a necessary component for the establishment of an ECOWAS-wide free trade agreement (FTA).

Equally worth noting is that the same ten-year delay has been recorded in the region's larger plan to achieve economic and monetary union, endowed with a single currency and a single central bank. The two initial start dates were 2010 and 2015. Recently, Kalilou Traore, ECOWAS Commissioner for Industry and Private Sector Promotion, declared that the commission is committed to implementing a single currency in West Africa by 2020.[1] However, at present, nothing guarantees that this objective will be achieved.

Building on a macro institutional framework in the broad integration literature that reflects cooperation and coordination problems (political and technical issues) in the region, this chapter argues that given the difficulties encountered in the implementation of the community convergence programme and the obstacles to real ownership at political level, ECOWAS will not achieve its goals until it is able to establish the most important trade obligation facilitator, which is the existence of a supranational institution as the primary decision-making body. Since collective deliberations are at the core of all regional integration decision-making, this means that member states legally cannot individually or collectively reverse or block a decision made by a regional integration organization.[2] Suffice to say that the degree of importance of a supranational institution is dependent on the level of regional integration. In this sense, such institutions could be nominally established without any assigned tasks. These offices, often known as secretariats, have no mandate other than to prepare and host meetings. These secretariats in other instances could be tasked with amending proposals. In yet other circumstances, they are given the ability to veto proposals, and finally, they could be used for the purpose of gathering information and offering advice.

Using primary and secondary sources of data, this chapter is structured as follows. Section two provides highlights of the provisions of the ECOWAS treaty for an economic and monetary union. Section three provides a summary of major ECOWAS common sectoral policies targeting the implementation of a common market and currency. Section four provides conceptual markers for understanding the coordination and cooperation problem in ECOWAS using the inability to introduce a single currency to facilitate trade as an example of the importance of having a supranational institution as the primary decision-making body. Section five concludes the chapter.

Highlights of the ECOWAS treaty (1975 and 1993)

The idea of regional economic arrangements as a strategic tool for overcoming the limitations of the post-colonial situation in Africa dates back to the immediate post-independence era under the umbrella vision of African Unity. However, it was not until the late 1970s and 1980s that firm steps were taken to establish economic integration institutions in all the sub-regions more in line with the successful global neoliberal economic paradigm as seen in Europe.

Originally inspired by the Declaration of Conakry by Presidents Kwame Nkrumah of Ghana and Ahmed Sekou Toure of Guinea, ECOWAS has progressed in stages from being a customs union of six countries to a regional economic body with the signing of a formal treaty on 28 May 1975 in Lagos, Nigeria. Comprising 15 member states in 2017, ECOWAS is considered one of the most promising regional integration experiments in Africa.[3] Under the original Lagos Treaty, its mission is to promote cooperation and economic integration through the elimination of customs duties; abolition of quantitative and administrative restrictions on trade among member states; harmonization of agricultural policies; establishment of common customs tariffs and commercial policies towards other developing states; abolition of obstacles to the free

Osaore Aideyan

movement of persons, services and capital among member states; and implementation of collective schemes for the development of industry, transport, telecommunications, energy, and other infrastructures.[4]

Due to structural constraints in the implementation of these objectives, the ECOWAS treaty was revised and signed on 24 July 1993 in Cotonou, Benin. A detailed summary of the main topics covered by the 1993 agreement from the World Trade Organization (WTO) Regional Trade Agreements Information System (RTA-IS) is provided below in Tables 30.1–30.4. Compared to the 1975 treaty the revised version is more comprehensive in content and more diversified in its provisions.

An important difference between the revised treaty and the 1975 treaty that is relevant to the focus of this chapter is the assertion in the Preamble that in furtherance of its goal to achieve an economic union of West Africa, it is necessary that member states be required to effect some transfer of sovereignty to the community within the context of a collective political will. It is not clear what 'political will' signifies in this context, but political and economic institutionalists are quick to direct attention to the absence of adequate market-enhancing governance architecture. Here we refer to institutional arrangements that are directed towards solving problems of collective action and the reluctance of regional political leaders to encourage the seeming erosion of national sovereignty and the emergence of a supranational authority. This would be necessary to co-ordinate and manage commitment problems in macroeconomic policy in the region.

Summary of trade and common sectoral polices

A review of various annual reports published by the ECOWAS Executive Secretariat and information provided on its official website reveals that over the past 42 years ECOWAS has strived to adopt protocols and to develop policies and programmes to cover almost all areas of integration that were identified in the initial treaty as well as in the revised treaty. The summary distilled here is restricted to policies that have immediate relevance to the implementation of a common market and currency. For a detailed review of major ECOWAS sectoral policies to ensure an economic and monetary union in West Africa, the reader is encouraged to look at the 2015 report of the ECA subregional office for West Africa of ECA.[5] As it is evident in the

Table 30.1 Background information

States parties	Benin, Burkina Faso, Cape Verde, Côte d'Ivoire, The Gambia, Ghana, Guinea, Guinea-Bissau, Liberia, Mali, Niger, Nigeria, Senegal, Sierra Leone and Togo.
Date of signature	24 July 1993
Date of entry into force	24 July 1993
Transition period for full implementation	Ten years as from 1 January 1990 (Article 35).
Date of full implementation	1 January 2000
Website addresses or points of contact	ECOWAS official website. Available at www.ecowas.int/
List of related GATT/WTO documents	WT/COMTD/N/21 Notification WT/COMTD/54 Agreement

Source: WTO (2017) RTA-IS database. Available at http://rtais.wto.org/UI/PublicAllRTAList.aspx (accessed 30 November 2017).

Table 30.2 Internal trade liberalization provisions

Import duties and charges	Article 35 (Liberalization of Trade) Article 36 (Customs Duties)
Export duties and charges	Article 3 (Aims and Objectives)
Non-tariff measures	Article 35 (Liberalization of Trade) Article 40 (Fiscal Charges and Internal Taxation) Article 41 (Quantitative Restrictions on Community Goods) Article 44 (Internal Legislation)
Sector-specific rules	Chapter IV (Cooperation in food and agriculture) Chapter V (Cooperation in industry, science and technology and energy) Chapter VI (Cooperation in environmental and natural resources) Chapter VII (Cooperation in transport, communications and tourism)
Product exclusions	None

Table 30.3 Common external tariff

Provisions	Article 35 (Liberalization of Trade)
	Article 37 (Common External Tariff)

Source: WTO (2017) RTA-IS database. Available at http://rtais.wto.org/UI/PublicAllRTAList.aspx (accessed 30 November 2017).

revised treaty, ECOWAS common market and currency initiatives are characterized by key policy changes such as the free movement of people, the elimination of tariff and non-tariff barriers to intraregional trade and procedural barriers to trade, and avoidance of import bans and levies and export tax and prohibitions.[6]

To enhance the protocol on the free movement of people, ECOWAS has made provisions for the adoption of a biometric identity card (common passport) as a travel document, in the place of the ECOWAS travel certificate which did not really work; withdrawal of the resident card (freedom of establishment granted to community citizens); and free access to employment in member states. In addition, it has set up a platform to harmonize immigration procedures and examine the introduction of applications for the ECOVISA (a Schengen-type visa), which will eliminate the need for multiple-entry visas for third-country nationals to enter member states, for tourism purposes or on business trips.[7] ECOWAS has also implemented measures to ease the movement of persons transported in private and commercial vehicles by harmonizing policies that enable vehicles to enter and temporarily reside in a member state for up to 90 and 15 days, respectively. Most ECOWAS member states have, in this regard, introduced the ECOWAS 'brown card', an insurance policy for motor vehicles that covers the civil responsibly of owners residing in the ECOWAS region.[8]

In 2013 the regional group established National Committees to adopt a single programme on the elimination of non-tariff barriers. It consists of a web-based system that member states can use to report non-tariff barriers and follow up on the elimination processes. ECOWAS also runs a customs connectivity programme whose aim is to link customs software and facilitate the data-sharing on the movement of goods in the region. To facilitate trade, ECOWAS has implemented one-stop border posts whose aim is to reduce delays at cross-border points, which are brought about by poor facilities and traffic flow, and manual, lengthy and non-integrated processes.

Osaore Aideyan

Table 30.4 General trade-related provisions

Provision	Relevant Article(s)	Additional information
Rules of origin	Article 38	The rules governing products originating from the Community shall be contained in the relevant protocols and decisions of the Community.
Standards-related measures	Article 3	The Community shall ensure the harmonization of standards and measures.
Sanitary and phytosanitary measures	None	
Safeguard mechanisms (intra-trade)	Article 49	In the event of serious disturbances occurring in the economy of a member state, the state concerned shall, after informing the Executive Secretary and the other member states, take the necessary safeguard measures pending the approval of the Council. These measures shall remain in force for a maximum period of one year and may not be extended beyond that period except with the approval of the Council.
Anti-dumping and counter-vailing measures	Article 42	Member states undertake to prohibit the practice of dumping goods within the Community. In the event of alleged dumping the importing member state shall appeal to council to resolve the matter.
Subsidies and state aid	None	
Customs-related procedures	Article 46	Member states shall, in accordance with the advice of the Trade, Customs Taxation, Statistics, Money and Payments Commission and the provisions of the Convention for Mutual Administrative Assistance in Customs Matters, take appropriate measures to harmonize and standardize their customs regulations and procedures to ensure the effective application of the Chapter and to facilitate the movement of goods and services across their frontiers.
IPR	None	
Government procurement	None	
Competition	None	
Investment	Article 3	The Community shall ensure the harmonization of national investment codes leading to the adoption of a single community investment code.
General exceptions	Article 41	A member state may introduce or continue to execute restrictions or prohibitions affecting the application of security laws and regulations; the control of arms, ammunition and other war equipment and military items; the protection of human, animal or plant health or life, or the protection of public morality; the transfer of gold, silver and precious and semi-precious stones; the protection of national artistic and cultural property; the control of narcotics, hazardous and toxic wastes, nuclear materials, radioactive; products or any other material used in the development or exploitation of nuclear energy.
Accession	None	

Provision	Relevant Article(s)	Additional information
Dispute resolution	Article 76	Any dispute regarding the interpretation or the application of the treaty shall be amicably settled through direct agreement without prejudice to the provisions of the treaty and relevant protocols. Failing this, either party or any other member states or the Authority may refer the matter to the court of the Community whose decision shall be final and shall not be subject to appeal.
Relation with other trade agreements	Chapter XVII, Chapter XVIII and Chapter XX	The integration of the region shall constitute an essential component of the integration of the African continent. Member states undertake to facilitate the coordination and harmonization of the Community's policies and programmes with those of the African Economic Community. In realizing its regional objectives, the Community may enter into cooperation agreements with other regional communities. The Community may conclude cooperation agreements with third countries. To this end, the Community shall also cooperate with the organization of African Unity, the United Nations and any other international organization.
Transparency	None	
Institutional provisions	Chapter III, Articles 52 and 53	Chapter III provides for the establishment of the following institutions: the Authority of Heads of State and Government; the Council of Ministers; the Community Parliament; the Economic and Social Council; the Community Court of Justice; the Executive Secretariat; the Fund for Cooperation, Compensation and Development; and Specialised Technical Commissions. It also details the composition and function of each of these institutions. The Agreement also establishes a Committee of West African Central Banks and a Movement of Capital and Capital Issues Committee.

Source: WTO (2017) RTA-IS database. Available at http://rtais.wto.org/UI/PublicAllRTAList.aspx (accessed 30 November 2017).

Note: Trade and tariff data are not available.

Quite early in its establishment, ECOWAS introduced its comprehensive Trade Liberalization Scheme (ETLS). Designed for implementation in 1979, it was not until 1990 after three deferments that the ETLS was launched. It stipulated an immediate and full liberalization of trade in unprocessed goods and traditional handicrafts; a phased liberalization of trade in industrial products, with the phasing reflecting the differences in the levels of development of three categories of member states; and the gradual establishment of a common external tariff. According to its schedule, all trade barriers were meant to have been eliminated by 1999, but this did not happen thus resulting in the heads of the member states resolving to adopt a fast-track approach to achieve the region's objective of economic integration. This ultimately led to the proclamation of the region as an FTA in 2000 and 1 January 2001 was set for its transformation into a customs union.

Osaore Aideyan

Unfortunately, not all these commitments to policy changes correspond to a high volume of trade in the region. The region's largest trade partner, the EU, accounts for 37.8 per cent of total trade. Meanwhile Nigeria, which has the largest economy in the region, exported only 2.3 per cent and imported less than 0.5 per cent from other West African countries in 2010.[9] Trade within ECOWAS remains very low because of the absence of a supranational institution that can help to create common policies needed to tackle cross-border externalities and their costs, which are heightened by both internal and external factors, principal among which are sharp differences in policy preferences and currencies across member states.[10] In their insightful review of these recent initiatives, De Melo and Tsikata note that the ECOWAS sub-region is not yet a fully fledged FTA. Like most PTAs in Africa, ECOWAS will need to surmount many hurdles on the way to what it calls a linear model of integration which is a stepwise creation of a customs union to a single market, followed by monetary union with a single currency, before talking of its ultimate goal of an economic union.

In the contested terrain of the political economy of regionalism and monetary union, this will involve the institutionalization of a set of political and economic measures that create incentives for member states to align their fiscal policies with other regional monetary institutions such as the European Central Bank (ECB). When applied to the ECOWAS project, we aim to have twin explanations that address the cooperation and coordination problems in the region that would not only strengthen individual economies, but also foster the region's global competitive position:

1   What will it take to get West African states to make credible commitment to policies consistent with the end goal of a common market and currency?
2   How do member states effect some transfer of national sovereignty in the field of monetary policy to any supranational body?

Conceptual markers for understanding the problem of coordination and cooperation[11]

This section provides conceptual markers of a culture of cooperation and coordination that are relevant to understanding the ECOWAS project. Since these attributes are not measurable quantitatively, I employ qualitative conceptual markers to capture the necessary institutional preconditions for a common market and currency to assess the ECOWAS experience. These markers are based on a macro-institutional approach developed by the author in a previous article[12] that seeks to explain the difficulty facing ECOWAS in achieving the proposed common currency, the Eco. In applying the framework, which draws inferences from the eurozone as well as other parts of the world, I first summarize the essential attributes of European monetary cooperation and coordination that are key to the successful implementation of a common currency and provide a short analysis based on a set of questions.

(i) There needs to be an existing institution that connects the past to the present and future in promoting sound monetary policies that are consistent with the goal of a common market and currency. Accordingly, the euro has evolved because of the substantial continuity between the European Monetary System (EMS, 1979–98) and the eurozone rather than a sudden beginning in 1999. As the evidence shows, the EMS has been used to attain consensus, which is in short supply in West Africa.

Indicators

(a) Does ECOWAS have an equivalent of the EMS, which is used for attaining consensus?

ECOWAS does not have an equivalent EMS for building consensus. However, in 2001 the West African Monetary Institute (WAMI/Institute) was set up to undertake technical preparations for the establishment of a common West African Central Bank and the launching of a single currency for the West African Monetary Zone (WAMZ). Formed in 2000, WAMZ is a group of six countries within ECOWAS. Member states include The Gambia, Ghana, Guinea, Liberia, Nigeria and Sierra Leone. WAMZ is dominated by Nigeria, thus reflecting its status as the region's largest market. All the members of the group are English-speaking countries, except Guinea, which is Francophone.[13]

In addition to monitoring the quantitative convergence criteria, the mandate of the Institute has been expanded over the years to include the adoption of measures that will facilitate trade integration, financial sector integration, payments system development and statistical harmonization. In fulfilment of its mandate, therefore, the Institute currently conducts biannual on-site and monthly off-site multilateral surveillance missions to monitor member states' compliance with both the quantitative and qualitative benchmarks.[14] The ultimate phase of the regional efforts would be a merger of the WAMZ arrangement with the West African Economic and Monetary Union (also known as UEMOA) which already has a common central bank, the Banque Centrale des Etats de l'Afrique de l'Ouest. The WAMI has not made enough progress in achieving this outcome because the UEMOA single currency, the CFA franc (mostly used by former French colonies) is pegged to the euro and is shored up by France during times of crisis. Consequently, there is no incentive for the Francophone countries to give up the CFA franc for another currency as French support in the interim seems more durable and credible for a currency that might not produce the same benefits for UEMOA states. Suffice to say that as one of the world's oldest monetary unions UEMOA should be a sufficient platform for achieving consensus by ECOWAS leaders, but their allegiance to the former colonies does not inspire this interchange.

(b) Based on the EU template, have member states sought the opinion of their citizens on the abolition of national currencies through a referendum or another medium of public opinion?

If it is assumed that the decision on whether to abolish a country's national currency when considering joining an economic and monetary union will formally be decided by a majority of nationals residing within the borders of a member state through a referendum, there is no evidence yet that any of the 15 member states of ECOWAS have had one, nor are there immediate plans to hold a referendum. The facts on the ground show pervading distrust and paranoia among most of the region's peoples against each other despite the positive pronouncements of the ECOWAS leadership and treaty.[15]

(c) What rules exist to prevent ECOWAS member states from joining other parallel agreements? Suffice to say that ECOWAS has negotiated an Economic Partnership Agreement with the EU as well as engaged in discussions with other zones and countries within and outside Africa (particularly Morocco) in a bid to conclude trade agreements with them.

The objective here is to commit all countries to achieving the goal of a common market and currency by making exit from the group very difficult. At present, the only instrument that resembles a step towards making exit difficult is the ECOWAS Monetary Cooperation Pro-gramme, where countries have demonstrated strong commitment to comply with the criteria for achieving an economic and monetary union. However, the absence of sanctions for non-compliance and poorly designed indicators has undermined the ability to implement the various protocols of the WAMZ.[16] As Yahya argues, there is much insincerity and a lackadaisical atti-tude in governments of member states towards implementing the vital protocols of monetary union. This could be explained by the fact that most Francophone countries in the region seem to have an effective alternative supporter in France, which for colonial historical antecedents, appears to provide them with significant benefits from their association with it rather than with their cohorts in the region. It should also be noted that Liberia and Cape Verde have in the past expressed reservations about plans for a new common currency but not a common market, which is difficult to understand in a region that aspires to be like the EU.[17]

(d) Does ECOWAS have an effective supranational bureaucracy with important regulatory powers?

Since its transformation from a secretariat to a commission the ECOWAS Commission has developed a vision for the development of a regional grouping committed to eliminating borders. However, it has yet to establish an effective region–wide agency that can regulate economic behaviour, a vital aspect of PTAs.

(e) Have regional powers sufficiently shown enough preference for a common market and currency?

Until recently when Ghana became a force to be reckoned with economically, Nigeria and Côte d'Ivoire were considered the economic and military powerhouses of the region, but there is no evidence that either of these two countries have shown any commitment to a swift implementation of a single market and currency for the region. As recently as October 2017 President Muhammadu Buhari of Nigeria, while drawing lessons from the EU, cautioned ECOWAS leaders against the pursuit of monetary integration because of what he appropriately termed the diverse and uncertain macroeconomic fundamentals of many countries in the region, among other reasons.[18]

(ii) Actors need a frame of reference in terms of which they can make sense of monetary and fiscal policy and help to define their preferences. In the case of the eurozone, Germany pro-vided the cognitive template that would eventually be emulated by other European policy-makers. The willingness of other European governments to follow the German example increased the chance that the EMS would hold together, because prior to the introduction of the euro the German Deutschmark served as its anchor.

Indicator

(a) Does ECOWAS have a German equivalent to emulate its monetarist policy?

The obvious answer is no. An equally obvious reason for this is that the dependence of many West African states on their former colonial powers have worked against their ability to use the experiences of either of the region's two economic powers, Côte d'Ivoire or Nigeria, as a template for West African policymakers. The absence of a lead country decreases the ability of the region to hold together in its efforts to achieve a common market and currency. As a regional hegemon with more than 70 per cent of the GDP of West Africa, other member states view Nigeria with suspicion.

(iii) The existence of formal and informal institutional processes and concepts that legitimize and validate the efforts to achieve a common market and currency. In the case of the eurozone, professionals in monetary policy have sought to legitimize the process through a neoliberal conception of the euro and globalization.

Indicator

(a) What neoliberal concept(s) exist for ECOWAS policymakers to rally around?

As specified in the framework, the legitimacy of an economic and monetary union is attained to the extent that there are rational bases to situate it in the context of the new global economic regime that has the potential to emasculate the power of the sovereign state. This is perhaps one of the attributes of the framework that has been attained by the region. In West Africa as well as across the continent, concepts like competitiveness, intra-African trade and FDI have been invoked to foster the cooperation needed to achieve deeper integration. It is instructive to note that while these are not uncommon ways to steer a sustainable path in an increasingly globalized world, the ECOWAS proposal has also received backing from the International Monetary Fund, the EU, the Economic Community of Africa, the ECB and the Bank of England. The significance of these external sources of support is that they help to address the high degree of uncertainty about the costs and benefits of economic integration among a group of weak states, which is needed in the current global economic regime that is driven by neoliberal ideas and institutions.

Conclusion

Despite some successes in using regional economic integration arrangements to achieve sustainable development in Africa within a neoliberal framework, the effectiveness of these subregional integration efforts like ECOWAS has been hampered through both domestic and external factors. In this chapter, I have tried to show that while leaders in ECOWAS are committed to addressing these problems, they must move beyond unfulfilled good intentions and develop a sufficiently sound governance structure that can help to resolve cooperation and coordination problems. For this purpose, the goal should be the creation of a supranational institution as a primary decision-making body. Since collective deliberations are at the core of all regional integration decision-making, this means that member states legally cannot individually or collectively reverse or block a decision made by a regional integration organization like a central bank. An independent central bank would be particularly relevant not just in ECOWAS, but within the whole of Africa, where credible institutional fixes are harder to implement.

Given the reality and experiences so far in ECOWAS, the difficulties that member states find in reaping the potential benefits of RTAs might persist until the leaders claim real ownership of the process at a political level.

Notes

1 'ECOWAS to Implement Common Currency in West Africa', *Vanguard*, 8 December 2015. Available at www.vanguardngr.com/2015/12/ecowas-to-implement-common-currency-in-west-africa-official/ (accessed 28 May 2016).

Osaore Aideyan

2 Gaspare Genna (2017) 'Measuring Integration Achievement in the Americas', in Philippe De Lombaerde and Edgar Saucedo Acosta (eds) *Indicator-Based Monitoring of Regional Economic Integration*, United Nations University Series on Regionalism 13, New York: Springer International.

3 Benin, Burkina Faso, Cape Verde, Côte d' Ivoire, Gambia, Ghana, Guinea, Guinea-Bissau, Liberia, Mali, Niger, Nigeria, Senegal, Sierra Leone and Togo.

4 Official ECOWAS website (2017). Available at www.ecowas.int/ (accessed 20 January 2017).

5 UN Economic Commission for Africa (ECA) and ECOWAS (2015–05). *An Assessment of Progress Towards Regional Integration in the Economic Community of West African States Since Its Inception*, Addis Ababa: ECA.

6 Caroline Ntara (2016) 'African Trading Blocs and Economic Growth: A Critical Review of the Literature', *International Journal of Developing and Emerging Economies*, 4(1), February: 1–21.

7 ECA and ECOWAS, *Assessment of Progress Towards Regional Integration in the Economic Community of West African States*, p. 51.

8 African Union (2013) *Status of Integration in Africa IV*. Available at www.au.int/ar/sites/default/files/SIA%202013(latest)_En.pdf (accessed 20 May 2017).

9 Tahiru Liedong (2017) Could West Africa Introduce a Single Currency? The Conversation. Available at www.cnn.com/2017/08/08/africa/single-currency-west-africa/index.html (accessed 8 August 2017).

10 Jaime De Melo and Yvonne Tsikata (2014) 'Regional Integration in Africa: Challenges and Prospects', FERDI Working Paper 93, February, Clermont-Ferrand: FERDI.

11 This section of the chapter draws heavily on my work on the eco, a common currency for West Africa.

12 Osaore Aideyan (2016) 'Political and Institutional Prerequisites for Monetary Union: Assessing Progress in the Economic Community of West African States', *ECOWAS, Politics and Policy*, 44(6), December: 1192–212.

13 Central Bank of Nigeria (CBN) 'International Economic Cooperations: The Economic Community of West African States (ECOWAS)'. Available at www.cenbank.org/monetarypolicy/ecowas.asp (accessed 12 June 2016).

14 The West African Monetary Institute (2001) *The Role and Functions of the West African Monetary Institute*, Accra: WAMI.

15 Yahya (2008) 'West Africa: Seven W/African Countries, One Bus Ride (i)', *Daily Trust*, 16 March.

16 O. J. Nnanna (2006) 'Economic and Monetary Integration in Africa', Paper presented at the G24 meeting in Singapore.

17 'Common Currency for West Africa', *Africa Business Pages*. Available at www.africa-business.com/features/currency.html (accessed 30 November 2014).

18 'President Buhari Calls for Caution in Implementing ECOWAS Single Currency', *Vanguard*, 24 October 2017. Available at www.vanguardngr.com/2017/10/president-buhari-calls-caution-implementing-ecowas-single-currency/ (accessed 24 October 2017).

31

SADC

Towards a deeper and wider union?

Donald L. Sparks[1]

Introduction

Southern Africa is home to a large number of overlapping regional economic intergovernmental organizations, hosts the world's oldest customs union (the Southern African Customs Union – SACU) and perhaps the continent's most effective currency union (the Common Monetary Area – CMA). By many measures, the 16-member Southern African Development Community (SADC) is the most important economic community on the continent: the SADC region accounts for roughly one-third of the membership of the African Union (AU), one-third of total continental gross domestic product (GDP), and one-third of the continent's total population. In addition, SADC is one of eight regional economic communities (RECs) recognized by the AU. The other seven RECs are the Arab Maghreb Union; the Common Market for Eastern and Southern Africa (COMESA); the Community of Sahel-Saharan States; the East African Community (EAC); the Economic Community of Central African States; the Economic Community of West African States (ECOWAS); and the Intergovernmental Authority on Development.[2]

Beginning during the region's anti-apartheid struggle, nine nations (then known as the frontline states) came together as a loose affiliation who shared a common goal of distancing themselves economically from apartheid-ruled South Africa, and since then the organization's membership has expanded to 16 member states and has evolved into a true economic and political community. While trade promotion is an important part of SADC, it views itself more as a development community than as a trade bloc.

This chapter will look at SADC's history, its current structure, goals and objectives as well as examining some of the challenges the organization faces for the future. The concluding question for this chapter is: does the community want to and can it become 'deeper' (i.e. experience increased convergence and harmonization in a variety of economic, political and social areas) and 'wider' through the addition of new additional members?

History

SADC's origin goes back to the 1960s and 1970s when the region's majority-ruled countries and liberation movements were working towards ending minority-ruled South Africa's apartheid

Donald L. Sparks

system of government.[3] In 1979 nine southern African neighbours (Angola, Botswana, Lesotho, Malawi, Mozambique, Swaziland, Tanzania, Zambia and Zimbabwe, sometimes knows as the frontline states) signed the Lusaka Declaration (Southern Africa: Toward Economic Liberation) which created the Southern African Development Coordination Conference (SADCC) the following year, in 1980.

It is important to recall that at that time South Africa's nearby neighbours, especially Botswana, Lesotho and Swaziland, were and in many ways still are economically dependent on the region's economic powerhouse. SADCC was established to foster regional economic and commercial cooperation between themselves and to lessen dependence on South Africa.

Initially, the organization had no formal structure or secretariat. Instead, it focused on a sectoral approach to regional development, with each SADCC member state taking the lead in an area where it had expertise. Angola, because of its important oil sector, for example, was the lead country for regional energy planning. Botswana took the lead for foot-and-mouth disease control and crop production research; Malawi for freshwater fisheries and wildlife; Mozambique for regional transport; Swaziland for manpower development and training; Tanzania for coordination strategy; and Zambia provided studies for a Southern Africa Development Fund. Each member state designated a ministry responsible for coordination, and these ministries undertook a number of studies in such fields as regional trade, farming and animal husbandry, health, natural resources, hydrological basins, mining, energy, environment, food security, and road, port and energy infrastructure.

SADCC's four principal objectives were to (1) secure international cooperation for the goal of economic liberation from South Africa; (2) reduce member state dependence on South Africa; (3) create linkages for regional integration; and (4) help members to implement national, interstate and regional programmes.

By the early 1990s it was becoming apparent that South Africa would finally achieve majority rule, which it did in 1994. In adopting the Windhoek Declaration and the subsequent treaty ratification by its founding members (along with newly independent Namibia), SADCC was converted into SADC in 1992. The new SADC initially provided socio-economic cooperation and political and security cooperation among its members. In addition to the original ten members (Namibia being the 10th), the other new members were South Africa (joining in 1994), Mauritius (1995), the Democratic Republic of the Congo (DRC) (1997), Seychelles (1997, left the organization in 2004 but rejoined in 2008) and Madagascar (2005, suspended in 2009 due to what SADC considered an unconstitutional change of government, but was reinstated in 2014) and Comoros in 2017. In 2000 SADC undertook a major restructuring of its organization and moved its secretariat to Gaborone, the capital of Botswana (where it still is located).

SADC's mission

As discussed above, SADC has expanded its original mission from trying to lessen economic dependence on minority-ruled South Africa to a more integrated regional community. Its current mission is 'to promote sustainable and equitable economic growth and socio-economic development through efficient, productive systems, deeper cooperation and integration, good governance, and durable peace and security; so that the region emerges as a competitive and efficient player in international relations and the world economy'.[4]

The community is guided by the 1992 SADC Treaty which includes 18 chapters and 44 articles. The major goals are delineated in Article 4 which includes five major principles: 'Sovereign equality of all member states; solidarity, peace and security; human rights, democracy and the rule of law; equity, balance and mutual benefit; and, peaceful settlement of disputes'.

SADC's major objectives, known as the Common Agenda, are specified in Article 5. They are to:

1 achieve development and economic growth, alleviate poverty, enhance the standard and quality of life of the people of Southern Africa and support the socially disadvantaged through regional integration;
2 evolve common political values, systems and institutions;
3 promote and defend peace and security;
4 promote self-sustaining development on the basis of collective self-reliance, and the inter-dependence of member states;
5 achieve complementarity between national and regional strategies and programmes;
6 promote and maximize productive employment and utilization of resources of the region;
7 achieve sustainable utilization of natural resources and effective protection of the environment; and
8 strengthen and consolidate the long-standing historical, social and cultural affinities and links among the people of the region.

SADC has 33 legally binding protocols (of which 27 have been signed, see Appendix A) dealing with issues such as defence, economic development, the illicit drug trade, free trade and the movement of people to name a few. In order for a protocol to enter in to force, two-thirds of the member states must ratify it. Any member state that had not initially become party to a protocol can assent to it later.

Organizational structure

The original SADCC Treaty created a number of official bodies but they were only intended to act as facilitators in a coordinating role (as described above). There was a growing consensus among the members that this organizational model could not achieve what they wanted (i.e. increased regional integration) and thus a restructuring was necessary to move towards a regional community. In 2001 the community undertook a major restructuring at its meeting in Windhoek where it amended the original treaty. These reforms established eight institutions, under Article 9 of the Treaty Amendment. Institutional decision-making is by consensus (typically carried out in Gaborone), except for the Tribunal (which is based in Windhoek). Since 2001 a few more bodies have been added and the structure now is as follows:[5]

Summit of Heads or State or Government

The summit is responsible for overall policy direction and thus it is the organization's policy-making institution, comprising all SADC heads of states or of government. It is managed on a troika system that comprises of the current SADC Summit chairperson, the incoming chairperson (the deputy chairperson at the time), and the immediate previous chairperson.

Summit Troika of the Organ

This is charged with steering and providing member states with direction regarding matters that threaten the region's peace, security and stability.

Donald L. Sparks

SADC Tribunal

The Tribunal was created to ensure adherence to, and proper interpretation of, the provisions of the SADC Treaty and to adjudicate disputes referred to it. After several judgements ruling against the Zimbabwean government, the Tribunal was de facto suspended at the 2010 SADC Summit.

SADC Council of Ministers

The Council oversees SADC's functioning and is tasked with ensuring that policies are properly implemented. The Council consists of ministers from each member state, usually from the ministries of foreign affairs, economic planning, or finance.

Sectoral and Cluster Ministerial Committees

These committees (consisting of ministers from member states) are responsible for overseeing the activities of what are considered the core areas of integration, and for monitoring the implementation of the Regional Indicative Strategic Development Plan. These core groups are trade, industry, finance and investment; infrastructure and services; food, agriculture, natural resources and environment; social and human development and special programmes (including HIV and AIDS, education, labour, employment and gender); politics, defence and security; and legal and judicial matters.

Standing Committee of Senior Officials

This a technical advisory committee to the Council of Ministers and consists of one Permanent/ Principal Secretary from each member state. The chairperson and vice-chairperson of the Standing Committee are appointed from the member states holding the chair and the vice-chair of the Council.

SADC Secretariat

This is the principal executive institution and is responsible for strategic planning, co-ordination and programme management. Headquartered in Gaborone, it is headed by an executive secretary and two deputy secretaries (one for regional integration and the other for internal finance and administration).

SADC National Committees

These national committees comprise key stakeholders from government, the private sector and civil society in each member state. They provide input in formulating regional policies and coordinating programmes at national level.

SADC Parliamentary Forum

The Forum tries to enhance regional integration through national parliamentary involvement and address a range of issues such as promoting of human rights, peace, security and stability; economic cooperation, development and informing SADC of the national perspectives on development issues. It is composed of members of parliament from SADC's member state

362

national parliaments and represents over 3,500 parliamentarians. It consists of a presiding officer and a maximum of five representatives elected by the national parliament of each member state.

SADC's Common Agenda: increased regional integration

SADC's most important – and most challenging– agenda clearly is to increase regional economic integration (which is expected to lead to increased economic development and poverty reduction). In that regard, it has ambitious goals (although generally not reached to date) in the area of regional trade and monetary affairs. Its agenda has been outlined in the Regional Indicative Strategic Development Plan (RISDP) which was revised in 2015. The RISDP comprises seven chapters with priority interventions in trade liberalization, infrastructure and peace and security. As the RISDP is set to expire in 2020, SADC is currently formulating a new blueprint for post-2020 development cooperation.

While SADC's Protocol on Trade calls for liberalization on intraregional trade, trade among members is not particularly high (see Table 31.1). Intraregional exports (as a percentage of total exports) range from 0.5 per cent in Seychelles to 81.6 per cent in Swaziland. This low level of trade is due largely to the fact that the members' major exports are low value-added primary products. Members do not need these types of imports from their neighbours – Tanzania does not need to import coffee from Malawi, for example. Intraregional imports range from 3.6 per cent in Tanzania to 81.2 per cent in Swaziland as again the region does not produce many finished products. Most of the intraregional trade is with South Africa (which does produce a variety of value-added products). In 2015 SADC members exported 24.8 per cent of their exports to other SADC members, and purchased 17.2 per cent of their imports from fellow members. Total intra-SADC trade was 20.9 per cent of the region's total trade. The level of trade between members has not increased significantly since 2000. While trade from the DRC and other members has increased dramatically, levels from five other members (Malawi, Mozambique, Seychelles, Zambia and Zimbabwe) have actually declined as a percentage of total trade.

However, Yayo and Asefa found that intra-SADC trade is growing in two sectors: fuels, minerals and heavy manufacturing (e.g. mining) while declining in agriculture and light manufacturing (e.g. home care products, furniture). Whether regional integration is in the economic interests of the participants depends upon the extent of trade creation as opposed to trade diversion. Trade creation occurs when low-cost producers within the free trade area replace high-cost domestic producers. Trade diversion occurs when higher-cost suppliers within the free trade and this appears to have happened at least in agriculture and light manufacturing. Yayo and Asefa concluded that 'SADC countries retained their openness and outward orientation'.[6]

Trade among members is hindered further by poor infrastructure (including bottlenecks) and lack of transport alternatives (nearly half of the members are landlocked as well). The Regional Infrastructure Development Master Plan, part of SADC's Infrastructure Vision 2017, seeks to streamline trade.[7] Border crossings are notoriously difficult and time-consuming (it can take a week for large trucks to clear customs at some member border posts). In 2009 SADC sponsored a One Stop Border Post between Zambia and Zimbabwe (which reduced transit time to less than 30 hours). The goal is to have 16 of the most important 35 border posts converted to one stop by 2020.[8] In addition, SADC has sponsored 18 regional transport corridors in the region. The most successful of these is the Maputo Development Corridor which has attracted more than US $5 billion in investment, including a $500 million investment in the port of Maputo, Mozambique.

SADC so far has followed the traditional linear integration model that called for a free trade area followed by a customs union with a common external tariff, a monetary union and a single currency cumulating in an economic union. Furthermore, it has joined two neighbouring

Donald L. Sparks

Table 31.1 Intra-SADC trade (% of total trade that is with members)

		2000	*2015*
Angola			
	Exports	0.2	4.1
	Imports	7.8★	6.1
Botswana			
	Exports	11.6	29.5
	Imports	80.9	80.7
DRC			
	Exports	1.2	81.5★★
	Imports	21	46.1★★
Lesotho			
	Exports	27.8	78.0★★
	Imports	79.6	78.1★★
Madagascar			
	Exports	3.1	5.8
	Imports	9.8	10.1
Malawi			
	Exports	11.8	5.4
	Imports	35.3	7.4
Mauritius			
	Exports	1.7	15.7
	Imports	15.8	9.9
Mozambique			
	Exports	55.5	25.8
	Imports	64.0	32.0
Namibia			
	Exports	33.9	54.5
	Imports	87.4	72.1
Seychelles			
	Exports	3.7	0.5
	Imports	90.4	12.5
South Africa			
	Exports	10.6	23.4
	Imports	1.3	6.1
Swaziland			
	Exports	85.3	81.6

		2000	*2015*
	Imports	94.7	81.2
Tanzania			
	Exports	7.2	10.6
	Imports	13.8	3.6
Zambia			
	Exports	29.3	23.1
	Imports	68.7	52.2
Zimbabwe			
	Exports	82.1	68.6
	Imports	63.6	42.4

Source: SADC Secretariat (2017). Available at www.sadc.int/documents-publications/show/5066.

Note: * refers to 2002; ** refers to 2014.

organizations, the ECA and COMESA, in a new cooperative venture and recently signed an economic partnership with the European Union (EU) which will be discussed below.

Free trade areas

Regional economic integration refers to agreements between countries (usually) in a geographic region, to reduce tariff and non-tariff barriers to the free flow of goods, services, and factors of production (including people and capital) between each other. The most basic form is a preferential trade area (PTA) whereby members reduce the tariff barriers between each other, but leave their respective external barriers against all other trade partners (example, the US-Canada PTA agreed in the 1980s). A free trade area (FTA) eliminates trade barriers between members but leaves their respective external barriers against all other trade partners (e.g. the North American Free Trade Agreement – NAFTA). A customs union adds the requirement that all members set a common trade policy against non-members (e.g. SACU) while a common market does the above, and adds the free movement of labour and capital and sets a common trade policy against non-members (e.g. the former European common market). An economic union requires members to harmonize their tax, monetary and fiscal policies, can include the creation of a common currency, and generally concedes some sovereignty to the larger organization (for example, the EU).

The political case for integration has two main points: (1) by linking countries together, making them more dependent on each other, and forming a structure whereby they regularly have to interact, the likelihood of violent conflict and war will decrease; and (2) by linking countries together, they have greater clout and are politically much stronger in dealing with other nations.

In 2005 the SADC Protocol on Trade was amended and called for the FTA to come into force in 2008 and in that year the trade area met SADC's minimum conditions that 85 per cent of intraregional trade among the partner states must be at zero duty. Of SADC's members 13 are part of the FTA, and of course five members are also members of SACU.

Malawi has been unable to implement its tariff phase-down schedules and is trying to reconcile its tariff rates with those of SADC and a rival trade bloc, the COMESA. Zimbabwe and Tanzania likewise had difficulties in implementing their tariff commitments, especially

Donald L. Sparks

concerning what they consider sensitive products. Mozambique is expected to comply by 2018, while Angola, Seychelles and the DCR remain outside the agreement.

Monetary union and a single currency

The final stage in deepening SADC's regional economic integration would be a single currency, which would effectively create an economic union. SADC's Regional Indicative Strategic Development Plan Implementation Framework targeted 2018 as the (unrealistic) implementation date of a monetary union. SADC's plans to establish a monetary union have been developed by the SADC Committee of Central Bank Governors. The goal is to improve regional monetary cooperation by reforming payment, clearing and settlement systems and harmonizing central banks' legal operational frameworks. The Committee working on a model central bank law and has developed a cross-border payment system.

The region sustains an effective monetary union, the Multilateral Monetary Area (MMA, known as the Rand Zone).[9] Prior to independence, Botswana, Lesotho and Swaziland used the South African Rand as their currency, and there was free movement of capital between them. Following independence in 1972, Botswana, Lesotho, Swaziland and South Africa began negotiations to make the system permanent, resulting in the Rand Monetary Agreement in 1974, when Botswana opted out. The Rand Monetary Area was replaced by the CMA in 1986 with the signing of the Trilateral Monetary Agreement (TMA) between South Africa, Swaziland and Lesotho. This revised agreement gave both Swaziland and Lesotho greater authority in determining their respective monetary policies, although in reality not much has changed. The TMA was in turn replaced by the MMA in 1992 when Namibia formally joined.

A number of scholars have looked at Southern African regional integration,[10] but there has been little research regarding the costs and benefits to members should SADC choose to establish a formal monetary area. As the literature shows, monetary unions themselves are not panaceas for solving economic development problems.[11] The conclusion of several studies on Southern Africa is that the necessary convergence criteria for a viable monetary union appears to be lacking. Until there is more convergence, the chances for a successful monetary union are low.[12]

The Regional 'Tripartite Strategy'

At the 'Tripartite Summit' in June 2011, SADC joined with COMESA and the ECA to establish the African Free Trade Zone (AFTZ) which includes all members from each organization. The AFTZ consists of 26 countries with a joint GDP of an estimated US $624 billion. The agreement should eventually ease access to commercial markets within the zone and end problems arising from the fact that most of the members belong to multiple groups.

The AFTZ, now known as the Common Market for COMESA-EAC-SADC, includes 26 regional countries with a combined population of nearly 600 million people and a total GDP of approximately US $1.0 trillion. The main objective of the COMESA-EAC-SADC is to strengthen and deepen economic integration of the region. Such integration is expected to be achieved through the harmonization of policies and programmes throughout the three RECs primarily in trade, customs and infrastructure.

The free trade zone is part of what is called 'Tripartite Cooperation' between the three RECs with the stated vision of improving 'the economic and social welfare of the citizens of the COMESA-EAC-SADC region, through the promotion of regional economic growth by creating an enabling environment for regional trade'.[13] The focus areas are market integration (through the reduction of tariff and non-tariff trade barriers), infrastructure (rail, road, ports and

366

customs posts) and industrial development. The groups also agreed to the introduction of a tripartite regional coordination mechanism (which harks back in some ways to the original mission of SADCC) and each REC has established a permanent unit to support coordination efforts within the respective groups.

SADC-EU Economic Partnership

In 2014 the EU and SADC established the Trade Related Facility with initial funding of €31.6 million. The agreement (which ends in 2019) will help SADC members to focus on customs cooperation, technical barriers to trade, rules of origin, trade promotion and development, and trade facilitation.[14]

Further to the goal of increased regional trade integration, SADC and the EU signed an economic partnership agreement (EPA) in 2016.[15] The EU is the largest trading partner of the SADC-EPA group, which to date only includes SACU members Botswana, Lesotho, Mozambique, Namibia, South Africa and Swaziland, with Angola as an observer (sometimes known as SADC-Minus). According to EU Trade Commissioner Cecilia Malmström, the deal aims to facilitate sustainable economic growth in Southern Africa and to reduce poverty in the region.[16]

The SADC-EU EPA will result in tariff- and quota-free access to the EU market for 100 per cent of exports (except for arms) from all SADC EPA countries except South Africa (which will have nearly 98 per cent of its tariffs lifted in full, and about 2 per cent in part). The agreement is important for development purposes, as the SADC members will enjoy easier access to European-produced fertilizers, seeds and farm-related machinery.

In turn, the SADC EPA countries will fully or partially lift tariffs on around 86 per cent of imports from the EU, allowing for some more sensitive items to retain their existing tariffs. This type of agreement is known as asymmetric liberalization and it should be noted that the EU has never before agreed to such a degree of asymmetry on any previous agreement.

The accord also provides some safeguards (or 'safety valves') to help to offset the flow of EU imports into the SADC EPA countries if the level of imports were to jeopardize domestic industries. In addition, newer industries in the SACU member states that may require more time adhere to the 2000 Cotonou Agreement's sustainable development provisions ('infant industry protection'). In any new deal it is required that no trade or investment liberalization shall result in the lowering of social or environmental safeguards. The agreement also boosts regional integration requiring that each SADC EPA member gives to its fellow SADC EPA countries any improved terms that it grants to the EU (similar to most-favoured-nation status).[17]

Other SADC initiatives

While economic integration and trade are at the heart of SADC, the organization has also established a range of other initiatives which are briefly discussed below:[18]

Politics, defence and security

The major areas of focus are politics and diplomacy (including maintaining good political governance); defence (mediating regional conflicts, but not providing military assistance); police (regional police chiefs meeting to help to combat cross-border crime); state security (trying to prevent conflict between member states); public security (cross-border operations combatting smuggling, for example); and, regional peacekeeping (with members contributing to United Nations and AU peacekeeping operations).

Donald L. Sparks

Disaster risk management

The region suffers from a variety of natural disasters (drought, floods, cyclones, etc.) that have regional impacts. Climate change is expected to exacerbate many of these risks and SADC has created a Climate Services Centre to help with early warning and mitigation.

Infrastructure

The region has varied levels of infrastructure development. It has long been recognized that improved regional infrastructure is key to increased trade, economic growth and development. Through its Infrastructure and Services Directorate, SADC has identified a group of related sectors as key priority areas such as energy, tourism, meteorology, telecommunications, water and sanitation, and ports.

Agriculture and food security

Agriculture remains a major economic player for most SADC member states (contributing between 4 per cent and 27 per cent of GDP). Due to dramatic climate changes (as discussed above), the lack of appropriate farming technology and investment, poor transportation infrastructure, state disincentives and a range of other related constraints, SADC has rightly focused on agriculture. Its Food, Agriculture and Natural Resources Directorate is responsible for food security, crop and livestock production and fisheries.

Natural resources

The region suffers from a host of unsustainable economic activities and SADC addresses natural resource challenges in forest, wildlife, cross-border conservation areas, water and fisheries.

Health

SADC's Protocol on Health entered into force in 2014 and is helping to make pharmaceuticals more available and fighting communicable and non-communicable diseases (HIV/AIDS, tuberculosis and malaria being the largest threats to the region).

Social and human development

As about half of the population in SADC live below the international poverty line of US $1.50 per day, the organization is trying to address challenges such as employment (especially youth), education, technological innovation and children at risk (including more than 17 million orphans).

Poverty eradication and policy dialogue

There are a number of interrelated challenges that contribute to poverty in Southern Africa (including, but not limited to, lack of resources, low levels of education, gender inequality, unsuitable public policies, lack of employment opportunities), and poverty reduction is SADC's ultimate goal. The SADC Council of Non-Governmental Organizations is the key player in implementing the Poverty and Development Programme.

Conclusion and Prospects

SADC has evolved from a loose affiliation of neighbouring states into an international organization with diverse and ambitious goals, as discussed above. SADC has a range of integration targets, some of which it has met and some that it may never reach. As discussed earlier, SADC's success is further imperilled by member states' participation in other regional, security schemes that may compete with or could undermine SADC's aims. However, the region has finally recognized this problem, and it is possible that the Tripartite Strategy will result in one very large regional FTA and will at some point reduce such competition. It also should be noted that SADC's record beyond the economic sphere has been mixed. For example, according to Human Rights Watch, 'SADC has been criticized for its laxity on making human rights compliance within its member states a priority'.[19]

It may well be that the traditional linear integration model (i.e. starting as a PTA and then evolving into a FTA, a customs union with a common external tariff, a monetary union and a single currency cumulating in an economic union, as discussed earlier) is not suited to Southern Africa.[20] Like regional trade blocs elsewhere, there are inherent conflicts when members have varying degrees of economic development, income, political stability, transportation infrastructure and governing philosophies. South Africa's GDP of US $740 billion is almost 300 per cent larger than that of Seychelles (with $2.5 billion), the group's smallest economy.[21] Levels of competency vary, as do levels of education (for example, the literacy rate in Seychelles is 97 per cent, compared to 65 per cent in Malawi). And, as discussed above, the region's output is mostly primary products with limited regional markets.

Another approach (which is more organic) and which may be more appropriate, is the variable geometry (sometimes called the development integration) approach. This allows much more flexibility and takes into account the various differences noted above. Indeed, this is the model the EU used when it created its monetary union as initial members were able to opt in but were not required to.

Many of the regional challenges (developmental, security, climate, diseases and natural disasters, to name but a few) cannot be solved effectively by individual members. Floods and drought know no boundaries. Wars spread across borders. Business now seek low-cost production and customers often without regard to nationalities. Southern Africa certainly needs increased regional cooperation. In that regard, the important question remains as to how deep and how wide should – and could– the community become?

The question of width is probably easier to answer. With the AU's recognition of regional economic communities, it is unlikely that few members of nearby groups (COMESA or ECA) will jump ship for SADC. The political and economic costs of such a move could be considerable, while the gains (at least in the short term) could be hard to measure. Officially, SADC does not seek to increase its membership, although Burundi has applied and Rwanda has expressed an interest in joining. And should the common market for COMESA-EAC-SADC ever become truly effective, then the idea of expansion would be answered by default.

The question of deeper integration is harder to resolve. As noted above, the group is in the process now of harmonization in a range of areas (even sports, for example, with the organization hosting its own multi-sport event, the SADC Games, which was first held in 2004 in Maputo and the seventh in 2016 in Luanda). Again, a strengthened and successful tripartite grouping would necessitate wider harmonization.

With 20 per cent of total trade, the intra-SADC share of total regional trade is relatively high compared to other economic communities in Africa. However, until the SADC countries' economies diversify there is little chance for significantly increased trade with each other, and

Donald L. Sparks

thus the deepening of economic relations remains unlikely. Few, if any, members are in favour of expansion and the smaller non-member neighbours might be reluctant to join owing to South Africa's overwhelming economic and commercial dominance. Perhaps this chapter's concluding question of moving towards a deeper and wider union is inappropriate: SADC has never sought to form a union like the EU. Ultimately, it will be the individual decision of each member state – and each potential member – to determine how deep and how wide the community should become.

Appendix A: SADC Protocols (dates signed)

- Protocol Against Corruption (2001)
- Protocol on Combating Illicit Drug Trafficking (1996)
- Protocol on the Control of firearms Ammunition and other Related Materials (2001)
- Protocol on Culture, Information and Sport (2001)
- Protocol on Education and Training (1997)
- Protocol on Energy (1996)
- Protocol on Extradition (2002)
- Protocol on the Facilitation and Movement of Persons (2005)
- Protocol on Finance and Investment (2006)
- Protocol on Fisheries (2001)
- Protocol on Forestry (2002)
- Protocol on Gender and Development (2008)
- Protocol on Health (1999)
- Protocol to the Treaty Establishing SADC on Immunities and Privileges (1992)
- Protocol on Legal Affairs (2000)
- Protocol on Mutual Legal Assistance in Criminal Matters (2002)
- Protocol on Mining (1997)
- Protocol on Politics, Defence and Security Cooperation (2001)
- Protocol on Science, Technology and Innovation (2008)
- Protocol on Shared Watercourses (2000)
- Protocol on the Development of Tourism (1998)
- Protocol on Trade (1996)
- Protocol on Trade in Services (2012)
- Protocol on Transport, Communications and Meteorology (1996)
- Protocol on Tribunal and Rules Thereof (2000)
- Protocol on Wildlife Conservation and Law Enforcement (1999)
- Revised Protocol on Shared Watercourses (2000)

Notes

1 Professor of International Economics, the Citadel and Management Centre, Innsbruck. Special thanks to Mubita Luwabelwa and his staff at the SADC Secretariat for their invaluable insights and up-to-date data. I would also like to thank the Citadel Foundation for supporting my travel to Gaborone in November 2017.

2 Such overlapping and multiple memberships can be positive if they complement the development process but negative if they divert scarce resources for compliance. Apparently, such overlapping has not had a significant negative impact on SADC. See Sylvanus Kwaku Afesorgbor and Peter A. G. Van Bergeijk (2014) 'Multi-Membership and the Effectiveness of Regional Trade Agreements in Western

and Southern Africa: A Comparative Study of ECOWAS and SADC', *South African Journal of Economics*, 82(4): 518–30, doi:10.2139/ssrn.1766522.

3 See Richard Gibb (2012) 'The Southern African Customs Union: Promoting Stability through Dependence', in Chris Saunders, Gwinyayi A. Dzinesa and Dawn Nagar (eds) Region-building in Southern Africa: Progress, Problems and Prospects, London: Zed Books, 148–64; and Konstantinos D. Magliveras (2007) 'The Southern African Development Community: The Organisation, its Policies and Prospects', *International Organizations Law Review*, 4(1).

4 See the 37th SADC Summit, SADC Secretariat, Gaborone, 2017.

5 For further details see www.sadc.int.

6 Mengesha Yayo and Sisay Asefa (2016) 'International Trade Effects of Regional Economic Integration in Africa: The Case of the Southern African Development Community (SADC)', *International Journal of African Development*, 3(2), Article 6. Available at https://scholarworks.wmich.edu/ijad/vol3/iss2/6/.

7 SADC Success Stories (Vol. 2) SADC Secretariat, Gaborone, 2017.

8 SADC Industrialization Strategy and Roadmap, SADC Secretariat, Gaborone, 2015.

9 D. L. Sparks (2013) 'The Future of Monetary Integration in Southern Africa: Should SADC Join the Rand Monetary Area?' in M. Malliaris and M. Anastasios (eds) *The Global Economy: Financial, Monetary, Trade and Knowledge Asymmetries*, Toronto, ON: APF Press.

10 See Ngila Mwase (1995) 'Economic Integration for Development in Eastern and Southern Africa', *Round Table*, 336, October. Merle Holden (1998) 'South African Economic Integration', *World Economy*, 21(4), June; R. McLymont (1999) 'Regional Pact Spurs Trade', *Journal of Commerce*, 29 December; and D. Collings (1983) 'The Rand Monetary Area', International Monetary Fund DM/83/6, February.

11 See P. Kenen (1969) 'The Theory of Optimal Currency Areas: An Eclectic View', in R. Mundel and A. Swoboda (eds) *Monetary Problems of the International Economy*, Chicago, IL: University of Chicago Press; M. Obstfeld and K. Rogoff (1995) 'The Mirage of Fixed Exchange Rates', *Journal of Economic Perspectives*, 9(4); and Xavier Debrun and Paul R. Masson (2013) 'Modelling Monetary Union in Southern Africa: Welfare Evaluation for the CMA and SADC', *South African Journal of Economics*, 81(2): 275–91, doi:10.1111/saje.12008.

12 See D. L. Sparks (2013) 'The Future of Monetary Integration in Southern Africa: Should SADC Join the Rand Monetary Area?' in M. Malliaris and M. Anastasios (eds) *The Global Economy: Financial, Monetary, Trade and Knowledge Asymmetries*, Toronto, ON: APF Press; G. Tavlas (2009) 'The Benefits and Costs of Monetary Union in Southern Africa: A Critical Survey of the Literature', *Journal of Economic Surveys*, 23(1): 1–43; and C. Pattillo (2005) *The Monetary Geography of Africa*, Washington, DC: Brookings Institution Press.

13 See www.sadc.int.

14 SADC Trade Related Facility: An Update, SADC Secretariat, Gaborone, 2016.

15 European Commission (2016) 'Economic Partnership Agreement (EPA) between the European Union and the Southern African Development Community (SDC) EPA Group', Brussels: European Commission, October.

16 Bridges Africa (2016) 'EU-Southern Africa Economic Partnership Agreement Takes Effect', 13 October.

17 Euractive (2016) 'New African Economic Partnership Enters into Force, Critics Still Unconvinced', 11 October.

18 SADC Secretariat.

19 Human Rights Watch (2016) 'SADC Urged to Address Rights at Summit', 14 August. Available at www.hrw.org/news/2014/08/13/sadc-address-members-rights-issues.

20 See Peter Draper (2010) 'Rethinking the (European) Foundations of Sub-Saharan African Regional Economic Integration', OECD Development Centre, Working Papers No. 293, Paris: OECD Publishing.

21 Central Intelligence Agency (2017) World Factbook, Washington, DC, 2017.

32
COMESA
A case study

B. Seetanah, R. V. Sannassee, S. Fauzel and Paul Okiira Okwi

Introduction

The last three decades have witnessed a proliferation of regional initiatives which have come about in view of the slow progress achieved at the level of the World Trade Organization (WTO), particularly after the debacle of the Doha Round. The underlying motives for an increased willingness to become a member of a regional bloc reside in the various benefits which potentially could be unlocked including trade creation, the provision of a platform from which to tackle regional issues and increasing bargaining power for individual member countries since negotiations at WTO level are usually done through a regional trading bloc.

The situation is no different in the case of African countries. There have been a number of initiatives by member countries towards promulgating regional trade agreements (RTAs) with a view to fast-tracking trade liberalization measures to foster increased trade both within the regional groupings and also with non-members. However, despite their best intentions and despite the implementation of numerous trade liberalization measures in member countries, the expected benefits from such groupings have yet to materialize in the case of African RTAs. There are many reasons for this including elements of multiple membership, similarities in countries' exports and the non-negligible detrimental impact of non-tariff measures.

In view of the above, the aim of this chapter is to provide a descriptive analysis of one of Africa's most important RTAs, namely the Common Market for Eastern and Southern Africa (COMESA) through a review of its performance since its inception and a discussion of the impact of the establishment of the continental free trade area (FTA) on its probable future performance.

The background to COMESA

COMESA was established in December 1994 and replaced the former Preferential Trade Area for Eastern and Southern African States which came into existence in 1981. Interestingly, COMESA was the first FTA to be launched in Africa on 31 October 2000 under the African Union. In addition, nine of its member states, namely Djibouti, Kenya, Madagascar, Malawi, Mauritius, Sudan, Zambia and Zimbabwe, eliminated their tariffs for products originating in

COMESA, in line with the tariff reduction schedule implemented in 1992. In January 2004 Burundi and Rwanda joined the FTA. As such, these 11 member states not only eliminated customs tariffs but also engaged in the eventual elimination of quantitative restrictions and other non-tariff barriers. The FTA comprises 13 member states trading on a full duty-free and quota-free basis, with the remaining countries at various stages of joining the FTA. This is shown in Table 32.1:

Table 32.1

COMESA FTA member states	COMESA non-FTA member states
Burundi, Comoros, Djibouti, Egypt, Kenya, Madagascar, Malawi, Mauritius, Rwanda, Seychelles, Uganda, Zambia, Zimbabwe	Democratic Republic of the Congo (DCR), Eritrea, Ethiopia, Sudan, Swaziland

Overall, COMESA comprises 19 member countries, namely Burundi, Comoros, DCR, Djibouti, Egypt, Eritrea, Ethiopia, Kenya, Libya, Madagascar, Malawi, Mauritius, Rwanda, Seychelles, Sudan, Swaziland, Uganda, Zambia and Zimbabwe. Unfortunately, however, COMESA also suffers from the issue of overlapping membership with seven countries and four COMESA members being also members of the Southern African Development Community (SADC) (the DRC, Malawi, Mauritius, Seychelles, Swaziland, Zambia and Zimbabwe) and of the East African Community (EAC) (Burundi, Kenya, Rwanda and Uganda), respectively.

Objectives of COMESA

> The main goal behind the agreement was to promote economic prosperity through regional integration.

According to Article 3 of the COMESA Treaty,[1] the aims and objectives of the common market are as follows:

a   to attain sustainable growth and development of the member states by promoting a more balanced and harmonious development of its production and marketing structures;

b   to promote joint development in all fields of economic activity and the joint adoption of macroeconomic policies and programmes in order to raise the standard of living of its peoples and to foster closer relations among its member states;

c   to cooperate in the creation of an enabling environment for foreign, cross-border and domestic investment including the joint promotion of research and adaptation of science and technology in prospective developments;

d   to cooperate in the promotion of peace, security and stability among the member states in order to enhance economic development in the region;

e   to cooperate in strengthening the relations between the common market and the rest of the world and the adoption of common positions in international fora; and

f   to contribute towards the establishment, progress and the realization of the objectives of the African Economic Community.

These objectives point to a number of prerequisites. First, the treaty stresses the need for the adoption of a common customs bond guarantee scheme, the simplification and harmonization

373

of trade documents and procedures, the establishment of conditions regulating the re-export of goods from third countries within the common market, and the introduction of rules of origin with respect to products originating in the member states. Moreover, the treaty also promulgates cooperation among countries in terms of transport and communications which would serve to facilitate trade among member states as well as the movement of persons. Moreover, appropriate regulations have been put in place to facilitate transit within the common market as well as the adoption of a Third Party Motor Vehicle Insurance Scheme.

Another specific undertaking of the treaty was in the field of industry and energy. The treaty stresses the need to eliminate rigidities in the structures of production and manufacturing so as to provide goods and services that are of high quality and are competitive in the common market. Moreover, the provision of an appropriate enabling environment for the participation of the private sector in economic development and cooperation within the common market was also highlighted. There was also the need to cooperate in the field of industrial development; to adopt common standards, measurement systems and quality assurance practices in respect of goods produced and traded within the common market; and to provide an enabling stable and secure investment climate.

Furthermore, cooperation in monetary and financial matters and gradually establishing convertibility of the member states' currencies was necessary, as was the need for the harmonization of member countries' macroeconomic policies. In the agricultural sector, the treaty emphasized the need for cooperation among the member states to develop this sector and on the need to adopt a common agricultural policy. Moreover, the coordination of the member countries' policies was also deemed crucial with respect to the establishment of agro-industries.

The treaty also emphasized the need to harmonize the methodology of collection, processing and analysis of information required to meet the objectives of the common market. Furthermore, the adoption of a regional policy that would address the economic problems that member states might face during the implementation of this treaty and propose ways and means of redressing such problems in a manner that would satisfy the conditions of equitable and balanced development within the common market was also included.

The future agenda of COMESA includes negotiating an agreement on trade in services, the establishment of a common market by 2015, the formation of a monetary union by 2018 and the launch of a COMESA community by 2025. After 2025 COMESA expects to be a single trade and investment area with no internal tariffs, non-tariff and other impediments to the movement of goods, services, capital and people.[2] COMESA is also actively engaged in the formation of a COMESA-EAC-SADC tripartite free trade area to promote regional trade involving 26 countries covering nearly half of the continent. This is motivated by the current overlap of membership among COMESA, SADC and the EAC. Of the 19 members of COMESA, seven are members of SADC and four are members of the EAC.

Economic performance of COMESA member countries

COMESA comprises countries of widely varying size ranging from very small island economies to very large nations. In addition, it also includes countries at different levels of industrialization including 12 least developing economies and seven middle-income countries. Per caput GDP (on a purchasing-power parity (PPP) basis) varies from US $777.96 for Burundi to $28,391.33 for Seychelles. A closer look at Table 32.2 shows considerable variations in the average GDP growth rate for member countries between 2005 and 2016. For instance, we can see that countries such as Burundi, Comoros, Eritrea and Libya have registered negative growth rates while other nations have experienced relatively smaller growth rates (less than 2 per cent),

Table 32.2 Average GDP growth rate for member countries between 2005 and 2016

Country	GDP per caput, PPP 2016	GDP growth rates 2005–16 average	Economic classification	Trade, % of GDP, 2015
Burundi	777.96	–0.14	L-LDC	35.7826689
Congo, Dem. Rep.	800.75	1.98	LDC	70.1296184
Comoros	1522.26	–0.22	LDC	62.6
Djibouti	2,631★	2.06	LDC	77.126051★
Egypt, Arab Rep.	11131.72	1.68	MIC	34.845943
Eritrea	1,451★	–0.40	LDC	33.8598276★
Ethiopia	1734.92	5.32	L-LDC	39.6561241
Kenya	3155.94	1.83	MIC	44.3775451
Libya	21,152★	–2.28	MIC	103.223082★
Madagascar	1506.01	0.15	LDC	78.9451151
Mauritius	21087.75	2.76	MIC	107.94581
Malawi	1169.31	1.56	L-LDC	65.1594143
Rwanda	1913.40	3.69	L-LDC	49.3451981
Sudan	4730.29	3.20	LDC	19.1008041
Swaziland	8342.71	1.12	MIC	96.9501632
Seychelles	28391.33	2.90	MIC	185.736169★
Uganda	1848.79	2.09	L-LDC	45.9296362
Zambia	3922.34	2.56	L-LDC	84.3155592
Zimbabwe	2006.37	0.57	MIC	60.2060235

Source: Author computation; data from world development indicators (WDI).

L-LDC, LDC and MIC refer to landlocked least developed country, least developed country and middle-income country, respectively.

namely the DCR, Egypt, Kenya, Madagascar, Swaziland and Zimbabwe. Meanwhile, a third category of member countries (Djibouti, Ethiopia, Mauritius, Rwanda, Sudan, Seychelles, Uganda and Zambia) have posted higher than average GDP growth rates.

Although these figures point to highly skewed growth rates among the member nations, nonetheless one can contend that the third group has been resilient in the face of the global economic downturn, despite the many challenges faced by them, and this may be due to improved macroeconomic management, market-based reforms and continued structural progress in many of these countries.[3]

In 2015 the overall GDP growth for the COMESA region was 6.0 per cent, with region-wide inflation increasing marginally from 6.0 per cent in 2014 to 6.8 per cent in 2015. Interestingly, however, it should be noted that lower global oil prices and the continuing decrease in food prices as well as prudent monetary policies have contributed to single-digit inflation in most member countries.

Share of value added to GDP, 2016

Figure 32.1 delineates the share in 2016 of value-added for industry in the various countries. Figure 32.1 clearly highlights the prominence of both the service and the agricultural sectors,

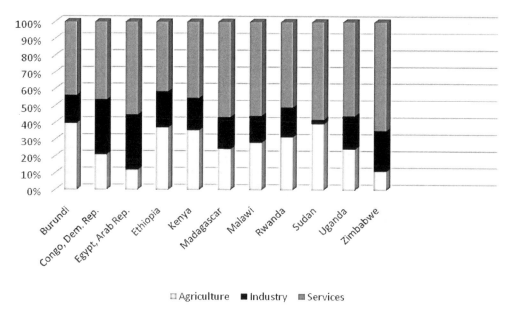

Figure 32.1 Share of value added to GDP, 2016
Source: Author computation with data obtained from world development indicators.

albeit that the latter displays lesser importance than the former. Undoubtedly, ensuring that discussions and positive outcomes result from any potential agreement on trade in services between member countries would be fundamental for the region to produce any trade creation benefits.

COMESA external trade

The figures shown in Table 32.3 demonstrate that trade between COMESA member states and the rest of the world increased from US $240 billion in 2011 to $233 billion in 2016, although external trade decreased in 2015 to $255 billion. Total exports for 2016 amounted to approximately $68.8 billion which represented a sharp contraction from the record high figure of $116 billion which was registered in 2012. The clear trend of declining export figures may be due to the very sharp fall in world commodity prices which has taken place over the last few years. Imports, on the other hand, have remained steady with figures approximating $165 billion in 2016.

Intra-COMESA trade

Table 32.4 shows that, with regard to intra-COMESA export trade, Egypt and Kenya recorded the highest figures in 2015, with a share of 22 per cent and 17 per cent, respectively. Zambia, the DCR and Uganda followed with 13 per cent, 12 per cent and 11 per cent, respectively. More specifically, Egypt exported products worth US $1.7 billion and Kenya $1.3 billion. The value of Zambia's exports was $977 million and those of the DCR $896 million.

Meanwhile, with regard to intra-COMESA import market share, Zambia registered the biggest share, at 24 per cent, with goods worth US $2.0 billion in 2015. The DCR, Sudan, Uganda, Libya, Kenya and Egypt followed with a share of 11 per cent, 10 per cent, 9 per cent,

COMESA

Table 32.3 Global COMESA trade, 2003–2016, values in US $ millions

	Exports	Re-exports	Total exports	Imports	Total trade
2005	53,701	2,093	55,794	62,309	118,103
2006	71,062	1,816	72,878	71,887	144,765
2007	73,777	2,100	75,877	88,642	164,520
2008	110,028	2,608	112,631	136,245	248,876
2009	82,841	2,469	85,310	118,489	203,799
2010	112,033	3,183	115,216	141,542	256,758
2011	92,735	3,691	96,426	144,290	240,716
2012	104,569	2,992	107,561	154,608	262,168
2013	112272.3	4024.4	116329.9	173149.4	289,479
2014	108507.4	5722.3	93930.1	190856.2	284,786
2015	72333.5	3406.9	75740.3	179476.4	255,217
2016	64103.7	2024	68817.7	164,821	233,639

Source: Data from COMSTAT and COMTRADE database. Available at http://comstat.comesa.int/ and https://comtrade.un.org/. [4]

Table 32.4 Intra-COMESA trade, 2015

Rank	Exporter	Value	% share	Importer	Value	% share
1	Egypt	1,672.8	22.1	Zambia	2,003.6	24.3
2	Kenya	1,309.1	17.3	Congo, Dem. Rep.	882.1	10.7
3	Zambia	976.5	12.9	Sudan	796.1	9.7
4	Congo, Dem. Rep.	896.4	11.8	Uganda	699.2	8.5
5	Uganda	835.9	11.0	Libya	624.1	7.6
6	Sudan	481.9	6.4	Kenya	612.6	7.4
7	Rwanda	321.5	4.2	Egypt	550.9	6.7
8	Mauritius	225.7	3.0	Zimbabwe	432.7	5.3
9	Malawi	212.0	2.8	Rwanda	394.8	4.8
10	Swaziland	174.3	2.3	Ethiopia	296.4	3.6
11	Ethiopia	162.1	2.1	Malawi	224.1	2.7
12	Zimbabwe	101.4	1.3	Mauritius	171.3	2.1
13	Libya	85.8	1.1	Madagascar	143.8	1.7
14	Burundi	48.0	0.6	Eritrea	99.1	1.2
15	Madagascar	45.9	0.6	Djibouti	93.8	1.1
16	Eritrea	9.2	0.1	Seychelles	84.9	1.0
17	Djibouti	6.8	0.1	Burundi	77.3	0.9
18	Comoros	2.2	0.0	Comoros	22.3	0.3
19	Seychelles	1.6	0.0	Swaziland	21.0	0.3
	Total	7,569.3	100.0	Total	8,230.0	100.0

Source: COMSTAT database in COMESA Summit bulletin, 2016[5].

8 per cent 7.4 per cent and 6.7 per cent, respectively. Zambia's intra-COMESA imports were mainly copper ores and concentrates and cobalt oxides and hydroxides from the DCR.

However, trade dealings among COMESA members are relatively weak when compared to the figures posted by other trading blocs (see Table 32.5) with figures approximating must US $9 billion compared with the North American Free Trade Agreement (NAFTA) countries, for example, where the value of intra-trade reaches almost $1,155 billion. Such findings support the analogy that trade openness through regional integration does not always result in significant increases in intra-trade, inter-trade, and economic growth unless certain prerequisites are present which include minimization of non-tariff measures, political will and export diversification. For instance, the study by Ebaidalla and Yahia[6] on intra-trade integration within COMESA found that COMESA member countries trade below their potential and perform poorly in terms of regional trade integration compared to Association of Southeast Asian Nations (ASEAN) member states[7]. Another study on COMESA by Tumwebaze and Ijjo[8] found that member countries experienced economic growth primarily because of population growth, increments in capital stock and global GDP, and increased openness to global trade. However, no significant increase in economic growth was registered for member states. Similarly, Seetanah et al[9], in their study of the trade-creating impact of three RTAs, namely SADC, COMESA and the EAC, and using a gravity model for the period 1996–2009, found that the co-efficient for the variable RTA was only significant for COMESA and the EAC albeit that the co-efficient was very small. They thus concluded that the trade creating impact of these RTAs was very minimal.

Table 32.5 Value of intra-group trade, 2015 (exports in US $ millions)

Rank	Trade bloc	Value	Value %
1	APEC	$5,767,009	69.29
2	European Union	$3,358,777	61.65
3	TPP	$1,902,513	50.35
4	NAFTA	$1,154,775	48.14
5	APTA	$358,011	24.45
6	ASEAN	$283,858	20.92
7	ARAB LEAGUE	$146,682	18.83
8	GCC	$75,288	16.67
9	MERCOSUR	$40,118	14.76
10	SADC	$30,620	14.59
11	SAARC	$23,187	14.48
12	ECOWAS	$10,024	13.36
13	COMESA	$8,889	12.20
14	CAN	$7,688	11.48
15	CEFTA	$4,018	10.84
16	EAC	$2,731	10.65
17	CARICOM	$2,635	7.99
18	EFTA	$1,981	7.00
19	ECCAS	$1,188	1.79
20	OECS	$62	0.49

COMESA export markets

With regard to COMESA's major export trade markets for the period 2003–12 (Table 32.6), it can be observed that the European Union (EU) is a major export destination for most COMESA member countries with countries such as the DCR, Madagascar, Mauritius, Uganda, Zambia and Zimbabwe being heavily reliant on EU countries as major exports destinations. In 2012 exports to the EU approximated US $33 billion, up from $31 billion in 2011. Products exported to the EU included petroleum oils and oils obtained from bituminous minerals from Libya. In addition, the People's Republic of China, South Africa and the USA were also major importers of COMESA products with the African Growth and Opportunity Act (AGOA) contributing to the figures achieved for the USA. In 2015 the EU was still ranked first with total exports from COMESA amounting to $21 billion in 2015 and these accounted for 26 per cent of COMESA's total exports. Major exports to the EU are petroleum oils and oils obtained from bituminous minerals, crude and natural gas in gaseous state primarily exported by Libya and Egypt. China was ranked as the second major export market for COMESA products after the EU in 2015. The COMESA region was ranked in third position with intra-exports worth $9.6 billion, recording an increase of almost 5 per cent from 2014 levels and accounting for 12 per cent of total COMESA exports. Figure 32.2 and Figure 32.3 show COMESA's major export trade market shares for 2015 and values for the period 2014–15.

COMESA and trade facilitation

As mentioned previously, trade facilitation is a crucial strategic concern for COMESA in that undeniably it can serve to boost intra-trade among member nations. Trade facilitation relates mainly to improvements in transport infrastructure, the modernization of customs administration and the removal of other non-tariff trade barriers. Trade facilitation, it may be argued, allows member countries to reap the benefits of open trade thereby contributing to economic

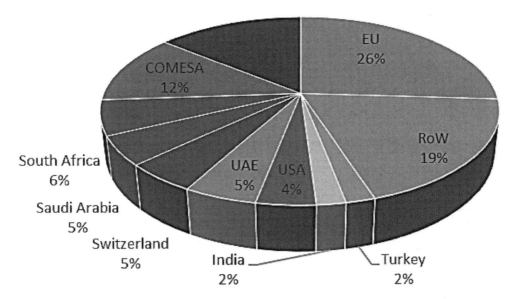

Figure 32.2 COMESA key export market shares, 2015
Source: COMSTA database.[10]

Table 32.6 COMESA's major export trade markets, 2003–12, values in US $ million

Rank	Market	2003	2004	2005	2006	2007	2008	2009	2010	2011	2012
1	EU	17,864	22,840	29,685	30,027	38,053	55,014	34,889	49,791	31,143	33,977
2	China	2,116	1,932	3,462	7,000	3,079	12,180	11,659	17,141	13,845	14,305
3	COMESA	2,145	2,335	3,208	2,970	4,520	6,772	6,621	9,040	10,134	9,263
4	Switzerland	948	1,266	1,823	3,214	3,714	5,791	3,930	4,909	5,550	6,471
5	South Africa	2,929	2,506	1,785	2,483	3,105	2,529	2,695	4,262	5,727	6,030
6	USA	1,516	2,071	3,548	4,865	5,201	6,350	4,285	4,950	3,697	5,833
7	United Arab Emirates	272	305	873	1,272	859	1,586	2,104	3,105	3,053	4,854
8	India	635	548	693	1,948	1,854	2,752	2,401	2,392	2,889	3,836
9	Saudi Arabia	408	524	764	754	903	1,695	1,827	2,152	2,402	2,333
10	Turkey	1,142	1,649	2,161	681	669	1,168	1,236	1,451	1,736	2,156
	Rest of the world	5,427	6,500	7,792	9,663	13,919	16,795	13,663	16,023	16,249	18,503
	Total	35,399	42,475	55794	72,878	75,877	112,631	85,310	115,216	96,426	107,561

Source: COMESA annual report 2012/13; data from COMSTAT database and UN COMTRADE database.

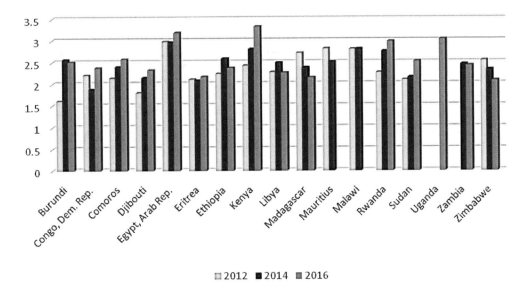

Figure 32.3 Logistics Performance Index, 2012–16
Source: Author computation with data from world development indicators.

growth and welfare maximization. By removing trade barriers, trade can be expanded. Also, more trade in countries provides economic opportunities for the population.

Trade facilitation mainly aims at harmonizing certain rules between countries to promote greater efficiency, transparency and predictability, based on norms, standards and internationally accepted practices, and may constitute a very important source of increased competitiveness for any given country, given its potential to reduce trade barriers and costs.[11] In addition, any improvement in processes and procedures that translates into greater trade facilitation may be beneficial to a country through (i) increased total factor productivity as a result of reduced levels of human and material input;[12] (ii) gains in trade, which can serve to increase income, which in turn may foster human development;[13] and (iii) greater offerings and choices to the public and to consumers as a consequence of the increase in trade. Taken together these benefits can only serve to enhance living standards.[14]

In this regard, the UNCTAD report on Trade Facilitation in Regional Trade Arrangements[15] showed that trade facilitation has been a crucial feature of regional integration in COMESA. A number of trade facilitation measures have been implemented (not necessarily by all member states) and these include air transport liberalization; the COMESA carriers licence; the Harmonized Axle Loading and Maximum Vehicle Dimension; the Regional Customs Transit Guarantee Scheme ratified by Burundi, Djibouti, Ethiopia, Madagascar, Malawi, Uganda, Zimbabwe, Kenya, Sudan and Rwanda; the Relaxation of Visa Requirement; the Protocol on Free Movement; common tariff nomenclature; the Protocol on Rules of Origin; the COMESA single customs declaration document; the implementation of common standards and capacity building with development of customs training modules.

With regard to the performance of individual COMESA countries in implementing trade facilitation measures, Figure 32.3 shows the logistic performance index for 17 COMESA member states from 2012–16. It can be observed that most countries have displayed an improved logistic performance index although countries such as Madagascar and Zimbabwe still need to promulgate more measures to foster trade facilitation.

Continental FTA: implications

In June 2015, at a meeting in Egypt, consensus was reached by members of three RTAs, namely SADC, COMESA and the EAC, to establish the Tripartite Free Trade Area (TFTA), a bloc which will undoubtedly change the whole spectrum of trade negotiations in the region. At the time of writing, of the 26 members who will need to ratify, 18 states have already signed the agreement and have already proceeded with implementing it.

The implementation of the TFTA is bound to have far-reaching consequences, in that it would comprise of a total population in excess of 630 million with a consolidated GDP of US $ 1.2 trillion. This entails the possibility for generating economies of scale, fostering greater competition, increasing the market attractiveness for potential investors inside and outside the region and increasing the potential for greater intra-regional trade. In addition, as posited by Mold and Mukwaya,[16] the potential benefits to be engendered from tariffs elimination are substantial with estimates of increases in intra-regional trade approximating 30 per cent. They also argued that the TFTA would be particularly beneficial for the manufacturing and food-processing sectors, which would in turn enhance export diversification and increased integration at the upper levels of global value chains. This can only serve to increase employment opportunities within the region with the resulting impact of increasing growth and fostering poverty alleviation.

Furthermore, it may also be contended that through the provision of a single economic area which promulgates harmonized trade policies embedded within a single regulatory framework, can only serve to alleviate the negative impact of multiple memberships, facilitate trade negotiations, reduce the costs of doing business and promulgates the potential for cross-border infrastructural projects.

However, in order for the expected benefits to materialize from such an enlarged FTA, there are certain fundamental lessons to be learnt. First, it has always been argued that African heads of state are always keen to ratify agreements, yet it has proved very difficult to implement them. As such, the political commitment to ensure the implementation of the various measures outlined in the agreement has to be there. Second, Africa, as a whole suffers from a critical lack of trade expertise to ensure the smooth implementation of agreements. To that end, it is fundamental that trade and trade-related capacity-building programmes are instituted to improve the technical capability of policymakers and those who tasked with implementing the such agreements. Third, there needs to be consensus with respect to eliminating non-tariff measures and barriers. Although the preservation of local interests might be fundamental in some instances, nonetheless, it is crucial that countries adopt a common approach geared towards the overarching aim of liberalizing trade and removing impediments to trade.

Conclusion

This chapter has sought to provide a descriptive analysis of COMESA, one of Africa's most important RTAs, through a review of its performance since its foundation and through a discussion of the impact of the establishment of the continental FTA on its probable future performance. The analysis showed that although such an agreement has led to increasing trade both among and vis-à-vis non-members, such benefits are highly skewed with some countries delineating very positive GDP growth rates while others have hardly progressed. Moreover, trade facilitation has been a crucial feature of regional integration in COMESA. Many of the member countries have indeed improved their trade facilitation index. However, regarding welfare indicators, it can be observed that there is growing and widespread poverty within the COMESA region, especially among the rural communities.

In addition, changes operating at global level are bound to have a major impact on the future of the trading bloc. For instance, the establishment of the TFTA, the withdrawal of the USA from the Trans-Pacific Partnership and Brexit (the UK's departure from the EU), both major trading partners of COMESA will undoubtedly influence trade flows between the latter and the two trading partners.

Irrespective of the above influential element, however, for member countries to further benefit from the treaty while ensuring more equitable gains, it is crucial that COMESA members strive to ensure that there is sustained improvement in political and economic governance and also sound economic management to enhance productivity in sectors where member countries possess comparative advantages.

Furthermore, it is crucial that measures are collectively implemented to foster increased regional sourcing which can serve to promulgate intra-trade. Nevertheless, what this requires is a general upgrading of the capabilities of the region's small and medium-sized enterprises which would effectively allow them to participate in regional higher value-added chains.

Last but not least, there are certain prerequisites which are fundamental for promoting trade. First, member countries should prioritize the diversification of their economies as this is crucial for enhancing regional trade. Second, continuous and sustained investment in infrastructure is essential since this is a vital ingredient for foreign direct investment from countries within the region and from non-member states. Finally, facilitating the movement of professionals and business persons, streamlining administrative procedures both at the border, even more so for landlocked nations, and at the ports in addition to sustained efforts geared towards trade liberalization and the removal of non-tariff measures can only lead to increased productivity, and thereby decreasing the cost of doing business and trade creation.

Notes

1 www.comesa.int/wp-content/uploads/2016/06/COMESA-Treaty.pdf.
2 www.comesa.int/wp-content/uploads/2016/06/comesa_annualReport-2011_12_final.pdf.
3 www1.uneca.org/Portals/rio20/documents/Workshop-Institutional-StrategicFrameworks/Day%20Two/COMESA-Presentation.pdf.
4 http://comstat.comesa.int/ and https://comtrade.un.org/.
5 www.comesa.int/summit2016/2016-summit-bulletins/.
6 E. M. Ebaidalla and A. M. Yahia (2014) 'Performance of IntraCOMESA Trade Integration: A Comparative Study with ASEAN's Trade Integration', *African Development Review*, 26(S1): 77–95.
7 C. K. Ntara, D. Njeje, W. Tenambergen, P. Opiyo, H. Kariuki, P. Kihara, T. Senaji, E. Njoka, B. Namiinda and J. Onyando (2005) 'African Trading Blocs and Economic Growth: A Critical Review of the Literature', *American Journal of Tropical Medicine and Hygiene*, 71(6): 765–73.
8 H. K. Tumwebaze and A. T. Ijjo (2015) Regional Economic Integration and Economic Growth in the COMESA Region, 1980–2010', *African Development Review*, 27(1): 67–77.
9 B. Seetanah, R. V. Sannassee and V. Tandrayen (2011) 'Regional Trade Integrations: A Comparative Study of African RTAs', Proceedings of the ICITI 2011 Conference , Mauritius.
10 http://comstat.comesa.int/.
11 F. Augusto and T. Scorza (2007) 'Trade Facilitation and Customs Procedures in WTO Negotiations: Outputs for Customs Law in Brazil', *Brasileira Magazine Foreign Trade*, 92: 44–58.
12 O. Canuto (2012) 'Facilitating Trade, Facilitating Development', *World Post*, 18 July.
13 J. S. Wilson, C. L. Mann and T. Otsuki (2003) 'Trade Facilitation and Economic Development: A New Approach to Quantifying the Impact', *World Bank Economic Review*, 17(3): 367–89.
14 B. Rippel (2011) 'Why Trade Facilitation Is Important for Africa', *Africa Trade Policy Notes*, 27.
15 http://unctad.org/en/PublicationsLibrary/dtltlb2011d1_en.pdf.
16 A. Mold and R. Mukwaya (2015) 'The Effects of the Tripartite Free Trade Area: Towards a New Economic Geography in Southern, Eastern and Northern Africa?' No. 15/04.

33

RCEP and Asian economic integration

Ganeshan Wignaraja[1]

Introduction

Negotiations are quietly proceeding in Asia on the Regional Comprehensive Economic Partnership (RCEP) amid a turbulent global trade policy landscape. Concerns about failing sectors and unemployment has made liberalization of trade unfashionable in the post-global financial crisis era. The World Trade Organization (WTO)'s Doha Round has effectively come to an end after years of negotiations. A more isolationist USA has left the ambitious Trans-Pacific Partnership (TPP) and is renegotiating the North American Free Trade Agreement (NAFTA). The UK's decision to leave the European Union (known as Brexit) has made EU trade policy uncertain and provides impetus for deglobalization.

Covering about three billion people across 16 diverse economies, RCEP is the largest free trade agreement (FTA) in the world. While concerns exist about the depth of the eventual preferential agreement, RCEP can support Asian economic integration and global recovery. A priori reasoning and model-based studies show that a comprehensive RCEP agreement can deliver notable economic gains for Asia and the world economy. However, several potential risks could reduce the extent of these gains.

This chapter assesses the role of RCEP in Asian economic integration. It covers several important issues in contemporary policy debates: (1) the framework for the RCEP negotiations including its aim, scope and time frame; (2) the contribution of RCEP to Asian economic integration; (3) quantitative assessments of the economic impact of RCEP and a discussion of risks; (4) case studies of India, which some argue is hesitant to liberalize its trade further and could be a stumbling block to the RCEP negotiations, and of Sri Lanka being omitted; and (5) pathways to multilateralizing RCEP.

The framework for negotiations

RCEP was launched at the East Asia Summit in November 2012 in Phnom Penh, Cambodia.[2] While it was envisaged that the partnership would expand ASEAN's role in coordinating regional trade, RCEP's key aim is to reconcile two long-standing proposals into a large, region-wide trade agreement. The two proposals being joined are (1) the East Asian Free Trade Agreement (or ASEAN+3), which includes the ten members of the Association of Southeast Asian Nations (ASEAN), the People's Republic of China, Japan and the Republic of Korea (South Korea); and (2) the Comprehensive Economic Partnership (or ASEAN+6), which has added Australia, New Zealand and India. The first was backed by China, and the second by Japan. RCEP neatly bridges the two proposals by adopting an open accession scheme so that any party that meets the template can join. Furthermore, ASEAN has been accorded the coordinating role for the RCEP process, which means better inclusion of the interests of smaller ASEAN economies.

The good thing about RCEP is that it is a step-by-step process, so any economy that meets the template can join. The states parties have declared that their goal is to achieve a modern and comprehensive trade agreement, and the negotiations are supposed to be guided by several key principles,[3] including:

- maintaining consistency with WTO rules, such as General Agreement on Tariffs and Trade (GATT) Article XXIV and General Agreement on Trade in Services (GATS) Article V;
- providing improvements over existing ASEAN+1 free trade agreements (FTAs);
- reflecting different levels of development of participating economies, and allowing for special and differential treatment for least developed countries; and
- ensuring an open accession clause to enable participation of any ASEAN FTA partner, as well as other external economic partners, at a future date.

The core of the RCEP negotiating agenda will cover trade in goods, services trade, investment, economic and technical cooperation, and dispute settlement. More specifically, RCEP seeks to achieve the following:

- gradually reduce tariff and non-tariff barriers on most trade in goods to create a free trade area;
- largely eliminate restrictions and discriminatory measures on trade in services for all sectors and modes of services;
- create an open and facilitative climate for investment;
- address the special needs of less developed ASEAN economies through early elimination of tariffs on products of interest to them, and through the provision of development assistance to narrow development gaps; and
- provide for a dispute settlement mechanism to effectively resolve trade disputes.

A three-year time frame for the RCEP talks was planned at the outset with formal negotiations beginning in May 2013 and scheduled to conclude by the end of 2015. But this ambitious time frame has slipped with the negotiations turning out to be more protracted than expected. Table 33.2 in the Appendix provides an overview of the various rounds and key discussion points distilled from official statements on the governmental websites of Australia and New Zealand. Between May 2013 and October 2017 as many as 20 rounds of RCEP negotiations were hosted by different members. Reflecting the optics of ASEAN centrality in the RCEP negotiations, half the rounds were hosted by ASEAN economies but poorer and smaller economies (e.g. Cambodia and Laos) did not host a single round. The hosts for the other were the richer and larger ASEAN dialogue partners with Australia, China, India, South Korea and Japan hosting two each. The most recent was held in Songdo, South Korea, in October 2017. The 21st round of RCEP negotiations was held in Yogyakarta, Indonesia, in February 2018.

The joint leaders statement issued at the first ever RCEP Leaders Summit in Manila in November 2017 instructed ministers and officials to intensify work in 2018 to conclude the RCEP negotiations (RCEP Leaders, 2017).[4] At the time of writing, the RCEP agreement was expected to be signed in November 2018 during the ASEAN Leaders Summit in Singapore. If this were to happen, a time frame of less than six years for concluding RCEP seems reasonable. It would be similar to the six years it took to conclude the ambitious TPP agreement among 12 states parties, dating from the formal start of negotiations in March 2010 to the signing of the agreement in February 2016. However, the USA withdrew from the TPP in January 2017 and the remaining 11 economies reached a partial agreement in November 2017, popularly termed the TPP-11. Meanwhile, the WTO Doha Round of trade negotiations among 164 members began in November 2001 but has been virtually abandoned after over 15 years of talks.

There is little official information on why the RCEP talks were not concluded by the end-2015 deadline. These talks are being conducted in secret in keeping with a trend followed internationally.[5] Media reports suggest that progress appears to have been made in the some-what less contentious areas of goods trade and trade facilitation. *China Daily* reported that the RCEP states parties reached preliminary agreements on tariff reduction schedules, rules of origin, customs procedures, and other trade facilitation measures.[6] Presumably agreement on these issues was somewhat easier as the RCEP provisions are fashioned on those of the five existing ASEAN+1 agreements with dialogue partners such as the ASEAN-China FTA, the ASEAN-Japan FTA and the ASEAN-India FTA. Furthermore, large exclusion lists on goods trade exist in sensitive areas like agriculture in most ASEAN+1 FTAs.

Meanwhile, negotiations have been slow and more contentious in the more difficult areas of barriers to services trade, investment rules and intellectual property rights (IPRs). This is partly due to differences in levels of development of the states parties, the negotiation positions of the states parties, and the influence of domestic lobbies. Some of these issues are discussed below with reference to India.

Contribution to economic integration

RCEP comprises of a heterogeneous group of economies. A handful of commodity-rich economies (like Brunei, Malaysia and Indonesia), co-exist among several largely resource-poor economies. As Table 33.1 shows disparities exist in world shares of gross domestic product (GDP) and trade as well as per caput income. RCEP includes some of the world's largest economies (e.g. China, Japan and South Korea) as well as smaller ones (e.g. Brunei, Laos and Myanmar). Furthermore, the grouping includes a mix of high-income economies (Australia, Brunei, South Korea, Japan, New Zealand and Singapore), middle-income economies (China, Indonesia, Malaysia, the Philippines and Thailand) and low-income economies (Cambodia, India, Laos, Myanmar and Viet Nam).

Levels of trade opening and FTA strategies also vary. Singapore has virtually no import tariffs, some have low tariffs of less than 10 per cent, while others have tariffs above 10 per cent. Approaches to FTA-led integration differ, with very active economies with bilateral and regional FTAs (e.g. Singapore, Japan, China and South Korea) alongside more passive economies (e.g. Cambodia, Laos and Myanmar) which rely on ASEAN regional FTAs.

It is noteworthy, however, that decades of rapid trade-led growth, outward-oriented development strategies particularly in East Asia, and demographics have propelled the diverse RCEP trade bloc to become more globally important than others in several respects. Figure 33.1 shows the RCEP members' world shares of population, GDP, total trade and foreign direct investment (FDI) inflows for 2016 compared with those of the TPP-11 and the EU. The RCEP

Table 33.1 Selected economic characteristics of RCEP members

	GDP per caput (PPP, current international US $, 2016)	Share of global GDP % (2016)	Share of global trade % (2016)	MFN Tariffs, simple average applied rates[a]	Number of FTAs as of 2017[b]
North-East Asia					
Japan	41,470	6.54	7.60	4.0	15
China	15,535	14.82	20.20	9.9	16
South Korea	35,751	1.87	5.34	13.9	16
ASEAN					
Brunei	77,441	0.02	0.05	1.2	8
Cambodia	3,736	0.72	0.70	11.2	6
Indonesia	11,612	1.23	1.70	7.9	9
Laos	6,186	0.02	0.05	8.5	8
Malaysia	27,681	0.39	1.85	5.8	14
Myanmar	5,773	0.09	0.14	5.6	6
Philippines	7,806	0.40	0.96	6.3	7
Singapore	87,856	0.39	4.60	0.0	20
Thailand	16,916	0.54	2.44	11.0	13
Viet Nam	6,424	0.27	1.82	9.6	10
Other					
India	6,572	3.00	4.39	13.4	13
Australia	46,790	1.59	2.35	2.5	12
New Zealand	39,059	0.24	0.47	2.0	11

Sources: Author's calculations based on World Development Indicators, World Bank. Available at https://data.worldbank.org/data-catalog/world-development-indicators; Asia Regional Integration Centre, Asian Development Bank. Available at https://aric.adb.org/beta; Tariff and Trade Map, WTO. Available at www.wto.org/english/res_e/statis_e/statis_maps_e.htm (accessed December 2018).

Note: a = Most-favoured-nation (MFN) tariffs are the most recent figures available, mostly for 2016; b = FTAs that have been signed and enforced.

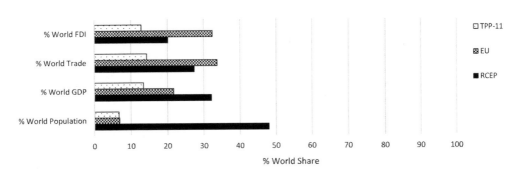

Figure 33.1 Global importance of RCEP, the TPP-11 and the EU in 2016

grouping covers as much as half of the world's population (48.1 per cent) and over one-third of its GDP (32.2 per cent). It also accounts for one-quarter of world trade (27.3 per cent) of world trade and one-fifth of world FDI inflows (20.2 per cent). The EU is smaller than RCEP in terms of world population (6.9 per cent) and world GDP (21.7 per cent) but is a larger global trader and larger destination for FDI with 33.7 per cent of world trade and 32.4 per cent of world FDI inflows. Meanwhile, on all the four indicators, the TPP-11 is smaller than RCEP and the EU.[7]

There are several a priori reasons why an RCEP agreement can contribute to the process of Asian economic integration. First, RCEP can help to insure against rising protectionist sentiments in the global economy if the new regional rules align with WTO agreements on goods and services. Non-tariff measures – e.g. import quotas, various government subsidies, arbitrary customs regulations, technical barriers to trade and sanitary and phytosanitary regulations – have been increasing since the global financial crisis including in Asia. The Trump Administration's America First approach seems to be tilting the USA towards isolationism and protectionist tendencies. Painstakingly collected data on non-tariff measures by Evenett and Fritz[8] show that the US Administration's approach is becoming more discriminatory towards the G20 and that others are beginning to resort to murky trade distortions.

Second, RCEP can help the spread of sophisticated global supply chains that make Asia the world's factory. If a comprehensive agreement can be reached, trade barriers impacting goods and services among RCEP members will fall. Rules governing the entry and operation of foreign firms should become more transparent and predictable. Market size will expand beyond national borders, and a larger regional market will facilitate the realization of economies of scale in production.

Third, in the area of investment rules – where there exists only a rather basic WTO agreement (the Trade Related Investment Measures, or TRIMs) – RCEP promotes easier FDI flows and technology transfers by multinational corporations. Reducing barriers to investment and supporting a regional, rules-based FDI regime will further facilitate regional supply chain trade.

Fourth, by simplifying trade rules, RCEP will also reduce the overlap among Asian FTAs and the risk of an Asian 'spaghetti bowl' of multiple trade rules.[9] Rules of origin, in particular, could be rationalized, made more flexible, and better administered through electronic means. This would reduce transaction costs for businesses, particularly for small and medium-sized enterprises (SMEs).

Fifth, despite likely exclusions on some sensitive agricultural items, falling trade barriers in the RCEP region will make available cheaper imports of food and consumer goods, which will significantly benefit consumers and low-income households in member countries. As food is a major item in the consumption basket of the poor, this will help to reduce poverty in RCEP economies.

Quantifying economic impacts and risks

Simulation modelling using computable general equilibrium (CGE) models are useful in quantifying the income effects of eliminating import tariffs on the trade in goods, and liberalizing cross-border trade in services through the formation of trade agreements. CGE models can trace economy-wide effects of policy changes and point to unintended economic consequences. CGE studies typically show that significant economic gains can arise from RCEP.

Gilbert et al.[10] provide long-term estimates of the gains from RCEP but assume only full liberalization of import tariffs. They show that full liberalization of goods trade under RCEP results in notable income gains to the world economy of US $127 billion. As Figure 33.2 shows, the more dynamic ASEAN economies see notable gains – Malaysia (1.7 per cent), Singapore (1.6 per cent), Viet Nam (1.4 per cent) and Thailand (1.2 per cent). The remaining

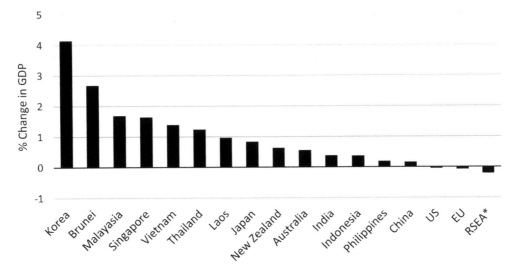

Figure 33.2 Gains from a goods-only RCEP
Note: RSEA (Rest of South East Asia).
Source: Author's presentation based on Gilbert *et al.*, 'The Economic Impact of the Trans-Pacific Partnership'.

ASEAN economies see mixed results, with Brunei and Laos achieving bigger gains than the rest of South-East Asia. In North-East Asia, South Korea (4.1 per cent) gains the most, China the least (0.2 per cent) and Japan (0.84 per cent) comes in between. Interestingly, India (0.4 per cent) records somewhat bigger gains than China. The other major global economies outside RCEP, such as the EU and the USA see relatively small loses. Thus, economies which are part of RCEP gain while economies outside of RCEP lose out from the agreement.

Factoring in liberalization of import tariffs, services barriers and trade costs gives more significant long-term estimates of the gains from RCEP. Kawai and Wignaraja[11] show that in such a comprehensive liberalization scenario, RCEP can offer large income gains to the world economy, reaching US $260 billion (or a 0.54 per cent change from baseline income).

Furthermore, as Figure 33.3 shows, all economies that are party to RCEP are projected to achieve gains. For ASEAN's dynamic members, projected gains are more significant and in a different order: Thailand (12.8 per cent), Viet Nam (7.6 per cent), Malaysia (6.3 per cent), and Singapore (5.4 per cent). For the rest of ASEAN – Cambodia, Indonesia, the Philippines and the remaining ASEAN economies – the gains are less than 3 per cent. Among the economies of North-East Asia, South Korea is projected to experience the largest gain under RCEP (6.4 per cent), while gains for Japan and China are less than 2 per cent. Meanwhile, the gains for India are 2.4 per cent, for Australia they are 3.9 per cent, and for New Zealand 5.2 per cent.

However, non-members of RCEP experience losses, and the magnitude of these losses differs by economy. For instance, the simulations show that the rest of South Asia – Bangladesh, Pakistan and Sri Lanka – are projected to lose out from RCEP.

The study also shows that the implementation of the RCEP scenario is likely to result in significant structural changes towards manufactures and services (and away from agriculture and other primary products) in Asia. There are also shifts within manufacturing. Among ASEAN's dynamic members, Thailand is projected to experience gains in electrical machinery and electronics, motor vehicles, and services; Viet Nam in textiles and clothing; and Malaysia in metals and metal products. In the rest of ASEAN, Cambodia sees losses in a key sector (textiles and

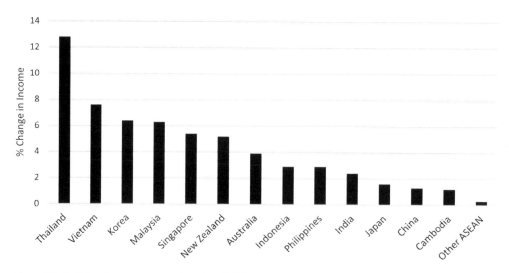

Figure 33.3 Gains from a comprehensive RCEP
Source: Author's presentation based on Kawai and Wignaraja, 'Policy Challenges Posed by Asian FTAs'.

clothing), and the Philippines in motor vehicles. Meanwhile, China achieves gains in electrical machinery and electronics, and India in services and metals. Japan and South Korea see gains in most manufacturing sectors. Strikingly, seven economies see declines in agriculture, and the others see negligible gains.

However, fully realizing the gains from RCEP will depend on addressing several risks during the negotiations and afterwards.[12] First, there are twin risks arising from the RCEP negotiating partners having different levels of development, global importance and interests. This creates the politically difficult challenge of respecting the central role of smaller ASEAN economies in driving the RCEP negotiations, amid the presence of Japan and rising Asian economies (China, South Korea and India). The related economic challenge is that granting exclusions to protect sensitive sectors will ultimately limit the scope of preferential liberalization and gains from RCEP. This risk seems more likely if low-income members press for differential speeds of opening up sectors.

Second, like all forms of trade liberalization, implementing RCEP preferential liberalization will bring gains and losses at sector level within members. The discussion of model-based studies below sheds light on countries that potentially stand to gain or lose as a result of RCEP. With wages and jobs at risk, adjustment costs may be higher than expected in declining economic sectors and new economic sectors may take time to emerge. The risk of significant losses in some sectors and economies could diminish public support for RCEP and prompt a backlash against Asian economic integration.

Third, there is a risk that firms, particularly SMEs, may underutilize RCEP tariff preferences due to a lack of international competitiveness and a poor understanding of its legal provisions. Unless SMEs can become subcontractors or suppliers to large firms, multinational corporations and large firms could gain disproportionately from RCEP. Fourth, the risk is that the spread of mega-regional FTAs like RCEP and the TPP-11 may exacerbate the divergence between regional and WTO trade rules, thereby causing the continuing erosion of the WTO's central role in global trade governance.

Accordingly, arguments for and moves towards RCEP are supported by economic modelling. The CGE analysis also reveals that some RCEP members and some sectors gain more than others and this issue should be addressed in policy discussions. There is a case for further narrowing development gaps by providing financial and technical support for low-income countries, particularly with respect to trade-related infrastructure, governance reforms, customs modernization, enhancing SME development, and capacity building. Providing transparent rules for non-members to join RCEP in the future is another important policy issue.

Case studies of India and Sri Lanka

India: an insider to RCEP

India is regarded as the new frontier in Asia's economic miracle story. Already accounting for 3 per cent of global GDP in 2016 (Table 33.1), the country has emerged as one of world's fastest growing economies with an expanding middle class in the post-global financial crisis era. Implementation of gradual trade and economic reforms by the government of Prime Minister Narasimha Rao in 1991 has resulted in a relatively open economy with simple average MFN applied tariffs falling to 13.4 per cent in 2016.[13] Agricultural goods (32.7 per cent) enjoy significantly higher tariff protection than industrial goods (10.2 per cent). India has also actively pursued FTA-led regionalism with East Asia.

Since 2013 India has been involved in the RCEP negotiations as an ASEAN dialogue partner. The country's involvement in building closer ties with East Asia dates to the Rao government's 1991 Look East policy to develop strategic and economic relations with the economically important region. However, critics have suggested that subsequent Indian governments emphasized forging strategic foreign policy partnerships and security cooperation with East Asian economies (particularly Japan and Viet Nam) at the expense of building economic relations. Eventually, efforts at fostering closer economic relations bore fruit. During the 2000s India concluded several FTAs with East Asia including a regional FTA with ASEAN in 2010, as well as bilateral agreements with Singapore in 2005, South Korea in 2010, Japan in 2011 and Malaysia in 2011. Bilateral FTA negotiations are also ongoing with Australia, New Zealand, Indonesia and Thailand.

In 2014 Prime Minister Narendra Modi announced a new Act East policy as a signature element of his government's economic strategy.[14] Modi's bold move signalled a more proactive approach to strengthening economic ties with dynamic East Asia. This soon translated into intensified Indian engagement in the RCEP negotiations. The Modi government felt that RCEP would fill in critical, missing FTA links between India and RCEP members by providing for India-China trade and India-Australia/New Zealand trade. In turn, Indian business would have greater opportunities to access a larger Asian market, to exploit India's relative strength in services with its vast pool of qualified professionals (including from sectors such as information technology), and to better integrate Indian manufacturing into global supply chains centred on East Asia (including in automotives, electronics and consumer goods).

However, three challenging issues have emerged during the RCEP negotiations. The first is liberalization of tariffs on goods trade. Relative to India, other RCEP members typically have a comparative advantage in key areas of goods trade. Several members have requested that import tariffs on agricultural and industrial goods be eliminated for more than 92 per cent of tariff lines.[15] Furthermore, some members have suggested reducing tariffs to 5 per cent on an additional 7 per cent of tariff lines taking total coverage of goods trade to as much as 99 per cent. This implies gradually phasing out tariffs in India and exposing both agriculture and industry to competition from RCEP members. Australia and New Zealand have demanded that India lower tariffs on dairy and wheat in particular and that tariff elimination should occur on items of significant trade value rather than just a large number of items.

The major concern for India is virtually free goods trade with China, where cheap imports are thought to have adversely affected import substituting manufacturing sectors in India.[16] Some argue that, due to pervasive state subsidies, Chinese firms have prices that few Indian firms can match. Concerns have also been expressed about opening up sensitive economic sectors and infrastructure to inward investment from China, particularly by state-owned enterprises that unfairly benefit from government subsidies.

India's counter-offer was tariff elimination based on a three-tier system with 42.5 per cent of tariff lines for China, Australia and New Zealand, 65 per cent for Japan and South Korea and 80 per cent for ASEAN.[17] However, other RCEP members rejected India's offer in favour of a single offer for all RCEP members. Despite fierce opposition from its farmers and industrialists, India made a new offer of eliminating tariffs on 70–75 per cent of goods with some deviations for China, Australia and New Zealand which are not FTA partners. But this has not satisfied other RCEP members, particularly Australia and New Zealand which are insisting on increased market access for dairy and wheat.

Agriculture remains a difficult area for RCEP negotiations as India wishes to protect the livelihoods of the rural poor who are electorally important. However, some Indian manufacturing exports have grown (including pharmaceuticals, the automotive sector, textiles, and food processing), and this trend is likely to continue under RCEP. The CGE projections indicate that India can achieve potential income gains of 0.4 per cent under a full tariff elimination scenario (Figure 33.2) which can rise up to 2.4 per cent under a comprehensive RCEP scenario (see Figure 33.3). Furthermore, WTO-compatible trade remedies such as temporary safeguards and anti-dumping measures are available to tackle import surges from China. Indian businesses should prepare for market openings under RCEP by investing in price, quality and delivery systems that meet international standards. The Indian government should also implement second-generation structural reforms, invest more in transport and energy infrastructure, invest in tertiary-level technical education, and strengthen technology institutions.

The second challenge concerns the liberalization of services trade. RCEP offers inroads for Indian services to China and the rest of East Asia, where India has achieved a comparative advantage on world markets.[18] These advantages include information technology, professional services, law, banking, and educational services. Moreover, India has seen increasing tourism arrivals from the Asia-Pacific region, and tourism services offer further opportunities for Indian businesses. India has been arguing for services trade liberalization in return for opening up of goods trade in the RCEP negotiations. In particular, India has been suggesting that there should be an easing of visa restrictions on the movement of skilled workers across RCEP borders for short-term work.[19]

Emulating the Asia-Pacific Economic Cooperation (APEC) Business Travel Card, it has proposed a RCEP Travel Card to facilitate visa-free travel for movement of skilled workers in areas such as information technology, engineering, training and investment banking. However, there have been few offers from RCEP members in this area.[20] ASEAN members have refused to offer even the limited level of openness that exists among the ten members of the grouping. ASEAN members are concerned that temporary movement of Indian skilled workers could become permanent with a loss of local jobs. Discussions are continuing over this issue.

The third challenge is IPRs rules. India has an internationally competitive pharmaceutical sector with strengths in manufacturing cheap generic drugs. It is also a global leader in using the WTO Agreement on Trade-Related Aspects of Intellectual Property Rights (TRIPS) safeguards to balance the rights of inventors with the health rights of the population. Leaked text from a 2015 draft of the RCEP agreement showed that Japan and South Korea were seeking strengthened protection for intellectual property raising concerns about reduced access to cheap generic drugs, high prices for non-generic drugs and adverse consequences for public health in low-income RCEP member states.[21] Civil society groups in India argue that the so-called TRIPS-plus standards in RCEP would increase protection for patent monopolies of multi-national corporations and enforcement mechanisms while simultaneously removing the ability of RCEP members, including India, to use TRIPS health safeguards.

Despite these challenges, India appears committed to supporting closer Asian economic integration through RCEP. RCEP can be achieved for India because it has the more ambitious India-Japan and India-Korea FTAs. Indian businesses, then, should embrace RCEP, as it includes all the ASEAN economies, as well as others. Modi's government has implemented a flurry of pro-growth measures since 2014 including investment climate reforms, a 'Make in India' initiative, and fiscal reforms, and has boosted public sector accountability and increased public infrastructure investment. It has upset some parts of business with two other measures – demonetizing large currency notes to fight corruption and introducing a general sales tax. But the economy is recovering from these shocks and the sales tax lays the basis for healthier future public finances. Sweeping domestic reforms over the next few years will make it easier for India to lock in the gains from trade by concluding an RCEP agreement

Sri Lanka: an outsider to RCEP

Until recently, none of the other South Asian economies expressed any interest in joining RCEP, but this is changing as policymakers are becoming concerned about the economic effects of being left out of the large regional integration group. This policy view is confirmed by academic research. A recent CGE-based study by Rahman and Ara[22] investigated the potential economic impact of tariff elimination under RCEP, the TPP and the Transatlantic Trade and Investment Partnership (TTIP). Their analysis revealed that under complete integration, in terms of tariff elimination under these three mega-FTAs, excluded South Asian countries could face significant negative impacts on their economies.

Sri Lanka – the first South Asian economy to adopt economic reforms in 1977 – is probably its most open. In 2015 the country's simple average MFN applied tariffs were 9.3 per cent with agricultural tariffs of 23.7 per cent and industrial tariffs of 6.9 per cent.[23] During the 2000s trade flows and inward FDI with RCEP economies increased significantly, particularly with China. Since 2015 a national government led by President Maithripala Sirisena and Prime Minister Ranil Wickremesinghe has pursued a more proactive FTA strategy including FTA negotiations with China, India and Singapore. There is also talk of an FTA with Thailand. After a relatively short period of negotiations requiring only eight rounds in under two years, the Sri Lanka-Singapore FTA was signed on 23 January 2018. This landmark FTA is Sri Lanka's first agreement beyond trade in goods and signals its serious intent to engage in FTA-led regionalism with East Asia.

However, Sri Lanka is excluded from RCEP as it is neither a member of ASEAN nor a Dialogue Partner. Sri Lanka's national government wishes to join the RCEP process and hopes that Singapore will use its influence as the 2018 ASEAN Chair to support its case. Joining RCEP offers Sri Lanka the prize of simultaneous access to a huge regional Asian market, attracting dynamic Asian FDI flows and entering global supply chains centred on East Asia. It is also arguably simpler to attain and is less draining on Sri Lanka's scarce trade negotiating capacity than separately negotiating bilateral FTAs with each of the 16 members.[24] Through its membership of the ASEAN Regional Forum, Sri Lanka is involved in informal multilateral discussions on security issues in Asia and the Pacific but not on economic issues. Observer status of ASEAN is an important first step in Sri Lanka's quest for RCEP membership and should be pursued through enhanced diplomatic efforts with ASEAN economies. Furthermore, think tanks in Sri Lanka should study the economic effects of RCEP on Sri Lanka and conduct a Track 1.5 dialogue with think tanks and other RCEP states parties.[25]

Pathways to multilateralization

With the demise of the WTO Doha Round, RCEP and the TPP are becoming even more central to Asia's trade architecture. While the TPP and RCEP are often portrayed as competing trading blocs due to US-China geopolitical rivalry,[26] how they might fit together is the weighty question facing Asia and the world economy today.

The rivalry between the TPP and RCEP stems from differences in their membership scope and level of ambition. Between 2010 and 2017 the USA led the TPP talks and was pivotal to the process. Following the departure of the USA, Australia and Japan are leading the TPP-11.

China – the world's second largest economy and the assembly hub of global supply chains – is not party to the TPP-11. Neither is rapidly growing India, which has a comparative advantage in information technology services and is fostering manufacturing development through its 'Make in India' initiative. Supported by China and India, ASEAN is driving negotiations for RCEP, which does not include the USA.

The TPP is an ambitious, 21st-century trade agreement dealing with complex behind-the-border regulatory issues.[27] Although the RCEP negotiations are ongoing, the TPP agreement is likely to be deeper than RCEP in two respects. First, with respect to the core issues covered by both RCEP and the TPP, the latter will have deeper commitments (e.g. faster and more comprehensive liberalization of goods trade). Second, the TPP will cover more areas than RCEP (by as much as 29 chapters) that aim to substantially reduce barriers to trade, as well as expand the rules to achieve regulatory coherence among members.

The TPP and RCEP are better seen as complementary pathways to a rules-based regional trading system in Asia.[28] First, some Asian economies enjoy certain advantages by being party to both trade pacts. These so-called overlapping members include four ASEAN members (Brunei, Malaysia, Singapore and Viet Nam) as well as Japan. For instance, their companies could enjoy TPP-11 tariff preferences when selling to Canada and Mexico, as well as RCEP tariff preferences when sourcing parts and components from China or India. Clearer regional trade rules including those on investment and dispute settlement would also be available. Eliminating tariffs and streamlining business regulations can translate into real cost advantages for companies in global supply chains. Moreover, if one agreement were to be derailed, the other could still be available. It therefore seems advisable for Asian countries to sign up to both agreements.

Open accession appears to be a feature in both pacts. The number of overlapping members could increase. Of the Asian countries, South Korea, Indonesia, the Philippines and Thailand expressed an interest in joining the TPP. Meanwhile, any ASEAN FTA partner that did not take part in the initial RCEP negotiations is able to join at a later date, provided that it meets the terms agreed with other participating economies.

The hope that China and possibly India might eventually join the TPP-11 would strengthen the coverage and economic benefits of the agreement. After all, China and India are gradually implementing their own long-overdue structural reforms. China has begun reforming its state-owned enterprises though mixed ownership of state firms and efforts to improve their corporate governance. India has loosened its regulations on equity limits for foreign investors.

Furthermore, it is possible that the TPP-11 and RCEP could be merged into a region-wide FTA – a Free Trade Agreement of Asia and the Pacific. At the APEC Summit in Beijing in November 2014, leaders launched a collective study on issues related to the realization of the region-wide FTA; the results of the exercise were reported at the APEC Summit in Peru in November 2015. Interestingly, this collective study was co-chaired by China and the USA, which may bode well for the future of Asia-Pacific trade. Despite the Trump Administration's criticisms of various trade deals, some suggest that a Bilateral Investment Treaty between China and the USA could be concluded in the next few years.

An optimal outcome would be a region-wide agreement that combines high-standard liberalization in the TPP-11, special and differential treatment for developing countries in RCEP and open accession. If designed well, such a comprehensive deal could rationalize the region's trade rules and effectively render the TPP-11 and RCEP redundant.

Conclusion

This chapter examined the role of RCEP in Asian economic integration. This is a difficult task as patchy official information exits on the progress of the RCEP talks. The ambitious three-year time frame for the RCEP talks has slipped but trade negotiators are under political pressure to reach an agreement in late 2018. Preliminary agreement on less contentious issues and a push by major regional economies have increased the chances of this happening.

RCEP is globally important as a trading bloc, and model-based studies suggest that it will generate notable income gains for Asia and the global economy. All RCEP members will benefit, but the magnitude of gains varies between economies. Structural changes induced by RCEP will shift economic activity toward manufactures and services. Outsiders to RCEP such as the EU and USA will lose out.

Realizing the benefits from RCEP depends on addressing risks during the negotiations and afterwards. These include ensuring ASEAN centrality in the RCEP process, supporting declining economic sectors, ensuring optimal use of RCEP trade preferences, and the erosion of WTO's role in global trade governance.

Rapidly growing India is keen to forge closer economic ties with East Asia through its Act East policy and RCEP. But various negotiation challenges have emerged on liberalizing goods and services trade as well as intellectual property rules. Some of these concerns seem overstated. Indian services and some areas of manufacturing stand to gain under RCEP. A renewed partnership between Indian businesses and government will help to prepare for market opening under RCEP. Sri Lanka risks losses from trade diversion from the advent of RCEP. The country has expressed an interest in eventually joining RCEP and its recently signed FTA with Singapore offers a stepping stone towards this end.

The way forward for the RCEP negotiations should be to take the best features of the existing ASEAN+1 FTAs[29] and to use them as a basis for negotiations to maximize the quality of RCEP and to observe the latest time frame for reaching an agreement. Afterwards, significant business support services would be needed for SMEs to improve their international competitiveness and lower the costs of using RCEP. Enhancing domestic structural reforms, investing in cross-border infrastructure, and streamlining trade facilitation would also help elicit a private sector response to he RCEP. Furthermore, adjustment assistance and social safety nets can help to mitigate the negative effects of trade liberalization under RCEP on affected sectors and jobs.

Finally, a WTO agenda on global supply chains and regionalism will facilitate greater coherence between mega-regionals like RCEP and WTO rules.

Appendix

Table 33.A1 Overview of RCEP negotiating rounds, 2013–17

Round	Place and date	Main discussion points
1	Bandar Seri Begawan, Brunei Darussalam 9–13 May 2013	• The round focused on developing a clear framework for negotiations on goods, services and investment. • The meeting established a Working Group on Trade in Goods, a Working Group on Trade in Services and a Working Group on Investment.
2	Brisbane, Australia 23–27 September 2013	• The meeting agreed to establish two new sub-Working Groups on rules of origin and customs procedures and trade facilitation to commence work at the third round.
3	Kuala Lumpur, Malaysia 20–24 January 2014	• The 16 RCEP participating countries made progress in Kuala Lumpur on core goods, services and investment issues. • The participating countries agreed at the third round to establish four new working groups on economic and technical cooperation, competition, intellectual property and dispute settlement.
4	Nanning, China 31 March–4 April 2014	• The 16 participating countries engaged in negotiations on goods, services and investment issues. • Participating countries hold a diversity of views. • They continued substantive work on intellectual property, competition, economic and technical cooperation and the approach to scheduling services and investment commitments.
5	Singapore 21–24 June 2014	• Negotiators focused on the scope of the RCEP agreement and the level of ambition for negotiations on tariffs, services and investment. • New negotiating groups on legal and institutional issues, sanitary and phytosanitary measures, and standards, technical regulations and conformity assessment procedures met for the first time.
6	Greater Noida, India 1–5 December 2014	• Around 550 officials continued negotiations across 12 negotiating groups and made progress on draft chapter text. • Negotiators worked to bridge differences on the level of ambition for market access commitments.
7	Bangkok, Thailand 9–13 February 2017	• Officials focused on expediting work on the core negotiating issues and draft chapter text.
8	Kyoto, Japan 5–13 June 2015	• Progress was made on narrowing differences between the participating countries on goods, services and investment leading into the Intersessional RCEP Ministerial Meeting to be hosted by Malaysia.
9	Nai Pyi Taw, Myanmar 1–7 August 2015	• Officials focused on the guidelines for initial market access offers for goods. • Officials commenced market access negotiations on services, with all countries having submitted their initial services offers. • The Working Group on Electronic Commerce met for the first time. Discussions on telecommunications and financial services started.

Round	Place and date	Main discussion points
10	Busan, Korea 12–16 October 2015	• Officials commenced market access negotiations on goods, services and investment. • The first substantive meetings of the Sub-Working Groups on Financial Services and Telecommunications were convened.
11	Bandar Seri Begawan, Brunei Darussalam 15–19 February 2016	• Officials worked constructively on market access in goods, services and investment throughout the week, making progress on draft chapter text and benchmarks for further improvements. • Officials working on rules of origin discussed product specific rules and draft text. • On services, all RCEP participating countries submitted their initial offers.
12	Perth, Australia 17–29 April 2016	• Made progress across a range of key issues, such as market access and draft chapter text. • Roundtable events with invited speakers were also held on financial services, e-commerce and investor aftercare with strong engagement and attendance from industry representatives. • Dialogue was also held with the East Asia Business Council Working Group on RCEP. • Countries are working on establishing regional standards and architecture that will promote trade and investment among RCEP participating countries into the future.
13	Auckland, New Zealand 12–18 June 2016	• All RCEP participating countries have now submitted initial offers for trade in goods and trade in services as well as initial reservation lists for investment. • Trade in services market access negotiations continue on a bilateral and plurilateral basis. In goods, negotiators continued to work on market access and progress on rules of origin was welcomed.
14	Ho Chi Minh, Viet Nam 14–19 August 2016	• The Trade Negotiating Committee focused its efforts on advancing market access negotiations, especially on the core areas of trade in goods, trade in services and investment to ensure a balanced, high-quality and mutually beneficial comprehensive economic partnership. • Discussions also focused on other outstanding issues, such as whether to include government procurement in the scope of the RCEP Agreement. • Text-based negotiations in other areas of negotiations were also discussed, including on competition, intellectual property, economic and technical cooperation, e-commerce and legal and institutional issues.
15	Tianjin, China 17–21 October 2016	• A key achievement of the negotiations in China was the conclusion of negotiations on the draft chapter text on Economic and Technical Cooperation. • The concluded chapter will complement existing economic partnerships among RCEP participating countries, by supporting effective implementation and utilization of the RCEP Agreement to accelerate the narrowing of development gaps and maximize mutual benefits among the RCEP participating countries.

Round	Place and date	Main discussion points
16	Tangerang, Indonesia 2–10 December 2016	• The Meeting welcomed the conclusion of the chapter on SMEs. • Likewise, negotiators had a stakeholder engagement session with representatives from 13 international, regional and local civil society organizations and took note of their views and concerns on a wide range of issues, including particular concerns regarding possible adverse impacts of some provisions in other agreements.
17	Kobe, Japan 21 February–3 March 2017	• RCEP participating countries made progress in Kobe across RCEP's three core market access areas (goods, services, investment), and on rules issues including intellectual property, electronic commerce and legal and institutional issues. • The Working Group on Economic and Technical Cooperation completed its work in previous negotiating rounds.
18	Manila, Philippines 2–12 May 2017	• The Meeting expressed shared commitment to work collectively and in a cooperative manner to progress the negotiations in a more accelerated way. • The negotiations made progress across the Working Groups on Trade in Goods and Trade in Services and their respective Sub-Working Groups, as well as the Working Groups on Investment, Intellectual Property, Competition, e-Commerce, and Legal and Institutional Issues. • The Working Groups and Sub-Working Groups continued their deliberations to further advance market access and text-based negotiations.
19	Hyderabad, India 18–28 July 2017	• The negotiations made progress across all Working Groups and Sub-Working Groups on market access and on rules. • The newly established Working Group on Government Procurement and Sub Working Group on Trade Remedies also met for the first time at this round. • The Meeting recognized the urgency of substantially advancing the RCEP negotiations and agreed on a set of key elements for significant outcomes in RCEP to be achieved by the end of 2017.
20	Songdo, Korea 17–28 October 2017	• During the negotiating round, progress was made on text negotiations across all areas. Negotiators focused their efforts to prepare for a further intensification of work in 2018. • Negotiators from the Trade Negotiations Committee (TNC), and the Working Groups on Trade in Services, Investment, Legal and Institutional Issues, Intellectual Property and Electronic Commerce met with representatives from international, regional and local civil society organizations. • In addition, the TNC also had a special session with Susana Malcorra, Chair of the 11th World Trade Organization Ministerial Conference (MC11), to exchange views on the importance of the multilateral trading system and achieving good outcomes at MC11.

Sources: Author's presentation based on Department of Foreign Affairs and Trade, Australia. Available at http://dfat.gov.au/trade/agreements/rcep/pages/regional-comprehensive-economic-partnership.aspx; Department of Foreign Affairs and Trade, New Zealand. Available at www.mfat.govt.nz/en/trade/free-trade-agreements/agreements-under-negotiation/rcep; ASEAN. Available at http://asean.org/?static_post=rcep-regional-comprehensive-economic-partnership.

Notes

1 Lakshman Kadirgamar Institute for International Relations and Strategic Studies (LKI), Colombo and Overseas Development Institute (ODI), London. The views expressed are mine and should not to be attributed to the LKI or the ODI. Pabasara Kannangara deserves thanks for efficient research assistance.

2 Sanchita Basu Das (2012) 'RCEP: Going Beyond ASEAN+1 FTAs', Singapore: Institute of Southeast Asian Studies, ISEAS Perspective, 17 August. Available at www.iseas.edu.sg/documents/publication/ISEAS%20Perspective_4_17aug12.pdf.

3 RCEP Ministers (2012) 'Guiding Principles and Objectives for Negotiating the Regional Comprehensive Economic Partnership'. Available at www.dfat.gov.au/fta/rcep.

4 RCEP Leaders (2017) 'Joint Statement on the Negotiations for the Regional Comprehensive Economic Partnership (RCEP), 14 November. Available at www.asean.org.

5 However, some like the European Union (EU) attempt to keep their citizens more informed about FTA negotiations to reinforce public trust and accountability. Before launching negotiations, the European Commission (EC) conducts a comprehensive impact assessment and carries out a 3-month public consultation process. During the negotiations, the EC publishes online proposals for legal texts and progress reports after each negotiation round. At the end of the negotiations, the negotiated text is also published before full legal revision is undertaken. See www.oecd.org/tad/events/ec-trade-comms-statement.pdf

6 See 'Backgrounder: The Regional Comprehensive Economic Partnership', *China Daily*, 31 March 2014.

7 The world shares of the TPP-11 are 6.7 per cent (population), 13.4 per cent (GDP), 14.3 per cent (trade) and 12.9 per cent (FDI inflows).

8 Simon Evenett and Johannes Fritz (2017) *Will Awe Trump Rules? The 21st Global Trade Alert Report*, London: CEPR Press.

9 Masahiro Kawai and Ganeshan Wignaraja (2013) 'Patterns of Free Trade Areas in Asia: A Review of Recent Evidence', East-West Center Policy Studies No. 65, Honolulu: East-West Center. Available at www.eastwestcenter.org/publications/patterns-free-trade-areas-in-asia.

10 John Gilbert, Taiji Furusawa and Robert Scollay (2016) 'The Economic Impact of the Trans-Pacific Partnership: What Have We Learned from CGE Simulation?' Asia-Pacific Research and Training Network on Trade (ARTNet) Working Paper No. 157.

11 Masahiro Kawai and Ganeshan Wignaraja (2014) 'Policy Challenges Posed by Asian FTAs: A Review of the Evidence', in Richard Baldwin, Masahiro Kawai and Ganeshan Wignaraja (eds) *A WTO for the 21st Century: The Asian Perspective*, Cheltenham: Edward Elgar.

12 Sanchita Basu Das, 'RCEP: Going Beyond ASEAN+1 FTAs'; Murray Hiebert and Liam Hanlon (2012) 'ASEAN and Partners Launch Regional Comprehensive Economic Partnership', Center for Strategic and International Studies website, 7 December. Available at http://csis.org/publication/asean-and-partners-launch-regional-comprehensive-economic-partnership. Masahiro Kawai and Ganeshan Wignaraja (2013) 'Patterns of Free Trade Areas in Asia: A Review of Recent Evidence', East-West Center Policy Studies No. 65. Honolulu: East-West Center. Available at www.eastwestcenter.org/publications/patterns-free-trade-areas-in-asia.

13 See www.wto.org/english/res_e/statis_e/statis_maps_e.htm.

14 Ganeshan Wignaraja (2016) 'India's Act East Policy: What Next?' in Yamini Chowdhuri and Anusha Diya Chowdhuri (eds) *Narendra Modi and the World: The Ring View Inside Out*, New Delhi: Bloomsbury India.

15 Amiti Sen (2017) 'Time for India to Exit the RCEP Trade Pact', *Business Line (The Hindu)*, 7 September.

16 Rahul Misra (2013) 'RCEP: Challenges and Opportunities for India', S. Rajaratnam School of International Studies, RSIS Commentaries No. 140, 25 July.

17 Sen, 'Time for India to Exit the RCEP Trade Pact'.

18 Ganeshan Wignaraja (2011) 'Economic Reforms, Regionalism and Exports: Comparing China and India', East-West Center Policy Studies No. 60, Honolulu: East-West Center.

19 S. Arun (2017) 'India to Flag Worry on the Pace of Services Talks at RCEP', *The Hindu*, 6 September.

20 Sen.

21 Tahir Amin (2017) 'Out of Sight RCEP Negotiations Threaten Public Health and Access to Medicines', *The Wire*, 25 July.

22 Mohammad Masudur Rahman and Laila Arjuman Ara (2015) 'TPP, TTIP and RCEP: Implications for South Asian Economies', *South Asia Economic Journal*, 16(1): 27–45.

23 See www.wto.org/english/res_e/statis_e/statis_maps_e.htm.

24 Ganeshan Wignaraja (2017) 'Better Late to the Party Than Never: The Regional Comprehensive Economic Partnership and Sri Lanka Policy Forum', Crawford School of Public Policy, Australian National University, 9 December. Available at www.policyforum.net/better-late-party-never/.

25 A Track 1.5 dialogue is an informal policy discussion often initiated by think tanks on topics such as negotiating an effective FTA. A broad range of government officials, executives and scholars participate in such events. The dialogue primarily intends to freely discuss issues relating to trade performance, trade barriers, sensitive sectors and pathways to preferential trade liberalization. A related aim is to build mutual trust and understanding on how each country approaches FTAs and to identify areas of potential cooperation.

26 Jeffrey D. Wilson (2015) 'Mega-Regional Trade Deals in the Asia-Pacific: Choosing between the TPP and RCEP?' *Journal of Contemporary Asia*, 45(2): 345–53.

27 Jeffrey J. Schott, Barbara Kotschwar and Julia Muir (2013) *Understanding the Trans-Pacific Partnership: Policy Analyses in International Economics*, Washington, DC: Peterson Institute for International Economics, 2013; and Akira Amari (2016) 'The Transpacific Partnership (TPP) Agreement', *Asia-Pacific Review*, 23(1): 11–20.

28 Shujiro Urata (2014) 'Constructing and Multilateralizing the Regional Comprehensive Economic Partnership: An Asian Perspective', in Richard Baldwin, Masahiro Kawai and Ganeshan Wignaraja (eds) *A WTO for the 21st Century: The Asian Perspective*, Cheltenham: Edward Elgar.

29 For a painstaking mapping of the features of the five ASEAN+1 FTAs, see Yoshifumi Fukunaga, and Ikumo Isono (2013) 'Taking ASEAN+1 FTAs towards RCEP: A Mapping Study', *ERIA Discussion Paper Series* DP 2013-2.

34

The TPP
Origins and outcomes[1]

Jeffrey J. Schott

The Trans-Pacific Partnership (TPP) was an international commercial agreement among 12 nations in the Asia-Pacific region representing about 38 per cent of the global economy. It included wide-ranging obligations to eliminate almost all tariffs and reduce other barriers to trade and investment in goods and services, new rules governing domestic policies that affect international commerce, and enforcement and dispute resolution procedures to promote compliance with the TPP provisions. In terms of the breadth and depth of the reforms agreed by the partner countries, the TPP was more comprehensive than any commercial accord since the ill-fated 1948 Charter for an International Trade Organization (ITO).

The USA was the lead architect of the TPP; the pact closely resembled and augmented previous US free trade agreements (FTAs) and required relatively minor changes in existing US law and practice. After almost six years of negotiations, the TPP agreement was signed on 4 February 2016. But despite the preponderant US influence on the treaty text, there still was strong opposition in the US Congress to specific provisions of the TPP, which delayed congressional action on the trade pact. As with the ITO, Congress never considered that the TPP would be implementing legislation in 2016. The new Trump Administration subsequently withdrew the US signature in late January 2017 for unspecified but largely political reasons.

Interestingly, the US withdrawal from the TPP did not kill the deal. Instead, the remaining signatories decided to go forward with a slightly revised pact, renamed the Comprehensive and Progressive Agreement for Trans-Pacific Partnership (CPTPP). The basic deal was kept intact with only minor revisions to the original substantive obligations and entry into force provisions. On 23 January 2018, the 11 remaining TPP signatories agreed to finalize work on the CPTPP provisions and to sign the revised deal in Chile on 8 March 2018.

The TPP: origins

The TPP can be best understood as the culmination of the long-standing pursuit of economic integration among Pacific Basin nations. The initial impetus for the TPP dates back more than two decades when leaders of the Asia-Pacific Economic Cooperation (APEC) forum committed to the long-term goal of free trade and investment in the Asia-Pacific region at their historic summit in Bogor, Indonesia, in November 1994. After a decade of limited progress in APEC

Jeffrey J. Schott

and other forums, four small countries (Singapore, Chile, Brunei and New Zealand), known as the P4, reinvigorated efforts by developing a new free trade pact – the Trans-Pacific Strategic Economic Partnership – that entered into force in 2006.

But the P4 had bigger goals. True to the strategic vision of Singapore's founding father, Lee Kwan Yew, the P4 wanted their pact to be the core of a broader regional initiative that included the USA. The P4 recognized that sustained US engagement was needed in the Asia-Pacific region to support economic development and deter the type of military adventurism that caused so much devastation in East and South-East Asia in the past century.[2] Accordingly, the deal had to be expanded to include the USA and accommodate its priority interests and concerns in the region.

In late September 2008, on the outskirts of the United Nations meetings in New York, the USA, Australia, Peru and Viet Nam agreed to join with the P4 to build on that pact and establish a more comprehensive deal called the TPP.[3] But late 2008 was not a propitious time to start new trade talks. The world economy was suffering from a major financial meltdown. Following the US election in November, the new Obama Administration focused first and foremost on domestic policies to reverse the sharp recession caused by the deepening crisis in world financial markets. Trade talks were shelved indefinitely.

Once the US economy had stabilized in the second half of 2009, US officials began to refocus, for both strategic and economic reasons, on the Asia-Pacific region. During his first official trip to Asia in December 2009 President Obama pledged that the USA would participate in new TPP negotiations. At the time, with low capacity utilization in US industry and high US unemployment, the TPP offered the prospect of increased US exports to the region producing the world's most dynamic growth. The TPP fit well into an emerging US trade policy response to the global financial crisis, the 'National Export Initiative', that Lawrence Summers (then Obama's chief economic adviser as head of the National Economic Council), and Michael Froman (then Summers' deputy and subsequently US Trade Representative), cogently argued could contribute to the US economic recovery.

The eight countries launched the TPP talks in Australia in March 2010.[4] Their vision was to craft a high-quality, 21st-century trade pact among a small group of like-minded countries that over time could attract participation by a larger number of Asia-Pacific nations. In the event, enlargement occurred even before the initial deal was struck. Unlike other trade negotiations, TPP membership changed and expanded over the course of the negotiations: Malaysia joined the talks during the third round of TPP negotiations in October 2010, Canada and Mexico began participating in late 2012, and Japan started negotiating in July 2013. After the US Congress passed legislation renewing trade promotion authority (according to expedited procedures for the passage of implementing legislation for US trade pacts) in mid-2015, US officials could proceed to finalize and accept the Asia-Pacific pact. The TPP negotiations concluded in October 2015 and the pact was signed by the 12 participating countries on 4 February 2016.

The TPP: like-minded but diverse participants

The TPP negotiations brought together countries with like-minded interests in building a comprehensive Asia-Pacific FTA. But the like-minded countries were not alike in terms of the size of their countries and economies and the level of their economic development. Finding common ground among countries as diverse as the TPP participants was a notable achievement.

Table 34.1 provides a snapshot of the key economic indicators of the countries that initially signed the TPP accord. Their diverse levels of development challenged the TPP negotiators in constructing a high-quality agreement that all countries could faithfully implement and enforce.

Table 34.1 Indicators of diversity, TPP-12, 2016

Country	GDP (billions of US $)[a]	Total population (millions)	Human Development Index[b]	RCEP member
Australia	1,204.6	24.1	0.939	Yes
Brunei	11.4	0.4	0.865	Yes
Canada	1,529.8	36.3	0.920	No
Chile	247.0	17.9	0.847	No
Japan	4,939.4	127.0	0.903	Yes
Malaysia	296.4	31.2	0.789	Yes
Mexico	1,046.0	127.5	0.762	No
New Zealand	185.0	4.7	0.915	Yes
Peru	192.1	31.8	0.740	No
Singapore	297.0	5.6	0.925	Yes
USA	18,569.1	323.1	0.920	No
Viet Nam	202.6	92.7	0.683	Yes
Total	28,720.3	822.4		

Sources: World Bank, available at https://data.worldbank.org/, and Human Development Report 2016, available at http://hdr.undp.org/sites/default/files/2016_human_development_report.pdf (accessed on 18 December 2017).

Notes: *a* measured in current US dollars; *b* the United Nations Human Development Index (HDI) is a summary measure of achievements in key dimensions of human development: a long and healthy life, access to knowledge, and a decent standard of living. The HDI is the geometric mean of normalized indices for each of the three dimensions. Data is for 2015.

The TPP-12 include large economies like the USA (*US $*18.6 trillion) and Japan ($4.9 trillion) but seven of the 12 have gross domestic products (GDPs) under $300 billion; three TPP members have populations of more than 100 million; and three have less than six million inhabitants. Most TPP participants are high-income or upper-middle-income countries.[5] In stark contrast, Viet Nam is the only lower-middle-income country; its Human Development Index (HDI), which measures relative levels of income and development, is significantly lower than that of the other developing country participants such as Malaysia, Mexico and Peru. These factors raise concerns about Viet Nam's ability to undertake and enforce domestic reforms required by TPP obligations, particularly disciplines on state-owned enterprises (SOEs), as well as rule-making obligations in sensitive areas such as labour, environment and the protection of intellectual property rights (IPRs).

Despite the wide diversity in size and level of development of the TPP countries, the pact requires signatories to accept common obligations with only limited exceptions for certain 'non-conforming measures' to be excluded from TPP disciplines in each detailed national schedule. But the pact recognizes that poorer countries face difficult challenges in implementing and enforcing TPP obligations, so the TPP sets out asymmetric implementation schedules that enable poorer countries to adopt TPP-mandated reforms during an extended but fixed transition period.

Unlike traditional trade pacts of the early post-war era, the TPP does not exempt poorer countries from most obligations through provisions on special and differential treatment for less developed countries (LDCs). The reason is straightforward: the more LDCs get a 'free pass' from undertaking critical domestic economic reforms, the harder it will be for them to compete for foreign investment. LDC negotiators argue that they need policy space or flexibility to

Jeffrey J. Schott

manage adjustment in their economies, especially in the face of staunch competition from the People's Republic of China in labour-intensive manufactures; however, history is replete with examples where special and differential treatment has abetted corruption and effectively impeded development prospects.

Although the TPP countries shared the same objectives of crafting a 21st-century trade pact, each approached the negotiations with different perspectives and priorities on product and sector specific liberalization, and on the desired scope of new rule-making obligations. Each country had 'no go' areas where attempts to change long-standing policies and practices, many of which discriminate against outsiders, would complicate or derail political support for the overall agreement. Such political economy considerations almost always drive negotiators to seek special treatment for their most politically sensitive products via long phase-outs for existing restrictions, partial liberalization, or even outright exemption from reform commitments. Almost all trade pacts contain exceptions in various forms. General Agreement on Tariffs and Trade (GATT) Article XXIV requires that customs unions and regional trade agreements cover 'substantially all' trade but most trade pacts are replete with exceptions in various forms. Compared to other FTAs, however, the TPP is the most consistent with the spirit and the letter of the legal obligations of GATT Article XXIV.

The TPP: broad objectives

While each TPP country entered the negotiations with different priorities and political constraints, they shared five broad policy objectives driven by both economic and strategic interests in deepening regional integration. These goals are comparable to those that underpinned the creation of APEC in the late 1980s and inspired the pursuit of deeper trade and investment relations among developed and developing economies in the region that has helped Asia-Pacific countries to modernize and to accelerate the pace of their economic growth.

First, as in any commercial accord, the partner countries sought to strengthen economic growth through policy reforms that would encourage trade and investment and spur innovation and productivity gains in each economy across the region. For some countries, the impetus to implement the necessary structural economic reforms at home was the real prize of the TPP initiative; indeed, Japanese Prime Minister Shinzo Abe justified TPP participation as critical to the successful achievement of structural policy reforms such as labour included in the 'third arrow' of 'Abenomics'. [6]

In retrospect, the TPP negotiators did a good job in meeting this core objective. According to the widely cited econometric analysis of the final TPP provisions by Petri *et al.*,[7] TPP reforms would contribute importantly to economic growth, raising the real income of TPP members by almost US $500 billion or 1.1 per cent of GDP once the deal was fully implemented (see Table 32.2). On average, non-TPP countries would benefit modestly as well because of higher growth in the TPP region and the fact that many TPP-mandated reforms would be implemented in a non-discriminatory manner.

Second, TPP members used the regional negotiations to efficiently upgrade existing bilateral FTAs with other TPP participants. While several FTAs among TPP members cover both goods and services and contain extensive obligations to reform domestic policies and regulations that can distort trade and investment, many of these pacts merely reference existing World Trade Organization (WTO) obligations in these rule-making areas and include only shallow commitments in key areas like investment, services, transparency and the movement of labour. The TPP substantially updated and augmented less comprehensive pacts between pairs of TPP countries, including most importantly the vintage North American Free Trade Agreement

404

Table 34.2 TPP-12 vs TPP-11: real income gains

| | TPP-12 | | TPP-11 | |
	%	billions in 2015 dollars	%	billions in 2015 dollars
World	0.4	492	0.1	147
TPP-12	1.1	465	n.a.	n.a.
TPP-11	2.2	334	1.0	158
USA	0.5	131	0.0	−2
ROW (non TPP-12)	n.a.	27	n.a.	−8

Source: Petri *et al.*

Notes: n.a. = not applicable/available; ROW = rest of world.

(NAFTA) between the USA, Canada and Mexico, as well as other more recent US FTAs such as the Korea-US or KORUS FTA. In addition, the TPP established new free trade obligations with countries where bilateral talks had not been successful in the past. Cementing US-Japan trade reforms was the most prominent example. Overall, the TPP effectively improved the quality, scope and economic pay-off of the FTAs of the TPP signatories.

Third, the TPP was designed to modernize the trade rulebook. It established new trade rights and disciplines that fill important holes in the WTO rulebook and that update and expand WTO obligations in other areas. Advances in TPP rule-making establish precedents for other regional and multilateral negotiations (covering issues such as the environment, e-commerce and disciplines on SOEs), and help to inform ongoing plurilaterial talks like those on trade in services. Some TPP provisions already have been transplanted into the current negotiations on a Regional Comprehensive Economic Partnership (RCEP).

Fourth, with its open-ended accession clause, TPP members sought to build an agreement that could set out a comprehensive template for broader Asia-Pacific economic integration and create the most viable pathway toward a Free Trade Area of the Asia Pacific (FTAAP) that APEC members have been pursuing for the past decade. Importantly, any country can join the pact, not just APEC members or other nations in the Asia-Pacific region.

Finally, as envisaged by Lee Kwan Yew, the TPP was designed to reinforce foreign policy and national security relations in the Asia-Pacific region. For Asia-Pacific nations that depend on open and secure sea lanes for their commercial prosperity, and those that face the threat of North Korean missiles and adventurism, the TPP was regarded as critically important to ensure strong US economic engagement and ongoing military presence in the region. US withdrawal from the pact in 2017 has had the opposite effect, raising questions about whether the USA can be considered a reliable partner.

The TPP: scope and coverage

The TPP is by far the most comprehensive trade accord involving developed and developing countries that has ever been negotiated in terms of scope of coverage and depth of commitments to trade liberalization and policy reform. Together, the 12 TPP countries accounted for almost 40 per cent of global output and one-quarter of world exports. The deal opened new opportunities for increased trade and investment in goods and services, including farm trade barriers that had long been resistant to reform. It upgraded the bilateral trade deals among individual members, deepened trade reforms at and behind borders, and limited exceptions so common in other FTAs. In so doing, the TPP architects created a cohesive and comprehensive template for trade reform that could be applied in other regional and multilateral negotiations.

The TPP participants committed to crafting a comprehensive agreement that dismantles barriers to trade in goods and services, breaks new ground on issues like labour, the environment, investment, competition policy, and SOEs, and develops a more coherent approach across sectors regarding regulatory policies that affect flows of trade and investment. TPP obligations also encourage good governance by promoting greater transparency of government policies and improvements in the quality of economic institutions in member countries. The goal was to create a trade regime that is 'state of the art' and sets a precedent for future trade negotiations.

As the 'gold standard' in terms of content and coverage, the KORUS FTA offered important precedents for the TPP negotiations. Provisions in the KORUS agreement in areas like IPRs, services and investment, labour, and the environment provided a detailed template for the elaboration of TPP obligations. For example, the KORUS agreement secured high levels of protection for copyright holders and trademarks by extending protection beyond the minimum requirements in the WTO's Agreement on Trade-Related Aspects of Intellectual Property Rights (TRIPS). Similarly, the KORUS FTA included precedent-setting provisions on the environment, including a list of multilateral environmental agreements whose obligations are enforceable under the FTA's general dispute settlement procedures.

Contrary to the Trump Administration critique, the TPP negotiators produced a noteworthy agreement and one that was favourable to US trading interests. The deal largely reflected US standards and practices, and would not have required Congress to legislate significant changes in US laws and regulations. The following summarizes key results of the trade agreement in terms of market access reforms and new rules that augment WTO disciplines.[8]

FTAs traditionally focus on improving market access for goods. In this area, the TPP negotiators had good results but left some distortionary practices on the table. The TPP required the quick elimination of most tariffs with very few exceptions. Most tariffs on autos and clothing were eliminated after a decade. The TPP made limited progress regarding non-discriminatory access to bidding on subnational public contracts but contained the first major opening of bidding on national government procurement by Viet Nam and Malaysia.

Like most FTAs, the TPP contained rules of origin to govern which products would qualify for tariff preferences. Because the pact credits content sourced in any of the member countries, the rules offer more flexibility regarding sourcing components across the Pacific Basin than bilateral or neighbourhood trade deals. Beyond this 'cumulation' effect, origin rules for autos and parts revamp and lower regional content requirements to levels well below comparable levels in NAFTA, a key point of contention in the US debate and one of the few specific issues cited by the Trump Administration in its rejection of the pact. In contrast, the TPP maintained the NAFTA 'yarn forward' rule for textiles and apparel, although it provided time-limited relief from this strict content rule for a specified list of products.

Unlike many agreements among Asian countries, the TPP participants agreed to comprehensive coverage of agriculture. Substantial cuts were made in farm trade barriers, tariffs as well as non-tariff measures such as sanitary and phytosanitary standards. The TPP agreement covered substantially all goods with the more import-sensitive products subject to a protracted liberalization schedule of perhaps ten to 15 years. For a narrow range of products, the TPP allows partial liberalization through expanded tariff rate quotas. With a nod to political reality, policies protecting sensitive farm products like rice, sugar and dairy remained largely in place; US sugar and US and Canadian dairy restrictions remained substantially intact. But no farm products were fully exempt from TPP reform, even sensitive Japanese products like rice, in contrast to the treatment of sugar in the US–Australia FTA and rice in the KORUS FTA.

The TPP also contained wide-ranging obligations on investment policy comparable or greater than those embodied in bilateral investment treaties. TPP countries applied a negative list approach to limit exceptions to commitments to accord foreign investors non-discriminatory treatment. The pact also restricted use of local content and other performance requirements and improved investor-state dispute settlement procedures (while reaffirming each country's right to issue regulations in the public interest that affect investor interests).

In services, liberalization commitments were much less demanding than in goods, although service providers will benefit from new TPP disciplines on foreign investment to ensure non-discriminatory treatment and to provide security and protection to foreign investors. In key infrastructure services like finance, insurance, telecommunications, air express delivery and other transport services, the TPP reforms targeted restrictions on commercial presence and established new disciplines on foreign investment to ensure non-discriminatory treatment, security, and greater transparency (for example, by removing or reducing limitations on foreign ownership and giving foreign individuals and firms the right to provide cross-border services without the requirement to establish a commercial presence). In financial services, for example, the pact provided greater access for portfolio management and payment/clearing services as well as partial constraints on state-run postal insurance systems.

The TPP did more than grant preferential access to member countries. New rule-making obligations constrain the use of industrial policy measures that discriminate against foreign suppliers and investors, including via government procurement preferences. Disciplines on subsidies and other preferential policies favouring SOEs go to some lengths to achieve competitive neutrality among public and private enterprises in the domestic market.

The new TPP rulebook included disciplines on issues like SOEs, competition policy, the environment and labour that incorporate and build on existing WTO commitments and FTA obligations. In brief, the TPP supplemented existing rules by extending obligations to areas not yet subject to WTO disciplines, augmenting current FTA commitments, and including development provisions to assist in enhancing human capital, technology transfer, capacity building and assistance for small and medium-sized enterprises. For example, the prevalence of significant SOEs in the economies of several TPP participants led negotiators to focus on crafting new rules in order to 'level the playing field' between private firms and SOEs, including new disciplines on the provision of public funds. The objective was not forced privatization but rather ensuring competitive neutrality between public and private firms in access to finance, factors of production, and distribution of goods and services in the marketplace.

The TPP also contained important, albeit controversial, provisions on IPRs. Perhaps most contentious were the new rules governing patents for pharmaceutical products, particularly the term for data exclusivity for certain biological products. Other TPP obligations covered patent linkages and patent term extension, and copyright protections, beyond those included in the WTO TRIPs accord. The agreement also strengthened enforcement of trade secrets, penalties for copyright infringement, including online and media products, and required criminal procedures and penalties for theft, including cyber theft.

The TPP also contained the most substantive chapter on trade-related environmental issues of any trade agreement. Among its key provisions, the environment chapter banned fish subsidies that were damaging, including those provided to illegal, unreported and unregulated fishing vessels; strengthened the enforcement of multilateral environmental agreements to which a country already is a party; promoted conservation programmes for specific marine species,

Jeffrey J. Schott

wetlands, and forest/fisheries management; and combated illegal taking and trafficking in wildlife and illegal logging. All these obligations were subject to the TPP's dispute settlement procedures.

In addition, the TPP included more explicit rules on labour practices than prior FTAs. The TPP labour chapter committed countries, *inter alia*, to maintain and enforce domestic labour laws, as well as the core labour rights of the 1998 Declaration on Fundamental Principles and Rights at Work of the International Labour Organization; called for new constraints on trade in goods made by forced labour; and mandated upgraded labour standards in export processing zones. Here again, compared to other FTAs, the TPP is notable for its significant new obligations regarding labour rights and protections, even if the negotiators did not include some far-reaching recommendations put forward by labour constituencies in various TPP countries.

The TPP also covered cross-cutting issues related to regulatory coherence, competitiveness and business facilitation. In that regard, TPP negotiators focused on streamlining supply chains, certification and regulatory processes, and improving coordination between the government and relevant stakeholders. These objectives were outlined in November 2011 by the leaders of the TPP countries, who endorsed a framework for the evolving trade pact that presaged 'a comprehensive, next-generation regional agreement that liberalizes trade and investment and addresses new and traditional trade issues and 21st-century challenges'.[9]

Finally, in parallel with the trade agreement, officials from the TPP countries adopted a Joint Declaration of the Macroeconomic Policy Authorities of Trans-Pacific Partnership Countries. The Declaration committed each TPP member to 'avoid persistent exchange rate misalignments' and 'refrain from competitive devaluation'. It also required each country to disclose foreign exchange reserves and interventions in spot and forward currency markets. Obligations under the Declaration were not subject to TPP dispute resolution procedures. The Declaration also established a new Group of TPP Macroeconomic Officials to monitor and assess exchange rate and macroeconomic policies.

While comprehensive, there still are areas that the TPP did not cover or did not cover well. For example, the TPP did not require major new services or procurement liberalization by the USA or disciplines related to global warming, particularly subsidies and other measures that distort demand for fossil fuels and renewable energy supplies. In addition, and importantly, national labour adjustment policies were not addressed. No support was given to countries struggling to manage adjustment to new competition in domestic markets.

Putting together such a comprehensive agreement among the diverse group of TPP economies seemed like a daunting task, but the negotiators did not start from scratch. In addition to the KORUS FTA, TPP countries built on the extensive network of bilateral and regional FTAs already in place among the TPP countries that included a variety of reform commitments. For example, TPP architects drew on provisions of the ASEAN (Association of Southeast Asian Nations)-Australia New Zealand FTA (AANZFTA), which incorporated valuable developmental elements such as different implementation periods for developing and advanced countries, and included provisions on FTA-plus issues like regulatory coherence, IPRs, transparency and competition policy.

Postscript: moving the TPP forwards without the USA

The Trump Administration's decision to withdraw from the TPP has had important implications for Asia-Pacific regionalism. It dealt a substantial setback to long-standing efforts towards an FTAAP, exacerbated trade frictions between the USA and its key trading partners in the region, and encouraged those countries to pursue other trade deals with regional partners, including China.

But, interestingly, after some initial hesitation when Trump took office in January 2017, the other 11 TPP signatories reassessed the value of the trade deal for their own economies and its precedential value for the world trading system. While the US withdrawal sharply reduced the economic footprint of the TPP, the other 11 signatories recognized that the deal still had considerable value even without US participation, although they all hoped that the USA would reconsider and participate in their new Asia-Pacific economic integration arrangement. Within weeks of Trump's action, the TPP-11 began working to salvage the fruits of their extensive negotiating efforts.

Why did the TPP-11 countries move forward without the USA on a deal that was largely based on the US FTA template? Three reasons should be mentioned.

First, the limited concessions opening the US market to other TPP members were only part of the deal's allure. Another large objective of these countries was to bolster their own domestic economic reform to become more efficient, productive and competitive in global markets. Adopting the TPP's demanding reform commitments would require each country to implement the necessary but politically contentious economic reforms that would help to boost productivity growth across the economy and generate significant real income gains for each country. That's why Japanese Prime Minister Abe initially joined the negotiations even as the talks were nearing completion and it is why he championed moving forward with the TPP even after the USA jumped ship – he recognized that the TPP would complement and provide impetus for the implementation of crucial structural economic reforms in the Japanese economy.

Second, the prospective real income gains from the trade pact are significant, even without US participation. As shown in Table 34.2, the TPP-11 countries still achieve increases in real income of around 1 per cent of GDP or US $158 billion above what would occur without the TPP reforms. That would be a big pay-off for any governmental action, albeit with less than half of the expected gains for TPP countries than if the USA also participated. Global income gains fall by 70 per cent without US participation but are still positive; the big loser from the US decision to withdraw from TPP is the USA, whose real income declines by $133 billion or 0.5 per cent of GDP compared to the TPP-12 outcome.

Third, the TPP established disciplines that address the new challenges affecting international commerce in the 21st century. Since the WTO was established in 1995, new technologies have changed the way in which goods and services are produced, exchanged, financed and delivered. TPP negotiators produced new guidelines and remedies for practices that were not prominent when the trade rulebook was last augmented, and they did not want to lose the progress that they had made in updating world trading rules.

In sum, the TPP countries went forwards with the pact – without the USA but in the hope that US officials would revisit the deal in the future – because they valued the trade and investment liberalization and reforms required by TPP obligations that spur productivity gains in their own economies, open new export and investment opportunities, encourage improvements in the quality and governance of economic institutions, and set comprehensive precedents for broader regional integration. With that common foundation, the 11 TPP signatories turned to the task of putting the regional pact into force.

Chile took the initial lead and organized an ad hoc High Level Dialogue on Integration Initiatives for the Asia Pacific on the sidelines of a meeting of the Pacific Alliance countries (Chile, Colombia, Mexico and Peru plus many observer nations) in Vina del Mar, Chile, in mid-March 2017. Attending were all 11 remaining TPP signatories plus China, Colombia, the Republic of Korea (South Korea) and the USA. In addition, the TPP-11 met separately and issued a statement noting that it regards the TPP's 'principles and high standards as a key driver for regional economic integration and promoter of economic growth'.

Jeffrey J. Schott

At the same time, however, many of the TPP signatories began to hedge their bets. Soon after the abrupt US withdrawal from the regional trade pact, many of them reassessed their substantial trade and investment ties with China and began to explore new or expanded bilateral FTAs and/or investment arrangements with China. Almost half of the TPP countries were also participating in the other major regional trade initiative (see Table 34.2), RCEP that included the ten member countries in ASEAN and their FTA partners (Australia, China, Japan, India, New Zealand and South Korea). Without the TPP, the predominant framework for regional integration would be RCEP, led by ASEAN, but driven by commercial ties with China. Salvaging the TPP and implementing its comprehensive body of rights and obligations was needed as a foil to RCEP and a response to Chinese commercial pressure.

At the APEC ministerial meetings in Da Nang, Viet Nam, in November 2017, leaders of the TPP-11 countries committed to finalizing a newly branded Comprehensive and Progressive Agreement for Trans-Pacific Partnership (CPTPP) largely comprised of the original TPP text. The entry into force provisions were recast and simplified to allow the pact to take effect 60 days after six of the signatories had ratified the new agreement. Each country's market access schedules would remain substantially intact. In addition, the TPP-11 agreed to resolve four specific issues prior to signing the pact, including a Canadian request for the inclusion of new provisions regarding exceptions for public support for cultural industries and specific exceptions to Malaysian commitments on SOEs.

The major difference between the CPTPP and its predecessor, besides the more awkward title, is the agreement to suspend, at least temporarily, the implementation of specific TPP provisions that the USA had insisted be included in the original pact despite widespread opposition from other countries; if the USA and others want to participate in the future, those obligations could be reactivated or revised as part of the accession compact. Prominent among the provisions suspended were the data exclusivity obligations regarding patents on certain pharmaceutical products, investment obligations and enforcement procedures related to investor-state arbitration, certain prohibitions on the illegal taking and trade in wildlife, and obligations and policy reforms covering express delivery services (see Annex II of the Trans-Pacific Partnership Ministerial Statement of 11 November 2017 for the complete list of suspended TPP provisions).

Once the CPTPP is up and running, the pact will be open to accession by other economies, including the USA. Prospective new members such as South Korea, Colombia and Taiwan began consulting with TPP-11 signatories about joining the CPTPP even before the final text of the revised pact was signed. Consequently, despite the absence of the USA and China at the outset, the TPP in its new incarnation is likely to be sustained as a viable framework for building a comprehensive economic integration arrangement in the Asia-Pacific region in the coming decade.

That said, it is hard to conceive of a comprehensive Asia-Pacific trade arrangement that does not eventually include China. TPP participants already have extensive trade and investment ties with China and have long been involved in working with China towards the long-term APEC goal of free trade and investment in the Asia-Pacific region. China, in turn, has committed to the regional integration strategy and championed initiatives to accelerate progress toward the formation of an FTAAP when it was chair of APEC in 2014.

To be sure, some observers have concluded that the TPP participants intend to exclude China from their integration arrangement because the bar is set so high in terms of transparency of domestic policies and the rigor of disciplines on government interventions in the marketplace. Others take this argument further and claim that the TPP is designed to 'contain China' in order to restrain its economic and political influence in the region. Such a strategy is implausible. However, the TPP countries do regard the reforms mandated by the trade pact as a vital part of their strategy to 'compete' with China, a factor overlooked by the USA in its hasty exit from the pact.

The US withdrawal from the TPP was a mixed blessing for China: it set back efforts to forge a US-China consensus on pathways to regional integration based on regional arrangements including the TPP and RCEP, but it also opened the door for China to assert a more pronounced leadership role in the region via its own bilateral trade pacts and regional investment arrangements like the Belt and Road Initiative. In the short term, however, China is more likely to prioritize deepening its ties with its Asian neighbours before engaging the TPP. Such restraint is basically due to a lack of readiness and willingness to pursue a trade accord as comprehensive as the TPP. But TPP accession is open to all countries who are willing to meet its requirements. At some point in the future, the queue for entry is likely to include the USA and China.

Notes

1 © Peterson Institute for International Economics (2018).
2 It is probably not a coincidence that Lee Kwan Yew advised President Barack Obama in November 2009 to maintain the US strategic presence in the region and to deepen economic relations by joining the TPP talks.
3 The US commitment to new trade talks was unusual at the end of a presidential term and amid a growing crisis in world financial markets. Given the protectionist rhetoric of the Democratic candidates for US president (Barack Obama and Hillary Clinton), the outgoing Bush Administration seemingly agreed to new trade talks to lock-in US participation before the expected victory by Barack Obama.
4 Viet Nam initially joined the talks as an 'observer'. It became a full participant during the fourth round of TPP negotiations in December 2010.
5 Country classifications are based on the World Bank's income classifications.
6 IMF (2015) 'Can Abenomics Succeed? Overcoming the Legacy of Japan's Lost Decades', Washington, DC: International Monetary Fund.
7 Peter A. Petri, Michael G. Plummer, Shujiro Urata and Fan Zhai (2017) 'Going it Alone in the Asia-Pacific: Regional Trade Agreements Without the United States', Peterson Institute for International Economics, Working Paper 17-10, October.
8 For a more comprehensive analysis of the TPP agreement, see Cathleen Cimino-Isaacs and Jeffrey J. Schott (eds) (2016) *Trans-Pacific Partnership: An Assessment*, Washington, DC: Peterson Institute for International Economics.
9 See TPP Leaders' Statement, Honolulu, 12 November 2011.

35

Japan's approach to preferential trade agreements

Gregory P. Corning

Economic multilateralism played a central role in Japan's post–Second World War economic growth. After decades of pursuing trade liberalization on an exclusively multilateral basis through the General Agreement on Tariffs and Trade (GATT), however, Japan began to explore the option of preferential trade agreements (PTAs) in the late 1990s. A number of changes in the global, regional and national economy help to explain this shift. At the global level, slow progress at the World Trade Organization (WTO) pushed developed economies to find alternative ways of expanding market access for their exporters. At the regional level, Japan's rejection of binding liberalization in the Early Voluntary Sectoral Liberalization Talks in 1998 made Asia-Pacific Economic Cooperation (APEC) less viable as a vehicle for regional liberalization. And following the Asian financial crisis in 1997–98, Japan also became more willing to explore regional projects that excluded the USA and more anxious about the growing regional profile of the People's Republic of China. Finally, at the national level, reformist policymakers saw PTAs as a way to help to extricate Japan from the years of economic stagnation that followed the collapse of the bubble economy of the late 1980s.[1]

This chapter examines the evolution of Japan's PTA policy. It begins by exploring the external pressures and internal constraints that shape policy. The chapter then traces the development of policy through bilateral, regional and finally mega-regional agreements. For almost two decades, Japan has pursued a cautious and reactive policy seeking agreements that eliminate trade diversion, offer minimal agricultural concessions, maintain access to resources, and respond to the rise of China. However, the Trump Administration's withdrawal from the Trans-Pacific Partnership (TPP) has unexpectedly thrust Japan into a leadership role in Asia-Pacific trade liberalization.

The political and social context of Japan's PTA policy

While the pressures of political and economic competition have pushed Japan to negotiate PTAs, the ambition of policy has been constrained by both weak political leadership and a strong farm lobby resistant to liberalization.

Drivers of PTA policy

Systemic pressures have played a decisive role in driving Japan's PTA policy. While economic factors such as the need to combat trade diversion or facilitate access to natural resources have been crucial in some cases, political competition and the desire to advance a preferred model of trade and investment cooperation have often been more important in shaping the contours of Japan's PTA policy.[2] In terms of economic competition, the defensive nature of Japan's PTA policy is clearest in the need to combat trade diversion – when a PTA diverts trade from a more efficient producer to a less efficient one. This puts pressure on excluded parties to negotiate their own PTAs to restore market access for their exporters. For example, Japanese firms have been vocal about trade diversion resulting from the North American Free Trade Agreement (NAFTA) and the Republic of Korea (South Korea)'s PTAs with the USA, the European Union (EU), and China. In response to the rise in Western investment in Asia following the Asian financial crisis, Japan also became more serious about negotiating trade and investment rules that would increase the reach and efficiency of its firms' regional production networks.

In terms of political and legal competition, both the rise of China and broader regional dynamics have shaped Japan's PTA policy. To be sure, policy has not been driven by the Sino-Japanese rivalry alone. Japan has negotiated several PTAs beyond East Asia and has not always pursued the most proactive or expeditious approach to balancing China. However, the spectre of China's growing influence is apparent in several aspects of Japan's PTA policy. Japan's decision to pursue a PTA with the Association of Southeast Asian Nations (ASEAN) followed quickly after China's announcement of such talks. Japan's 2006 proposal for the negotiation of a Comprehensive Economic Partnership for East Asia – that would include Australia, India and New Zealand – was conceived largely as a means to balance China's growing influence in Asia. And Japan's eventual support for the TPP aimed not only to cement relations with the USA but to advance a liberalizing model of economic integration – with WTO-Plus disciplines in areas such as intellectual property rights (IPRs), investment, services and state-owned enterprises (SOEs) – for which China was not ready.

At a broader level, the proliferation of PTAs in the region produced a 'political domino effect' whereby governments feared being excluded from a new form of economic diplomacy.[3] The primacy of political concerns in driving this proliferation is reflected in the choice of PTA partners and the small economic impact of many PTAs. Not only do bilateral PTAs allow discretion in the selection of partners but the weak disciplines in GATT Article 24 allow flexibility in the breadth and depth of sectoral coverage. Thus, Japan was able to negotiate PTAs with smaller trade partners, some of whom already had low tariffs. These agreements offered modest economic gains but provided preferential access for Japanese multinationals while protecting vulnerable import-competing sectors like agriculture.[4]

While systemic forces may have prompted Japan to incorporate bilateral PTAs into its foreign economic policy, lobbying by business helped to shape the development of that policy. Japan's post-war economic growth was driven by four industries that are heavily dependent on exports: automobiles, electronics, machinery and steel. Facing increasing competition in the global market at the turn of the century, firms in these industries actively lobbied for PTAs to secure or expand access to foreign markets. Japan's most influential business association, Keidanren, has played a pivotal part in organizing and articulating corporate interests. Keidanren's influence as a source of campaign donations and votes declined somewhat following electoral reforms in 1994 that introduced public subsidies for political parties as well as single-member districts that forced politicians to take a broader view of constituent interests. Nevertheless, Keidanren's influence on PTA policy is visible in three distinct roles. It has worked as a pressure group trying to shape

Gregory P. Corning

the preferences of bureaucrats and politicians through direct lobbying; as a provider of information to these actors through the publication of numerous position papers and participation on high-level advisory boards; and as an interest coordinator at the private level, both within Japan and with counterpart organizations in potential PTA partners.[5]

Constraints on PTA policy

One of the commonly cited motivations for negotiating PTAs is the desire to advance domestic reform efforts. In the case of Japan, however, this motivation has been more rhetoric than reality. Weak political leadership and bureaucratic sectionalism have led to a less than ambitious PTA policy. With perhaps the exception of Prime Minister Shinzo Abe, Japanese prime ministers have neither made PTAs a foreign policy priority nor championed the institutional reforms necessary to overcome the path dependence created by vested interests.[6] The weakness of political leadership on PTAs is a function of both a lack of centralized authority within the Prime Minister's office as well as political instability resulting from the short tenure of most prime ministers during the period 2001–12.

Japan did not establish a vision for PTA policy until the government of Prime Minister Junichiro Koizumi (2001–06), by far the longest-serving prime minister of the decade. However, the ability to realize this vision was limited by two factors. First, Koizumi was more focused on privatizing the postal system and revitalizing the alliance with the USA than on negotiating PTAs. Second, he failed to establish clear executive authority over PTA policy. In 2003, for example, Koizumi established the Council of Ministers on the Promotion of Economic Partnerships under the deputy chief cabinet secretary. The Council issued the 'Basic Policy towards Further Promotion of Economic Partnership Agreements' in 2004 which set out the economic rationale for negotiating PTAs and laid out criteria for identifying potential partners.[7] However, the Council had no authority to coordinate the diverse interests and agendas of the ministries and agencies represented and so the document reflects the lowest common denominator of policy across ministries. Likewise, in 2006, the Koizumi Cabinet set a target for trade with PTA partners to reach 25 per cent of the value of Japan's total trade by 2010.[8] However, the Cabinet had no institutional mechanism to orchestrate progress towards this goal.

The basic challenge posed by the lack of strong, centralized leadership on PTA policy was exacerbated by major instability in the political system. From 2006 to 2009 three Liberal Democratic Party (LDP) prime ministers held office for only one year each – with all three lacking the time and approval rating to undertake any bold policy initiatives. The LDP then lost power to the Democratic Party of Japan (DPJ) which encountered even more political turmoil including heightened tensions over US bases in Okinawa, as well as the response to the March 2011 Tohoku earthquake/tsunami and the Fukushima Daiichi nuclear disaster. From 2009 to 2012 three DPJ prime ministers held office for only one year each. The DPJ paid lip service to the importance of PTAs but policy did not progress until the LDP returned to power in 2012, with Shinzo Abe serving once again as prime minister. Mounting pressure on Japan to join the TPP negotiations and Abe's desire to reverse decades of economic stagnation would put PTAs at the centre of Japanese foreign economic policy.

Without strong political leadership during the 2000s, Japanese PTA policy was further undermined by turf battles among ministries. The greatest tension existed between the protectionist Ministry of Agriculture, Forestry and Fisheries (MAFF) and the more internationalist Ministry of Economy, Trade and Industry (METI) and the Ministry of Foreign Affairs. Heavily influenced by the agricultural lobby and politicians from rural areas, MAFF resisted even the inclusion of agricultural goods in PTA talks. In contrast, METI and the Ministry of Foreign

Affairs saw a need to increase Japan's PTA activity and pushed for reforms in the agricultural sector that would facilitate the negotiation of such agreements. Even among the internationalist ministries, however, rivalry and clashing visions also hampered effective PTA policy. METI was the first ministry to begin discussion of PTAs, partly in an effort to strengthen its policymaking role relative to the Ministry of Foreign Affairs. Responding to the needs of the business community which sought a more unified market in East Asia, METI also emphasized a regional approach to PTAs. Meanwhile, the Ministry of Foreign Affairs prioritized the negotiation of bilateral agreements to reinforce specific diplomatic relationships and to avoid alienating the USA.[9] With bilateral deals easier to reach and a lack of urgency behind METI's multilateral agenda, Japan's PTA policy initially defaulted to an emphasis on bilateral agreements.

The major societal constraint on Japan's PTA policy has been the power of the agricultural lobby. Japan Agricultural Cooperatives (JA) is the group name for the almost 700 regional cooperatives in Japan that supply members with production inputs such as fertilizers as well as transportation, marketing and financial services. JA is managed by a national headquarters, JA-Zenchu (Central Union of Agricultural Cooperatives), which oversees government relations. Since the GATT era, JA-Zenchu has focused on restricting imports. Maintaining tight internal cohesion and cultivating close ties with both MAFF and the LDP, it was able to exert a strong pull against liberalization with arguments about the importance of food security and maintaining rural communities. The power of JA-Zenchu has declined over time owing to deregulation measures including the elimination of its monopoly on rice distribution, a cleavage between full-time and part-time farmers, and the impact of the 1994 electoral reforms on campaign finance. Despite this weakening, however, the organization has still been a major factor constraining the ambition of Japan's PTA policy.

Japan's bilateral and regional PTAs

Like the USA and the EU, Japan has pursued the negotiation of WTO-Plus PTAs with provisions that move beyond WTO commitments in areas like IPRs, investment and services. Japan's PTAs also put considerable emphasis on economic cooperation such as capacity building for less developed partners. Indeed, the Japanese government uses the term economic partnership agreement although many dismiss the term as a euphemism for a low-quality PTA that promises economic cooperation to compensate for limited agricultural concessions.[10]

As of May 2018, Japan has PTAs in force with Singapore (2002), Mexico (2005), Malaysia (2006), the Philippines (2008), Chile (2007), Thailand (2007), Indonesia (2008), Brunei (2008), ASEAN (2008), Viet Nam (2009), Switzerland (2009), India (2011), Peru (2012), Australia (2015) and Mongolia (2016). It also has PTAs at various stages of negotiation with Canada, Colombia, the EU (negotiations finalised in December 2017), the Gulf Cooperation Council (suspended) and Turkey, and is part of the Regional Comprehensive Economic Partnership (RCEP), the Comprehensive and Progressive Trans-Pacific Partnership (CPTPP) signed in March 2018, and trilateral talks with China and South Korea. Japan's first PTAs were driven largely by political expediency or the need to eliminate trade diversion but over time geopolitical imperatives and the Sino-Japanese rivalry became increasingly important in Japan's thinking.

Cross-regional bilateralism

The agreements with Singapore and Mexico are representative of Japan's early PTAs. In what is widely viewed as a trial run for more challenging negotiations, Japan concluded its first PTA with Singapore in 2002. Initially sceptical about diverging from its focus on multilateral liberalization, Japan responded hesitantly when Singapore first broached the possibility of a PTA in

415

Gregory P. Corning

1999. Yet as developed economies and important trading partners with an interest in balancing Chinese influence in South-East Asia, the two nations shared both economic and political motivations for pursuing a PTA. The decisive factor for Japan in driving the agreement was the fact that Singapore is a small city-state with few agricultural exports. The parties were thus able to sidestep several of the common obstacles encountered in tariff negotiations and negotiate a 'new age partnership' emphasizing the facilitation of trade in services and the movement of capital, information and skilled workers.

Mexico represented the first genuine test for Japan's PTA policy. Mexico is an agricultural exporter and its farm sector was intent on increasing exports to Asia to compensate for the import competition created by liberalization under NAFTA. The difficulty of this test was mitigated, however, by two factors. The volume of bilateral farm trade was relatively small and Mexico had already signed a PTA with the EU that exempted sensitive farm goods from liberalization.

The Ministry of Foreign Affairs and a large part of the Japanese business community were initially not convinced about the importance of a PTA with Mexico as they prioritized an agreement with South Korea. Nevertheless, working through Keidanren, firms with operations in Mexico – including major trading, auto and electronics firms – pushed vigorously for an agreement. For these firms, the primary goal of the PTA was to eliminate the trade diversion created by NAFTA which was estimated to cost them approximately ¥400 billion (US $3.6 billion) per year.[11] Unsurprisingly, MAFF and the farm lobby strongly opposed any significant opening of the agricultural sector. Facing both the cost of significant trade diversion and the collapse of the 2003 WTO Ministerial Conference in Cancún, however, the Koizumi government became more assertive about the need to reach an agreement. Nevertheless, the protectionist impulse was still strong. Japan succeeded in excluding rice and sugar from negotiations and committed to only low-tariff quotas for other sensitive goods.

By the mid-2000s Japan's PTA policy expanded to include more cross-regional negotiations with partners in Latin America and the Middle East as well as negotiations with more developed countries. There is no systematic pattern, however, to this expansion. The agreements reflect a mix of motivations including responding to trade diversion and geopolitical imperatives, as well as the opportunity to conclude deals quickly. Japan reached its first agreement outside the Asia-Pacific with Switzerland in 2009. Like the earlier PTA with Singapore, this was very much a trial run for more challenging PTAs with developed countries. The economic stakes for Japan were relatively low in terms of potential costs and benefits. With both partners focused on issues like electronic commerce rather than agricultural liberalization, negotiations moved swiftly.

In contrast, the negotiation of a PTA with Australia proved much more challenging. Australia is a major agricultural exporter that had negotiated more liberalizing PTAs than Japan. And as a developed country, it was much less willing to accept Japanese promises of economic cooperation as a side payment to compensate for minimal agricultural concessions. Despite the strong opposition of the farm lobby, however, both economic and political imperatives made signing the PTA a priority for the Japanese government. To begin, the Australia-US PTA (2005) had put Japanese multinationals at disadvantage relative to their US competitors, especially in the auto sector. Japan also wanted to bolster political ties with Australia – a key provider of energy and mineral resources, and a security partner that had helped to protect members of the Japanese Self-Defense Force carrying out humanitarian work in Iraq.[12]

A halting embrace of regionalism

The ASEAN-Japan Comprehensive Economic Partnership (AJCEP) represents Japan's first attempt to move beyond bilateral PTAs. The AJCEP provides evidence of the importance of regional competition in driving PTAs in East Asia as well as Japan's limited ambition in negotiating such agreements.[13] Regional competition figured heavily in Japan's decision to launch negotiations and its eventual rush to conclude them. When China and ASEAN agreed to launch PTA negotiations in November 2001, Japan proposed its own negotiations with ASEAN just two months later. Rather than seeking a single agreement with ASEAN from the outset, however, Japan negotiated bilateral agreements with the objective of combining those agreements into a single AJCEP – an approach that would provide Japan with greater leverage to control the opening of its agricultural sector across the separate negotiations. While Japan made steady progress in bilateral negotiations, regional developments would make reaching a deal with ASEAN a much higher priority. With rapid progress made on a PTA between South Korea and ASEAN in 2006, Keidanren became more vocal about the threat to the competitiveness of Japanese multinationals in South-East Asia.

Despite the push to conclude the AJCEP, the results of the agreement were quite limited. Importantly, the agreement made minimal progress in liberalizing and harmonizing the rules of origin governing the content of goods eligible for preferential treatment. The AJCEP applies rules to fewer categories of goods but the rules applied are still very restrictive. Moreover, the parties have the freedom to apply the rules form their prior bilateral agreement if those are more favourable. In short, Japan did not take decisive action in the AJCEP to liberalize or rationalize trade with ASEAN.

Japanese policy was even more cautious in North-East Asia. It took many years for Japan to think seriously about the possibility of a trilateral PTA with South Korea and China. Deeply rooted historical tensions and competition across key economic sectors help to explain the fact that Japan has not signed bilateral PTAs with these two neighbours that are among its largest export markets. In terms of history, relations with South Korea and China have been plagued by territorial disputes and the legacy of Japanese imperialism. Japan and South Korea both claim sovereignty over the Takeshima/Dokdo Islands while both Japan and China lay claim to the Senkaku/Diaoyu Islands. Meanwhile private and public actors in South Korea and China have criticized Japan for failing to deal in a forthright manner with past transgressions, including depictions of colonial history in textbooks approved by the Japanese government and official visits to the Yasukuni Shrine which entombs the spirits of those who died in the service of Imperial Japan, including 14 Class-A war criminals. The periodic flare-up of such conflicts has often disrupted diplomatic relations. For example, the annual trilateral summit established in 2008 was suspended between 2012 and 2015 owing to heightened tensions. Against this backdrop of diplomatic rancour, however, there has been a strong element of pragmatism; trade and investment relations have deepened over time and the negotiations for a trilateral PTA, discussed below, proceeded without interruption.

Although diplomatic tensions have dominated the headlines, economic concerns have created just as great an obstacle to PTA negotiations. As Japan began to explore bilateralism in 1998, the government identified South Korea as its initial priority in PTA negotiations believing that it would be easier to win support at home for an agreement with an Asian nation. Yet after five years of study group consultations and six rounds of negotiations during 2003–04, the two countries had made little progress. Worried that the PTA could exacerbate its long-term trade deficit with Japan, South Korea was concerned about Japan's modest offer on agriculture, ongoing challenges with non-tariff barriers in Japan's distribution system, and the ability of firms in sectors such as industrial machinery to compete with their Japanese rivals. While Japan did little to break the impasse with South Korea, it was even less proactive regarding China. When China first made overtures about a trilateral PTA in 2002, Japan responded that China would first have to meet all obligations associated with its 2001 accession to the WTO.

Gregory P. Corning

Towards the end of the 2000s, however, Japan's calculus regarding the importance of a trilateral PTA began to change. With China continually ranking as their preferred destination for expansion of research and development, production and sales, Japanese multinationals became more vocal about the need for a PTA with China.[14] And their concerns would become only more intense following the signing of a bilateral PTA between South Korea and China in 2015. METI also warmed to the idea of a trilateral PTA but considered a trilateral investment agreement, signed in 2012, as a prerequisite for PTA negotiations. The shift towards serious consideration of mega-regional PTAs also focused attention on the need for a trilateral PTA. Moving forward with an ASEAN+6 PTA would necessitate an agreement among Japan, China and South Korea. And nesting trilateral negotiations within a broader regional framework could facilitate those negotiations in two important ways. It would not only take the spotlight away from bilateral diplomatic tensions but would also expand the potential pay-offs for more vulnerable sectors that would lose under a trilateral agreement.

A shifting focus to mega-regional agreements

The same elements of diplomatic necessity, economic need and political expediency that have driven Japan's bilateral and regional PTAs also explain its interest in the negotiation of three mega-regional agreements: the TPP, RCEP and the Japan-EU PTA.

The Trans-Pacific Partnership

The 12 countries that signed the TPP in February 2016 aimed to craft a '21st-century' agreement that moved beyond market access issues to a range of regulatory policies impacting trade and investment. The TPP presented Japan with three major opportunities. First, Japan would be able to collaborate with the USA in building a trade architecture for the Asia-Pacific without the participation of China which was not ready for the degree of liberalization envisioned in the TPP. Second, for a mature economy like Japan, the WTO-Plus emphasis on issues such as IPRs, services, investment, and tighter controls on SOEs would help to boost growth as well as level the playing field with 'state-capitalist' systems. According to the World Bank, a TPP that included the USA would have boosted Japanese GDP by 2.7 per cent by 2030, more than twice the average for all members, with deregulation and the lowering of non–tariff barriers facilitating the operation of global value chains and expanded business opportunities in the TPP area.[15] Third, the TPP could help Prime Minister Abe to advance his structural reform agenda with foreign pressure to open the heavily protected agricultural sector.

Despite the many potential benefits, Japan was slow to embrace the TPP; it only joined the negotiations in July 2013 almost two years after they had begun. The agricultural sector led a fierce and sophisticated campaign against the TPP, coordinating efforts with other interest groups such as the Japan Medical Association. This campaign and the publication of dozens of anti-TPP books fed into deeper and broader concerns about how the TPP could change Japan's economy and society. Although the anti-TPP campaign was unsuccessful in preventing Japan from signing or ratifying the agreement, it did help to prevent a major shock for the agricultural sector. Despite the farm sector being one of the key target targets of structural reform under 'Abenomics',[16] the concessions made in the TPP were relatively modest. Japan agreed to abolish tariffs on only 81 per cent of agricultural, forestry and fisheries goods by category. This was more than in any previous Japanese PTA but still far less than the 98.5 per cent average for other TPP members.[17] Moreover, Japan succeeded in maintaining tariff-rate quotas on a significant percentage of imports under the five most sensitive categories of farm goods: rice, wheat, beef and pork, dairy products and sugar.

418

The political victory for the Abe government was short-lived, however, as the Trump Administration withdrew from the TPP in January 2017. Although the prime minister initially despaired that the TPP would be meaningless without the USA, his government moved quickly to ratify the trade agreement despite a boycott by several opposition parties. This was more than a symbolic gesture as the TPP text could serve as a template for bilateral deals that would maintain the momentum of liberalization. There was also the possibility of moving ahead with a TPP-11 in the hope that the USA might be encouraged to rejoin at a later date. Even without the USA, however, a TPP-11 agreement could still have important economic benefits for Japanese firms. New rules for e-commerce, reduced restrictions on foreign invest- ment, and greater disciplines on the operations of SOEs would improve investment opportu- nities for a range of Japanese retailers and service providers. By one estimate, a TPP-11 agreement would still boost Japan's real GDP by 1.1 per cent.[18] However, the push for the TPP was not driven by broad public or business support. Only 38 per cent of the Japanese public supported ratification while 35 percent opposed it.[19] And although TPP remained important for Japan's leading export industries, surveys showed most Japanese manufacturing and services firms were more interested in expanding business opportunities in China, the USA and Thailand than in the TPP-11 area.[20]

Nevertheless, Abe remained anxious to maintain the momentum for the TPP negotiations. His government moved ahead with new spending intended to facilitate structural adjustment in the face of rising imports anticipated under the original TPP deal. And, more importantly, it played a leading role in bringing together the TPP-11 to push ahead with the pact. Members of the TPP-11 initially requested the suspension of 60 provisions in the TPP-12 text on the grounds that their concessions had been motivated by the promise of increased access to the US market. In last-minute negotiations at the November 2017 APEC Summit, however, Japan played a decisive role in bringing the group back closer to the original agreement. At the summit, the TPP-11 announced basic agreement on the CPTPP. Although the parties will not revisit any tariff-related concessions, they decided to freeze 20 provisions in the TPP-12 text— concerning mostly intellectual property and trade-related investment rules—which were cham- pioned by the USA. Signed in March 2018, the CPTPP will certainly be less ambitious than the TPP but still a state-of the-art agreement and an important achievement for Japan. It will enter into force if ratified by six of the members and set a higher standard of liberalization than the competing RCEP.

The Regional Comprehensive Economic Partnership

Japan has been part of RCEP since the launch of negotiations in May 2013 but the initiative took a backseat to the TPP. RCEP promises fewer economic benefits for Japan and lacks the geopolitical dimension that made the TPP so appealing. RCEP brings together ASEAN, China, Japan, South Korea, Australia, New Zealand and India — a grouping that accounts for roughly 30 per cent of global GDP and half the world's population. However, given the political and economic diversity of the participating countries, RCEP has set much more modest goals for tariff elimination and deregulation than the TPP. Rather than expanding the depth and scope of coverage of WTO-Plus issues, RCEP is essentially a developmental PTA intended to ratio- nalize the tangle of 34 PTAs that already connect RCEP members. Nonetheless, Japan can benefit from RCEP in two important ways. First, any progress in harmonizing rules of origin will facilitate Japanese production and supply networks. Second, RCEP can facilitate PTA negotiations with South Korea and China. RCEP provides a larger forum that shifts the focus away from bilateral, diplomatic tensions and allows a broader range of trade-offs in balancing

Gregory P. Corning

the gains and losses of economic liberalization. After the 22nd round of negotiations in May 2018, however, the group still has yet to announce agreement on any major topic of negotiation. Although the announcement of basic agreement on the CPTPP may provide impetus for RCEP to reach its own deal, any such deal will set lower standards than the CPTPP.

The Japan-EU PTA

Japan and the EU are important trade and investment partners. In 2016 the EU accounted for roughly 11 per cent of Japan's exports and 23 per cent of its overseas investment stock.[21] The value of a PTA became apparent to Japan after the entry into force of the South Korea-EU PTA in 2011 as Korean auto firms captured a rising share of the EU market. Japan began negotiations with the EU in 2013 but progress was slow until 2017 when developments in the world economy pushed the agreement to the top of the agenda. The PTA allowed both parties to take a rhetorical stand against the neo-mercantilist rhetoric of the Trump Administration. It also provided an important political victory for the Abe government following the US withdrawal from the TPP and for the EU prior to the start of the Brexit negotiations that were made necessary by the UK's decision in 2016 to leave the EU.

Japan and the EU reached basic agreement on a PTA in July 2017 and set a target date of early 2019 for its entry into force. As the core bargain, the EU agreed to eliminate tariffs on autos and auto parts while Japan agreed to significant opening up for select agricultural products. On the agricultural front, concessions were much easier for Japan than in the TPP. Whereas TPP partners were focused on highly sensitive commodities like rice, the EU was more interested in opening the market for specialty items like wine, chocolate and cheese which faced tariffs ranging from 15 per cent to 40 per cent.[22] As a WTO-Plus agreement between two developed economies, the Japan-EU PTA also includes important liberalization commitments in financial and telecommunications services, government procurement in the Japanese railway sector, and increased regulatory transparency and coordination. It is also the first PTA to include a specific commitment to the Paris Climate Accord. However, the July agreement also left some important issues to be addressed – most notably investment – with Japan resisting EU pressure to abandon the standard investor-state dispute settlement system and adopt a new investment court system staffed by public officials.

Conclusion

At the end of the 1990s systemic forces pushed Japan to begin the negotiation of bilateral PTAs. Two decades later, external pressures are once again pushing Japan into a more proactive trade policy – a policy necessary to confront major domestic challenges. The election of Donald Trump thrust the global trading system into a period of uncertainty. Today, Japan's PTA policy functions as a coping strategy to help to bolster growth amid this tumult. Faced with a dwindling population and shrinking domestic demand, Japan must become more engaged with the world economy. Pending ratification as this chapter goes to press, the CPTPP will be a major part of Abe's legacy but questions remain regarding Japan's pivotal economic relationship with the USA.

Although Vice-President Pence and other cabinet officials have made public statements about the importance of a US-Japan PTA, the Trump Administration made no public mention of plans for such a bilateral during the president's November 2017 visit to Japan. This was no doubt a relief for Japan because a bilateral would be a distant second best compared to a mega-regional involving the USA. First, a bilateral PTA would do less to constrain China's influence in the East Asian regional economy. Second, a bilateral PTA would not have the same regional impact in simplifying rules of origin. And, finally, it is likely that the Trump Administration would push for a better deal than the TPP, exerting pressure on several fronts including agriculture, autos and restrictions on currency manipulation.[23] For these reasons, it seems prudent for Japan to play a waiting game. US engagement with the CPTPP seems highly unlikely without a change in political leadership, and even then is far from certain. Although it would be very difficult to reject a US request for bilateral talks, Japan sees advantage in waiting for the Trump Administration to renegotiate existing agreements like NAFTA before moving forward with negotiations.

Against this backdrop of uncertainty, the LDP victory in the October 2017 Lower House election suggests a basic continuity in Japan's foreign economic policy over the next few years. Although the LDP retained its majority because of the splintering of the opposition rather than strong support for the prime minister's leadership, Abe appears to have strengthened his position within the LDP. Abe will be more focused on security issues, but he will still need to maintain the momentum in the negotiation of trade deals that bolster growth. This imperative was clear in Japan's leadership in moving the TPP-11 forwards. Japan has employed a cautious and calculated approach to PTA policy during the last two decades but the trade policy of the Trump Administration has, nonetheless, thrust Japan into the ironic role of leading talks to liberalize trade and investment in the Asia-Pacific.

Notes

1 Mireya Solis (2011) 'Japan and East Asian Economic Regionalism', in Alisa Gaunder (ed.) *Routledge Handbook of Japanese Politics*, London: Routledge, pp. 297–300.

2 Mireya Solis and Saori N. Katada (2009) 'Explaining FTA Proliferation', in Mireya Solis, Barbara Stallings and Saori N. Katada (eds) *Competitive Regionalism: FTA Diffusion in the Pacific Rim*, New York: Palgrave Macmillan, pp. 15–22.

3 John Ravenhill (2010) 'The New East Asian Regionalism: A Political Domino Effect', *Review of International Political Economy*, 17(2): 178–208.

4 Saadia M. Pekkanen, Mireya Solis and Saori N. Katada (2007) 'Trading Gains for Control: International Trade Forums and Japanese Economic Diplomacy', *International Studies Quarterly*, 41(4): 959–62.

5 Hidetaka Yoshimatsu (2005) 'Japan's Keidanren and Free Trade Agreements', *Asian Survey*, 45(2), March/April: 261–62.

6 Hidetaka Yoshimatsu (2012) 'Political Leaders' Preferences and Trade Policy: Comparing FTA Politics in Japan and South Korea', *Asian Politics and Policy*, 4(2): 198.

7 Office of the Prime Minister (2004) Council of Ministers on the Promotion of Economic Partnerships, 'Basic Policy towards Further Promotion of Economic Partnership Agreements', 21 December. Available at http://japan.kantei.go.jp/policy/index/keizairenkei/041221kettei_e.html (accessed 12 July 2017).

8 Office of the Prime Minister (2006) 'Basic Policies for Economic and Fiscal Management and Structural Reform 2006', 7 July. Available at www5.cao.go.jp/keizai-shimon/english/publication/pdf/060802_basic_policies_summary.pdf (accessed 15 July 2017).

9 Takeshi Terada (2010) 'The Origins of ASEAN+6 and Japan's Initiatives', *Pacific Review*, 23(1): 78–79.

10 Solis, 'Japan and East Asian Economic Regionalism', p. 304.

11 Keidanren (2003) 'Request for Bilateral Negotiations on a Japan-Mexico Economic Partnership Agreement', 16 June. Available www.keidanren.or.jp/english/policy/2003/060.html (accessed 17 July 2017).

12 Hidetaka Yoshimatsu and Patrick Ziltener (2010) 'Japan's FTA Strategy toward Highly Developed Countries', *Asian Survey*, 50(6), November/December: 1058–81.

13 Gregory P. Corning (2009) 'Between Bilateralism and Regionalism in East Asia: The ASEAN-Japan Economic Partnership', *Pacific Review*, 22(5): 640.

Gregory P. Corning

14 Japan External Trade Organization (2009) 'Survey on the International Operations of Japanese Firms FY 2008', 23 March. Available at www.jetro.go.jp/ext_images/en/reports/survey/pdf/2009_02_biz.pdf (accessed 4 August 2017).

15 World Bank (2016) *Global Economic Prospects*, Washington, DC: World Bank, January, p. 227. Available at www.worldbank.org/content/dam/Worldbank/GEP/GEP2016a/Global-Economic-Prospects-January-2016-Implications-Trans-Pacific-Partnership-Agreement.pdf.

16 IMF (2015) 'Can Abenomics Succeed? Overcoming the Legacy of Japan's Lost Decades', Washington, DC: International Monetary Fund.

17 Aurelia George Morgan (2015) 'What Does the TPP Mean for Japan's Agricultural Sector?' East Asia Forum, 19 November. Available at www.eastasiaforum.org/2015/11/19/what-does-the-tpp-mean-for-japans-agricultural-sector/ (accessed 1 December 2015).

18 Kenichi Kawasaki (2017) 'Emergent Uncertainty in Regional Integration: Economic Impacts of Alternative RTA Scenarios', National Graduate Institute for Policy Studies, Japan, Discussion Paper 16–28, January, p. 9. Available at https://econpapers.repec.org/paper/ngidpaper/16-28.htm (accessed 15 August 2017).

19 'Japanese Split on TPP: Nikkei Poll', *Nikkei Report*, 31 October 2016.

20 Japan External Trade Organization (2017) 'Survey on the International Operations of Japanese Firms FY 2016', 8 March, p. 11. Available at www.jetro.go.jp/ext_images/en/reports/survey/pdf/business_201703.pdf (accessed 5 August 2017).

21 Japanese Ministry of Foreign Affairs (2017) 'Japan-EU EPA', July. Available at www.mofa.go.jp/files/000013835.pdf (accessed 10 July 2017).

22 European Commission (2017) 'EU-Japan Agreement Explained', July. Available at http://ec.europa.eu/trade/policy/in-focus/eu-japan-economic-partnership-agreement/agreement-explained/ (accessed 10 July 2017).

23 'Analysts Pitch New and Improved TPP, Clash over Bilaterals', *Inside US Trade*, 24 February 2017, 35(8).

36

Australia's approach to PTAs

Richard Pomfret

For most of the 20th century, Australia's trade policy centred on a high protective tariff for manufactured goods, accompanied by preferential trading under British imperial preferences. The United Kingdom was the major trading partner in the first half of the 1900s, but its relative importance declined rapidly after 1945.[1] The British market was especially important for Australian farmers and pastoralists, until British accession to the European common market in 1973 led to Australian agricultural exporters facing poorer access than European competitors.

In 1966 Australia was the first country to introduce preferential tariffs on imports from developing countries in anticipation of the Generalized System of Preferences (GSP) that would be ratified in 1971. Australia signed a free trade agreement (FTA) with New Zealand in 1965 and offered preferential tariff treatment on imports from Pacific Island economies in the 1981 South Pacific Regional Trade and Economic Cooperation Agreement (SPARTECA), both of which were regionally important but globally minor.[2]

The high tariff regime was increasingly anachronistic. In 1983 Australia embarked on a major economic reform agenda that included reducing import tariffs to very low levels by the end of the century. At the same time Closer Economic Relations (CER) were established with New Zealand, extending the FTA into deeper integration. Apart from the CER and tariff preferences to developing countries under the GSP, SPARTECA and the 1991 Papua New Guinea-Australia Trade and Commercial Relations Agreement, Australian trade policy in the late 1900s was based on non-discriminatory multilateralism. Australia was a charter member of the World Trade Organization (WTO) in 1995, and at that time appeared to have become a pillar of the liberal global trading system based on unconditional most-favoured-nation (MFN) treatment.[3]

The first decade of the 21st century saw a policy shift away from multilateralism as Australia signed bilateral trade agreements with Singapore, Thailand, the USA and Chile. The move towards bilateral agreements accelerated in the 2010s. Australia also participated enthusiastically in negotiations towards mega-regional trade agreements such as the Trans- Pacific Partnership (TPP) that involved twelve countries from across the globe, and the Regional Comprehensive Economic Partnership (RCEP) that is still under negotiation.

The first two sections of this chapter examine the longer-standing Pacific Island relations, before turning to the 21st-century pattern of proliferating trade agreements outside the WTO. The pattern will be placed in a wider setting of Australia's desire for economic diversification

423

Richard Pomfret

beyond primary product exports and of global production being fragmented along ever more complex international value chains.

Preferential trade agreements with developing countries

In 1966 Australia was the first country to offer preferential tariffs on imports from developing countries. The scheme was simplified in 1986, and applied to all dutiable goods. The Australian scheme is based on a five percentage-point margin of preference: when the Australian MFN tariff is 5 per cent or higher, the tariff on products from beneficiary countries is reduced by five percentage points, and when the MFN rate is 5 per cent or less the preferential rate is zero.[4] Since 1991 countries have been graduated and some goods have been removed from the scheme. The government has indicated its intention to restrict beneficiaries to the least developed countries (LDCs) and some Pacific Island territories, although in practice the Australian government has been reluctant to remove GSP beneficiaries from the list. One reason for negotiating bilateral agreements with middle-income countries has been to ease transition from GSP status.

In 1981 more generous unilateral tariff preferences were offered in SPARTECA, which covered specified products originating from the developing island member countries of the Pacific Islands Forum. When Papua New Guinea (PNG) became independent in 1975, a trade agreement was negotiated such that PNG goods entered Australia duty-free, and in 1981 PNG was included in SPARTECA.[5] SPARTECA was valuable because it covered textiles, clothing and footwear goods, which faced high MFN tariffs in Australia but were excluded from the country's GSP scheme. The 14 beneficiary countries were the Cook Islands, Fiji, the Federated States of Micronesia, Kiribati, the Marshall Islands, Nauru, Niue, Palau, PNG, Samoa, Solomon Islands, Tonga, and Tuvalu and Vanuatu.

Establishment of the WTO in 1995 with its dispute settlement mechanism posed a fundamental challenge to non-reciprocal tariff preferences outside the GSP. SPARTECA and the European Union's Lomé Convention with African, Caribbean and Pacific developing countries were clearly contrary to the General Agreement on Tariffs and Trade (GATT)'s non-discrimination principle and fell under none of the permitted exceptions. While third countries had tolerated these preferential arrangements before 1995, in the new environment they would inevitably face judicial challenge. Termination of the EU's Lomé Convention with its one-way preferences and its replacement by the reciprocal Cotonou Agreement encouraged Australia and New Zealand to do the same with SPARTECA.[6] In 2001 Australia, New Zealand and the Pacific Island countries signed the Pacific Agreement on Closer Economic Relations (PACER), a framework agreement to deepen trade and investment liberalisation in 2001, committing all members to begin negotiations towards an FTA by 2011 at the latest. However, PACER negotiations progressed slowly[7] in large part due to dissonance between the position of Australia and New Zealand, who envisaged a WTO-consistent trade agreement that would not create precedents of exceptional treatment, and the Pacific Islands that expected exceptional treatment.[8]

In August 2008 Australia advocated a 'PACER-plus' agreement, in lieu of the originally envisaged FTA. PACER-plus negotiations were launched in October 2009 and concluded in Brisbane on 20 April 2017. The Agreement was signed in Nuku'alofa, Tonga, on 14 June 2017 by Australia, New Zealand and eight Pacific Island countries (Cook Islands, Kiribati, Nauru, Niue, Samoa, Solomon Islands, Tonga and Tuvalu); Vanuatu signed in September 2017. PACER-plus covers goods, services, investment, labour, sanitary and phytosanitary measures, and other issues. Unlike SPARTECA's one-way preferences offered on the Pacific Island developing countries' exports to Australia and New Zealand, PACER-plus requires all signatories to eliminate tariffs on trade among PACER-plus partners. Each country has a schedule of specific goods tariff commitments. Tariff reductions for all countries will mostly take place in the first ten years, apart from the LDCs (Kiribati, Solomon Islands, Tuvalu and Vanuatu), whose tariff reductions begin in 2028 unless these countries graduate from LDC status. Tariffs in the other eight signatories must fall to zero by 2042, 25 years after the entry into force of the agreement.

The impact of these agreements on trade in the 21st century is small. Reductions in Australian tariffs have eroded GSP margins, and imports with significant tariffs are likely to be excluded from GSP treatment (or be irrelevant to low-income countries). Pacific Island links are important to the partner countries which are mostly dependent on Australia and New Zealand for transport and trade, but these are small economies (Table 36.1). The most populous, PNG and Fiji, have had politically fraught relations with Australia, while the other countries have a combined population of a little over one million.[9]

Regional integration with New Zealand

Australia's deepest preferential trading arrangement is with New Zealand. Bilateral agreements date back to a first agreement signed in 1922, although bilateral trade was small between economies that were competing rather than complementary and conflicts over non-tariff trade barriers were frequent. The 1965 New Zealand-Australia FTA was characterized by its restricted coverage and limited impact.[10] The 1983 CER agreement led to much deeper integration.

All tariffs and quantitative import or export restrictions on trade in goods originating in the free trade area are prohibited under the CER. Since 1 July 1990 all goods meeting the CER rules of origin criteria can be traded across the Tasman free of duty and quantitative import

Table 36.1 Australia's Pacific Island partners

	PTAs		*GDP per caput (US $, 2016)*	*Population in thousands, 2016*
Cook Islands	S	P	n.a.	12★
Federated States of Micronesia	S		3,069	45
Fiji	S		5,153	899
Kiribati	S	P	1,449	114
Marshall Islands	S		3,449	53
Nauru	S	P	7,821	13
Niue	S	P	n.a.	2★
Palau	S		13,626	22
Papua New Guinea	S		2,183[a]	8,085
Samoa	S	P	4,028	195
Solomon Islands,	S	P	2,005	599
Tonga	S	P	3,689	107
Tuvalu	S	P	3,084	11
Vanuatu	S	P	2,861	270
New Zealand	S	P	39,427	4,693

Source: GDP per caput and population from World Bank, *World Development Indicators* (accessed 17 September 2017), apart from * CIA Factbook.

restrictions. The Trade in Services Protocol brought services into the CER from January 1989, allowing most services to be traded free of restriction with limited exclusions. The CER includes measures to minimize market distortions in trade in goods, including through domestic industry assistance and export subsidies and incentives. With most of the trade goals met, the Australian and New Zealand governments decided to take a single economic market approach to closer economic relations, aiming to harmonize the two economies to enable business, consumers and investors to conduct operations across the Tasman in a seamless, regulatory environment.

The CER is supplemented by more than 80 government-to-government bilateral treaties, protocols and other arrangements covering trade and the movement of people, investment, aviation, business law coordination, mutual recognition of goods and professions, taxation, health care, social security, superannuation portability, food standards and government procurement. The Protocol on Investment entered into force on 1 March 2013, benefiting investors in both countries through lower compliance costs, higher screening thresholds and greater legal certainty when investing in their Trans-Tasman neighbour. The harmonization of Trans-Tasman food standards through the Australia New Zealand Food Authority Agreement of 1995 means lower compliance costs for industry, fewer regulatory barriers and more consumer choice. Mutual recognition of goods and occupations removes technical barriers to trade and impediments to the movement of skilled personnel between jurisdictions without the need for complete harmonization of standards and professional qualifications.

The degree of economic integration in the CER reflects the strong historical and cultural ties between Australia and New Zealand. New Zealand (and Fiji) participated in Australasian colonial conferences in the 1800s, but when federation became a serious prospect following the decision to unite Australia's six colonies in 1899 New Zealand decided not to join.[11] Nevertheless, ties remained close, e.g. in the 1908 and 1912 Olympic Games Australia and New Zealand competed as a joint Australasian team. The Australian and New Zealand Army Corps (ANZAC) was formed in 1914 and operated at Gallipoli in the First World War. In the Second World War ANZAC was re-established during the 1941 Battle of Greece, and remains a potent symbol even though foreign policies have diverged and there has been little discussion of political unification since 1945.

Bilateral trade agreements

Since the turn of the century, Australia's bilateral trade agreements have proliferated (Table 36.2). The Singapore-Australia FTA was negotiated in 2001–02 and entered into force in July 2003. The Thailand-Australia FTA and the Australia-US FTA both entered into force in January 2005, and the Australia-Chile FTA in March 2009. Australia and New Zealand signed a joint agreement with the Association of Southeast Asian Nations (ASEAN) in 2009 that entered into force between 2010 and 2012. Trade agreements with the Republic of Korea (South Korea), Japan and the People's Republic of China entered into force in 2014, 2015 and 2016, respectively, while agreements with India and Indonesia were under negotiation at the time of writing.[12]

Analysis of the utilization rate for Australia's six preferential trading arrangements in the period 2000–09 reveals a pattern of declining ratios of imports receiving preferential tariff treatment to the total value of bilateral imports. In 2000 over half of Australian imports from New Zealand, the Pacific Island Forum economies, Thailand and Chile claimed preferential treatment under the GSP, SPARTECA or the CER, but all of these trading partners had lower utilization rates by 2009. Using high-quality disaggregated customs data, Pomfret et al.[13] show that low utilization is primarily because of the increasing number of zero MFN tariff lines. When Australia's MFN tariffs are positive, preferential tariffs are utilized and preferred trading

Australia's approach to PTAs

Table 36.2 Australia's 21st-century trade agreements, to the end of 2016

Partner	Entry into force
Singapore	28 July 2003
Thailand	1 January 2005
USA	1 January 2005
Chile	6 March 2009
ASEAN	1 January 2010[a]
Malaysia	1 January 2013
South Korea	12 December 2014
Japan	15 January 2015
China	20 December 2016

Notes: *a* = 1 January 2010 for Australia, New Zealand, Brunei, Malaysia, Myanmar, the Philippines, Singapore and Viet Nam; 12 March 2010 for Thailand; 1 January 2011 for Laos; 4 January 2011 for Cambodia; 10 January 2012 for Indonesia.

partners pay lower customs duties, but erosion of preference margins as a result of multilateral trade liberalization has reduced the raw utilization rates. Positive utilization rates indicate that tariff preferences do have an impact, and the exporters claiming the preferential tariff rate are better off than they would be in its absence. However, preferential tariffs are becoming less and less useful as Australia's tariffs have been reduced or eliminated. Preference erosion applies a fortiori to Australia's GSP scheme, where the preference margin has effectively fallen to zero on most included goods.

Given the diminishing value of preferential tariff treatment why does Australia continue to negotiate trade agreements? For some Australian exporters, primarily in the agricultural sector, tariff and non-tariff barriers to trade remain significant. These barriers may be reduced by offering relevant non-trade concessions to trading partners, as in, for example, the US trade agreement.[14] More generally, Australia's 21st-century trade agreements focus on deep integration issues, and in particular trade facilitation.

Relations among the ASEAN+6 countries illustrate the point. When Australia and New Zealand negotiated a trade agreement with ASEAN, they effectively created a classic FTA with zero tariffs on goods traded among the signatories.[15] Bilateral agreements with ASEAN members Singapore, Thailand and Malaysia moved beyond tariff issues, to the extent that the ASEAN agreement is seen as a framework rather than the end product. Meanwhile, negotiations towards a RCEP are seeking to harmonize the network of agreements among the ASEAN countries, Australia, China, India, Japan, South Korea and New Zealand (the ASEAN+6) by extending tariff-free trade, standardizing rules of origin and moving on deeper integration issues. These pathways involve different speeds of integration as RCEP follows the convoy principle of moving at the speed of the most reluctant partner, while bilateral agreements among Australia, New Zealand, Singapore, Malaysia and Thailand reflect the aspirations of the ASEAN+6 countries most committed to regional trade liberalization and economic integration.

Why have 'deeper' integration agreements flourished since the turn of the century? This has been a regional phenomenon, as ASEAN moved from lugubriously pushing an ASEAN free trade area in the 1990s to enthusiastically creating an ASEAN economic community in the 21st century. The crucial change has been recognition that international competitiveness in an increasing number of goods derives from producing along a global value chain (GVC) with ever finer levels of fragmentation of the production process.[16] GVCs require ease of doing business

427

Richard Pomfret

and, especially, ease of crossing borders, i.e. facilitation of trade in terms of cost, time and certainty.[17] Failure to facilitate trade increases the need to carry inventories of parts that undermine a country's attractiveness as a GVC participant.

East Asia has played the leading role in GVC formation, characterized by the label 'Factory Asia', although in practice a handful of Asian countries have been heavily involved in GVCs and many Asian countries have been absent.[18] The process of creating international value chains can be traced to Japan moving car and electronic assembly offshore when the yen appreciated after 1985, with Thailand as a preferred location, and also to the offshoring of labour-intensive activities by Hong Kong and Singapore when they lost their comparative advantage in the 1980s, with southern China, Malaysia and Indonesia as preferred locations. With China's rapid growth and internationalization of the Chinese economy in the 1990s and accession to the WTO in 2001, China increasingly became the preferred location for final assembly. These patterns are reflected in Singapore, Thailand, Malaysia, and more recently China and Indonesia, taking the leading role in negotiating trade facilitation agreements.[19]

How does the GVC phenomenon affect Australian trade policies? Australian firms participate in some GVCs, but overall participation is small.[20] Australian governments, supported by analysis from the Productivity Commission, seek to increase this participation. The embracing of trade agreements can be seen as a logical continuation of Australia's trade liberalization since 1983. Once tariffs had been reduced to minimal levels, the next step in encouraging competitive participation in the global economy was to reduce the costs of international trade through trade facilitation measures. At the same time, the government seeks to open up markets for agricultural exports, although these represent a small and declining share of Australian exports.

Negotiating mega-regionals

When the WTO was established in 1995, following the end of the Uruguay Round of multilateral trade negotiations, the GATT agenda of a liberal world trade regime had been achieved in essentials. Further steps to introduce elements such as investment measures, intellectual property rights, or trade facilitation would be more difficult, a fact that explains the interminable Doha Development Round negotiations. In order to avoid the consensus necessary for binding WTO obligations, countries wishing to pursue the WTO+ agenda may sign voluntary plurilaterals, such as the Information Technology Agreement (ITA), or join like-minded countries in reaching agreement on deeper integration issues. Australia has followed both tracks, signing the ITA and participating in mega-regional trade negotiations.[21]

The highest profile mega-regional was the Trans-Pacific Partnership (TPP), launched in 2011. The 12 countries that negotiated the TPP – Australia, Brunei Darussalam, Canada, Chile, Japan, Malaysia, Mexico, New Zealand, Peru, Singapore, the USA and Viet Nam – represent around 40 per cent of the global economy and one-quarter of world trade. They include the most active countries in international value chains in North America and in East Asia, apart from China, as well as other countries such as Australia, New Zealand and Chile that are committed to liberal international trade policies. By setting common rules and promoting transparency of laws and regulations, the TPP is intended to provide certainty for businesses and to reduce costs and red tape for traders, service suppliers and investors. Schott et al.[22] describe the TPP as 'the most comprehensive trade deal ever negotiated between developed and developing countries'.

After five years of negotiations the Trans-Pacific Partnership Agreement was concluded in October 2016. Conclusion of the TPP negotiations was seen as the first concrete step towards realising the long-term vision of a free trade area of the Asia-Pacific, with membership open to other Asia-Pacific economies and a commitment to expanding TPP membership over time. However, following the US election, President Trump announced in January 2017 that the USA would not ratify the agreement, throwing the TPP's future into doubt. Some of the 11 remaining signatories wanted to press ahead with ratification, while others felt that they had made concessions primarily in return for access to the US market and were less willing to ratify an 11-member TPP.

RCEP, launched in November 2012, involves the ASEAN+6 countries. A basic aim is to reduce 'spaghetti bowl' effects by harmonizing the existing ASEAN+6 agreements, which vary in coverage and in definition of rules of origin.[23] Negotiations are, however, going beyond trade in goods, although RCEP is weaker than the TPP insofar as it seeks less deep integration. The key TPP-RCEP differences centre on the scope of new disciplines in TPP such as labour and environmental policies, e-commerce and cross-border data flows, and state-owned enterprises, and on RCEP's consultative versus the TPP's binding dispute settlement procedures. RCEP is sensitive to national sensitivities and to differences in levels of development, permitting exemptions for sensitive products and special preferences and flexibility for poorer members. RCEP is also likely to have a smaller impact on third countries.[24] Commentators have differed as to whether the two mega-regionals are complementary, because both could be way stations en route to a free trade area of the Asia-Pacific, or perhaps in competition, because the TPP excludes China but China is a major player in RCEP.

Australia has embraced both the TPP and RCEP. The TPP is seen as a harbinger of deeper integration, and originally involved the USA, a major trading partner with which Australia has a significant bilateral trade deficit. RCEP is a natural step beyond the Australia-New Zealand-ASEAN FTA, harmonizing preferential trade treatment with and among the other ASEAN+6 countries, and also taking steps towards deeper integration.

The Australia-Europe-Asia Triangle

In April 2017 Australia and the EU announced that they had concluded a joint scoping exercise on a future FTA between the two economies. This is a key step towards the launch of negotiations, after which both sides will work through their domestic processes to secure approval of a negotiating mandate. According to official announcements, a comprehensive, high-quality Australia-EU FTA is intended to ensure that the bilateral trade and investment relationship reaches its full potential by removing barriers to trade in goods, by expanding services linkages and investment ties, and by enhancing regulatory cooperation in specific sectors of interest to business.

Negotiations for an Australia-EU trade agreement could move relatively quickly because the Comprehensive Economic and Trade Agreement (CETA) between the EU and Canada provides a blueprint. CETA, signed in 2016 and provisionally implemented in September 2017, was the first trade agreement signed by the EU with a high-income country outside Europe, and was seen as a forerunner of an agreement with the USA; the latter hope is on hold since the 2016 US election, but could equally apply to an agreement with Australia. WTO+ areas such as trade in services and investor-state dispute settlement were eventually agreed, and ratified by all 28 EU member countries.[25] Agriculture was difficult, and will be for EU-Australian negotiations, even though the EU's policy is much reformed since 1972 and for both partners agriculture accounts for a small share of total trade. CETA's terms include elimination of tariffs on 98 per cent of Canada-EU trade, mutual recognition of professional qualifications in many areas (e.g. architecture, accounting, engineering), and easier transfer of professional staff between offices in Canada and Europe.

Richard Pomfret

For Australia, a deep integration agreement with the EU will complement progress towards the mega-regionals described in the previous section. An EU agreement and Australian agreements with the Pacific Alliance and Hong Kong, with both of whom negotiations were launched in July 2017, would complete a network of WTO+ agreements with all of Australia's significant trade partners committed to an integrated global economy. The pattern is a logical continuation of Australia's trade policies since the turn of the century.

An EU agreement may also help Australian firms to find niches in GVCs. Although the term GVC is in common use, most international value chains have been regional, centred on East Asia, the EU or North America. As trade costs continue to decline the regional value chains are starting to link up. Given the unpredictability of US policy since the 2016 presidential election, this process is likely to be strongest between the EU and China.[26] Australia hopes to join this process as the third point of a triangle.[27]

Conclusion

Australia's approach to preferential trade agreements has changed dramatically since 2000. In the final decades of the 20th century Australia abandoned the high-tariff policy that it had implemented for most of the 1900s. Tariff barriers to trade were rapidly removed on a multilateral basis. The only exceptions were the GSP scheme and preferential treatment of trade with Pacific Islands, and in both cases the value of tariff preferences was eroded as Australia's MFN tariff rates fell towards zero. The most important Pacific partner was New Zealand, with which integration went deeper in the CER arrangements.

In the 21st century Australia has combined a low MFN trade regime with an increasing number of bilateral trade agreements. Some of the early agreements sought to ease GSP graduation, but the agreements have mostly focused on WTO+ areas. In the 2010s the dominant pattern has been to negotiate mega-regional agreements among groups of countries (the TPP, RCEP, the EU) sharing the desire to go beyond the WTO into areas such as trade facilitation, services, investment, intellectual property and so forth. For Australia, a driving force behind this pattern has been the goal of diversifying the economy beyond dependence on commodity exports, and a view that this is best done by embracing globalization and participating in global production networks.

Finally, it is worth noting that the 21st-century agreements are largely non-preferential. For example, if customs regulations are simplified by agreement among the signatories, it is unlikely that non-signatories will be forced to use the previous more cumbersome arrangements. In general, agreement to simplify regulations are likely to be non-preferential. Specific commitments, e.g. mutual recognition of qualifications, may favour nationals of the signatories, but do not necessarily leave other countries' nationals worse off. However, there are concerns that mega-agreements may pre-empt standard setting to the advantage of signatories and the disadvantage of others.[28]

Notes

1 The share of Australian exports going to the UK fell from 36 per cent in 1951–55 to 11 per cent in 1968–72, while the East Asian share increased from 14 per cent to 38 per cent. The composition of exports also changed dramatically in this period; the share of rural products in exports fell from 86 per cent in 1950/51 to 44 per cent in 1970/71, while the shares of fuels and minerals increased from 6 per cent to 28 per cent and of services from 5 per cent to 16 per cent. See K. Anderson (1995) 'Australia's Changing Trade Pattern and Growth Performance', in R. Pomfret (ed.) *Australia's Trade Policies*, Melbourne: Oxford University Press, 29–52.

2 Australia's other preferential arrangements within the British Commonwealth lost importance in the 1960s following the UK's application to join the European Community. Limited tariff preferences under the 1960 Canada-Australia Trade Agreement were superseded by multilateral tariff reductions negotiated in GATT rounds.

3 Australia was a charter member of the WTO in 1995, and has also participated in WTO plurilateral arrangements (i.e. voluntary commitments not required of all WTO members) such as the 1997 Information Technology Agreement. The evolution of Australian trade policy is analysed in greater detail in Pomfret (2015).

4 UNCTAD (2000) *Generalized System of Preferences: Handbook on the Scheme of Australia*, United Nations Conference on Trade and Development Technical Cooperation Project on Market Access, Trade Laws and Preferences, UNCTAD/ITCD/TSB/Misc.56, Geneva: UNCTAD, p. 5.

5 PNG is by far the largest recipient of Australian aid, but trade relations have not flourished and economic agreements have had little impact. The Agreement on Trade and Commercial Relations between the Government of Australia and the Government of Papua New Guinea (PATCRA II) was signed and came into force in 1991. The Australia–Papua New Guinea Economic Cooperation Treaty was signed by Prime Minister Abbott and Prime Minister O'Neill on 21 March 2014.

6 R. Pomfret (2016) 'Multilateralism and Regionalism in the South Pacific: WTO and Regional Fora as Complementary Institutions for Trade Facilitation', *Asia and the Pacific Policy Studies*, 3(3): 420–29.

7 W. Morgan (2014) 'Trade Negotiations and Regional Economic Integration in the Pacific Islands Forum', *Asia and the Pacific Policy Studies*, 1(2): 325–36.

8 Attempts to include labour migration as a distinctive feature with favourable treatment for Pacific Islanders were rebuffed by Australia and New Zealand, which preferred separate migration protocols rather than treaty obligations. A separate Australia-Fiji Trade and Economic Relations Agreement (AFTERA) was signed in 1999, but bilateral relations became tense when Australia imposed sanctions on Fiji following the 2006 coup; relations have improved since 2014.

9 Their political status is mixed. The Cook Islands and Niue are self-governing dependencies of New Zealand.

10 I. McLean (1995) 'Trans-Tasman Trade Relations: Decline and Rise', in R. Pomfret (ed.) *Australia's Trade Policies,* Melbourne: Oxford University Press, pp. 178–80.

11 However, the door was left open. Section 6 of the Preamble of the Australian Constitution reads: '"The States" shall mean such of the colonies of New South Wales, New Zealand, Queensland, Tasmania, Victoria, Western Australia, and South Australia, including the northern territory of South Australia, as for the time being are parts of the Commonwealth, and such colonies or territories as may be admitted into or established by the Commonwealth as States; and each of such parts of the Commonwealth shall be called "a State"'.

12 Negotiations on the Australia-India Comprehensive Economic Cooperation Agreement began in May 2011, and on the Indonesia-Australia Comprehensive Economic Partnership Agreement in September 2012. Negotiations on an FTA with the Gulf Cooperation Council (GCC) started in June 2007 with four rounds of negotiations by June 2009, but since then negotiations have remained on hold while the GCC reviews its trade agreement policies. Launches of negotiations for trade agreements with Hong Kong and with Peru were announced in May 2017 and with the Pacific Alliance (a trading bloc made up of Mexico, Chile, Peru and Colombia) in July 2017.

13 R. Pomfret, U. Kaufmann and C. Findlay (2010) 'Use of FTAs in Australia', RIETI Discussion Papers Series 10-E-042, Research Institute of Economy, Trade and Industry, Tokyo.

14 The most controversial non-trade chapter of the US agreement concerned investor-state dispute resolution. When the Australian government introduced laws on cigarette packaging to highlight health risks, a US tobacco company sought redress for reduced profits through the arbitration panel mandated in the Australia-US trade agreement.

15 AANZFTA included chapters on investment, services, and competition policy, as well as annexes incorporating bilateral commitments on labour and the environment. The investment chapter sought to include the best elements of ASEAN members' bilateral investment treaties, and also has a compulsory investor-state dispute settlement process, including safeguards against frivolous claims and to mitigate claims infringing legitimate policy space. Service commitments were more specific, with eight ASEAN members making WTO-plus commitments, including commitments in accounting, transport, tourism, education, legal services, engineering, environmental services, urban planning, landscape architecture, health, construction, and a range of business services (consulting, advertising, technical testing, and others (Vitalis, 2015, 10–11). AANZFTA also contains a general commitment to

transparency and to acceleration of authorization and licensing procedures and to limitation of use of such measures as informal barriers to competition. However, these WTO+ elements are shallower than in the mega-regionals described in Section 4 below.

16 A turning point in attitudes occurred when Malaysia ceased to seek exclusion from the ASEAN FTA for its car industry, acknowledging that an integrated national industry could no longer match cars produced along GVCs, and clearing the way for progress towards free trade in goods in the ASEAN Economic Community.

17 R. Baldwin (2016) The Great Convergence: Information Technology and the new Globalization, Cambridge, MA: Harvard University Press.

18 R. Pomfret and P. Sourdin (2018) 'Value Chains in Europe and Asia: Which Countries Participate? International Economics', *International Economics*, 153, May: 34–41.

19 The Asian Development Bank (ADB) monitors members' free trade agreements, being negotiated or in force, see https://aric.adb.org/fta (accessed 17 September 2017). Despite some double-counting and inclusion of dormant FTAs, the Asian Regional Integration Center's tracking captures the proliferation of trade agreements and their distribution across countries (in Table 6). The largest numbers are for the ASEAN countries most active in GVCs (Singapore 33, Thailand 23, Malaysia 22, Indonesia 17, Viet Nam 16) and for the +6 partners (China 24, Japan 24, South Korea 26, India 28, Australia 22, New Zealand 19); only one other ADB member (Pakistan, 18) has more than 15 FTAs. By contrast, the Philippines has 11 FTAs, Cambodia eight and Timor-Leste zero.

20 P. Athukorala and T. Talgaswatta (2016) 'Global Production Sharing and Australian Manufacturing', Office of the Chief Economist, Department of Industry, Innovation and Science, Commonwealth of Australia, Canberra.

21 With respect to the other two WTO plurilaterals, Australia has been negotiating accession to the WTO's Government Procurement Agreement since September 2015, and has not signed the Agreement on Civil Aircraft. Australia is leading negotiations to introduce an Environmental Goods Agreement, and is negotiating the Trade in Services Agreement (TiSA), a services-only trade agreement jointly led by Australia, the EU and the USA.

22 J. Schott, C. Cimino-Isaacs and E. Jung (2016) 'Implications of the Trans-Pacific Partnership for the World Trading System', Policy Brief 16–8, Washington, DC: Peterson Institute for International Economics, p. 1.

23 Urata provided a stock-taking of existing ASEAN trade agreements, examined the feasibility of consolidating the ASEAN+1 FTAs into a Regional Comprehensive Economic Partnership, and discussed possible ways to multilateralize RCEP. He highlighted the varying degrees of comprehensiveness of tariff elimination and the differing rules of origin in the ASEAN+6 agreements. See S. Urata (2013) 'Constructing and Multilateralizing the Regional Comprehensive Economic Partnership: An Asian Perspective', ADBI Working Paper No. 249, Tokyo: Asian Development Bank Institute.

24 The TPP with its range of external tariffs and more restrictive product-specific rules of origin (e.g. the USA insisted on particularly restrictive rules of origin in labour-intensive sectors such as textiles and apparel, including the notorious 'yarn-forward' rule) could have more adverse trade diversion impacts than RCEP. Schott *et al.* ('Implications of the Trans-Pacific Partnership for the World Trading System', p. 13; emphasis in the original) conclude that 'On balance, the net global economic impact of the TPP is positive, but the *distribution* of benefits among rich and poor countries varies and could disadvantage some developing countries in Asia, Africa, and Latin America.' In the most-cited quantitative study, Petri and Plummer estimated that TPP would bring net benefits for the rest of the world; losses to non-TPP countries mainly resulted from goods provisions, while benefits to excluded countries arose from the services and investment provisions. See P. Petri and M. G. Plummer (2016) 'The Economic Effects of the TPP: New Estimates', in *Assessing the Trans-Pacific Partnership*, vol. 1: *Market Access and Sectoral Issues*, Washington, DC: Peterson Institute for International Economics.

25 The framework was announced in 2004, negotiations were launched in 2009 and concluded in August 2014, and the 1,634-page text was published in September 2014 and signed by the 28 EU members, although it has still not been fully translated into the 24 EU languages. Application is provisional because CETA is still subject to challenges at the European Court of Justice. Major sources of popular protest in Europe concerned perceived weakening of EU food standards with respect to genetically modified crops and growth hormones in beef.

26 One symptom has been the rapid development of rail connections between China and Europe since 2011, driven by the needs of GVC participants such as electronics and automobile companies for faster and more reliable links than sea transport and at lower cost than air freight. Although commentary

often focuses on the geopolitical implications of China's Belt and Road Initiative, the rail landbridge preceded China's 2013 announcement of a Silk Road Economic Belt and has been driven by the commercial interests of rail companies, freight forwarders and their customers. See J.-P. Larçon (ed.) (2017) *The New Silk Road: China Meets Europe in the Baltic Sea Region*, Singapore: World Scientific Publishing Company.

27 J. Drake-Brockman and P. Messerlin (eds) (forthcoming*) Potential Benefits of an Australian-EU Free Trade Agreement: Key Issues and Options*, Adelaide: University of Adelaide Press.

28 Australia has been concerned that the EU-China FTA includes agreement on use of specific geographical indicators of origin that seem to give 'prosecco' such status, even though prosecco is a grape variety and not a place and hence should not qualify as a geographical indicator. The interpretation in the FTA will force Australian prosecco exporters to relabel their wine with a name unfamiliar to Chinese consumers or a simple generic such as 'sparkling'.

Index

AANZFTA (Association of Southeast Asian Nation-Australia New Zealand FTA) 408, 431–2n15

Abe Shinzo 404, 409, 414, 418, 419

Acemoglu, Daron 13, 16n10

ACP (Africa-Caribbean-Pacific) group 52n7, 118, 183, 185–6, 335–6, 337–8, 342, 343, 345–6

ADB (Asian Development Bank) 432n19

Adly, Amir xiii, 322–34

Afesorgbo, S.K.R. and Van Bergeijk, P.A.G. 370–71n2

Africa: AFTZ (African Free Trade Zone) 366; ITAs in force in (1948–2017) 48; participation of RTAs in 21; *see also* AU (African Union); COMESA; ECOWAS; SADC 48

AfT (Aid for Trade) 118

Agenda 21 of Rio Summit Plan of Action 123

Agricultural Cooperatives (JA) in Japan 415

agriculture: agricultural market access, TTIP and 265–6; comprehensive coverage of, TPP and 406–7; difficult area for RCEP 392; SADC food security initiative 368

Aideyan, Osaore 348–58

AJCEP (ASEAN-Japan Comprehensive Economic Partnership) 416–17

ALADI (Latin America Integration Association) 198–9, 200, 207n31, 219, 228n3, 250n7, 308

ALBA (Bolivarian Alliance for the Peoples of Our America) 6, 241–50; alliance, development of 243; contestation, movement to content from 243; economic and political upheaval, vulnerability to 241–2; emergence of 242–3; FTAA 241; future integration, prospects for 249–50; innovative ideas, implementation of 243–4; irregular implementation, impact of 248–9; Pacific Alliance 230; People's Trade Treaty 244–5; Petrocaribe 247–8; SUCRE trade volumes (2010–2016) 246; Unified Regional Compensation Scheme 245–7

Algeria: Bahraini exports to (2015) 314; EU-Algeria trade agreement (2004) 102

Allee, T. and Lugg, A. 27–8n31

alliances and conflict, international trade and 92–3

Alschner, Wolfgang xiii–xiv, 79–90

Amari, Akira 399n27

American Journal of Political Science 104

Amin, Tahir 399n21

Amiti, M. and Davis, D. 66n45

Amiti, M. and Konings, J. 65n27

Anderson, James 57, 64n6

Angola 7; intra-SADC trade (2000 and 2015) 364; SADCC membership 360

anti-apartheid struggle 359

'anti-globalization' movements 138; *see also* neoliberal globalization, anti-globalization and

ANZAC (Australian and New Zealand Army Corps) 426

APEC (Asia-Pacific Economic Cooperation) 234, 235, 392, 395, 401–2, 404, 405, 410, 412, 419; Business Travel Card 392; intra-group trade, value of (2015) 378; Japan and 412; Pacific Alliance and 233; TPP and 401–2, 404

APTA intra-group trade, value of (2015) 378

Arab League 331; intra-group trade, value of (2015) 378

ArabMaghreb Union, SADC and 359

Argentina 6, 10, 199, 204, 207n31, 218, 220, 225, 227, 228n1–2, 234, 242, 249, 315; Mexican bilateral investment treaty (BIT) with 195

Arkolakis, Costas 62, 66n48

Armenia 6; corruption in (2007–2017) 288; democracy in (1994–2012), Polity IV project and 284; EaP (Eastern Partnership initiative) 282; ease of doing business in (2007–2017) 287; EU, exports to and imports from (2005–2014) 292; exports of goods and services (1995–2016) 290; freedom of the press in (1995–2012) 285; manufactures, exports of (1995–2016) 290; market economy in, transition determinants (2012) 286; trade, direction of (2012) 291; trust in (2007–2017) 289

Arun, S. 399n19

ASEAN (Association of Southeast Asian Nations) 55n74; ASEAN+1 agreements, RCEP, Asian economic integration and 386; Australia and 426, 427, 429, 431–2n15–16; Australian trade agreement with (2010) 427; intra-group trade, value of (2015) 378; Japan and 413; Japan PTA with (2008) 415; Pacific Alliance and 233

Asian financial crisis (1998) 137

Athukorala, P. and Talgaswatta, T. 432n20

Atkinson, T., Luttrell, D. and Rosenblum, H. 143n5

AU (African Union): ACP (Africa-Caribbean-Pacific) group and 335–6, 337–8, 342, 343, 345–6; Association Agreements 335–6; AU-EU partnership and agency for progressive action to contest 'trade reciprocity' 342–5; COMESA and 372–3; Cotonou Agreement (2000–2020) 335, 344; DCFTAs and moral economy of trade reciprocity in Maghreb 335, 339–41; deindustrialization, job losses and 338–9; EPA agenda, factsheet (2017) 336–7; EPA agenda, moral economy of EU trade reciprocity as embodied in 335, 336–9; EPA Development Programme (EPADP) and 341; EU (European Union) and 7, 335–46; EU-Tunisia Action Plan 339–3–40; European Development Fund and 335; Joint Africa-EU Joint Strategy (2007) 336; Kenya, EEC and 335–6; Lomé Conventions (1975–2000) 335; moral economy of EU trade reciprocity as embodied in EPA agenda 336–9; 'reciprocal' trade content 335; SADC and 359; SSA (Sub-Saharan Africa) and 335–6, 339, 341, 342, 343–4, 345; Sustainability Impact Assessments (EU, SIAs) 338–9, 340–41; trade liberalization, European Commission pursuit of 345–6; Yaoundé Accords (1963–75) 335

Auckland negotiations (RCEP, 2016) 397

Augier, Patricia 14, 16n12

Augman, Rob 142n1

Augusto, F. and Scorza, T. 383n11

Australia: AANZFTA (Association of Southeast Asian Nation)-Australia New Zealand FTA) 408, 431–2n15; ANZAC (Australian and New Zealand Army Corps) 426; ASEAN (Association of Southeast Asian Nations) and 426, 427, 429, 431–2n15–16; Australia-Europe-Asia Triangle 429–30; Bahraini imports from (2015) 314; bilateral trade agreements 426–8; bilateral trade agreements, policy shift from multilateralism to 423; CER (Closer Economic Relations) Agreement with New Zealand (1983) 423, 425–6; CETA (Comprehensive Economic and Trade Agreement, EU-Canada) and 429; Chile-Australia FTA (2009) 426; China, trade agreement with (2016) 427; Cook Islands, MFN tariffs with 424; diversity indicators, TPP-12 (2016) 403; economic characteristics (2016–17) 387; EU-China FTA, concerns about 433n28; Fiji, MFN tariffs with 424; gain from comprehensive RCEP 381; goods-only RCEP, gains from 389; GSP (Generalized System of Preferences) 423; GVC (global value chain) phenomenon and 427–8, 430, 432n16; high-tariff regime, anachronistic nature of 423; ITA (Information Technology Agreement) 428; Japan, trade agreement with (2015) 427; Japan negotiation of PTA with 415–16; Kiribati, MFN tariffs with 424; Malaysia, trade agreement with (2013) 427; Marshall Islands, MFN tariffs with 424; Mexican bilateral investment treaty (BIT) with 195; Micronesia, MFN tariffs with 424; Nauru, MFN tariffs with 424; negotiating mega-regionals 428–9, 430; New Zealand, regional integration with 425–6; Niue, MFN tariffs with 424; PACER (Pacific Agreement on Closer Economic Relations) and 424; Palau, MFN tariffs with 424; Papua New Guinea, MFN tariffs with 424; preferential tariffs for developing countries (1966) 423, 424–5, 431n2; PTAs, experience with 8, 423–30; RCEP (Regional Comprehensive Economic Partnership) and 423, 427, 429, 430, 432n23–4; regional integration with New Zealand 425–6; Samoa, MFN tariffs with 424; Singapore, trade agreement with (2003) 427; Singapore-Australia FTA (2003) 426; Solomon Islands, MFN tariffs with 424; South Korea, trade agreement with (2014) 427; SPARTECA (South Pacific Regional Trade and Economic Cooperation Agreement) 423, 424, 426; Thailand, trade agreement with (2005) 427; Thailand-Australia FTA (2005) 426; Tonga, MFN tariffs with 424; TPP (Trans Pacific Partnership) and 423, 428–9, 430, 432n24; trade agreements, 21st century (to end of 2016) 427; Trump, Donald A (and administration of) and 429; Tuvalu, MFN tariffs with 424; UK trade with 423, 430n1; United States, trade agreement with (2005) 427; United States-Australia FTA (2005) 426; Vanuatu, MFN tariffs with 424; WTO charter member (1995) 423, 431n3

Austria, Mexican bilateral investment treaty (BIT) with 195

autarkic economies 94

Autor, David 13, 16n10, 61, 65n43

Axelrod, Robert 99n6

Azerbaijan 6; corruption in (2007–2017) 288; democracy in (1994–2012), Polity IV project and 284; EaP (Eastern Partnership initiative) 282; ease of doing business in (2007–2017)

Index

287; exports of goods and services (1995–2016) 290; freedom of the press in (1995–2012) 285; manufactures, exports of (1995–2016) 290; market economy in, transition determinants (2012) 286; trade, direction of (2012) 291; trust in (2007–2017) 289

Azevêdo, Roberto 113

Baccini, L. and Chow, W.M. 110n20
Baccini, L. and Dür, A. 54n42
Baccini, L. and Urpelainen, J. 19, 110n17
Baccini, L., Dür, A. and Elsig, M. 109n12
Baccini, L., Osgood, I. and Weymouth, S. 107, 111n36
Baccini, Leonardo xiv, 101–11
Baetens, Freya 90n56
Baggs, Jen 33, 59, 60, 65n21
Bagozzi, B. and Landis, S.T. 99–100n10
Bagwell, K., Bown, C.P. and Staiger, R.W. 28n33
Bahrain 7; economic growth rates (1980–2016) 310; export and import volumes (2015) 314; GCC and case of 310–12; Indian trade with (2014–2016) 318; Mexican bilateral investment treaty (BIT) with 195; telecommunications liberalization in 108
Baier, Scott 57, 64n8
Balassa, Bela 52n20
Balcuinaite, V. 120n8
Baldwin, John 60, 65n28
Baldwin, R. and Jaimovich, D. 53n33
Baldwin, Richard 16n2, 22, 25, 26, 27n16, 28n33, 83, 89n33, 432n17
Bandar Seri Begawan negotiations: RCEP, 2016 397
Bangkok negotiations (RCEP, 2017) 396
Barbieri, Katherine 99n3
Barroso, José Manuel 262
Basu Das, Sanchita 12, 399n2
Baudenbacher, Carl 281n7
Baunsgaard, A. and Keen, M. 77n22
Bearce, D.H., Eldredge, C.D. and Jolliff, B.J. 110n29
Beck, S. 269n2
Beijing World Conference (1995), gender rights and 115
Belarus 6; corruption in (2007–2017) 288; democracy in (1994–2012), Polity IV project and 284; EaP (Eastern Partnership initiative) 282; ease of doing business in (2007–2017) 287; exports of goods and services (1995–2016) 290; freedom of the press in (1995–2012) 285; manufactures, exports of (1995–2016) 290; market economy in, transition determinants (2012) 286; Mexican bilateral investment treaty (BIT) with 195;

trade, direction of (2012) 291; trust in (2007–2017) 289
Benin, ECOWAS membership 350–51
Berden, K., Francois, J., Thelle, M., Wymenga, P. and Tamminen, S. 270n16
Berg, Aslak xiv, 271–81
Berger, Axel 89n31
Berghahn, V. and Young, B. 258n14
Bergkamp, L. and Kogan, L. 130n6
Bergman, M.S. 89n18
Bergsten, C. Fred 24, 27n27
Bergstrand, Jeffrey 57, 64n8
Berlingieri, Giuseppe 63, 66n55
Bernard, A., Jensen, B., Redding, S. and Schott, P. 65n20
Bernard, Andrew 60, 65n20
Bhagwati, J. and Panagariya, A. 54n43
Bhagwati, Jagdish 5, 8, 13, 14, 16n2, 18, 26n3, 43, 52n5
Bianco, Giuseppe 89n32
Biersteker, Thomas 136, 137, 143n15
Bilal, S., Dalleau, M. and Lui, D. 77n21
bilateral agreements: Australia 426–8; Australia, policy shift from multilateralism to 423; CARICOM 187–8; dispute propensity 92–3; economic effects of 58–9, 61–2; GCC 309–10; Japan 415–18; TPP upgrading of 404–5
Biological Diversity, Convention on 123
BITs (bilateral investment treaties): investment component of trade agreements 79, 81, 82, 85, 86; PTIAs and, differences, overlap and interaction between 87
Blecker, Robert A. xiv, 147–65
BLEU (Belgium-Luxembourg Economic Union) 195
Blyde, J., Estevadeordal A. and Suominen, K. 12
Blyth, Mark 17, 143n2
Bogor Summit (1994) 401–2
Bongardt, Annette xiv–xv, 296–306
Bonnitcha, J., Waibel, M. and Skovgaard Poulsen, L.N. 88n3
Border Environmental Cooperation Commission (US-Mexico) 127
Bordo, M.D., Eichengreen, B. and Irwin, D.A. 143n18
Bordo, Michael D. 143n4
Botswana 7; intra-SADC trade (2000 and 2015) 364; SADCC membership 360
Bouazizi, Mohamed 141
Bouteflika, Abdelaziz 102
Bové, Jose 140
Brander, James 60, 65n33
Brander, James A. 98, 100n21
Branstetter, L., Fisman, R., Foley, C.F. and Saggi, K. 40n22
Brazil 6; advocate for a multipolar global order 224; Bahraini imports from (2015) 314;

CARICOM trade partner (2014) 182; Omani imports from (2015) 315; patent rights in 34; 'Plano Real' in 219

Breidlid, J. and Vahl, M. 281n11

Breinlich, Holger xv, 56–66

Brexit, trade agreements, regional integration and EU after 7, 8, 296–304; application of lessons 73–5; Brexit, peculiar case in international trade context 297; challenges facing UK and EU outsider 300–301; deep FTAs prompt qualitative change in EU trade 302–3; EU and Brexit 297–9; EU position on Brexit 301; EU trade dynamics 296–7; post-Brexit EU-UK trade relationship, prospective arrangements for 299–300; regulation in internal and external trade, issue of 303–4

Brisbane negotiations (RCEP, 2013) 396

Broda, Christian 62–3, 66n53

Broude, Tomer 89n17

Brunei: diversity indicators, TPP-12 (2016) 403; economic characteristics (2016–17) 387; goods-only RCEP, gains from 389; Japan PTA with (2008) 415; P4 (Singapore, Chile, Brunei, New Zealand) 402

Bryn, K. and Einarsson, G. 280n3

Bueno de Mesquita, B., Smith, A., Siverson, R. M. and Morrow, J.D. 102, 109n3

Burkina Faso, ECOWAS membership 350–51

Burundi: COMESA membership 373; GDP growth rate as member of COMESA (2005 and 2016) 375; intra-COMESA trade (2015) 377; logistics performance index (2012–2016) 390; share of added value to GDP (2016) 376

Busan negotiations (RCEP, 2015) 397

Bush, George W. 223, 241, 262

Bustos, Paulo 59–60, 65n26

Büthe, T. and Milner, H.V. 109–10n15

Cadot, O. and de Melo, J. 55n73

Cadot, O. and Gourdon, J. 55n75

Cadot, O. and Ing, L.Y. 55n70

CAFTA (Central American Free Trade Agreement) 105–6

CAFTA-DR (Central American Free Trade Agreement-Dominican Republic) 5, 166–77; consequences, first decade of 168–73; Costa Rica, divergent trajectory of 175; deeper integration, prospects for 176–7; demographic characteristics 171; Dominican Republic, divergent trajectory of 175; Economic Freedom Index 169; economic indicators by country (2005–2014) 172; employment indicators by country (2005–2014) 173; environmental indicators (2015) 174; environmental oversight 177; foreign balance of goods and services 169; gender rights and trade agreements 118; goods and services, foreign balance of 169; Guatemala, divergent trajectory of 176; inequality, vulnerability and (2015) 174; infrastructure expansion 176–7; national trajectories, divergencies in 173–6; negotiations 167–8; Nicaragua, divergent trajectory of 175; Northern Triangle, divergent trajectory of 175–6; opposition 168; precursors to 166–7; ratification 168; regional integration 166–7; securitization 176; trade partners (2015) 170; United States, divergent trajectory of 173–4; United States, trade balance with 170; US relationships with Central America 167

Cambodia: economic characteristics (2016–17) 387; gain from comprehensive RCEP 381

Cameron, James 13, 131n8

Cameron, M.A. and Tomlin, B.W. 107–8, 111n42

CAN (Andean Community of Nations) 223, 224, 234–5, 242, 244, 245, 249; intra-group trade, value of (2015) 378

Canada 5, 15, 18–19, 20, 47, 97, 103, 105, 128; Caribbean-Canada Trade Agreement (CARIBCAN) 184–5; CARICOM trade partner (2014) 182; CETA interests 212–13; Chile-Canada FTA (1997) 119; CUSTFA (US-Canada comprehensive economic agreement) 59–60, 61, 82; diversity indicators, TPP-12 (2016) 403; US-Canada FTA (1988) 59, 81, 82; see also CETA; NAFTA

Canuto, O. 383n12

Capaldo, Jeronim 267, 270n21

Cape Verde, ECOWAS membership 350–51

capital controls, removal of 137

Cardoso, Fernando Henrique 219–20

Caribbean: Caribbean Basin Initiative (CBI) 184; EU-Caribbean Economic Partnership Agreement (EPA) 70; ITAs in force in (1948–2017) 48; participation of RTAs in 21

CARIBCAN (Caribbean-Canada Trade Agreement) 184–5

CARICOM (Caribbean Common Market) 5, 181–90; bilateral agreements 187–8; Caribbean Basin Initiative (CBI) 184; CARIFORUM-EU EPA (2008) 186; Columbia, bilateral agreement with 187; Costa Rica, bilateral agreement with 188; Cotonou Agreement (2000) 185–6; Cuba, bilateral agreement with 188; Dominican Republic, bilateral agreement with 187–8; Economic Partnership Agreements (EPAs) 185–6, 188–9, 190; establishment of 181; exports, shares to trading partners (2007–2016) 190; intra-group trade, value of (2015) 378; Lomé Convention (1975) 185–6; regional characteristics 181–4; tariff liberalization schedule (CARIFORUM) 186; trade agreements, assessment of involvement in 188–9; trade agreements, involvement in

184–8; trade partners (2014) 182; Venezuela, bilateral agreement with 187

Cartagena Protocol on Biosafety (2000) 123

Cartes, Horacio 227

Cashore, Benjamin 143–4n31

Castro, Fidel 6, 241, 242

CEC (Commission for Environmental Cooperation) 127

CEDAW (UN Convention on the Elimination of all forms of Discrimination Against Women, 1979) 114–15, 119

CEFTA intra-group trade, value of (2015) 378

CELAC (Community of Latin American and Caribbean States) 198, 226; ALBA (Bolivarian Alliance for the Peoples of Our America) and 249; Pacific Alliance and 230, 234, 235

Central America: ITAs in force in (1948–2017) 48; Mexican trade with (2016) 194; participation of RTAs in 21

CER (Closer Economic Relations) Australia-New Zealand (1983) 423, 425–6

CETA (Comprehensive Economic and Trade Agreement) 5, 209–17; Australia and 429; Canadian interests in 212–13; cracks in European trade coalition 214–16; economic potential, identification of 210; ERT (European Round Table of Industrialists) and 214; EU motivations for 213–14; *Europe 1990: An Agenda for Action* (ERT) 214; European Commission mandate for negotiation 213; investment component of trade agreements 81, 83–4; JCC (Joint Cooperation Committee) 209–10; MRAs (mutual recognition agreements) 211; NAFTA (North America Free Trade Agreement) and 210, 212; NMR (negotiation of mutual recognition) 211; political miscalculation 215; political problems 211–12; pre-history 209–10; Quebec Summit (2008) 210; rationale for development of 211–12; Strategic Partnership Agreement (2017) 210; trade policy 212–13

Charnovitz, Steve 132n49

Chase, Kerry A, 111n35

Chávez, Hugo 6, 226, 241, 242, 249

Chen, M.X. and Sumit, J. 53n40

Chen, Y. and Puttitanun, T. 40n23

Cheong, J., Kwak, D.W. and Tang, K.K. 54n51, 65

Chile 6, 9, 10, 15, 30, 37, 47, 51, 105, 106; Australia-Chile FTA (2009) 426; diversity indicators, TPP-12 (2016) 403; Japan PTA with (2007) 415; Mexican trade with (2016) 194; P4 (Singapore, Chile, Brunei, New Zealand) 402; Uruguay-Chile FTA (2016) 118

China 8; Australian trade agreement with (2016) 427; Bahraini imports from (2015) 314; CARICOM trade partner (2014) 182;

COMESA export trade to (2003–2012) 380; economic characteristics (2016–17) 387; environmental provisions in RTAs 129–30; gain from comprehensive RCEP 381; goods-only RCEP, gains from 389; Mexican bilateral investment treaty (BIT) with 195; Omani exports to (2015) 315; Omani imports from (2015) 315

Chu, Ben 143n3

CIS (Commonwealth of Independent States): ITAs in force in (1948–2017) 48; participation of RTAs in 21

Clinton, Bill 24, 127, 241

Clunan, Anne L. xv, 134–44

CMA (Common Monetary Area), SADC and 359

Cole, Tony 90n49

Collings, D. 371n10

Collor de Mello, Fernando 218, 219

Colombia 6, 15, 20, 51, 59, 67, 105, 106, 108; banking and insurance liberalization in 108; bilateral agreement with CARICOM 187; CARICOM trade partner (2014) 182; exports from CARICOM to (2007–2016) 190; Mexican trade with (2016) 194

Colyer, Dale 131n31

COMESA (Common Market for Eastern and Southern Africa) 7, 55n74, 372–83; AU (African Union) and 372–3; Burundi, member state 373; COMESA-EAC-SADC tripartite free trade area 374; common customs bond guarantee scheme 373–4; Comoros, member state 373; continental FTA, implications of 382; Djibouti, member state 373; DRC (Democratic Republic of Congo), non-FTA membership 373; economic development and cooperation 374; economic performance of member countries 374–5; Egypt, member state 373; Egypt and 329; energy strategy 374; Eritrea, non-FTA membership 373; establishment of 372–3; Ethiopia, non-FTA membership 373; export market shares (2015) 379; export trade markets (2003–2012) 379, 380; external trade 376; GDP growth rate of members (2005 and 2016) 375; global level change, impacts on 383; global trade (2003–2016) 377; harmonization of trade documentation 373–4; Harmonized Axle Loading and Maximum Vehicle Dimension 381; industrial strategy 374; intra-COMESA trade 376–8; intra-group trade, value of (2015) 378; Kenya, member state 373; macroeconomic policies 374; Madagascar, member state 373; Malawi, member state 373; Mauritius, member state 373; member states 373; monetary and financial cooperation 374; objectives 373–4; prerequisits for trade promotion 373–4, 383; Regional Customs Transit Guarantee Scheme 381; rules of origin 374; Rwanda, member state 373; SADC and 359, 365–6, 366–7; Seychelles, member state 373; share of value added to GDP (2016) 375–6; Swaziland, non-FTA membership 373; Third Party Motor Vehicle Insurance Scheme 374; trade facilitation 379–81; trade liberalization measures 372–3; TTFA (Tripartite Free Trade Area) 382; Uganda, member state 373; WTO (World Trade Organization) and 372; Zambia, member state 373; Zimbabwe, member state 373

Common Agenda of SADC 363–7

Community of Sahel-Saharan States, SADC and 359

Comoros 7; COMESA membership 373; GDP growth rate as member of COMESA (2005 and 2016) 375; intra–COMESA trade (2015) 377; logistics performance index (2012–2016) 390; SADC membership 360

The Company States Keep (Gray, J.) 104

comparative advantage, Ricardian model of 94, 96–7

Comprehensive Economic Partnership for East Asia 413

Connelley, W.E. 143n8

Cook Islands: Australia, MFN tariffs with 424; partnership with Australia (2016) 425

copyrights 31; limitations and exception (L&Es) on the scope of 34

Corning, Gregory P. xv, 412–22

corporate power, TTIP and protection of 269

Correa, Rafael Vicente 106, 241

Costa Rica: bilateral agreement with CARICOM 188; demographic characteristics (2005–2015) 171; divergent trajectory of, CAFTA-DR and 175; economic freedom index for 169; economic indicators (2005–2014) 172; employment indicators (2005–2014) 173; environmental indicators (2015) 174; exports from CARICOM to (2007–2016) 190; foreign balance of goods and services for 169; inequality, vulnerability and (2015) 174; insurance sector liberalization in 107; top trade partners (2015) 170; trade balances with US (2000–2015) 170

Costinot, Arnaud 62, 66n48

Côte d'Ivoire, ECOWAS membership 350–51

Cotonou Agreement (2000): AU (African Union) and 335, 344; CARICOM and 185–6; gender rights and trade agreements 118; SADC and 367

CPTPP (Comprehensive and Progressive Agreement for Trans-Pacific Partnership) 8; investment component of trade agreements 86, 87; Japan and 415; TPP and 401

Crawford, Jo-Ann 23

credible commitment, developing countries and 101, 103, 104–5, 108, 109n14, 354

cross-regional bilateralism 415–16

Cuba: bilateral agreement with CARICOM 188; exports from CARICOM to (2007–2016) 190; Mexican bilateral investment treaty (BIT) with 195

cultural autonomy 5, 136, 138, 139–40

Cusack, Asa xvi, 241–50

CUSFTA (Canada-US Free Trade Agreement): economic effects of FTAs 59–60, 61; investment component of trade agreements 82

Cutting the Gordian Knot of Economic Reform (Baccini, L. and Urpelainen, J.) 104–5, 110n21

Czech Republic, Mexican bilateral investment treaty (BIT) with 195

Dabène, Olivier 250n3

Dai, M., Yotov, Y.V. and Zylkin, T. 54n48

Dam, Kenneth 18

data insights, spread of ITAs 47–9

Davos World Economic Forum 138

DCFTAs (Deep and Comprehensive Free Trade Agreements) 7, 282; effect on trade of EaP (Eastern Partnership initiative) 293–4; moral economy of trade reciprocity in Maghreb and 339–41; qualitative change in EU trade and 302–3; successful negotiation of 283

De la Mora Sanchez, Luz Maria xvi, 192–208

De Loecker, J., Goldberg, P., Khandelwal, A. and Pavcnik, N. 60, 65n31

De Loecker, Jan 60, 65n29

De Mestral, Armand 89n25

De Ville, Ferdie 270n5

Debrun, X. and Masson, P.R. 371n11

Deere, Carolyn 11, 39n6

'defeminization' of employment 114

defence economics 93–4

Deibert, Ronald 144n32

Della Porta, Donatella 144n33

democracy: dissemination of 46; free press and 284–5; Polity IV project, EaP and 284

Denmark, Mexican bilateral investment treaty (BIT) with 195

Desiderá Neto, Walter Antonio xvi, 218–29

Desta dataset 107, 110n18

Destler, I.M. and Noland, M. 27n12

Deutscher Richterbund 270n27

developing countries, economic reform and service liberalization in: Algeria-EU trade agreement (2004) 102; Bahrain, telecommunications liberalization in 108; CAFTA (Central American Free Trade Agreement) 105–6; Colombia, banking and insurance liberalization in 108; Costa Rica, insurance sector liberalization in 107; credible

Index

commitment 104–5; economic powers, benefits of PTAs with 104–5; economic reform, trade agreements and 103–4; GATS (General Agreement on Trade in Services) 107; Honduras, financial services liberalization in 108; international cooperation and domestic reform, relationship between 102; international economic organizations, state of 106; liberal microeconomic policies 102; Mexico, financial sector liberalization in 107–8; most-favoured-nation (MFN) and preferential tariffs 102, 103; NAFTA (North American Free Trade Agreement) 103, 105, 107–8; neoliberal economic reforms, opposition to 102; non-traditional gains from PTAs, analysis of 103–4; OECD (Organisation of Economic Co-operation and Development) 107; political economy of reform 102–3; power, role of 105–6; PTAs (preferential trade agreements) 101–2; reform, problem of 102–3; reform, PTAs and 101, 104–5, 107–8, 108–9; services, evidence from US PTAs on reform of 107–8; signalling 104; south-south regional agreements 106; timing, reform problem and 103; United States services, political engagement of 107; window dressing 106–7; WTO (World Trade Organization) 102, 107

Dhingra, Swati 63, 66n55

Dilma, Rousseff (and administration of) 225, 226, 227

DiMascio, Nicholas 90n42

Discrimination (Employment and Occupation) Convention (1958) 117

distributional impacts of trade: myths and misconceptions about RTAs and 13; NAFTA (North American Free Trade Agreement) and 158–61

Djibouti: COMESA membership 373; GDP growth rate as member of COMESA (2005 and 2016) 375; intra-COMESA trade (2015) 377; logistics performance index (2012–2016) 390

Doha Development Round (WTO) 3, 18, 25–6, 184, 193, 203, 224, 296, 302, 372, 384–94, 428; GCC trade agreements and 307, 312–19; myths and misconceptions about RTAs 10; spread of international trade agreements (ITAs) 45

Dolzer, Rudolf 90n47

Dominican Republic: bilateral agreement with CARICOM 187–8; demographic characteristics (2005–2015) 171; divergent trajectory of, CAFTA-DR and 175; economic freedom index for 169; economic indicators (2005–2014) 172; employment indicators (2005–2014) 173; environmental indicators (2015) 174; exports from CARICOM to

(2007–2016) 190; foreign balance of goods and services for 169; inequality, vulnerability and (2015) 174; top trade partners (2015) 170; trade balances with US (2000–2015) 170; *see also* CAFTA-DR

Donner, Abreu M. 54n69

Dorn, David 13, 16n10, 61, 65n43

DPJ (Democratic Party of Japan) in 414

Drake-Brockman, J. and Messerlin, P. 433n27

Draper, Peter 371n20

DRC (Democratic Republic of Congo) 7; COMESA non-FTA membership 373; GDP growth rate as member of COMESA (2005 and 2016) 375; intra-COMESA trade (2015) 377; intra-SADC trade (2000 and 2015) 364; logistics performance index (2012–2016) 390; SADC membership 360; share of added value to GDP (2016) 376

Duhalde Maldonado, Eduardo Alberto 220

Dür, A., Baccini, L. and Elsig, M. 110n18

Dür, A., Baccini, L, and Haftel, Y.Z. 89n30

Dyson, Kenneth 259n36

EAC (East African Community) 55n74; economic development, trade agreements and 70; intra-group trade, value of (2015) 378; SADC and 359, 366–7

EaP (Eastern Partnership initiative) 6, 282–94; Armenia 282; Azerbaijan 282; Belarus 282; corruption 287–8; DCFTAs, effect on trade of 293–4; DCFTAs, successful negotiation of 283; democracy, free press and 284–5; directions of trade 291–2; ease of doing business 286–7; European Neighbourhood Policy 282; exports, levels and composition of 289–90; Georgia 282; Global Strategy (EU) 282; market economy, transition to 285–6; Moldova 282; potential of trade with EU, significance of 294; Prague summit (EU, 2009) 282; quality of institutions in EaP countries 283–9; Russia, underestimation of democratic values 294; trade negotiations 282–3, 292–3; trade patterns 289–93; trust 288–9; Ukraine 282; Ukraine, Association Agreement with 283

East Asia: Comprehensive Economic Partnership for 413; East Asia Summit, Phnom Penh (RCEP, 2012) 384–5; ITAs in force in (1948–2017) 48; participation of RTAs in 21

Ebaidalla, E.M. and Yahia, A.M. 378, 383n6

Ebell, Monique 59, 64n18

Eberhardt, P. 270n26

ECCAS intra-group trade, value of (2015) 378

ECJ (European Court of Justice) 126

Economic Community of Central African States, SADC and 359

economic development, trade agreements and 4, 67–76; anticipated effects of trade agreements

440

68; assessment of impacts, problems of 70–72; Brexit, application of lessons and 73–5; Caribbean-EU Economic Partnership Agreement (EPA) 70; claims about potential impacts 67; cost of utilizing FTA provisions 69; development impact analyses 67; EAC (East African Community) 70; European Commission 67; expected effects of agreements and why they might not happen 69–70; GATT (General Agreement on Tariffs and Trade) Article XXIV 70; global value chains 69; government revenue, effects on agreements on 72–3; GSP (Generalised System of Preferences) 74–5; harnessing opportunities, concerns about 70; ITC (International Trade Center) 72; knowledge gaps 71; liberal case for development, criticism of 68; limited evidence of non-trade impacts 71–2; link between UK and EU-27 policies, asymmetrical nature of 74; NAFTA (North American Free Trade Agreement) 73; OECD (Organisation for Economic Co-operation and Development) 72; policy space, loss of 68; protectionism 69; rules of origin 69; scale of effect, factors influencing 75–6; trade barriers 70; trade creation 68; trade diversion 68; United States Congressional Research Service report on economic impact of trade agreements 70–71; variability in outcomes 69; WTO (World Trade Organization) 67; WTO (World Trade Organization) Enabling Clause 74

economic effects of FTAs 4, 56–64; bilateral trade and agreements 58–9, 61–2; company performance measures 59; consumer price effects of trade agreements 63; CUSFTA (Canada-US Free Trade Agreement) 59–60, 61; economic welfare, effects on 62–3; EEA (European Economic Area) 59; endogeneity, country-pair fixed effects to control for 57; EU (European Union) 63; firm-level impacts 60; firms, effects on 59–62; General System of Preferences 56; gravity equations 56–7, 58; gravity estimation methods 57; labour markets, effects on 61; MERCOSUR 59–60; meta-analysis (World Bank, 2005) 57; NAFTA (North American Free Trade Agreement) 61; OECD (Organization of Economic Co-operation and Development) 58–9; Poisson pseudo-maximum likelihood estimation (PPML) statistical test 57, 58–9; productivity (and productivity enhancement) 59–60; reciprocal free trade agreements (FTAs), surge in 56; regulatory harmonization, effects of 64; selection, issue of 57; stock market reactions to unexpected FTA-related announcements 60; trade, effects on 56–9; trade creation and trade diversion, effects of

58; trade flows 56–7; trade in services, exclusion from analyses 58; US-Vietnam Bilateral Trade Agreement (2001) 61; welfare gains, measurement of 62–3; WTO (World Trade Organization) and 56

Economic Freedom Index, CAFTA-DR and 169

Economic Partnership Agreements (EPAs) 185–6, 188–9, 190

The Economics of Defense in the Nuclear Age (Hitch, C.J. and McKean, R.N.) 18, 96, 100n13

ECOWAS (Economic Community of West African States) 7, 348–57; Burkina Faso membership 350–51; Cape Verde membership 350–51; common currency, case for 348; common external tariff 351; coordination and cooperation, conceptual markers for understanding problem of 354–7; Côte d'Ivoire membership 350–51; economic and monetary union, achievements in 348–9; economic powers in, need for leadership from 356–7; ECOWAS treaty, highlights of (1975 and 1993) 349–50; EMS for, prospects of 354–6; Gambia membership 350–51; Ghana membership 350–51; Guinea-Bissau membership 350–51; Guinea membership 350–51; international trade liberalization provisions 351; intra-group trade, value of (2015) 378; Liberia membership 350–51; Mali membership 350–51; neoliberal concepts for policymakers, question of 357; Niger membership 350–51; Nigeria membership 350–51; SADC and 359; Senegal membership 350–51; setbacks 348–9; Sierra Leone membership 350–51; Togo membership 350–51; trade and common sectoral policies, summary of 350–54; trade-related provisions 352–3; trade within, low levels of 354; UN Economic Commission for Africa (ECA) 348

ECSC (European Coal and Steel Community), extablishment of 91

EFTA (European Free Trade Association) 6, 271–80; dual structure 271; EEA (European Economic Area) Agreement 273–4; EEA functioning 276–7; EEA future challenges 279; EEA two-pillar structure 274; establishment of 271–2; EU-EFTA relations beyond free trade 273–4; EU relations, development of 272–3; facilitation of cooperation purpose for 271; GCC accords with 317; intra-EFTA relations, development of 275–6; intra-group trade, value of (2015) 378; investment component of trade agreements 81; Mexican trade with (2016) 194, 198; third country policy, creation of 274–5; third country policy, development of relations beyond EU 277–9; third country policy, future challenges for 279–80; trade in goods (2016) 278

Index

Egger, P. and Larch, M. 53n40

Egger, P., Larch, M., Staub, K.E. and Winkelmann, R. 64n11

Egger, Peter, H. 17, 58–9, 64n11

Egypt: Bahraini exports to (2015) 314; COMESA and 329; COMESA membership 373; Euro-Egyptian Association Agreement 326–8; feigned reorientation, PTAs and 332–3; GAFTA 330–32; GDP growth rate as member of COMESA (2005 and 2016) 375; intra-COMESA trade (2015) 377; liberalization-cum-PTAs, curious case of 322–3; literature review on case of 324–6; logistics performance index (2012–2016) 390; PTAs, experience with 7, 322–33; QIZ (Qualified Industrial Zones) 329–30; share of added value to GDP (2016) 376

El-Agraa, Ali M. 53n22

El Salvador: demographic characteristics (2005–2015) 171; economic freedom index for 169; economic indicators (2005–2014) 172; employment indicators (2005–2014) 173; environmental indicators (2015) 174; foreign balance of goods and services for 169; inequality, vulnerability and (2015) 174; top trade partners (2015) 170; trade balances with US (2000–2015) 170

Elliott, Kimberly Ann xvi–xvii, 17–28

endogeneity, country-pair fixed effects to control for 57

energy strategy at COMESA 374

enforcement expectations for IPRs 32–3

environment and trade agreements 4, 122–30; Agenda 21 of the Rio Summit's Plan of Action 123; Asia, RTAs and environment in 128–30; Biological Diversity, Convention on 123; Border Environmental Cooperation Commission (US-Mexico) 127; Cartagena Protocol on Biosafety (2000) 123; CEC (Commission for Environmental Cooperation) 127; China, environmental provisions in RTAs 129–30; ECJ (European Court of Justice). 126; Europe, RTAs and environment in 125–6; European Commission 122–3; FAO (Food and Agriculture Organization, UN) 123; Fish Stocks, UN Agreements on (1995) 123; GATT (General Agreements on Tariffs and Trade) Article XX 124, 125, 130; globalization, precautionary principle and 124–5; Maastricht Treaty (EU, 1992) 125; Marrakesh Agreement (1994) 122, 130n1; Mexico, Pollutant Release and Transfer Registry law in 127; Montreal Protocol on Substances that Deplete the Ozone Layer (1987) 123; NAFTA (North American Free Trade Agreement) 125, 127–8; National Environmental Policy Act (US, 1969) 123;

North America, RTAs and environment in 127–8; North American Development Bank 127; precautionary principle 123–5; precautionary principle, politics of 126; Rio Declaration on Environment and Development (1992) 123; RTAs, environment and 125–30; Sanitary and Phytosanitary Measures (SPS Agreement) 124; Technical Barriers to Trade, Agreement on (WTO) 122; UN Framework Convention on Climate Change 123; WTO (World Trade Organization) 122, 125, 126, 130

environmental oversight at CAFTA-DR 177

environmental standards, EU mandate for 265

EPAs (Economic Partnership Agreements) 7; agenda of, moral economy of EU trade reciprocity as embodied in 336–9

EPZs (export processing zones) 113

Equal Pay Act (UK, 1970) 115

Equal Remuneration Convention (1951) 117

Eritrea: COMESA non-FTA membership 373; GDP growth rate as member of COMESA (2005 and 2016) 375; intra-COMESA trade (2015) 377; logistics performance index (2012–2016) 390

Erogbogbo, V. 120n13

Estevadeordal, A. and Suominen, K. 16n2, 16n4

Estonia: exports of goods and services (1995–2016) 290; manufactures, exports of (1995–2016) 290

Ethier, Wilfred J. 109n11

Ethiopia: COMESA non-FTA membership 373; GDP growth rate as member of COMESA (2005 and 2016) 375; intra-COMESA trade (2015) 377; logistics performance index (2012–2016) 390; share of added value to GDP (2016) 376

EU (European Union) 4, 5, 6, 251–8; Armenia, exports to and imports from (2005–2014) 292; AU (African Union) and 7, 335–46; Brexit and 7, 8, 296–304; CETA and, motivations for 213–14; challenges to global trade position 252; China-EU FTA, Australian concerns about 433n28; COMESA export trade to (2003–2012) 380; East African Community EPA with 118; economic effects of FTAs 63; EFTA-EU relations beyond free trade 273–4; EU-Tunisia Action Plan 339–3–40; exports from CARICOM to (2007–2016) 190; Georgia, exports to and imports from (2005–2014) 292; global financial crisis, impact of 254–6; Global Strategy 282; global trading power 251; goods-only RCEP, gains from 389; intellectual property rights, trade agreements and 29; intra-group trade, value of (2015) 378; Japan-EU PTA 420; Lamfalussy Committee 255; Mexican trade with (2016)

194; Mexico 197–8; Mexico-EU Global Agreement (2000) 118; Moldova, exports to and imports from (2005–2014) 292; position on Brexit 301; post-Brexit perspectives 256–8; RCEP, Asian economic integration and 384; relations with EFTA, development of 272–3; SADC-EU Economic Partnership 367; trade agreements, regional integration and EU after Brexit 297–9; trade dynamics 296–7; trade policy coordination, challenge of 252–4; Trump, Donald A (and administration of) and 254; TTIP and, mandate for negotiation 262–5; *see also* EaP (Eastern Partnership initiative)

Europe: Euro-Egyptian Association Agreement 326–8; ITAs in force in (1948–2017) 48; participation of RTAs in 21; promotion of integration in 18; RTAs and environment in 125–6

European Commission 422n22; economic development, trade agreements and 67; environment and trade agreements 122–3

European Neighbourhood Policy 282

European Union (EU): improved market access, TTIP and EU mandate for 263–4

Evans, Peter 135–6, 141, 143n11

Evenett, S. and Fritz, J. 399n8

Faiola, Anthony 258n19

Fairtrade movement 112

Fajgelbaum, P. and Khandelwal, A. 66n58

Falvey, R. and Reed, G. 16n6

FAO (Food and Agriculture Organization, UN) 123

Fauchald, O.K. and Vennemo, H. 77n3

Fauzel, Sheereen xvii, 372–83

feigned reorientation, PTAs and 332–3

Felbermayr, G.J., Heid, B. and Lehwald., S. 270n17

Fergin, Elina 52n15

Ferguson, Y.H. and Mansbach, R.W. 144n38

Fernandes, Ana 59, 65n24

Fernandez, R. and Portes, J. 103, 109n13

Fernandez, R. and Rodrik, D. 109n8

Fiji: Australia, MFN tariffs with 424; partnership with Australia (2016) 425

Fink, C. and Maskus, K.E. 39n9

Fink, C. and Reichenmiller, P. 39n7

Finland, Mexican bilateral investment treaty (BIT) with 195

Finley-Brook, Mary xvii, 166–80

Fish Stocks, UN Agreements on (1995) 123

Fontagné, L., Gourdon, J. and Jean, S. 270n11

Fontanelli, Filippo 89n32

Foster, Caroline E. 16, 131n9

France, Mexican bilateral investment treaty (BIT) with 195

Franco, Itamar 219

Francois, J. and Hoekman, B. 111n33

Frankel, Jeffrey 9, 23, 24, 27n2

free trade areas, SADC and 365

free trade in GCC, case for 313–16

Freund, C. and Ornelas, E. 54n62

Frias, J., Kaplan, D. and Verhoogen, E. 66n45

Friendship, Commerce and Navigation (FCN) Treaty (1859) 81–2

Froman, Michael 402

FTAA (Free Trade Area of the Americas) 6, 167, 183, 193, 205n11, 220, 223, 224, 312; ALBA (Bolivarian Alliance for the Peoples of Our America) and 241, 242, 244, 249

FTAAP (Free Trade Area of the Asia Pacific) 405, 408, 410

Fukunaga, Yoshifumi 400n29

Fukushima Daiichi nuclear disaster 414

Funk, Lothar 258n14

future prospects: ALBA (Bolivarian Alliance for the Peoples of Our America) 249–50; EEA (European Economic Area) 279; gender rights and trade agreements 119–20; NAFTA (North American Free Trade Agreement) 162; SADC (Southern African Development Community) 369

Gabon, CARICOM trade partner (2014) 182

GAFTA (Greater Arab Free Trade Area), Egypt and 322, 323, 330–32

Gaines, Sanford 131n21

Galgoczi, Bela 258n12, 260n47

Gallagher, Kevin P. 127, 132n48

Gambia, ECOWAS membership 350–51

Gann, Pamela B. 89n19

Ganslandt, M. and Maskus, K.E. 39n12

Gao, Henry 133n65

García, Alan 235

Garcia, Ryan xvii, 91–100

Gardini, Gian Luca xvii, 230–40

Gasiorek, Michael 14, 16n12

GATS (General Agreement on Trade in Services): developing countries, economic reform and service liberalization in 107; investment component of trade agreements 80; myths and misconceptions about RTAs 10–11; neoliberal globalization, anti-globalization and 137; RCEP, Asian economic integration and 385

GATT (General Agreement on Tariffs and Trade): establishment of (1947) 82; Japan and 412, 413; national security, trade agreements and 93; neoliberal globalization, anti-globalization and 136; spread of international trade agreements (ITAs) 41

GATT (General Agreement on Tariffs and Trade) Article XXIV: economic development, trade

Index

agreements and 70; myths and misconceptions about RTAs 10–11, 16n3; spread of international trade agreements (ITAs) 41; TPP and 385, 404

GATT (General Agreements on Tariffs and Trade): Article XX 124, 125, 130

GCC (Gulf Cooperation Council) 7, 307–19; Bahrain, case of 310–12; bilateral FTAs 309–10; creation of 307; economic growth rates (1980–2016) 310; economic integration goals 308–9; EFTA, accords with 317; free trade in, case for 313–16; FTA accords with partners 316–19; India, negotiations with 317–19; Indian trade with (2014–2016) 318; intra-group trade, value of (2015) 378; Oman, case of 312–13; Singapore, accords with 316–17; trade activities, coordination of 307–8

GDP (gross domestic product): growth rates as members of COMESA (2005 and 2016) 375; national security and 96; share of value added to GDP (2016) 375–6

gender rights and trade agreements 4, 112–20; AfT (Aid for Trade) 118; Beijing World Conference (1995) 115; CAFTA-DR 118; CEDAW (UN Convention on the Elimination of all forms of Discrimination Against Women, 1979) 114–15, 119; Chile-Uruguay FTA (2016) 118; codification of gender rights 115–19; Cotonou Partnership (2000) 118; 'defeminization' of employment 114; Discrimination (Employment and Occupation) Convention (1958) 117; EPZs (export processing zones) 113; Equal Pay Act (UK, 1970) 115; Equal Remuneration Convention (1951) 117; EU-East African Community EPA 118; EU–Mexico Global Agreement (2000) 118; Fairtrade movement 112; future directions in gender-aware trade policies 119–20; gender-aware trade policies, calls for 114–15; *Gender Aware Trade Policy* (WTO, 2017) 116; Gender Focal Point (WTO, 2017) 117; gender rights in trade agreements, contested processes 112; gender-trade nexus 112–15; gendered impacts of liberalization, global scale of 114; Grown by Women 112; Human Rights, UN Declaration of 115; ICESCR (UN International Covenant on Economic, Social and Cultural rights, 1966) 115; ILO (International Labour Organization), explicit aims on gender equality 117; ILO (International Labour Organization) Action Plan on Gender Equality and Gender Mainstreaming 115–16; ILO (International Labour Organization) Declaration on Fundamental Principles and Rights to Work 117; LGBTQ community, differential impact of trade on 114; Millennium Development Goals (UN) 116; NAFTA (North American Free Trade Agreement) 118; segregation of women into unskilled positions 113–14; Sex Discrimination Act (UK, 1975) 115; Sustainable Development Goals (2015) 116; trade liberalization, assumptions underpinning 112; trade liberalization, positive assessment of 113; UNCTAD (UN Conference on Trade and Development) 118; Women and Development Network 113–14; Workers with Family Responsibilities Convention (1981) 117; WTO (World Trade Organization) 112–13, 116–17

General System of Preferences 56, 148

geographical indications: intellectual property rights, trade agreements and 31–2; TTIP (Transatlantic Trade and Investment Partnership) 266

geopolitical stability, quest for 46

Georgia 6; corruption in (2007–2017) 288; democracy in (1994–2012), Polity IV project and 284; EaP (Eastern Partnership initiative) 282; ease of doing business in (2007–2017) 287; EU, exports to and imports from (2005–2014) 292; exports of goods and services (1995–2016) 290; freedom of the press in (1995–2012) 285; manufactures, exports of (1995–2016) 290; market economy in, transition determinants (2012) 286; trade, direction of (2012) 291; trust in (2007–2017) 289

Germany: Bahraini imports from (2015) 314; Mexican bilateral investment treaty (BIT) with 195

Ghana, ECOWAS membership 350–51

Gibb, Richard 371n3

Gilbert, J., Furusawa, T. and Scollay, R. 388–9, 399n10

Gill, Stephen 268, 270n24

Glenday, G. 78n27

global financial system: collapse of (2007–8) 134; cost of rescue of 134–5; crisis in, impact on EU of 254–6

global social justice, demand for 140–41

Global Strategy (EU) 282

global supply chains 11, 13, 22, 23–4, 25, 26, 27n25, 112, 134, 162; spread of 388, 391, 393, 394, 396

globalization: local enterprise and 139–40; precautionary principle and 124–5

Goldberg, P. and Pavenik, N. 65n37, 66n50

Goldberg, Pinelopi 60, 65n29

Goldberg, P.K. and Pavenik, N. 55n72

Gonzalez, Elizabeth 250n5

Gowa, J. and Mansfield, E.D. 9, 93, 99n6

Grant, J.H. and Lambert, D.M. 53n34

gravity equations (estimation methods) 56–7, 58

Gray, Julia 30–31, 104, 106, 110n16
The Great Convergence (Baldwin, R.) 83
Great Recession 141, 142
Greater Noida negotiations (RCEP, 2014) 396
Greece, Mexican bilateral investment treaty (BIT) with 195
Greenaway, David 52n13
Grossman, G.M. and Lai, E.L.-C. 39n4
Grown by Women 112
Gruber, Lloyd 105, 110n22
Gryzmala-Busse, Anna 144n48
GSP (Generalized System of Preferences): Australia and 423; economic development, trade agreements and 74–5
Gu, Wulong 60, 65n28
Guatemala: demographic characteristics (2005–2015) 171; divergent trajectory, CAFTA-DR and 176; economic freedom index for 169; economic indicators (2005–2014) 172; employment indicators (2005–2014) 173; environmental indicators (2015) 174; foreign balance of goods and services for 169; inequality, vulnerability and (2015) 174; top trade partners (2015) 170; trade balances with US (2000–2015) 170
Guinea, ECOWAS membership 350–51
Guinea-Bissau, ECOWAS membership 350–51
Guy, Paul 131–2n32
Guyana, CARICOM trade partner (2014) 182
GVCs (global value chains): economic development and 69; importance of 83; phenomenon of, Australia and 427–8, 430, 432n16

Haiti, Mexican bilateral investment treaty (BIT) with 195
Hakobyan, Shushanik 61, 65n38
Haldane, A., Aikman, D., Kapadia, S. and Hinterschweiger, M. 143n6
Haldane, Andy 134–5
Handl, Gunter 131n10
Hanson, Gordon 13, 16n10, 61, 65n43
harmonization of trade documentation, COMESA and 373–4
Harmonized Axle Loading and Maximum Vehicle Dimension 381
Harris and Suominen 14
Harrison, A. and Rodriguez-Clare, A. 64n19
Hathaway, Oona A. 109n5
Haughton, Tim 259–60n44
Hausman, D. 66n59
Hayakawa, K., Fukunari, K. and Laksanapanyakul, N. 16n11
Head, Kenneth 13, 58, 64n10
health initiative of SADC 368
Heckscher and Ohlin (H-O) model 95, 96–7
Heiligendamm 134

Held, David 144n37
Henry, Lester xvii–xviii, 181–91
Hernández, José Gregorio 243
High Level Dialogue on Integration Initiatives for the Asia Pacific, TPP and 409
Hillman, Arye L. 51n2
Hinnebusch, Raymond 144n46
Hitch, Charles 93, 96, 100n13
Ho Chi Minh negotiations (RCEP, 2016) 397
Hofmann, C., Osnago, A. and Ruta, M. 64n2
Holden, Merle 371n10
Honduras: demographic characteristics (2005–2015) 171; economic freedom index for 169; economic indicators (2005–2014) 172; employment indicators (2005–2014) 173; environmental indicators (2015) 174; financial services liberalization in 108; foreign balance of goods and services for 169; inequality, vulnerability and (2015) 174; top trade partners (2014) 170; trade balances with US (2000–2015) 170
Hsieh, C.-T., Li, N., Ossa, R. and Yang, M.J. 66n54
Hübner, Kurt xviii, 209–17
Hufbauer, G., Cimino-Isaacs, C. and Moran, T. 16n9
Hufbauer, G.C. and Schott, J.J. 27n12
Hull, Cordell 17
Humala, Ollanta 235
Human Rights, UN Declaration of 115
Hur, J., Alba, J.D. and Park, D. 54n49
Hyderabad negotiations (RCEP, 2017) 398

Iceland 6; Mexican bilateral investment treaty (BIT) with 195
ICESCR (UN International Covenant on Economic, Social and Cultural rights, 1966) 115
ICSID (International Centre for Settlement of Investment Disputes) 86
IDB (Inter-American Development Bank) 232–3
ILO (International Labour Organization): Action Plan on Gender Equality and Gender Mainstreaming 115–16; Declaration on Fundamental Principles and Rights to Work 117; explicit aims on gender equality 117
IMF (International Monetary Fund) 422n16; neoliberal globalization, anti-globalization and 136, 137, 139, 140–41, 142
India: Bahrain, trade with (2014–2016) 318; Bahraini exports to (2015) 314; Bahraini imports from (2015) 314; COMESA export trade to (2003–2012) 380; economic characteristics (2016–17) 387; gain from comprehensive RCEP 381; GCC, negotiations with 317–19; GCC, trade with (2014–2016) 318; goods-only RCEP, gains from 389; Japan

Index

PTA with (2011) 415; Kuwait, trade with (2014–2016) 318; Mexican bilateral investment treaty (BIT) with 195; Oman, trade with (2014–2016) 318; Omani exports to (2015) 315; Omani imports from (2015) 315; Qatar, trade with (2014–2016) 318; RCEP, Asian economic integration and case study of 391–3, 395; Saudi Arabia, trade with (2014–2016) 318; UAE (United Arab Emirates), trade with (2014–2016) 318

Indonesia: economic characteristics (2016–17) 387; gain from comprehensive RCEP 381; goods-only RCEP, gains from 389; Japan PTA with (2008) 415

inequality, vulnerability and (CAFTA-DR, 2015) 174

intellectual property rights, trade agreements and 4, 29–38; Brazil, patent rights and 34; challenges, dispute settlement and 34–5; compulsory licences, issue of 33, 34; confidential test data 32; copyrights 31; dispute settlement 34–5; enforcement expectations 32–3; EU (European Union) 29; exhaustion, treatment of 33; geographical indications 31–2; IPRs as regulatory devices, principles of 30; lagal standards 30; limitations and exception (L&Es) on the scope of copyrights 34; major requirements of TRIPS 30; non-voluntary licences, issue of 33; parallel imports, treatment of 33; patents 31; precise specifications, determination of 30; protectiveness 30; PTAs (preferential trade agreements), importance of 29; PTAs (preferential trade agreements), role of 36–9; PVRs (plant variety rights) 32; residual policy space 33–4; TPP (Trans-Pacific Partnership) and 37; trade secrets 32; trademarks 31–2; TRIPS, WTO and 29–35; TRIPS-Plus agenda 36–9; UPOV Treaty (1978) 32; WCTs (WIPO copyright treaties) 36; WIPO (World Intellectual Property Organization) 29, 36; WPPT (WIPO Performance and Phonograms Treaty) 36

Internet of Things, technological innovations and 14–15

investment component of trade agreements 4, 79–88; BITs and PTIAs, differences, overlap and interaction between 87; BITs (bilateral investment treaties) 79, 81, 82, 85, 86; Canada-US FTA (1988) 81; CETA (Comprehensive Economic and Trade Agreement) 81, 83–4; common origins 81–2; convergence 82–3; core investment protection provisions 85; CPTPP (Comprehensive and Progressive Agreement for the Trans-Pacific Partnership) 86, 87; CUSTFA (US-Canada comprehensive economic agreement) 82; distinct paths followed 82; EFTA (European

Free Trade Association) 81; Friendship, Commerce and Navigation (FCN) Treaty (1859) 81–2; GATS (General Agreement on Trade in Services) 80; GATT (General Agreement on Tariffs and Trade), establishment of (1947) 82; global value chains, importance of 83; ICSID (International Centre for Settlement of Investment Disputes) 86; investment facilitation provisions 80–81; investment rules in agreements 80–81; investor-state dispute settlement 83, 86–7; ISDS (investor-state dispute settlement) 80; legal debate about investment rules 84–5; legal issues in PTIA investment chapters 85–7; most-favoured nation (MFN) treatment 82, 84, 85; NAFTA (North American Free Trade Agreement) 79, 80, 81, 82–3, 84, 87; New York Convention on the Recognition and Enforcement of Foreign Arbitral Awards 86; OECD (Organisation for Economic Co-operation and Development) 82; political economy debate about investment rules 83–4; PTIAs (preferential trade and investment agreements) 79, 80, 81, 83, 85–7, 88; regulation of investment protection with trade agreements 81–5; scope of investment provisions in agreements 80–81; substantive protection provisions 85–6; TRIMs (trade-related investment measures) 80; typology of agreements with investment provisions 81; UNCTAD (UN Conference on Trade and Development) 85; WTO (World Trade Organization) 79

investment facilitation provisions: investment component of trade agreements 80–81; Investment Facilitation Initiative (Pacific Alliance) 233

IPRs (Intellectual Property Rights): as regulatory devices, principles of 30; TPP ans 407

ISDS (investor-state dispute settlement) 80, 83, 86–7

Israel, Mexican trade with (2016) 194

ITA (Information Technology Agreement) in Australia 428

Italy: Mexican bilateral investment treaty (BIT) with 195; Omani imports from (2015) 315

ITC (International Trade Center) 72

ITO (International Trade Organization) Charter (1948) 401

Ivus, Olena 40n22

JA-Zenchu (Central Union of Agricultural Cooperatives) in Japan 415

Jackson, John 7, 10, 12, 19, 26n1

Jamaica, CARICOM trade partner (2014) 182

Japan: Agricultural Cooperatives (JA) in 415; AJCEP (ASEAN-Japan Comprehensive

Economic Partnership) 416–17; ASEAN, PTA with (2008) 415; ASEAN (Association of Southeast Asian Nations) and 413; Asia-Pacific Economic Cooperation (APEC) and 412; Australia, negotiation of PTA with 416; Australia, PTA with (2015) 415; Australian trade agreement with (2015) 427; Bahraini imports from (2015) 314; bilateral and regional PTAs 415–18; Brunei, PTA with (2008) 415; CARICOM trade partner (2014) 182; Chile, PTA with (2007) 415; Comprehensive Economic Partnership for East Asia 413; constraints on PTA policy 414–15; CPTPP (Comprehensive and Progressive Trans-Pacific Partnership) and 415; cross-regional bilateralism 415–16; diversity indicators, TPP-12 (2016) 403; DPJ (Democratic Party of Japan) in 414; drivers of PTA policy 413–14; economic characteristics (2016–17) 387; economic multilateralism and growth of 412; EU-Japan PTA 420; External Trade Organization 20, 422n14; Fukushima Daiichi nuclear disaster 414; gain from comprehensive RCEP 381; GATT (General Agreement on Tariffs and Trade) and 412, 413; goods-only RCEP, gains from 389; India, PTA with (2011) 415; Indonesia, PTA with (2008) 415; JA-Zenchu (Central Union of Agricultural Cooperatives) in 415; Keidanren, influence of 413, 416, 417, 421n11; LDP (Liberal Democratic Party) in 414; MAFF (Ministry of Agriculture, Forestry and Fisheries) in 414, 415, 416; Malaysia, PTA with (2006) 415; mega-regional agreements, shifting focus to 418–20; METI (Ministry of Economy, Trade and Industry) in 414–15; Mexican trade with (2016) 194; Mexico, Japanese PTA policy and 416; Mexico, PTA with (2005) 415; Mongolia, PTA with (2016) 415; NAFTA (North American Free Trade Agreement) and 413, 416; North-East Asia, Japanese policy towards 417–18; Omani exports to (2015) 315; Peru, PTA with (2012) 415; Philippines, PTA with (2008) 415; political and social context of PTA policy 412–15; Promotion of Economic Partnerships 414; PTAs, experience with 8, 412–21; RCEP (Regional Comprehensive Economic Partnership) 415, 419–20; regionalism, halting embrace of 416–18; Singapore, PTA with (2002) 415; South China Seas, sovereignty issues in 417; Switzerland, PTA with (2009) 415; systemic forces, bilateral PTAs and 413; Thailand, PTA with (2007) 415; TPP (Trans-Pacific Partnership) and 412, 413; Trump, Donald A (and administration of) and 412, 419, 420–21; TTP (Trans Pacific Partnership) 418–19; Vietnam, PTA with (2009) 415; Voluntary Sectoral Liberalization Talks (1998) 412; WTO-Plus PTAs, negotiation of 415; WTO (World Trade Organization) and 412; Yasukuni Shrine 417

Johnson, Renee 132n41

Joint Declaration of Macroeconomic Policy Authorities of Trans-Pacific Partnership Countries 408

Jonas, Hans 130

Juncker, Jean-Claude 258

Juris, Jeffrey S. 144n32

Kannangara, Pabasara 399n1

Kawai, M. and Wignaraja, G. 11, 399n9

Kawasaki Kenichi 422n17

Kéchichian, Joseph A. xviii, 307–21

Keck, M. and Sikkink, K. 143n30

Keidanren, influence in Japan 413, 416, 417, 421n11

Kenen, P. 371n11

Kenya: COMESA membership 373; EEC and 335–6; GDP growth rate as member of COMESA (2005 and 2016) 375; intra-COMESA trade (2015) 377; logistics performance index (2012–2016) 390; share of added value to GDP (2016) 376

Keohane, Robert O. 99n6

Keynes, John Maynard 18, 136

Khagram, Sanjeev 144n53

Kim, Inkyoung xviii–xix, 122–33

Kimura, F., Kuno, A. and Hayakawa, K. 54n58

Kimura, Fukunari 58, 64n16

Kirchner, Néstor Carlos 220–21, 242

Kiribati: Australia, MFN tariffs with 424; partnership with Australia (2016) 425

Klotz, Audie 143–4n31

Kobe negotiations (RCEP, 2017) 398

Koizumi Junichiro 414, 416

Kok, Wim 255, 259n25

Kollman, K. and Prakash, A. 143–4n31

Korea, Republic of, Mexican bilateral investment treaty (BIT) with 195

KORUS FTA 405, 406, 407, 408

Kovács, Oliver 259–60n44

Kovak, Brian 61, 65n42

Krasner, Stephen D. 143n21

Krishna, Pravin 23, 27n23

Krugman, Paul 53n32

Kuala Lumpar negotiations (RCEP, 2014) 396

Kuwait 7; Bahraini exports to (2015) 314; economic growth rates (1980–2016) 310; Indian trade with (2014–2016) 318; Mexican bilateral investment treaty (BIT) with 195

Kyle, M.K. and Yi Qian 40n24

Kyoto negotiations (RCEP, 2015) 396

447

Index

labour markets, effects of FTAs on 61
labour practices, TPP and 408
labour reallocation, RTAs and 12
labour standards, TTIP and 266
lagal standards, IPRs (intellectual property rights) and 30
Lai-Tong, C. 16n12
Lamesch, Joe 51n1
Lamfalussy Committee (EU) 255
land transport, TTIP and 266
Langan, Mark xix, 335–47
Laos: economic characteristics (2016–17) 387; goods-only RCEP, gains from 389
Larch, Mario 17, 58–9, 64n11
latent military capability 93, 94, 95–6, 98, 99
Latin America: left-leaning governments in 230; Mexico and 198–201
LDCs (less developed countries), TPP provisions for 403–4
LDP (Liberal Democratic Party) in Japan 414
Le Pen, Marine 142
Lease, Mary Elisabeth 135
Lee, Hyun-Hoon 58, 64n16
Lee, J.-W., Park, I. and Shin, K. 54n55
Lee, S.H., Park, K.S. and Seo, Y.W. 54n47
Lee Kwan Yew 402, 405, 411n2
Lesotho 7; intra-SADC trade (2000 and 2015) 364; SADCC membership 360
Levitsky, Steven 144n48
LGBTQ community, differential impact of trade on 114
liberal capitalism, resurgent ethos of 136
liberal case for development, criticism of 68
liberal microeconomic policies 102
Liberia, ECOWAS membership 350–51
Libya: GDP growth rate as member of COMESA (2005 and 2016) 375; intra-COMESA trade (2015) 377; logistics performance index (2012–2016) 390
Liechtenstein 6
Lileeva, Alla 59, 65n25, 66n46
Lima Declaration (2011) 230
Limão, Nuno 9, 64n5
Lipow, Jonathan xviii, 91–100, 93, 100n14
Lipsey, R.G. and Lancaster, K. 94, 100n15
Lipsey, Richard 52n11
Lithuania, exports of goods and services (1995–2016) 290
Lloyd, P.J. 16n6
logistics performance index (2012–2016) 390
Lomé Conventions (1975–2000) 185–6, 335
Long, A.G. and Leeds, B.A. 99n8
Looney, Robert E. xiii, 3–8
Lugo, Fernando 226
Lula da Silva, Luis Inácio 220–21, 242
Lusaka Declaration (1979) 360
Luwabelwa, Mubita 370n1

Maastricht Treaty (EU, 1992) 125
McCaig, Brian 61, 65n40
McGillivray, F. and Smith, A. 109n4
McGinnis, Michael D. 99n6
McGowan, L. and Phinnemore, D. 259n38
McKean, Roland 93, 96, 100n13
McLaren, John 61, 65n38
McLean, I. 431n10
McLymont, R. 371n10
Macri, Mauricio 227, 249
macroeconomic policies of COMESA 374
Madagascar 7; COMESA membership 373; GDP growth rate as member of COMESA (2005 and 2016) 375; intra-COMESA trade (2015) 377; intra-SADC trade (2000 and 2015) 364; logistics performance index (2012–2016) 390; SADC membership 360; share of added value to GDP (2016) 376
Maduro, Nicolás 242, 249–50
MAFF (Ministry of Agriculture, Forestry and Fisheries) in Japan 414, 415, 416
Magee, Christopher S.P. 8, 52n4
Maggi, G. and Rodriquez-Clare, A. 109n14
Maghreb 7, 335, 336, 339–40, 341, 342, 343–4, 345, 359
Magliveras, Konstantinos D. 371n3
Mahbubani, Kishore 143n25
Malawi 7; COMESA membership 373; GDP growth rate as member of COMESA (2005 and 2016) 375; intra-COMESA trade (2015) 377; intra-SADC trade (2000 and 2015) 364; logistics performance index (2012–2016) 390; SADCC membership 360; share of added value to GDP (2016) 376
Malaysia: Australian trade agreement with (2013) 427; diversity indicators, TPP-12 (2016) 403; economic characteristics (2016–17) 387; gain from comprehensive RCEP 381; goods-only RCEP, gains from 389; Japan PTA with (2006) 415
Mali, ECOWAS membership 350–51
Malmström, Cecilia 9, 251–2, 254, 258n4, 367
Mandela, Nelson 102
Manger, Mark 108, 110n29
Manila negotiations (RCEP, 2017) 398
Mansfield, E., Milner, H. and Rosendorff, P. 53n38
Mansfield, E.D. 16n2
Mansfield, E.D. and Bronson, R. 99n7
Mansfield, E.D. and Reinhardt, E. 99–100n10
Mansfield, E.D., Milner, H.V. and Rosendorff, B.P. 109–10n15
Maputo Development Corridor 363
Markell, David L. 132n53
Marrakesh Agreement (1994) 122, 130n1
Marshall Islands: Australia, MFN tariffs with 424; partnership with Australia (2016) 425

Martin, P., Mayer, T. and Thoenig, M. 53n39, 93, 99n5

Martínez-Zarzoso, Immaculada xix, 282–95

Maskus, Keith E. xix, 29–40

Masungu, Sisule 39n16

Mattli, Walter 110n32

Mattoo, A., Mulabdic, A. and Ruta, M. 12, 16n7

Mauritius 7; COMESA membership 373; GDP growth rate as member of COMESA (2005 and 2016) 375; intra-COMESA trade (2015) 377; intra-SADC trade (2000 and 2015) 364; logistics performance index (2012–2016) 390; SADC membership 360

Mayer, Thierry 13, 58, 64n10

Mayes, David 259n29

Meade, James 44, 53n28

mega-regional agreements: Australian negotiating of 428–9, 430; Japan and shift in focus to 418–20

Melitz, M. and Trefler, D. 66n57

Melitz, Marc J. 109n7

Menem, Carlos Saúl 218

MERCOSUR 5–6, 218–27; Asunción, Treaty of (1991) 219, 220; Brazil, advocate for a multipolar global order 224; Brazil, 'Plano Real' in 219, 220; CASA (South American Community of Nations) 223; CCMASM (Coordination Commission for Social Affairs Ministers) 222; Chinese presence, progressive growth of 225–6; consolidation of common market (1991–1994) 219; Constitutive Protocol of Mercosur Parliament (2005) 222; coordination and integration process 223–4; 'Customs Union Consolidation Programme' 221; economic-commercial phase (1991–2002) 218–20; economic effects of FTAs 59–60; economic models based on artificial parity with US dollar 220; external shocks 224–5; foundation of 218; Guayaquil Summit (2002) 223; IIRSA (South American Regional Infrastructure Integration Initiative) 222, 223; Interregional Cooperation Framework Agreement between Mercosur and European Union (1995) 220; intra-group trade, value of (2015) 378; Itaipu-Corpus Issue 218; Las Leñas Timetable (1992) 219; liberalization processes 219; MHR (High Representative-General), creation of (2010) 222; Montevideo work programme (2004–2006) 221; Ouro Preto Protocol (1994) 219; Parlasur 222; Productive Integration Programme (2008) 221–2; social, political, participatory and distributive phase (2003–2010) 220–24; UNASUR (Union of South American Nations) and 223; uncertainty phase (2011-) 224–7

Merkel, Angela 253, 262

METI (Ministry of Economy, Trade and Industry) in Japan 414–15

Mexico 6; Asia-Pacific 201–3; Australia, bilateral investment treaty (BIT) with 195; Bahrain, bilateral investment treaty (BIT) with 195; Belarus, bilateral investment treaty (BIT) with 195; Chile, trade with (2016) 194; China, bilateral investment treaty (BIT) with 195; Colombia, trade with (2016) 194; compensation (hourly) of Mexican production workers (1994–2016) 161; Cuba, bilateral investment treaty (BIT) with 195; Denmark, bilateral investment treaty (BIT) with 195; diversity indicators, TPP-12 (2016) 403; ECAs under ALADFI, network of 199; EFTA 198; EFTA, trade with (2016) 194; EU 197–8; EU, trade with (2016) 194; exports of goods to other NAFTA members (1993–2016) 154; FDI inflows (1980–2016) 156; financial sector liberalization in 107–8; Finland, bilateral investment treaty (BIT) with 195; France, bilateral investment treaty (BIT) with 195; FTA network 193; Germany, bilateral investment treaty (BIT) with 195; Greece, bilateral investment treaty (BIT) with 195; Haiti, bilateral investment treaty (BIT) with 195; Iceland, bilateral investment treaty (BIT) with 195; imports of goods to other NAFTA members (1993–2016) 155; India, bilateral investment treaty (BIT) with 195; Israel, trade with (2016) 194; Italy, bilateral investment treaty (BIT) with 195; Japan, trade with (2016) 194; Japan PTA with (2005) 415; Japanese PTA policy and 416; Korea, Republic of, bilateral investment treaty (BIT) with 195; Kuwait, bilateral investment treaty (BIT) with 195; labour productivity (1950–2014) 160; Latin America 198–201; manufacturing employment (2007–2016) 151; NAFTA, trade with (2016) 194; NAFTA (North American Free Trade Agreement) 193–6; Netherlands, bilateral investment treaty (BIT) with 195; network of BITs 195; open regionalism of, challenges to 203–4; Pacific Alliance, trade with (2016) 194; Panama, bilateral investment treaty (BIT) with 195; Panama, trade with (2016) 194; Peru, trade with (2016) 194; Pollutant Release and Transfer Registry law in 127; Portugal, bilateral investment treaty (BIT) with 195; PTAs, experience with 5, 192–205; Singapore, bilateral investment treaty (BIT) with 195; Slovakia, bilateral investment treaty (BIT) with 195; Spain, bilateral investment treaty (BIT) with 195; strategy of creating network of RTAs 192; Sweden, bilateral investment treaty (BIT) with 195; Switzerland, bilateral investment treaty (BIT) with 195;

trade with RTA partners (2016) 194; Trump, Donald A (and administration of) and 192, 196, 203, 204–5; Turkey, bilateral investment treaty (BIT) with 195; UK, bilateral investment treaty (BIT) with 195; Uruguay, bilateral investment treaty (BIT) with 195; Uruguay, trade with (2016) 194

Micronesia: Australia, MFN tariffs with 424; partnership with Australia (2016) 425

Middle East: ITAs in force in (1948–2017) 48; participation of RTAs in 21

MILA (Business Council and the Integrated Latin American Market), Pacific Alliance and 232, 234, 236, 238

military power, battlefield performance and 93

Millennium Development Goals (UN) 116

Milner, H.V. and Kubota, K. 109n5–6

Milonvic, Branko 143n26

Ministerial Conference, Cancún (WTO, 2003) 416

Misra, Rahul 399n16

Mittleman, James H. 143n30, 144n47

MMA (Multilateral Monetary Area), SADC and 366

Modi, Narendra 391, 393

Mold, A. and Mukwaya, R. 383n15

Moldova 6; corruption in (2007–2017) 288; democracy in (1994–2012), Polity IV project and 284; EaP (Eastern Partnership initiative) 282; ease of doing business in (2007–2017) 287; EU, exports to and imports from (2005–2014) 292; exports of goods and services (1995–2016) 290; freedom of the press in (1995–2012) 285; manufactures, exports of (1995–2016) 290; market economy in, transition determinants (2012) 286; trade, direction of (2012) 291; trust in (2007–2017) 289

Molle, Willen 53n23

monetary and financial cooperation at COMESA 374

monetary union and SADC 366

Mongolia, PTA with Japan (2016) 415

Montreal Protocol on Substances that Deplete the Ozone Layer (1987) 123

moral economy of EU trade reciprocity as embodied in EPA agenda 336–9

Morales, Evo 241

Morgan, Aurelia George 422n17

Morgan, W. 431n7

Morocco, Bahraini exports to (2015) 314

Morris, Danielle 90n44

Moser, Christoph 60, 65n35

most-favoured-nation (MFN): preferential tariffs and 102, 103; trade on basis of, RTAs as hindrance to 10; treatment, investment component and 82, 84, 85

Moudachirou, D. and Mukhtar, H. 133n71

Mousseau, Michael 143n28

Mozambique 7; intra-SADC trade (2000 and 2015) 364; SADCC membership 360

Muhr, Thomas 250n2

multilateralism: RCEP as pathway to 394–5; RTAs as hindrance to 10, 11; WTO (World Trade Organization) and 3

Mwase, Ngila 371n10

Myanmar, economic characteristics (2016–17) 387

myths and misconceptions about RTAs 4, 9–15; architecture of RTAs 15; benefits of RTAs 12; distributional impacts of trade 13; Doha Round (WTO) 10; effect of RTAs on WTO 10–11; employment, RTAs and 12–13; formation of RTAs, technological change and 15; formation of RTAs, WTO and 10; GATS (General Agreement on Trade in Services) 10–11; GATT (General Agreement on Tariffs and Trade) Article XXIV 10–11, 16n3; global trading system, RTAs and Balkanization of 14; goodwill, generation of 12; Internet of Things, technological innovations and 14–15; intra-RTA sourcing 11; labour reallocation 12; literature 12, 16n2; most-favoured-nation (MFN) trea, hindrance to 10; multilateralism, hindrance to 10, 11; NAFTA (North American Free Trade Agreement) and 9, 12, 14, 15; Pacific Alliance and 12, 15; plurilateral agreements 14; political contentiousness of RTAs 9–10; political economy, changes in 10; proliferation of RTAs 9. 10; RCEP (Regional Comprehensive Economic Partnership) and 9; renegotiation of RTAs 14–15; restrictive regulations of commerce 11; rules, differences in 13; 'spaghetti bowl' of multiple overlapping RTAs 13–14; TiSA (Trade in Services Agreement) 14; TPP and 9; trade deal upgrading 15; trade diversion, RTAs and 11–12; Trump, Donald A (and administration of) and 9, 14; TTIP (Transatlantic Trade and Investment Partnership) and 9; wage bargaining power 12

NAFTA (North American Free Trade Agreement) 5, 8, 147–62; compensation (hourly) of Mexican production workers (1994–2016) 161; content of agreement 149–53; controversial nature of 147–8; debate about 148–9; developing countries, economic reform and service liberalization in 103, 105, 107–8; developmental impact 159–61; distributional impact 158–61; economic development, trade agreements and 73; economic effects of FTAs 61; economic impact 153–61; employment effects 157–8;

environment and trade agreements 125, 127–8; future, post-Trump potential for 162; gender rights and trade agreements 118; intra-group trade, value of (2015) 378; investment component of trade agreements 79, 80, 81, 82–3, 84, 87; Japan and 413, 416; Mexican exports of goods to other members (1993–2016) 154; Mexican FDI inflows (1980–2016) 156; Mexican imports of goods to other members (1993–2016) 155; Mexican labour productivity (1950–2014) 160; Mexican manufacturing employment (2007–2016) 151; Mexican trade with (2016) 194; Mexico 193–6; motives and visions for, divisions over 147–8; myths and misconceptions about RTAs and 9, 12, 14, 15; national security, trade agreements and 92, 99; neoliberal globalization, anti-globalization and 138, 142; origins 148–9; productivity gains 158; ratification of 149; RCEP, Asian economic integration and 384; SADC and 365; TPP and 404–5; trade and investment effects 153–7; trade balances of members with non-NAFTA countries (1993–2016) 156; Trump, Donald A (and administration of) and future for 162; welfare effects 158

Nai Pyi Taw negotiations (RCEP, 2015) 396

Namibia 7; intra-SADC trade (2000 and 2015) 364; SADC membership 360

Nanjing negotiations (RCEP, 2014) 396

national committees in SADC 362

National Environmental Policy Act (US, 1969) 123

national security, trade agreements and 4, 91–9; aggregate income, latent military power and 95–6; alliances and conflict, international trade and 92–3; autarkic economies 94; B-S model 97–8; bilateral trade, dispute propensity and 92–3; classical economic analysis of trade agreements 93–5; comparative advantage, Ricardian model of 94, 96–7; defence economics 93–4; ECSC (European Coal and Steel Community), establishment of 91; GATT (General Agreement on Tariffs and Trade) 93; GDP (gross domestic product), national security and 96; Heckscher and Ohlin (H-O) model 95, 96–7; latent military capability 93, 94, 95–6, 98, 99; military power, battlefield performance and 93; NAFTA (North American Free Trade Agreement) 92, 99; neoclassical economic analysis of trade agreements 95–7; 'new trade' theory analysis of trade agreements 97–8; pacifying qualities of international trade 92–3; Schuman Declaration (1950) 91; security-related objectives, explicit and tacit nature of 91–2; TPP (Trans-Pacific

Partnership) 91–2; trade and conflict literature 93; WTO (World Trade Organization) 93

natural resources initiative at SADC 368

Nauru: Australia, MFN tariffs with 424; partnership with Australia (2016) 425

neoclassical economic analysis of ITAs 95–7

neoliberal concepts for ECOWAS policymakers, question of 357

neoliberal globalization, anti-globalization and 4–5, 134–42; 'anti-globalization' movements 138; Asian financial crisis (1998) 137; capital controls, removal of 137; collective well-being, globalization and 141; critical history of neoliberal globalization 136–8; critiques of resistance to neoliberal globalization in action 141–2; cultural autonomy, demand for 139–40; Davos World Economic Forum 138; GATS (General Agreement on Trade in Services) 137; GATT (General Agreement on Tariffs and Trade) 136; global financial system, collapse of (2007–8) 134; global financial system, cost of rescue of 134–5; global social justice, demand for 140–41; globalization, local enterprise and 139–40; Great Recession 141, 142; Heiligendamm 134; IMF (International Monetary Fund) 136, 137, 139, 140–41, 142; liberal capitalism, resurgent ethos of 136; NAFTA (North American Free Trade Agreement) 138, 142; neoliberal economic reforms, developing countries' opposition to 102; neoliberal globalization, challenges to 135–6; neoliberalism, dominance of 137; popular representation, demand for 139; populism 135, 138–9, 141, 144n48; progressive counter-hegemonic movement against globalization 135–6; public anger at liberal capitalism, long history of 135; public outcry, galvanization of 135; resistance to neoliberal globalization 134–6; resistance to neoliberal globalization, critiques of 138–41; Seattle, 'Battle' of (1999) 137; Sustainable Development Goals (UN) 142; TPP (Trans-Pacific Partnership) 138, 142; TRIMs (Trade-Related Investment Measures) 137; TRIPs (Trade-Related Aspects of Intellectual Property Rights) 137, 142; Trump, populism and 135–6; TTIP (Trans-Atlantic Trade and Investment Partnership) 138; Washington Consensus 137; World Bank 136, 137, 139, 140–41, 142; World Social Forum 138, 139; WTO (World Trade Organization) 137, 139, 140–41, 142; WTO (World Trade Organization) Development Agenda 137–8

Netherlands: CARICOM trade partner (2014) 182; Mexican bilateral investment treaty (BIT) with 195; Omani imports from (2015) 315

Index

'new trade' theory analysis of trade agreements 97–8

New York Convention on the Recognition and Enforcement of Foreign Arbitral Awards 86

New Zealand: diversity indicators, TPP-12 (2016) 403; economic characteristics (2016–17) 387; gain from comprehensive RCEP 381; goods-only RCEP, gains from 389; P4 (Singapore, Chile, Brunei, New Zealand) 402; partnership with Australia (2016) 425; regional integration with Australia 425–6

Newcombe, Andrew 90n47

Nicaragua: demographic characteristics (2005–2015) 171; divergent trajectory, CAFTA-DR and 175; economic freedom index for 169; economic indicators (2005–2014) 172; employment indicators (2005–2014) 173; environmental indicators (2015) 174; foreign balance of goods and services for 169; inequality, vulnerability and (2015) 174; top trade partners (2014) 170; trade balances with US (2000–2015) 170

Niger, ECOWAS membership 350–51

Nigeria, ECOWAS membership 350–51

Niue: Australia, MFN tariffs with 424; partnership with Australia (2016) 425

non-traditional gains from PTAs, analysis of 103–4

North America: ITAs in force in (1948–2017) 48; NADB (North American Development Bank) 127; participation of RTAs in 21; RTAs and environment in 127–8

North-East Asia, Japanese policy towards 417–18

Northern Triangle of CAFTA-DR, divergent trajectory of 175–6

Norway 6

Ntara, C.K., Njeje, D., Tenambergen, W., Opiyo, P. *et al.* 383n7

Obama, Barack (and administration of) 20, 24, 402, 411n2

objectives: COMESA 373–4; RCEP, Asian economic integration 385; SADC 361; SADCC 360; TPP 404–5

O'Brien, R., Goetz, A.M., Scholte, J.A. and Williams, M. 143n30

Obstfeld, M. and Rogoff, K. 371n11

Oceania: ITAs in force in (1948–2017) 48; participation of RTAs in 21

OECD (Organisation for Economic Co-operation and Development): developing countries, economic reform and service liberalization in 107; economic development, trade agreements and 72; economic effects of FTAs 58–9; investment component of trade agreements 82

OECS, intra-group trade, value of (2015) 378

Oh, Cecilia 39n16

Ohlin, Bertil 100n17

Okediji, Ruth L. 39n17

Oman 7; Bahraini exports to (2015) 314; Brazil, imports from (2015) 315; China, exports to (2015) 315; China, imports from (2015) 315; economic growth rates (1980–2016) 310; export and import volumes (2015) 315; GCC and case of 312–13; India, exports to (2015) 315; India, imports from (2015) 315; Indian trade with (2014–2016) 318; Italy, imports from (2015) 315; Japan, exports to (2015) 315; Netherlands, imports from (2015) 315; Qatar, imports from (2015) 315; Saudi Arabia, exports to (2015) 315; Saudi Arabia, imports from (2015) 315; Singapore, exports to (2015) 315; South Korea, exports to (2015) 315; South Korea, imports from (2015) 315; Thailand, exports to (2015) 315; UAE (United Arab Emirates), exports to (2015) 315; UAE (United Arab Emirates), imports from (2015) 315; United States, exports to (2015) 315; United States, imports from (2015) 315; Yemen, exports to (2015) 315

open-ended accession clause (TPP) 405

open regionalism of Mexico, challenges to 203–4

origins: CAFTA-DR (Central American Free Trade Agreement-Dominican Republic) 166–7; CARICOM (Caribbean Common Market) 181; CETA (Comprehensive Economic and Trade Agreement) 209–10; COMESA (Common Market for Eastern and Southern Africa) 372–3; EFTA (European Free Trade Association) 271–2; GATT (General Agreement on Tariffs and Trade) 82; NAFTA (North American Free Trade Agreement) 148–9; SADC (Southern African Development Community) 360; TPP (Trans-Pacific Partnership) 401–2

Ortino, Federico 90n51

P4 (Singapore, Chile, Brunei, New Zealand), TPP and 402

PACER (Pacific Agreement on Closer Economic Relations), Australia and 424

Pacific Alliance 6, 230–38; achievements of 232–3; ALBA (Bolivarian Alliance for the Peoples of Our America) and 230; APEC 233; ASEAN 233; CELAC 230; chal;lenges, new initiatives and 235–7; functioning of 231–2; IDB (Inter-American Development Bank) 232–3; Investment Facilitation Initiative 233; Latin America, left-leaning governments in 230; Lima Declaration (2011) 230; Mexican trade with (2016) 194; MILA 232; myths and misconceptions about RTAs and 12, 15;

nature of 231–2; rational for 231; regional integration as national strategy 233–5; UNASUR 230

pacifying qualities of international trade 92–3

Palau: Australia, MFN tariffs with 424; partnership with Australia (2016) 425

Panagariya, Arvind 52n13

Panama: Mexican bilateral investment treaty (BIT) with 195; Mexican trade with (2016) 194

Pandey, Sanjay 52n10

Papua New Guinea: Australia, MFN tariffs with 424; partnership with Australia (2016) 425

Papyrakis, E., Cocarrubias, A. and Verschoor, A. 114, 121n4

Paradell, Lluís 90n47

Paraguay 6

parallel imports, treatment of 33

Pareto optimality 45, 63n29

Park, I. and Soonchan, P. 54n46

parliamentary forum of SADC 362–3

patents 31

Pattillo, C. 371n12

Pauly, Louis 144n34

Pauwelyn, Joost 90n42

Pavcnik, Nina 59, 65n23, 66n44

Pekkanen, S.M., Solis, M. and Katada, S.N. 421n4

Pelkmans, Jacques 53n23

Pence, Mike 420–21

People's Trade Treaty, ALBA and 244–5

Péridy, N. and Roux, N. 77n7

Perth negotiations (RCEP, 2016) 397

Peru 6; diversity indicators, TPP-12 (2016) 403; Japan PTA with (2012) 415; Mexican trade with (2016) 194

Petri, P.A., Plummer, M.G., Urata, S. and Zhai, F. 404, 411n7

Petrocaribe 247–8

Pevehouse, Jon. C. 109–10n15

Philippines: economic characteristics (2016–17) 387; gain from comprehensive RCEP 381; goods-only RCEP, gains from 389; Japan PTA with (2008) 415

Phillips, N. and Mieres, F. 143–4n31

Pinochet, Augusto 242

Pitschas, Christian 269n2

Plummer, M.G., Cheong, D. and Hamanaka, S. 77n6

plurilateral agreements 9, 14, 15, 16n1, 18, 19, 25, 26, 51, 266, 397, 428, 431n3

Poisson pseudo-maximum likelihood estimation (PPML) statistical test 57, 58–9

Polachek, Solomon W. 5, 92, 99n4

Polanyi, Karl 12, 135, 136, 140, 143n7

policy dialogue initiative at SADC 368

policy space 124, 161, 247, 303, 403–4; loss of 68, 72, 75, 431–2n15; residual 33–4

Pollack, Mark A. 269n3

Pomfret, R, and Sourdin, P. 432n18

Pomfret, R., Kaufmann, U. and Findlay, C. 431n13

Pomfret, Richard xix–xx, 423–33

populism 135, 138–9, 141, 144n48; representation, demand for 139

Portugal, Mexican bilateral investment treaty (BIT) with 195

post-Brexit perspectives 256–8, 299–300

Prague summit (EU, 2009) 282

precautionary principle 123–5, 126

Price, Daniel M. 89n23

Price, Sophia xx, 112–21

productivity (and productivity enhancement) 59–60, 158

Promotion of Economic Partnerships in Japan 414

protectionism: corporate power, TTIP and protection of 269; economic development, trade agreements and 69; insurance against 388; intellectual property rights, trade agreements and 30; investment protection 81–5, 264–5, 266

Protocols (SADC) 370

Prusa, T.J. 27n19

Przeworski, Adam 109n10

PTAs (preferential trade agreements) 3, 4; Australia, experience with 8, 423–30; Australian experience with 8, 423–30; developing countries, economic reform and service liberalization in 4, 101–9; Egypt, experience with 7, 322–33; Egyptian experience with 7, 322–33; importance for intellectual property rights 29; Japan, experience with 8, 412–21; Japanese experience with 8, 412–21; Mexican experience with 5, 192–205; Mexico, experience with 5, 192–205; role in protection for intellectual property rights 36–9

PTIAs (preferential trade and investment agreements) 4; investment component of trade agreements 79, 80, 81, 83, 85–7, 88

public outcry, galvanization of 135

Puerto Rico, CARICOM trade partner (2014) 182

Puig, Sergio 90n41

PVRs (plant variety rights) 32

Qatar 7; Bahraini exports to (2015) 314; economic growth rates (1980–2016) 310; Indian trade with (2014–2016) 318; Omani imports from (2015) 315

QIZ (Qualified Industrial Zones) in Egypt 329–30

Index

Rahman, M.M. and Ara, L.A. 393, 400n22

ratification of: CAFTA-DR 168; NAFTA (North American Free Trade Agreement) 149

rationale for development of: CETA 211–12; Pacific Alliance 231; spread of international trade agreements (ITAs) 45–6

Ravenhill, John 421n3

Raza, W., Grumiller, J., Taylor, L., Tröster, B. and Von Arnim, R. 270n19

RCEP (Regional Comprehensive Economic Partnership), Asian economic integration and 7–8, 384–98; agriculture, difficult area for 392; America First Approach of Trump and 388; ASEAN+1 agreements 386; Asia-Pacific Economic Cooperation (APEC) Business Travel Card 392; Auckland negotiations (2016) 397; Australia and 423, 427, 429, 430, 432n23–4; Bandar Seri Begawan negotiations (2013) 396; Bandar Seri Begawan negotiations (2016) 397; Bangkok negotiations (2017) 396; barriers to trade, reduction of 388; Brisbane negotiations (2013) 396; Busan negotiations (2015) 397; East Asia Summit, Phnom Penh (2012) 384–5; economic gains 388–9; economic impacts and risks, quantification of 388–91, 395; economic integration, contribution to 386–8; EU (European Union) and 384; framework for negotiations 384–6; GATS (General Agreement on Trade in Services) 385; global importance as trading bloc 386–8, 395; global supply chain spread 388; Greater Noida negotiations (2014) 396; Ho Chi Minh negotiations (2016) 397; Hyderabad negotiations (2017) 398; India, case study of 391–3, 395; investment rules 388; Japan and 415, 419–20; Kobe negotiations (2017) 398; Kuala Lumpar negotiations (2014) 396; Kyoto negotiations (2015) 396; losses of non-members 389; Manila negotiations (2017) 398; multilateralization, pathway to 394–5; myths and misconceptions about RTAs and 9; NAFTA (North American Free Trade Agreement) and 384; Nai Pyi Taw negotiations (2015) 396; Nanjing negotiations (2014) 396; negotiating rounds (2013–2017) 396–8; negotiation rounds (2013–2017) overview 396–8; negotiations, way forward 384–6, 395–6; objectives 385; Perth negotiations (2016) 397; principles, negotiating agenda and 385; protectionism, insurance against 388; services liberalization, challenges for 392; Singapore negotiations (2014) 396; Songdo negotiations (2017) 398; 'spaghetti bowl' of multiple trade rules, risk of 388; Sri Lanka, case study of 393–4; Tangerang negotiations (2016) 398; Tianjin negotiations (2016) 397; TPP and 403, 405, 410–11; TPP

II, China and 394–5; TPP (Trans-Pacific Partnership) and 384; trade rule simplification 388; TRIMS (Trade Related Investment Measures) 388; TRIPS (Trade-Related Aspects of Intellectual Property Rights) 392–3; Trump, Donald A (and administration of) and 395; TTIP (Transatlantic Trade and Investment Partnership) 393; WTO (World Trade Organization) and 384

Reagan, Ronald 136

real income gains (TPP-12 *vs.* TPP-11) 405

reciprocal free trade agreements (FTAs), surge in 56

RECs (Regional Economic Committees) at SADC 359

Redding, Stephen 60, 65n20

reform, problem of 101–2, 102–3, 104–5

regional/bilateral agreements, WTO and 4, 17–26; Africa, RTAs in force (2018) 21; Bretton Woods arrangements 18; Caribbean, RTAs in force (2018) 21; Central America, RTAs in force (2018) 21; CIS (Commonwealth of Independent States), RTAs in force (2018) 21; comprehensive liberalization 24–5; customs unions, FTAs and 23; deep integration agreements 25; discrimination against outsiders 23; Doha Round (WTO) 18, 25, 26; East Asia, RTAs in force (2018) 21; economic welfare, trade effects of regionalism and 22–6; Europe, RTAs in force (2018) 21; fragmented global supply chains, impact of RTAs upon 23–4; GATT (General Agreement on Tariffs and Trade) Article XXIV 17–19, 21–2, 23, 24; IMF (International Monetary Fund) 17; ITA (Information Technology Agreement) 19; ITC (information and communications technology), revolution in 17; Japan-Mongolia FTA (2016) 20; mega-regional agreements 24; MFN (most-favoured-nation) principle 17, 19; Middle East, RTAs in force (2018) 21; NAFTA (North American Free Trade Agreement) and 20, 23; non-discrimination and multilateralism in post-war trading system 17–19; North America, RTAs in force (2018) 21; Oceania, RTAs in force (2018) 21; proliferation in RTAs 20; proliferation in RTAs, WTO responses to 21–2; regionalism, implications of 22; regionalism, systemic implications of 24–6; regionalism, trends in 19–21; South America, RTAs in force (2018) 21; 'spaghetti bowl' of complexity, danger of 22; Tokyo Round (GATT, 1973–79) 20; TPP (Trans-Pacific Partnership) and 20; trade effects of regionalism, economic welfare and 22–6; trade policy, question of whither 26; Trump, Donald A (and administration of) and 20, 25;

TTIP (Transatlantic Trade and Investment Partnership) and 20; West Asia, RTAs in force (2018) 21; World Bank 17; WTO (World Trade Organization) 4, 17–26; WYO-X areas 26

Regional Customs Transit Guarantee Scheme at COMESA 381

regional integration: CAFTA-DR 166–7; as national strategy, Pacific Alliance and 233–5; New Zealand-Australia 425–6; SADC agenda for increase in 363–7, 369–70

Reichman, J.H. and Hazensahl, C. 39n14

Reitan, Ruth 143n10

Ricardo, David 45, 94, 95

Rio Declaration on Environment and Development (1992) 123

Rippel, B. 383n14

RISDP (Regional Indicative Strategic Development Plan) at SADC 363

Robson, Peter 53n21

Rodríguez-Clare, Andrés 62, 66n48

Rodrik, Dani 48, 100n11, 139, 144n35

Roffe, P. and Spennemann, C. 39n7, 40n20

Rolfe, Ralph 93, 100n12

Romei, Valentina 258n5

Rose, Andrew 60, 65n35

Ross, Wilbur 254

Roy, M., Marchetti, J. and Lim, H. 111n39

Roy, Martin 111n44–5

RTAs (regional free trade agreements) 3; Africa, participation of RTAs in 21; architecture of 15; Asia, RTAs and environment in 128–30; benefits of 12; Caribbean, participation of RTAs in 21; Central America, participation of RTAs in 21; China, environmental provisions in RTAs 129–30; CIS (Commonwealth of Independent States), participation of RTAs in 21; distributional impacts of trade and 13; Doha Development Round (WTO) and 10; East Asia, participation of RTAs in 21; effect on WTO of 10–11; employment and 12–13; environment and 125–30; Europe, participation of RTAs in 21; Europe, RTAs and environment in 125–6; formation of, technological change and 15; global trading system, RTAs and Balkanization of 14; intra-RTA sourcing 11; labour reallocation and 12; Mexico, strategy of creating network of RTAs in 192; Middle East, participation of RTAs in 21; most-favoured-nation (MFN), RTAs as hindrance to 10; multilateralism, RTAs as hindrance to 10, 11; myths and misconceptions about 4, 9–15; North America, participation in RTAs of 21; North America, RTAs and environment in 127–8; North American RTAs and environment in 127–8; Oceania, participation of RTAs in 21; political contentiousness of 9–10; proliferation of 9, 10; renegotiation of 14–15; rules, differences in 13; security-related objectives, explicit and tacit nature of 91–2; South America, participation of RTAs in 21; 'spaghetti bowl' of multiple overlapping RTAs 13–14; trade diversion, RTAs and 11–12; West Asia, participation of RTAs in 21

Ruggie, John G. 136, 143n14

rules of origin: COMESA 374; economic development, trade agreements and 69; TPP 406

Russett, B. and Oneal, J. 92–3, 99n5

Russian Federation: CARICOM trade partner (2014) 182; corruption in (2007–2017) 288; democracy in (1994–2012), Polity IV project and 284; democratic values, underestimation of 294; ease of doing business in (2007–2017) 287; exports of goods and services (1995–2016) 290; freedom of the press in (1995–2012) 285; manufactures, exports of (1995–2016) 290; market economy in, transition determinants (2012) 286; trust in (2007–2017) 289

Rwanda: COMESA membership 373; GDP growth rate as member of COMESA (2005 and 2016) 375; intra-COMESA trade (2015) 377; logistics performance index (2012–2016) 390; share of added value to GDP (2016) 376

Rybczynski, T. M. 100n17

SAARC, intra-group trade, value of (2015) 378

Sachs, Wayne 88–9n16

SACU (Southern African Customs Union), SADC and 359

SADC (Southern African Development Community) 7, 55n74, 359–70; AFTZ (African Free Trade Zone) 366; agriculture and food security initiative 368; Angola, SADCC membership 360; anti-apartheid struggle 359; ArabMaghreb Union and 359; AU (African Union) and 359; Botswana, SADCC membership 360; CMA (Common Monetary Area) 359; COMESA and 359, 365–6, 366–7; Common Agenda 363–7; Community of Sahel-Saharan States and 359; Comoros, SADC membership 360; Cotonou Afreement (2000) 367; council of ministers 362; disaster risk management initiative 368; DRC (Democratic Republic of Congo), intra-SADC trade (2000 and 2015) 364; DRC (Democratic Republic of Congo), SADC membership 360; EAC (East African Community) and 359, 366–7; Economic Community of Central African States and 359; ECOWAS and 359; EU-SADC Economic Partnership 367; free trade areas 365; future prospects 369; health initiative 368; historical perspective 359–60;

infrastructure initiative 368; intra-group trade, value of (2015) 378; intra-SADC trade (2000 and 2015) 363, 364–5; intraregional imports 363; Lesotho, intra-SADC trade (2000 and 2015) 364; Lesotho, SADCC membership 360; Lusaka Declaration (1979) 360; Madagascar, intra-SADC trade (2000 and 2015) 364; Madagascar, SADC membership 360; Malawi, intra-SADC trade (2000 and 2015) 364; Malawi, SADCC membership 360; Maputo Development Corridor 363; Mauritius, intra-SADC trade (2000 and 2015) 364; Mauritius, SADC membership 360; mission 360–61; MMA (Multilateral Monetary Area) 366; monetary union 366; Mozambique, intra-SADC trade (2000 and 2015) 364; Mozambique, SADCC membership 360; NAFTA (North American Free Trade Agreement) and 365; Namibia, intra-SADC trade (2000 and 2015) 364; Namibia, SADC membership 360; national committees 362; natural resources initiative 368; objectives 361; organizational structure 361–3; parliamentary forum 362–3; policy dialogue initiative 368; politics, defence and security initiatives 367; poverty eradication initiative 368; Protocols 370; RECs (Regional Economic Committees) 359; regional challenges 369; regional integration, agenda for increase in 363–7, 369–70; RISDP (Regional Indicative Strategic Development Plan) 363; SACU (Southern African Customs Union) and 359; SADC intra-SADC trade (2000 and 2015) 364–5; SADCC, objectives of 360; SADCC (Southern African Development Coordination Conference) 360; secretariat 362; sectoral and cluster ministerial committees 362; senior officials, standing committee of 362; Seychelles, intra-SADC trade (2000 and 2015) 364; Seychelles, SADC membership 360; single currency 366; social and human development initiative 368; South Africa, intra-SADC trade (2000 and 2015) 364; South Africa, SADC membership 360; summit of heads of state or government 361; Swaziland, SADCC membership 360; Tanzania, intra-SADC trade (2000 and 2015) 365; Tanzania, SADCC membership 360; TMA (Trilateral Monetary Agreement) 366; trade, protocol on 363, 365; tribunal 362; Tripartite Strategy 366–7, 369; troika of the organ 361; Windhoek Declaration (1992) and establishment of 360; Zambia, intra-SADC trade (2000 and 2015) 365; Zambia, SADCC membership 360; Zimbabwe, intra-SADC trade (2000 and 2015) 365; Zimbabwe, SADCC membership 360

SADCC (Southern African Development Coordination Conference), SADC and 360
Saguier, Marcelo I. 250n4
Salacuse, Jeswald W. 89n24
Salamanca, L.J.G., Gómez, F.B. and Landínez, I. C. 77n4
Samoa: Australia, MFN tariffs with 424; partnership with Australia (2016) 425
Samper, Ernesto 249
Sannassee, R.V. xx, 372–83
Santos Silva, J. M. C. 57, 64n7
Saudi Arabia 7; Bahraini exports to (2015) 314; Bahraini imports from (2015) 314; COMESA export trade to (2003–2012) 380; economic growth rates (1980–2016) 310; Indian trade with (2014–2016) 318; Omani exports to (2015) 315; Omani imports from (2015) 315
Schamis, Hector E. 109n5
Scherrer, Christoph xx, 261–70
Schiff, M. and Winters, A. 53n35
Schiff, M. and Winters, A.L. 16n2
Schill, Stephan W. 89n20, 90n48
Schmalesee, R. 65n34
Schmidt, Christoph 93, 100n12
Schneider, Gerald 99n3
Schott, J., Cimino-Isaacs, C. and Jung, E. 432n22
Schott, Jeffrey J. xx–xxi, 401–11
Schott, J.J., Kotschwar, B. and Muir, J. 399n27
Schott, Peter 60, 65n20
Schreuer, Christoph 90n47
Schuman Declaration (1950) 91
Schweiger, Christian xxi, 251–60, 258n10, 259n37
Scott, James C. 141, 144n47
Scott, R.E. 270n18
sea transport, TTIP and 266
Seattle, 'Battle' of (1999) 137
secretariat of SADC 362
securitization, CAFTA-DR and 176
Seetanah, B., Sannassee, R.V. and Tandrayen, V. 378, 383n9
Seetanah, Boopen xxi, 372–83
segregation of women into unskilled positions 113–14
Seiermann, Julia 89n29
Sell, S.K. and Prakash, A. 144n52
Sen, Amatrya 144n43
Sen, Amiti 399n15
Senegal, ECOWAS membership 350–51
services: evidence from US PTAs on reform of 107–8; liberalization of, challenges for RCEP in 392
Sex Discrimination Act (UK, 1975) 115
Seychelles 7; COMESA membership 373; GDP growth rate as member of COMESA (2005 and 2016) 375; intra-COMESA trade (2015)

377; intra-SADC trade (2000 and 2015) 364; SADC membership 360

Shadlen, Kenneth C. 105–6, 110n23

Sierra Leone, ECOWAS membership 350–51

signalling 104

Sinclair, Scott 132n59

Singapore: Australian trade agreement with (2003) 427; diversity indicators, TPP-12 (2016) 403; economic characteristics (2016–17) 387; gain from comprehensive RCEP 381; GCC, accords with 316–17; goods-only RCEP, gains from 389; Japan, PTA with (2002) 415; Mexican bilateral investment treaty (BIT) with 195; Omani exports to (2015) 315; P4 (Singapore, Chile, Brunei, New Zealand) 402; RCEP negotiations (2014) 396; Singapore-Australia FTA (2003) 426

Sirisena, Maithripala 393

Skougarevskiy, Dmitriy 89n29, 90n57

Slapin, Jonathan J. 106, 110n30

Slovakia, Mexican bilateral investment treaty (BIT) with 195

Smith, Adam 45

Snorrason, Thomas S. 29, 53n24

Solis, M. and Katada, S.N. 421n2

Solis, Mireya 421n1

Solomon Islands: Australia, MFN tariffs with 424; partnership with Australia (2016) 425

Song Kim 111n40

Songdo negotiations (RCEP, 2017) 398

Soobramanien, T.Y. and Razzaque, M.A. 78n30

Sorgho, Zakaria xxi–xxii, 41–55

Soto, D., Aguilar-Manjarrez, J. and Irde, E. 131n15

South Africa 7; COMESA export trade to (2003–2012) 380; intra-SADC trade (2000 and 2015) 364; SADC membership: SADC 360

South America: ITAs in force in (1948–2017) 48; participation of RTAs in 21

South China Seas, sovereignty issues in 417

South East Asia goods-only RCEP, gains from 389

South Korea: Australian trade agreement with (2014) 427; economic characteristics (2016–17) 387; gain from comprehensive RCEP 381; goods-only RCEP, gains from 389; Omani exports to (2015) 315; Omani imports from (2015) 315

south-south regional agreements 106

'spaghetti bowl' of multiple overlapping RTAs 13–14, 43, 46–9, 388

Spain: CARICOM trade partner (2014) 182; Mexican bilateral investment treaty (BIT) with 195

Sparks, Donald L. xxii, 359–71

SPARTECA (South Pacific Regional Trade and Economic Cooperation Agreement) 423, 424, 426

Spence, Barbara J. 98, 100n21

spread of international trade agreements (ITAs) 4, 41–51; Africa, ITAs in force in 48; Caribbean, ITAs in force in 48; Central America, ITAs in force in 48; CIS (Commonwealth of Independent States), ITAs in force in 48; comparative evolution of ITAs and intra-trade within blocs (1995–2016) 49; data insights 47–9; democracy, dissemination of 46; Doha Round (WTO) 45; East Asia, ITAs in force in 48; economic welfare of ITAs 44–5; empirical studies 46–7; Europe, ITAs in force in 48; GATT (General Agreement on Tariffs and Trade) 41; GATT (General Agreement on Tariffs and Trade) Article XXIV 41; geopolitical stability, quest for 46; global evolution of ITAs (1995–2016) 42; global trade, increase in 42; ITA (international trade agreement), developments prior to WTO 41–2; ITA (international trade agreement), multilateralism, threat to 43; ITA (international trade agreement), wide-ranging nature of 41; Middle East, ITAs in force in 48; North America, ITAs in force in 48; Oceania, ITAs in force in 48; overlapping of ITAs 47; political economy of ITAs 43–6; reasons for 45–6; South America, ITAs in force in 48; 'spaghetti bowl' phenomenon, evidence of 43, 46–9; spread of ITAs, reasons for 45; state interventions affecting global trade per year (2009–2017) 50; trade agreements in force by region, including intra- and cross-regional ITAs (1948–2017) 48; trade diversion, vulnerability to 48–9; trade flows, ITAs and positive impact on 42–3; welfare theoretic analysis of trade blocs 44–5; West Asia, ITAs in force in 48; WTO (World Trade Organization) and 41

Springford, J., Tilford, S., Odendahl, C. and McCann, P. 259n41

SPS Agreement (Sanitary and Phytosanitary Measures) 124

Sri Lanka, RCEP and case study of 393–4

SSA (Sub-Saharan Africa) 7, 329, 335–6, 339, 341, 342, 343–4, 345

state interventions affecting global trade per year (2009–2017) 50

Staub, Kevin E. 17, 58–9, 64n11

Stevens, C. and Kennan, J. 32, 78n29

Stevens, C. and Massa, I. 77n20

Stevens, C., Irfan, M., Massa, I. and Kennan, J. 9, 14, 77n5, 78n33

Stevens, Christopher xxii, 67–78

Stevens, Mary 131n12

Index

Stiglitz, J.E. and Charlton, A. 39n5
Stiglitz, Joseph 139, 144n36
Stolper, W.F. and Samuelson, P.A. 100n17
Strange, Susan 143n22
SUCRE (Unified Regional Compensation System) 243, 245–8, 350; trade volumes (2010–2016) 246
Sudan: COMESA non-FTA membership 373; GDP growth rate as member of COMESA (2005 and 2016) 375; intra-COMESA trade (2015) 377; logistics performance index (2012–2016) 390; share of added value to GDP (2016) 376
Summers, Lawrence 402
Suominen, Kati xxii–xxiii, 9–16
Sustainable Development Goals (UN): gender rights and trade agreements 116; neoliberal globalization, anti-globalization and 142
Swaziland 7; COMESA non-FTA membership 373; GDP growth rate as member of COMESA (2005 and 2016) 375; intra-COMESA trade (2015) 377; intra-SADC trade (2000 and 2015) 364; SADCC membership 360
Sweden, Mexican bilateral investment treaty (BIT) with 195
Switzerland 6; COMESA export trade to (2003–2012) 380; Japan PTA with (2009) 415; Mexican bilateral investment treaty (BIT) with 195
Sykews, Alan O. 90n43

Tangerang negotiations (RCEP, 2016) 398
Tanzania 7; intra-SADC trade (2000 and 2015) 365; SADCC membership 360
Tarrow, Sidney 143n29
Tavlas, G. 371n12
Taylor, Adam 144n50
Technical Barriers to Trade, Agreement on (WTO) 122
Temer, Michel 227, 249
Tenreyro, Silvana 57, 64n7
Terada Takeshi 421n9
TFTA (Tripartite Free Trade Area) 382–3
Thailand: Australian trade agreement with (2005) 426, 427; economic characteristics (2016–17) 387; gain from comprehensive RCEP 381; goods-only RCEP, gains from 389; Japan, PTA with (2007) 415; Omani exports to (2015) 315
Thatcher, Margaret 136, 256
Thornton, Phil 22, 27n16
Tianjin negotiations (RCEP, 2016) 397
TiSA (Trade in Services Agreement) 14, 432n21
Titi, C. 90n55
TMA (Trilateral Monetary Agreement) 366
Togo 358n3; ECOWAS membership 350–51

Tonga: Australia, MFN tariffs with 424; partnership with Australia (2016) 425
Topalova, Petia 61, 65n41
Torres, Francisco xxiii, 296–306
TPP (Trans-Pacific Partnership) 5, 7–8, 401–11; agriculture, comprehensive coverage of 406–7; APEC (Asia-Pacific Economic Cooperation) and 401–2, 404; Australia and 423, 428–9, 430, 432n24; bilateral FTAs, upgrading of 404–5; Bogor Summit (1994) 401–2; comprehensive agreement objective 406; CPTPP (Comprehensive and Progressive Agreement for Trans-Pacific Partnership) 401; diverse participation 402–4; diversity indicators, TPP-12 (2016) 403; environmental issues 407–8; foreign policy and national security reinforcement 405; GATT (General Agreement on Tariffs and Trade) Article XXIV 385, 404; High Level Dialogue on Integration Initiatives for the Asia Pacific 409; intellectual property rights, trade agreements and 37; intra-group trade, value of (2015) 378; investment policy obligations 407; IPRs (Intellectual Property Rights) 407; ITO (International Trade Organization) Charter (1948) 401; Japan and 412, 413, 418–19; Joint Declaration of Macroeconomic Policy Authorities of Trans-Pacific Partnership Countries 408; KORUS FTA 405, 406, 407, 408; labour practices 408; LDCs (less developed countries), provisions for 403–4; myths and misconceptions about RTAs and 9; NAFTA (North American Free Trade Agreement) and 404–5; national security, trade agreements and 91–2; neoliberal globalization, anti-globalization and 138, 142; objectives 404–5; open-ended accession clause 405; origins 401–2; P4 (Singapore, Chile, Brunei, New Zealand) 402; participants, like-minded but diverse 402–4; RCEP, Asian economic integration and 384, 403, 405, 410–11; real income gains (TPP-12 vs. TPP-11) 405; regulatory coherence, competitiveness and business facilitation 408; rulebook and disciplines 407; rules of origin 406; scope and coverage 405–8; subsidies, disciplines on 407; talks about, launch of (2010) 402; TPP II, China and 394–5; trade rulebook, modernization of 405; Trans-Pacific Strategic Economic Partnership 402; TRIPS (Trade-Related Aspects of Intellectual Property Rights) 407; Trump, Donald A (and administration of) and 52n7, 401, 406, 408–9; United States National Export Initiative and 402; United States participation, moving on without 408–11
trade rule simplification, RCEP and 388

trade rulebook, TPP and modernization of 405
trade secrets 32
trademarks 31–2
Trans-Pacific Strategic Economic Partnership 402
Trefler, Daniel 25, 59, 61–2, 65n22, 66n46, 109n9
TRIMs (Trade-Related Investment Measures): investment component of trade agreements 80; neoliberal globalization, anti-globalization and 137; RCEP, Asian economic integration and 388
Trinidad & Tobago: CARICOM trade partner (2014) 182; Mexican bilateral investment treaty (BIT) with 195
Tripartite Strategy of SADC 366–7, 369
TRIPs (Trade-Related Aspects of Intellectual Property Rights) 4; neoliberal globalization, anti-globalization and 137, 142; RCEP, Asian economic integration and 392–3; TPP and 407; TRIPS-Plus agenda 36–9; WTO and 29–35
Trommer, S. and Hannah, E. 120n14
Trump, Donald A (and administration of) 5, 6, 8, 135, 141–2, 227; America First Approach 388; Australia and 429; EU (European Union) and 254; Japan and 412, 419, 420–21; Mexico and 192, 196, 203, 204–5; myths and misconceptions about RTAs 9, 14; populism and 135–6; RCEP, Asian economic integration and 395; TPP and 52n7, 401, 406, 408–9; TTIP, withdrawal from 261
TTIP (Trans-Atlantic Trade and Investment Partnership) 6, 261–9; academic and societal critique of 267–9; agricultural market access 265–6; consent and dissent areas between EU and US 265–6; corporate power, protection of 269; employment aspect, bias in studies of 267; environmental standards, EU mandate for 265; EU mandate for negotiation 262–5; geographical indications 266; government procurement 266; improved market access, EU mandate for 263–4; investment protection 264–5, 266; investment rules 269; labour standards 266; land transport 266; myths and misconceptions about RTAs 9; negotiations, 15 rounds of 261–2; neoliberal globalization, anti-globalization and 138; public services, encroachment on 268; RCEP, Asian economic integration and 393; regulations and non-tariff barriers, EU mandate for 264; rules, EU mandate for investment protection and 264–5; sea transport 266; social standards 266; social standards, EU mandate for 265; Trump administration and withdrawal from 261
Tumwebaze, H.K. and Ijjo, A.T. 378, 383n8

Tunisia, EU-Tunisia Action Plan 339–3–40
Turkey: COMESA export trade to (2003–2012) 380; Mexican bilateral investment treaty (BIT) with 195
Tusk, Donald 254
Tuvalu: Australia, MFN tariffs with 424; partnership with Australia (2016) 425

UAE (United Arab Emirates) 7; Bahraini exports to (2015) 314; Bahraini imports from (2015) 314; CARICOM trade partner (2014) 182; COMESA export trade to (2003–2012) 380; economic growth rates (1980–2016) 310; Indian trade with (2014–2016) 318; Omani exports to (2015) 315; Omani imports from (2015) 315
Uganda: COMESA membership 373; GDP growth rate as member of COMESA (2005 and 2016) 375; intra-COMESA trade (2015) 377; logistics performance index (2012–2016) 390; share of added value to GDP (2016) 376
UK (United Kingdom) 6, 7; Australia, trade with 423, 430n1; Bahraini imports from (2015) 314; CARICOM trade partner (2014) 182; Mexican bilateral investment treaty (BIT) with 195; see also Brexit
Ukraine 6; corruption in (2007–2017) 288; democracy in (1994–2012), Polity IV project and 284; EaP, Association Agreement with 283; EaP (Eastern Partnership initiative) 282; ease of doing business in (2007–2017) 287; exports of goods and services (1995–2016) 290; freedom of the press in (1995–2012) 285; manufactures, exports of (1995–2016) 290; market economy in, transition determinants (2012) 286; trade, direction of (2012) 291; trust in (2007–2017) 289
UN (United Nations): Economic Commission for Africa (ECA) 348; Framework Convention on Climate Change 123
UNASUR (Union of South American Nations): ALBA (Bolivarian Alliance for the Peoples of Our America) and 249; Pacific Alliance and 230, 234, 235, 238
UNCTAD (UN Conference on Trade and Development): gender rights and trade agreements 118; investment component of trade agreements 85
Unified Regional Compensation Scheme (ALBA) 245–7
United States 4, 5–6, 8; Australia-US FTA (2005) 426; Australian trade agreement with (2005) 427; Bahraini exports to (2015) 314; Bahraini imports from (2015) 314; CAFTA-DR and 167; CARICOM trade partner (2014) 182; COMESA export trade to (2003–2012) 380; Congressional Research Service report on

459

economic impact of trade agreements 70–71; demographic characteristics (2005–2015) 171; divergent trajectory of CAFTA-DR 173–4; diversity indicators, TPP-12 (2016) 403; economic freedom index for 169; economic indicators (2005–2014) 172; employment indicators (2005–2014) 173; environmental indicators (2015) 174; exports from CARICOM to (2007–2016) 190; foreign balance of goods and services for 169; goods-only RCEP, gains from 389; inequality, vulnerability and (2015) 174; National Export Initiative, TPP and 402; Omani exports to (2015) 315; Omani imports from (2015) 315; services, political engagement of 107; top trade partners (2015) 170; TPP participation, moving on without 408–11; trade balance with CAFTA-DR 170; US–Vietnam Bilateral Trade Agreement (2001) 61

UPOV Treaty (1978) 32

Urata, Shujiro 400n28, 432n23

Uruguay 6; Chile-Uruguay FTA (2016) 118; Mexican bilateral investment treaty (BIT) with 195; Mexican trade with (2016) 194

Uruguay Development Round (WTO) 4, 21, 25, 45, 130n1, 149, 150, 193, 196, 204, 275, 311–12, 324, 428

Vahl, Marius xxiii, 271–81

Van den Broek, Naboth 90n44

Van Staveren, I., Elson, D., Grown, C. and Catagy, N. 120n2

Van Wincoop, Eric 57, 64n6

Vandevelde, Kenneth J. 16, 88n14

Vanek, Jaroslav 53n25

Vanuatu: Australia, MFN tariffs with 424; partnership with Australia (2016) 425

Venezuela 6, 167, 183, 200, 207n31, 238; ALBA (Bolivarian Alliance for the Peoples of Our America) and 241–4, 245–50; bilateral agreement with CARICOM 187; CARICOM trade partner (2014) 182; exports from CARICOM to (2007–2016) 190; MERCOSUR and 224, 225, 226, 227, 228n22, 229n29

Vicard, Vincent 53n37

Vietnam: diversity indicators, TPP-12 (2016) 403; economic characteristics (2016–17) 387; gain from comprehensive RCEP 381; goods–only RCEP, gains from 389; Japan, PTA with (2009) 415

Villarreal, M.A. and Fergusson, I.F. 77n16

Viner, Jacob 44, 52n9, 53n25

Voluntary Sectoral Liberalization Talks (1998) in Japan 412

Voss, Jürgen 88n2

Vreeland, James Raymond 109–10n15

Walker, Herman 16, 88n15

Waltz, Kenneth 100n16

Washington Consensus 137, 138, 339

Webber, Douglas 260n45

Weinstein, David 62–3, 66n53

welfare effects, NAFTA and 158

welfare gains, measurement of 62–3

welfare theoretic analysis of trade blocs 44–5

West Asia: ITAs in force in (1948–2017) 48; participation of RTAs in 21

Whalley, John 53n36

Whitehouse, Mark 144n49

Wickremesinghe, Ranil 393

Wiener, J.B., Rogers, M.D., Hammitt, J.K. and Sand, P.H. 133n72

Wiersema, Annecoos 131n11

Wignaraja, Ganeshan xxiii, 384–400, 399n14, 400n24

Wilson, Jeffrey D. 399n26

Wilson, J.S., Mann, C.L. and Otsuki, T. 383n13

Windhoek Declaration (1992) and establishment of SADC 360, 361

Winfield, Mark 132n52

Winters, L.A. 16n2

WIPO (World Intellectual Property Organization): intellectual property rights, trade agreements and 29, 36; WCTs (copyright treaties) 36; WPPT (WIPO Performance and Phonograms Treaty) 36

Women and Development Network 113–14

Woolcock, Stephen 126, 130–31n7

Workers with Family Responsibilities Convention (1981) 117

World Bank 16n2, 17, 57–8, 64n4, 77n10, 109n1, 111n37, 115, 156, 193, 309, 310, 387, 403, 418, 422n15; Eastern Partnership initiative (EU) and 286, 287, 290; Egypt, PTAs and 322, 324, 331, 332, 333; neoliberal globalization, anti-globalization and 136, 137, 139, 140–41, 142; Pacific Alliance and 233, 237, 239n22

World Social Forum 138, 139

World Trade Report (WTO, 2011) 23, 25, 26, 27n11, 30

Worth, Owen 143n9

WTO (World Trade Organization): Australia, charter member (1995) 423, 431n3; COMESA and 372; developing countries, economic reform and service liberalization in 102, 107; Development Agenda 137–8; Doha Development Round 3, 10, 18, 25–6, 45, 184, 193, 203, 224, 296, 302, 307, 312–19, 372, 384–94, 428; economic development, trade agreements and 67; economic effects of FTAs 56; Enabling Clause 10, 70 74, 207n32; environment and trade agreements 122, 125, 126, 130; gender rights and trade agreements

112–13, 116–17; investment component of trade agreements 79; Japan and 412; Ministerial Conference, Cancún (2003) 416; multilateral approach 3; national security, trade agreements and 93; neoliberal globalization, anti-globalization and 137, 139, 140–41, 142; RCEP, Asian economic integration and 384; regional/bilateral agreements and 4, 17–26; spread of international trade agreements (ITAs) 41; Uruguay Development Round 4, 21, 25, 45, 130n1, 149, 150, 193, 196, 204, 275, 311–12, 324, 428; WTO-Plus PTAs, Japan and negotiation of 415

Yackee, Jason Webb 89n36, 90n40
Yaoundé Accords (1963–75) 335
Yasukuni Shrine 417
Yayo, M. and Asefa, S. 363, 371n6

Yemen 330; Omani exports to (2015) 315
Yi Qian 40n23
Yoshimatsu H., and Ziltener, P. 421n12
Yoshimatsu Hidetaka 421n5–6

Zambia 7; COMESA membership 373; GDP growth rate as member of COMESA (2005 and 2016) 375; intra-COMESA trade (2015) 377; intra-SADC trade (2000 and 2015) 365; logistics performance index (2012–2016) 390; SADCC membership 360
Zimbabwe 7; COMESA membership 373; GDP growth rate as member of COMESA (2005 and 2016) 375; intra-COMESA trade (2015) 377; intra-SADC trade (2000 and 2015) 365; logistics performance index (2012–2016) 390; SADCC membership 360; share of added value to GDP (2016) 376